Praise for *Common Purpose*

"Diligent in its research an[...]
—*Washington Post Book* [...]

"*Common Purpose* deals m[...]w
in print with the social pr[...]nd
points the way toward solutions. Research-based, practical
and incisive, it is a landmark book, required reading for everyone concerned to reweave our rapidly unraveling social fabric."
—JOHN W. GARDNER,
   former Secretary of Health, Education and Welfare

"Tough, cerebral, informed—and sanguine but not quixotic
about the possibilities of injecting flexibility and imagination
into the policies that govern welfare, child protection, and education."
—*Kirkus Reviews*

"[Starred Review] Schorr's thoughtful book offers compelling
arguments for keeping measurable outcomes in focus . . .
Highly recommended."
—*Library Journal*

"This terrific book helps all of us know what can be done
about the staggering problems faced by children today. Lisbeth
Schorr has carefully explored what does work and how to
make it work for every child in our rich nation. Read and act
on this important book."
—MARIAN WRIGHT EDELMAN

"This prodigiously researched study is an optimistic and well-
thought-out call to action."
—*Publishers Weekly*

"*Common Purpose* explores a social frontier that breaks traditional political boundaries and transforms our most challenged
neighborhoods into communities of hope. The evidence is
compelling, the message is clear: change is possible."
—BILL BRADLEY

Lisbeth B. Schorr

Common Purpose

Strengthening Families and Neighborhoods to Rebuild America

ANCHOR BOOKS
DOUBLEDAY
New York London Toronto Sydney Auckland

AN ANCHOR BOOK
PUBLISHED BY DOUBLEDAY
a division of Bantam Doubleday Dell Publishing Group, Inc.
1540 Broadway, New York, New York 10036

ANCHOR BOOKS, DOUBLEDAY, and the portrayal of an anchor
are trademarks of Doubleday, a division of Bantam Doubleday Dell
Publishing Group, Inc.

Common Purpose was originally published in hardcover by Doubleday in 1997.

Book design by Paul Randall Mize

Excerpt from *Before Their Time: Four Generations of Teenage Mothers* copyright © 1992 by
   Joelle Sander, reprinted by permission of Harcourt Brace & Company.
Excerpt from "Upon this age that never speaks its mind" by Edna St. Vincent Millay. From
   Collected Poems, HarperCollins. Copyright © 1939, 1967 by Edna St. Vincent Millay and
   Norma Millay Ellis. All rights reserved. Reprinted by permission of Elizabeth Barnett, liter-
   ary executor.

The Library of Congress has cataloged the hardcover edition of this work as follows

Schorr, Lisbeth B.
Common purpose: strengthening families and neighborhoods
to rebuild America / Lisbeth B. Schorr.
p.   cm.
1. Human services—United States. 2. Public welfare—United States.
3. Community development—United States. 4. Social programs—United States.
5. United States—Social policy—1997
I. Title
HV91.S2945   1997
361.973—dc21   97-11595
CIP

ISBN 0-385-47533-O
First Anchor Books Trade Paperback Edition: August 1998

10 9 8 7 6 5 4 3 2

To Dan,
whose many gifts to me
made this book, and much else, possible.

Contents

Foreword

William Julius Wilson

GIVEN THE CURRENT RETREAT from using social policy to fight inequality, this important book could not be more timely. Declining confidence in our political institutions to address social ills combined with "rampant antipathy toward government" represents, in the words of Lisbeth Schorr, "perhaps the greatest obstacle to the development of strategies to bring all children and families into the American dream." If the nation is to reverse the course it has taken in recent years, it is essential that thoughtful books such as *Common Purpose* be widely read and publicly discussed.

Schorr's goal is explicit. She wants to move the nation beyond the programmatic agenda of replicating model, but limited, social programs toward a more comprehensive long-term strategy "that could combat a wide range of social ills, including those that are separating the haves ever further from the have-nots."

The loss of trust in our political institutions, the nation's limited view of the effectiveness of large-scale antipoverty programs, the social basis of inner-city poverty and joblessness, and the need to have faith in systematic social reform are all extensively discussed and explained in this book. More importantly, *Common Purpose* draws upon an impressive array of evidence to demonstrate how families could be strengthened, whole systems—child protection systems, family support systems, and school systems—could become more effective, and how troubled neighborhoods could be revitalized and regain their social control and enhance their social organization.

However, the evidence presented in this book is not based on the prevailing evaluation approaches upon which many policy makers rely. Indeed, Lisbeth Schorr persuasively argues that the nation's distrust of the effectiveness of social programs and the belief that "nothing really works" stems in part from evaluation methods that fail to capture the true effects of some social interventions. Moreover, traditional evaluation models have been ineffectual in helping to understand which aspects of a program are having a desired effect and which components are weak and ineffective.

Because of the heavy reliance on an experimental method that only includes variables that are easily quantifiable, complex community-based interventions tend to be ignored in conventional evaluation studies. This results, as Lisbeth Schorr notes, in a lot of "rigorous" information on what is not working, but little useful knowledge of "what might work." Important data that could be derived from interventions that are multifaceted, interactive, and broad (e.g., school reform, early childhood supports, and improved links to employment) and that are designed to produce multiple outcomes (e.g., school achievement, rates of employment, and a reduction of solo parent family formation) are often too cumbersome for traditional evaluation designs.

Moreover, most traditional evaluation studies lack a strong conceptual and theoretical framework that would explain how and why a social intervention might achieve a desired outcome. Theory-based evaluation provides what statistical analysis alone cannot furnish: conceptual specification of underlying causal mechanisms through which a program is thought to operate. "By combining outcome measures with an understanding of the process that produced the outcomes," states Schorr, theory-based evaluation "can shed light both on the extent of impact and on how the change occurred."

Fortunately, the heavy reliance on the traditional evaluation methods is on the wane. Ms. Schorr reveals that new evaluation methods are allowing social scientists to observe the more complex and promising programs. These innovative approaches are not only guided by a strong conceptual and theoretical base, they also employ multiple research techniques, including both quantitative and qualitative methods, to capture and document the full complexity of the social intervention.

By going beyond the narrow confines of evaluation studies, Schorr is able to discuss comprehensive and long-range strategies, including those demonstrating that even a dysfunctional bureaucratic model can be modified and made more effective. It is with social intervention at the institutional level, especially where government is involved, that we have experienced our most serious difficulties and disappointments. Schorr reveals how public purposes can be enhanced and neighborhood and front-line discretion can be achieved through post-bureaucratic models of accountability and new public-private partnerships. Moreover, Schorr makes evident the importance of encouraging schools, especially schools in depleted neighborhoods, to become partners in neighborhood efforts to build communities and reform services. Indeed, the success of neighborhood schools depends not only on formal and specialized services, it "also depends on the creation of informal helping networks, including church and social ties, family support services, youth development programs, mentoring, recreational opportunities, and strong bonds among adults."

Instead of focusing on limited problems with circumscribed solutions, Lisbeth Schorr demonstrates the need to take a broader and long-range view. We can, for example, effect positive change in a neighborhood or in a neighborhood-based institution. However, the problems in depleted inner-city neighborhoods cannot be overcome by relying on neighborhood resources alone. On the one hand, "effective neighborhood transformation requires that community-based organizations be able to draw on funding, expertise, and influence from outside, and that outsiders be able to draw on information, expertise, and wisdom that only can come from the neighborhood itself." However, few of the complex interventions can solve problems overnight. Ms. Schorr wants us to take a longer view and be prepared to build for a future that our generation may not see. This kind of practical advice, backed up by the systematic presentation of evidence and thoughtful arguments on what works and how it works, is what this country needs now more than ever.

Introduction

ALL OVER THIS COUNTRY, right now, some program or some institution is succeeding in combating such serious problems as high rates of single parenthood, child abuse, youth violence, school failure, and intergenerational poverty. Yes, successful programs exist, but they have, in the main, been small and scarce. Why?

That question has long been haunting me. Why do models of excellent schools, effective job training, and wonderful early childhood programs remain only models? Why do interventions that actually change the odds for their high-risk participants succeed briefly and in miniature, and fail the moment we try to sustain them or expand them? Why were the small successes I described in my earlier book, *Within Our Reach,* only rarely sustained or expanded?

As I surveyed the current scene, it became clear that *we have learned to create the small exceptions that can change the lives of hundreds. But we have not learned how to make the exceptions the rule to change the lives of millions.*

I wanted to know what stopped us from turning the exceptions into the rule, and what we could do about it.

In my search for answers, I looked at both successes and failures in going from small to large, from model to mainstream. And I listened. I asked, What makes the difference in whether your wonderful demonstration can thrive outside the hothouse? Is it money? Is it one leader's charisma? Is it luck?

Those all matter, came back the answer, but only superficially. What *really* matters, my informants said—assuming one knew what they meant—is "the system." Whether you can get around it or manipulate it or beat it or change it, or whether—as is most likely—it ultimately defeats you.

"The system"? What are all these people talking about when they name the system as villain? The principal who says he can't hire the teachers who will improve student achievement because "the system" downtown won't let him. The director of a neighborhood center that can't send home visitors to provide both parent support and immunizations because "the system" won't permit mingling the grant funds. The child care director who can't read with the children because she has to spend her time meeting "the system's" paperwork requirements. The counselor who can't work with a thirteen-year-old runaway because "the system" limits her services to children who have been certified as abused. The child welfare worker who has to send three siblings to three different faraway foster families because "the system" won't let her keep the siblings together and in their own neighborhood. The president of a community development group that can't run a teen center because it doesn't meet "the system's" definition of an eligible sponsor. The chair of a new county board on children and families that has just spent a year raising $20,000 in grant funds for a new health outreach program, while "the system" has withdrawn twenty million dollars from the children's medical care budget.

Each of these people means something slightly different by "the system." But they all know that it is something beyond their own control that keeps them from accomplishing valued social purposes. All have seen successful models flourish briefly in splendid isolation, only to disappear or be diluted when the special funding or special political protection ends, or when they run out of leaders who are willing to lie, cheat, and connive in order to make their interventions work in the face of a hostile system.

So, I set out to understand how the system got in the way of sustaining and scaling up effective programs, how the system kept interventions that had succeeded with hundreds from reaching millions. I searched for real-life examples of successes that had thrived beyond the hothouse, and found many more than I had dared to hope. In Indiana, Iowa, Missouri, Michigan, and Oregon, in Los Angeles, New York City, Baltimore, and Savannah, I found people scaling up from small successes. I found people changing institutions and systems to support new and more effective ways of working with children and families.

Now I was ready to tell the stories of how major systems were being made hospitable to programs that once thrived only in hot-house conditions. I could describe what could be done—what was being done—to translate small successes into large ones, and to put many small successes together to change entire neighborhoods. I could offer a vision of the possible, rooted in the valiant, everyday experience of heroic systems change pioneers.

The story of these triumphs has gone largely untold, because most observers fail to see how they combine to portray a more hopeful future.

The journalists and others who take the trouble to search out what's working do indeed find inspiring examples of local successes. They showcase the model programs, sometimes even on the evening news, that were founded by a wizard who is some combination of Saint Francis of Assisi, Machiavelli, and a CPA, and that operate with special funding or under the protection of a powerful political figure. They treat success as a one-time curiosity and miss the recurring pattern. The media's (and perhaps their audiences') preference for simple, circumscribed stories means little attention to complexities of success that cannot be conveyed with sound bites or reduced to a horse race.

The idealogues and the politicians, happy to accommodate the media's inclination toward polarization, obscure the hopeful signs with sterile debates about public versus private, entitlement versus charity, top-down versus bottom-up, and markets versus bureaucracies.

Academics, in their turn, operate within narrow disciplines that also produce only limited understanding. Too many use their accumulated knowledge to belittle what others think they know, and endlessly document the problem while neglecting solutions that lack scientific certainty. Evaluators of social programs, too, often put a higher priority on elegant and precise statistical manipulation than on producing usable knowledge.

People at the front lines in local communities, be they school-teachers, outreach workers, or community organizers, are so over-whelmed with meeting mushrooming needs with diminishing resources that they cannot take time off to record their inspiring stories.

But before I could finish my book to tell their stories, the stakes had escalated: An unprecedented cynicism about the capacity of government to help solve our most serious social problems was casting a terrible pall over our national life.

The prevailing belief that the federal government was helpless to act on America's most serious domestic problems had, by August of 1996, led to the repeal of the federal guarantee of welfare benefits and major cutbacks in other safety-net programs—programs that many regarded as actually doing harm. The reigning conviction that anything we set out to do collectively on a large scale was doomed to failure was paralyzing those who were looking for alternatives to inaction and indifference.

The collapse of confidence in our political institutions and the rampant antipathy toward government that emerged in the mid-1990s represented perhaps the greatest obstacle to the development of strategies to bring all children and families into the American dream. Citizens certain that nothing works, or that nothing done by government works, were turning into reluctant taxpayers and noisy cynics. They rejected societal solutions to the problems of the inner city and the poor—especially those that cost money—less out of meanness than out of the conviction that no one knew how to help.

Polls found that the proportion of the public who would trust the government in Washington to do what is right most of the time or always fell from 76 percent in 1964 to 25 percent in 1995.

What I call the Trust Deficit—pervasive distrust of our most important institutions—had become more of a threat to the nation's ability to act on its problems than the budget deficit.

Equally ominous, the gap between America's haves and have-nots was continuing to grow and becoming more entrenched. We were sorting ourselves out in America, and the differences in how winners and losers live, and in their children's life prospects, were growing exponentially. The risk factors that increase the chances of "rotten outcomes"—too-early childbearing, juvenile violence, and high rates of school failure—were being compounded far beyond our capacity to intervene.

By 1994, the gap between rich and poor had become the widest since the Census Bureau began keeping track in 1947. The U.S. now has the greatest income disparity of any modern democratic nation. Except for countries overthrown by revolution or military defeat, no country has ever experienced such a sharp shift in the distribution of earnings as has America in the last generation.

Never before have median wages of American men fallen steadily for twenty years, with consequences exacerbated by U.S. tax and transfer policies, which stand virtually alone in the industrialized world in how little they cushion the effects of harsh economic forces.

As a direct result, proportionately more children live in poverty in the U.S. than in any other industrialized nation.

The polarizing effects of growing income inequality are intensified by racial, ethnic, and class differences and solidified by a dramatic upsurge in geographic separation. At one end of town are the fortunate fifth, "quietly seceding from the rest of the nation" in walled-off privacy. Across town, the losers live in ever greater isolation, in neighborhoods steeped in violence and despair, with a majority of adults not working, not married, not succeeding in any activity society values, and with a life expectancy lower than that of their counterparts in Third World countries.

I looked at these trends and saw I would have to expand my aspirations for my book.

My agenda could no longer be solely programmatic. It would not be enough to show that we could indeed replicate this or that model program. I would also have to be able to show that entire systems— school systems and child protection systems and family support systems—could be made to work, that families could be strengthened, and that devastated neighborhoods could be transformed. It would take that kind of evidence to counter the nihilism of a skeptical public. I would have to be able to show that continued funding cutbacks need not be the only policy option on the horizon, and that there were valued purposes to be achieved through governmental action, even government initiatives that cost money. It would take solid evidence of success that went beyond the programmatic to counter the nihilism of a skeptical public and to overcome our sense of helplessness. The long-term strategies that could combat a wide range of social ills, including those that are separating the haves ever further from the have-nots, would not be adopted until Americans were convinced our problem-solving capacities could once again be harnessed for shared purposes, and would ultimately accomplish more good than harm.

So if I was to persuade my readers that the needed fundamental changes were possible, I had to counter at least four prevailing beliefs that would otherwise undermine the arguments and evidence I present.

First, that the prevailing distrust of government is a permanent condition of our national life. Second, that past efforts at social reform have failed far more than they have succeeded. Third, that most of the people who are stuck in the inner city are there primarily as a result of individual, personal failings. And last, that large-scale social reform that does more good than harm is simply not possible.

I will briefly examine and try to refute each of these beliefs in this introduction.

Is the prevailing distrust of government a permanent condition? The conviction that our social institutions are simply incapable of responding effectively to fast-changing conditions pervades our lives.

Whether cynical Americans have become mean-spirited Americans is in dispute. I lean toward columnist William Raspberry's position when he writes, "What we are seeing is not a lack of desire to solve these dreadful problems . . . but doubt that the funds we're asked to provide will solve them. What we call laziness, selfishness and bigotry are frequently nothing more than the people's transcendent doubt that anything they do will make any real difference."

Opinion surveys support that conclusion. A national poll sponsored by *The Washington Post,* the Kaiser Family Foundation and Harvard University found that respondents unwilling to pay more in taxes for increased spending on the poor and minorities said this was not because they opposed all government assistance for the poor, but because "the federal government can't do the job right."

The erosion of confidence in our public institutions goes far beyond the suspicion of government that has been traditional among Americans. We came out of World War II with an enormous burst of energy and sense of pride in our national capacity. Americans had worked double and triple shifts to produce more weapons than all Allied and Axis powers combined. They had served in the armed services and made sacrifices to the plaudits of a grateful nation. Veterans came back to be educated on the GI Bill and to buy houses and build the suburbs on government-guaranteed mortgages, and we had a sense of unity and common purpose.

Then came a war lost and lied about, economic forces that induced pessimism about the future, and promises to resolve deep-seated social problems not kept because the money had gone to the Vietnam War. Distrust and alienation from government exploded. Americans lost confidence in their ability to control their own destiny and came to believe that their institutions were no longer capable of change and renewal. "For the first time in their national history," writes Alice Rivlin, "Americans came to see themselves as helpless victims of circumstance, unable to take charge of their future."

Increasingly, through the 1970s and 1980s, Americans came to see government as part of the problem, not part of the solution. By 1994, two thirds of American adults were telling the Roper Poll that big government is the country's gravest peril. Sixty-six percent said that government is almost always wasteful and inefficient. Sixty-nine percent said government creates more problems than it solves.

Dr. Robert Blendon, public opinion expert at the Harvard School of Public Health, has concluded that a major reason for the distrust is that "most people believe that government has failed in the things that they care about" because it seems to have been unable to control violent crime and to assure that their children will be prosperous and do better than they have done.

The press may also play an important role in feeding distrust by the way it provides information about governmental affairs and public issues. James Fallows, editor of *U.S. News and World Report,* contends that mainstream journalism tends to portray issues that affect the collective interest of Americans—crime, health care, education, economic growth—mainly as arenas in which politicians fight. He writes that "by choosing to present public life as a contest among scheming political leaders, all of whom the public should view with suspicion, the news media helps to bring about that very result."

These findings suggest that if government begins to succeed in achieving results that citizens care about (by reducing crime, increasing rates of children succeeding at school, etc.), trust can be rebuilt. Even the press is beginning to examine its own contribution to spreading cynicism. But it will require authentic success in achieving results, as well as attention to disseminating word of those successes before today's Trust Deficit will be overcome.

Did past efforts at reform fail more often than they succeeded? Along with their general distrust of government, many Americans are convinced that past efforts to reduce poverty and address other social problems have sent the deficit soaring and have made everything that's gone wrong worse.

Our convictions about what should be done are powerfully shaped by our beliefs about what has been done, especially about what has been spent. And it turns out there is a lot of misinformation about social spending. A poll taken on election night 1994 found that 46 percent of voters thought that either welfare or foreign aid was the biggest item in the federal budget—although the basic welfare program, AFDC, and foreign aid each actually accounted for only about 1 percent of the federal budget.

The actual numbers and proportions for 1995, in rank order, were as follows:

Social Security	$336 billion	22%
Defense	272	18%
Interest on the debt	212	15%
Medicare	157	10%
Medicaid	88	6%
Food stamps	27	1.8%
Federal welfare (AFDC)	17	just over 1%
Foreign aid	13	just under 1%

Hobart Rowen, the late economics correspondent of *The Washington Post,* wrote that he considered voter misinformation of this magnitude to have been carefully nurtured by the congressional Republican "Contract with America" campaign, anxious to convey the impression that "government spending had mushroomed for programs on which the public has soured, notably welfare and foreign aid." The public deficit that mushroomed in the 1980s, and that has so constrained the ability of the federal government to respond to social needs, was the legacy, as E. J. Dionne put it, of "the acquisitive, materialistic, and self-indulgent ethos of the 1980s." It was not the result of spending on the poor, and it was not an accident. "Reagan's real innovation," wrote historian Arthur Schlesinger, "was to use tax reduction and defense spending to create vast budgetary deficits and then to use deficits to force the cutback of social programs."

The second big misunderstanding is about who has benefitted from rising social expenditures and from the social programs that were begun in the 1960s. Of the sharp rise in government spending over the past thirty years, only a minor portion went to poor families with children. More than four fifths (81 percent) of the increased social spending of the 1970s and 1980s was targeted on the aged and disabled, "precisely the group that the legislators hoped would benefit," observes social policy analyst Christopher Jencks.

The widespread belief that the antipoverty initiatives of the Great Society were a failure was more than a misreading of the numbers. When it comes to fighting poverty, there is an "abiding national assumption that everything has been tried and nothing has worked," wrote Jason DeParle in *The New York Times.* Actually, the abiding national assumption goes farther: It is that everything that has been tried has made things worse.

Many Americans accepted President Reagan's contention that "we fought a war on poverty and poverty won," despite the facts that

- We won the war against poverty of the aged, which dropped from 35.2 percent in 1956 to 12.2 percent in 1993.
- We shrank the health gap between the haves and the have-nots. In 1965, there were 25 infant deaths per 1,000 live births; in 1995, there were 7.5; the differential between blacks and whites was reduced by half. Before 1965, the poor made 20 percent fewer doctor visits than the rest of the population, although they were much more likely to need medical care. By 1980, income no longer had any effect on the chances that someone who was sick would see a doctor.
- Medicaid, Head Start, nutrition programs, and community health centers dramatically reduced death and suffering in pockets of concentrated poverty. In Beaufort, South Carolina, for example, infant mortality was reduced from 62 per 1,000 births in 1969 to 10 per 1,000. (Community activist William Grant says that in 1969 he showed Senator Ernest F. Hollings and his colleagues "poverty in the raw." When Hollings came back in 1995, extreme poverty was gone, and no one knew of anyone who was going hungry or suffering from worms or other parasites or from the nutrition-related diseases that he showed the Hollings group in 1969.)
- Compensatory education, together with Head Start, began to close some of the gaps between the educational haves and have-nots. Twice as many black and Hispanic children could read proficiently in 1990 as in 1975, and the proportion of seventeen-year-olds with very low reading and math scores has fallen substantially since the early 1970s. The gap between black and white students' proficiency in both reading and math narrowed at each age level between the early 1970s and 1992.
- Head Start changed the face of some of the nation's poorest areas. In Mississippi, for example, parents who had been tenant farmers, sharecroppers, laborers, and domestics were trained to become teachers and administrators. The Head Start experience enabled them and their children to achieve new levels of education and prosperity, and strengthened them in registering to vote without fear of losing their jobs.

I do not cite the success of many of the antipoverty programs of the 1960s to suggest that it was all done right. It wasn't, by a long shot. The investment was never great enough to realize the promises made, and after the first two years funding was severely cut back to finance the escalating Vietnam War. But it was a noble chapter in our history, reflects Hyman Bookbinder, one of its architects, "because the country as a whole, starting with its president, was saying, 'We will not tolerate a situation where the many who are okay say it's not their business to be concerned about those who are not.' " And that is probably its most important legacy. For those of us who were part of the War on Poverty, it represented a shining alternative to social indifference.

Of course it is true that the cornerstone of the Great Society was an economy so robust that it was possible to commit a larger share of prosperity to the public sector without anyone feeling a loss. It is also true that the Economic Opportunity Act was enacted in a climate of confidence in the possibilities of social change. People could imagine an America where poverty would no longer exist.

But because poverty was not defeated, the public began to wonder whether those who remained poor might not be themselves at fault and undeserving of our help. Which brings us to the next question.

How did so many people get stuck in the inner city? Rush Limbaugh says that if you can't make it in America, it's your fault. If he is right, then there is little reason for taxpayers to help those who aren't making it—be it with income support, food stamps, compensatory education, preschool programs, health care, or job training.

Those who believe that the problem of the inner city comes down to poor people having too many children they can't support and don't know how to raise, flouting cherished American values of hard work and responsibility, have reason to be wary of proposals to help—especially with taxpayers' money.

To understand why so many Americans have gotten stuck in concentrated poverty, one has to go back to the years following World War II, when everyone could get good work. Even minorities who were in other ways discriminated against, even recent migrants from the South could get good work. They might lack skills, they might encounter racial slights, but they could support their families. Sylvester Monroe, now with *Time* magazine, whose family was part of the massive black migration north from Mississippi in the 1950s, remembers Chicago as "this land of opportunity, where if you had a strong back and willingness to work, you could make it. There were jobs, jobs, and jobs. And that was the key, that you could get work. And if you could get work, you could make it."

By contrast, the economic growth that occurred after 1973 was a disaster for those at the bottom because it failed to provide jobs for the unskilled that paid enough to support a family. Together, the decline in manufacturing, higher skill requirements for decent jobs, and globalization (meaning that anything can now be made anywhere and sold everywhere) reversed the universal economic progress of earlier decades. Average wages and household incomes dropped, the number of Americans living in poverty increased, the share of national income obtained by the lowest fifth of the population plummeted, the number of persons without health insurance increased, and unemployment among the unskilled exploded.

The days when strong backs and a willingness to work translated into jobs with a living wage were over. "Everything used to be mechanical," says Dennis Walsh, director of training at Swift Textiles in Columbus, Georgia. "If it didn't work you got a bigger hammer." Mechanics who used to lug around a thirty-pound tool belt to manually repair broken machinery now use a hand-sized terminal to diagnose problems on computer-driven equipment. The work that requires little skill is being performed in countries that most of us can't find on a world map.

The economic upheavals have been most disastrous for those with the least education. In the early 1970s, the 2.5 million members of the United Auto Workers and United Steel Workers were earning a good living, although 76 percent had not completed high school. Today, the only young men hired by Ford and GM are engineers or systems analysts. U.S. Steel in Gary, Indiana, hasn't hired anyone from the local high schools in years.

Young families, unskilled workers, and minorities bore the biggest brunt of the economic and technological revolution.

Because economic prospects for the unskilled diminished just as opportunities for those with training expanded, young people of color in a position to do so moved up and out of the ghetto. But the unskilled black males who once needed only to demonstrate their skill and stamina now encountered a labor market that didn't need their ability to do strenuous work. Employers increasingly saw young black males as "uneducated, unstable, uncooperative, and dishonest." Poverty quickly became more concentrated and more persistent. The jobless ghetto of the inner city was being created. Residential segregation and the social disinvestment that accompanies it soon hastened the deterioration of the ghetto.

Heated controversy surrounds efforts to understand these most depleted neighborhoods and the people who live in them. Some see inner-city decay as caused primarily by structural factors: high levels of joblessness, disinvestment, and lack of economic opportunity. Others see the causes as almost entirely psychological and cultural.

The controversy is heated because of its implications for remedies.

If the psychological/cultural school is right, the remedies begin and end with the carrots and sticks that would change the attitudes and behavior of individual inner-city residents. If the economic school is right, the remedies are economic growth and development. A third school regards the interaction of economic and social forces as critical, and would use an array of remedies, including incentives, economic development, job training, better links to jobs, and better preparation for economic opportunity through more effective schools, strengthened families, and more supportive communities.

William Julius Wilson, the sociologist who did more than any other to call attention to the alarming conditions in ghetto neighborhoods, has shown how the sharp increase in joblessness among black males has had a devastating effect on family life in the inner city, as black women have found fewer men likely to be reliable economic providers. Sociologist Elijah Anderson, who spent much of the past twenty years with the residents of a low-income Philadelphia neighborhood, says that many of the young men he got to know don't get married because they feel they can't "play the roles of men in families in the way they would like. . . . To be that upstanding husband and father, you need resources, you need money." He says that the men he interviewed were convinced they couldn't get the family-sustaining jobs. He believes their lack of hope and inability to form a positive view of the future is behind their seeming "lack of responsibility and wantonness," as they seek to prove their manhood through machismo and sexual prowess.

Racial discrimination exacerbates the effects of joblessness, as illuminated by the work of Ron Ferguson of Harvard's Kennedy School of Government. He has documented how black youngsters, especially boys, are warped by the messages that society fears and distrusts them, that society has low expectations of them, and that their parents are powerless. Some youngsters are protected from the full negative impact of these messages by the hope and positive self-image that parents and others instill in them, by being taught enough about racial bias to allow them not to take these messages personally, or by being imbued with a sense of purpose or religious faith. But for those who are not so protected, the separate messages come together into one big message: "You will not find much satisfaction in conventional settings, pursuing conventional goals."

In response, explains Geoffrey Canada in his illuminating book, *fist stick knife gun,* young black males often adopt a "face-saving defensive posture," which includes the determination not to conform, to resist low-wage work, and to adopt an anti-achievement ethic at school. They do not trust teachers, social workers, and other "helping" professionals. They refuse to be part of the system because they feel the system has rejected them.

Elijah Anderson says that many of the children lose interest in attempting to negotiate the mainstream system. They attach enormous value to objects like jackets and sneakers to shore up their identity. They invest in and live by a code of the streets, where they assert themselves and make sure they are granted the deference they feel they deserve.

The higher rates of employment among recent immigrants than among blacks—often cited as evidence that high rates of joblessness among blacks is their own fault—reflect differences in employer perceptions and practices, and in how well the two groups are positioned to take advantage of employment opportunities.

From the perspective of youngsters coming of age in the inner city, individual effort and hard work often seem to go unrewarded, and conventional symbols of success (be they luxury cars, jewelry, or expensive sneakers) seem to be reserved for those with access to illegal means to achieve them. Lack of jobs and opportunity become part of a self-reinforcing causal cycle. They interact to make it less likely that employers will be inclined to hire inner-city young people and that inner-city children will grow up prepared for good jobs.

This picture presented by Wilson and others of life in the jobless ghetto is very unattractive, writes Harvard social critic Nathan Glazer, "even if one understands the forces that have created it." Glazer fears that this unattractive picture could keep the majority of Americans from supporting the remedies that might change the situation. My own view is that understanding the forces that have created the jobless ghetto also makes it possible to intervene constructively, with interventions that impact both opportunity and preparation to take advantage of opportunity.

Which brings us to our last question.

Is systematic social reform actually possible? Doubts about the possibilities of systematic social reform have been around since the French Revolution and have recently reached new heights of popularity.

Charles Murray joins earlier conservatives in seeing reforms as either perverse, because they will backfire and have the opposite of their intended effect, or futile, because they are powerless to alter the natural order of things or because the expansion of any reform will ultimately overwhelm and defeat it.

The obvious conclusion that it is better to leave things alone ignores the possibility of learning from the past and of adapting social policies and programs in the light of new evidence—be it evidence of unanticipated needs or unintended consequences, or of new and better ways of accomplishing common purposes.

In advocating strategies that would actually change lives *and* counter the skepticism about our collective ability to do so, I do not minimize the difficulty of the task.

I believe, just as the conservatives do, that changing life trajectories requires relationships that reach the intimate terrain where teachers, health professionals, child care workers, home visitors, recreation leaders, welfare workers, and community police interact with the children, youth, and families they hope to touch. I agree with Charles Murray that most successful "attempts to solve the problems of the inner city . . . are local, small-scale, initiated and run by dedicated people, and operated idiosyncratically and pragmatically." I further agree that public contexts have, with some notable exceptions, been inhospitable to such programs. But I don't agree that it must be ever thus, that relationships of trust and mutual respect are only possible in nongovernmental settings, financed by charitable donations or governed by market forces. The standardization and rigidity that have characterized publicly financed programs may indeed have made it impossible to deliver effective services, supports, and schooling in the past. But that stifling degree of standardization and rigidity need not be *inherent* in programs operating under public auspices.

"I don't know where this idea has come from," says educator Deborah Meier, "that we can't collectively use our intelligence to create strong and effective public institutions."

I have assembled in this book some of the evidence to show that we can.

And what makes me believe that the evidence will persuade the cynics?

I base my faith on a conviction and a hope:

My conviction is that Americans who still believe that fairness, justice, and opportunity for all will ultimately triumph will join with those who want a workforce that can win the international economic competition. Together they could be a powerful force in support of the changes now needed—once they come to believe that our major helping systems can be made to work.

My hope, and the hope of many portrayed in the following chapters, is that leaders, national and local, will emerge to convey to the American public a new understanding not only about the depth of our disarray and the disasters it portends but also about the remarkable accomplishments we are now capable of because we have so much of the knowledge we need.

This book is intended to assemble some of that knowledge, inspired by the words of Edna St. Vincent Millay:

> Upon this gifted age, in its dark hour,
> Rains from the sky a meteoric shower
> Of facts . . . they lie unquestioned, uncombined.
> Wisdom enough to leech us of our ill
> Is daily spun; but there exists no loom
> To weave it into fabric . . .

One of the most thrilling discoveries in writing this book has been how readily the facts culled from successful experience can be woven into fabric. In going from model to mainstream, across domains and disciplines, the threads become patterns and reinforce one another.

Some of the stories of systems change pioneers will strike the reader as so extraordinary as to raise the question of their larger significance. If it takes a miracle worker to accomplish the needed changes—and it often has—will there be enough miracle workers to bring off miracles in the numbers needed? The answer is that we must learn from the breakthroughs these local heroes have made to establish conditions in which well trained, committed, persevering but otherwise ordinary people can achieve the ends it once took a miracle worker to reach. The systems change pioneers like those carving out new frontiers in any realm, can make it possible for others, in much greater numbers, to follow. Every community in America already offers living proof that individuals of talent are ready, willing, and able to take on the formidable challenges of the years ahead.

The evidence collected in *Common Purpose* shows that the United States is rich in resources, ideas, and even in goodwill. We *can* resolve our most urgent domestic problems. Virtually all the elements that are part of the solution can be identified and described; they are a reality today, somewhere in this country. Taken to scale, these elements could be combined into a powerful Public Purpose Sector.

Combining the best in our public and private sectors, the experiences assembled in this book point the way to the strategies that utilize our individual and collective strengths at the national, state, and local levels. The experiences assembled in this book show it is possible to strengthen families and neighborhoods to improve the prospects of all Americans, especially our children. The experiences assembled in this book show how all Americans can join to restore our trust in one another and in our institutions, and to heal the rifts that threaten our life together as a nation. They show that we have a Common Purpose and that our Common Purpose can be realized.

Part I

Spreading and Sustaining Success

In the next five chapters, we will see that it is possible
to spread and sustain what works. We will see examples
of new approaches to replication, tamed bureaucracies,
the shift to results-based accountability, and efforts to
expand our understanding of what works and why. We
will see how citizens, practitioners, administrators, and
legislators have created environments that allow effective
interventions to flourish.

1

What Works and Why We Have So Little of It

IT WAS A FRONT-PAGE STORY in *The New York Times:* A "one million dollar experiment" had produced "some of the most remarkable results for poor youths since the test runs for Head Start." A follow-up editorial cited rigorously documented statistics showing that "careful investments in disadvantaged youths can work."

What caused the stir this time was the Quantum Opportunities Program (QOP), financed by the Ford Foundation. Over a period of four years it had provided randomly selected high-risk youth with all the mentoring, caring, and nurturing that are known to help. The results? In each of four cities, significantly more participants ended up graduating from high school, avoiding teenage pregnancy, and not in trouble with the law than a control group who didn't get the intervention. In one city, the QOP group had one fifth as many high school dropouts as the control group and three times as many youngsters in college. In another, only 7 percent of the participants had babies as teenagers; the control group, over four times as many.

We read the good news, rejoice that something works to change outcomes we had heard were intractable, and shake our heads because the interventions that work seem to touch so few and are rarely heard of again.

The flicker of hope generated by the school, the program, the miracle worker singled out for having heroically changed lives remains just a flicker. Neighborhoods don't become more peaceful. Juvenile violence and idleness don't diminish. Single-parent families continue to form. The successes remain isolated if they remain at all.

We know that isolated successes are no match for the powerful forces that are destroying children, families, and neighborhoods, but we don't seem to be able to get beyond the isolated successes.

In my previous book, *Within Our Reach,* I described a pilot nurse home-visiting program for high-risk babies and their mothers in Elmira, New York. It had succeeded in reducing prematurity, child abuse, and accidents among the babies, and subsequent pregnancies and welfare dependence among the mothers. A careful evaluation had made clear that the intensiveness of the intervention was key to its success. The relationship between mother and nurse began during pregnancy and continued until the baby was two years old. Home visits were frequent and lasted long enough to allow time to address not only the nurse's but the young mother's agenda.

Nevertheless, on the day the program went from university-sponsored demonstration to Medicaid-funded health department program, the nurses' caseloads were doubled, the duration of their visits curtailed, and families dropped from the rolls when the baby was four months old. Public health administrators felt that with limited funds they had to spread the benefits of home visiting as widely as possible. Since funds for evaluation were also eliminated, no one knew for sure how the dilution had affected outcomes. But all the nurses in the original program left, convinced by their own experience and available research that the watered-down program could not achieve its intended purposes.

In *Within Our Reach,* I also described the South Carolina Resource Mothers Program providing supportive prenatal care to high-risk pregnant teenagers. It was a pilot program operated in three South Carolina counties under the auspices of the Medical University of South Carolina. Its success was documented by a significant reduction in babies born at low birth weight. When it went from pilot project to large-scale service program, the effective pilot became ineffective. The scale-up to sixteen counties by the state health department was implemented over the next three years with larger caseloads, fewer visits, shorter client contact, less linkage with the community, less training, and less intensity. An extensive follow-up found the scaled-up program had had no impact on the incidence of low birth weight.

If we are to move beyond discovering one isolated success after another, only to abandon it, dilute it, or dismember it before it can reach more than a few, we must identify the forces that make it so hard for success to survive.

We begin that exploration with an examination of exactly what makes for successful interventions—the Seven Attributes of Highly Effective Programs.

1. *Successful programs are comprehensive, flexible, responsive, and persevering.* As I have traveled the country, describing my findings about the distinctive attributes of programs that work, I often found myself quoting Sister Mary Paul, the diminutive nun who ministers to the families of Sunset Park in Brooklyn. She says that in her program, "No one ever says, this may be what you need, but it's not part of my job to help you get it." That struck me as the key, not only to her success but the success of many others. That simple statement of a flexible, unbureaucratic approach characterized what I had observed in dozens of effective programs. When I repeat Sister Mary Paul's words in lectures, people often come up to tell me their own stories showing that this broadly responsive attitude has been the key to *their* successes or, conversely, they tell me that they recognize their inability to adopt this stance as the biggest reason for their failure.

In auspices and origin, Sister Mary Paul's Brooklyn program couldn't be more different from the Quantum Opportunities Program that caught *The New York Times*'s attention. But its success is built on similar foundations.

Like Sister Mary Paul, QOP found that it takes not just services but "caring, compassion, and especially patience" to change lives. The staff's persistence, dogged determination, and commitment to stay with the youngsters, no matter what, was crucial. In the words of one QOP worker, "These youngsters were permitted to get away with nothing, but nothing they could do would be bad enough to be expelled from the program." The young people came to feel they belonged to an extended family whose sole purpose was to nurture their success. As one of the participants put it, "With an entire support system rooting for our success, it was more difficult to give up." Program administrators willing to go the extra mile could motivate youngsters to go the extra mile, too.

Successful programs, such as Sister Mary Paul's and the Quantum Opportunities Program, respond not with a fistful of referral slips or phone numbers. Rather their front-line staff are able to exercise enough discretion so they can help people get what they need when they need it.

A new breed of worker in an experimental Oregon program helping former welfare recipients to remain self-sufficient may, on a typical day, "counsel a depressed client about a deteriorating relationship with a boyfriend; find a tutoring program for a client's child who is failing in school; help a recently unemployed participant look for a job."

Successful programs do not, in fact, provide everything to everyone, but they are all flexible in offering more than a single strand of service or support. Prenatal-care outreach workers help find housing for a family when they discover that a pregnant woman is threatened with eviction. The effective early childhood program finds a way to respond to the sudden revelation of a parent's drug problem.

The staff in successful programs take on an extended role in the lives of the children and families they work with. They think beyond professional services and help families to strengthen bonds with neighbors and churches and other natural networks of support. They respond to the needs of families at places and times that make sense to the family—often at home, at school, or in neighborhood centers and at odd hours—rather than offering help only in places that may be convenient for agency staff but are far removed geographically and psychologically from those who use them. Many of these programs make sure that staff members are available twenty-four hours a day so that family members have some place to turn in a time of crisis.

Many successful programs provide their front-line staffs with a pool of flexible funds that they can use at their discretion to help a family buy a wheelchair or a washing machine or to get the car repaired.

Staff in successful programs persevere, even when progress is slow or unsteady. They know that child care arrangements can fall apart; the first job placement may not last; there are many hoops to jump through before referral to a specialist actually solves a problem.

In their responsiveness and willingness to hang in there, effective programs are more like families than bureaucracies. You don't lose your "eligibility" at a family support center. The welfare-to-work program Cleveland Works says, "We will be there for our clients forever," unlike most training and employment agencies, which stop at training and placing a client, even though a high proportion of first jobs end within six months.

Five pioneering state agencies that undertook successful child-health initiatives all emphasized the importance of persistence in working with families distrustful of the existing service system. All told of continuing to make home visits until rapport with the family was finally achieved, opening the way to a relationship crucial in motivating family change.

2. *Successful programs see children in the context of their families.*

They know that strong families are the key to healthy children, so they work with two and often three generations in a household. Head Start programs and family support centers echo the thought expressed by Gilda Ferguson, the director of Family Focus in Chicago's North Lawndale neighborhood: "We nurture parents so they can nurture their children."

These programs focus on family strengths but recognize that frequently, intensive individual treatment may be necessary to deal with serious problems, including substance abuse and mental illness.

Effective programs, whether they work primarily with children or adults, are alert to the family context. They are aware that whether children's emotional and intellectual needs will be met usually depends on their parents coping abilities, mental health, and social and economic resources. They know a hungry child may mean there is trouble at home; a depressed parent makes them think about what is happening to the children.

Schools increasingly recognize the need for deeper parent involvement. They are aware that enlisting the overwhelmed and overstressed parents of today as collaborators requires more skill and ingenuity than ever before. In many communities the new partnership transforms schools into community centers. In others, schools join forces with community institutions to help strengthen families— be it through family support services, school-based health or social services, the child welfare system, or churches. Successful programs, then, do not substitute for strong families, but they have the ability to support families' capacities to raise strong children.

3. *Successful programs deal with families as parts of neighborhoods and communities.* Successful programs grow deep roots in the community and respond to the needs identified by the community. One of the most difficult lessons for policy makers to learn is that most successful interventions cannot be imposed from without. There is no simple model that can just be "parachuted" in. Rather, successful programs are shaped to respond to the needs of local populations and to assure that local communities have a genuine sense of ownership.

The Council of State Policy and Planning Agencies, conducting field research into "best practices" in antipoverty programs, "peeled away the layers of the onion, asking why some programs worked and others did not." The working group found very little that held true regardless of context. At their core, "Successful programs recognize and respond to the needs of the community; they reflect the character of its people; . . . they build capacity in people and in neighborhoods. . . ." The council concluded that " 'best practices' are whatever works in a given context."

Being community-based means more than being located in the neighborhood. Increasingly, successful programs are not just *in* but *of* the community. Even programs that see themselves as primarily providing services mobilize community members to participate as more than clients. The Children at Risk substance abuse prevention project attributes much of its success to the fact that each of its six sites has produced its own version of the program, "drawing on its own history, perspectives, and resources."

Successful service programs take into account the real world of those they serve. As part of the community, practitioners recognize the many problems that are rooted in a lack of resources or supports rather than a "client's pathology."

Staff of a preschool center where children are routinely exposed to neighborhood violence see the children's fear as presenting both internal and external problems. They may organize a neighborhood safe zone, in addition to providing counseling to the children and their parents.

4. *Successful programs have a long-term, preventive orientation, a clear mission, and continue to evolve over time.* Many programs are successful because they attack the preventable risk factors that occur at an early age and are implicated in later "rotten outcomes" of too early childbearing, school failure, and delinquency. That's why many successful programs focus on the period from pregnancy through elementary school as the most productive time to intervene, and why the programs that work with young adults in difficulty also try to work with their children.

Successful programs create an organizational culture that is outcome oriented rather than rulebound. They combine a highly flexible mode of operation with a clear sense of mission, which everyone associated with the organization can articulate in simple terms. Like the successful corporations described in Peters and Waterman's *In Search of Excellence,* they are "tight" about their mission and simultaneously "loose" about how the mission is carried out. They don't abandon their fundamental mission for the fad of the moment. Successful schools, for example, do not simply pile each new reform one upon the other but build a sense of shared purpose and values to create a compelling ethos.

Those responsible for these programs have no illusion that they can implement the perfect model program—at once or ever. The programs evolve in response to the changing needs of individuals, families, and community, and to feedback from both front-line staff and participants. Because so many of these programs operate in areas where there is little scientific certainty, it is particularly important that they be able to continue evolving, learning from their successes and failures, and finding new and better ways to achieve their goals.

They maintain a stable core because they share common beliefs based on research, theory, and experience. They hold their goals steady but adapt their strategies to reach those goals. This often requires a program to expand its reach beyond the provision of services. When a program finds it is futile to do parent education with mothers who can't provide their children with a safe place to crawl, explore, or sleep, or that housing and public safety issues must be addressed before family support services begin to have an impact, it often finds itself catapulted into helping "clients" to become activists to change the conditions in which they live.

5. *Successful programs are well managed by competent and committed individuals with clearly identifiable skills.* Managers of successful programs don't do it by magic or charisma but by using identifiable management techniques to create a coherent, outcome-oriented organizational culture. They inspire their staffs with a shared view of the validity and value of the organization's principal goals and tasks.

The widespread belief that behind every successful program is a miracle worker—a leader of such charismatic power that there are no more than a handful of such magical persons to be found in the land—is not borne out by the evidence. It is true that miracle workers are often the only ones who can overcome the most formidable systems obstacles, especially in jurisdictions and domains where it's never been done before. But as experience with slaying the systems dragons accumulates, those skills, too, can be taught. Many successful initiatives have found that when their mission is inspiring, they are able to attract people with the courage, ingenuity, and skills the jobs call for.

It is also significant that leaders of prize-winning public programs have many skills in common that are not mysterious and can be learned. These include the willingness to experiment and take risks; to manage by "groping along"; to tolerate ambiguity; to win the trust simultaneously of line workers, politicians, and the public; to respond to demands for prompt, tangible evidence of results; to be collaborative in working with staff; and to allow staff discretion at the front lines.

Managers of successful programs create supportive settings stable enough to permit staff to learn from the latest research—and from their own mistakes. Front-line workers in these programs receive the same respect, nurturing, and support from their managers that they are expected to extend to those they serve.

6. *Staffs of successful programs are trained and supported to provide high-quality, responsive services.* Effective programs are aware that the greater discretion given to front-line staff, the greater the importance of excellent training, monitoring, and supervision—to ensure that the discretion is exercised in keeping with mission goals and high standards of quality.

The importance of competence and quality among staff and institutional settings is so obvious as to be sometimes overlooked. Successful programs recognize that competence and quality are the crux of effective services. Versatility and flexibility build on competence; they are not a substitute for it. While a pregnant teenager who is poor, frightened, depressed, perhaps addicted, and possibly homeless requires much more than conventional obstetrical care to have a healthy baby, she does need care of high quality. No matter how alert to the patient's larger environment, the nurse-midwife cannot produce good outcomes if she has three times as many patients as she can handle and if she cannot call on a competent obstetrician when she is faced with a pregnancy or delivery beyond her capacity.

7. *Successful programs operate in settings that encourage practitioners to build strong relationships based on mutual trust and respect.* It is the quality of these relationships that most profoundly differentiates effective from ineffective programs and institutions. But life-transforming relationships do not exist in a vacuum—they must be sustained by supportive institutions.

Reports on successful change efforts from every domain—from prenatal care to early child development, from elementary schooling to school-to-work transitions, from child protection to welfare-to-work efforts—find a special kind of relationship to be at the core.

At Last Chance Ranch, where Florida's most serious juvenile offenders are rehabilitated in record-setting numbers, Philip Adams, the man in charge, says relationships are at the heart of his success. "I believe in discipline, I believe in kids doing exactly what I tell them to do. But what changes kids, what makes them act the right way when I'm not around, is that I love them, and they know that I love them, and they know that I care about them. If those kids can respect me and my set of values, and adopt those values as their own, then they're going to do what's right when nobody's around."

Karen Pittman, one of the nation's leading youth development advocates, says that many years ago, when she began looking for successful pregnancy prevention programs on behalf of the Children's Defense Fund, she would often stumble onto dropout prevention programs and delinquency prevention programs. She soon realized that all of the apparently successful efforts were doing much the same thing, regardless of the disaster they were funded to prevent. But what was most striking, she said, was that caring and relationships seemed to be the most important aspects of the programs—although rarely explicitly stated.

The National Academy of Science's Panel on High Risk Youth surveyed programs that had been effective with adolescents growing up in high-risk environments. It found that the opportunity to develop sustained, trusting relationships with caring adults was central to their effectiveness. Psychiatrist and school reformer James Comer says that relationship issues are particularly important among low-income people who have given up on helping systems.

Ron Ferguson of Harvard's Kennedy School of Government, who has studied a wide variety of efforts to improve the prospects of minority youth, concluded that "to incur the costs and take the risks that pursuing conventional success may require," minority adolescents need a close relationship with an adult who combines caring about him or her with being an effective confidant, guide, broker, advocate, and disciplinarian. Caring relationships are critical to efforts to change life trajectories because they compensate, in some degree, for lost affiliation and influence with the old peer group.

A study of Head Start concluded that a critical factor in its success is that "Head Start staff enter into a compassionate partnership with each Head Start parent to shape the future of their Head Start child." Case managers find that families known to an alphabet soup of agencies remain unhelped until someone finally is there long enough and is close enough and persevering enough to forge the kind of authentic relationship that helps to turn lives around.

An extensive study of effective schools by Stanford researcher Milbrey McLaughlin found that teachers' ability to connect with their students' families and life outside of school mattered more than any other single factor in students' willingness to work hard toward academic goals and in improving student achievement. (A fourth grader told University of North Carolina researchers, "If a teacher doesn't care about you, it affects your mind. You feel like you're nobody and it makes you want to drop out of school.")

Smallness of scale at the point where professionals interact with their pupils or clients or participants helps a lot. Large schools, large classes, massive outpatient clinics, and large caseloads vastly complicate the job of personalizing interventions. Phil Adams says about Last Chance Ranch that not having more than twenty youngsters there at any one time is crucial to his success in rehabilitating juvenile offenders.

Settings that encourage trusting relationships provide a warm, welcoming climate that conveys a sense of safety and security. Successful programs are not "lean and mean," although clear rules and discipline provide predictability often missing in the lives of high-risk young people.

In view of the growing interest in mentoring and other supports and services provided by nonprofessionals, it is striking how many of the characteristics of effective professional practice also apply to the involvement of volunteers. Extensive and systematic studies have now shown effective mentors and volunteers are not free-lancers who bypass all the structural impediments that have made it difficult to provide effective services in formal systems. Quite the contrary, they too are dependent on supportive structures to be effective. "You can't turn volunteers and kids loose, and hope for the best," says Marjorie Wilkes of New York Mentoring. "It's plain unrealistic to assume mentoring is easy, or that you can do it on the cheap." The strongest conclusion of a synthesis of seven years of research on mentoring was that effective mentoring requires program structures that support mentors in their efforts to build trust and develop positive relationships with youth. "Most volunteers and youth cannot be simply matched and then left to their own devices." Programs must provide the infrastructure—including screening, training, and ongoing supervision—to foster the development of effective relationships.

A New Practice and a New Practitioner?

In talking with researchers and practitioners about the importance of relationships, I have concluded that I have been observing the evolution of a new form of professional practice, often at odds with more conventional ways of working.

The new practice has emerged, more pragmatically than ideologically, from many disciplinary origins, often in opposition to professional traditions. The touchstones of the new practice are new professional skills, new professional norms, new power relationships, and a new mind-set about what it means to be a professional. Far from "coddling" their clients, which worries conservative politicians, the new professionals aim, quite consciously, to strengthen the ability of clients, students, young people, and families to make the journey toward independence and to take greater control over their own and their children's lives. To this end, practitioners elicit client strengths and assets rather than pathology.

The family support movement has been one impetus behind the development of a new relationship between helper and helped, encouraging transactions that become "a problem-solving exchange between mutually respecting persons."

The same evolution in professional practice is now occurring in many different contexts. In his study of efforts to debureaucratize special education in Madison, Wisconsin, law professor Joel Handler found that the most profound change occurred in professional norms. "The professional task was redefined. . . . Parents were seen as part of the solution rather than the problem. Everyone . . . could comfortably concede to the views of the other, confident that the matter was still open for renegotiation." Teachers, students, and parents were working together to achieve shared goals.

Homebuilders, which shaped early family-preservation initiatives, is another source for the new form of practice, for redefining the meaning of professionalism, and for encouraging staff to "push the boundaries of their job description." At a Homebuilders staff meeting I attended, a therapist told of appearing at the front door of a family in crisis, to be greeted by a mother's declaration that the one thing she didn't need in her life was one more social worker telling her what to do. What she needed, she said, was to get her house cleaned up. The Homebuilders therapist, with her special training and mind-set, responded by asking the mother if she wanted to start with the kitchen. After working together for an hour, the two women were able to talk about the out-of-control teenager who had set off the family's difficulty. It was an unorthodox way of forging what the mental health professionals call a therapeutic alliance, but it worked!

The new collaboration with families is authentic, reflecting the readiness of the professional to attribute expertise to the family. MIT organizational theorist Don Schön finds that the new practitioners' collaborative stance involves a willingness on occasion to be uncertain about what to do, as well as looking for the strategic moment "to act on their own sense of what needs to be done." Having studied social work practice in several societies, including the U.S. and Israel, Schön says this represents a major departure from traditional social workers, who listen "in such a way as to mold what clients say to fit pre-existing categories," disregarding the messages that do not fit these categories on the explicit or implicit premise that they know what is best for the client. The new practitioners are driven by their commitment to making a difference in the lives of the families they serve, although their professional training would dictate a more judgmental, distanced posture.

It is striking how often effective practice is characterized precisely by how it departs from traditional norms about what is considered "professional." Shawn Satterfield, seventeen, says that what was special about Project Roadmap in Baltimore, and why it worked for him when previous interventions had not, was that in other programs "they never put their personal feelings in it; it was just like a nine to five type thing." At Project Roadmap, it seemed that everyone wanted to help. "These people . . . they care and they deliver . . . they are in it with their heart."

Dorothy Stoneman, founder of YouthBuild (whom we meet at greater length in the next chapter), says that YouthBuild encourages staff to go to funerals and hospitals, to give out their phone numbers, and to be on call twenty-four hours a day. But Stoneman says that staff never forget that "these young people are not our children, and we can't treat them as if they were and will be our children until the day we die." She says that because participants need to become independent, "we have to say, 'Do it, I'm your counsellor. I care very much about you, but I won't be able to be your mother. But you will be able to create the family of your dreams as an adult when you choose to make a commitment of your own.' "

An early YouthBuild evaluation stressed the importance of achieving balance between developing the relationships that establish trust and challenging youth to perform. "When staff simply do what they are paid to do, trainees remain agnostic or negative concerning whether the staff really care . . . and can be trusted not to betray or to abandon them." Trainees learn to trust when they see staff going above and beyond the call of duty. A YouthBuild staff member cites an example from the first week of orientation, when the three-month-old brother of a trainee died. "The family knew nothing about arranging a funeral—who to call, where to get flowers, any of that. Three of us [teachers] got together and made the telephone calls, and we helped the family make the other arrangements. I mean, you would have thought that it was our family that had a death."

Such an obvious show of caring is an important signal to participants that this time it will be different from previous experiences characterized by excessive formality and social distance. Positive outcomes seem to be greatest, the YouthBuild evaluators found, when these trusting relationships were used to help young people "to find conventional goals that have moral legitimacy and to find moral legitimacy in conventional goals," and when they were used to push youth to perform, observe the rules, and persevere.

These are obviously tricky waters. The balance between being supportive and being challenging, between providing security and new worlds to master, between building on family strengths without forgetting that family pathology also requires a competent response, is hard to achieve and maintain. So it is not surprising that many effective programs report that to achieve this balance, they pay careful attention in recruitment to personal characteristics and relevant life experience as well as formal education.

The new practitioner, then, especially in working with populations that have been disconnected from the supports traditionally provided by families and neighbors, is able to help reduce dependency and strengthen families by adopting a new, empowering, and collaborative mode of professional practice.

In no sense do these new professionals operate under norms where anything goes if it feels right. Their skills include a rigorous understanding of the theory that underlies practice. The new practitioners operate within the boundaries of well-developed theory about effective practice, while pushing the constraints imposed by job descriptions and bureaucracies.

A Spiritual Dimension?

A growing number of observers and people at the front lines are calling attention to a spiritual dimension to the relationships that seem to foster change.

In Opportunity to Succeed, a program for drug abusers discharged from prison run by the Center on Addiction and Substance Abuse (CASA), participants say that recovery would be impossible without their religious faith. "We need spirituality in order to begin to develop that trust in another human being or that higher power," says one participant. "There's got to be something greater than me to guide me to be more constructive and productive," says another. Joe Califano, a lifelong liberal Democrat and CASA's founder and president, recognizes that religion and spirituality are often an important part of successful drug abuse treatment, and defends the use of public funds in the Opportunity to Succeed program. "It has nothing to do with separation of church and state. . . . I think we ought to fund programs that help people get better, and if God is involved in those programs, we shouldn't recoil . . . and say, 'Oh my God, we can't put any federal funds into this.' "

Frank Farrow, of the respected mainstream Center for the Study of Social Policy, says that many new neighborhood-based service reforms are incorporating a spiritual approach to helping in a way that traditional social services have avoided. He believes that by addressing the spiritual aspects of an individual's experience, these efforts—some under public auspices that have contracted with faith-based neighborhood agencies—are showing they can be an important key to change.

Robert L. Woodson, founder and president of the National Center for Neighborhood Enterprise, takes this point further. He says that because social workers are trained not to get emotionally involved and to "always remain in charge," the kind of healing relationships that make a real difference in people's lives can occur *only* in settings with a spiritual or religious base and a "leader with a strong element of spirituality." As evidence of the need for a spiritual foundation, Woodson quotes a young man describing his relationship with Philadelphia's Sister Fatah: "She was always available for me—for family funerals, when my mother was sick, on a Friday night at ten o'clock when I was feeling frustrated . . . even when I rejected her she didn't reject me."

The importance of going to funerals and persevering in the face of rejection seems to be agreed upon. The difference is that Woodson ascribes to the spiritual auspice what others think of as the new professional practice. Philosopher Michael Sandel suggests that conservatives may turn away from the idea of redemption through secular means because they believe that absent an appeal to spiritual and religious precepts, there would be little hope of teaching ghetto youths to abstain from sex, drugs, and violence. He cites conservative academic Glenn Loury's observation that "successful efforts at reconstruction in ghetto communities invariably reveal a religious institution, or set of devout believers, at the center of the effort."

Often, perhaps, but not invariably. When Cokie Roberts interviewed Eva Oliver in Baton Rouge for the Christmas Day, 1994, *This Week with David Brinkley* television show, the former welfare recipient told of how proud she was to be earning good money as a mechanic first class. "I weld, I pipefit, I fix pumps, I break lines. And it just makes you feel great. It gives you your pride and your dignity back." Oliver explained that many earlier attempts to acquire the skills that would allow her to leave welfare had failed, but that at last she had found a program that worked. It worked, she told Roberts, because "the staff gave us a lot of love. They made you believe in yourself. It was a time of learning and a time of healing."

In a subsequent conversation with Cokie Roberts, I speculated with her as to what kind of job training agency it might have been that was remembered by a client as providing love and healing. Roberts thought that perhaps it had been "the nuns down there in Baton Rouge." We were equally surprised when, after some further checking, I found that it was not some obscure, faith-based agency that was responsible for the love and healing, but the Building and Industrial Trades Training Program of the Louisiana Governor's Office of Women's Services.

My own conclusion, after reviewing available evidence, is that it may be easier to establish strong relationships in settings with a spiritual or religious foundation than in secular settings, but faith-based auspices are not the only ones that can cultivate transformative relationships. Even in highly secular Los Angeles County, there are probation officers who are regarded by their former probationers as the fathers they never had, and who speak of their own personal journeys as the basis for believing in the possibility of redemption.

Unquestionably, the sense of being part of a movement that transcends the individual's material needs contributes to success. This is particularly true, as the hardheaded evaluators at Public/Private Ventures note, when the movement springs from "religious, political, ideological, ethnic, or other deep-seated forces, themselves rooted in some larger underlying concept."

Paul Light of the Pew Charitable Trusts, in his review of innovating organizations, concluded that one "cannot underestimate the importance of faith as a core value," providing the extra element that makes it possible to persevere in the face of the stress and uncertainty and to overcome the "disappointments involved in pressing against the prevailing wisdom of the public good." This faith, Light found, may be "rooted in formal religion, culture, one's own vision of a just society, or simply confidence in human capacity."

A compelling ethos that can rival that of a spiritual or religious auspice can be created by organizations with a strong commitment to other ideals that provide shared meaning and purpose. Many of the national and community service efforts, such as City Year and others operating with support from AmeriCorps, are examples. Organizations that support the new practitioner, that are shaped by a well-defined sense of mission, and that advocate practical steps to idealistic goals are showing that secular organizations can have transformative effects.

If the Seven Attributes of Highly Effective Programs Are So Great, Why Are They So Scarce?

The attributes of success that I have described, now widely agreed upon and supported by theory, a convergent body of research, and front-line experience in many different disciplines, are not counterintuitive or surprising. Practitioners know that effective programs are characterized by flexibility, comprehensiveness, responsiveness, front-line discretion, high standards of quality and good management, a family focus, community rootedness, a clear mission, and respectful, trusting relationships. This is the stuff that people on the front lines know works—the stuff they know is important, and the stuff that many fight to sustain amid pressures designed to move them in exactly the opposite direction.

Marc Tucker of the National Center on Education and the Economy says, "When you find an individual school that works, it's almost always because it's running against the grain. You find a teacher or a principal who really doesn't give a damn about the system. They are willing to ignore or subvert every rule in the book in order to get the job done for the kids." A retired administrator of the New York City school system reached the same conclusion after a meeting with ten principals who had been given outside recognition for their achievements. All said that they had succeeded because they had "beaten the system"—that is, broken the board of education's rules.

You can hear the same thing from child protection workers, staffs of job training programs, and every other kind of human-services provider.

It is now absolutely clear that the attributes of effective programs are undermined by their systems' surroundings, especially when they attempt to expand to reach large numbers.

The mismatch between the attributes of effective programs and the imperatives of prevailing systems is what stands in the way of successful demonstrations becoming part of the mainstream. It is what stands in the way of reaching millions with what has proved to work with hundreds. Unless we come to grips with this mismatch, successful models will continue to flourish briefly and then disappear or be diluted or dissected when special funding and special political protection end, or when the initiatives can no longer find leaders who are both wizard and saint.

This is the great hidden paradox. Agreement around the elements of successful programs has grown, and yet policy and practice have not recognized how poorly matched are the attributes of effectiveness and the requirements of institutions and systems within which programs must operate if they are to reach millions instead of hundreds. We have not acknowledged that the attributes of effectiveness are consistently undermined by the institutions and systems on which they depend for funding and legitimation. And, because this mismatch has gone unrecognized, people continue to be surprised that wonderful programs, having demonstrated their achievements, rarely become part of mainstream systems. Thus, the nation's rich body of knowledge about improving the life prospects of disadvantaged children remains largely unutilized.

The history of efforts to replicate, sustain, and scale up from effective programs is dismal. The single most important reason, in my view, is the failure to understand that the environment within which these programs have to operate, and which these programs depend on for long-term funding, skilled professionals, and public support, is profoundly out of sync with the key attributes of success. Scaling up effective services requires conditions that are still exceedingly rare.

That is why effective programs have flourished only under some form of protective bubble, outside or at the margins of large public systems. Protective bubbles can be created by foundation funding, by a powerful political figure, by a leader who is a wizard, by promises that the effort will be limited in scale and time, or by some combination of all of these. The problems arise when the successful pilot program is to expand and thereby threatens the basic political and bureaucratic arrangements that have held sway over the decades.

When the model is expected to become the norm, it can no longer evade the barriers of traditional financing, accountability, governance, and public perception. Failure to recognize this fact has seriously impeded efforts to scale up. When effective programs aiming to reach large numbers encounter the pressures exercised by prevailing attitudes and systems, the resulting collision is almost always lethal to the effective programs. Their demise can be prevented only by changing systems and public perceptions to make them more hospitable to effective efforts to change lives and communities.

Otherwise we will continue to experience the familiar story of pilot programs found effective enough to be considered worthy of large-scale implementation within mainstream systems with public funding, only to be diluted into ineffectiveness. Many, perhaps most local programs figured out long ago what it takes to provide effective services, but that knowledge does nothing for them if they are prevented from doing what it takes by inadequate funding, rigid rules, hierarchical management techniques, and other constraints.

Unless there is a protector on the scene providing a buffer against systems pressures, especially at a time of massive funding cutbacks and a tendency to demonize the people who need help, effective programs cannot be sustained.

A Maryland boot camp offering intensive rehabilitation to juvenile offenders that had been universally considered successful was closed in 1996. According to a state official, Maryland's juvenile services was looking for places to cut back, having lost $10 million of federal aid in the previous two years, and this program "stood out in terms of cost." Ignoring the studies showing that the intensity of the program, including follow-up mentoring and monitoring, was responsible for its success, negotiations were underway to replace the program with a less expensive version—shorter stays, more beds, fewer staff, and less follow-up support.

The state's secretary of juvenile justice invoked the funding crisis as the reason for the closing, stating, "We have to drive a Chevrolet instead of an Oldsmobile."

He missed the point. You can get where you're going driving either a Chevy or an Oldsmobile. You can't get where you're going in a youth program divested of the attributes that made it effective.

Allowing Success to Survive

If the successes of the past and present that flourished as demonstration programs depended on the protection of philanthropies, godfathers, and miracle workers, and if prevailing methods of financing, regulation, management, and assessment undermine a successful program's ability to operate in the mainstream, what is to be done?

We must now extract from our successes the lessons that will show us how to support the attributes of effectiveness wherever they are needed—in schools, child protection, juvenile justice, welfare-to-work, school-to-work, drug treatment, child care, mentoring, family support, and community building—so that our systems will no longer subvert our best efforts to improve outcomes for children, families, and neighborhoods.

The following chapters are an attempt to do that. They identify the fundamental changes that must be made, and set forth the evidence showing that they can be made. They show that somewhere in this country they are, in fact, being made. The attributes of effectiveness described in this chapter are being spread and sustained. The stories of new approaches to replication, to bureaucracy, to accountability and evaluation are stories of systems being changed to reverse unacceptable rates of youth crime, childbearing by single mothers, school failure, youth idleness, long-term welfare dependence, and the growing polarization of our society.

2

Spreading What Works Beyond the Hothouse

THE NINE OUTLETS that made up the McDonald's fast-food chain when Ray Kroc took over as franchising agent in 1954 had become 18,400 in ninety countries some forty years later. Kroc "achieved wealth beyond his wildest dreams," and McDonald's became a symbol, like the Model T Ford, of American ingenuity, based on finding a winning model and making sure it's copied faithfully. The key to Kroc's success, David Halberstam explains in his memoir of the fifties, was that once he discovered McDonald's, he immediately understood that he had to set clear standards and impose his will on independent owners. Kroc told the McDonald brothers, founders of the enterprise, that in franchising you cannot trust "people who are nonconformists, you cannot give them an inch. . . . The organization cannot trust the individual; the individual must trust the organization."

The early McDonald's handbook stipulated that the McDonald's hamburger would cost 15 cents and contain a patty 3 and 5/8 inches in diameter of commercial-grade ground chuck weighing 1.6 ounces, to be served with a quarter ounce of onion, a teaspoon of mustard, a tablespoon of ketchup, and a pickle one inch in diameter. Kroc didn't allow McDonald's to serve hot dogs because "people were determined to have hot dogs their own way." The hamburger, by contrast, could and would be assembled on Kroc's terms, so that a hamburger in California would be an advertisement for one in Chicago or New York.

Peter Drucker, the management guru, explains that with the franchise model, there's nothing to be done but to follow clear instructions. "It doesn't require any training. It requires a checklist. It enables incompetents to do a first-class job. You use human beings as robots. . . . Not only do you not expect them to handle unexpected situations, you don't want them to."

Much of what we revere in this country's past tells the same glorious story. You find what works—to feed American families, transport them, or cure their pneumonia. You standardize it and replicate it widely and faithfully—improving the lives of millions, the entrepreneurs' most of all.

So it should come as no surprise that there is a great yearning to follow a similarly straightforward path to meet the nation's other needs: Identify what works, define it clearly, and the rest comes down to communication, persuasion, and the right incentives.

Indeed, in the loftiest realms of academe, the word goes out to gather great minds to solve the replication problem. A memo circulated around Harvard University urged the Children's Initiative of the American Academy of Arts and Sciences to "find ways to mass produce the delivery of health and human services to children and those who care about them." It argued that as "Henry Ford made it possible for all of us to have an automobile by creating interchangeable parts and interchangeable production," so in human services must access be expanded by faithful replication so that "variance in the product or service" will be reduced, and delivery personnel will require "less extensive knowledge and skill."

The task, then, would seem to be to find the schools that work and replicate them, the job training programs that work and replicate them, the child abuse prevention programs that work and replicate them.

But is it really that simple? President Clinton frequently points out, "You can find virtually every problem in our country solved by somebody somewhere in an astonishingly effective fashion. . . . The challenge for us is to figure out how to replicate that. . . ."

The day before his first inauguration, Clinton told the nation's governors that his number-one disappointment as governor had been that it was so hard to "take something that works to the next level." He said he "could never figure out a way to make the exception the rule, and that is our enduring problem in America in public life."

The president's interest in replication even surfaces in *Primary Colors*, the fictionalized portrayal of the 1992 Clinton campaign. After hearing the candidate's description of his visit to a widely praised adult literacy program in New York's Harlem, the candidate's wife explains to their traveling companions that they often argue about how to spread social programs. "He's a sucker for inspirational leaders. He figures you can parse genius, analyze it, break it down and teach others how to do it. My feeling is . . . you can't teach inspiration. What you do is come up with a curriculum. Something simple, direct. Something you don't need Mother Teresa to make happen—and that's what you replicate."

The governor counters, "But you can't sell anything if the teacher is a dud. You've gotta figure out a way to make great teachers. If you can really liberate them, reward them for creativity, they'll make their own programs."

Both the fictional governor and the real president are on to something important. How do you spread what works? How do you convert the innovative exception into the prevailing rule?

The problem is not that success in education and human services can't be built upon to reach millions rather than hundreds, but that we have been very late recognizing that the McDonald's hamburger and the Model T Ford are not the images that can point the way.

In complicated interactions between human beings involving teaching and learning, growth and development, pain and suffering, life and death, isolation and connectedness, you cannot simply clone good ideas. You cannot find out what works to improve lives and build communities as though operating in a laboratory. And if those delicate interactions are to take place within large institutions or encrusted systems, you have to worry about their survival in a harsh climate.

The Hidden Ceiling on Scale

Time was when scaling up from success was less an issue because it was generally assumed that successful programs contained the seeds of their own replication. The notion that promising models would automatically spread provided the rationale for funding of demonstration projects over the years.

But these beliefs have not been supported by experience. For many years, foundations, and even public agencies, funded pilot programs and discovered many that seemed successful, only to find them coming to a quick end when the demonstration funds ran out. The ones that worked disappeared or were diluted into ineffectiveness at much the same rate as those that didn't work.

Looking back, David Racine of Replication and Program Services,

Inc. says, "We thought the way to produce social change was to test a model scheme in a few places and, if it worked, to then send it into the intergovernmental system by way of federal edict and financial incentives." There were early indicators that this idea might work as planned: The Ford Foundation's Gray Areas Program became the basis for the OEO's community action agencies in 1964. The foundation-funded experiments in community mental health were written into the Community Mental Health Centers Act of 1964. The early childhood programs that began with foundation support in the early 1960s provided the impetus and justification for incorporating Head Start into the War on Poverty.

Evidence that this comfortable arrangement was not continuing to work as expected surfaced gradually and was initially widely ignored. The interventions that worked turned out to be more complicated and local settings more diverse than anyone had thought. And for a combination of ideological and budgetary reasons, the federal money for "taking to scale" what had been learned from successful demonstrations dried up beginning in the mid-seventies.

Foundations were slow to adjust to this new reality and continued, as Michael Rubinger, then with the Pew Charitable Trusts, pointed out, "to fund models and demonstrations without a clear idea of what we will do with them if they prove successful." Federal agencies, for their part, adopted "the language of 'demonstration,' 'experiment,' and 'pilot project' . . . to mask their disinvestment in social programs, and to justify the funding of programs that were so small in scope that they could hardly be expected to have any effect."

We saw the beginnings of what I have come to think of as a Ceiling on Scale—made up of a series of elaborate rationalizations that keep us from acting on the implications of what we learn from pilots and demonstrations. Few challenged the idea of continuing demonstrations without ever taking them to scale and without finding out anything new. We deluded ourselves into thinking we didn't know enough, when what actually has kept us from going to scale was an unwillingness to invest the necessary resources or a reluctance to disturb the status quo. We celebrated innovations and ignored their lack of impact on the big systems where the big money was.

Public and private funders collaborated in hiding the Ceiling on Scale and maintaining the fiction that the earlier rationale for funding demonstrations remained unchanged by not focusing on the fact that successful demonstrations weren't being replicated. Some reconciled themselves to a succession of aborted demonstrations as they stopped funding the pilot programs that had proved their worth and let them die out. Others continued funding successful demonstrations even after they had served their demonstration purpose.

When I asked around to find out what had happened to the Quantum Opportunities Program that had caused all the excitement in 1994, I was stunned to find that the heir to what had been hailed as such a successful demonstration was . . . another demonstration. The original sponsors of the demonstration (the Opportunities Industrial Centers of America and the Ford Foundation) had enlisted a third partner, the U.S. Department of Labor, to engage in a national replication. But the "national replication" that had been promised when the original success was announced turns out to be at only seven sites.

And if this additional round of demonstrations proves to be a success, would the program then be taken to scale? The responsible Department of Labor official told me there would be no way to do that—QOP was much too expensive an intervention. (The OIC representative I spoke to scoffs at that idea. "Ten thousand dollars per kid over a four-year period too expensive? When we have no trouble spending a hundred thousand to send them to boot camp or jail?") I asked the Labor Department person why, if it's too expensive to scale up from, they would be doing the demonstration at all. She replied that perhaps people could learn something from it that might enable them later to replicate pieces of the intervention. Given that the evaluators of the original intervention had concluded that it was the interaction of its multiple components that accounted for its success, this struck me as one more rationalization for doing *something* without actually breaking through the Ceiling on Scale when resource constraints got in the way of the real scale-up that seemed to be justified by the demonstration evidence.

Another way we keep the Ceiling on Scale hidden, is when we comfort—and delude—ourselves by not acting on the implications of how often model programs succeed by beating the system. They do so by going around the system, getting their people first in line in overcrowded clinics, developing personal relationships with professional colleagues to avoid the lack of responsiveness of other institutions, and by sending advocates along to make the system respond in ways it does not do under ordinary circumstances. They take advantage of whatever opportunities they find to maneuver between and around existing barriers.

Many reform efforts thus achieve results, in the words of one study, essentially by "tricking the system into giving what is needed to operate, without changing it fundamentally." In this way, model projects are able to innovate at the margins and attract demonstration funds and serve, as Heather Weiss of the Harvard Family Project has pointed out, as "the safety valve to stave off systems change." Gerald Smale, the British social innovation expert, goes further, saying that pilot programs, by providing enough exposure to the proposed change to allow the rest of the system to inoculate itself, often make the system actually more resistant to change.

But, most important, the techniques that work to beat the system when the model program is small and marginal can no longer help when it is time to expand and break through the Ceiling on Scale. As educator Deborah Meier points out, others operating within the system become resentful that favored innovators are not being held to the same constraints they chafe under. Efforts to reach greater numbers bring greater visibility, and greater visibility creates new demands to comply with old rules. That is why innovative programs cannot grow and thrive in an unchanged system.

Foundations became increasingly aware in the early 1990s that they were overemphasizing innovation for its own sake and ignoring the challenge of funding implementation on a significant scale. The Charles Stewart Mott Foundation and several others began to focus directly on the replication issue. In 1993, the Pew Charitable Trusts and the Robert Wood Johnson Foundation joined to provide start-up funding to Replication and Program Services, Inc. to promote the replication of programs serving social and community purposes. And Pew, together with the Rockefeller Foundation, support the Boston-based Going to Scale Project.

But acting on the finding that effective demonstrations so frequently bumped into the Hidden Ceiling on Scale would be no simple matter. Demonstrations don't make waves. Moving them into mainstream systems does. Moving demonstrations into the mainstream requires, to use T.S. Eliot's words, a willingness to "disturb the universe," because it means breaking the Hidden Ceiling on Scale by changing the legislative, funding, and regulatory foundations on which the replications are expected to operate.

Past Misunderstandings

Enough successes in expanding the reach of effective interventions are now underway that the mistakes in earlier replication efforts are becoming apparent: franchising, mass production, and biomedical science turn out to be misleading analogs; we underestimated the importance of local variation, local ownership, and the subtleties of effective interventions; and we ignored the critical role of the external environment. Our lack of understanding cost dearly in missed opportunities to build on success.

We didn't realize that people-centered interventions can't be turned out like widgets. Most front-line staff in successful programs can testify that while they operate on a body of shared knowledge and skills, a significant portion of what they do cannot be standardized. The good ones are forever responding to contingencies. The home visitor comes in ready to teach the new mother how to take the baby's temperature and finds that the landlord has just delivered an eviction notice or the abusive boyfriend has returned. There is no protocol to cover every eventuality. The home visitor must have the capacity and the authority to respond. Her instructions must leave her free to meet the family at home or at the Laundromat, or to give mother and baby a ride to the hospital.

Even less standardization is possible in neighborhood transformation efforts. Leaders of these initiatives are very clear that they must have the capacity to adapt to changing circumstances. If the local police department is ready to partner with the community in efforts to restore public safety, or jobs open up that residents could seize if transportation were available, they cannot be constrained in responding to these opportunities by having to adhere to a model developed elsewhere.

The lack of standardization also complicates the process of determining what makes a program worth replicating. Sir Alexander Fleming discovered quickly that his bread mold contained a substance unlike any known before, that it killed bacteria and was nontoxic to human cells. Alas, neither human services nor community building work with the uniformity of penicillin. The most promising interventions rely on at least some components that change from one site to the next, and that evolve with considerable variations over time.

We didn't realize that local people may have to reinvent parts of the wheel. Even when local people set out to replicate someone else's intervention, they find they have to adapt it to local conditions to make it work. Veterans of successful community-based programs agree that people implementing programs in new settings must be able in fundamental ways to make them their own.

The importance of local reinvention and adaptation varies depending on what is being replicated. Having stipulated that, and having rejected the cookie-cutter model of replication, one still finds considerable disagreement about the ideal mix between replication and reinvention. David Racine, who worries about this matter full-time at Replication and Program Services, Inc., has found that "people will often commit to a model or approach imported from outside the community if it meets an important local need, they believe it works, and they are able to collaborate with the program's developer in ways that allow local experience to be reflected in the ongoing refinement of the model."

We underestimated the subtleties of effective interventions. Even the best practitioners often can't give usable descriptions of what they do. Many successful interventions reflect the secret the fox confided to Saint Exupéry's Little Prince: What is essential is invisible to the eye. The practitioners know more than they can say. In the words of MIT professor Don Schön, they operate with an "iceberg of tacit knowledge and artistry beneath the surface of readily accessible descriptions" of effective practices. For this reason, Toby Herr, founder of Project Match, counsels "going both deep and wide": deep to understand successful interventions and wide to disseminate them. "With depth but no wideness, no one beyond the doers learn anything. With wideness but no continued depth, the danger is that many people will learn the wrong things."

We failed to see that you can't grow roses in concrete. Human service reformers and educators alike thought the challenge was to develop new ideas, not to change institutions. They assumed an innovation or a "good product" would become part of a mainstream system because of its merit, unconstrained by the system's funding, rule making, standard setting, and accountability requirements—all of which are likely to be inconsistent with the innovation.

Perhaps we failed to appreciate the importance of context because early thinking about replication was based on the model of the agricultural agent disseminating the news of the new weed killer. Once the weed killer had been shown to be effective in increasing productivity and innocuous in its side effects, the agricultural agent simply disseminated the appropriate information to opinion leaders, who in turn spread it to the ultimate users, and the job was done.

We also underestimated the importance of context because many of our ideas about spreading innovations came from the private sector, where context is simpler. In the private sector, the context is the market, and profit is the measure of success. Rules and regulations may intrude, but they stop short of prescribing the very essence of what the enterprise does and how it does it. By contrast, human services, education, and community building are shaped by highly complex systems that specify what you may or may not do. (You may see your clients in the office but not in their homes, after 9 A.M. but not after 6 P.M.) They determine what your institution will be paid for. (Medicaid reimburses for EKG's and CAT scans, but not for outreach workers.) They define for what you will be rewarded or penalized. (Reducing eligibility errors is valued, but connecting with an alienated adolescent isn't.)

The roses that thrived in the hothouse *can* be bred to grow in huge numbers in well-tended fields for commercial harvesting, but not in concrete. Programs carefully developed under protective bubbles cannot be sustained in the arid soil of bureaucracies that value equity but not intensity; standardization but not flexibility; routine procedures but not discretion; categorization but not comprehensiveness; professional authority but not collaborative relationships; reduction of errors but not responsiveness to urgent human needs.

Replication efforts that ignore context are destined to remain forever outside the big systems (education, social services, work training, health care, family support, criminal justice, etc.)—in which society has placed the bulk of its investments in human and community renewal. Failing to recognize how powerfully the forces of inertia, cultural norms, and bureaucracy congeal into the concrete where no roses can grow means repeating the pattern over and over again.

Failure to recognize those forces also makes the task of spreading what works seem more intractable and mysterious than it has to be. Ronald Haskins, senior Republican staff member of the House Ways and Means Committee, says, "We have seen over and over that even if you can produce good results with small programs, when you expand to a national level, the effect often disappears." Ann Lieberman, early-childhood expert at Columbia Teachers College, says, "What we don't know yet is what you have to do to not lose the essence of these things when you scale up."

I submit that we *do* know how to keep the effect from disappearing and how to avoid losing "the essence of these things." You do that by not ignoring the institutional context, and by not leaving the responsibility for creating a more hospitable context to the front-line people, who are not in a position to change the wider environment.

We failed to see that public reluctance to invest in the poor led to the dilution of effective programs. The national ambivalence about helping the poor significantly hampers the spread of effective programs. Citizens who will support providing intensive, high-quality services to a few dozen poor and minority families as part of a demonstration balk at the investments required to make such services widely available. Thus, the proven effectiveness of intensive individualized services is routinely diluted—and destroyed—by the pressure to reach large numbers with inadequate resources.

I believe that our national reluctance to invest in programs targeted on poor or minority populations explains some of the mystery of our inability to learn from experience (illustrated by the South Carolina Resource Mothers, Elmira home visiting, and Maryland boot camp stories in Chapter 1) that when effective programs are diluted, they become ineffective.

Administrators, policy makers, and funders acquiesce in a great deception when they unthinkingly agree to scale up from a proven success by diluting it. They may say—they may even believe—they are replicating an intervention that works, but they hide from themselves and from the public that when they increase caseloads, decrease professional time, or give the job to less well-trained personnel, they are not replicating a proven intervention. If their gamble on multiplying effective programs on the cheap doesn't pay off, they not only fail to improve outcomes, they contribute to the prevailing cynicism that nothing works.

But we may not be doomed forever to repeat the mistakes of the past. We may slowly be learning to think and act anew: first, to take the Ceiling on Scale out of hiding, and then to break through it.

The following tales of successful replication suggest we may be learning that if we mean to spread what works beyond the pilot stage in order to reach large numbers with effective interventions, we must keep from stripping them down, diluting or dismembering them, standardizing them, and plopping them into inhospitable surroundings.

Tales of Successful Replication

Everywhere in this country there are valiant people trying to protect the fragile attributes of successful programs while trying to extend their reach. Media attention still goes to the individual, telegenic programs that transform individual lives, but misses the emerging drama of efforts to scale up from small successes that transform lives and sometimes neighborhoods *and* change the norms that prevail in large institutions and systems.

We will examine four successes in breaking the Ceiling on Scale: one trains young people with high-risk backgrounds to become accomplished in the construction trade and as community leaders, a second makes home visits to support high-risk families with newborn infants, a third makes it possible for neighborhood-based organizations to shine the beacon of community from schools in the poorest areas of New York City, and a fourth makes it possible for schools to assure that no child will leave third grade without basic reading skills.

YOUTHBUILD, TESTING WHETHER HUMAN RECLAMATION CAN SURVIVE IN A FEDERAL AGENCY

Dorothy Stoneman is the founder of YouthBuild, a program *The New York Times* described as "a wellspring of human reclamation." YouthBuild combines building low-income housing with teaching construction skills to unemployed urban youngsters with helping them acquire academic and leadership skills—and ultimately greater control over their lives. Stoneman says that "scaling up one of these enterprises is really an evolving art form," that she is figuring out as she goes.

Neither Stoneman's modest demeanor nor her simple office in Somerville, Massachusetts, signal that this is the woman who has taken a unique vision from its beginnings in the shadows of East Harlem, to replication first in five and then in fifteen cities, to its present incarnation as a new federal program that by January 1997 had awarded more than $100 million to grantees in thirty-four states. The passion and wisdom she conveys in explaining her life's work may help to explain her 1996 "genius" award from the MacArthur Foundation.

Soon after her 1963 graduation from Radcliffe College, she joined the grassroots New York Harlem Action Group in organizing rent strikes. A year later, while studying for a master's degree in early childhood at the Bank Street College of Education, she set up a summer preschool program in Harlem. Soon she was teaching second grade in a Harlem public school. ("I wanted to see for myself if the public schools were as bad as I had heard. They were.") Next she became a teacher and then executive director of the East Harlem Block Schools, a school network started and controlled by a group of East Harlem parents as an alternative to the public schools. It showed "just how effective community organizing can be if it's done right."

In that setting, she learned what she considers a critical skill—how to be accountable to and follow the policy decisions of a community-based parent board. Learning to function in changed power relationships was fundamental to her later work with young adults. "When you put young people in charge of significant things, adults have to treat them differently, and that releases all sorts of positive energies that would otherwise remain dormant."

In that spirit, she set out to organize East Harlem teenagers, asking what changes they wanted to make in their community. "Behind their cynical distance was a desire to do something. They wanted to have a better life." One group had expressed an interest in renovating housing. They were accustomed to hearing adults say no. When Stoneman offered to help them get the necessary resources, they became energized and "began to overcome their deep feelings of powerlessness." That was the beginning of the Youth Action Program that Stoneman founded in 1978, initially as a volunteer, later with funding from the Law Enforcement Assistance Administration's Community Anti-Crime Program.

Youth Action undertook seven highly visible community improvement projects. The first, designed and governed by youth, was the renovation of an abandoned tenement, which became the prototype for YouthBuild.

By 1988, when Stoneman and her family moved to Boston, others in New York City tried to build on what she had done, but their replication efforts turned out to be severely hampered by the lack of capacity to provide the needed technical assistance. At this point Stoneman started to think about developing a national intermediary organization that could support the spread of the YouthBuild idea to other sites.

The name YouthBuild symbolizes allowing youth to build and building youth. As the idea has evolved, young people spend half their time building and renovating low-cost housing. They are trained by journeymen in construction skills and the personal habits and qualities that contractors seek in entry-level workers. The other half of their time goes to obtaining the education and leadership skills that, together with job skills, will help them rebuild their own lives and provide them with the prospect of a decent future.

YouthBuild puts great emphasis on leadership, which it defines as taking responsibility for making things go right for one's self, one's family, and one's community. Every YouthBuild program has a policy committee, and no staff person is hired without the policy committee's agreement. "This dramatically reverses the disrespect with which low-income young people have been treated, and is central to the culture of YouthBuild," says Stoneman. There are stiff penalties, ranging from loss of pay to dismissal, for disruptive behavior, absences, or use of drugs or alcohol. Trainees who successfully finish the program are helped in finding jobs—usually in construction, often as apprentice electricians, carpenters, painters, or plumbers, but also often in social services. Some go on to college.

A number of local YouthBuilds are beginning to add training in other than construction skills, but Stoneman says, "Building housing will always be the centerpiece of YouthBuild as long as there is housing needed in low-income communities. Young people want to produce something that is visible, tangible, and important to their communities. They care about homelessness. Furthermore, the construction trades are well paid and highly respected. It's also very male. In a society which has devalued low-income men, especially young men of color, and made them marginal, YouthBuild set out to do something that would pull them back into a more central role in their communities."

"YouthBuild graduates won't all go to the construction trades," says John Bell, director of leadership development in YouthBuild USA, and Stoneman's partner and husband. "But whatever time they have with us, we want to help build a foundation for their lives, so that whatever they decide to do in life, they'll have more skills, more self-esteem, more confidence, more knowledge."

Because YouthBuild happens on the street, residents see young people who six months ago looked either threatening or lazy now doing something positive. "That gives a lot of people hope," says Stoneman. "There is a desperate need for a visible, tangible, positive role for poor, inner-city and rural young people who have dropped out of school and out of society because they don't see anything out there for them other than drugs, jail, work at McDonald's, or getting killed."

The first full replication of the YouthBuild idea occurred when a young community organizer, Tim Cross, had set out to make something like Youth Action in New York work in Boston. Stoneman was able to help him with the development of YouthBuild Boston while working on the establishment of YouthBuild USA, which would become a national intermediary, providing local programs with needed expertise.

YouthBuild Boston accepted its first group of thirty trainees, ages sixteen to twenty-four, in the fall of 1990, after interviewing four times as many applicants and selecting those that seemed most serious about the program and its opportunities. In its second year, YouthBuild Boston was already showing a 65 percent retention rate and an 87 percent attendance rate. Boston construction manager

David Lopes says that "even on a freezing day, *everyone* is at the site on time."

Stoneman says that "what was actually happening with YouthBuild Boston was so fabulous that my conviction that this was my life's work was confirmed."

Soon there were YouthBuilds in San Francisco, Cleveland, Tallahassee, and Gary, Indiana. Data from these sites showed 85 percent attendance and 67 percent completion of the program, among a population that was 80 percent minority males and 56 percent parents; 65 percent had a juvenile record; 33 percent had been jailed for felonies. Even among those who had been in prison, the completion rate was 58 percent. Data from four more sites showed that 70.5 percent of participants completed the program. Of these, 95.6 percent went on to college or were placed in jobs paying an average of $7.06 an hour.

Probably nothing distinguishes YouthBuild more dramatically from conventional job training programs than its emphasis on community and on relationships. Stoneman believes that every young person needs to belong to a family and a community, and that for an alienated young person to make the journey into the American mainstream, "you need a community that has values and aspirations and support systems and opportunity systems." She believes programs that are run right can fill some of the gaps for young people who never had an adequate support system.

Stoneman says that staff people spend a lot of time discussing the extent to which making a program feel like family is appropriate. She points out that anyone who has had professional social work training has been "trained to keep their distance." Most YouthBuild counselors don't have social work training, "and they are going whole hog and being tremendously supportive. . . . But there's always a pull on professionals, a pull away from something that's too personalized, too exposing, or might seem to be overpromising." She says that she is always amazed at how quickly young people would call her their mother. "But you can get into trouble and you can be feeding your own needs when people hook on you their fantasy of their ideal mother or ideal father. Our response has to be, 'I'm actually not your mother; I care very much about you, but I won't be able to be your mother.' " The point, says Stoneman, is to build a mini-community in which that need for family is at least partly met.

No program raises the replication issue more poignantly than one like YouthBuild, which puts such a heavy emphasis on relationships, has so much the feel of a movement, and involves so fundamental a departure from the conventional. The confidence that Dorothy Stoneman and her colleagues and board had in their ability to spread the program came in part out of the experience of finding "people at the local level who are inspired by the comprehensiveness of the program, its philosophy of youth leadership, and its vision of doing something that has a potentially big impact."

"I'm finding so many wizards," she says, "and I can begin to refute the many people who've said, 'It all depends on you.' But it doesn't depend on me, it depends on having a set of program ideas that are sound and well-developed through experience, on being able to teach those ideas, and being able to inspire local leadership of very high quality with those ideas."

As one probes, one finds a highly strategic approach to the process of replication and the provision of ongoing support to the sites. Stoneman believes that the purpose of replication cannot be to reproduce something that already exists, but rather "to build on previous experience and improve it." New program operators must develop a sense of mission, of belonging to something larger than one's own isolated efforts, and must have access to people who have successfully implemented the program. "Someone must be always available to provide direct, consistent, easily obtainable, flexible, wise, and wholly supportive consultation at every point of difficulty or of question. Technical assistance must always be rendered with a sense that there are new frontiers to be explored, new solutions to be thought of, and that nothing about the idea can be allowed to become static."

In practice this conception means that each of the sites relates to a single program adviser, who is on the staff of YouthBuild USA and located in Boston, and whom the sites can call anytime—days, nights, and weekends, because "directing a YouthBuild program is so tough." Stoneman says that directors have to be able to run an alternative school, build housing on schedule, counsel young people who have been in deep trouble in the past, operate the whole thing in partnership with youth, and raise a lot of funds from many different sources. At a retreat for directors, one told her, "We urgently need a place of safety in YouthBuild USA, where we can admit the struggle we're having, where we don't have to front, where we can support each other."

The lessons of the first few years of getting multiple sites up and running successfully were becoming clear: It takes time, and requires the opportunity for staff of the many sites to get together for reflection, the freedom to make constant modifications based on new understanding, and the availability of ongoing and intensive support and technical assistance of a kind that could hardly be called technical. It was also clear that the greatest difficulties were being encountered by those programs operating under the auspices of another organization for which YouthBuild concerns did not come first. They were hobbled by constraints imposed from outside, usually because they were dependent on money that came with strings.

But at the same time something else was becoming apparent: Operating with the sources of funding then available, YouthBuild could not hope to raise enough money to meet the need as Stoneman and her colleagues perceived it. In the face of diminishing federal funding for the inner-city poor that had been occurring throughout the eighties, YouthBuild leaders felt that young people in low-income communities had to have a stronger voice.

"We thought we could build a voice around YouthBuild, because YouthBuild unites people who care about young people with people who care about homelessness and poverty and education," Stoneman said. "Because it's a comprehensive program, you can build a lot of political support, more than if it had been just one thing or another."

YouthBuild USA set its sights on a goal of $200 million of federal funds to support YouthBuild programs in two hundred communities. They agonized about whether to try for a staged expansion, in a setting where they could exercise substantial control, before going to the $200 million level. They contemplated operating under the private, nonprofit Neighborhood Reinvestment Corporation, but as funding would have been limited to $20 million, they risked "being stuck there forever, and therefore staying small forever, no matter how good it was." That risk, Stoneman and colleagues ultimately concluded, seemed roughly equivalent to "the risk of putting it in a big federal agency and seeing it distorted and not handled well."

As auspices for the scaled-up program, they considered several federal agencies, including Labor, Health and Human Services, Housing and Urban Development, and later the Commission for National Service. They began leaning toward HUD, knowing that HUD had the capacity to run a large program combining housing and employment training, that the department's purpose included broad community development and alleviation of poverty, and that funding was likely to be available at a high enough level.

At the time they began their conversations, Stoneman recalled, HUD was headed by Jack Kemp, "who at least dared to talk about a war on poverty." HUD also had Anna Kondratas, an assistant secretary, with whom Stoneman hit it off. "We found we were both talking about responsibility, and we both emphasized that people should have an opportunity to take responsibility, to become self-sufficient, and to be trained. Anna said she believed in democratic capitalism, and if democratic capitalism is to succeed, it has to do a better job of eliminating poverty. She said she was a radical conservative, and I said I was a conservative radical, and we agreed there was no reason we couldn't work together."

Then Stoneman and her many supporters went to Congress, where Senator John F. Kerry of Massachusetts and Representative Major Owens of New York became their champions and the sponsors of their bill. Together they drafted legislation authorizing $200 million of HUD funds to support two hundred projects in which high-risk young people would spend half their time in education and half in housing construction.

In 1994, looking back on that process, Stoneman confessed to having had "a certain kind of naive hope" that was the result of never having dealt with a big federal agency. "Was I convinced at the time that we were really ready to turn YouthBuild over to some federal agency that we couldn't control? Not at all. But I *was* convinced that we had to get enough resources into local communities so that many more people at that level could do something, and the only way to do that was to risk the involvement of the federal government. We could try to influence how the federal government would be involved, we could try to give the federal government sufficient assistance so that maybe they could do it better than they had in the past, but we had to take a big risk."

Soon after passage of the legislation, Stoneman recalls, mid-level HUD officials told her, "Hey, we're not replicating your project design. Your program design is just one way to do it. The legislation is much broader; we're going to let people do it all sorts of ways. We've learned that the federal government shouldn't be too prescriptive."

At that point, Stoneman was still suspending judgment, hoping it would turn out all right. "Maybe we don't want to force people to follow our program design. We're not sure that someone else might not think of something better."

At the instigation of the directors of the fifteen then existing YouthBuild sites, a formalized network was established within YouthBuild USA to set standards and protect the core vision of YouthBuild against whatever destabilizing influences HUD funding might produce. (The directors were anticipating that scores of opportunists, who didn't really care about YouthBuild or the young people, might swarm in to scoop up the federal money.) Although HUD was unwilling to impose YouthBuild USA's standards, it had no objection to the establishment of the YouthBuild USA Affiliated Network. YouthBuild USA was able to raise $1.9 million in private funds to support the Affiliated Network and to provide additional technical assistance to the sites that voluntarily joined.

In the early days, HUD officials rarely consulted with YouthBuild. In selecting sites, they took great pains to show no favoritism to existing YouthBuild sites or to sites in the districts of their congressional supporters. In the first round of funding, 809 community-based organizations applied. *Youth Today* reported that YouthBuild headquarters and affiliates were "heartbroken" that only four of thirty-one implementation grants went to operating YouthBuild sites, and that "critics suspected that HUD put a premium on public housing know-how" over youth development.

Stoneman, as ever, rolled with the punches. Adopting the dual roles of technical assistance provider for HUD and choreographer of the voluntary Affiliated Network, YouthBuild was able to exercise its influence and bring its experience to bear. "We had no formal power," says Stoneman. "Our power to shape the field was almost entirely dependent on how well we could persuade and inspire both HUD and the grantees to embrace our philosophy, best practices, and performance standards."

Trying to sustain congressional support in an era of massive cutbacks in domestic programs soon became an enormous challenge. The greatest setback occurred when Congress threatened, after the 1994 election, to rescind YouthBuild's appropriations and/or incorporate them into job training block grants to the states. Stoneman says the rescission battle was won (ending up with a 70 percent expansion in 1995) because the young adults in YouthBuild programs, "unbelievably passionate about how the YouthBuild experience has transformed their lives," were able to ignite support among both Democratic and Republican legislators and staff.

By January 1996, Stoneman pronounced the collaboration with HUD as "solid" and characterized by "trust, respect, and cooperation." Most notably, when thirty grantees faced defunding six weeks after receiving their award letters because of a new $10 million congressional rescission, HUD program staff worked with YouthBuild staff and directors to avert catastrophe. In what Stoneman called "a tiny miracle of mutual commitment . . . unprecedented in anyone's memory of government and community relations," the ninety-eight organizations that had received YouthBuild grants agreed to take a voluntary 12.8 percent cut in order to prevent the thirty other programs from being eliminated.

Stoneman says the relationship with HUD requires constant nurturing and vigilance because internal staff changes and external political pressures at HUD are a constant source of potential disruption. Nevertheless, by 1996, four years after passage of the initial authorizing legislation, one hundred YouthBuild programs were operating in thirty-four states. Some 2,400 young men and six hundred young women were in YouthBuild classrooms earning high school diplomas or GEDs, and on work sites building housing for the homeless and other low-income people and acquiring construction skills. Equally important, they were learning what it feels like to belong to a community.

Stoneman says that if she had to do it over again, she would do it the same way, but with more awareness up front about the likely difficulties and complexities of going to scale in partnership with a federal bureaucracy. But lately Stoneman has been reassured by the enthusiasm generated in the field by both the program design in the YouthBuild legislation and the energy of the Affiliated Network. "The network does seem to be becoming a center of gravity in the universe of YouthBuild programs," she observed. "It says we stand for certain philosophies, certain program design, certain outcomes that we're trying to reach."

Stoneman sees her challenge as continuing to ensure that all YouthBuild sites work well, that those that don't work well "are either corrected or eliminated," and that YouthBuild USA provides enough good training and technical assistance to allow the maximum number of sites to thrive.

Stoneman's determination seems to have enabled her to surmount every obstacle. She has inspired a national network of committed people to "show what's possible, to achieve the highest standards, and to fight for the resources to do it right." She feels they have a moral responsibility to say to a skeptical nation that we do know what works. "It's so important that the tendency of the society to say that nothing works is really overcome by what we do."

HOME VISITING MAKES THE JOURNEY FROM HAWAII
TO THE MAINLAND

Healthy Families Indiana is living proof that effective replication requires as much wisdom and skill as effective program design.

In January 1992, Peggy Eagan, director of the Indiana chapter of the National Committee to Prevent Child Abuse (NCPCA), traveled to Honolulu at the invitation of her national organization to learn about a Hawaii program called Healthy Start that had been successful in significantly reducing child abuse by making home visits to high-risk families with newborn babies. Because the NCPCA had already figured out that any hope of scaling up from a local success is enhanced if a team, rather than a single individual, becomes interested in replication, Peggy Eagan came as part of a state delegation that also included Nancy Edgerton of the Hamilton Mental Health Center and Doree Bedwell of the State Family and Social Service Administration.

What the three learned in Hawaii built on what they already knew: that home visiting is not a single, uniformly defined service but a strategy for providing services and family support, and that it had been used in many settings and many countries to promote healthy births and healthy child development as well as to prevent child abuse.

The trio came home convinced that some form of the Hawaii program would work in Indiana. Nine months later they were ready to invite associates from public and private agencies throughout the state to a meeting to learn about Healthy Families America, the initiative developed by NCPCA to help states and local communities nationwide to set up comprehensive home visiting programs for families with newborns. The turnout of two hundred far exceeded expectations. Eagan warned that they were starting with an exciting idea but no money. "We don't have a dime and I don't know if we ever will have a dime." What they did have were statistics showing that almost every week one Indiana child died as a result of abuse or neglect, and impressive evidence that something could be done to reduce that tragic number.

The evidence came from a variety of small projects around the country, but most dramatically from the Hawaii project. Healthy Start had shown that a comprehensive and intensive home visiting program, beginning at birth and continuing for several years, linking families to comprehensive services, teaching parenting skills, and providing parents with ongoing support, could make amazing inroads on the incidence of child abuse. The initial experimental project, serving a group of 241 families with newborns that had been selected for their high-risk status, had succeeded in reducing the reported incidence of abuse or neglect over a three-year period to an entirely unexpected zero.

When these results first became public in 1988, one of those paying attention was Anne Cohn Donnelly, executive director since 1980 of the NCPCA, the nation's best-known child abuse prevention organization. Donnelly had come to this position with advanced degrees in medical sociology and health administration and planning. After her academic training, she had worked in the office of Representative Albert Gore, Jr. as a Congressional Science Fellow and the following year for the secretary of Health and Human Services as a prestigious White House Fellow. This combined background in research and policy may have put her in a unique position in 1991 to seize the opportunity created by an unusual convergence of events: The NCPCA had recently begun to question whether its agnostic support of whatever preventive efforts a community proposed was having much effect. Child abuse rates were continuing to increase and the NCPCA's leadership was ready for a reappraisal. At the same time, Hawaii's Healthy Start released its home visiting results, a General Accounting Office report came out pointing to the benefits of home visiting, and the U.S. Advisory Board on Child Abuse and Neglect issued its report concluding that the most promising form of child abuse prevention was home visiting along the lines pioneered by Hawaii.

"At that moment," recalls Donnelly, "the Ronald McDonald House Charities came to us and said, 'Child abuse is an issue we care about; we want to put some major dollars into child abuse prevention, and we'd love to work with you.' They told us they wanted to fund something already proven to be successful, that was replicable, that would have national implications, that was noncontroversial, and that would be easy to describe within the corporate world." Donnelly says that in a conversation with Gail Breakey, cofounder of the Hawaii program, "the idea just kind of hatched." The Ronald McDonald representatives agreed that it made sense to try to spread the Hawaii program to the mainland and offered a million dollars toward that end.

The Hawaii people were more than ready. Already planning a conference for January 1992, they were glad to move to larger rooms at Honolulu's Sheraton Waikiki Hotel to accommodate the expanded audience that NCPCA would bring.

They had quite a story to tell.

It began when Dr. Cal Sia, one of Hawaii's most honored pediatricians, discovered that he and health planner Gail Breakey agreed that it was unacceptable that Hawaii's parents and children had to be in serious difficulty before they could "qualify" for help from the health or social service systems. They succeeded in obtaining federal demonstration funds from the Children's Bureau to establish a Family Stress Center, launching a program to support new parents on the island of Oahu *before* they got in trouble.

Their initial effort targeted Leeward, a multiethnic, mixed urban and rural Oahu community with a litany of social problems, including high rates of substandard housing, unemployment, substance abuse, mental illness, domestic violence, and child abuse and neglect.

They began in the local hospital. Well-trained paraprofessionals screened families immediately after the birth of a baby to determine the extent of the family's risks and stresses. The assessment is based on a family stress checklist that has turned out to be a good predictor of the potential for child abuse.

Every family scoring high on the stress checklist was offered the help of a home visitor, and 241 high-risk families were enrolled. Families reluctant to accept the services became candidates for "creative outreach," which could involve weeks of drop-in visits, notes, phone calls, and other forms of gentle persuasion, sometimes proffered through a locked screen door. The home visiting was done primarily by paraprofessionals, working under frequent supervision from master's degree–level professionals. The home visitors were trained to be compassionate and respectful and to develop a nurturing, caring relationship with the family. This essential trusting relationship, according to one home visitor, comes "from deep in the heart; there has to be a string from my heart to theirs; then when they tug on it, I'm there." This invisible "string" links families to the program and to a network of essential services. The visits are weekly or more often in the beginning, and taper off in frequency as families learn to care more competently for themselves. Home visitors also provide access to an array of services tailored to each family's needs, including a dependable source of medical care for parents and children, job training, housing applications, parent education, child development assessments, any indicated treatment, and crisis intervention, day and night. In addition, home visitors make a commitment to follow the family's progress for as long as five years.

The program's three-year experience—not a single report of abuse or neglect among the 241 enrolled families—was more spectacular than the founders had dreamed possible. But, as with similar pilot programs, success did not shield Hawaii's Healthy Start from the threat of extinction. As federal demonstration funds dried up in the early 1980s, Sia and Breakey, along with Hawaii's newly organized

Statewide Council on Child Abuse and Neglect, began a campaign to transform their demonstration program into a stable, state-funded program. Armed with evidence of dramatic reductions in abuse and neglect, the founders and their supporters persuaded key state legislators to sponsor legislation to underwrite the expansion of Healthy Start to all five Hawaiian islands.

Thus Healthy Start managed the difficult transition from single-site pilot project, with short-term funding, to a statewide program with public funding, strong political backing, committed citizen support, and a permanent administrative home in Hawaii's Department of Health.

This was the story that Gail Breakey and Cal Sia were ready to tell their mainland colleagues in January 1992. NCPCA had invited every mainland state to send a team to the Honolulu conference. Their participation would be funded by NCPCA under the Ronald McDonald grant if they would send representatives of both public and private agencies and commit themselves in writing to go home to apply what they had learned. Twenty-four state teams came.

Gearing up to work with state and local representatives, NCPCA established Healthy Families America (HFA). In collaboration with the Hawaii group, HFA developed a strategic plan and an initial training capacity to nurture homegrown varieties of Healthy Start throughout the country. A crucial early decision was that HFA would not advocate exact replication of Hawaii's winning recipe. Leslie Mitchell Bond, who became director of Healthy Families America, explained, "We wanted to build on local strengths and strengthen existing collaborations. So all our programs look different from one another, but they share a common core." Critical program elements include a standardized assessment tool, intensive services over three to five years with well-defined criteria for increasing or decreasing the frequency of services, limited caseloads, and intensive training and supervision of service providers.

HFA has trained a cadre of certified trainers, who impart HFA's planning procedures, principles, values, and philosophy to state administrators, community leaders, service providers, and local trainers. Leslie Bond says they are developing the leadership, training the trainers, providing the inspiration and the tools so that states and communities can develop their own individual programs. "We are selling an approach, not a model."

By early 1997, this process of dissemination through intensive training, technical assistance, workshops, conference calls, newsletters, and self-assessment questionnaires had produced 250 local sites in thirty-five states, each a unique response to a particular community.

As local sites become more sophisticated and proficient, dependence on the national office is expected to diminish, but HFA recognizes its crucial role in assuring high-quality services, especially in the face of rapid growth. Reconciling high standards and local flexibility is central to HFA concerns, as with most conscientious replication efforts. Working together with its sites, trainers, and a network of researchers, HFA is designing a strong system of quality controls. This includes a continuing role in training through its own certified master trainers, arranging for an ongoing dialogue between the sites and a network of fifty researchers funded by the Carnegie Corporation, providing assistance for the sites to undertake self-assessments, and, beginning in January 1997, certifying programs by granting or withdrawing the use of HFA's trademarked name.

Through a national campaign of newspaper advertising and television and radio public-service announcements in partnership with the Advertising Council, the NCPCA is seeking to shape public receptivity to the idea that early intervention, when done right, can help stop abuse before it starts.

Which brings us back to Peggy Eagan and her Indiana collaborators. Convinced they had learned at the Hawaii meeting of a program ripe for implementation in Indiana, they formed a statewide group that met over a period of six months to develop strategies for initiating Healthy Families throughout the state.

Within six months, four state agencies had ingeniously found a way to pool sufficient funds to support Healthy Families projects in six communities. Soon a Healthy Families Fund of over $2 million was created by an imaginative and unusual blending of federal moneys awarded to state agencies for such programs as substance abuse treatment, sexual offense prevention, criminal justice, and maternal and child health. An official of the U.S. Department of Health and Human Services says he considers this a remarkable achievement that could serve as a model for how states can make uncategorical use of categorical funds.

The speed with which Healthy Families took root was probably due, in part, to the single-minded determination of Peggy Eagan and her collaborators, and in part to the existence of another statewide children's initiative, Step Ahead. Launched in 1991 by Governor Evan Bayh to ensure that all children start school ready to learn, Step Ahead had already laid the groundwork for the collaboration that would be necessary, especially to support prevention. Bob

Franklin of the State Bureau of Child Protection says that children's advocates had already "used Step Ahead to 'infiltrate' the bureaucracy, so that when Healthy Families came along, turfism subsided and we all signed on." Peggy Eagan's leadership and credibility were also instrumental. "She made us feel like the New Frontier all over again, like there really was something we could do to change things."

In an innovative solution to the governance problems raised by multiagency partnerships, the Step Ahead councils also serve as the governance mechanism for the Healthy Families project.

Indiana is now one of twenty-one states with its own team of certified HFA trainers, having found that state-based training is not only more economical than national training but better at responding to local concerns. Walking a tightrope between what is essential and what is left to local creativity, Eagan sees training as the prime way to "guard against adaptations that violate the vision."

Healthy Families Indiana has been successful in maintaining the vision during a period of extraordinary expansion. A year and a half after the first six HFI sites opened in September 1993, there were programs in twenty-two counties. State officials predict—with a mixture of pride and amazement—that there will be HFI projects in all ninety-two counties by 1998. "Healthy Families hit this state like a flash fire," said one child welfare administrator. "Instead of asking, 'Who is going to pay for it?' for the first time bureaucrats were asking, 'What can we do to help?' "

HFI is currently operating with local funding and the pooled federal grants administered by state agencies. The leadership had decided to bypass the state legislature, at least for several years, to give Healthy Families time to produce substantial outcome data that can be used to win support and counter opposition. Peggy Eagan believes that flexible, discretionary federal funding gives the program far more latitude than it would have been given by the conservative state legislature, which she feared would be leery of a program that could be pictured by opponents as "potentially interfering with something as sacred as the family."

But evidence of the program's ability to strengthen families was already coming in. Allen County (which includes Fort Wayne) served 125 high-risk families with 312 children in its first year. All of the children were linked to medical care, all received immunizations and developmental screening. At the end of the first year, 97 percent of the families had no reported incidents of abuse or neglect.

The strength of the program and of its team approach to leadership are also confirmed by its undiminished effectiveness after the departure of Peggy Eagan in mid-1996 to lead the Children's Services Network of North Carolina.

Summing up the state's long-term view, the supervisor of the juvenile division of Indiana's Criminal Justice Institute, John Krause, says that the state officials involved have all recognized that the investment in Healthy Families is to Indiana's vested interest. "Our prisons are filled up; we met our prison quota long ago. We have to stem the tide, reach these kids earlier. This is the best way we know to do it."

SCHOOLS AS BEACONS OF HOPE

New York City's Beacon schools have become a beacon of hope not only to the children and families in the forty New York City neighborhoods where they operate but also to communities around the country hoping to emulate their success. They offer a two-tiered replication story: adaptation of one idea in many local sites, and the potential for subsequent national replication.

The Beacon idea built on experience with collecting multiple services in one place to make them more accessible (one-stop shopping and full-service schools) and attaching health and other services to schools (school-based clinics, family support centers, and school-based social service centers). But the Beacon idea was more ambitious because it promised also to make the school-based services part of a community-building venture. The Beacon concept is particularly interesting in the replication context because it was not a single model but an idea that would be implemented in different ways in different places.

The idea surfaced in New York City in 1990 when a commission, appointed by Mayor Edward Koch and chaired by former Attorney General Nicholas Katzenbach, recommended to incoming Mayor David Dinkins a new anti-drug strategy for the city. Recognizing that substance abuse—like delinquency, academic failure, promiscuity, and other "rotten outcomes"—is deeply tied to the conditions of the community, the commission identified the need for safe havens for children, youth, and families in troubled city neighborhoods.

Specifically, the commission recommended that the city target nine neighborhoods, in which resources would be strengthened and coordinated for the immediate purpose of reducing drug use and for the long-range purpose of providing a vehicle for community organization and development. The centerpiece of that effort would be "schools transformed into community centers, available to children and adults 365 days a year."

In response, Dinkins allocated $10 million from his 1991 "Safe Streets, Safe Cities" budget to establish ten school-based community centers. Aware as he was of the crushing problems the seedling program would face in the bureaucratically encrusted board of education, Dinkins decided that instead it would be housed in the Department of Youth Services (DYS) and would be operated at the local level entirely by community-based nonprofit agencies. To run the DYS, he appointed Richard Murphy, who had been an influential consultant to the Katzenbach commission and had worked extensively with the city's most disadvantaged families. It was Murphy who came up with the name "Beacons."

"The beauty of the Beacons is that it is pretty basic and pretty simple," Murphy says. "The program is designed to keep what in most communities is the only decent building for young people open literally three times as many hours as it was before, and to provide a wide range of opportunities for them and their families."

The rest was left to the communities.

The only requirements imposed on applicants were that they be community based with a community advisory council, that they keep school buildings open into the evenings and all year round, and make available needed services, supports, and an array of safe and constructive activities. No one specified the services to be included. Applicants were advised to collaborate as widely as possible with other local agencies and to be as comprehensive and creative as they could in addressing the needs of community residents. DYS would pay custodians to keep the school buildings open for as many hours as the Beacon programs requested, so long as they offered programming that attracted the participation of community residents.

Ultimately, more than fifty community organizations responded to the Beacon solicitation. In June 1991, ten initial Beacons were selected, including at least one from each of the city's five boroughs.

I have had the good fortune to visit two of the original sites, including an extensive visit to Countee Cullen in Harlem, operated by the Rheedlen Centers under the direction of its dynamic president, Geoffrey Canada.

Canada had risen from a hard-scrabble childhood in the South Bronx to earn a graduate degree in education from Harvard University before becoming president of the Rheedlen Centers for Children and Families, a social service agency for needy New York families. He has written about his extraordinary journey, and his hopes for the children to whom he has dedicated his life, in a marvelous book called *fist stick knife gun* that both moved and educated me.

Among Canada's many wonderful stories is one about how eager he was to get one of the Beacon grants for his organization—for two reasons: First, he wanted a place ("a watering hole, a meeting place") that could engage everyone in the community and provide a safe haven for its children. He saw the opportunity to do more than just assemble "a bunch of services for children and families." He saw it as the basis for a community development strategy. He wanted it to be a place where the community residents were involved from the beginning in developing plans, and where well-trained and caring adults could stand side by side with children "in the war zones" of America's inner cities. He has also come to see it as a place to bring more men into the lives of children. He recently told *New York Times* columnist Bob Herbert, "We want the kids to know that they can count on men—not only to be strong, not only for protection, but also to give them a hug, to hold their hand."

The second reason Canada was so eager for a Beacon grant is that he saw the Beacons as a way of going to scale. He says that if we want to deal with violence, educational failure, teenage pregnancy, drug and alcohol abuse, lack of employment, crime, and AIDS, the real problem is not one of individual program design but of scale. He says, "We cannot design a few small demonstration projects and expect to have any real impact on any of these issues. We can't expect to make a difference unless we are willing to talk about comprehensive services for massive numbers of children *and* their families."

He saw the Beacon schools as one way to accomplish this, and his organization got one of the original grants.

So it was with considerable enthusiasm that Geoff Canada welcomed me to the Countee Cullen Community Center at P.S. 194 in Central Harlem. He introduced me to the two veteran Rheedlen youth workers, Shawn Dove and Joseph Stewart, who are the center's codirectors.

Named after revered Harlem poet Countee Cullen, the center's doors are, as promised, open seven days a week from nine in the morning until 11:00 P.M. or midnight. Youth workers help with homework and conduct afterschool sports and recreation programs for about two hundred children from 3 P.M. to 6 P.M.

The youngsters are taught conflict resolution and that they have a responsibility to the community. Perhaps most important, the staff responds to the youngsters' need for structure. "The young people want limits established for them," says Stewart. "We set those limits."

Services for high-risk families are integrated into other Beacon activities. Social workers may co-lead a recreational or rites of passage group to help youngsters on their caseloads to break their isolation and to develop new coping skills. The informal atmosphere is nonthreatening, and because social workers often lead the activities, young people do not stereotype them or the youngsters they counsel. (When Tarsha Black came there as a summer youth worker, she said she thought the whole staff were recreation specialists until she overheard two of them talking about a "case." That was how she found out they were social workers.)

In the Beacon office on the third floor, I saw a lot of informal counseling and consultation between staff and both children and parents. The codirectors had their own stories about how much it helps to get to know the children in this setting, where "you don't have to be pregnant or addicted to get services. You can just walk in." And just being there helps knowledgeable staff figure out which youngster needs a little extra attention, and what it means when a parent confides, "If somebody doesn't help me out I'm going to kill this kid!" Countee Cullen social workers help prevent children from being placed unnecessarily in foster care and to work with both youngsters and parents, offering counseling, case management, referrals, and whatever else will help families solve problems.

Between 5:30 P.M. and 6 P.M., parents arrive to pick up their children and to participate in parent support groups. Some come to share a family night dinner with their children in the school cafeteria. At seven o'clock, about forty teenagers show up to participate in youth leadership activities while parents and children gather in the gymnasium for a joint African dance class.

Programs for adults, including Alcoholics and Narcotics Anonymous, aerobics, and educational workshops, have brought more and more community adults into the school and allowed the center to "take on more of the values of the larger community and fewer of the values of the adolescents in that community."

Before I left, Shawn Dove and Joe Stewart told me they wanted me to meet the president of the teen youth council, Victor G. Cherry. Dove said that he first noticed Victor, then fourteen, during a summer basketball game, when he kicked the ball over the fence in reaction to a call against him. "If I don't play, nobody plays," he shouted. During the next eighteen months, he was repeatedly suspended from center activities for cursing, threatening, and fighting.

He had recently seen two close friends killed. His ambition seemed clear: the *G* in Victor G. Cherry stood for "Gotti." He had chosen the name of a notorious mob kingpin and wanted to follow in his footsteps. Canada believes that the Countee Cullen Community Center turned this young man around. Dove says he was able to watch Victor transform his pain into poetry. When I met him, we chatted about the work of the youth council, and he delighted me by giving me a copy of his poems in book form.

Just weeks before, when Attorney General Janet Reno came to visit Countee Cullen, he had presented her with flowers and a Rheedlen basketball shirt on behalf of the youth council. Canada writes in his book that he was stunned when Victor handed Janet Reno the flowers and the shirt, told her that he was really touched that the attorney general had come to Harlem, and then hugged her. "She hugged him back," writes Canada, "unaware that this was a person who only a short time before had considered all law enforcement people as the enemy."

Beacon staff also work hard to alter the traditional, one-sided relationship between neighborhood parents and school personnel. Before the Beacon program, "parents would come into the building only for crisis situations—their child was suspended, in a fight—or to curse out the principal," recalls Dove. "Lots of times the parents feel really intimidated by the teachers." But slowly, as more and more parents became involved in the Beacon programs, they would start "to come to our office, to whomever they had developed a relationship with, and say 'I'm here to see the principal,' or, 'I'm here to see this teacher. Do you have any words of advice, or will you come with me?'" Stewart adds that staff now often mediate between parents and teachers, even though the conflict between school and community can be intense. "It took us eighteen months to get on the same chapter," says Dove, "and two years to get on the same page."

Today, tensions inside P.S. 194 have eased. Academic performance at the school has improved dramatically, rising from 580th out of 620 city elementary schools in reading achievement in 1991 to 319th three years later. Attendance has also improved, and police report fewer felony arrests among neighborhood youth. While these achievements are part of an encouraging citywide trend, and the school principal believes that most are the result of school initiatives and not the Beacon, Stewart and Dove report that an atmosphere of mutual acceptance has emerged.

Activities for adolescents in the late evenings and on weekends have turned out to be a particularly important Beacon contribution, providing an alternative to the streets. There are classes in drama, dance, video, community service, job readiness (interviewing, résumé writing, job shadowing), and computer skills. Boy Scouts meet on Thursday afternoons, and Friday is Teen Movie Night.

Sixty junior high and high school students participate in the Countee Cullen youth council. Together they run a voter registration booth in the entryway to P.S. 194, part of a drive that has added two thousand Harlem residents to the voting rolls, and they intend to open a newsstand on a nearby street corner currently dominated by drug dealers. Canada writes, "They've led hunger drives for the homeless, clothing drives for poor people, and anti-violence demonstrations to get the message out that . . . they want the opportunity to grow up."

The youth council's biggest project thus far has been creating a safe playstreet for neighborhood children during the summer months. Youth council members spearheaded a petition drive to convince local residents and merchants to keep their cars off the street in front of the school. They regularly sweep the street, sidewalk, and playground, have planted trees in front of the school, and have led a successful campaign to replace a billboard on the corner advertising cigarettes with a promotion for the United Negro College Fund.

"If you don't train leadership and homegrown service providers, then what you end up doing really is making that community less empowered and less developed," Canada says. "[Countee Cullen] looks less like a place where outsiders are coming in to do something for you and more like a place where you are coming together to do something for yourselves."

The other Beacons in New York have similarly dramatic tales to tell, although each Beacon is very different from the others, and each is responding to the needs and strengths of its particular neighborhood in a unique way.

The MOSAIC (Maximizing Opportunity, Service & Action in the Community) Beacon in the South Bronx neighborhood of Highbridge, for example, represents a community-wide network of agencies pulled together under the aegis of Bronx Community College. MOSAIC has reached out to parents with adult education classes, hired parents as Beacon staff members, and offered others the opportunity to lead activities and classes for other parents and for children. One of its particular successes has been attracting alienated teen girls to become part of community activities.

The Beacon in Sunset Park, Brooklyn, at P.S. 314 operates under the leadership of Sisters Mary Geraldine and Mary Paul, directors of the Center for Family Life. The Center for Family Life is about as close to an old-fashioned settlement house as exists today, and this atmosphere combines with that of a summer camp to set the tone for the nonschool hours at the local elementary school housing the Beacon. On my visit I was able to observe a conscientious thirteen-year-old counselor-in-training run a writing class for second and third graders, eager grandmothers painting with a group of preschoolers, a homework-help workshop for parents held in English, Spanish, and Mandarin Chinese, and the bustle of parents coming in and out for their own activities or to pick up children, clearly feeling very much at home in the school. And I heard from the assistant principal how delighted the school people were with the new role models the children were being exposed to, and the closer relationships between the school and community parents that the Beacons had helped to bring about.

Richard Murphy believes that one of the reasons there has been a nearly uniform record of success among the thirty-seven Beacons, even though they differ greatly one from the other in every other way, is that none was left to its own devices to start from scratch and to cope in isolation with the difficulties that came up.

This was probably due in large part to the foresight of Michele Cahill, a leading scholar and advocate in the youth development field. She had watched the early development of the Beacons initiative and saw a crucial void. "Initially, there were no means for them to get together," Cahill recalls, "no mechanism for them to have a common vision." There was no way to provide systematic assistance to the community organizations to help them deal with the enormously complex tasks they were undertaking in a way that would be in accord with a shared vision.

So Cahill approached Murphy with a proposal to create an entity to work with and support the emerging Beacons, to serve as their hub and a source of ideas that could respond to the common challenges facing local Beacon grantees. Murphy agreed, and by the time the first ten Beacon programs were selected in June 1991, the city's Department of Youth Services had joined with the Fund for the City of New York to support a new entity, the Youth Development Institute (YDI).

YDI became a continuing source of support, technical assistance, and documentation to the Beacons. It helped the community organizations with Beacon grants to pool and learn from their experiences, and to deal with some of the knotty questions they all faced: How could Beacons, all situated in dangerous neighborhoods, ensure security while maintaining a friendly and welcoming environment? How could they find and train a cadre of skilled and committed youth development professionals to staff their programs sixteen hours a day? How is it possible to utilize categorically funded programs without losing the holistic Beacon vision? How could the Beacons encourage community participation and stimulate neighborhood development? How could they get parents involved and train them to become more effective agents and advocates for their children's education? And, perhaps most difficult of all, how were they going to work out their relationships with their host schools?

Each of these questions posed a critical challenge to the emerging Beacons, with no easy answers in sight. Through YDI, however, leaders of the emerging Beacons had a forum in which to look for and develop solutions. "It wasn't top down, a matter of depositing information into people's heads," Cahill says, "but getting a dialogue going about findings from research and practitioner experience, and how to apply these in difficult situations. And then sticking around to work it through."

Since 1991 YDI has hosted monthly daylong meetings for the Beacon directors. YDI also brings in consultants and researchers to lead seminars for Beacon staff on issues they want help with.

And, although it has had to shift approaches somewhat to accommodate the growing number of programs, YDI's role has continued to be vital in working with the twenty-seven additional Beacons added to the initiative in 1992 and 1993.

"It was against everybody's advice" to expand the program so quickly, Murphy recalls. "They all said we shouldn't do it, we couldn't do it. But I had all of these communities coming to me saying, 'We don't have a Beacon, give us a program' . . . I knew it had to be a bigger initiative. It would have been killed if it stayed small. The more the administration invested in it, the less chance they would kill it." Murphy says that "once the decision to expand rapidly was made, technical assistance became more critical than ever," because "some of the agencies we were now working with weren't as strong as the initial Beacons, and we had to really work with them."

"Having thirty-seven directors coming together who are doing the same thing, facing the same challenges, has been invaluable," according to Murphy. "Comparing notes on the different problems they face. Even comparing bills. And the knowledge that they're not alone out there."

YDI has also been an effective ambassador for the Beacons with city government agencies. For example, YDI helped broker an inter-agency agreement between the DYS and the city's Child Welfare Administration to site foster care prevention services within the Beacon programs. In 1996, the City of New York also added $3.7 million in city tax levy funds to sustain this program when New York State cut its foster care prevention funds in moving to block-grant its child welfare funding.

The importance of YDI's contribution was borne out perhaps most dramatically during the mayoral transition following David Dinkins's defeat by Rudolph Giuliani in November 1993. As outgoing DYS commissioner, Murphy worked hard to ensure a warm reception for the Beacons in the new administration, staying on an extra week to host a Beacons conference for incoming Giuliani officials. However, Murphy says, without the work that had been done from the beginning by YDI and the Fund for the City of New York, it might not have been possible to sustain the Beacons during the transition. The firm grounding in a common vision and a guiding framework that had been achieved by the Beacons, its documented accomplishments, and its enthusiastic constituencies of parents, school personnel, and young people, all helped the Beacons to escape the 1994 and 1995 budget cutbacks largely intact, and to become the major youth initiative of the Giuliani administration.

Both YDI and Murphy, now at the Academy of Educational Development's Center for Youth Development in Washington, D.C., remain involved in helping spread the Beacon concept to other cities. Initiatives are underway in several cities, including Chicago, Little Rock, Oakland, and San Francisco, to replicate the Beacon model or institute Beacon-like programs. Murphy believes that the Beacons have established a beachhead for an old-fashioned idea of bringing back a sense of community. He sees Beacons becoming the village green, "re-creating that feeling that there's a place in the community that you can go to just because you want to go, not because you have a problem."

They have also established a beachhead for the idea that with a mandate to reflect local needs and a highly capable intermediary entity to provide support, it is possible to "replicate" a strong framework and a few clearly defined principles, while allowing—indeed encouraging—the most profound local variations.

SUCCESS FOR ALL IN LEARNING TO READ AND LEARNING TO REPLICATE

My last example of successful replication draws on the lessons that Robert E. Slavin extracted from efforts to disseminate widely Success for All, the program he and his Johns Hopkins colleagues developed with the objective of finding a way to make sure that all children would learn to read before they left the early elementary grades. The educators who designed the model (including Slavin and his wife, Nancy Madden) are also the ones engaged in its replication, and have paid as much systematic attention to removing the mystery from effective dissemination as they have to developing the original intervention.

Success for All had its origins in a question posed to Slavin in 1986 by Kalman Hettleman, the hyperkinetic special adviser to the president of the Baltimore school board and to the Baltimore school superintendent. Slavin already had a considerable reputation for rigorous and thoughtful work on cooperative learning, class size, and ability grouping. Now Hettleman wanted to know from him what it would take to assure that every child in the inner city of Baltimore would succeed at school. He said to Slavin, "Forget about cost, about regulations, about the way we've always done things. Just tell me what it would take."

After a thorough review of the literature and extensive consultations with school district staff, Slavin and his Johns Hopkins colleagues designed a program based on two essential principles: first, that major learning problems must be prevented by providing children with the best available classroom programs and by engaging parents to support school success; second, that when learning difficulties do appear, corrective interventions must be immediate and intensive.

The original design was piloted in one Baltimore elementary school, Abbottston Elementary, in the 1987–88 school year. It has been refined since, but its major elements have stayed constant. It is still aimed at assuring that all students will reach third grade with basic reading skills, and it is still designed for schools serving large numbers of children at risk for school failure.

While Success for All is designed to be "always adapted to the needs and resources of each school using it," Slavin says it is "not reinvented from scratch for each school staff." The core of Success for All is the combination of three essential components: changes in the entire school's approach to teaching reading, supported by intensive professional development; a family support team in each school to help parents ensure their children's school success; and deployment of specially trained certified teachers as one-on-one tutors to students who are behind their classmates in reading.

"If you left out one of the elements, it would leave a hole through which the gains of the other two elements would leak out," says Slavin. His conviction that all three elements are essential makes him skeptical about proposals that would rely on volunteer tutors to teach young children to read. "It makes no sense to have kids sit six hours in school and not be taught effectively, then to think that reading after school with a tutor is going to make everything right."

Success for All brings about fundamental changes in how reading is taught in the classroom. In preschool and kindergarten, Success for All emphasizes oral language development and pre-reading skills. In grades one, two, and three, students are divided into small groups that read at the same level, and classroom teachers emphasize stories, cooperative learning, and writing. Students learn decoding and comprehension from shared books and stories.

Children are assessed every eight weeks to determine whether they are making adequate progress in reading. This information is used to suggest alternate teaching strategies to teachers in the regular classroom, to match teaching strategies to student needs, and to determine the need for individual tutoring. The one-on-one tutoring is closely coordinated with regular classroom instruction, takes place twenty minutes daily during times other than reading periods, and focuses primarily on first graders.

All children are required to read books of their own choosing for twenty minutes at home every evening. The family support teams make home visits, arrange parenting workshops, ask parents to work at school as volunteers, and help parents develop strategies to help their children at home. When they find a child who has vision trouble, they work with the family to solve the problem. If it means replacing a pair of broken glasses that Medicaid won't pay for, they find a way to make sure the child somehow gets new glasses.

Slavin says that his model is based on the conviction that "substantial positive change in student learning can only come about on a broad scale when major changes take place in the daily interactions of teachers and students." To bring about these changes, Success for All requires each school to employ at least one tutor and a full-time facilitator, who works with teachers to help implement the reading program, manages the eight-week assessments, assists the family support team, makes sure that all staff are communicating with one another, and helps the staff as a whole to ensure that every child is making adequate progress.

After its initial tryout at Abbottston Elementary, Success for All was expanded in 1989 to five other schools in Baltimore and one in Philadelphia. It continued to be carefully monitored and to spread farther.

By 1993, results were in from Charleston, Memphis, Montgomery, Fort Wayne, and Caldwell, Idaho, as well as Baltimore and Philadelphia. Evaluations in fifteen schools in seven states found that students in Success for All schools achieved higher reading levels throughout the elementary grades, had better attendance, and were less likely to be placed in special education or retained in their grade than comparison groups. Longitudinal studies now include schools in Modesto and Riverside, California, where a Spanish version and an English-as-a-second-language version are showing similarly positive results.

The greatest significance of the evaluation findings, says Slavin, is in "demonstrating that an effective program can be replicated and can be effective in its replication sites, and that success for disadvantaged students can be routinely ensured in schools that are not exceptional or extraordinary."

By 1996, Success for All had spread to more than 450 schools in ninety districts in thirty-one states.

Conceptually, Success for All is a fairly simple model, but because it requires substantial changes in teaching, curriculum, and family support, and because facilitators, tutors, family support team members, and principals must all learn new roles, replication is a complicated proposition. Slavin and his colleagues believe it is essential that the whole school makes a free and informed choice to incorporate the model and to participate in extensive professional development activities. Success for All requires that at least 80 percent of the school's professional staff vote by secret ballot for its adoption. There is much emphasis on professional development over an extended period of time, including continuing follow-up. The follow-up includes feedback to teachers, help to facilitators with problem solving, an implementation review, visiting classes, and looking at outcomes together with teachers, family support teams, and tutors. Slavin considers a long-term commitment between schools and disseminators to be essential: "We must be prepared to be engaged with schools for many years, perhaps forever."

Slavin believes that the Success for All dissemination strategy has found the right balance between prescriptiveness and flexibility. He says that those who worry that it may be too prescriptive are usually reassured as they come to appreciate, in the course of implementation, the opportunities for adaptation on the one hand, and the completeness of materials and guidance they receive on the other.

Because the Johns Hopkins group has been able to identify some consistent principles in the instructional programs that support reading success for all children, the reading program is only minimally adapted in each school they work with. Slavin says, "We expect to see our materials in use every day by every teacher in every Success for All school. Schools do make adaptations of various kinds, but you would never fail to recognize our program in any school doing a good job of implementing Success for All." He notes that innovative, skilled teachers can go beyond the model, but his objective is to provide a program that can be used successfully by every teacher in high-poverty schools. "We want to be sure that even the least skilled have something that will work well."

In terms of fidelity to the original, he draws a distinction between the reading program and the family support team. He believes the latter is, and must be, substantially adapted to local needs. He says it wouldn't make sense to have the same family support activities in inner-city Philadelphia, inner-city Houston, rural Idaho, and the Navajo reservation in Arizona. "Even schools next to each other vary enormously in needs, resources, capacities, and interests in family support and integrated services."

Slavin's main worry at this time is how to maintain the integrity of the model when training requirements are so extensive and pressure to scale up quickly so great. He says quality control and rigorous enforcement of high standards of practice are a constant preoccupation. "Whatever dissemination strategy we use, constantly checking on the quality of training, implementation, and outcomes is essential. Without it, all programs fade into nothingness." He also believes that for innovations and reforms to be sustained over time and "survive the inevitable changes of superintendents, principals, teachers, and district policies," school staffs need to feel that there is "a valued and important group beyond the confines of their district that cares about and supports what they are doing."

He and his colleagues have explored a variety of strategies to solve the problem of scale-up in professional development, including collaborations with regional training sites, universities, and state departments of education. Not all attempts have been successful; they are most optimistic about expanding their capacity to hire regional trainers and to engage staffs of successful, experienced schools in training and follow-up in new schools. "School-to-school mentoring lets the real experts—the teachers, facilitators, and principals in successful Success for All schools—share their wisdom of practice and hard-won experience." By allowing a high proportion of learning to occur through observation—shadowing, mentoring, and apprenticeship—Slavin bypasses at least some of the problem of translating into written materials what teachers actually do. Because there is provision for professionals to watch one another work, many of the essentials can be communicated without being articulated.

Slavin believes he has gone far toward figuring out the nub of the replication question: how to expand effective programs "without losing their integrity or the elements that made them effective and without blindly imposing solutions developed in one place on situations that are quite different."

The Elements of Successful Replications

The very diverse scale-up efforts chronicled in the preceding pages are all part of the "occasional, private, ad-hoc entrepreneurial efforts" at scaling up that characterize the current scene. But they have in common several elements that could help to make scale-up more a matter of deliberate public policy.

They combine the replication of the essence of a successful intervention with the adaptation of many of its components to a new setting or new population. These examples reflect wide variation in the proportion of the intervention that is replicated and the proportion that is adapted. All of these initiatives have used intelligence, experience, and wisdom to sort out the components that can be defined and disseminated centrally and those that must be crafted to fit local needs and strengths.

So Dorothy Stoneman says that the purpose of the replication of YouthBuild is not to reproduce something that already exists but rather "to build on previous experience and improve it." So Leslie Mitchell Bond of Healthy Families America says that all the HFA programs share a common core but are not exact replications of Hawaii's program because they build on local strengths and existing collaborations. So Geoff Canada saw that spreading the Beacon schools *idea* was a way to get comprehensive services to massive numbers of children and their families nationwide. So Robert Slavin insists that it is foolish for reformers to shy away from being as prescriptive as experience permits in specifying the elements that make an intervention effective.

All have rejected the top-down, one-size-fits-all, cookie-cutter model of replication. But in doing so, all are also aware that the clearer the understanding, description, and specification of effective practices and interventions, the more likely their spread to improve outcomes among massive numbers of children and their families nationwide. Their successes suggest that time, money, and energy can be saved even in reinventing the wheel when outsiders provide local entrepreneurs with the formula for calculating the circumference of the wheel and with information about the materials that go into sturdy spokes. Local programs can make use of imported designs and parts, but the human-service and community-building wheels that work tend to be of local construction.

They have had the continuous backing of an intermediary organization that offered expertise, outside support, legitimation, and clout to help sustain the scaled-up intervention. Every one of the systems and institutions on which these scale-up efforts have tried to gain a foothold contains features "that force reformers back toward the status quo and eventually exhaust them." Intermediary organizations and the networks of reformers supported by intermediaries strengthen the reformers in countering those pressures.

YouthBuild USA provides YouthBuild sites around the country with consultation "at every point of difficulty" and was able to persuade Congress and an executive agency to launch a large initiative embracing its philosophy, best practices, and performance standards.

The National Committee to Prevent Child Abuse not only identified the Hawaii home visiting program as a useful model to scale up from and obtained funding to disseminate the idea, it also developed a strategic plan and the initial training capacity to nurture the development of homegrown varieties of the program throughout the country and maintains control over quality and training.

The Youth Development Institute supports Beacon schools by promoting a youth development approach to community building and serves as a forum in which to look for and develop solutions to the common challenges facing local grantees. It has become a continuing and valued source of support, technical assistance, and documentation for the Beacon schools. It has also been able to speak for the Beacons with city agencies and is involved in helping spread the Beacon concept to other cities.

Success for All's base at Johns Hopkins University promotes the dissemination of the model, monitors the quality of training, implementation, and outcomes, and continues to explore strategies to solve the problem of scale-up in professional development, shadowing, mentoring, and apprenticeship. It has established networks among participating school staffs to enable them to interact and to ensure that they feel part of an esteemed national enterprise.

They recognize the importance of the systems and institutional context. They are fully aware of how readily the institutional or systems environment can interfere with any fundamental change in practice. They know that if they cannot solve the problem of context, their innovations will remain outside the mainstream and be deprived of the public funding that supports mainstream efforts. Depending on the circumstances, they adopt one of three strategies to make certain of a hospitable environment:

- They seek out settings where their interventions will be welcome. Innovative early-childhood and welfare-to-work programs have found new homes in comprehensive community initiatives, with climates that are more flexible, less rulebound, and more hospitable to a human development orientation.
- They seek out institutional vacuums, devoid of a thicket of rules and other constraints. Head Start could begin as a parallel system with direct federal funding because there were few institutions already on the scene offering a preschool experience to poor families. National service programs such as City Year and Public Allies began that way. Healthy Families Indiana is operating largely outside the public system, though the initial program in Hawaii and other replications of the same program have become part of state systems.
- They invest effort and resources to create a hospitable institutional or systems climate to assure that the intervention will be sustained over the long term. To support New York City's Beacon schools, both the city youth commissioner and the Fund for the City of New York worked to assure that the idea of community schools would be broadly accepted by people with a wide range of political views. This helped to sustain them during a period of fundamental political change in city government. Reflecting its strategic approach to social change, when the Edna McConnell Clark Foundation recognized that intensive family preservation services would not become part of public systems unless significant obstacles were removed or overcome, it methodically went about making systems more hospitable. It supported new kinds of training for front-line staff and managers, offered technical assistance to states to reform their child welfare financing, held conferences for

family-court judges, and helped states and cities change employee work rules, union contracts, relations with the courts, and public accountability.

They recognize the importance of the people context. They make sure that those who will be implementing the program believe in it, believe in its importance, and are committed to making it work. That's why Robert Slavin's Success for All requires 80 percent of a faculty to agree on inviting the program to their school. That is Toby Herr's conclusion after participating in several efforts on both coasts to replicate programs developed at Chicago's Project Match. She found that one essential component of a successful replication is that those implementing the program not only want it to work, but feel they have a lot riding on its working.

They use an outcomes orientation to judge success. All judge success by how effectively their scale-up efforts—whether they are replicating concepts, principles, or models—improve the outcomes achieved by children, families, and communities. None claims success purely based on the fidelity with which the original has been copied or on the number of replications.

Here is where the greatest distinction occurs between replication in the Public Purpose Sector and market sector. The measure of success in the business world is the *fact* of replication. Starting with nine McDonald's outlets and ending up with 18,400 is success. But success in the Public Purpose Sector lies in changing the world in some desired way. If one program is easy to replicate because it is simple and circumscribed, and another is hard to replicate because it is complicated, a market-oriented decision would surely choose the first for replication. Only in considering social purposes (what are we accomplishing in doing this?) does it become clear that if the hard-to-replicate program is more likely to have a significant impact on outcomes, it will be preferable to struggle with all the complexities of trying to spread it. Similarly, if one successful program is easy to replicate because it plans to operate outside mainstream systems, but another is hard to replicate because it aims to reach much larger numbers by operating within a state or county child welfare system, the public purpose is better served by the second program's replication plan.

Replication experts who advise, as some do, that nonprofits should not contemplate replication in an environment that is hostile ignore the public purpose to be achieved. When they urge funders to bet only on the replications most likely to succeed, and discourage them from taking on the hard cases, which require a fundamentally changed environment to succeed, they redefine the problem into something more readily solved but miss the chance of more significant impact.

They tackle, directly and strategically, the obstacles to large-scale change. Effective replication efforts recognize that successful scale-up of significant social interventions happens when program people and funders, in philanthropy or government, develop the strategies, make the investments, take the risks, and support the disruptions of the status quo that large-scale change entails. Almost all are grappling with environments that have been highly successful at resisting change—especially when the innovation comes close to the core of an institution or system.

Some, but not all, of the replicator/adapters whose stories I have told are facing or will ultimately face the reality articulated by Laurence E. Lynn, Jr. of the University of Chicago that in order to replicate an intervention or program "of true significance," you have to change "deep structures . . . permanently." Lynn believes that those who would spread interventions "of true significance" must be prepared to undertake or make room for a "disruptive, and fundamental transformation" in the host organization or system, or they will end up with a stifled, diluted, or distorted version of what was once a success.

That is the crux of the replication problem, and the reason that significant public purposes will not be achieved simply through the dissemination of information about discrete innovations and effective practices. Breaking the Ceiling on Scale is so hard because all the forces aligned against change drag innovations back to the status quo. If effective interventions are not to be limited by the short-term funding they can attract from peripheral sources, if they are not to stay stuck at the margins of public policy and at the margins of people's lives, replicators and their supporters must recognize and resolve the contradictions that effective interventions pose to prevailing institutions and systems.

When that happens, much else will fall into place. When the leaders of effective interventions no longer have to spend most of their energy and ingenuity in battling their hostile surroundings, the problem of having to rely on the Mother Teresas and Local Heroes will begin to recede. We will begin to see well-trained, competent, persevering but otherwise ordinary people reach the goals that only miracle workers used to achieve.

3

Taming Bureaucracies to Support What Works

WE ARE SO EAGER, as a body politic, to eliminate the possibility that public servants will do anything wrong that we make it virtually impossible for them to do anything right.

The restraints we impose on those entrusted with public funds to help us educate our young, keep them healthy, protect them from abuse and neglect, keep our streets safe and our communities livable, and buffer families against economic distress may keep them from doing bad things but will more surely keep them from doing good things. We have pretty much set it up so that only risk-takers and saints are able to accomplish public purposes.

Two stories, one about the price we pay for bureaucratic constraints and the other about the benefits of settings where bureaucracies have been tamed, will illuminate the point.

First consider the story of Leticia Johnson and her quest for drug treatment, as described by her grandmother, Rena Wilson.

> Leticia was here at the apartment for a few days, even though legally I'm not supposed to let her stay. [The Bureau of Child Welfare has allowed Leticia's grandmother to care for Hazela, Leticia's daughter, but only on condition that Leticia would not live there.] But Leticia said she wanted to go to Beth Israel Hospital for detoxification, so I thought it would be better if she stayed here until we went. We had gone there this past Saturday, and they said they did have a bed for her. But she didn't have her Medicaid card.
>
> We went to the Medicaid office to get an emergency card, but they wouldn't give it to her because she didn't have proof of where she lives.

A rent receipt, a telephone bill. The problem is, she doesn't have an address. I can't let her use mine because then I could lose Hazela. So we put down she was staying with her great grandmother. But they checked with her, and she didn't want to sign anything. Leticia's mother couldn't provide an address because she lives in a project and she'd have to get a letter of permission from management to let anyone stay with her officially.

The people at the Medicaid office finally did give us a temporary card, and the woman told us that if Leticia goes into the hospital she would be able to use it. The woman told us to be at the hospital at 7 a.m. sharp. So we left home at 5:45. When we got there, we found out the clinic didn't open until 9. They had a bed, but they said she had to have more than a temporary Medicaid card and that she had to have an address. When we explained that Leticia couldn't get any documentation of an address, she told her to go to a shelter and use that as her address.

Meanwhile, Leticia was suffering with these pains in her stomach, so we went to the emergency room. The doctor told her she had a bad vaginal infection and gave her a prescription to be filled. But they wouldn't give her the medicine because I didn't have enough money with me, and they said we didn't have the right card. "The other office made a mistake in giving it to you. You'll have to come back with the proper one."

Next day, Leticia called from the shelter. "Gramma, I can't get a letter for the hospital before 7 a.m. tomorrow morning. Beth Israel said I had to be there before 6 tonight or they'd give up the bed." And she said she was afraid to spend any more time at the shelter. "If I'm laying there, maybe somebody would kill me." She left the shelter without the letter.

When I next saw Leticia, ten days later, she was becoming more and more desperate. She had gone to Harlem Hospital to see if she could apply for a Medicaid card there. The woman at the hospital gave her a form to fill out and told her she needed a lease or a telephone bill for proof of address. She had just been through all that! So Leticia went out on a binge. She got high. I didn't see her again until the next Monday.

When she came here, I could tell she had been using drugs. She couldn't sit down. She kept jumping up, and she was swaying back and forth. It was difficult to understand her, but she said she had been sexually assaulted. Then she left. That night at three in the morning there was this loud bang on the door. It was Leticia. She was mumbling and crying. "My stomach is hurting me. My feet are all swollen up. I can't walk. Can't you let me in?" I told her, "No."

When she left, I looked outside and saw her go over to one of the benches outside. I was up the rest of the night, thinking about her. I said to myself, if she's really trying to get help, this is not helping her. In the morning she was still on the bench. I went downstairs and told her to come up. "We'll try to call one more place and get you into a program." And she said, "Gramma, that's what I want to do. I can't control myself anymore."

I'll tell you, if Leticia really wants to get into a drug program, if there was anything I could do to help her, I'd be the first one, because she would be helping herself. I know Leticia's scared to death. But I'm also upset with her. It's her own fault she doesn't have all these papers. I said to her, "I guess you're too much into crack." And she said, "Gramma, you're right." But then, even so, when a person is down like that, how do they get up? I personally feel if someone is doing something detrimental to themselves and they seek help, they should be given it.

So we called another place, and they told us they had a long waiting list. That she should sign up but that it would take weeks, possibly months, before there would be a place for her. That night she was back on the street again.

Contrast this dismal story with the story of Tisha James, another poor woman seeking drug treatment, who was fortunate enough to luck into a nonbureaucratic setting.

One afternoon at quarter after five at Chicago's North Lawndale family support center, counselor Judy Weber got a call from a nurse she knew at a nearby health clinic, asking whether anyone there could see Tisha James, a pregnant woman who had just decided she was ready to get off drugs. The nurse worried that her patient couldn't do it alone and that her good intentions might not survive a delay. Because the health clinic was about to close, the nurse hoped that the family support center, with its more flexible hours and staff, might be able to help.

Weber walked over to the clinic, brought James back with her to the center, and listened to her story. She had been using drugs, off and on, for six years. Now, at 21, she was expecting her third child and was determined to get help to get clean and stay clean. The counselor worked the phone for over an hour that evening until she had located a place in a residential treatment center that would be available the next morning and would accept Medicaid payment. Then she drove the young mother home and helped her work out arrangements with friends and relatives to care for the 2-year-old and 4-year-old while James was in treatment. Then Weber helped the young woman to assemble the documentation and the clothes she would need and promised to return next morning to drive her to the treatment center. She stayed with James at the treatment center to smooth out the inevitable snags she knew would surface in the admissions process. She left only after James was fully settled in.

Which is what made Judy Weber late to work the next morning, and how I happened to hear the story, because I was visiting the Lawndale family support center that day. Even before I heard her describe what she was able to do for Tisha James, I knew this was a program where managers, funders, and staff believe the mission is more important than the rules. In a more traditional setting Weber couldn't have done what she did. She would have been violating the rules that have everyone keeping the same office hours, and the rules that would protect the agency if there had been a car accident. Her job description would not have allowed her to go to a client's home to help her pack or to spend the time it took to stay with James through the admissions process. Her actions would have raised the equity question of whether the agency planned to do the same for every drug-abusing woman in the neighborhood seeking treatment, and procedural questions of why she didn't notify Child Protective Services so that Tisha James's two children could be put into foster care.

It is stories like these that suggest we must recalculate the costs and benefits of the bureaucratic constraints we now live with.

As Harvard's Steven Kelman writes, "The maze of rules, clearances, and limits on discretion and judgment that comprise the bureaucratic paradigm exact a terrible toll. Seeking to root out corruption by tightening the noose of supervision and suspicion comes at a cost . . . [that is] too high."

If bureaucracies fail to provide a human touch, it is because they are designed not to provide a human touch. "Bureaucracy develops the more perfectly the more it is 'dehumanized,'" taught Max Weber. "The professional bureaucrat is only a small cog in a ceaselessly moving mechanism which prescribes to him an essentially fixed route of march."

But today in America the mechanism is no longer "ceaselessly moving." It has gotten stuck because dehumanized services cannot meet human needs.

Bureaucracy as villain is a comfortable position for conservatives because it seems so closely intertwined with governmental efforts to help. It lends great urgency to calls for shrinking government. Liberals are not at all sure they should acknowledge the problems of bureaucracies. Even if true, why say it? The information could fall into the wrong hands. Acknowledging the weaknesses and failures of bureaucracy could lead—has led—large numbers of people to believe that government can't do anything right and that only individuals, acting alone in the private sector, can solve social problems.

Let me be precise about the aspects of government at issue here. This is not about the tension between business and consumer interests (as in regulation of food and drugs) or the tension between property and environmental interests (as in protection of public lands or regulation of toxic emissions into air or water). Specifically, this is about tensions that arise *when government gets in government's way*—when efforts to pursue the public interest are thwarted in a collision with rules and regulations that no longer serve a useful purpose, or whose useful purpose is overshadowed by how much they interfere with getting the job done.

This is about reconciling the public interest in protecting employees from auto accidents with the public interest in a clinic nurse driving a pregnant woman to enroll in a drug treatment program, and about reconciling the public interest in helping a family get help for an out-of-control twelve-year-old before he "qualifies" by committing a crime or being abused.

The re-sorting that is now needed to maintain the essential protections that bureaucracy provides while unshackling public servants and their agencies enough so they can do their job must begin with an understanding of the origins of existing bureaucratic constraints.

The Reasons for Bureaucracy: To Every Rule There Is a Purpose

America's preeminent scholar of bureaucracy, James Q. Wilson, points out that every restraint, every rule, and all red tape arises from someone's demand for it.

Bureaucracy to control corruption and patronage. In nineteenth-century America, government operating decisions were usually based on partisan political considerations. Appropriations were made without benefit of budgets. Political bosses ran America's cities as their private fiefs, "robbing the public as they cemented their political control." Tribute flowed into their coffers from office seekers, contractors, public utilities, railroads, prostitutes, gamblers—anybody who happened to need protection or favors. George Washington Plunkitt of Tammany Hall happily explained, "I seen my opportunities and I took 'em."

When the Progressive Era arrived, it was "infused with determination to root out 'corrupt' forms of party patronage and machine democracy." Reformers advocating merit hiring, objective criteria for contracting, and an end to clubhouse rule began to prevail in the early twentieth century as the country evolved from a decentralized, agrarian society to an urban, industrialized nation that required efficient government. The bureaucratic reform vision became a compelling system of beliefs that placed the highest value on impersonal exercise of public authority and consistent application of universal rules.

If the reformers of the Progressive Era recognized that the standardization and routinization they so ardently advocated exacted a price in operational effectiveness, their priorities were clear: They loathed corruption more than they loved efficiency. They welcomed whatever restrictions had to be imposed to avoid scandal and assure that all citizens were treated equally. There was little challenge to the dominant beliefs that public benefits must be centrally standardized and routinized, and that lower-level discretion and flexibility would threaten the integrity of public institutions and agencies.

Cumbersome procedures for contracting, procurement, and establishing eligibility were seen as unambiguously preferable to the possibility that a crony would land a contract, that a fruitcake lacking the specified number of maraschino cherries would be served to a soldier at holiday time, or that a destitute mother would collect welfare benefits without the requisite birth certificate to prove that the hungry baby she was carrying was indeed hers.

Bureaucracy as a response to intergovernmental mistrust. If good government reforms laid the groundwork for today's bureaucratic rules, the next layer was imposed by lack of trust.

The Founding Fathers were nervous about lodging too much power in any central authority, but by the end of the nineteenth century there was broad support for the federal government to rein in monopolies and to regulate food adulteration, child labor, and other excesses of the market. Alice Rivlin, then a Brookings Institute expert on federal-state relations, wrote that the Great Depression reinforced the conviction that "new national institutions were needed to strengthen the economy and perform functions that states could not be expected to perform on their own." By the 1960s, it also became clear that states were "shortchanging the poor, urban dwellers, and minorities," and lacked the capacity and the will to respond to most modern domestic problems. Congress, or at least its liberal majority, feared that federal tax money turned over to lower levels of government without strict guidelines would be misused, and that state and local governments would underfund programs (such as pollution control or compensatory education) when benefits went beyond the jurisdiction that funded them or were targeted on a minority. Efforts in the 1960s to right past wrongs with the Civil Rights Act and the War on Poverty, followed in the 1970s by sweeping environmental legislation, increasingly constrained state and local autonomy.

Reflecting back on the Great Society, Joseph Califano, one of its architects, said he thinks now that "many federal laws were written in far too much detail" because the civil rights struggle left the federal government "deeply and often unjustifiably suspicious of the motives and intentions of institutional and middle America," with the result that "regulation writers cast aside the great American common law principle that every citizen is presumed to obey the law." Quite the contrary, he says, "We wrote laws and regulations on the theory that each citizen would seek to circumvent them. We became victims of the self-defeating and self-fulfilling premise that, unless we were protected by a law or regulation, we were vulnerable, and our regulations got into too many nooks and crannies of American life. . . ."

Resentment of federal interference escalated in the 1980s and 1990s as the competence of state and local governments increased and as the federal government's fiscal position weakened. Rivlin explained, "The federal government's own fiscal weakness has not made it any less eager to tell states and localities what to do. . . . [It] turned increasingly to mandates as a means of controlling state and local activity without having to pay the bill." These mandates (which could be requirements to comply with certain rules, or conditions attached to the receipt of federal funds) increasingly became a source of state and local indignation as states and localities saw themselves forced to pay for implementation of complex and costly regulations they had no say in creating.

In addition and regardless of party, neither Congress nor the White House trusted the federal agencies, seeming to prefer agency paralysis to agency independence. As more constraints are imposed, rigidities fixing agencies in their established ways intensify. Failures in responding to controls increase, so more controls and clearances follow. Sixty-three layers of decision making separate a nurse working in a Veterans' Administration hospital from the top of the agency. Sixty-nine units of the Department of Commerce are responsible for setting the guidelines affecting a specific international trade transaction.

Members of Congress micromanage the agencies to get benefits for their districts and, to assure interest groups that neither side's enemies would prevail, impose labyrinthine procedures that further limit agency discretion.

When the White House and Congress are of different parties, the opportunities for creating both mischief and paralysis are particularly great. The story is told that soon after being appointed secretary of Housing and Urban Development in 1993, Henry Cisneros visited a comprehensive community initiative on whose board he had served. He explained that providing HUD support to this initiative in the form of funding and technical assistance would be completely consistent with HUD's purposes under the new administration, but that he had virtually no authority to commit HUD resources. His hands were tied, ironically enough, by constraints imposed by a Democratic Congress seeking to limit the department's discretion during the Reagan and Bush administrations.

Bureaucracy to protect agencies and staffs. Bureaucracies guard agencies against scandal and protect agency staffs from being overwhelmed by demands to which they are unable to respond.

The rules that encumber public agencies are meant to minimize the chances of scandal—be it the death of a child known to child welfare authorities, a heinous crime by a furloughed prisoner, or a contract with a corrupt provider. Agencies operating with federal funds are the most encumbered. "In Washington's highly politicized world," writes Vice President Al Gore, "the greatest risk is not that a program will perform poorly, but that a scandal will erupt. Scandals are front-page news, while routine failure is ignored. Hence control system after control system is piled up to minimize the risk of scandal." He goes on to explain that "the budget system, the personnel rules, the procurement process, the inspectors general—all are designed to prevent the tiniest misstep."

It is not always easy to distinguish between what it takes to guard against "the tiniest misstep" and what it takes to prevent genuine disaster. Granted that many lawmakers and administrators impose new regulations for important policy and programmatic purposes—they may genuinely expect that a new child welfare rule, for example, will protect children from grievous harm. But often what gets guarded against is a mistake in procedural details. A former inspector general says that "no matter how gross the corruption, one would still find the paper work in order."

Bureaucratic rules also protect agency staffs from being overwhelmed by demands they cannot meet. Rules that narrowly define the obligations of front-line workers may tie their hands and make it hard for them to do their job well. But those same rules are a great boon to multitudes of professionals who feel they are asked to contend with unmet needs of such magnitude with so few resources that their only consolation is that at least they're doing what their job description calls for. Rules and clearances provide comfort to workers who yearn to be rescued from ambiguity and discretion, especially when they don't have enough training, resources, and supervision to do the complex jobs to which they are assigned. When professionals are horrified at their inability to keep bad things from happening, it is consoling to be able to announce that at least "all the procedures were followed."

Bureaucracy to protect clients. Perhaps the most important purpose of bureaucracy is to protect powerless persons from the excesses and arbitrariness of powerful government agencies. Even without the video evidence of the Rodney King beating and the audio evidence of Mark Fuhrman's racism, there is no overestimating the terror that discretion in the hands of omnipotent police officers, prison guards, housing inspectors, welfare workers, and psychiatric attendants can strike in the hearts of those at their mercy.

The resistance to front-line discretion has deep roots in the American constitutional tradition, which "assigns the highest priority to keeping government power in check" and sees discretion as "an open invitation to abuse of citizen rights, corruption, favoritism, racial and ethnic discrimination, and sloth."

As bureaucracies became more important in people's lives, especially in poor people's lives, it seemed that fairness lay in imposing ever firmer constraints on their power. At a time when welfare caseworkers made unannounced searches of welfare recipients' homes, looking for an able-bodied man or even a telephone—grounds for cutting off benefits—advocates for the poor sought rules limiting what caseworkers could do or decide. And, if such constraints on professionals and agencies were found to result in new and unforeseen problems, new rules were added specifying new responses to special circumstances.

The existence of counterproductive rules should not, of course, lead anyone to underestimate the importance of rules needed to protect recipients from being harmed. Child care centers and family day care homes are examples where the problem has been not too many rules and standards, but too few.

Bureaucracy resulting from pressure to achieve other valued purposes. The idea that government activity should improve life for all Americans took hold during the New Deal and accelerated as part of the Great Society of the mid-1960s. New rules were added to government programs to achieve valued social purposes unrelated to the purpose of the program itself. The objectives of these rules included environmental protection, veterans and minority preferences in hiring and contracting, preference for American-made products, protection of unionized workers and civil servants, access for the disabled, and assurance of due process.

Bureaucracy resulting from categorical funding. Categorical grant programs grew most dramatically in the 1960s, when the federal government was perceived to have the resources, the capacity, and the will to undertake a major expansion of domestic public services. The states and localities were viewed as appropriate agents.

The expansion of categorical funding has been one of the most remarkable governmental trends of the century, and especially of the past thirty years.

It was fueled first by the progressives' view of specialization as the way to achieve efficiency. As problems became more complex, they were sliced into ever smaller parts.

Categorical funding also gives advocates the opportunity to protect and make visible client groups and problems that might otherwise be neglected. Categories range from the broad (like Head Start for three- and four-year-olds from poor families) to the narrow (like child care for HIV-infected two-year-olds from homeless families) to the incremental (like expanding Medicaid to cover additional categories of pregnant women). Categorical programs typically receive intense political support from citizens groups to whom the issue is highly salient (be it the American Association of Retired Persons, the National Alliance for the Mentally Ill, or parents of developmentally disabled children). Interest groups can lobby for separate programs without having to add up their total impact on the budget. In defending categorical allotments over time, they also help lock the status quo into place.

As new needs and new opportunities arise, the very American—very pragmatic—answer has been to add yet another circumscribed response. As Ralph Smith, vice president of the Casey Foundation, puts it, "When we see a need in human services, we just Velcro another project grant or case management system or collaborative on top of what now exists." University of California at Fullerton decategorization scholar Sid Gardner says that when existing arrangements seem too cluttered and cumbersome to respond to urgent new needs, "we bypass the more important—and difficult—task of systemic change or of making old programs more effective. When we are moved by the discovery of a new (or renamed) target group like abused children, dropouts, teen parents, crack babies . . . our desperation and intensity lead us to create new, narrowly defined programs *just for those children.*"

"The vending-machine approach to social change" is what John Gardner, secretary of Health, Education and Welfare in the Johnson administration, labeled it. You respond to a social problem by inserting a coin that delivers a law expected to solve the problem.

Joseph Califano, domestic policy advisor under President Johnson, described the process this way:

> We seemed to have a law for everything. Fire safety. Water safety. Pesticide control for the farm. Rat control for the ghetto. Bail reform. Medical libraries. Presidential disability. Juvenile delinquency. Safe streets. Tire safety. Age discrimination. Fair housing. Corporate takeovers. International monetary reform. Sea grant colleges.
>
> When we discovered that poor students needed a good lunch, we devised legislation for a school lunch program. When we later found out that breakfast helped them learn better, we whipped up a law for school breakfasts. When a pipeline exploded, we proposed the Gas Pipeline Safety Act. When we needed more doctors, or nurses, or teachers, we legislated programs to train them. When my son, Joe, swallowed a bottle of aspirin, President Johnson sent Congress a Child Safety Act.

The new federal agenda may have reflected a "crazy quilt" design rather than an orderly pattern, wrote Peter Edelman and Beryl Radin twenty-five years later, but "in the optimism of the time, many assumed that a coordinated system would emerge." If there were signs that no such coordinated system was emerging, that was less important than that categorical funding suited legislators and philanthropists, eager to attach visible victories to their names, to take political credit for defining a new problem and a new program to solve it, although funding might be only at token levels. A Nixon administration official called categorical grant programs "the porkiest of the pork" because they delivered identifiable program benefits to narrowly drawn constituencies for which members of Congress could take credit. Modest and incremental improvements, adding yet one more category, whether or not it fit with what was already there, became particularly attractive to legislators, program people, and advocates as the chances for new universal programs and major new spending dimmed in the 1970s and 1980s and virtually ended in the 1990s.

The Trade-offs

In our eagerness to guard against scandal and malfeasance, to achieve equity and uniformity, and to solve problems one visible problem at a time, we are sacrificing the discretion, flexibility, responsiveness, and coherence essential to success. To find a new and better balance between rules that protect valued public purposes and rules that prevent valued public purposes from being achieved, we must understand the trade-offs.

Rules to assure equity can undermine responsiveness. To assure equity, bureaucratic rules decree uniformity. But uniformity gets in the way of responsiveness.

That quandary was brought home to me by way of a washing machine. Speaking to a group of community leaders in Charlotte, North Carolina, I told of having recently heard a family preservation professional explain to her colleagues at a Homebuilders staff meeting why the program should come up with $200 to help a family buy a washing machine.

The staff person, who had been virtually living with the family during the past two weeks, explained that a washing machine would do far more to reduce daily stress for this mother caring for an infant, two toddlers, and an incontinent aunt than the more expensive mental health counselor or homemaker's aide that city social services would routinely authorize. The contribution toward purchase of the washing machine was approved by her colleagues, experts on the connection between overwhelming stress and the probability of child abuse and other disasters.

A young lawyer, director of Legal Services in Charlotte, approached me after my talk to say he wasn't sure that this was such a wonderful story. He wanted to know whether other families in the Homebuilders caseload would also get $200 toward purchase of a washing machine.

I told him about the McKnight Foundation's finding that the front-line worker's ability to come up with cash to help individuals cope with unexpected contingencies—be it a car repair or a rental deposit—seemed to be critical to the success of the welfare-to-work program it was funding in Minnesota. We talked about how, over the past twenty-five years, many of us may have overestimated the extent to which equity and even quality could be safeguarded by regulation. We may not have recognized how much strict rules, strictly interpreted, could undermine responsiveness in the provision of human services.

Rules to assure quality can also undermine responsiveness. Quality standards also have the potential of interfering with responsiveness to individual families and communities. After spending three years as federal commissioner for the Administration of Children, Youth and Families, Olivia Golden concluded that one of the hardest parts of her job was reconciling her mandate to safeguard quality with her commitment to make Head Start and other federal programs responsive to children and families. She sought to develop a mix of rules and regulations that would assure quality without undermining local variation and responsiveness, while satisfying all stakeholders, including Congress. She is constantly struggling to find a balance between rules that will prevent failure and shoddy quality by setting minimum health and safety standards, classroom ratios, and training requirements, and the rules that will have the effect of stifling quality, responsiveness, and creativity.

Rules to assure equity undermine effectiveness when resources are inadequate. The equity issue also arises in the context of how thinly inadequate resources are often spread. When equity collides, as it often does, with limited resources, the usual result is the dilution of quality and effectiveness. Particularly for services and supports whose effectiveness is a product of their intensity, the pressure to reach large numbers often results in their being so diluted that the purpose of the intervention is defeated.

As we saw in the stories of several diluted programs in Chapter 1, equity is often undermined by insufficient resources. Another example comes from a successful demonstration in Missouri of a family-support and early-education program called Parents as Teachers. Having found identifiable gains in parents' knowledge of child development and early detection of developmental problems after monthly home visits, Missouri decided to make the program statewide. But in the initial replication, an "equitable" distribution of utterly inadequate funds meant that the program could pay for only four home visits a year! Many local communities scrambled for funds to supplement the state funds, but whether four home visits in the course of a year made any difference at all remained an unanswered question. (Since then, Parents as Teachers has spread to forty-seven states, and typically makes monthly home visits.)

Controls meant to protect against wrongdoing interfere with discretion. Centralized control is the key to efficiency in the bureaucratic construct, "the lifeblood of efficient administration." Accounting systems, audits, personnel manuals, hierarchical lines of authority, reporting requirements, and regulations are all designed to reduce discretion and increase compliance where it counts—at the point where the client is counseled, the student taught, and the patient treated. Front-line discretion and local variation in program design and implementation are seen as a necessary evil at best, and by most policy makers as illicit. Managers guard against discretion by writing ever-more-elaborate and cumbersome rules to control their subordinates.

"We assume we can't trust employees to make decisions, so we spell out in precise detail how they must do virtually everything, then audit them to ensure that they have obeyed every rule," observes Vice President Al Gore.

Bureaucratic traditions reinforce the idea that public servants exercise too much discretion. But experience suggests that most exercise too little, and that variability and discretion at the delivery level are often assets. This does not mean that anyone should be free to disregard standards of quality and fairness or professional norms. It does mean *maximizing discretion* at the point where the problem must be solved, while providing the supports, guidance, and supervision to assure that the discretion will not be misused.

But no one should underestimate how fundamentally discretion in program design and front-line practice goes against the bureaucratic grain.

I remember being invited by the lieutenant governor of Illinois to a meeting to consider statewide human service reforms. My presentation was to follow a film on the family support centers recently established in Kentucky. The film emphasized the significant variations in design and operations in each of the seven centers shown. Before I could begin to speak, the lieutenant governor interrupted to ask whether I supported the local variation that the film seemed to be promoting. When I indicated—to his horror—that I did, he said, "Now look here, we have one hundred and two counties in Illinois; surely you're not saying that the State of Illinois should fund one hundred and two family support centers, each of which would look different from the others? That would be an administrative nightmare!"

I suggested that family support centers were indeed more likely to accomplish their purpose if they were shaped by local communities to reflect local needs and strengths. I also suggested he might be able to turn a nightmare into a dream by replacing centralized micromanagement from his office with new and better ways to hold local programs accountable.

Despite the evidence that supports maximizing discretion at the point where the problem is most immediate, it is the rare public official who dares to rely on discretion to improve the effectiveness of local programs. But standardized solutions, developed far away, have turned out to be notoriously unreliable because they reduce reliance on local knowledge and skill and limit the flexibility of people at the front lines to solve the problems they encounter.

Harvard education reformer Richard Elmore points out that when policies designed to assure uniformity and consistency come up against situations that policy makers failed to anticipate, adaptation "consists either of subversive, extralegal behavior or a complex procedure of hierarchical clearance." The tighter the structure of hierarchical relationships, the greater the number of checks and decision points required to assure compliance, the more opportunities for delay and diversion from the mission, and the less likely that the ideas of people who know what's really going on will be heard and become the basis for making change.

In the business world, companies are rushing to abandon hierarchical forms of organization and to celebrate individual autonomy, creativity, and employee initiative. "The age of the hierarchy is over," declared James Houghton, late chairman of Corning Glass. Corporations are discovering that the old command and control forms of top-down leadership don't achieve the results they seek.

But these insights have not generally been adopted in the public sector, which continues to dwell on the need to limit discretion to guard against disaster. As Vice President Gore and his colleagues in the National Performance Review will testify, it is hard to make inroads on the bureaucratic belief that front-line staff would subvert the public interest if not strictly controlled by central authorities.

The struggles that have recently absorbed the public sector—more government or less, privatizing or not, vesting authority in federal, state, or local officials—may not have left room for the equally important search for new ways of giving front-line people broader discretion while holding them accountable for results.

The accumulation of rules leads to paralysis. Reflecting what James Q. Wilson calls this nation's "profound bias toward solving problems by adopting rules," the rules that define how most large institutions conduct themselves have built up over the decades. The problem was already apparent when de Tocqueville wrote of how "a network of small complicated rules, minute and uniform, through which the most original minds and the most energetic characters cannot penetrate . . . compresses, enervates, extinguishes, and stupefies."

The rules have become so elaborate and technical that they are, in the words of former Stanford law school dean Bayless Manning, "beyond the understanding of all but a handful of Mandarins." As rule systems become more complex, more staff are needed to administer and update them. As constraints grow, more managers are needed to enforce them. Eventually, agencies find themselves choking on their own regulations and procedures. Their capacity to tackle new problems is sapped. Ultimately, they become paralyzed.

After hearing from federal, state, and local agencies nationwide, Vice President Gore wrote, "Before long, simple procedures are too complex for employees to navigate, so we hire more budget analysts, more personnel experts, and more procurement officers to make things work. By then, the process involves so much red tape that . . . simple travel arrangements require endless forms and numerous signatures. Straightforward purchases take months; larger ones take years. Routine printing jobs can take dozens of approvals."

Teachers commiserate with one another's paperwork stories (sign-in sheets, absence slips, textbook requests, ethnic and language surveys, field trip requests, parental conference reports, etc.) and share tales of principals more concerned that the lesson plan be filed than that the lesson be good. They give up trying to get services for a child or family because the paperwork has become too burdensome.

A Columbia University study of nonprofit preventive services agencies in New York State found that the paperwork demands were a serious morale-breaker for professional people who felt they were being scrutinized as if they were incapable of doing the right thing.

Rules that stem from hyper-categorization interfere with coherence and prevention. Ask people who have tried putting together a comprehensive community-based intervention about their biggest impediment. The answer will be categorical funding.

Ask people who believe in intervening early to prevent risks from turning into intractable problems why there are so few preventive interventions. The answer will be categorical funding.

Ask families who have tried to get help from prevailing systems about the biggest impediment they have faced. The answer will be fragmented programs.

Not all of these people will define categorical funding or fragmentation the same way, but all will agree that funders, be they federal, state, or local governments or private philanthropies, put fences around their money that make it very hard to use it to strengthen children, families, and communities. Judgments may differ on which restrictions are the most destructive: narrow definitions of who can benefit (public housing residents but not their neighbors, children who have been abused but not those in danger of abuse); conflicting eligibility requirements (Head Start has one set of income criteria, Medicaid another); or bewildering definitions of covered services (a psychological assessment by a school psychologist is reimbursed, but the same assessment by a psychologist on the staff of a mental health center is not—or vice versa). But judgment among the rule-scarred veterans does not differ on the fact that the conditions tied to categorical funding, each with its own rationale, add up to chaos.

Few persons who have not specifically looked for evidence of fragmentation and proliferation of small categorical programs are aware of their extent. Sid Gardner *did* go out to look, and found 238 separate programs for Los Angeles students defined as being at risk. Planning groups involved in California's recent expansion of school-based services documented "several hundred thousand dollars of staff, allocated in small increments of one day per week or less, in schools in which counselors and support staff are overburdened by caseloads that far exceed any definition of reasonable." Gardner says that through small, circumscribed, widely dispersed grants, programs to prevent delinquency, drug use, alcohol use, tobacco use, child abuse, teen pregnancy, gangs, and violence "have created categorical bureaucracies in some high schools that literally line the corridors with separate offices." Of course, not only are the offices separate, so are the rules covering eligibility and the labels assigned to participating students to reflect their presumed deficits. Depending on which program she stumbles into, a student may be classified a learning problem, a mental health problem, a potential runaway, or a "person in need of supervision." The services she gets may depend more on the label she is assigned than her needs.

Categorical funding that divides services into small, isolated pieces has made it almost impossible to prevent trouble before it occurs.

In many jurisdictions money is available to pay the exorbitant costs of placing families into run-down hotels and shelters, but not to help families find and pay for permanent housing.

A Massachusetts family with an out-of-control teenager could not get help from the probation department because he had not yet committed a crime. Nor could the family get help from the local mental health center because "his mental illness had not yet progressed far enough."

Even a child welfare unit in the midst of a reform effort aimed at putting greater emphasis on prevention sent away a family that walked into one of its new neighborhood outstations asking for help. The agency head later commented that old ways die hard. "This family's appeal should have been welcomed as a sign the unit was being seen by the community as a source of support, not just as 'child snatchers.' But the 'walk-in' was turned away because this family's problems simply lacked relevance to a system geared to referrals that prompt an investigation."

New York City taxi driver Jose Sanchez, Sr., raising his son alone in East Harlem, asked school officials for help because the boy was failing in school, and he was convinced he was losing his son to the streets. The school authorities said there was nothing they could do. When his son reached thirteen, Sanchez asked the city child-welfare authorities for help. A caseworker came to the home and told him there were no grounds for intervening because the father was doing nothing "wrong."

In early 1995, the Washington, D.C.-based Institute for Educational Leadership invited federal and state legislators and their staffs to step into the shoes of a hypothetical working poor family in San Diego, and apply for help from the major federal, state, and local programs they were presumably eligible for. It turned out that "none of the Ph.D.s, lawyers, elected officials, administrators, or assorted policy wonks participating in the exercise could deal competently with the mounds of paperwork that would face the barely literate Hernandez family." It also turned out that "just about everyone participating in the exercise lied, cheated, or purposely withheld information (because) it seemed like the only sensible thing to do."

Workers concentrating on specialized functions often lose sight of the family as a whole. As Milwaukee child welfare director John Hagedorn found, the most immediate problem may not be dealt with at all. Hagedorn tells of sitting in on a meeting with three professionals working with one family. The social worker from the Department of Social Services was complaining about the teenager's gang activity, the school social worker was concerned about how often the seven-year-old was absent from school, and the school nurse said that when the children did come to school their clothes were not clean. When Hagedorn asked the mother about her concerns, she said that it was the electricity. It turned out that all three professionals had been aware that the family had been without electricity for six weeks, and each explained that it was not in her job description to intervene with the electric company to get the lights turned back on.

Many sources of child care funds are categorized by the reason a family needs subsidized child care. As a result, children may be moved from one child care setting to another every time a parent's situation changes—from training to employment, from one pay level to another. In the IEL demonstration, the hypothetical Hernandez family found that each of their children would be eligible for a different child care program, each in a different location, each with different operating hours.

Under prevailing rules accountability is almost always at odds with achieving the mission. What auditors count has, until now, been related only tenuously to the purpose to be served. And what auditors count (usually at the behest of legislators) is what workers are held responsible for and therefore pay attention to. Child protection workers report that they spend far more time talking with their supervisors about getting their paperwork filled out and submitted on time (which the auditors check) than about whether the children in their caseloads are safe and thriving (which the auditors don't keep track of).

The state of Maryland relies on twenty forms in the welfare application process "to keep its error rates low" and to have as "evidence to check against records like state car registrations to make sure that recipients aren't cheating." Jessie Hall, assistant district manager of social services in Baltimore, says, "Our case-workers do an excellent job, but there is not time to spend with the human being. We're dealing with eligibility standards. . . . We don't have time to discuss with the client . . . that she should hang in there."

Margaret Dunkle of the Institute for Educational Leadership says her studies have convinced her that these problems are consistent across all public social service agencies. "Front-line workers spend from 70 to more than 90 percent of their time on record keeping and documentation . . . they spend their time double-checking eligibility, calculating error rates, and weeding out the deceptions that the system encourages in the first place. [It is] a paranoid system that would rather prevent one audit exception than enable 20 families to get their feet on the ground."

Why the Bureaucracy Problem Must Be Solved

We have seen, then, the many ways that bureaucracies operate to obstruct the delivery of effective human services and education.

Conservatives proclaim, and liberals grant, that changing long-term outcomes requires individualized, trusting relationships in the "exquisitely specific contexts" where teachers, health care professionals, child care workers, home visitors, recreation leaders, welfare workers, volunteer mentors, and community police interact with the children, youth, and families they seek to reach. The question is whether these intimate relationships are possible only in nongovernmental settings, financed by charitable or other private-sector funds.

The belief is widely shared that public agencies, and nonpublic agencies operating with public funds, cannot be responsive and supportive of relationships of trust and respect with vulnerable families. Former *New York Times* columnist Anna Quindlen wrote that government agencies are of little help in strengthening disintegrating families because agencies rarely manage to deal with individuals individually. "Families are as unique as fingerprints," she said, "while the rubber stamp is the escutcheon of government."

Could a citizenry that has equipped its public servants only with rubber stamps choose to equip them with different tools?

More and more citizens and decision makers are coming to believe that the bureaucratic constraints defining most public institutions may have been valid once, but now create an unworkable system. But where to go from there? As Princeton professor Paul Starr notes, "To condemn bureaucracy is easy; to find the means that will actually avoid it is the trick."

Conservatives would devolve authority from the federal government to states and localities, and from the public to the private sector.

Liberals, after defending the hard-won gains of the past thirty or sixty years, would hope to bypass the worst of the fragmentation resulting from categorical funding by encouraging service integration and collaboration. Many would join the conservatives in trying to make government more entrepreneurial and innovative.

How likely are these strategies to solve the bureaucracy problem?

DEVOLUTION WILL NOT SOLVE THE BUREAUCRACY PROBLEM

Current efforts to redistribute power from the federal government to the states are driven primarily by a conviction that reduction of federal power and federal spending will, in and of itself, solve urgent national problems. In exploiting voter distrust of Washington, the partisans of devolution argued that since the federal government has not been able to solve mounting social problems, the solution lies in turning tax dollars back to the fifty states. The premise is that state and local governments are by nature more efficient, more responsive, and more knowledgeable than the federal government about how tax moneys should be spent and services provided. Whatever the problem or the program, the Republican revolution said "devolve it." Its biggest victory was the 1996 welfare law.

Supporters of devolution stressed that block grants would bring decision making closer to the people, and government would become more responsive and flexible. That, presumably, was the reasoning behind President Clinton's argument that "this mighty river [of money and responsibility that] has flowed in the direction of Washington, D.C. . . . should instead flow toward our families, schools, communities, and states."

Since federal legislation and regulations have indeed created at least part of the bureaucratic rigidities that interfere with effectiveness, the key question now is whether changing the locus of authority will solve the problem. Will devolving authority to states decrease bureaucracy and increase responsiveness? Or do block grants simply reallocate power among unresponsive bureaucracies?

The evidence suggests that there is nothing about devolution per se that will reduce bureaucratic rigidities. State agencies can match federal agencies in dumb and counterproductive rules. State rules can do as much as federal rules to make agencies more bureaucratic. City halls and state capitals can work every bit as poorly as Washington, D.C. Steve Goldsmith, Republican mayor of Indianapolis, says that "replacing a bloated, unresponsive Federal bureaucracy with bloated, unresponsive state bureaucracies will not do much to help the urban poor."

Anna Kondratas, senior fellow at the conservative Hudson Institute and a federal housing official in the Reagan and Bush administrations, says that if simplification is the reason for devolution to the states, that could be accomplished more easily at the federal level. As a former block grant administrator, she says, "I can confidently state that block grants will certainly not reduce bureaucracy and regulations."

Devolution does not mean fewer government employees, does not lessen the influence of special interests, and does not reduce paperwork.

As for the impact of block grants on making services less fragmented, the prospects are also dim. In a study of five communities that were specifically funded and provided with technical assistance to help them put services together as part of a child health initiative of the Robert Wood Johnson Foundation, the evaluators were struck by how little progress the five sites were able to make in decategorizing funds and services. They concluded that even when federal programs are combined into block grants and delegated to the states, "state and local governments are likely to continue to impose restrictions on the use of block granted funds." Several local grantees even found states *re*categorizing funds that the federal government had decategorized. Moreover, the evaluators pointed out, some services needed for specific populations of children and families may require funding from several different block grants. They concluded that "fragmentation will not be eliminated simply by the reorganization of programs into federal block grants," and that when block grants incorporate spending cuts, the chances of decategorization may be diminished, since program administrators are much less willing to pool resources when money is scarce.

If devolution does not *guarantee* debureaucratization, does it provide *opportunities* for debureaucratization and greater flexibility?

Optimists on this score are influenced by Justice Louis Brandeis's theory of states as places where social experiments can be designed and evaluated. That is exactly how much of America's social insurance evolved, to be adapted into national policy by the New Deal. Since then the world has become more complicated, but state governments have also become more competent. Alice Rivlin points out that, in a period of twenty-five years, states have, for the most part, turned themselves into modern, responsive governments with vastly strengthened capacity.

Still, there is room for skepticism about how the poor, the cities, and minorities will fare at the hands of states in the future. There is reason to doubt the ability of the states to weather economic turbulence in a global economy. And the states have not always exercised their powers justly.

State power, as E. J. Dionne has written, was used by southern states first to defend slavery and later segregation. "It took federal action to overturn both, and this bred into liberals a deep skepticism of devolutionist arguments." Early in the twentieth century, it took federal power to curb unfettered profit seeking, scandalous health, safety, and labor practices, and other excesses of big business—not solely because states were unwilling to take on the "malefactors of great wealth," but because they lacked the power to do so.

States will find it harder than the federal government to maintain a floor of protection under needy families, as we shall see in Chapter 6 on welfare reform. To vindicate Justice Brandeis's vision, states would have to set out, thoughtfully and systematically, to adopt policies and programs designed to achieve agreed public purposes rather than to shore up outmoded bureaucracies.

If states are to be at the forefront of creating a better life for Americans in the twenty-first century, governors, state legislators, and administrators must grasp the difficulty of the task. They have to distinguish between the flexibility of rules that enable a child welfare worker to provide a housing voucher to an evicted family instead of taking the children away and the "flexibility" of civil service rules that allow a worker "to go from feeding animals at the zoo one day to investigating sexual abuse complaints the next day," without regard to training. They must recognize that "outstationing" staff into neighborhoods and establishing "one-stop" human service centers in the community will not improve outcomes unless they are combined with changes enabling the people on the front lines to respond to family and community needs much more effectively than they do now.

Devolution offers no assurance in itself that anything will go better in the encounter between teacher and pupil, between physician and patient, or between child welfare worker and family. Shuffling administrative and fiscal responsibilities among various levels of government will not improve outcomes unless bureaucracies themselves are reconstructed to support what works.

SERVICE INTEGRATION AND COLLABORATION WILL NOT SOLVE THE BUREAUCRACY PROBLEM

The fragmentation of services caused by bureaucratic specialization and categorization is probably the single most obvious obstacle to delivering effective services and supports for families most in need of outside help.

Because fragmentation is so destructive and because changes at the funding source have seemed so unlikely, the bulk of human-services-reform energy of the past two decades has gone into efforts to integrate services at the point of delivery. The enormous difficulty of this task—of getting local agencies competing for shrinking resources to collaborate instead—has resulted in service integration coming to be seen as an end in itself rather than as a means to achieve improved outcomes. The difficulty of the task also has deflected attention from the possibility that the services being integrated may be inappropriate, of mediocre quality, rendered grudgingly, and wholly inadequate to actual needs.

Inherent in the push for service integration is acceptance of the legitimacy and value of each of the collaborating programs, even though some may be deeply flawed. Agencies that pride themselves on responsiveness may be expected to integrate with others not sharing that orientation. Those that have found they can serve clients more effectively by providing services at the site of their job training, family support center, or afterschool recreation program may, in the interest of not duplicating services, be expected to ask clients to use services located elsewhere that they consider inadequate. For example, the comprehensive Beethoven Project in Chicago's Robert Taylor Homes was told to refer pregnant women to a nearby health department clinic for prenatal care instead of providing care directly, on site. They were unwilling to do so because they knew that the clinic did not treat patients with the respect that the Beethoven Project considered essential to effective care.

Purely local attempts at service integration have not been able to solve the fragmentation problem. They cannot overcome the complexity of existing financing streams and administrative practices, the sheer insufficiency of needed services, the absence of informal supports, and the isolation of the service sector from the community or economic conditions that created many of the needs for services.

Even the Manpower Demonstration Research Corporation, which generally tries to encourage incremental reforms, reported in 1994 that service integration, or simply making connections between schools and social services, does not reorient services toward prevention, does not result in individualizing services, does not make services family centered, and does not make services more flexible.

Although service integration could do very little to actually improve outcomes, it became the reform of choice in the 1970s, 1980s, and early 1990s. It was so popular because it offered the opportunity to do something without requiring new funds, and without requiring changes in existing bureaucracies. Efforts to integrate services often seemed most compelling when what was actually needed were new social policies.

PRIVATIZATION AND ENTREPRENEURSHIP WILL NOT SOLVE THE BUREAUCRACY PROBLEM

Proponents of privatization look to it to reduce the costs, size, and scope of government. If the bureaucratic constraints of the public sector are the problem, says James Q. Wilson, "the solution is not to seek an alternative form of government operations, but to reduce reliance on government." Privatization has become the 1990s elixir. It has been advanced, as Paul Starr points out, as "a sovereign cure for virtually all ailments of the body politic," mainly by people who are convinced that government is evil or—at best—"incurably incompetent."

The most committed privatizers would turn over to the private sector as much of government as possible and would encourage as much competition as possible for what must remain in public hands, especially by contracting out public functions to the private sector.

A less strident and more optimistic version of the privatization argument is made by David Osborne and Ted Gaebler in their influential 1992 book, *Reinventing Government.* Their analysis was embraced by President Clinton, who said their book should be read by every elected official in America.

The diagnosis in *Reinventing Government* is surely on target: "The kind of governments that developed during the industrial era, with their sluggish, centralized bureaucracies, their preoccupation with rules and regulations, and their hierarchical chains of command, no longer work very well." But the prescribed cure—an infusion of the entrepreneurial spirit—promises more than it can deliver.

Much good work has resulted from the push toward making government more entrepreneurial and innovative. At the federal level, entire volumes of rule books, with purchase specifications for items ranging from ashtrays to fruitcakes, have been scrapped with great fanfare. Outcomes and missions have been elevated to unprecedented prominence—at least in rhetoric—and economic incentives for excellent performance have been adopted. Cities are putting services out for bids, with some, like Indianapolis, allowing city workers to compete with private business on everything from repairing engines to fixing potholes.

But, as we shall see, what works for fixing potholes may not work for strengthening families.

Contracting Out Won't Solve the Bureaucracy Problem

The most frequent form of privatization is when a government agency contracts with a private nonprofit agency or a business to do the work the government agency is responsible for. It has become the trendy bipartisan answer to every challenge, including demands for lower costs, greater flexibility, and more responsiveness.

So dominant a pattern has contracting out become that most of the public money for social services is spent through private nonprofit contractors, and government has become the principal source of nonprofit human service agency financing.

So why has contracting out not solved the problems of bureaucracy?

Human services differ too profoundly from such government functions as trash collection, where contracting out *has* solved the problems of bureaucracy. Human services only rarely meet the conditions that make competition a solution.

Contracting out brings benefits, theorists and practitioners agree, if and only if the task or product can be specified with precision in advance, the contractor's performance can be evaluated immediately after the fact, and contractors can be easily replaced if performance is unacceptable.

But these conditions of meaningful competition are unlikely to prevail in the provision of human services. The contracting agency cannot issue clear and unchanging specifications in advance, evaluate effectiveness quickly, and shift contracts among easily replaceable bidders without disrupting the consistency, continuity, and stability of its services.

The lack of qualified providers inhibits competition, and the system easily becomes provider dominated. "The monopolistic behavior of government, which lay at the core of the privatization argument," writes Donald Kettl, "has been replaced by monopolistic behavior on the part of its contractors." Indianapolis Mayor Stephen Goldsmith, who has pushed privatization hard, says, "If you bring in a private contractor with a monopoly, you're not going to be any better off—maybe worse." The result, says Kettl, is that "whatever advantages contracting out for social services might produce, greater efficiency through market tested competition is not one of them."

When contracting out brings savings and the greater flexibility it promises, it is usually the result, writes UCLA law professor Joel Handler, of "less unionization, younger workers, lower wages, lower benefits, less job security, and less due process. . . ."

As the public sector came, in the past twenty years, to dominate the private human service sector, the unsolved problems of the public sector were simply duplicated in the private sector. As public money flowed to private providers, the demands for standardization and for accountability through compliance with prescribed procedures resulted in "an inexorable shift away from flexibility." Private agencies with major public funding become bureaucratized and increasingly resemble public agencies. In many cases, Handler has found, "the organizations are indistinguishable."

A foundation-funded grantee attempting to spread school-based health centers in Colorado says that as soon as the search for long-term, nonfoundation financing began, both corporate and public sector prospects made it clear that the model had to be standardized and made uniform throughout the state.

Thus, if the claimed advantages of the voluntary sector disappear because nonprofit agencies must conform to public sector norms to get public funding, we cannot escape the necessity of changing public sector norms.

Reliance on Markets Won't Solve the Bureaucracy Problem, and Leaves Public Purposes Unattained

The siren call to rely on the market rather than government for essential services, including schooling and social services, is being heeded in the 1990s not just by laissez-faire conservatives but also by traditional liberals. Citizens fed up with bureaucratic inefficiency, gridlock, and lack of accountability find it tempting to think that the bureaucracy problem could be solved if we were willing to become a nation of customers. Employees of the Department of Motor Vehicles would become more attentive and teachers more dedicated because they and their institutions would be in competition for satisfied, sovereign consumers.

It takes more than market pressures to make institutions act responsively. Students at the University of California at Berkeley are treated no less respectfully than students at Stanford University, although one is a state institution and the other private. They are treated well at both institutions because, as students in prestigious universities, they have high standing in the society. When it comes to providing education or social services for powerless and undervalued people, the value of their voucher is unlikely to make them into such powerful customers that schools and health clinics and child welfare agencies will reform and become effective at last. It is only when institutions and agencies deliberately set out to change norms, to treat even nonpowerful clients with respect, and to remove the bureaucratic obstacles that have kept them from being effective in the past that we will see the changes which improve outcomes. And that can happen under public, private, or mixed auspices, as we shall see in the examples of debureaucratization that follow.

There is very little about privatization—or even about introducing a more entrepreneurial culture—that makes agencies and front-line workers more effective. Privatization offers no strategy for helping front-line workers to manage situations over which they have little control. Privatization does offer the promise of less restrictiveness, but how much restrictiveness we want to impose on public institutions is not a given. Why should we not be having a national conversation to debate this question, rather than running away from it in the hope that the market will offer a way out?

Privatization leaves unsolved the problem of defining organizational values and missions. If one of the objectives of privatization is to "empower" clients by turning them into sovereign customers, we must be aware how often those needing the service are not the customers. Health care providers depend on insurers more than on patients, and for-profit day care centers serve their owners' bottom line more than children or their parents.

Handler concludes from his study of privatization that "the claims of enhanced consumer autonomy or empowerment under privatization are simply not plausible" because even with privatization and contracting out, "clients are simply not important stakeholders."

We are brought back to the question of achieving public purposes.

Businesses are more easily managed than government agencies (as a bevy of CEOs who have gone from large corporations to government have testified) precisely because they do not have to meet a complex array of public purposes.

To contend that valued public purposes cannot be achieved with reforms that rely on unleashing market forces is not to say that these valued public purposes are currently being attained within the public sector. It is to say that they will be attained only by reforms specifically designed to achieve these valued common purposes, be they an educated citizenry or safe streets or strong families.

Publicly funded programs—from Medicaid and the public schools to Head Start and college loans—exist in America precisely because, in some areas of our lives, private markets are not adequate to serve our common purposes. The market by its very nature distributes benefits on the basis of economic power. Government, on the other hand, is not just one participant among others in a lively market; it is the participant vested with intrinsic responsibility for pursuing the public interest.

Public institutions offer a "countervailing logic to the logic of markets," writes Robert Kuttner, editor of *The American Prospect*. Public institutions remind us that our nation is more than a giant market, that there is an American commons to protect. We give up at our peril community institutions, like public schools, libraries, parks, community centers, public transportation, and national service, in which the classes mix and income is irrelevant.

That makes it imperative that we focus on making public institutions, in Kuttner's words, as "nimble, innovative, decentralized, and accountable as their entrepreneurial suitors."

Reliance on Charities Also Leaves the Bureaucracy Problem Unsolved and Public Purposes Unattained

After the Republican congressional victories of 1994, new and old proposals surfaced to turn over responsibility for helping the poor to private charities as a means of reducing both government power and government spending.

Most private charities were appalled. They recognized that they could not possibly come up with the magnitude of resources to meet the needs of those who cannot fend for themselves. Some politicians were also appalled, asking how a democracy can cede to the affluent the decision of who shall be helped. Former Governor Mario Cuomo said, "Your ability to help those millions of people who are in terrible trouble would depend upon the willingness of the rich people in this society to make contributions . . . to their favorite charity. . . . You can't conceivably imagine that that would meet the need. What you're really doing is finding an excuse not to help those people."

The United States is unique among nations in the generosity of private donors, but most of the money raised by charities goes to support the services that donors themselves use—symphonies, the ballet, museums, and the universities they expect their children to go to. Most recent data show cultural contributions are up, while donations to organizations providing human services are down.

Sharon Daly, lobbyist for Catholic Charities USA, says that the agency expects calls on its help "will just about double" as it faces "a drop in direct government support for charitable organizations just as demand for their help surges because of simultaneous cuts in federal entitlement programs."

Even agencies operating with very little public money, like the largest emergency food pantry in Utah, dread the impending federal cuts. Glenn Bailey, who runs that agency, said, "There is no way that churches and private charities are going to be able to make up billions of dollars. There is no way private giving can handle that . . . And that will become painfully obvious to average Americans when they see levels of pain and suffering never anticipated."

After the 1996 repeal of federal welfare guarantees, expectations escalated that private charities could somehow take up the slack. But it became increasingly common to read in the morning paper that one more coalition of religious leaders had tried to explain that its congregations could not make up for governmental abandonment of the "intricate and often chronic needs of the poor."

Analyses prepared for Independent Sector show that between 1997 and 2002, nonprofits are likely to lose a cumulative total of $89.1 billion of federal revenues. To offset these cuts, private giving would have to increase by 57 percent—nineteen times faster than its projected rate of increase.

Radical proposals to remove government entirely from any efforts to help the poor and cede that responsibility exclusively to private charities became increasingly popular among a conservative reform fringe. This idea, which most historians believed was buried with the nineteenth century, was revived in a 1992 book, *The Tragedy of American Compassion,* by University of Texas journalism professor Marvin Olasky. It was rescued from obscurity by House Speaker Newt Gingrich in 1995, and subsequently by the ultraconservative doyenne Arianne Huffington, both touting it as a blueprint for replacing the welfare state.

The keys to fighting poverty successfully, according to Olasky, are to avoid depersonalizing the helping process and to emphasize Christian religious conversion. Social conservatives believe that private charities, especially religious ones, can do what publicly financed agencies can't do: They can stress the personal responsibility, discipline, and spiritual values that could transform the needy.

The reader will recognize that I agree with Olasky about the centrality of the personal touch in the helping process. As we saw in the first chapter, human relationships are central to effective interventions, and a spiritual dimension is often an important component as well. Many of those most concerned about these delicate aspects of effective interventions have given up on a governmental role in operating, even funding, such interventions.

I differ with Olasky in that I believe that close personal relationships, and even a spiritual component, *can* be parts of programs that operate with public funds. The public standards that must be observed in providing publicly funded services can be reconciled with a highly individualized approach; the front-line worker can exercise discretion in whether a parent needs help with cultivating job prospects, learning how to be a better parent, or overcoming a drug habit without being free to favor white homeless men over black, or being allowed to require the acceptance of religious guidance as a condition for help.

TAMING BUREAUCRACIES, RENEWING THE PUBLIC SECTOR

As a society, we have no choice but to figure out how to reconcile the protections provided by traditional bureaucracies with more flexible approaches that would enable large institutions and systems—even those in the public sector—to operate more effectively. But what good is such an assertion when bureaucratic theory says that it can't be done?

James Q. Wilson, preeminent scholar of bureaucracy, says less bureaucracy in large public institutions may well be desirable, but it can't be achieved. He knows exactly what makes for strong and effective public institutions and concludes that we can't have them: "If an agency is to have a sense of mission, if constraints are to be minimized, if authority is to be decentralized, if officials are to be judged on the basis of the outputs they produce rather than the inputs they consume, then legislators, judges, and lobbyists will have to act against their own interests . . . [and] it is hard to imagine this happening."

I wonder if that will be forever true. I wonder if we really have to accept the idea that the interests of legislators and judges (leave the lobbyists aside for the moment) are so divergent from the common interest. Aren't we all beginning to see that strong and effective public institutions are indeed in the public interest, and that the nation's common purposes cannot be achieved without strong and effective public institutions at every level of government, without strong and effective partnerships among public and private institutions and the communities they serve?

It is true, as another scholar of bureaucracy, the Harvard Kennedy School's Alan Altshuler, points out, that in government authority is typically fragmented, value conflicts are endemic, employee socialization is haphazard, and bureaucratic innovation is risky. But must it remain so forever?

The public sector *can* be renewed, says bureaucracy scholar Steven Kelman, if we are willing to break with the traditions that value the bureaucratic virtues of regularity and impartiality above all else, and if we are willing to abandon the "tangles of rules and clearances [that] discourage innovation and lead public employees to believe they have done their jobs as long as they have adhered to the rules." Instead, he says, "We need a new model of human service management that relies less on rules and more on discretion, judgment, and creativity."

Is that sheer fantasy or could that actually happen? The only convincing answer would have to come from actual experience. The stories that follow show that a beginning is being made.

TALES OF SUCCESS IN TAMING BUREAUCRACIES

In the following pages we examine evidence that bureaucracies are actually being tamed and that a postbureaucratic model is actually evolving. These are stories of bureaucracies in the process of being transformed—some from inside, some from outside—into institutions within which flexible ways of working are gaining a foothold. New ways of working with mainstream funding are slowly being developed, with the prospect of being sustained.

None of the initiatives whose stories I tell in the following pages has slain all the bureaucratic dragons I have described. But all have made progress in that direction. All show that tamed bureaucracies need not be dismissed as a pipe dream.

The first example, Walbridge Caring Communities, is the product of an unprecedented partnership among five state agencies and several local communities and school districts in Missouri. The second is the story of a group of reformers in New York City developing a system capable of supporting and holding accountable more than a hundred schools, each distinguished by its uniqueness. The third is the story of a state protecting children by supporting new partnerships between public and private agencies and new ways of working intensively with families.

MISSOURI'S CARING COMMUNITIES

They come from all over to learn from Missouri's Walbridge Caring Communities. The perceptive ones leave knowing that all of it— Walbridge itself and current efforts to expand its principles statewide—happened because a bureaucracy dared to do things differently.

In the Walnut Park section of North St. Louis, crack dealers are gradually going out of business. Mothers and fathers have received help in giving up drugs, families are being reunited, neighborhood violence is receding, schoolchildren needing extra attention are getting it in and outside the classroom. Restless teenagers have places to go and someone to turn to for help in channeling their energies, in developing discipline through sports and study, and for recreation, companionship, and mentoring. Police, citizens, social workers, and principals are joining hands to combat crime and cultivate dreams.

Caring Communities, the initiative behind these developments, was launched in May 1989 and built around the Walbridge Elementary School in St. Louis. Five months later, a second Caring Communities project was added in Missouri's rural Knox-Schuyler counties region. By 1995, with a $24 million shot in the arm from the Missouri legislature, Caring Communities had expanded to some fifty new sites around the state.

The program's early successes in St. Louis and its later expansion statewide reflect the rare vision and risk-taking spirit of a group of state agency leaders who sowed the seeds, set the ground rules, made a commitment to flexibility that involved adjusting and readjusting course as necessary, and then stepped back. In the process of expanding a successful model, the state of Missouri simplified procurement, changed traditional budgeting and financing practices, and state officials—in a virtually unprecedented move—relinquished traditional centralized controls so that local leaders could give the program a form and flavor reflecting the needs and strengths of individual neighborhoods and communities.

To understand this departure from the traditional, one has to go back to the late 1980s, when Keith Shafer, then director of the state department of mental health, approached Bob Bartman, commissioner of education, about his concern that youth and family problems were undermining communities and eating away at agency budgets. Shafer suggested they think about a pilot project that could keep these problems from always reaching crisis proportions before help became available.

The two officials decided to approach social services director Gary Stangler, who already had a reputation for doing whatever it takes to get the job done, even if that meant major departures from long-standing practice. The social services department was also known for its ingenuity in obtaining funding from new sources to expand child and family services.

The three department heads went on to enlist the director of the state health department. Together they gained the backing of the St. Louis schools and the St. Louis-based Danforth Foundation.

Looking for an urban site to house their vision of blended services around a school-community collaboration, the partners approached the Walbridge school. Located in a poor, urban, primarily African-American area in North St. Louis, the school serves a neighborhood with high rates of unemployment, family disruption, substance abuse, and drug dealing. Since the late 1970s, Walbridge had been operating as one of several school-community centers that offered neighborhood outreach services. Its principal, James Ewing, was already committed to collaboration, and its community-school coordinator, Khatib Waheed, embraced the opportunity to push state officials toward a broader vision of seamless services, community safety, and family well-being. Waheed had already established a reputation as an effective youth leader, role model, and charismatic community activist—with an uncanny knack for building alliances and a round-the-clock commitment to making them work.

The state agency leaders were prepared to support his vision, recalls Waheed, now the director of Caring Communities in St. Louis. Together they set broad goals, such as keeping children in school, off the streets, and out of the juvenile-justice and foster-care systems. But the state officials understood that to accomplish these goals, they needed to go into partnership with the neighborhood.

The partnership crafted by Waheed, using his own community connections, included block-association captains and community activists, families who had never had a voice in policy matters, as well as the usual institutional stakeholders. The group drew its power from a local advisory board of parents, school staff, community leaders, and funding partners.

Realizing that the local people could not succeed wholly on their own, the state officials established an interagency team of middle-level managers from each department to help them cut through red tape and help make sense of the systems they had to work within, "to make happen whatever needed to happen for this to be successful," says Jan Carter of the state department of mental health.

Boundaries between educators and service providers were made easier to cross by ensuring that principals and teachers had a pivotal role in the planning process.

Families in crisis are linked with intensive in-home supports and services. Children having difficulty at home or in school can get special tutoring and attend afterschool programs and summer camps. For older children, the community center offers fitness classes, homework help, Ping-Pong and pool, and Saturday night dances. Karate classes instill discipline and allow older students to mentor and demonstrate their mastery to younger ones.

Mary Lewis, a sixty-two-year-old grandmother caring for her grandson, Jason, because of his mother's drug problems, says the counseling and companionship helped to pull Jason out of his despondency over his mother's absence.

A coherent set of support services is available, from short-term financial help to pre-employment training, GED classes, and respite nights—pizza parties and well-supervised all-night slumber parties for children—to give overburdened parents some time to themselves. Many parents have become active in school parent organizations and volunteer work, and some hold jobs in the school. Others have come to see it as a refuge and comfortable place to spend time.

Patricia Fedrick, who was helped to overcome her grief after her eighteen-year-old son was shot and killed over a gold necklace, is now president of the parent-teacher organization at Walbridge and chairwoman of the Caring Communities advisory board. Denise Bailey, whose family got twenty-four-hour-a-day support for months after their home was fire-bombed by drug dealers, has a part-time job as a school crossing guard, while her husband works at the teen center.

Perhaps the most striking part of the St. Louis program is how successfully professionals are working with community residents to purge the community of drug influence. Caring Communities has its own substance-abuse counselors, who patiently but persistently try to gain parents' trust and steer those who need it toward treatment and rehabilitation. Working closely with the local police—who have gone from passive skeptics to steadfast supporters—the program has staged periodic drug marches. The marchers carry placards and chant menacing anti-drug messages, courageously zooming in on suspected crack houses. Police credit the program with helping to shut down more than twenty crack houses.

Waheed points to the cultural and spiritual foundation of Caring Communities as an important factor in its success—one which would surely have been impossible in a more bureaucratic climate. The program is grounded in Afrocentricity, emphasizing the history and contributions of African-Americans, and using Swahili principles. But Waheed emphasizes that the approach is not exclusionary. Children are taught to appreciate the contributions of all peoples and to try to correct their own failings while assuming collective responsibility for their families and communities.

Continuing to expand the partnership's purview, Waheed recently launched a series of meetings with influential adult males in the community to map out a plan to coax local gang members into Caring Communities activities and away from their more destructive pursuits.

"A lot of this [success] has to do with Khatib and what he brings to it as a person—his consistency, his visionary nature in terms of children and families," says Jan Carter of the mental health department. "But all those involved acknowledge that Waheed's magical touch wouldn't have been enough without the deft behind-the-scenes support of the state agencies, and without their determination that existing rules and regulations would not undermine the local work."

Hoping to preclude unnecessary placement of children in out-of-home care, Caring Communities staff established a school-based team to intervene early with families of troubled or troubling children. They designed their own intervention model, based on both family preservation and mental health approaches. This required intricate changes in state policies and in contracts with local mental-health providers. With their clear mandate from above to surmount whatever barriers stood in the way, the newly flexible bureaucrats were able to proceed with the program even before the policy details had been formally approved.

When Waheed and some of the social service professionals were asked about the barriers they had to overcome to work out of a school, they seemed perplexed. "We just did it," they said—which is precisely how those doing the behind-the-scenes maneuvering to overcome bureaucratic obstacles want it to be perceived.

State officials are full of stories about quandaries ranging from who should get billed for the pizza on respite night to how to finance the installation of school telephones to enable teachers and Caring Communities staffers to stay in touch. "At first, every time an invoice came in, everyone asked which department was going to pay for this," recalls Kathy Martin of the department of social services. They all agree it's becoming easier, and are no longer nervous about what the state auditor might say. They make clear to a visitor from Washington that the group was scrupulous about never doing anything illegal, but that they were under clear instructions to solve problems in ways that would allow them to get the job done.

The initial success of Walbridge Caring Communities persuaded Governor Mel Carnahan to issue an executive order in November 1993 to institutionalize the changes, creating a new alliance to further the collaborative efforts of the agencies involved. Called the Family Investment Trust, it has a board of directors that includes five state cabinet officers as well as community leaders. The trust is now a policy-setting body that serves as the vehicle for collaborative decision making and for technical assistance to help state agencies support community partnerships. Its goals are to achieve better results for children and families by revamping the way services are delivered, decisions made, and dollars spent.

Kathy Martin, who had been working with Caring Communities since 1989, was designated as chief operating officer for Caring

Communities statewide. Based in Gary Stangler's social services department, Martin is the point person for the integration of finances and services among all the departments involved in the partnership.

In its biggest feat of boundary-crossing yet, the original four agencies developed the first multiagency budget proposal ever submitted to the Missouri legislature, and in 1993 lobbied jointly for its approval. In an action that Stangler considers one of the group's major triumphs, the legislature approved an unprecedented $4 million package to expand the Walbridge program to eight other sites in the state.

In 1994, the Family Investment Trust board took another remarkable step. In response to the urging of a St. Louis businessman, Reggie Dixon, it decided to expand the goals of Caring Communities to include parent employment and invited the Department of Labor and Industrial Relations to join the partnership.

In 1995, the group upped the ante further and gained the legislature's support for a $24 million cross-agency expansion of Caring Communities to some thirty to sixty new sites in fiscal 1996. In this go-around, the agencies not only increased their financial commitments but agreed to a unified, decategorized budgeting process that no longer hinged on separate invoices and separate payments.

Now, Gary Stangler explains, the initiative had reached a new stage. It should no longer have to depend on the hand-crafted, ad hoc arrangements made behind the scenes among individual government officials. If the promising but fragile front-line innovations were to be protected, they would have to become part of a broader strategy to reform human services across the state. The state agency leaders sought and obtained specific authorizing legislation for their Caring Communities activities.

In their scale-up efforts, the partners drew a lesson from one of their few disappointments. There had been less progress than hoped in school achievement among Walbridge students. While an early evaluation showed marked improvements in reading, mathematics, work habits, and behavior among those children who got the most intensive services through Caring Communities, the rest did not make significant gains in standardized test scores. Waheed and others contend that it was more important at the beginning for the school to initiate community-building activities and to set in motion a service-delivery system that would address the urgent needs of families than it was to take on a massive school-restructuring effort. As one teacher observed, test scores may not go up for several years, but motivation and learning are bound to thrive when children and families have a basic sense of security and support.

But now, in the expansion phase, officials took care to select schools willing to make a commitment to education reform strategies, such as Accelerated Schools, being pursued under the state's Outstanding Schools Act. "These new sites will have the dual benefits of support systems in place for families as well as changes in the classroom," says Bob Bartman. "We've also gotten a little bit more refined about outcomes and more thoughtful about putting systems in place to measure those achievements," adds Kathy Martin.

In what could be a textbook illustration of how debureaucratizing and shifting to outcomes accountability go hand in hand, Stangler explains that a critical element of the expansion has involved setting benchmarks as the basis for results-based accountability. The process has become a two-way conversation in which the state agency partners bring to the table basic categories of results to be achieved, and the benchmarks are set with the full input of the community. "We are not just block granting," Martin emphasizes. "We are definitely at the table working with them."

The commitment to encouraging local variation and to allowing local programs to evolve over time remains unchanged—partly out of necessity. The politics of the big cities are very different from those of small communities, says Stangler. The Afrocentric model that works so well in St. Louis, for example, would not fit sites with different demographics. But ensuring that programs in those communities draw on their own cultures is considered just as critical.

In some communities, neighborhood safety is a paramount concern; in others, it's finding constructive activities for latchkey children or providing adults with continuing education or job-seeking skills. Stangler makes the ultimate unbureaucratic observation, "I think you could say that we're becoming comfortable with the idea that it's okay for those developments to look different from one community to another."

At the state level, officials are wary of federal cutbacks, which could shake at least some of the foundations on which Caring Communities was built. "The governor and the state directors have said this effort will continue as a priority," declares Phyllis Rozansky, director of the Family Investment Trust, even though, "depending on the actions of Congress, it could get tough."

But Caring Communities has maintained its momentum and its funding through a shift from a Republican to a Democratic governor, through changes in state legislative leadership, and changes at the helm of the state departments of health and mental health. Support has transcended politics and personality, and there are many signs that the bureaucratic innovations it has brought about have indeed been institutionalized.

NEW YORK NETWORKS FOR SCHOOL RENEWAL: ACCOUNTABILITY
WITHOUT CRIPPLING CONSTRAINTS

Deborah Meier is one of a handful of the nation's famous school principals. She became famous for founding and heading one and then ultimately four successful public schools in East Harlem. Her story became legend. In a school district with the worst attendance, highest rate of suspensions, and poorest ranking in reading and math of the thirty-two school districts in New York City, with half the population living below the poverty line, Deborah Meier, Anthony Alvarado, Sy Fliegel, and other pioneers turned things around.

When I went to see her in 1986 so I could describe her achievements at Central Park East in *Within Our Reach,* Deborah Meier was reluctant to generalize from her experience. "You can't replicate a school any more than you can replicate a family," she said. "Education is not like manufacturing an automobile. One must have respect for the uniqueness of education."

Over the next several years she was pushed by the national turmoil around school reform, and by colleagues, particularly education reformer Ted Sizer, to expand her one-school-at-a-time focus. She was pushed to extract principles from her experience that would make it easier for others to succeed. Her book, *The Power of Their Ideas,* about her life as a teacher and principal, hinted that she was beginning a new stage, waking up each morning "worrying about 'other people's' schools," not only her own. In her last chapter she wrote that if schools were not to "drive out the best educators and undermine the natural drive to do one's best that lies at the heart of good parenting and good schooling," bureaucracies must change. She was beginning to generalize from her experience, identifying the conditions that foster good teaching as "small schools, schools of choice, school autonomy over the critical dimensions of teaching and learning, lots of time for building relationships and reflecting on what's happening, along with a culture of mutual respect for others and a set of habits of mind that fosters inquiry as well as responsibility."

It did not come as a complete surprise, then, to learn, in the summer of 1994 that Deborah Meier had been named an Annenberg fellow and was becoming associated with a new school reform effort in New York City, to be funded in large part with money from America's biggest financier of education reform, Walter Annenberg. And it was no surprise at all to learn that it would plow new ground in large-scale reform because its hallmark, according to Meier, would be "cherishing and celebrating the idiosyncratic."

What makes this venture so fascinating is that Meier and her new colleagues were as committed to solving the bureaucracy problem as they were to promoting their own approaches to educating children and organizing schools. They knew that, to be taken seriously, they would have to be able to demonstrate that no matter how idiosyncratic, their schools would improve student achievement and could be held to account for doing so in an equitable and fiscally responsible fashion.

This bold effort to revitalize public education was designed to build on the experience of a body of effective small schools already in existence at the time it formally began, in 1994. These included the New Visions Schools, established under the auspices of the Fund for New York City Public Education at the invitation of the then chancellor, Joe Fernandez. The Fund had been asked, in 1992, to come up with a workable alternative for a school system "overwrought by fiscal, structural, and societal challenges." The first fifteen New Visions schools were all small, academically rigorous, and collaboratively designed and supported by teams of educators and community representatives. They obtained waivers from the board of education and the teachers' union to exercise greater freedom in selecting faculty so they could match their skills and interests with those of the schools, students, and parents. An unusually open process of soliciting proposals and choosing from among them succeeded in bridging the gaps between school and community and enhancing public participation.

Under Meier's leadership, the Fund for New York City Public Education, the Center for Educational Innovation of the Manhattan Institute (a conservative think tank), the progressive grassroots organization ACORN, and the Center for Collaborative Education (the New York City affiliate of the Coalition for Essential Schools) joined to create the New York Networks for School Renewal. Each of the sponsors had impressive track records of restructuring existing schools or creating small schools. When they first met together in the spring of 1995, they realized that, among them, they had nearly eighty small schools already underway, some going back many years.

Building on their earlier experience, the sponsoring organizations found they shared the fundamental conviction that good schools are learning communities that challenge both staff and students to use their minds thoughtfully and rigorously. They believed that because a school community is best served when participants choose to be there, students, families, teachers, school leaders, and other school staff should be able to select their school on the basis of its educational approach. They were deeply committed to public schools and knew that if they were to succeed in creating a critical mass of effective small schools within the public school system, they had to enlist not only teachers and parents but also union leadership and policy makers. They were able to persuade New York's mayor and school chancellor, as well as the presidents of the board of education and the United Federation of Teachers, to join the partnership.

The reformers were acutely aware that up to now, the development, operation, and expansion of effective schools were hampered by their leaders having to spend too much of their time, energy, and resources "trying to get around the system." They were determined to create a structure that would be less cumbersome, while still holding the schools accountable for the essentials.

They knew they would have to explore a variety of ways of turning around existing schools, of making new schools out of old ones. They knew they would have to make it possible for real authority to be vested in local schools, opening the door to meaningful parent and community involvement. They knew they would have to enable new schools to break down traditional barriers isolating them from other schools by introducing technological and other solutions so that they could learn from one another.

In April of 1995, Douglas H. White, former New York State commissioner of human rights, became the project's director. He and Meier led intensive workshops, retreats, and discussions that produced ideas and draft documents for exchange among the project sponsors and project partners.

The administrative structure that evolved is designed to be lean and primarily supportive to the individual schools. It consists mainly of those working at the school level—not an extra layer of separate and distant administrators. Schools sharing similar pedagogical principles or close geographic proximity would be organized into networks supporting one another. Networks would lend the expertise of established schools to new ones. Each network would be unique. (For example, one consists of four middle schools within the same school district; another includes several high schools for limited English-proficient students; a third consists of several schools going from kindergarten through twelfth grade.) Schools are expected to work together within networks to share resources, insights, and effective practices and to develop standards and accountability mechanisms. Common indicators, including "quick and dirty" data like graduation rates and attendance, would be collected on a centralized basis.

The sponsors would provide technical assistance to the individual schools and the networks and—perhaps most important—would negotiate with the city, the state, and the unions on behalf of the schools and networks for relief from prevailing rules, regulations, and procedural requirements.

That was the easy part. The hard part was to figure out how to assure quality and accountability in dozens, perhaps hundreds of unique institutions. If the reformers were to be successful in helping more than one school at a time to escape from traditional hierarchical controls, they couldn't do it by just saying to the public, "Trust us!" They would have to be able to demonstrate that the exceptional models of the past, which worked because they were able to buck the system, could henceforth become part of a new system—a "system of exceptions" that would support and sustain them. This system would indeed cherish and celebrate the idiosyncratic, but it could, at the same time, be held publicly accountable for fiscal integrity, equity, and student achievement.

The New York reformers' invention that reconciles accountability with freedom from crippling bureaucratic constraints is the Learning Zone.

Essentially, the Learning Zone reviews the networks and certifies them as credible and reliable, doing the job they set out to do, and acting in the public interest and achieving public purposes. Once admitted to the Learning Zone, a network continues to be monitored but is immediately granted greater freedom from regulation, more direct access to its share of public resources, and greater autonomy in decision making.

A fundamental belief of the participants in the New York Networks for School Renewal is that "those closest to and most knowledgeable about schools should have the most important and critical decision-making role." (Deborah Meier says that "does not ensure that wise decisions are always made, but it stacks the deck, in the long run, in favor of wisdom and fairness.") But they also believe that "given the public nature of the enterprise," decision making by the immediate users needs to be balanced by "other publics than the immediate users." So admission to the Learning Zone must be approved by a "blue ribbon review panel of State and City education officials, educators, parents, and community leaders," which assesses the network's reliability, credibility, and capacity to conduct its business.

The Learning Zone represents a new way of balancing the need to assure the public that public funds are being spent to achieve broad public purposes with the need to allow institutions to evolve with minimal outside constraints. I believe that this group of reformers was able to achieve this new balance because they trusted each other ("We're built on trust, not on a worst scenario of schools engaged in a conspiracy to rip off tax payers, children, or school staff."), because they shared a profound commitment to the children they would be educating, and because they were willing to be accountable to the skeptics.

MICHIGAN'S STATEWIDE MOVE BEYOND BUREAUCRACY
TO PROTECT CHILDREN

Several stellar examples of governmental debureaucratization have come out of recent efforts to reform child welfare, and that is no accident.

From the mid-1980s, child welfare agencies have been in crisis, overwhelmed by escalating reports of abuse and neglect, by the numbers of children needing protection and families needing support, by the severity and complexity of family problems, and by their limited capacity to respond. Both public and private agencies had few alternatives to removing children from their families when something went wrong.

During the late 1980s and the early 1990s, the conviction spread in the child protection field that more flexible, intensive, and comprehensive services were needed. But it quickly became clear that the most promising new tools represented massive departures from prevailing practice and prevailing mind-sets. If they were not to be consigned to the margins of mainstream child welfare systems, deliberate efforts to debureaucratize would be required. Michigan took those steps.

It began in the mid-1980s, when Michigan child welfare officials heard about intensive family-based services, or "family preservation" services, as they became known, as an alternative to automatic removal of children to out-of-home care. Homebuilders in Tacoma, Washington, had shown that in many situations children could be protected without having their lives disrupted by being removed from home if their families could receive immediate intensive supports, services, and supervision from professionals trained to work with families in new ways.

In the Homebuilders model, a professional meets with families on their own turf, spends as much as twenty hours a week with a single family over a period of four to six weeks, and has a caseload of no more than two or three families at any one time. Homebuilders staff are trained to protect and monitor the safety of children while providing a mix of counseling and help with practical problems to respond to each family's unique situation.

Michigan child welfare leaders were particularly impressed by evidence that by averting unnecessary out-of-home placements, states might be able to save as much as three times the cost of family preservation services. (Residential care, also reduced by family preservation services, often costs more than ten times as much as family preservation services.) Since about 80 percent of the families that received family preservation services did not have a child removed within a year of the intervention, family preservation services could be shown to represent a substantial saving.

In 1987, the expectation of possible long-term savings persuaded the Michigan legislature to redirect $5 million from the foster care budget to a family preservation demonstration project. The Department of Social Services had requested the transfer of funds to determine whether family preservation services could bring about a reduction in the steep, 20 percent annual increase in the cost of foster care.

One Michigan legislator had become a supporter of the demonstration after having heard from his sister, Susan Kelly, how ineffectively state agencies were dealing with some of the families she was meeting as a volunteer at a soup kitchen for the homeless. Kelly, an Anglican Dominican nun since 1961, was teaching in the psychology department of the University of Michigan, also working as a therapist in a student counseling center, and volunteering at the campus soup kitchen. Concerned about the increasing number of homeless families, especially those threatened with losing their children to foster care because they could not afford adequate housing, Kelly complained to her brother the legislator about "the inhumane policies that punished families for being poor." As she recalled recently, he replied that "I should consider putting my money where my mouth was."

He told her about the newly funded demonstration program, which as yet had no director, and urged her to apply for the job. She did so after determining that working in the Department of Social

Services would be "completely compatible with the mission of the sisterhood to seek peace and social justice." She worked first as a contract employee in the exploratory phase of the project and, in due course, was appointed to the newly created job of family preservation program manager.

Kelly found that she not only had a large sum of money at her disposal, but also eighteen months for planning. "Time to plan was as great a gift as the five million dollars," she said. "So often people don't learn from what has gone before." After persuading Ken Visser, well-respected Department of Social Services insider, to work with her, a relatively unknown outsider, Kelly scoured the state, visiting protective service offices in every county. "We read case files on literally thousands of children, talked to social workers—especially black social workers, many of whom were convinced that foster care was unnecessarily destroying black families—and went with protective service workers to investigate allegations of abuse or neglect."

The months spent in reviewing files revealed that 70 to 80 percent of Michigan's foster children were taken into care because of neglect related to poverty or because of a drug problem, which was assumed to mean neglect.

"The majority of parents were not abusing their kids," Kelly said. "They were people with incredible strengths who needed help getting out of poverty, learning parenting skills, and enrolling in drug treatment."

During this early planning phase, the Edna McConnell Clark Foundation helped Michigan with its planning process, arranging for Kelly and Visser to meet with leading practitioners nationwide and attend training sessions at the Behavioral Sciences Institute, the technical assistance arm of Homebuilders. Visser recalls, "We asked questions, shared experiences and visited programs in Washington State, New York, New Jersey, and Maryland. We had a lot of wisdom going in."

One piece of advice Kelly and Visser rejected was to start small and go slow. Visser said the experts "were afraid that a big failure would set all of us back." But Kelly and Visser feared that, with $5 million to spend, if they couldn't point to a significant impact within two years, the skeptics in the legislature and the Department of Social Services would never give them another chance. The gamble paid off.

Calling their program Families First, they contracted with twenty nonprofit agencies to provide front-line services. Kelly believes it would have been impossible to maintain the flexible operating conditions and "model fidelity" required by Families First without contracting out. She was particularly concerned that hiring decisions not depend on seniority. "We want people who can operate as team members, who don't come into a home with answers, but can listen, and can learn new ways of relating to families."

Kelly and Visser also stipulated that the agencies implement a clearly defined service model with a clearly defined population. The discretion workers at the front lines could exercise in responding to family needs would be coupled with rigor in adherence to key principles, assessment of child safety, and methods of service delivery. Finally, the program would make a major investment in oversight and monitoring and in training and evaluation to prevent "model drift"—deviations from Families First quality standards.

As time went on, Kelly became ever more firmly convinced that model drift posed a serious threat to keeping children safe. In particular, the apparent failure of several family preservation programs in Illinois convinced her that unless standards were rigorously enforced and low caseloads maintained, quality could be diluted and the safety of children jeopardized. The decision as to which children could remain safely in their own homes if their families received intensive services, and which had to be removed, had to be made in accordance with the highest quality standards.

Having made these judgments about program design, there remained the formidable task of convincing local departments of child protective services—and the agencies they would be contracting with—to try Families First.

Jim Beougher, director of Lenawee County Department of Social Services, says, "Susan Kelly brought us more than persistence. She had a complete package: There were protocols, staffing requirements, extensive training, consultation, computer tracking and evaluation systems, a management team, contract specifications, and high-level backing from the governor's office. That's what instilled confidence in us to give it a try."

But it wasn't just the public agencies that had to be persuaded; so did the private agencies. Edna Walker, director of Lutheran Child and Family Service of Michigan, explained her initial hesitation. "We are an old-line agency, founded in 1899 and steeped in the tradition of child protection, which meant child removal. We saw our job as saving children, not saving their families." But she says now that the agency has found the new approach reconciles keeping children safe and strengthening families, they are committed to it.

Although Families First services are provided by private agencies under contract to local departments of social services, clients must be referred or approved by the local departments' foster care staff. Initially there was some concern that this arrangement might produce antagonism between the public and private sectors. Instead, showing that a shared focus on outcomes and on more flexible ways of working can result in new connections in support of the community's children, the shared responsibility has encouraged a trusting, collaborative partnership that did not exist before Families First.

Families First staff take responsibility for linking families with the assistance essential to reducing their level of stress and despair, be it in locating safe and adequate housing, confronting landlords failing to provide heat in winter, evicting an abusive boyfriend, finding adequate child care, or even repairing a leaking toilet. In each case, Families First workers solve problems collaboratively *with* family members, not *for* them, so that parents will then have the ability to solve problems on their own. This is one more way that Families First instills hope. As Ladora Barnett, director of Caregivers in Detroit, observed, "We don't just talk about hope, we give them the resources to make hope a reality."

In another departure from bureaucratic tradition, Families First gives in-home staff the discretion to spend $300 to $400 per family for repairing or replacing a refrigerator or a washing machine or buying a tire or a stroller. "It's smarter, kinder, and cheaper to help a family purchase these essentials if the alternative is putting the kids in foster care and the parents into a homeless shelter," one worker explained. At the same time, families are helped to link up with long-term resources in the community, such as health care, drug treatment, self-help, or a religious organization that can continue to provide support after the crisis abates.

By 1992, it became clear that the Families First intervention, together with other reforms in Michigan's human services, was reducing the number of children in foster care. This evidence, coupled with moving testimony from families who had completed the program, encouraged state officials to expand the program statewide.

To support expansion without sacrificing quality, Families First has made a major investment in administrative oversight and quality control. Kelly insists that program managers provide front-line workers with the same kind of supportive caring, concern, and advice that the workers, in turn, are expected to provide to families. One in-home staff worker explained that even though "I work solo with a family, I never feel I am alone. The whole agency is backing me up." Not only do program regulations require that this backup be available twenty-four hours a day, seven days a week, but front-line staff are encouraged to seek out extra consultation and supervision as often as they need it.

Families First requires that front-line workers participate in at least one hour a week of formal, individual supervision and also participate in a weekly case consultation, which gives the entire team an opportunity to review the status of each family the agency is responsible for. In addition to these two weekly meetings, supervisors regularly accompany front-line workers on home visits to assess firsthand the competence of the services and supports they are providing and—if necessary—to suggest alternative methods of handling difficult situations. The major focus of all the supervision and oversight is to ensure child safety, always the first priority.

By 1995, Families First had expanded geographically to include all eighty-two counties in the state, and had succeeded both in changing lives and changing systems. It had become stimulant to as well as beneficiary of statewide human service reform efforts. These include a mandate to decategorize funds, creation of a "Barrier Busters Board" to grant waivers to remove regulations that hinder collaborative service delivery, and a requirement that every community create a multipurpose board to coordinate all human services within the community, to achieve "collaborative, seamless, locally-controlled and family-friendly systems of services."

Kelly says that because "good programs die every day because attention has not been paid to their context," she is convinced that "changing the systems on which programs depend is really crucial to their survival."

Families First has also become the catalyst for reforming other state service systems. Kelly has been able to convince other human service agencies to train together, using the tested Families First training curriculum. This has helped to strengthen the alliance between Families First and other providers, resulting in a widespread shift in philosophy. "We treat families with respect and the respect has become contagious."

In addition, Families First has expanded its services to include others beyond the initial target group, and now serves families experiencing domestic violence, families whose children have recently returned from foster care, teenage parents living independently, families whose stability is threatened by a child's mental illness or developmental disability, and families with delinquent youths.

As its most direct effect on families and children, Kelly points to the 83 percent of children still safely living at home one year after intensive services ended and a 28 percent decrease in out-of-home placements that occurred in Michigan between 1993 and 1995, a period when the number of children in out-of-home care increased in almost every other state. The state legislature endorsed the new ways of working with families by increasing the annual appropriation for Families First to $23 million in 1995.

Susan Kelly believes that now Families First is operating throughout the state, it has had a dramatic effect even beyond the families receiving intensive services. It has changed assumptions and practices in domestic violence shelters, public health clinics, the family court system, public schools, juvenile detention facilities, and departments of child protective services. Even state legislators, she says, have become more sophisticated about how to protect vulnerable children and families.

Lessons for Moving Toward the Post-Bureaucratic Era

Trailblazers in Missouri, New York City, and Michigan are showing that it is possible to tame bureaucracies. A critical mass of influential officials recognized that the public sector had made it too difficult to achieve common purposes and initiated a series of public decisions to impose fewer restrictions on how key public sector institutions would go about their work. Rather than turn public functions over to the private sector and hope for the best, they addressed the bureaucracy problem head-on.

These small miracles of debureaucratization, already operating in mainstream institutions and using mainstream sources of funds, are thriving outside the hothouse. They have shown that it is possible to find new ways to balance equity, quality, visibility, and accountability with flexibility, discretion, responsiveness, and effectiveness.

In each of these examples, public officials and administrators have recognized the distinction between the functions that must be standardized from the top down and those whose effectiveness hinges on being responsive to specific individuals, families, and communities. They recognize that in agencies charged with educating children and keeping them healthy, with strengthening families and communities, the centralized procedural orthodoxy underlying much of modern government, far from guaranteeing effectiveness, has undermined it. Through good management, good training and technical assistance, and new policies and practices, they are assuring quality, equity, and accountability without sanctioning arbitrariness.

In each of these examples, effective leaders succeeded in cultivating a shared view of the nature and importance of the organization's reframed and restructured tasks among front-line professionals who saw themselves as part of a voluntary community of shared beliefs, values, and norms. Managers had the time to plan, evolve, and learn from their experience. They were able to elicit from their staffs a commitment to high-quality performance that superseded pressures to serve their narrow self-interest, and freed them to exercise their discretion.

In none of these examples were those who created the bureaucratic changes left to fend for themselves. All were able to draw on outside intermediaries that offered clout and expertise—and sometimes extra funds.

Efforts to build on these examples will use their lessons and generate new ones because there is no single model of successful debureaucratization. All such efforts will find that achieving a new balance between constraints and effectiveness becomes harder as the scale of the effort becomes larger, more visible, and more threatening to the status quo. And all will continue to require help from outside to lubricate the wheels of change.

The empirical evidence from these and similar reform efforts goes far to weaken the argument that "it can't be done." It demonstrates that the bureaucratic model that has grown dysfunctional at the end of the twentieth century can indeed be modified. With the creation of new public-private partnerships and post-bureaucratic models of public accountability, the heavy hand of bureaucracy can be gentled, neighborhood and front-line discretion can be achieved, and public purposes can be realized.

4

A New Focus on Results

THE NATION'S ABILITY to know whether programs, policies, and tax dollars are achieving their intended purpose is in the midst of a revolution.

Accountability is no longer the sole domain of auditors. The focus is shifting. What counts is no longer confined to whether rules are being complied with. Instead, accountability procedures are beginning to reflect common sense: what matters is whether public purposes are being accomplished.

For a long time, the main thing anyone could know about publicly financed programs was how much money they were spending and whether the people who staffed them were complying with the rules. We had no way of knowing whether they were achieving their intended purposes.

"What is the bottom line when there is no 'bottom line'?" asks Peter Drucker about the public sector. If profits are not the measure of value, what is? How are we to differentiate what works from what doesn't?

Much of the current debate about whether anything works and whether government does anything right is ideological. But that does not diminish the need for rigor in distinguishing between actual success and failure in achieving public purposes. Most legislators want to know what works when they vote on laws and appropriations; parents want to know how well their children are being educated; foundations want to know about the impact of their support; and the staff of social programs want to know how effective they are.

Taxpayers, having given up on compassion, demand to know whether public funds are accomplishing what their proponents promise.

As a result, improving the ability to judge the success of agencies and programs in achieving agreed-upon outcomes is becoming a major reform strategy, both in efforts to strengthen children, families, and communities and in efforts to restore confidence in our public institutions—from schools to initiatives to rebuild neighborhoods.

The new attention to results signals a profound shift, because it moves us beyond technocratic concerns with procedural protections to focus on the purpose of what we choose to pursue. If we as a nation are serious about efforts to strengthen children, families, and depleted neighborhoods, we must know the outcomes we're after and we must be continually able to monitor progress—and face up to failures as well.

The way it used to be. Until recently, anyone who wanted to know whether tax or philanthropic dollars were being spent to good purpose was offered one of three unsatisfactory responses: The most traditional response was to assume that what mattered were processes and resources. The family service agency was doing its job if its budget was increasing, if its monthly parent education sessions were well attended and supervised by a certified social worker, and if the paperwork documented that eligibility had been properly determined and that the services billed for had been rendered.

A second, more recent response has been to say that if you really want to know what's working, you have to privatize the function and let the marketplace become the judge of effectiveness. ("Shift the burden of evaluation from the shoulders of professional evaluators to the shoulders of clients, and let them vote with their feet," advises UCLA professor James Q. Wilson.)

In a third possible response, providers of health, education, and social services say, "Trust us. What we do is so valuable, so complex, so hard to document, so hard to judge, and we are so well intentioned, that the public should support us without demanding evidence of effectiveness. Don't let the bean counters who know the cost of everything and the value of nothing obstruct our valiant efforts to get the world's work done."

Since the mid-1980s, a fourth answer has emerged: accountability for results.

We have already seen that effective programs have clear missions, usually defined by the outcomes they are pursuing. The momentum with which results-based accountability is now moving, from offbeat programs to mainstream systems, reflects a growing belief that public support for social investments depends on legislators, citizens, and communities being able to hold the providers of services, supports, and education accountable for achieving the results that citizens value. Results-based accountability is also emerging as the key to freeing human services from a straitjacket of rigid rules and centralized micromanagement. And it focuses attention on whether the magnitude of investments matches the tasks to be accomplished.

The Problems That Outcomes-based Accountability Can Solve

The public wants proof of results. Increasing numbers of Americans are convinced that their taxes are not being spent wisely, and are frustrated by not knowing what they are getting for their money.

The 1995 Senate hearings on the confirmation of Dr. Henry Foster as surgeon general featured lengthy and often confused exchanges on the impact of the teenage pregnancy prevention program that Dr. Foster had founded in Nashville, Tennessee. After much discussion about the meaning of several program evaluations, Senator James Jeffords of Vermont finally said, in some exasperation, "We're fooling ourselves to think these programs are good because they feel good, when the evidence of impact isn't there."

Citizens, philanthropists, and government officials are calling for better and more usable tools to make judgments about what is working.

Attention to outcomes rather than inputs is central to the "reinventing government" proposals of David Osborne and Vice President Al Gore. But they were hardly the first to preach the outcomes gospel. Two decades before becoming budget director in the Clinton administration, Alice Rivlin was calling for better measures to assess the success of social programs, because public concern with ineffectiveness of human services was already running "very high indeed." She concluded, "All the likely scenarios for improving the effectiveness of education, health, and other social services dramatize the need for better [outcome] measures. No matter who makes the decisions, effective functioning of the system depends on measures of achievement. . . . To do better, we must have a way of distinguishing better from worse."

Outcomes accountability can free human service programs from rigid regulation. An outcomes orientation allows and encourages people to think about the results they are trying to achieve rather than the procedures they must comply with. Outcomes accountability is the best alternative to the top-down, centralized micromanagement that holds people responsible for adhering to rules so detailed that they impose an enormous paperwork burden—rules that focus attention on complying with regulations instead of on responding effectively to a wide range of urgent needs.

For better or worse, an outcomes orientation focuses everyone, from front-line worker to authorizing legislator, on why they do what they are doing. As President Clinton put it, "If the government rewards writing citations and levying fines more than safety, then there's a good chance that what you get is more citations, more fines, and no more safety."

Outcomes accountability requires clarity about goals. A lack of clarity about goals leaves no alternative to holding employees accountable for procedural correctness. In a study of federal community development grant programs, University of Wisconsin professor Donald F. Kettl found that the responsible federal agency had virtually no useful knowledge about what was going on in the communities that had received its grants. Because of "all the ambiguity over goals . . . federal investigators tended to make sure the files were well organized instead of probing to see what the programs actually accomplished."

Whereas the bureaucratic paradigm assumes that control can be exercised only through rules, an outcome orientation allows employees to channel their energies into solving problems. Staff performance improves when employees feel accountable because they regard their intended work outcomes as consequential to other people. An outcomes orientation also encourages staff to think less categorically as they become more aware of the connection between what they do and the results they seek.

Outcomes accountability becomes essential when local agencies and front-line staff are given greater discretion. When intelligently and thoughtfully implemented, outcomes accountability can become the key to flexible provision of high-quality interventions. Barbara Dyer, a veteran of both state and federal governmental reform efforts, sees outcomes accountability, with its focus on results, replacing the deeply rooted presumption of mutual distrust that runs throughout our entire governmental system, with a new attitude of trust-but-verify.

A recent dramatic illustration of how a focus on outcomes has accomplished extraordinary results comes from the New York City Police Department. The mayor and police commissioner both attribute the dramatic drop in New York City homicide rates between

1990 and 1996 to a new culture of policing in the city, founded on "giving the precinct police more discretion in their neighborhoods while holding them strictly accountable for results."

Information about outcomes enables communities to be more deliberate in support of shared purposes. "In the long run, men hit only what they aim at," said Henry David Thoreau. Agreement on a common set of goals and outcomes helps to promote a community-wide "culture of responsibility" for children and families and spurs momentum for change. The rallying cry for investment in early intervention and prevention—such as when police chiefs advocate early education and expanded recreation opportunities to prevent youth crime—becomes more credible when investments can be reliably linked to outcomes.

The flip side of Alice in Wonderland's insight that if you don't know where you're going, any road will get you there, is that knowing where you are going will minimize expenditures of energy, political capital, and funds on empty organizational changes and ineffective activities that won't get you there.

An outcomes orientation illuminates whether investments are adequate to achieve expected results. The new conversation about results may, as its most profound effect, inject a strengthened ethical core into human service systems that have often focused more on the fate of agencies and programs than on helping people. The new outcomes focus promises (or threatens, in the eyes of some) to end a conspiracy of silence between funders and program people by exposing the sham of asking human service providers, educators, and community organizations to accomplish massive tasks with wholly inadequate resources and tools.

Over the past thirty years reformers seldom faced up to the fact that those who would help disadvantaged children, families, and neighborhoods were being asked to do a very expensive job on the cheap. Equipped with the strength of a wimp, they were expected to do the job of a Hercules. Not only did resources not match aspirations, but in the eagerness to do *something* about the injustice of poverty amid plenty, we lied to ourselves—and to those who would have been helped had our interventions not been so feeble.

Attention to results forces the question of whether to expect less from limited investments or to invest more in order to achieve promised outcomes.

In the past, parent education classes have been funded in the vague expectation that they would somehow reduce the incidence of child abuse, although a few classroom sessions have never been shown to change parenting practices among parents at greatest risk of child abuse. Similarly, outreach programs to get pregnant women into prenatal care were supposed to reduce the incidence of low birth weight in the vague supposition that outreach programs are a good thing regardless of the quality of the available prenatal care.

Especially in circumstances requiring a critical mass of high-quality, comprehensive, intensive, interactive interventions to change outcomes, an outcomes orientation can help funders and program people to resist the temptation to hide the limitations of so many current efforts. A focus on outcomes could end the prevalent practice of grantees pleading with funders and evaluators to document just their efforts and not their results because it wouldn't be fair to hold them accountable for real changes in outcomes when they're doing the best they can with what they have.

Results-based accountability helps to make clear that dilution regularly transforms effective model efforts into ineffective replications. It helps to clarify that a single, circumscribed intervention may not be sufficient to change outcomes. It helps to make the argument for adequately funding a critical mass of promising interventions.

Fears of a Faustian Bargain

Critics of the push toward outcomes accountability range from skeptical to appalled. Commenting on pressures to incorporate outcomes accountability in early childhood programs, Sue Bredekamp of the National Association for the Education of Young Children says it is but "one more opportunity and justification to 'blame the victims,' because the children who are in greatest need of services demonstrate the poorest outcomes."

Skeptics see the willingness of service providers to be held accountable for achieving specified outcomes as a Faustian bargain—even when they agree that a shift toward outcomes accountability might solve serious problems. They believe that in their eagerness to obtain more funding and to escape over-regulation, human service professionals who agree to be held responsible for outcomes become unwitting tools in the wars against government, against the vulnerable, and against all public sector activities grounded in morality and social justice.

Those who resist the push to outcomes accountability have at least five specific fears.

First, they fear that *programs may be distorted.* Knowing that what gets measured gets done, they fear that what will get done will be what is most easily measured and has the most rapid payoff rather than what's really important. They point out that most communities have aspirations for their children that greatly exceed currently measurable results, especially when funders demand quick evidence of success. They worry that community health clinics will raise immunization rates at the cost of cutting support for chronically ill children, that preschool programs will deprive children of the opportunities for play that stimulate creativity and teach empathy in order to reserve more time for the flash cards whose mastery shows up on "school readiness" tests.

Second, they fear that *even effective programs will seem to accomplish less than they actually do.* Will an inner-city consortium that was funded to improve employability of youngsters coming out of high school be judged a failure if they don't get jobs as quickly as the funders had hoped? Will the consortium be held responsible for achieving citywide improvements in outcomes even though they were able to work with only 150 youngsters and their families—and the local GM plant just closed?

This fear is compounded by the possibility that outcomes-based accountability will soon lead to such hard-edged consequences as outcomes-based budgeting. An outcomes orientation may be promoted initially to serve such benign functions as creating pressures for reform and sharpening the focus of managers and practitioners on accomplishing their missions rather than preserving their turf. But outcomes can be used in the actual allocation of funding. Will a program or agency be shut down because it could not provide evidence of its contribution to achieving agreed outcomes, or will it be helped to improve its intervention?

Third, they fear that in the complex, interactive strategies that are the most promising, *responsibility for both progress and failure cannot be accurately ascribed.* No one agency, acting alone, can achieve the most significant outcomes. If raising the number and proportion of children ready for school at the time of school entry depends on the effective contributions of the health system, family support centers, high-quality child care, nutrition programs, and Head Start, as well as on communitywide and informal supports to families, will agency accountability be weakened as attention shifts to communitywide accountability efforts? How are individual agencies to be held accountable for outcomes over which no single agency has control?

Fourth, they fear that *the determinants of outcomes are often outside the control of those being held accountable.* If the avoidance of school-age childbearing is significantly affected by the prospect of good jobs at decent wages (as indeed it is, at least in the most depleted communities), how can youth workers and family planning clinics be held accountable for achieving this desirable outcome when they have no control over the community's employment prospects?

Fifth, they fear that *outcomes accountability could become a screen behind which protections for the vulnerable are destroyed.* Especially in an antiregulation era, rock-bottom safeguards against fraud, abuse, poor services, and discrimination based on race, gender, disability, or ethnic background could be demolished. The new outcomes orientation could lead to abandonment of the input and process regulations that now restrict the arbitrary exercise of frontline discretion by powerful institutions against the interests of powerless clients.

Minimizing the Dangers and Maximizing the Benefits of an Outcomes Focus

Every one of the fears I have described is legitimate, and must inform the movement toward greater reliance on outcomes. The process of choosing and applying outcome measures and of identifying reliable interim milestones must be done carefully and thoughtfully, involve all stakeholders, and draw on the time, skills, and resources to do this job at the highest level of competence.

Choosing the right outcomes. The initial challenge is to get everyone who has a stake, including skeptics, to agree on a set of outcomes considered important, achievable, and measurable. When all concerned actually agree on outcomes they consider important, the outcomes become the constants, making possible experimentation and even disagreement about means: whether parents helping children with their school work is a more effective form of parent involvement in their children's education than parents participating in governance or as classroom aides; what kinds of police-neighborhood partnerships are most likely to bring safe streets. By being fixed on the ends, it is possible to stay flexible on the means.

Complicating the process of choosing outcomes is our lack of experience in this country in thinking together about the substance of what we are really after. We are much more comfortable agreeing on procedural protections than substantive goals.

We have long been more opportunistic than deliberate about measuring success. We reach for what is easiest to measure rather than what accurately reflects a program's purpose. Thus the Westing-house Learning Corporation, under a government contract in 1969 to assess the effects of the earliest years of Head Start, measured only changes in the IQ of participating children—this although IQ is one of the least malleable of human characteristics and although Head Start had other aims from the outset: improving health, nutrition, social skills, and school readiness of participating children, empowering their families, and strengthening their communities. Some thirty years later, IQ remains the outcome most frequently assessed in early childhood programs because it is such a handy measure. Even today there is talk of evaluating family support programs on the basis of their effect on the IQ of participating children.

Rigorous thinking about purposes and results means asking anew what is worth doing and to what end. The outcomes most amenable to agreement are those on which judgments are least subjective and where most people agree on the desirable direction of change—even if they do not agree on what they would give up to achieve such change, how to achieve it, or which outcomes are most important.

The outcomes conversation means becoming explicit about everything, including multiple, even conflicting goals. Disciplined thinking about results means acknowledging that while the greatest impact of Head Start may be on rates of school readiness, it also provides jobs to local residents, frees Head Start parents to pursue training or employment, and decreases their social isolation.

Having observed many recent efforts to agree on outcome measures in a wide variety of settings, I have become convinced that it helps when participants start with the following premises: Goals may be more ambitious than measurable outcomes; outcomes selected for accountability purposes should be easy to understand and persuasive to skeptics; outcomes selected for accountability purposes should clearly reflect the purposes to be achieved; outcome measures should be distinguished from process measures; and sometimes it will be important to incorporate outcomes in a broader accountability context.

Ambitious goals and measurable outcomes. When communities, parents, practitioners, policy makers, and advocates are asked about their goals for their children, they talk about wanting all children to grow up in loving, nurturing, and protective families, to be connected to those around them, and to achieve their personal, social, and vocational potentials. They want youngsters to feel safe, to have a sense of self-worth, a sense of mastery, a sense of belonging, a sense of personal efficacy, to be socially, academically, and culturally competent, and to have the skills needed for productive employment.

Goals such as these can become a framework within which outcome measures can be selected for accountability purposes, with the understanding that only some aspects of these goals can currently be measured with available data and with outcome measures around which it is possible to gain broad agreement. Goals and outcome measures serve different purposes: Goals represent what the community is striving for. Outcome measures represent what the community will be held accountable for—by public and private funders and perhaps by higher levels of government. The goals can be general, but the outcome measures must be so specific, the public stake in their attainment so clear, and their reliability so well established that the community would ultimately be willing to see them influence resource allocation decisions.

Outcomes that are easy to understand and persuasive to skeptics. Outcome measures must be consistent with common sense and compelling not only to experts and not only to those who already support the program.

Efforts to agree on school achievement standards, which we examine at greater length in Chapter 8, were briefly discredited when a few proponents overreached and failed to distinguish between what parents wanted for their children and what they could hold their schools, teachers, and children accountable for.

State bodies proposed draft standards that included such items as "All students understand and appreciate their worth as unique and capable individuals and exhibit self-esteem; all students act through a desire to succeed rather than a fear of failure while recognizing that failure is a part of everyone's experiences." From the perspective of many parents, these might have been reasonable hopes for their children. But it was unrealistic to think that such goals could be agreed on as the measurable objectives that schools would be held accountable for.

One clear lesson of the education experience is that, in the outcomes selection process, it is lethal to ignore the distinctions between outcomes persuasive only to supporters and those also persuasive to skeptics.

Outcomes that authentically reflect the purposes to be achieved. There is no disputing that, for better or worse, what gets measured has a great effect on what gets done. In one way or another, teachers teach to the test, just as social workers pay attention to what the auditors count. So the trick is to devise measures that come as close as possible to reflecting authentically what ought to get done. If you want children to learn to reason in math, you go beyond multiplication tables in assessing their performance. If you want children with defective eyesight to be treated, you don't measure the number of vision screenings that took place, but the number of untreated vision defects that remain.

In efforts to select the right outcomes, no one should be under the illusion that any one set of outcomes or outcome measures will be perfect. They will have to be refined always, sometimes renegotiated, and evolve continuously.

Distinguishing between outcomes and processes. The failure to distinguish between process measures describing what is going on and outcome measures describing what is being accomplished results in what David Osborne calls "process creep." When process creep occurs, means and ends become confused and the focus on what actually happens to people as a result of the activity is lost. Many people participating in a new neighborhood coalition may be the product of a great deal of effort but is not evidence of progress toward stipulated outcomes unless there is good reason to link the activity to desired outcomes.

The confusion about process measures is not only conceptual but political. There is a constant temptation to fall back on process measures as evidence of progress, even when there is no basis for linking them to outcomes. Process measures so often become substitutes for outcome measures because they provide comforting evidence of activity—they demonstrate that *something* is happening.

Typically, both funders and program people contribute to process creep. It happens in the early stages of implementation, when everyone involved suddenly becomes afraid that hopes for the project may not be realized. It also happens when funders encounter hostility to outcome accountability from grantees, who fear that outcome measurement will not do justice to their underfunded intervention.

In responding to these fears, funders often find it easier to move or remove the goalposts than to strengthen the players. The typical forget-about-the-goalposts conversation takes place a few months into the implementation phase. The funder says to the grantee: "We gave you the grant in the hope that you would reduce teenage pregnancy and youth violence in this community, and now you say that was really an unrealistic expectation? You may be right. But we do need some hard evidence that our grant is making some sort of difference, so let's get an evaluator to design a survey that will show how many youngsters come to your meetings and classes, or whether you have increased the number of teenagers who think it's a bad idea to become sexually active and carry a gun when they're younger than fifteen."

While it defeats the purpose to substitute process measures for outcome measures, process measures will continue to be important in an outcomes-oriented world to guard against fraud, corruption, and inequities or discrimination based on race, gender, disability, or ethnic background. Procedural protections will have to be maintained and monitored wherever there is no other way to restrict the arbitrary exercise of front-line discretion by powerful institutions against the interests of powerless clients. Existing process measures will continue to play a role in holding agencies, communities, and systems accountable, especially during the period of transition, because the present capacity to use outcome measures to judge program effectiveness is still primitive, and because it takes so long for outcomes to improve in response to even the most effective interventions. As more information becomes available about the interim measures that predict long-term success, it will be possible to rely increasingly on outcome measures.

Process measures are also essential to understanding whether a program or intervention has actually been implemented according to plan. (For example, is the family support center in operation for the number of hours its funders expect? Is it being utilized by the expected number of families? Does the home visiting program reach the expected proportion of high-risk families?)

Outcomes in a broader accountability context. Even at its best, outcomes-based accountability may not always capture the full effects of some excellent interventions.

Someone who has struggled mightily to develop new ways to maintain public accountability while protecting the fragile aspects of the best of interventions is educator Deborah Meier, whom we met in the last chapter in connection with the debureaucratization efforts of the New York Networks for School Renewal. She and her colleagues have been trying to devise mechanisms of public accountability that put a strong emphasis on outcomes but would also incorporate other ways of knowing what works. She calls for an accountability system based on "the responsible exercise of collective human judgment," in which all the participants—parents, assessors, legislators, and the public—would have access to a shared body of credible outcomes information, including actual student work as well as statistical data, upon which to build their judgments. The new forms of accountability she would add to "pure" outcomes accountability would include peers who could examine each other's work. For high schools, for example, accountability processes would include judgments of external committees composed of college faculty, parents, community members, other high school teachers, and networks of sister schools. They would include formal review panels composed of critical friends and more distanced and skeptical publics, demanding convincing evidence that the institution or program under review was on the right track and acting responsibly.

Multifaceted accountability systems of this kind are now under development in a variety of settings. Leaders of these efforts hope to show that it is possible to protect both the public interest in results-based accountability and the activities that will always be hard to measure. But even this more complicated and nuanced approach to accountability relies on shared goals. What Meier says about schools pertains to every institution meant to serve a shared purpose: "A really good school does depend on parents, teachers, and students coming to terms about what they are trying to achieve and holding themselves accountable for it. If that doesn't exist, the school will not succeed. . . ."

Who Decides? Who Is Responsible?

In determining who selects the outcomes to be achieved, there is much controversy about "top-down" versus "bottom-up" processes. On the one hand, there are certain essential outcomes (such as healthy births, school readiness, children learning to read and do math, reduction in single parenting, safe neighborhoods, etc.) in which society has so much at stake that a local process is not required in identifying the outcomes to be achieved.

There are other areas, such as efforts at strengthening families and neighborhoods in supporting healthy youth development and keeping children safe, where the process of selecting outcome measures can best gain legitimacy through a local consensus-building process. When all of those affected—as legislators, taxpayers, providers, beneficiaries, or participants—have some role in selecting the outcome measures they will use, decision making will become more outcome oriented.

An outcomes orientation can be applied at many different levels, from individual institution to community and beyond. When a state or community coalition shifts its lens from a focus on program outcomes (did the youngsters who participated in the mentoring program benefit?) to measuring population outcomes (are all the youngsters in the neighborhood that initiated the mentoring program and a new afternoon activities center better off?), it moves from the programmatic to the strategic. If a community's rates of pregnancy among unmarried teens reflect not only the extent of information about sex and contraception and the availability of contraceptives, but also community norms and the extent to which young people in the community find reasons to postpone childbearing, then outcomes cannot be attached to a single program or agency. It would make no sense to assign entire responsibility for decreasing teenage pregnancy to a school-based clinic. One would also have to consider as factors the availability of jobs opportunities, of schools and community centers that engage the interests of early adolescents, and the community networks that support norms that discourage early childbearing.

Communities using an outcomes orientation to strengthen their capacity to think strategically may make more progress than those that see outcomes accountability as a simple yes or no mechanism in deciding to fund or defund specific programs or institutions. Community agencies that join together to deliberate about the strategies most likely to lead to improved outcomes, are in a good position to analyze whether failure to achieve a given outcome resulted from a wrong strategy, a right strategy poorly implemented or inadequately financed, unanticipated outside forces, or faulty data. A community could learn from this process what it would take to provide the needed midcourse corrections and then mobilize the missing ingredients—in the form of technical assistance, new kinds of training, more careful monitoring, or moving resources from ineffective to effective strategies—not simply to make an agency or program more effective, but to achieve the results of greatest moment to community and society.

What's Missing?

Communities, agencies, collaboratives, and even states moving to outcomes-based accountability would be able to improve performance and judge success much more effectively if they could obtain more relevant and timely data and if there were better understanding of the links among interventions, interim milestones, and long-term outcomes.

Mismatch between data needed and data available. There is a severe—and at first blush, strange—paucity of data to help answer urgent questions about how well efforts to change vulnerable lives are actually helping.

The disconnect between the data needed for outcomes accountability and the indicator data currently being collected exists because of pressures to cut back on publicly funded data collection and analysis, especially at the federal level, and because data collection was not designed for this purpose. Rather, it has been shaped primarily by the need for administrative data for use in managing programs and policies and by the research needs of social scientists.

Data that could document the effects of intentional interventions on the well-being of children, families, and communities is hard to come by, and until recently was not much in demand. Participants in Oregon's pathbreaking effort to switch to outcomes accountability (which we examine in detail later in this chapter) say that finding the right data turned out to be so difficult, they called it their "Achilles' heel."

Much new work is now needed, and some has begun, spurred by growing demands for data-based judgments about extensive investments in new kinds of interventions—and about new policies, including those that have suddenly ended traditional guarantees of government help.

- Work is under way to make it easier to use, collect, and analyze data in units corresponding to the small areas, such as neighborhoods and school catchment areas, that are often the optimal targets of intervention. Work is also in progress to make data available in a more timely way to make it more policy- and practice-relevant.
- Work is being done to identify components of child and family functioning and well-being that can be measured without extensive individual observation.
- Measurement experts are just beginning to catch up with the burgeoning interest in understanding community change, especially the effects of deliberate efforts to build community. A number of groups are now hard at work on defining meaningful measures of community change that could shed light on efforts of Empowerment Zones and comprehensive community initiatives to affect the social and economic well-being of residents in a given neighborhood; the physical conditions of a neighborhood; residents' sense of security, safety, and personal efficacy; access to employment opportunities; and the extent of positive interactions among neighbors and neighborhood organizations.

A Human Intervention Mapping Project to chart the links among interventions, interim milestones, and long-term outcomes. The greatest single obstacle to realizing the benefits of shifting to results-based accountability is the lack of reliable information about the connections among interventions, interim milestones, and long-term outcomes.

Much progress has recently been made on helping communities and funders (public and private) to identify long-term outcome measures, such as healthy births, school readiness and school success, and employment, that can help to assess the effects of interventions not only within but across the domains of health, education, child welfare, juvenile justice, community development, economic development, and job training.

But sorely missing is the identification of interim milestones that could show reliably that reform efforts are on track toward their long-term goals. Local communities, agencies, and programs struggling to reform their services or rebuild neighborhoods are clamoring for interim outcome indicators. The most frequently cited lesson from major current reform efforts is that they take so much more time than expected—both to launch the initiative and to reach the point of showing an impact on real-world outcomes. They desperately need new tools that would allow them to demonstrate their short-term achievements. They need to be able to get interim information *very quickly*—often long before a program is "proud," long before it has had a chance to make an impact on rates of school readiness, child abuse, teenage pregnancy, violence, school success, and employment.

Otis Johnson, director of Savannah Youth Futures Authority, says you cannot expect community people to stay engaged with an initiative that will not reach its goals for twenty years; you have to be able to celebrate interim accomplishments, and we need to know more about which interim milestones are reliable markers.

Although initiatives should have a say in which indicators are used to judge its success, program funders and managers should be able to pick from interim milestones identified and described under other auspices, on the basis of past experience and social science research. *These interim indicators should not have to be produced individually and ad hoc by every local agency or institution, community coalition, or neighborhood transformation initiative.*

Interim indicators that can predict later outcomes may represent a short-term manifestation of long-term outcomes (for example, children reading by third grade have a substantially increased chance of avoiding later troubles at school), or they may represent a community's capacity to achieve identified long-term outcomes (the availability of a high-quality home visiting and family support program may predict a later reduction in the incidence of child abuse; a community that is investing in effective efforts to increase neighborhood safety is likely to see an increase in economic and social activity that strengthens neighborhood bonds and thereby improves outcomes for children and families).

The need for short-term indicators of movement toward long-term outcomes has long been recognized. But it has not been met, perhaps because progress in linking interventions with strategies, interim markers, and long-term outcomes involves a higher ratio of judgment to certainty than most social scientists are comfortable with. For many of the best minds working in this area, the fact that causal connections cannot be established with certainty is reason enough to stay away from the quest.

But the high stakes may justify efforts to overcome the formidable obstacles. Significant progress in designing, implementing, evaluating, and holding accountable what are probably the most promising kinds of interventions to improve outcomes for children, youth, and families will be very difficult in the absence of progress on systematically identifying promising links along the many chains that lead to improved outcomes. It makes no sense for each local initiative and collaborative, for every city council or county board of supervisors, for each state legislative committee, to try to figure out on its own which strategies are most promising and whether it is established, probable, disproved, or unknown that full-service schools have an impact on school achievement, that investment in school-to-work connections results in higher youth employment, or that communities that are forging greater personal connections through community building experience a drop in crime.

I believe that the time has come to undertake a major national effort as ambitious as the Human Genome Mapping Project now under way under the auspices of the National Institutes of Health, with such spectacular results from many centers of research and learning. The task would be to achieve a more systematic understanding of the links along the chains that connect interventions and outcomes by examining systematically the research and experience that can provide a more rigorous and deeper understanding of established and probable connections among interventions and short-term and long-term outcomes.

In several senses a Human Intervention Mapping Project would be even more ambitious than its genome analog. This is in part because of the primitive current state of research and evaluation, which has produced only limited data even about the natural history of how human development interacts with changing social environments, and about the intricate developmental pathways to healthy and unhealthy outcomes. The data on complex, comprehensive interventions aimed at changing development trajectories is still scarcer. As forbidding as the shortage of rigorous data is the fact that intervention in human and social development is so complex that one can never rely exclusively on "scientific" certainty.

But these difficulties do not make it impossible to produce usable knowledge. Investment in such an undertaking would produce knowledge that promises to enhance vastly society's capacity to improve outcomes for disadvantaged populations now living under high-risk conditions.

Early Adventures in Applying an Outcomes Orientation: Oregon Benchmarks and the Oregon Option

The most ambitious experiment in using outcomes to structure decision making has been taking place in the state of Oregon. "No other state," says Vice President Gore, "has gone so far down the road to results-driven governance."

The pioneering effort began under the leadership of Oregon's Governor Neil Goldschmidt, whose visionary 1989 document, "Oregon Shines," called for specific improvements in the state's economy, natural environment, and quality of life. Since then, Oregon citizens and policy makers have been working together to define benchmarks of progress toward family stability, school readiness, student achievement, affordable housing, air and water quality, reduced crime, and full employment. In 1991, the state legislature created the Oregon Progress Board, headed by the governor, to identify measurable indicators that could be used to monitor implementation and assess progress toward the broad goals of "Oregon Shines."

"The legislature asked us to do something that no other state has done before," says Duncan Wyse, the board's first executive director. "A lot of states have written strategic reports, but no state has ever translated that plan into a set of measurements to focus where government programs need to head. They built plans, but never created accountability for getting results."

In setting the indicators, called Oregon Benchmarks, the board solicited participation from an unprecedented number of organizations and citizens through town meetings, electronic voting, and other means. Governor Barbara Roberts, who led the 1992 "Conversation with Oregon," says, "We learned that when voters demand efficiency, they don't mean just cut programs—they mean spend my tax dollars better. We learned people do care about the future, the kind of a state their children and grandchildren will live in. And we learned how thirsty they are for information and participation." The governor particularly appreciated that participants were eager to focus on goal setting. She told a Washington, D.C., audience that when the discussion targeted teenage pregnancy, "no matter what you thought the solution was, whether you thought the answer was abstinence, contraception, or greater job opportunities, you had a place at the table, and you could agree on the goal of reducing pregnancies among Oregon teenagers." In a 1994 report, the board stated that "never before has a state brought together so many public, private, and nonprofit organizations to pursue a shared vision and to measure progress toward that vision."

There are currently 259 Benchmarks. Among those labeled urgent are increased school readiness and school skills, the reduction of teen pregnancy, poverty, drug and alcohol use among school-age children, and juvenile crime.

In the initial stage, the Benchmarks were used primarily as a framework for policy discussions, to set priorities, and to get people to think about resource allocation from a longer-term perspective. But the Benchmarks were used in budgeting when the state budget had to be cut by 20 percent, and agencies could recapture some of their funding for programs directly tied to the Benchmarks. The Oregon Community Foundation, Portland United Way, and nine local governments are building on the state Benchmarks with their own local process. By late 1996 there was considerable evidence that some of the smaller counties around the state had been able to mobilize citizens in unprecedented collaborative action toward several of the outcomes identified as urgent by the Benchmarks.

Probably the greatest accomplishment so far of the Oregon Benchmarks process is that it led to the Oregon Option, an unprecedented marriage between a federal government bent on reinvention and a state that was ready. It combines the shift to outcomes accountability with a new kind of intergovernmental partnership, testing the proposition, according to Barbara Dyer, "that multiple levels of government can align their efforts to achieve results that matter to people."

The first intergovernmental relationship of its kind, Oregon Option was launched on December 5, 1994, by Governor Roberts and other state and local Oregon officials, together with Vice President Gore. Under the Oregon Option, federal, state, and local officials have agreed to work together to define and measure the results they wish to achieve with federal dollars. In return, states and localities will have greater autonomy, freedom from paperwork, and fewer restrictions on how they achieve these results. Federal agencies have committed themselves to consolidate funding and to cut red tape through a Federal Interagency Action Team, which includes federal officials from the Domestic Policy Council, the Office of Management and Budget, and the Departments of Agriculture, Commerce, Education, Justice, Labor, HHS, and HUD. All are focused on goals broader than those of any single agency, program, or even level of government.

Governor Roberts predicted that this kind of cooperation would prove to a cynical public that government can work. "This is a giant step toward good government, smart government, and government our citizens can believe in," she said. Alice Rivlin, then budget director, agreed. "By focusing on results and the measures for achieving them in a way that is mutually agreed by the states and the federal government, you can free the states from preoccupation with whether they're filling out forms correctly and give them considerable latitude to do their own thing. That's a much better idea than block grants, which have the effect of giving the states a blank check with no accountability."

When Governor Roberts did not run for reelection in 1994, some feared for the future of Oregon Benchmarks and the Oregon Option. But virtually every aspect continues to evolve, as funding streams are merged and partners are held jointly accountable for results. Both continue to thrive under Robert's successor, John Kitzhaber. Alan Altshuler of Harvard's Kennedy School believes this is one of several indications that the new processes have been institutionalized beyond identification with any single administration or party.

OUTCOMES ACCOUNTABILITY AS THE BASIS FOR NEW INTERGOVERNMENTAL PARTNERSHIPS?

The early success of the Oregon Option suggests that an outcomes orientation could be the basis for new kinds of relationships among state and local governments and the federal government. William A. Morrill, president of Mathtech, and HHS assistant secretary for planning and evaluation in two Republican administrations, has written about institutionalizing the principles of the Oregon Option through legislation that would establish a process by which states and localities could negotiate five-to-ten-year contracts that exchange increased flexibility for outcomes accountability. All outcomes would have to be measurable, with a baseline no worse than current levels, and with specified improvements during the life of the contract in the outcomes for vulnerable individuals, families, and communities. Morrill points out that this proposal has some of the presumed virtues of block grants but corrects one of the major defects: the lack of accountability. It gives states and localities considerably more say about how funds will be used while leaving existing legislation in place until sufficient evidence is collected to make sure that the alternative is an improvement over current arrangements.

The appeal of this proposal across ideological lines was put to the test in 1996, when Republican Senator Mark Hatfield of Oregon, introduced the Empowerment and Local Flexibility bill, with provisions accepted by the Clinton administration, for generic waivers of certain federal regulations in return for proof of performance. The bill never emerged from the committee, probably because enough watchdog groups expressed concern that the Congress would be ceding too much authority over individual federal programs.

However, with the prodding of Vice President Gore's National Performance Review, other federal efforts are well under way to change the way federal agencies do business, shifting their focus from program compliance and financial audits to program outcomes. In addition, community collaboratives, representing the public sector, nonprofits, business, and community representatives, are increasingly taking responsibility for achieving community-wide outcomes.

Could Mother Teresa Survive in an Outcomes-Oriented World?

Many committed practitioners, as we have seen, harbor a visceral unease about the whole idea of outcomes accountability. Early childhood educators, youth workers, and health and mental health professionals ask with particular intensity, "Why should we have to prove to hostile critics that our work is valuable?" They say that those who would shred the safety net and dismantle the entire infrastructure of public and nonprofit services and institutions aren't arguing efficacy but principle. These practitioners, along with many parents, community leaders, and other advocates also wish to stand *their* ground on principle, and assert that feeding young children and providing them with lovely places to play is enough justification; that comforting a frightened adolescent needs no further rationale; that every expectant mother is entitled to the highest quality prenatal care—whether or not these pay off in higher rates of school readiness, employability, or healthy births. Other countries, after all, don't make public support for basic services for children and families contingent on proof of efficacy. In France, Germany, Britain, and Japan, publicly supported child care and maternal and child health care, paid family leaves, and universal child protective services are taken for granted and require no evidence of effectiveness.

Many American human service practitioners see themselves as part of a tradition of service to the vulnerable, whose ultimate value is independent of its effects. They cite Mother Teresa's explanation of perseverance despite the enormity of world poverty: "God has called on me not to be successful, but to be faithful." They cite Gandhi's teaching, "It is the action, not the fruit of the action, that is important."

My own belief is that the moral underpinnings for social action, especially by government, are not powerful enough in the cynical closing years of the twentieth century to sustain what needs to be done on the scale that it needs to be done. In this era of pervasive doubt, public investment of the needed magnitude will be forthcoming only on evidence of achieving its purpose and contributing to long-term goals that are widely shared. And the chances of developing the responsive bureaucracies that can support effective programs will increase to the extent that accountability for results replaces accountability inscribed in rigid rules.

Judging the Effects of Large Social Policy Changes (Like Welfare Repeal)

Senator Daniel Patrick Moynihan called the 1996 repeal of the federal welfare guarantee the largest gamble in social policy made in the twentieth century. The legislation set in motion actions and reactions that pose an unprecedented challenge to the weak national capacity to assess the effects of large changes in social policy. The problem of inadequate capacity to monitor the changes that actually take place, and to measure their impact, is vastly compounded by the political dynamite contained in the findings—whatever they may be.

Will entire families become homeless and freeze to death on city grates? Will the threat of benefit cutoffs succeed in converting a population of borderline disabled mothers into workforce self-sufficiency? Will frustration over inability to find work under pressure of time-limited benefits explode into violence against young children? Will additional stigmatizing of welfare dependency and childbearing by unmarried girls and women reduce teenage pregnancy and single parenting? Will 2.6 million additional Americans fall into poverty, as the Urban Institute predicts? Will states use their new freedom to reduce spending on the poor or become ingenious in their efforts to help them become self-sufficient? Will the youngest children be permanently damaged by poor-quality custodial day care? Will youngsters get into ever more serious trouble because there is no one at home to supervise? Will minority children become ever more alienated from a society that has sent the ultimate message of uncaring by allowing them to go hungry? Will economic and social effects interact to send inner-city neighborhoods into a steeper downward spiral?

The policy changes that raise these questions were not driven by data or rational analysis. But everyone wants answers to these questions, and everyone wants to use the answers to make political points. The demands for reliable information are enormous, growing, and unlikely to be met by a diminished data-gathering and analysis capacity within the public sector.

In response, the Annie E. Casey Foundation and the Henry J. Kaiser Family Foundation are supporting the Urban Institute to undertake the largest project in its history to monitor, document, and assess the effects of the welfare changes and other experiments in decentralization of social programs, and to make the results widely available. The Urban Institute will collaborate with Child Trends, Inc., a Washington, D.C., research organization, in monitoring changes in the well-being of children and their families. They hope to test and measure possible causal links between changes in government programs and changes in such indicators of well-being as labor force participation, access to health services, teenage fertility, family stability, and overall poverty rates. Other for-profit, not-for-profit, academic, and advocacy organizations are undertaking major monitoring and assessment efforts. The Institute for Research on Poverty at the University of Wisconsin, the Center for Children in Poverty at Columbia University, and the Office of the Assistant Secretary for Planning and Evaluation at the U.S. Department of Health and Human Services have all been convening major participants, encouraging a thoughtful allocation of resources and talent, and trying to ensure that as much rigorous information as possible would be available to all the many stakeholders.

Knowing the limits of statistical data analysis, virtually all the researchers involved in these efforts are also urging journalists to use their vantage point to learn and write about the massive policy changes over the next several years, especially their effects on children and families.

Evaluation Research in an Outcomes-Oriented World

There was a time when the worlds of outcomes accountability and evaluation were entirely separate. The accountability world was ruled by administrators and auditors, who made sure that the proper procedures were being followed and that moneys, especially public moneys, were being responsibly spent. The evaluation world was ruled by social scientists, who used obscure techniques to describe circumscribed interventions and sometimes to judge their effectiveness.

Two forces are bringing these worlds together: The accountability world is moving from monitoring processes to monitoring results. The evaluation world is being demystified, its techniques becoming more collaborative, its applicability broadened, and its data no longer closely held as if by a hostile, foreign power.

As results-based accountability becomes the norm and not the exception, as outcomes become an important part of the everyday way people think about programs, policies, and reform initiatives, the role of the evaluator and of evaluation research will undergo significant change. This is especially true in the evaluation of complex, multisystem, multidisciplinary interventions that are expected to impact children, families, institutions, and entire communities.

When desired outcomes are specified (whether by a community, state, program, or some other entity), it is reasonable to judge the effect of an intervention on those outcomes. The evaluator would then no longer assume the responsibility for selecting (or negotiating with program people to select) the outcomes on which the effort would be evaluated. Furthermore, the outcome measures used for accountability purposes will overlap with those already being collected for other purposes, usually by official agencies (e.g., rates of low birth weight, immunization, arrests, school completion, employment, etc.), and are therefore more likely to be widely recognized for their "real world" significance than measures showing performance on scales constructed by researchers primarily for research purposes.

This would also reduce evaluation costs, whether measured in money, time, intrusiveness, or required expertise.

The result could be a demystification and democratization of both outcomes accountability and the evaluation process, encouragement of citizen monitoring of the welfare of children, families, and neighborhoods, greater access to information about results and effectiveness, an increase in usable knowledge, and a vastly improved capacity to intervene effectively.

As we shall see in the next chapter, some of these changes are actually now occurring in the evaluation world.

5

Finding Out What Works

A NEW EVALUATION MIND-SET is emerging that promises to expand vastly our understanding about what works.

The old evaluation mind-set was key to a 1960s study of schooling, one of the largest social science research projects ever undertaken to that point. Senator Daniel Patrick Moynihan, then assistant secretary of labor, tells about learning of the results in 1966 when he returned to Harvard to attend a Faculty Club reception. His friend and former colleague, sociologist Seymour Martin Lipset, greeted him with the question, "You know what Coleman [James S. Coleman, then professor of social relations at Johns Hopkins University] is finding, don't you?"

"What?" asked Moynihan.

"All family," replied Lipset, referring to the findings from Coleman's research that the measurable elements of schooling accounted for very little of the variation in student achievement. All that really mattered, Lipset reported, was the student's family background.

Thirty years later, Moynihan wrote admiringly about Coleman's courage in coming out with his "politically incorrect" data showing that "social change was going to be far more difficult than anyone had thought." The Coleman findings, in fact, challenged the entire basis on which American public schools were founded. If schools couldn't counteract the influence of family origins, what happens to Horace Mann's 1848 claim to the Massachusetts State Board of Education that "education, beyond all other devices of human origin, is a great equalizer of the conditions of men—the balance wheel of the social machinery?" Was social science now confirming the cynics' worst suspicions, that schools were not, in fact, springboards to opportunity, that they simply reinforced the advantages and disadvantages that children started out with?

Today we know that schools are able to change outcomes among children from profoundly disadvantaged family backgrounds. We also know where the Coleman team went wrong. It was the old evaluation mind-set that led them to take into account only the most readily quantifiable data, such as per-pupil expenditures and the number of books in school libraries, components of schooling that would turn out—years later—not to be critical factors in changing outcomes. We shall see in Chapter 8 on education how powerfully schools can impact life trajectories, as documented by evaluators using a new mind-set. But the Coleman story shows how deeply evaluators' choices of what to count and what to study affect what they are likely to find out about what works.

The new evaluation mind-set does more than change what evaluators count. It will also change what all the rest of us think of as worth knowing and worth doing.

The Methods, Mind-Sets, and Influence of Traditional Evaluation

Evaluation became increasingly important over the past thirty-five years as policy makers came to believe that the methods of social science should guide their decisions about social programs and social policy.

The evaluation profession spawned by that belief exerts its influence through its promise to use the scientific method to figure out what works. That promise underlies its considerable influence over social policy.

And this influence, in my view, has been predominantly destructive. I don't want to minimize the contributions of traditional evaluation to our understanding of certain circumscribed interventions. In welfare-to-work programs, for example, evaluations have led to much greater insight into specific aspects of what works. But when it comes to broad, complex, and interactive interventions (early childhood supports, school reform, and better links to employment, for example) aimed at changing multiple outcomes (such as school success, employment rates, and a reduction in the formation of single-parent families), traditional evaluation has been of scant help.

Prevailing evaluation methods have not provided the knowledge needed to make good judgments about the very social programs that hold the most promise.

I believe the national conviction that nothing works owes a lot to the fact that the evaluations on which most policy makers rely overwhelmingly favor activities where one circumscribed problem is addressed by one circumscribed remedy. And that, of course, is not where the answers lie.

Columnist Mary McGrory, reporting in 1995 on a Senate Finance Committee hearing on welfare reform and teenage pregnancy, wrote, "One certainty, and only one, emerged. . . . No one has the faintest idea of what to do about unwed teenage mothers. . . . After two hours of articulate and thoughtful testimony from a panel of four experts who had all the latest data and theories in hand, Moynihan said humbly . . . 'This morning we have learned how little we know and how much we have failed and how much we have denied our failure.'"

This time Senator Moynihan's conclusion was simply wrong. He was misled by relying on studies that looked at only the narrowest of interventions, because these are the only kinds of interventions that have been evaluated by methods he considers "scientific."

Legislators, other policy makers, and program people have, in my view, all been relying on an outmoded approach to evaluation that has had us looking for answers in all the wrong places.

The conventions governing traditional evaluation of program impact have systematically defined out of contention precisely those interventions that sophisticated funders and program people regard as most promising. They consider only interventions with the following characteristics to be "evaluable":

- They are standardized and uniform. A single intervention protocol is implemented across several different sites and remains constant over time.
- They are sufficiently circumscribed that their activities can be studied and their effects discerned in isolation from other attempts to intervene and from changes in community circumstances. (Ascertaining the effects of a new family support center requires a neighborhood that is making no other intentional changes affecting young children and their families and experiencing no other "contaminating" changes, such as a significant increase or decrease in employment opportunities during the period of the experiment.)
- They are sufficiently susceptible to outside direction so that a cen-

tral authority is able to design and prescribe how participants are recruited and selected in accordance with the evaluator's protocol.

But, of course, these are precisely the conditions that are least likely to characterize effective programs.

So how did we get into this mess, where the very conditions that make for good programs render them "unevaluable"?

As long ago as 1976, Alice Rivlin—then a Brookings scholar, later budget director, now member of the Federal Reserve Board—warned, "Maybe the whole evaluation movement started off on a couple of false premises—that there is such a thing as a social program in the sense of a treatment, which applied [equally] to [all] people, which can then be evaluated to see if it works or not. Most of the evaluations . . . assumed that we were providing something to people, that we could say what it was, that we could define some sort of output, and that we could measure whether it took place or not." There have been few challenges to this evaluation mind-set in the intervening years.

In my view, the origin of the problem was the fledgling evaluation industry's reliance on the biomedical, experimental model as the basis for understanding social and human service programs. This model, as described by the Rensselaerville Institute's classic *Outcome Funding,* assumes the presence of a premade treatment that need only be administered in the right dosages to ensure success for interchangeable customers. "The client may—indeed should—remain patient and passive until his or her medicine arrives. . . . What is given is presumed equivalent to what is received, and what is received is equal to what is used. Use is then equated to gain."

The requirements imposed by the biomedical model of evaluation make sense if one assumes a standardized treatment. It then makes sense to require randomized recruitment and selection of subjects (allowing for unambiguous comparisons between those receiving the "treatment" and a statistically similar group who do not). It makes sense to hold a standardized intervention constant across sites and over time. It makes sense to dismiss the effects of variations in neighborhood environments as "contaminants."

But given the nature of the most promising interventions, the traditional approach to evaluation does not make sense. As Yale researcher Sharon Lynn Kagan puts it, "We simply cannot fit the square peg of conventional evaluation into the round hole of comprehensive, community-based efforts."

The evaluation industry's traditional stance might represent a regrettable peccadillo were it not for its devastating effect on programs most likely to change outcomes. What if interventions that change only one thing at a time fail, as Henry Aaron of the Brookings Institution suggests, *because* they change only one thing at a time? Then the evaluators have defined out of evaluation consideration precisely the interventions most likely to have an impact. The multipronged, interactive, custom-tailored, evolving interventions that draw on many disciplines and systems to impact not only individuals but also neighborhoods, institutions, and systems are anathema to the traditional evaluator. They were therefore subject to a process evaluation only, which meant there would be no information about their impact—that is, whether they "worked." (Process evaluations describe how interventions are implemented. Impact evaluations assess whether they have the hypothesized effect.)

I believe that the big funders, public and philanthropic, whose pressures were shaping evaluation might have long ago questioned the evaluation industry's assumptions had they not been captivated by the aura of science and the glitter of certainty that surrounded traditional evaluation. The idea that social science could be as precise as the physical and biological sciences, using an experimental approach approximating a laboratory setting, was so seductive that private and public funders went for years without seeing how much the requisites of traditional evaluation were skewing program design and failing to produce usable knowledge on which to build new and more effective interventions.

Congressional authorization of programs began to require that they be evaluated as a condition for continued funding and that evaluations use an experimental design with randomly assigned control groups. In that way, policy makers could be confident that the observed impacts were indeed the result of a designated treatment. If that left no room for comprehensive initiatives, for community building, for unique responses to unique circumstances, and the possibility that the whole of the intervention would turn out to be more than the sum of its parts, the assumption was that little would be lost. By 1988 the Urban Institute's Isabel Sawhill was writing that "a consensus seems to be emerging that . . . random assignment should be the *sine qua non* of future evaluations."

Skewed Program Design and Lack of Useful Information

The narrow limits of what has traditionally been considered "evaluable" have had a pernicious effect on program design. Evaluators told program people that if their program did not fit into the procrustean evaluation bed, they should simplify, narrow, standardize, or otherwise change their design. Pressures to make the intervention evaluable often distorted program design before the intervention ever got off the ground.

A recent example comes from a 1990s undertaking to demonstrate the effectiveness of early intervention in reducing mental retardation among high-risk infants. A pilot program conducted in the 1980s had succeeded in raising the IQs of babies born at low birth weight and prematurely. In 1984, visiting several participating sites, I had become aware of the tension between the evaluators' pressures for uniformity across sites and the program implementers' beliefs that their interventions would work better if they were adapted to local circumstances.

Assuming that much had been learned from this experience, I was horrified to find in 1994, as a member of the advisory committee to the new effort, building on the earlier one, that once again a single model was to be tested in ten sites. "Standardized curricula" would be provided to both home visitors and center teachers at all sites, coupled with monitoring to minimize "the possibility for one or more sites to deviate from the intended intervention." Any attempt to introduce "variation in the implementation" would be subject to "approval by the Government." When I asked if we hadn't learned by now that program effectiveness was directly related to the implementer's ability to engage in local adaptation and provide for ongoing responsiveness to evolving needs, I was told that all this was probably true, but allowing for significant local variation would render the intervention neither evaluable nor replicable.

The mismatch between prevailing evaluation approaches and the most promising kinds of social interventions has resulted not only in skewing of program design away from complex, community responsive interventions, but also in a lack of reliable information about many interventions that may have been successful but were considered "unevaluable."

Harvard law professor Martha Minow tried to understand why there was so little "social scientific evidence" to document the effectiveness of home visiting programs to families with infants. Her review led her to believe these programs had been highly successful in providing support at times of stress, improving the health status of children, and increasing the economic independence and self-reliance of parents. But social science findings were not providing policy makers with the kind of evidence they needed to gain public support to scale up home visiting. She concluded that "the very cautiousness of social science undermines its usefulness in policymaking" by limiting what counts as reliable knowledge and rejecting as untrustworthy studies that fail to use randomized assignment.

And, of course, it is caution and skepticism that attract respect, not just among academics but also among legislators. The mantle of rigor is more readily bestowed on those adding to our knowledge of what isn't working than those contributing to our knowledge of what might work.

But the near-unanimous acceptance of prevailing research and evaluation approaches may be nearing an end. When I heard Harold Richman, director of the influential Chapin Hall Center for Children at the University of Chicago, tell a group of grant makers that the attempt to "shoehorn these complex new initiatives into old evaluation methods has become obscene," it seemed to me that the funeral bells were beginning to toll. As more and more researchers, practitioners, and funders came to appreciate the importance of the interaction among interventions, the crucial contribution of neighborhoods, and the difficulty of measuring the effects of community-building and institutional reforms, it became glaringly apparent that any method of evaluation which excluded such factors as "contaminants" could not long be considered the sole legitimate source of information about what works.

After all, if an adolescent's chances of being arrested decrease if he has a *neighbor* who is a churchgoer, as demonstrated by Anne Case and Lawrence Katz, the individual "treatment" mind-set had to go.

New Approaches to Evaluation to Supplement the Old

A number of efforts are now under way to combine a variety of evaluation approaches to generate more usable information and greater understanding of complex interventions.

But it will not be easy to break with the dogma of experimental designs using random assignment as the only source of reliable knowledge. Swarthmore economics professor Robinson G. Hollister, a leading figure in evaluation circles since the mid-1960s, says that experimental designs are "like the nectar of the gods: once you've had a taste of the pure stuff it is hard to settle for the flawed alternatives." And the nectar of the gods of experimental design have intoxicated not only evaluators but also policy makers and funders.

The "flawed alternatives" may provide less certainty about what, exactly, caused the observed effects but do offer a broader range of information that may turn out to be more useful in making judgments about what really matters. The new evaluators embrace both the old and the new, in the belief that there is knowledge worth having and acting on even if it is not absolutely certain knowledge. They do not reject—on grounds of messiness or complexity—information that can shed light on real-world efforts that promise to improve outcomes.

The new approaches to the evaluation of complex interventions share at least four attributes: They are built on a strong theoretical and conceptual base, emphasize shared interests rather than adversarial relationships between evaluators and program people, employ multiple methods and perspectives, and offer both rigor and relevance.

Weapon against chaos: A strong theoretical and conceptual base. The broader evaluation mind-set is strongly guided by theories about how and why an initiative works. Using theory as a starting point is in the finest tradition of social science. The activist/academic John W. Gardner points out that "most striking about the enormously useful work of people like Darwin and de Tocqueville, is that they came to their observations with very well-developed concepts. [They got away from the] fruitless efforts to measure precisely the variables which were not relevant or to answer questions which did not reflect a theory of change. . . . They knew what they were looking for."

Evaluator Michael Knapp explains that in comprehensive initiatives, so much is going on "that even if we can document change or improvement, we have little idea what to attribute it to . . . the integrated early childhood program, the Blue Cross managed care experiment, a new charter school . . . the family preservation funds . . ." That is why, he says, we must construct "conceptual maps that link one thing to another." The conceptual maps act as a weapon against chaos.

Especially when it comes to disentangling such complex forces as the effects of neighborhoods on individuals, "the most powerful tools . . . are not statistical but conceptual." Which is why it is essential to ground both design and measurement in theoretical orientations.

Carol H. Weiss, professor at the Harvard Graduate School of Education, is one of the pioneers of applying theory-based evaluation to comprehensive community initiatives. She explains that behind every intervention there are theories about why it should work. Theory-based evaluation helps to figure out what's working in situations where statistical analysis alone can't provide the needed answers. By combining outcome measures with an understanding of the process that produced the outcomes, it can shed light both on the extent of impact and on how the change occurred. Evaluators who are using theory-based evaluation believe it can help people on the front lines to think more rigorously about what they are doing, help them improve their programs, allow others to learn from their successes, and persuade the skeptical funder, legislator, and taxpayer that the purposes of the initiative are being achieved.

In applying a theory-based approach, evaluators begin by working with program people to articulate what they are doing and why. The conversation will probably go in both directions—backward from outcomes sought to the interventions being used, and forward from the interventions being used to the outcomes sought. To be most helpful, the evaluators should probably come to the conversation equipped with theories that have emerged from research and from experience elsewhere. It is certainly easier for the people operating an initiative to recognize a theory approximating their own thinking and to modify that theory to apply precisely to their own situation than it would be to generate theories from a blank slate. (Progress on the Human Intervention Mapping Project described in the last chapter would considerably expedite this task.)

The process of identifying theories of change may strike the reader as self-evident. But it will often be a difficult undertaking. Many reform efforts are led by individuals who have not had occasion to think rigorously about their goals and the strategies that could accomplish those goals. One evaluator reports that of twenty-nine directors of youth development projects in the midwest asked about the theory behind their projects, only one responded with anything resembling a theory. This continued to be true after the evaluator explained the concept of theory "as a set of premises or generalizations from which one could deduce—or hypothesize—likely actions and consequences." With the one exception, the project directors' justifications for their projects focused on "some combination of conventional wisdom, pragmatics, personal affinity, or 'it just seemed like a good idea.'"

To illustrate how a theory-based approach could illuminate both the design and evaluation of an early childhood program, here is an example of a rough theory of change: Children whose experiences during infancy and early childhood equip them to enter school "ready to learn" are more likely to succeed at school than children who enter school not "ready to learn." More children will be ready for school learning if the community can reduce early deficits in health care, nutrition, child care, and preschool experiences; if families feel safe and protected in the neighborhood; and if the community is able to support families in ways that contribute to children's developing trust, curiosity, self-control, and the ability to interact with others.

Once theories have been articulated, evaluators work with program people to identify, on the basis of experience and research, what needs to be in place to accomplish the agreed-upon outcomes. In the case of the "ready to learn" theory, the steps leading to school readiness might include the availability to all low-income families of accessible, responsive, high-quality health care for infants, children, and pregnant women; child care that combines developmentally appropriate care, education, and family support; child protective services; family support programs; adequate nutrition; adequate income; and supportive community norms. Interim outcome measures, which would be apparent before long-term outcomes, might include higher rates of pregnant women receiving prompt and continuing prenatal care; higher rates of infants and preschool children receiving preventive health care, including immunizations; higher rates of three- and four-year-olds in Head Start and other high-quality child care/education settings; higher rates of infants and toddlers receiving care in high-quality settings; fewer confirmed and repeat instances of child abuse and neglect; and lower rates of inappropriate out-of-home placements.

A pathbreaking application of a theory-based evaluation has been designed by the Manpower Demonstration Research Corporation (MDRC) to understand the effects of Jobs-Plus, an initiative launched by MDRC in 1996, in partnership with the U.S. Department of Housing and Urban Development and the Rockefeller Foundation, providing "saturation-level employment opportunities for working-age residents of public housing." Both the intervention and the evaluation are shattering precedents because they embrace rather than shun the challenge of implementing and evaluating rigorously an intervention that will vary across sites, "reflecting their local preferences and constraints." The evaluators are prepared to test whether synergy among three strategies that have heretofore never been studied in combination will produce the expected major changes in residents and the public housing and communities in which they live. The three strategies that are to be combined are state-of-the-art employment and training services, financial incentives to promote work, and the creation of "a public housing community that actively supports work through resident groups and other local organizations." The fact that the sponsors have been able to come up with a rigorous, theory-based research design to measure the impact of such a complex intervention is good news. It bodes well for all who are looking to a broader evaluation mind-set as a source of reliable information about initiatives that count on both synergy and local adaptation as crucial components of effectiveness.

The theories-of-change approach to evaluation, then, has evaluators, practitioners, and researchers working together to construct a conceptual map that links the most important parts of an intervention together. As these conceptual maps accumulate, are refined through experience, and systematically analyzed, they will provide an ever richer and more reliable understanding of all the links along the causal chain leading to improved outcomes for children, families, and communities.

Shared interests rather than adversarial relationships: new roles for evaluators. The new evaluators are finding ways to build on shared interests with the program people and funders with whom they engage in a problem-solving process to improve outcomes.

They are aware that in the past, people responsible for programs, whether as teachers, social workers, Head Start staff, youth workers, or neighborhood residents, have often viewed evaluation research as an "unfriendly act."

Charles L. Usher of the University of North Carolina explains that the adversarial roots of evaluation stem from two sources—the traditions of financial auditing, basically an "investigative approach to evaluation," and "training in social science methods and philosophy, [which has] tended to reinforce the detachment of evaluators from program managers and policy makers." Usher suggests that many social scientists put a higher value on their mantle of scientific objectivity than on their ability to make a contribution to an informed policy debate or better program design. He believes that the traditional adversarial relationship between evaluators and program people is premised on the questionable assumption that the judgment of program managers and staff is inherently biased, because all they are interested in is expanding the resources allocated to programs they control. Usher and colleagues are persuaded that it is more likely that program managers and staff sincerely want to do a good job and avoid embarrassing mistakes, and that "those who develop programs and provide services are in the best position to know what their intents are and have the greatest interest in improvement." Consistent with this outlook, Usher and colleagues are promoting a concept they call self-evaluation, which has a number of elements in common with the theory-based approach to evaluation. They put a heavy emphasis not only on collaboration between evaluators and program people, but on explicit efforts to demystify evaluation, to help program people develop the capacity to monitor and assess their own performance, to enable them to detect problems and make midcourse corrections before the results of errors escalate, and to transform evaluation from a threatening event to an ongoing supportive process.

Ron Ferguson of Harvard's Kennedy School believes that many kinds of interventions, but especially complex community initiatives, need someone whom he calls an "inside evaluator" who can act as coach and confidant for senior staffers and leaders, and sometimes even as an honest advocate. In his experience, most local staff of comprehensive community initiatives were never trained for their jobs and "welcome the collegial, frank and timely evaluative feedback . . . that an inside evaluator can provide during both planning and implementation."

The danger, of course, is that the evaluator who does not maintain his or her distance from the initiative being evaluated will lose objectivity and become a cheerleader for that initiative, regardless of its merits. But that problem begins to recede as an outcomes orientation becomes the norm. When accountability is based on achievement of agreed-upon outcomes, the evaluator will no longer be the sole arbiter of the extent to which outcomes were realized. Evaluators will be free to focus more on the "why" and "how" as opposed to the "whether." They can position themselves better to obtain an accurate and nuanced understanding of the nature of interventions and how they link to the desired outcomes. They can move toward an explicit posture of helping practitioners learn from their daily experience and thereby improve their practice and their intervention. The new evaluator can provide feedback to practitioners for midcourse corrections, enhancing their capacity to reflect and to do on-the-spot experimentation. Evaluators can help practitioners think more carefully about both the theory and practice of what they are doing. Ultimately, they could develop a new evaluation culture leading to a greater understanding of successful interventions and how they are related to outcomes. Evaluators would become collaborators with reflective practitioners in the interest of improved programs.

We may want to try out a new image of the evaluator as cheer-leader. The evaluator would become a declared partisan, not of a particular initiative or intervention but of *solving the problem,* fully legitimized as an engaged participant in the quest for better ways to improve outcomes.

Employing multiple methods and perspectives. The new evaluators are not seeking to substitute a single new methodology for the experimental method based on random assignment. In their effort to be, as Usher puts it, "constructively critical rather than simplistically judgmental," they are using multiple methods and perspectives.

They welcome the opportunity to use the experimental method where its application does not distort the intervention. They welcome the opportunity to link quantitative approaches to the work of ethnographers and other trained observers who will document and describe successes, failures, and processes through narrative.

Their use of multiple approaches makes possible the kind of research that education scholar Anthony Bryk has been doing, subjecting "a very soft idea—that good schools have a sense of community"—to rigorous specification and empirical scrutiny. Bryk warns of the dangers of ignoring the factors that cannot be captured in statistical analysis or summarized with numbers. He believes that a true renewal of our educational institutions requires "melding insights from scientific pursuits with inspiration from our evocative traditions."

Rigor without certainty: better relevant than elegant. The new, multipronged approach to evaluation is gaining adherents today because it promises to provide more usable information about a wider array of interventions than can be obtained through experimental designs alone to answer the question of what would have happened had there been no intervention. It can be applied in situations where many of the influences that might affect results do not "stand still" long enough to permit certainty about what caused the observed effect.

The new evaluation, even when it cannot provide certainty about which component of intervention *caused* the improved results, can provide critical information. It can allow outsiders to distinguish between those who have implemented the intervention and those who have not, and to make "a well-reasoned and supported case that the results of the intervention are moving in the desired direction, probably because of the intervention. . . ." The new evaluation promises sufficiently timely answers so that the questions on which it sheds light will still be relevant. It provides tools to combat what MIT's Don Schön describes as "epistemological nihilism in public affairs," the view that nothing can be known because the certainty we demand is not attainable.

The thoughtful observer's informed understanding, based on a wide array of data about what happened and about what might have happened under a different set of circumstances, especially when combined with understanding of similar interventions and events, can ultimately build a strong and useful knowledge base. Although offering less certainty about causation, the new evaluators can bring information to the table that is not only rich but rigorous, and that can lead to effective action on urgent social problems.

There can be no scientific certainty about remedies for youth violence or alienation, family dissolution, school failure, or growing childhood poverty. But there *can* be systematic learning about all the promising ways to intervene. The systematic learning now needed must encompass a more generous approach to science, combining logic and evidence with hunch, analogy, insight, and creativity—a combination that Nobel prize–winning molecular biologist David Baltimore identifies as the basis for "the most fundamental progress in science."

Richard Darman, President Bush's director of the Office of Management and Budget, writes in a provocative essay that the great Washington scandal is that the federal government embarks on domestic programs without reliable empirical evidence that they could work. He complains that although "Americans across the political spectrum want to improve education, reduce violence, eliminate substance abuse, strengthen families, restore traditional values and increase opportunity," we have never organized a sustained effort to learn from our efforts to accomplish these ends. He blames American impatience and wariness of the "experts" who would do the evaluations. He calls on President Clinton to "end the era of policy corruption" by initiating a set of bold research trials focused on major policy initiatives. Darman envisions a long-term process that would guide social policy in the twenty-first century.

If Darman's proposal is to build a body of knowledge rather than to get simple yes-or-no answers to what works, he is on to something very important. Analytic rigor and objectivity cannot continue to be the monopoly of those who believe that nothing works. When the current spasm of cynicism relinquishes its hold on the body politic, the people who believe that well-designed, thoughtfully implemented interventions can indeed change lives and promote common purposes must be able to produce rigorous, usable knowledge. Such knowledge can become the foundation for large-scale support of policies and programs that would restore hope to the children and families most at risk in the nation today.

Part II

Reforming Systems

In the following three chapters, we focus directly on three systems—welfare, child welfare, and schools—established to reduce poverty, to safeguard children from abuse and neglect, and to educate our children. We will see how each of these systems has become archaic. We will see that although today's systems change pioneers are hampered by cutbacks in public funding and skepticism about public institutions, some have overcome even these obstacles. They show how systems can accomplish public purposes by reaching beyond formal boundaries to establish partnerships with citizens and communities. They provide examples of institutions becoming unchained from the rigidities of the past. They provide the evidence that interventions that strengthen families and neighborhoods can thrive, even within formal systems.

6

Beyond Welfare Repeal:
Real Welfare Reform

WHATEVER ELSE the "welfare reform" of 1996 did, one thing it did not do—reform welfare. It didn't put in place the portfolio of remedies that would promote family self-sufficiency, decrease the formation of single-parent families, and break the cycle of poverty. That remains to be done.

The underlying assumption of the 1996 welfare repeal legislation was that guaranteed cash benefits to welfare families established perverse incentives to depend on government handouts and to have babies outside marriage. The idea of ending the entitlement and setting time limits for cash benefits attracted enormous enthusiasm from politicians and the public. Other measures, arguably more effective, to increase family self-sufficiency—supporting the move into employment, making sure there are jobs, making work pay, and stronger enforcement of child support—never made it onto the legislative or public radar screen.

The law enacted in August 1996 abolishes the sixty-year-old federal guarantee of support for poor children, sets rigid work requirements, and mandates a five-year lifetime family limit on the receipt of assistance. The legislation may prod some beneficiaries—no one knows how many—to get organized and to seek and keep a job. It may even give a few young people occasional pause about bringing children into a harsher world. But it also removed for hundreds of thousands of children the thin layer of protection from destitution. Remaining to be tested is the premise that large numbers of actual and potential welfare recipients would become self-supporting once they could no longer count on government support. Remaining to be seen is how much harm will come to children, with less adult care and supervision, increased evictions, more crowded housing with its potential for family violence, and perhaps the return of hunger.

How Did the Welfare Repeal of 1996 Happen?

The welfare system that was repealed in 1996 was fundamentally flawed and urgently in need of repair. It had been designed for the social and economic conditions of the 1930s, essentially providing permanent cash assistance to families whose breadwinner—almost always the father—had died or been disabled. Permanent support for widows and orphans made sense in an era when few mothers worked outside the home. But sixty years later conditions had changed and norms had changed. Most of the children receiving Aid to Families with Dependent Children (AFDC) had living fathers, and mothers at all income levels were expected to work.

As the welfare reform discussion heated up between 1992 and 1996, hardly anyone defended the welfare system. Not the beneficiaries, not welfare administrators, not conservatives, not liberals, and taxpayers least of all.

So it was no wonder that, in 1992, presidential candidate Bill Clinton found that his biggest applause line was his promise to overhaul welfare. When his campaign was in trouble, Gloria Borger wrote in *U.S. News and World Report,* "his tough-on-welfare TV ads boosted his poll numbers. When he promised crowds to 'end welfare as we know it,' they went wild." One campaign aide estimated that 40 percent of Clinton's paid campaign advertising mentioned ending welfare. The welfare reform pitch pleased everyone, none more than the candidate's supporters in the centrist Democratic Leadership Council. They considered time-limited welfare benefits crucial in legitimating Clinton's claim to be a New Democrat.

I have no doubt that originally Clinton was committed to real reform that would reduce poverty and make life better for people at the bottom of the American economy. As governor, he was a major supporter of the Family Support Act of 1988, a modest, underfunded, and undervalued effort to make the welfare system more work oriented. As candidate and as president, he embraced the welfare reform ideas of David Ellwood, the highly respected welfare expert at Harvard's Kennedy School of Government.

Ellwood's 1988 book, *Poor Support,* argued that the welfare system had to be radically changed if it was to succeed in reducing poverty and accord with strongly held American values. The centerpiece of welfare reform would be work, and financial support had to be provided to people with low incomes without reducing their incentive to work and to help themselves. And one had to help single parents without encouraging single parenthood.

The Clinton welfare proposal, as it emerged during the campaign, featured time limits on welfare payments that would be coupled with the supports to enable people to leave welfare for work without harm to their children. The responsibility of welfare offices would be converted from check-writing to helping recipients make it on their own in the world of work. Employment would be made into a reasonable alternative to welfare by making work pay. Child support obligations would be enforced, and no one trying but unable to find a job would be abandoned.

The question that everyone asked later was whether the president should have known that his "screaming, whistling, foot-stomping audiences were cheering something quite different from the detailed plan that Mr. Clinton's aides were handing out to more thoughtful observers." Whether, in fact, Clinton was responsible for unleashing the political firestorm that followed.

I believe that Clinton made two serious mistakes. First, he talked about welfare in ways that validated distorted views of the nature of the problem and the solution. Second, having caught the voter's attention, he failed to use his unique opportunity to educate the American public about what it would really take to "fix" the welfare system. At a time when the political cost might not have been prohibitive, he did not fight vigorously for what he knew to be right.

Clinton's promise to "end welfare as we know it" was ambiguous enough to allow liberals to expect a full array of supports to help people to make the journey from welfare to work and permit conservatives to believe that the welfare system would soon be dismantled. For a politician to make promises susceptible to contradictory interpretations is a standard and forgivable practice. What is not easily forgiven is encouraging middle-class Americans to believe that high rates of female-headed families and teenage parenthood were problems primarily under the control of individuals who were making poor choices, and to attribute the welfare problem to the irresponsible behavior of poor women, with lines like "So, I say to people up and down the line that we will help you, but we want you to change."

During the campaign and as president, Clinton sought to avoid the "big spender" label by not talking about what it would cost to convert to a real work-based system. The cheering campaign audiences did not know, wrote *New York Times* columnist Bob Herbert, "that the detailed plan, which provided for education, job training, job placement, even job creation, would cost much, much more than welfare as we knew it." Borger wrote in *U.S. News* that the "nasty secrets"—that the plan could be "very expensive," would require a massive jobs bill, child care, and federally guaranteed child support—were never mentioned during the campaign.

Most tellingly, Ellwood says that while he always summed up the administration's proposal as "two years and you work," the president started out saying "two years and you work," and switched to "two years and you're out." The two slogans tested equally well in focus groups, Ellwood told me in October of 1995, not long after he left the administration. But the president seemed reluctant to use the "work" slogan, lest it focus attention on the need for public service jobs and their cost. So the president passed up the opportunity to tell his receptive audiences about the high short-run cost of the transition from welfare to work.

The president might have been able to bring the public along. In a November 1993 poll for *U.S. News,* 93 percent of respondents said they would favor a plan to "require job training for those on welfare and after two years require them to work." Asked whether they would favor such a plan if it became necessary to put people to work in government jobs, 82 percent of respondents still approved. A May 1994 *Los Angeles Times-Mirror* poll found 91 percent would support a plan that incorporated the basics of the administration proposal to Congress—a two-year limit on welfare, with recipients thereafter getting a job or taking a job the government would give them, with training and child care provided.

The president, and the American people, paid dearly for his failure to use the bully pulpit to rally the voters to support and fund the fundamental changes that I believe he genuinely favored. Clinton's unwillingness to make clear how complex were the causes of welfare dependency—with their implications for a significant federal role to support the journey from welfare to work—sanctioned a simplistic view of poverty as the result of individual failings, and of its cure as greater individual effort.

Of course, the president was not alone in encouraging this view. It fit well with the conservative push to cut back on government. And the press also contributed to the perception of poverty as a matter of individual failings. The personal drama, after all, makes a better story than root causes and economic trends. As Michael Massing wrote in *The New Yorker,* "The very qualities that make today's journalism so compelling—the seamless narrative, the eye for detail, the blend of empathy and candor—serve also to highlight the behavior of the poor, making it seem the cause of their poverty rather than the other way around." Even the best journalistic accounts tend to leave out the "larger economic, political, and even cultural factors that lie beyond the ghetto and the behavior of its residents—in boardrooms, say, or in Washington."

It thus becomes more understandable, that, in the mid-1990s, inchoate frustration among so many Americans coalesced to target, like a heat-seeking missile, the welfare system, welfare recipients, unmarried teenage mothers, and "irresponsible behavior." Christopher Jencks and Katherine Edin write that Americans came to regard welfare recipients as "irresponsible and incompetent parents living in communities that breed lawlessness and promiscuity . . . as black idlers who live off the labor of industrious whites."

By the time the Clinton Administration unveiled its welfare reform plan in 1994, a bidding war was already on to see who could be the toughest and most punitive, who could make the deepest slashes, whose proposal could go further in divesting the federal government of any protective role. A small band of House Democrats who were appalled by the prospect of time-limiting welfare benefits "begged" the administration to postpone action, reported Elizabeth Drew, "because they were struggling to win congressional approval of Clinton's health care proposal, because the Hispanic and Black Caucuses felt that the welfare proposal was racially targeted, and other liberals were squeamish about it."

Then came the November elections, and a changed world.

The new speaker of the house, Newt Gingrich, was determined to take the welfare issue away from Clinton, and ultimately to smash the welfare system. To that end, Gingrich, along with Robert Rector of the Heritage Foundation and William Kristol and William Bennett, the new conservative gurus, agreed that the focus of the welfare debate had to be shifted from work to illegitimacy.

I remember attending an Urban Institute meeting on welfare reform exactly one week after the 1994 election. All eyes were on Ron Haskins of the House Ways and Means Committee, who had been suddenly catapulted from obscurity to become the ranking staff person responsible for crafting the new legislation, to be known as the Personal Responsibility Act. The first words he uttered when the session began were "This bill is going to be about illegitimacy, not about work!" The proposed cure was denial of welfare benefits to the families of illegitimate children.

The Republicans also reframed the "welfare" debate to include all government programs and policies serving vulnerable children and families. One brush, dipped in the unpopularity of AFDC, could be used to taint them all. *New York* magazine columnist Jacob Weisberg wrote, "By invoking with a sneer the phrase welfare state, Gingrich implies that collective action is typified by welfare." At the heart of the Republican strategy, wrote E. J. Dionne, was discrediting government.

Tragically, the president made no effort to change the distorted picture voters were getting. No one told the stories of struggling families saved from destitution, whose children were able to make it into the American mainstream because they had welfare support. No one got through the din to explain that the causes of long-term welfare dependence were more complex than that cash benefits carried perverse incentives. Instead, the president seemed to climb on the Republican bandwagon. A month after the Republican midterm sweep, Clinton said in a radio address, "There's less disposable income for most working Americans than there was just a decade ago. Many people can't even imagine being able to afford a vacation anymore, let alone send their children to college. *And I'm talking about hardworking Americans, who play by the rules; they're tired of watching their earnings benefit people who don't.*"

Ultimately the welfare repeal of 1996 became possible because, without strong leadership to guide middle-class anxieties in a different direction, the more punitive the legislative proposals got, the more they resonated with a frustrated public.

Soon the public became convinced that the budget deficit was largely caused by huge government spending on the poor, that ending the federal guarantee of benefits would "rescue millions of Americans out of a corrupt welfare system," and that time limits on benefits would get millions of welfare recipients into jobs and stop unmarried teenagers from having babies.

That the new Republican proposals might also increase the number of children living in poverty seemed unimportant and unpersuasive—even to most Democratic legislators and ultimately to the president, in the light of the popularity of even the harshest of the pending bills.

Here lay a grim irony. President Clinton had started with a plan to prod welfare recipients to go to work. To make work a realistic alternative, he had proposed to accompany time limits with provisions to make work pay and to make sure the jobs were available. But, faced with radicalized Republicans, he was unwilling to go to bat for a program that would cost $10 billion more than current federal spending to ensure that children would not be harmed nor families driven into deeper poverty. He was left to sign a bill that withdrew $55 billion of federal aid to the poor, and shredded the sixty-year-old federal safety net under poor families with children.

As the president, preparing for his reelection battle, signed the bill, Jason DeParle of *The New York Times* observed that this legislation would end welfare as we know it, and perhaps poverty as we know it—by making both worse.

Real Welfare Reform: Strategies for Self-sufficiency

When it became clear that the president intended to sign the 1996 welfare bill, Bishop Felton E. May of the United Methodist Church asked, "If we, as individuals, would be willing to give a hungry child our last loaf of bread, as I believe we would, how can we, collectively—as a national government—turn our back on any child in poverty?" I think the answer is that we are sure the loaf of bread we give the hungry child will feed him, but we have been persuaded that government programs will not. Conservative Republicans even persuaded us that the old programs may have hurt hungry children, and that—as a nation—we don't know enough to devise better ones.

When President Clinton signed the Republican welfare legislation in August 1996, it had become conventional wisdom that the federal government was right to get out of the minimum-income-assurance business because it didn't know what it was doing.

I don't agree. I believe we knew then what to do, and we know now, although it will be more difficult under the new ground rules, which constrain both state and federal authority and funds. But acting on what we know requires vigorous leadership to persuade a skeptical public and cynical legislators that we do know what to do, that it can be done, and that it's worth doing—even if it costs more in the short run.

We start with the widely shared goals of helping poor people to become self-sufficient and regain control over their lives while assuring that their children get a good enough start in life to break the cycle of inherited misery. A second widely shared goal is to reduce childbearing among unmarried women without causing suffering among the children they do have. These goals can be reached in ways consistent with American values of responsibility, hard work, strong families, compassion, and a willingness to help those who are prepared to help themselves.

The strategies to accomplish these goals extend well beyond replacing the AFDC system. They would assure that more adults, both men and women, will become self-sufficient by supporting the move from unemployment or welfare to work, making sure jobs are available, making work pay, and strengthening child support. A second set of strategies would combine with these to reduce the number of single-parent families.

Before examining these strategies, we should pause for a moment to try to understand what these issues look like from the perspective of one who lives them. A Chicago woman named Mary Ann Moore is typical of the many women who live precarious lives and work miserable jobs for little pay, struggling to stay off welfare and doing the best they can for their children.

Moore was one of several women interviewed by *New York Times* reporter Jason DeParle in the fall of 1994. Assigned to cover welfare reform, DeParle had set out to hear directly from some of the women around whom the controversy was swirling. Toby Herr, director of Project Match, invited several Chicago women she knew to meet DeParle.

Months later, he still couldn't shake from his mind the story Moore had told him of how, after working steadily for a while, she wanted to use her meager savings to buy a bicycle for her fourteen-year-old, six-foot son. But her son had dissuaded her, saying it was no use because the gangs would just take it. She told DeParle that the gangs were also the reason she couldn't let him go outside by himself. DeParle kept thinking about what that said about the life this family led, and resolved to try to do a follow-up profile of Moore for *The New York Times Magazine*. DeParle's editors agreed, Moore agreed, and DeParle returned to Chicago to get his in-depth story of one struggling family.

He hadn't quite figured out how he was going to do the story, because some of it was about how Moore gets up every morning at three-thirty, rousing her four children, dressing the younger ones, giving them breakfast, taking them in her decrepit car to her mother's apartment on the other side of town, and getting to her job as cook at a Salvation Army homeless shelter by 6:00 A.M. Wondering whether *he* could get himself up in a hotel room in time to reach the Moores' apartment to witness the start of their day, he had brought a sleeping bag to Chicago, just in case. He was relieved when Moore invited him to bring his sleeping bag to her place. DeParle bunked with the Moores, sharing their life for ten days.

Moore worked a fifty-two-hour week at her Salvation Army cook's job, including a thirteen-hour shift on Saturdays and Sundays. Before that, Moore had landed and lost some twenty jobs since receiving her first welfare check thirteen years earlier at the age of nineteen, eleven of those jobs just in the previous five years. "She has driven trucks and peddled nuts, fried eggs and bathed invalids," wrote DeParle. "She has cruised the aisles of a mail-order warehouse on roller skates to fill customer orders, she has strapped a revolver onto her six-foot frame to guard the high-rises at Cabrini Green where she was raised." Moore's experience typifies that of a high proportion of women leaving welfare for work, who lose their jobs within the first six months. Child care arrangements fall apart, someone gets sick, the car breaks down, a supervisor imposes demands that seem unacceptable or rules that seem outrageous. Moore's example of the last is the ban on incoming phone calls that prevented her, several months earlier, from learning that her mother had had a heart attack.

During his stay with the Moores, DeParle watched fourteen-year-old Marchello dribbling an imaginary basketball down the hallway and shooting fake jump shots at the ceiling because his mother was determined to keep him indoors, safe from the gangs. DeParle also shared an episode of food poisoning that felled him for twenty-four hours, but hit the exhausted Moore much harder. Her illness lasted two weeks and started one more downward spiral that cost her yet one more job, leaving her complicated life to fall apart yet one more time.

DeParle was awed by the energy and determination it took for Mary Ann Moore to keep her life and family together. But his biggest new insight was about the role played by men in many women's welfare-to-work dramas, the "jealous interference," or even physical assault, by boyfriends who feel threatened by the prospect of their financial independence. In Moore's case it was a boyfriend who tried to sabotage her victories. But there is almost always a boyfriend or husband or father who feels endangered when the woman's prospects begin to improve. "It's the untold story," Herr told DeParle. "The men are not working, and they don't want the women feeling better. They don't want to think they're not needed anymore." Herr thinks that no welfare reform will work unless it finds ways to also improve employment of men. They have perhaps not been "corrupted" by welfare subsidies, but they "have wound up even poorer and more wretched" than the women.

DeParle's profile of Mary Ann Moore concludes that, as the details of her life accrue, "welfare itself seems to shrink in importance, compared with the surrounding problems, like low wages, unaffordable rents, gangs, violence, rickety cars, drugs and irresponsible men." He also notes that whatever else welfare may have done, the fact that cash assistance was available when Moore was unable to find work "has managed to keep Marchello and his siblings with a mother they clearly adore."

Mary Ann Moore is someone who could well be hurt by the new welfare laws. On the other hand, her efforts to help herself might help much more if the self-sufficiency strategies we now examine were adopted.

Supporting the Move from Welfare or Unemployment to Work

The states now have the action on designing the supports to help people move from welfare to work, some of whom are, at best, only marginally employable.

They have to take account of three groups of welfare recipients with quite different needs and widely varying capacities.

- *Families in transition.* The largest single category of past welfare recipients are those who need and have been receiving only temporary support. Historically, half of all recipients have left AFDC within a year of becoming eligible. Three quarters left within the first two years. Three quarters of those reentering welfare exited again, 50 percent within twelve months. These families are suffering temporary economic difficulties as a result of losing a job, death, divorce, or abandonment, or because of the illness of a child or parent. They may need help with job search and placement, and they need income support to get back on their feet, but these are the families whose behavior and life choices are not a subject of great concern, because they are likeliest to regain on their own the capacity for self-support.

- *Families whose adult breadwinners are not motivated or willing to do what it takes to prepare for, obtain, and hold jobs.* These are the families whom Americans are most angry about. In 1996, it appeared that most citizens thought this was the category that applied to most welfare recipients—and the men who fathered their children. But the public overestimates the number who *choose* not to work. Most women on welfare with skills to earn a living wage are already working, says Judith Gueron, president of the Manpower Demonstration Research Corporation. Most of the rest face "real obstacles to employment," like clinical depression or substance abuse. "This is not a group that just needs a good kick to get their act together," Gueron said.

Those who have studied in depth mothers dependent on welfare have concluded that most would not endure an existence so miserable if they had better options. One study of welfare mothers in Chicago concluded, "Single mothers do not turn to welfare because they are pathologically dependent on handouts or unusually reluctant to work. They do so because they cannot get jobs that pay better than welfare."

- *Families where the adult breadwinner lacks the skills, support, or capacity to find and keep work that pays enough to get the family out of poverty.* A significant number of adult welfare recipients leave the welfare rolls but, like Mary Ann Moore, cycle back on— 45 percent of them within a year, and almost two thirds within three years. Jobs are a lot easier to get than to hang on to, as Mary Ann Moore explained to Jason DeParle: "I always get 'em, it's keeping 'em that's the thing."

In a Kansas City survey of 599 workers placed in jobs in which employers were paid a wage supplement and workers had access to case managers, 363 had quit within a year. "You can have someone who really wants to work, but if Grandma gets sick, or child care falls through, or you get a flat tire . . . all those things can throw a person out of a job," said Gayle Hobbs, executive director of the Local Investment Commission, which coordinates social services in Kansas City.

For many long-time welfare recipients, leaving welfare is so onerous not because they have become "addicted" to a dependent way of life, but because they lack the education and personal qualities, including interpersonal skills, needed to obtain and hold on to a job paying a decent wage. Some lack the cognitive ability or the "emotional competence" required not to hold a job, but to hold most jobs over time. As Christopher Jencks and Kathryn Edin explained, "For every schizophrenic who is completely out of touch with reality, there are half a dozen other adults who have trouble getting along with a boss or coworkers and therefore don't hold any job for a long period. Likewise, for every victim of Down's syndrome who cannot write her name, there are half a dozen others who can read and write, but have trouble figuring out what their boss would want them to do in an unfamiliar situation. Such people are employable, but they will be the last hired and the first fired."

Low cognitive capacity is a barrier to getting and holding a job for many. Researchers Nick Zill of Westat and Gary Burtless of the Brookings Institution have tried to figure out how many, using the scores on the Armed Services Qualifying Test, given to a huge sample of twenty-five-year-old women, including AFDC recipients, who were part of the National Longitudinal Survey of Youth. Zill found that fully 68 percent of "long-term" AFDC recipients (individuals receiving three or more years of benefits within the previous five years) scored in the bottom quarter, so low that none of these women would be considered eligible for the armed forces. Burtless, using a slightly different calculation, found that 72 percent of women who had received AFDC payments during all of the previous twelve months scored in the bottom quartile.

University of Wisconsin Poverty researcher Robert Haveman estimated that up to one quarter of welfare recipients encountered "insurmountable barriers to employment," including chronic mental and physical health problems, lack of basic skills, or serious language deficiencies.

No one knows precisely how many families or potential bread-winners there are at various points along the spectrum of employability. There are few reliable estimates, especially in the drug abuse arena. However, estimates from three respected sources agree that at least one in five current welfare recipients are significantly handicapped in obtaining job training and employment by their abuse of alcohol and/or illicit drugs.

Another significant group of women have been unable to leave welfare for work for lack of transportation, stable day care for their children, or the encouragement of another adult.

Many women are in settings that undermine rather than encourage their struggle toward self-sufficiency. In a nationwide survey of welfare-to-work programs, the Taylor Institute found extensive evidence of a pattern of male violence that undermined women's efforts to become economically independent. Many poor single women, struggling to combine work and child rearing, have men in their lives with a stake in keeping their female partners dependent and isolated from outside relationships and influences. Unwilling to let these women succeed on their own, they may, the night before a key test or job interview, engage their partners in nightlong quarrels, leaving the women unable to perform well;

they may batter them in the hope they will be too embarrassed about their bruises or too injured to show up; they may promise to provide child care or transportation, only to become drunk or disappear when needed.

The high-quality child care that is essential to enable most mothers to work has not been available and affordable, even for mothers already working: Texas and California, two states that kept track, had waiting lists for subsidized day care of 40,000 and 225,000 poor children, respectively.

BUILDING ON WHAT WE KNOW ABOUT HOW TO HELP

It is too early to know how many states will succeed in designing policies and programs that will move people with all these varied needs from welfare and unemployment to self-sufficiency, and how many will compete with one another to do the least for their most vulnerable citizens. It is too early to know how many have learned and will act on the recognition that the systems that are effective in moving both men and women from unemployment or welfare to work must, in the words of Indianapolis's Republican Mayor Stephen Goldsmith, have "flexibility and heart," It is too early to tell how many have learned that to be effective, welfare-to-work systems must support the same Seven Attributes of Highly Effective Programs identified in Chapter 1, which account for success in all the other domains of human service. It is too early to know how many have learned that the road from unemployment or welfare to work is not smooth or straight, and how many are therefore devising realistic supports for the transition to work.

In assessing the extent to which states are building on what is known, one is struck by how impervious the 1996 welfare legislation was to empirical information about what had worked and not worked in the past.

While most of the changes that ultimately became part of the legislation were a leap into the unknown—so unprecedented that there was no knowledge base to draw on—the information that *was* available was never considered. "The remarkable thing about the [1996] welfare bill . . . is that it ignores just about everything we've learned about the subject during the past 35 years," said Paul Offner, formerly Senator Moynihan's welfare expert and now commissioner of health care finance for the District of Columbia.

Available information would have shown that the employment targets set by the legislation were unrealistic. Available information would also have pointed to the link between the deteriorating economic status of young men and the plight of single mothers, and focused attention on helping unemployed and alienated young men enter the world of work. In contrast with "the enormous amount of argument about what we need to do to equip, train, cajole, or compel mothers to make this transition to work," observed Douglas Nelson, executive director of the Casey Foundation, "fathers are virtually invisible."

Offner says that if we don't soon start paying attention to the economic prospects of poor men, the poor neighborhoods of the future will be places where "welfare mothers pack their lunch buckets and head off to work while the fathers of their children lounge around the street corners, watching them go."

Improving the work prospects of unemployed men would help to get men back into the lives of their children, reducing the pressures that cause so many to abandon their parenting responsibilities in the first place. "I walked away because my job situation didn't allow me to be the provider I needed to be," says one young father. The anecdotal evidence is confirmed by the statistics showing that between 1969 and 1993, the number of households headed by women increased at virtually the same rate that the economic fortunes of young men declined.

It is unlikely that the states will make better use of existing knowledge of what works than did Congress, since many of the most effective interventions cost more than the present system. In addition, the states have not had time for the careful planning required to take advantage of accumulating experience of both community-based programs and state reforms, including those that have come out of state experiments under federal welfare waivers.

PROJECT MATCH: THE NONLINEAR JOURNEY FROM WELFARE TO WORK

Among the most promising initiatives trying to discover, develop, and then describe new ways of helping welfare recipients to become more self-sufficient is Project Match in Chicago, and one of its offspring, which is becoming part of the state system in Oregon.

For those designing supports for the journey from welfare to self-sufficiency, the biggest obstacle, according to welfare-to-work expert Toby Herr, is a linear mind-set. "The underlying assumption of the standard welfare-to-work model is that leaving welfare is a predictable, orderly process that can be accomplished relatively quickly: A person participates in an education, training, or other job preparation program, finds employment, leaves AFDC, keeps working, and never returns to welfare." Project Match found that this model did not fit the real world.

What actually happens, says Herr, is that welfare recipients who find jobs are likely to lose them and to need help finding subsequent ones. They may need help returning to school or getting additional training or in making different child care arrangements—or in getting rid of an abusive boyfriend. Because no two persons take exactly the same route out of welfare, the nature and timing of their need for support will vary and services must be individualized. Post-employment services become as important as pre-employment ones. Setbacks must be seen as normal, not as failures, and assistance in overcoming them must be immediately available.

Part of the problem is that few appreciate how long change takes. The latest findings from a long-term follow-up study of Project Match participants show that while after a year in the program only 26 percent were working year-round, by the end of five years, 54 percent had worked a full year. Herr worries that programs are not designed to reflect the fact that "entering the workforce is really the starting point," not the end point. "For people with limited work experience and complicated lives, it takes a long time to become a steady worker."

Herr's experience suggests that the conventional linear model, putting all the services at the front end and letting the support wither away at the point of first employment, is "massively flawed." She has concluded that "leaving welfare is not a one-step process about getting a job, but rather a long and difficult process about human growth and development." Watching women who have never been part of the work force gradually become steady workers has convinced Herr that "we have to create a welfare-to-work system that reflects what we know about how people learn and grow." That is why participants must have choices about sequences and why the program must fit the individual's time commitments. "Some will do education first, some will work first. You have to be flexible around sequencing, you have to be flexible around time commitments. Some people could start on their GED, but they can't do it twenty hours a week. Most people need to work first. You don't want to send the high school dropout right back where she failed. And, for many people, the standard activities are not the right ones. They're too structured, they're too demanding."

When Project Match researchers studied the pathways of 225 participants, they found that about half had made either unsteady or no progress in the first three years. "That's when I realized that, although we were flexible on sequencing and we were flexible around time commitments, we also needed to be flexible about how we defined the lowest rung on the ladder."

Project Match learned to redefine work preparation, redefine progress, and put new rungs on the bottom of the ladder. "Now we view doing things for your kids as work preparation. Because the same parents that can't get themselves on time to anything, including a job, also never got their kids to school on time, never got their kids to extracurricular activities. Getting there on time is a learned competency. So we write into their employability plan, you're going to take Johnny to Scouts once a week, you're going to get Mary to Head Start, and you'll get there on time. You're going to get organized, get involved. And that's a realistic beginning to the journey from welfare to work. Next you'll volunteer at the Head Start center. That's progress we can capture and dote on and celebrate! What you do is broad and negotiable, but we make sure that everybody is always engaged in something that represents progress for that person. And, equally important, this is a way we can do welfare reform and help kids at the same time—because, by getting your act together to be a good parent, you're also getting your act together to be employable."

Herr's story immediately raises the question, of course, of whether a flexible, nonlinear intervention like Project Match could be sustained as part of a public system. She sought and found an opportunity to address that question when the State of Oregon decided to build a demonstration on Project Match's post-employment experience.

Post-Employment Services in Oregon

In 1993 the U.S. Department of Health and Human Services funded four state demonstrations aimed at helping former welfare recipients to keep their jobs or find new ones promptly. Oregon was one of the four grantees. Because Project Match was one of the first welfare-to-work programs to recognize the importance of working with welfare recipients *after* they had begun a job, Toby Herr was invited to help the Oregon demonstration get under way.

Under the terms of the demonstration, participants would be able to receive an array of services for up to two years after starting on their first post-welfare jobs. These services would supplement the transitional child care, Medicaid, and work-related payments for which all Oregon AFDC recipients were eligible for ninety days after leaving AFDC. They would be provided through one of four post-employment case managers, called "retention workers," a position newly created for the purpose of the demonstration.

The retention worker would make contact with each person in her caseload (randomly selected from welfare recipients who had found jobs) to let her know about the services and assistance available, find out how she was doing in her job, and whether she was experiencing problems at home or at work that might threaten her keeping her job. The retention worker was trained "to be responsive to whatever people are preoccupied with at a particular moment without losing sight of the larger mission of keeping people in the labor force."

The four retention workers all spent a great deal of time trying to establish close relationships with their clients. They found that a high degree of trust and intimacy was needed to enable a client to reveal a personal problem that led to loss of a job, or for a client to accept feedback on how she dressed or behaved. Because clients usually could not talk on the phone from their jobs, the retention workers shifted their working hours to be able to talk to their clients evenings and weekends.

The sponsors of the demonstration recognized that the retention workers would need a great deal of discretion, since no one knew the most effective strategies to keep people in the labor force. They became convinced that even after the demonstration period, flexibility would still be needed in almost every aspect of program operations. Staff discretion seemed to be particularly important in disbursement of work-related payments and in adjusting the level of contact with clients over time.

Here, too, a linear model didn't fit. The level of a client's need fluctuated with events in her life. "Early on we thought people would need a lot of attention at first, and then not a lot, but that's not the case," said one retention worker. "It's not a matter of needing a lot up front and, after that, only maintenance. At any time there might be the need for a lot of contact."

Reporting on the demonstration, Herr and her colleagues observe, "Like good parents and teachers, the retention workers have had to be discerning judges of when it's appropriate to step back and let clients go along on their own and when to intervene more directly and forcefully." They also noted the constant tension between providing social support and social control. They echoed policy analyst Lawrence Mead's observation that "case managers appear to motivate their clients with a combination of help and hassle." In each contact with a client, the worker has to feel her way on what mix of sanctions, encouragement, and just plain intensive listening the client needs. Herr and colleagues wrote that "the workers are extraordinarily helpful and caring, but they also clearly communicate the expectation that everyone can and should work."

An analysis of the first year's experience in the four demonstration sites by Mathematica Policy Research and the Urban Institute finds that the part of the intervention most valued by clients has been the moral support and encouragement of staff, which the evaluators say is made possible by retention workers and case managers who are freed from "excessively bureaucratic or rigid procedures." One client said, "My worker has come through for me in the last couple of months more than anybody else in my life. I called her at midnight, I called her at eight in the morning. She has been calling me. She has really gone out of her way. And obviously she has done that for other people, too." Another called her case manager a "miracle worker" for the way she was able to resolve conflicts with the bureaucracy about benefits. An Oregon client says, "It seems like the retention people not only help you with resources, like financial and stuff, but they really help you emotionally. You know, they're not just 'these are the rules.' They're there to support you in any way they can."

While the Oregon post-employment services experiment was able to enrich the services and supports made available to former welfare recipients, it was, like most demonstrations that are inserted into an existing bureaucracy, constrained by existing policy and administrative structures that did not support the new mission. What the Oregon agency was unable to do, making it harder to provide effective post-employment services in that setting, was to change the bureaucratic context in which the demonstration operated.

"They kept bumping into the old policies that did not support the new post-employment services," Herr found. New services were put in place, based on a more flexible understanding of what it takes to help welfare recipients make a permanent attachment to the workforce, but the system didn't make the accommodation that would have made the new services most effective.

Among the constraints the Oregon experiment "kept bumping into," three seemed to be most important. First, the pressures to preserve organizational neatness produced rules that undermined organizational effectiveness. If a demonstration participant lost her job and wanted to reapply for AFDC, she had to go through the local welfare office. That rule was never modified, even though everyone knew it interfered with effectiveness by causing weeks of delay before the retention worker—who was geared up to provide prompt support, before demoralization set in—could work again with her client.

A second barrier was the inability of the bureaucracy to encompass two such diverse ideas as that the relationship with a case manager can be essential, but that it is not *always* essential. "I'm not going to tell you that I screwed up on the job or that I have a drug problem unless I know you well and trust you," Herr explains. "But a job lead doesn't require a relationship. Updating your résumé doesn't require a relationship. Sometimes all that is needed is access to a 'resource room.'"

Herr recalls that for many years, case management wasn't part of the welfare-to-work process. "Then, all of a sudden, it's case management or nothing." Once it became apparent that client-case manager relationships could make an essential contribution, new rigidities were locked in. "If the particular help people need is not relationship based, we shouldn't put procedures in place as though it were."

A third barrier was the inability of the welfare system to encourage—even allow—people to use resources informally, on an "as needed" basis. In the Oregon experience, the "resource room" became the central tool for getting people back into the workforce, with its job developers, who know the local labor market; a continuous supply of job orders; word processors for updating résumés; telephones and copying and fax machines; and staff to assist those who needed help. But ways of providing quick and easy access to the resource room, including on evenings and weekends, perhaps with a computerized card that would entitle participants to a stipulated amount of services, have so far remained outside the reformers' grasp.

Herr recognizes that there are no precedents for a "twenty-four-hour Kinko's" for job seekers. Programming and funding are not organized "so that people can come in and out." Funders want to know in advance how many people will be served, who will be a client and who won't, and who is on the caseload and who isn't. "That's an unnecessary set of complications to put around something you want people to access quickly, easily, and unbureaucratically."

Oregon's resource centers are especially interesting in that they respond to the heretofore unmet employment-related needs of persons long outside the mainstream labor market.

"In a lot of inner-city neighborhoods," says William Julius Wilson, "the informal jobs network system has broken down because so many people are not working. The informal network system is characterized by friends, relatives, acquaintances passing on word to their employers about somebody that they know who lives in the neighborhood who could work in one of the jobs that they're involved in and they recommend these people. But if nobody's working, you're not in a position to do that, and so a lot of people don't find out about jobs through the informal network system." That is why he considers job information centers crucial, and most helpful if they can mobilize other missing supports, including the creation of van pools and car pools when public transportation can't get people where the jobs are.

Wilson would also charge the job information and placement centers with the task of helping persons who have been out of the labor force to become job ready "so that a prospective employer would be assured that a worker understands and appreciates employer expectations such as showing up for work on time and on a regular basis, and accepting the orders of supervisors. . . ."

LESSONS FOR SUPPORTING THE TRANSITION TO WORK

A review of the most promising experiments in supporting the transition to work suggests a set of lessons that should inform the efforts of states and of community agencies aiming to help more men and women move from unemployment or welfare to work.

1. The journey from unemployment or welfare to work hardly ever moves in a straight line, and each person is likely to travel a unique and often bumpy path. Systems and agencies meant to assist people in making this journey must have the flexibility to respond to a wide range of needs and capacities and to modify their policies and practices in the light of experience.

2. Effective job-training, search, and placement are well-connected to specific employers and to labor market needs. Effective efforts recognize that employers look not only for specific job skills, but also for workers who are punctual, efficient, cooperative, and ready to pick up more skills.

3. Many individuals who are difficult to place face barriers that require intensive interventions, including treatment for substance abuse or mental illness. Many individuals will not become self-sufficient without long-term, intensive, committed personal support, especially during major transitions.

4. Welfare-to-work programs that focus on prompt job placement have better short-term outcomes, but may not be effective in help-

ing individuals lacking solid educational foundations to achieve self-sufficiency in the long run.

5. Welfare-to-work programs must be prepared for a greater demand for child care than most had expected. They must be prepared to make special efforts to help families make provisions for care of infants, for care during evenings and weekends, and for care of sufficiently high quality that it will not harm the future prospects of young children.

Jobs, Jobs, Jobs: Where Will They Come From?

The welfare debate has been waged as though "behavior" were the problem, as though just getting the incentives right, and getting the people at the bottom properly motivated, would end the need for welfare support. The assumption has been that there would be enough jobs at the end of the line, stable enough and paying enough to make former welfare recipients and their families economically independent. That assumption is far-fetched at best, and probably just plain wrong.

The biggest obstacle to achieving a work-oriented welfare system and reducing poverty lies in a job market that doesn't need low-skilled workers. And when it does offer work to the low-skilled, the work is likely to be unstable. The Mary Ann Moores who blame themselves for being unable to hang on to a job—and the many observers who blame their personal failings—fail to see that cost-conscious employers have little reason to hang on to unskilled workers when demand is slack or when they miss work because their child is sick.

That is why the second essential component of real welfare reform is making sure there are jobs—decent jobs.

Some academics estimate that the number of poor jobless workers currently exceeds the number of vacancies by at least six to one. Wilson believes that the supply of low-skilled workers compared with the number of available jobs is so large that it would take ten to fifteen continuous years of economic expansion to absorb them— and, he adds, "We've never had a period of sustained economic growth that has lasted that long."

As three Yale University professors have written, "The labor market is a giant game of musical chairs in which there aren't enough seats for everyone who is actively seeking work, let alone for all those the public thinks should work." A Milwaukee study found about 75,000 persons needing jobs were going after a total of

30,635 positions. They conclude that it's not just good jobs there aren't enough of, "there aren't enough bad jobs either."

Another study found that in Harlem, fourteen people were pursuing every new $4.25-an-hour fast-food-restaurant job. After looking for a year, 73 percent of them still didn't have a job. The job market was already glutted with people who were better qualified than most welfare recipients. For example, while more than half of the people working at fast-food jobs in Harlem have high school diplomas, only one third of long-term welfare mothers do. The researchers observed, "The jobs once considered solely the province of high school dropouts just starting in the world of work are now dominated by workers in their mid- and late-20s trying to support families on $170 a week."

In their interviews with Harlem employers, the researchers learned that employers favor job applicants who commute from distant neighborhoods—they worry that people living in the immediate area will bring problems, such as friends who badger them for free eats. Employers also said they prefer immigrants to Americans, explaining that newcomers from poor countries value low-wage jobs more than Americans do. Of job applicants who were legal immigrants, 40 percent were hired; of applicants who were U.S.-born African-Americans, 14 percent were hired. Wilson reports similar findings from Chicago, where employers who advertise entry-level jobs in newspapers often choose ethnic and immigrant newspapers that bypass black neighborhoods.

Economists in New York City estimated that if the city's growth continued at the rate it has experienced since the 1992 recession, and if *every* job gained by the local economy were given to a New Yorker on welfare, it would take twenty-one years for all 470,000 adults receiving welfare support to be absorbed into the economy. As if to bring the economists' projections to life, four thousand hopeful applicants stood in lines that formed well before dawn on March 18, 1997, in response to a tiny classified advertisement in New York's newspapers announcing the Roosevelt Hotel was reopening in midtown Manhattan and would be filling seven hundred jobs.

It is indeed paradoxical, as economists Sheldon Danziger and Peter Gottschalk observe, "that so much attention has been focused on changing the labor-supply behavior of welfare recipients and so little has been given to changing the demand side of a labor market that has been increasingly unable to employ less-skilled and less-experienced workers." The potential of private sector initiatives and new public-private partnerships remains to be fully exploited. These range from strengthening the job creation possibilities of Empowerment and Enterprise Zones to the proposal of Hugh Price, president of the National Urban League, that employers reserve "training slots and real jobs for residents of neighborhoods or census tracts with high unemployment rates." They also include new pleas from President Clinton to employers—including the federal government—to hire former welfare recipients.

Why we lack a national jobs strategy today, why we put all our emphasis on changing the behavior of welfare recipients and not on changing the labor market, may be paradoxical, but it is not mysterious. A jobs strategy is expensive.

President Clinton is not the first politician who has been unwilling to face up to the investment a real jobs-based antipoverty strategy would require.

In 1964, in the midst of a booming economy, President Johnson turned down proposals to make a massive jobs program the centerpiece of the war on poverty, because it would have required new taxes.

Senator Moynihan recently recalled the 1964 Cabinet meeting when the planning group for the war on poverty presented its proposal for the centerpiece of the new federal initiative—a massive jobs program, to be financed by a cigarette tax. "President Johnson listened for a moment or two, and announced that in that election year we were cutting taxes, not raising them. He thereupon picked up the telephone attached to the Cabinet table, called someone, somewhere, about something else." Moynihan believes that at that moment, "The war on poverty was lost before it began."

A year later, Moynihan—then Assistant Secretary of Labor—wrote the report, "The Negro Family: The Case for National Action," highlighting the problem of black family disintegration, but offering no solution. Moynihan has long been known as better on defining problems than solutions. But this time, according to critic Mickey Kaus, it "wasn't because he had no solutions in mind." Kaus believes that at the time Moynihan favored "a large federal jobs program to provide employment to black men." But because President Johnson had already rejected the idea of funding a jobs program, the loyal Moynihan left the jobs proposal out. Without a remedy, the report was subject to devastating criticism for blaming the victims of racial discrimination and lack of opportunity for their fate. The report left the body politic free to conclude that single-parent families and unmarried childbearing were simply the product of unwise individual choices and imprudent individual behavior.

What are the chances that this time the nation will turn boldly to the task of job creation—first in the private sector, and where necessary in the public sector? Perhaps this time, with the new welfare law, the alternatives are sufficiently grim: women and children living in bus stations and freezing on grates, turning to prostitution or the drug trade, or clinging to abusive boyfriends; allowing the nihilism among inner-city people to increase and spread as they take increasingly desperate measures to survive, with cities becoming "almost unlivable."

I believe that, given some vigorous leadership, the many Americans who lack the stomach for seeing that happen can be mobilized to support new policies that would assure that everyone prepared to work could get a job.

Peter Edelman, who resigned as HHS assistant secretary over the welfare legislation, points out that a simple replication of the Depression's Works Project Administration, ambitious though it would be, won't meet the need in this very different era. The WPA never had to contend with providing work for millions without skills and without any attachment to the labor market. That is why Edelman proposed, in the March 1997 issue of *The Atlantic Monthly,* a combined public and private sector job creation effort, closely tied to job training and job readiness programs, open to both men and women.

Yes, such an initiative would be expensive. But we've always known that the cash benefits of AFDC were the cheapest alternative, and we did away with the cheapest alternative. Now we must invest what it takes to enable everyone ready to work to do so.

MAKING WORK PAY

They have become sound bites, but they make sense: If you work you shouldn't be poor. Work must pay, so that those who play by the rules are not losing the game. These are also achievable goals on which liberals and conservatives can agree.

The largest group of the poor in America today are families already doing a great deal to help themselves by working full- or part-time. Many are single parents trying to be both nurturer and economic provider to the family.

The long-term decline in wages, especially at the bottom of the income distribution, has made it harder than ever to earn enough to support a family and leave welfare. The long-term decline in wages has also interfered with family formation, because fewer low-skilled men earn enough to support a family. Thus, the goal of making work pay requires an extension of the Earned Income Tax Credit, subsidized child care, and health insurance for families with children who are working but not covered by their employers' insurance.

Of 165 poor single working mothers interviewed by researchers Kathryn Edin and Laura Lein in Boston, Chicago, San Antonio, and Charleston, *none* was able to live on earnings alone. Most were able to work only because their child care needs were met by a relative or friend or through some other below-market-rate arrangement. Most also would not have been able to stay off AFDC without financial help from absent fathers, boyfriends, or family members.

Health insurance and better pay for people in low-wage employment would make welfare unnecessary for a substantial proportion. The single most frequent reason for women being forced back on welfare has been the need for health insurance, which they typically don't get as part of their marginal employment. One study found that if health insurance benefits were available to all female workers, welfare caseloads would go down by 20 to 25 percent.

The Earned Income Tax Credit (EITC) has received very little public visibility, considering that it is the largest federal program for assisting low-income working families, with benefits totaling twice the amount the federal government spends on AFDC. As economists Barry Bluestone and Teresa Ghilarducci point out, "It is life support for the permanently low-wage worker; it is earnings insurance for the middle class."

President Reagan called it "the best anti-poverty, the best pro-family, the best job creation measure to come out of Congress." Its continued expansion could not only make it easier for women to move from welfare to work, but it could have a substantial effect on the employment prospects of low-skilled men.

STRENGTHENING ENFORCEMENT OF CHILD SUPPORT

A fourth strategy to help achieve self-sufficiency is strengthening enforcement of child support from absent fathers, and supplementing these payments when they prove undependable as a source of monthly income. Where the father has low earnings, a system of child support assurance would supplement the father's contribution and ensure that mother and children received a minimum amount of support.

Making sure that these funds go to the children these men have fathered would go far to ease the burden on one parent trying to do the job of two.

In 1992, the House Ways and Means Committee held hearings on but failed to report out a Child Support Enforcement and Assurance Act. Under the bill, which was—reflecting its bipartisan appeal—cosponsored by liberal Tom Downey and conservative Henry Hyde, the federal government would assume responsibility for collecting child support payments, primarily through wage withholding, and would guarantee a minimum level of income support for children where a parent has failed to meet a support order.

Strengthened child support enforcement would draw attention not only to the father's responsibility, but to the plight of low-income males and how they could better provide both economic and other supports to their children.

CAN THE STATES DO THIS JOB?

In the 1995–96 debate over devolving federal authority to the states, the issue repeatedly arose of whether governors and state legislators *cared* as much about children and the poor as the federal government. That was the wrong question; the welfare legislation, as enacted, involves a political calculus in which "caring" by state officials does not figure.

The stern reality is that moving people from welfare to work costs more, not less, than supporting them on welfare; the interplay of political interests within the states will not protect poor children; and states have to compete to keep tax burdens low. No amount of "caring" by governors or legislatures can change these realities.

Moving people into the workforce costs more than supporting them on welfare. The cheapest thing to do with chronic welfare-dependent families is simply to leave them as they are. Helping a welfare client into the workforce is labor intensive, costly, and problematic, says Senator Moynihan. Wisconsin's experience with welfare reform confirms that. Princeton welfare scholar Lawrence Mead found that the high performing areas of Wisconsin's welfare reform feature "relentless follow-up of clients to see that they stay on track." The costs of that kind of effective employment support, including job search, job placement, and employment monitoring can run up to $5,000 per year per recipient, estimates Robert Haveman.

For those who don't understand why the process should be expensive, Haveman suggests thinking about what middle-class people do for their children to make sure that they will succeed in the labor market. "First they give their children lots of education, with monitoring and advice and expectations and parental participation in schools. When schooling is done, they may support them for a time while they 'get their act together.' Parents may actively, one to one, help with job search, helping their children prepare résumés, putting them in touch with friends and acquaintances, preparing them for job interviews—all so they can find their own niche in the world of work." Obviously, it takes a lot more than that to work with young, and not so young, people whose main life experiences have been defeats.

The interplay of political interests within the states will leave poor children unprotected. Without some basic national guarantees, "children will be the certain losers when state governments divide up a shrinking pot of federal funds," says Republican political consultant John D. Deardourff. Deardourff's conclusion is based on an extensive eighteen-month study of how children fare at the hands of state governments. He says he is not suggesting "that most governors and state legislators don't care about poor children or families in their states. Most do care. But . . . politics is politics, and when the horse-trading starts in state capitols, poor children are often left far behind. . . . In state after state children's advocates are outgunned by richer and more powerful interests, whether homebuilders, truckers, nursing home operators, trial lawyers, veterans, or the elderly." A legislative leader from a large midwestern state put it to Deardourff bluntly: "Hell, funeral home directors have more clout in our state than child advocates." The speaker of the house in a large eastern state was even more explicit: "If we have $20 million and the choice is between spending it for senior citizens or poor kids, it's no contest. The seniors get the money every time."

Many states seem to be unable to protect the most vulnerable children and families. Thirty-six states have so badly underfunded child care help for poor working families that they maintain substantial waiting lists of children needing such help. Twenty-one states are partially or totally under court supervision for having mishandled foster care and other programs to protect children from abuse or neglect.

Mary Jo Bane, the other assistant secretary of HHS who resigned over the 1996 welfare legislation, doubts that the states will use their new flexibility to develop innovative ways to support welfare recipients in the transition to work. She writes, "All the incentives are there for them to cut assistance, impose shorter time limits, and use . . . freed-up state funds for more politically palatable programs." The pressures to put less money into job development, job training, and worker support will be compounded by the for-profit firms bidding to run state welfare systems, who will be driven primarily or exclusively by cost considerations.

"Spiraling parsimony" will occur as states compete to keep tax burdens low. Without a continuing federal role, it can be assumed, Isabel Sawhill explains, that "any one state, acting generously, risks the possibility that its neighbors will not follow suit and that it will be left with disproportionate responsibility for the poor."

As states become freer to construct their own programs, their fear of becoming "welfare magnets" inhibits their generosity. Most of the experts predict a "race to the bottom." George E. Peterson, senior fellow at the Urban Institute, foresees "a competitive scramble to cut benefits and limit eligibility" for fear of "migration of the poor (or of the affluent in response to the costs of providing for the poor)." He calls it "spiraling parsimony," and considers it the almost inevitable outcome "as every state scrambles to avoid becoming a welfare haven that treats the poor more generously than its neighbors."

When you add to these pressures on states, their new freedom to shift funds to other, more popular causes, you begin to see why states will find it more attractive to cut benefits than to move people to work. You begin to understand why more than a third of the states by early 1997 had already adopted time limits more restrictive than the ones Congress mandated.

Urban Institute estimates indicate that the benefit cutting and time limiting the states are likely to do would ultimately deny benefits to about 42 percent and reduce benefits for another 30 percent of the 4 million families, including 9 million children, who were receiving AFDC benefits in 1996. The Urban Institute further estimates that unless the states provide the necessary training, supports, and jobs, as many as two thirds of these adults could remain unemployed.

Yes, We Can Reduce High Rates of Illegitimacy

The Republican decision, after the 1994 election, to reframe the welfare debate as being about illegitimacy found great public resonance. The idea that illegitimacy was the single most important social problem of our time, and that the welfare system was the fundamental cause of illegitimacy, was not a hard sell. The proposed cure, the denial of welfare benefits to the mothers of illegitimate children, wasn't either.

Conservatives and liberals could agree that effective strategies to reduce single parenting would be an important component of welfare reform. They differed on what those strategies should be. The new conservative construction dismissed fears that the withdrawal of guaranteed income support would put the well-being of millions of children in jeopardy, but held that to the extent it did, it was a price worth paying to reduce high rates of illegitimacy.

Illegitimacy and teenage childbearing symbolize moral decline. For many Americans, the large number of babies born to unmarried mothers, especially teenagers, represents the decline of traditional values and the failure of government programs. Concerns about high rates of unmarried motherhood, especially among teenagers, reinforced the impression that American values are disintegrating, and that government is either impotent or part of the problem. The AFDC program came to be seen as the prime example of government not working. Taxpayers were convinced that the welfare benefits to which they contribute so reluctantly actually encourage the behavior they condemn. It's one thing to help people in need, says an angry talk show host, "but I don't want my tax dollars to pay for the sexual pleasure of irresponsible adolescents."

Feelings about disintegrating values run deep, and probably originate in post–World War II affluence, when Americans began to revel in expanding their life choices and pursuing self-expression and self-fulfillment. Bonds of commitment to marriage, family, children, job, community, and country were loosened. Changes in values were soon reflected in changed lives: sharp rises in divorce, a spectacular growth in cohabitation as a prelude or substitute for marriage, a significant weakening of the link between marriage and childbearing, and a rise in drug use.

But it was not long before one could discern a growing discomfort with the values shift. By the mid- to late-eighties, more people were having trouble reconciling the traditional values they grew up embracing with new ones they had more recently adopted. They enjoyed fewer restriction on adult behavior but worried that the decline of marriage might be bad for children. They worried most about the increasing openness of sexuality among the young. They realized that the social norms that rationed youthful sex to a few uncomfortable places and that produced shotgun weddings and lifetime marriages might cause adults a lot of misery, but they also provided the assurance that almost every child had a claim on some adult male's earnings and protection. So it was that single and teenage parenting became an increasing source of concern, as well as "a convenient lightning rod for the anxieties and tensions in Americans' lives."

The serious consequences of illegitimacy and teenage childbearing. A child's life chances are markedly diminished if he or she is born to a single mother, and even more so if the single mother is a teenager.

Child rearing today is simply too hard for anyone to undertake successfully alone, and even harder for someone not fully grown-up herself. Especially in the first two years, the predictable nurturing and consistent protection that babies need require economic, social, and emotional resources far greater than most single parents can mobilize, particularly if they are still adolescents. A teenager struggling to get her own needs met finds it almost impossible to give ungrudgingly of herself to a dependent creature without asking anything in return, to put the needs of her dependent baby ahead of her own, especially in the face of the poverty and curtailed parental education that usually accompany single and teenage parenthood.

With one adult trying to act both as provider and caretaker, with scant financial and other supports, it is no wonder that children of unmarried teen mothers have a higher incidence of low birth weight and childhood health problems, and lower levels of language development, impulse control, and academic achievement. They are also more likely to suffer from physical abuse, abandonment or neglect, to end up in foster care, to run away from home, and to drop out of school. The daughters of adolescent mothers are more likely to become mothers themselves before age eighteen, and the sons of teen mothers are more likely to end up behind bars.

The political symbolism of teenage parenthood as a drain on tax moneys as well as a breakdown of family structures and a threat to the entire moral order was made more vivid by the research that confirmed early childbearing as an important antecedent to subsequent poverty and dependency. More than half (52 percent) of adults receiving welfare benefits had their first child as a teenager, and more than half (53 percent) of AFDC funds were going to families in which the first birth occurred in the teenage years.

Single parenting adds additional risks. Regardless of the mother's age when her children were born, if she is single, the prospects for her children may be sharply curtailed, economically and otherwise. Children who spend all or part of their childhood in a single-parent family (as an estimated 60 percent will) are more likely than other children to drop out of school, to divorce, to become teen mothers and unmarried mothers, and to spend time in jail, and they are less likely to be in paid employment as adults.

Mothers raising children alone find their authority undermined by their single status and have more difficulty controlling their children. With less adult support, they have less time to supervise their children's school lives and to be involved in their church and recreational activities. Research confirms that the greater the number of adults committed—rationally and irrationally—to a child's well-being, the brighter that child's prospects.

How big a problem? Although teenagers had been having babies at a pretty consistent rate for most of the century, teen pregnancy began to be defined as an epidemic in the late 1970s, when advocates for expanding access to contraception sought to dramatize their cause by focusing on providing teenagers the means to avoid pregnancy.

Concern about births to teenagers mounted further as the number and proportion of all births outside marriage exploded. Between 1960 and 1994 there was a greater than fivefold increase both in the proportion of births to all unmarried mothers (from 6 percent to 33 percent), and in the proportion of births to unmarried teenagers (from 15 percent to 76 percent).

These changes in family composition are not unique to the United States. Every other Western country has experienced similarly large changes in family structure. While trends in out-of-wedlock births in the U.S. are very similar to those of other countries, this nation is unique in three respects. First, in other countries, most births outside marriage are to cohabiting couples who live very much like married couples. Second, the American response to family change has been unique. Other nations have avoided our cultural warfare over the family and have adapted their policies to provide greater support to all families raising children, regardless of income or marital status. Single-mother families in the U.S. are economically much worse off compared with such families elsewhere, in large part because our country is so much less successful in reducing poverty through income-transfer programs. This is a particularly important point, since researchers believe that about 50 percent of the negative consequences associated with single parenthood are accounted for by low income.

The third big difference between the U.S. and other countries is that our teen birthrate is higher than that of any other industrialized nation (twice as high as the United Kingdom's, and ten times as high as Japan's). And contrary to popular belief that high U.S. rates are accounted for by the high proportion of minorities in the U.S. population, America's number-one position among Western democracies holds when one counts the teen birthrate among whites alone.

Causes and the remedies they imply. Deep social and economic forces have combined with changed norms throughout Western society to produce current high rates of teen and single childbearing. Prevailing inducements to early sexual activity have driven the age of initiation of sexual activity steadily downward—for men since the 1950s, for women since the 1960s. But, unlike the fifties and sixties, the pregnancies that occur today do not usually result in marriage.

The link between early childbearing and marriage began to weaken in 1973; today the connection has become so loose that *only 15 percent of all teen pregnancies end with an in-wedlock birth.* Although a smaller proportion of teens today bear children than in the 1950s, the great majority of these teen mothers do not marry the fathers of their children either before or after the birth.

The massive increase in single-parent families occurred among both the middle class and the poor. But the negative effects have been much more severe at the bottom of the ladder. The bleaker economic outlook of the unskilled has dimmed prospects for a future structured around marriage and self-sufficiency, especially among minorities. Fewer employed males with decent incomes has meant fewer marriages; women are finding fewer men who are likely to be reliable economic providers.

A trend originally most apparent among minorities began to hit all the unskilled. Ethnographer Mercer Sullivan found that, while family formation among whites and blacks once operated very differently, the patterns became more similar as good jobs became less available to the unskilled of all races. Sullivan found that before the virtual disappearance of manufacturing in the northeast, a teenager who got a girlfriend pregnant was more likely to marry her if he was white than black or Hispanic. But as well-paying blue-collar jobs diminished, "the behavior of the young white men increasingly came to resemble that of the blacks and Hispanics: they became less likely to marry their pregnant girlfriends as their future came to seem more uncertain, and they began to encounter more problems with drugs and alcohol, which surely made them less attractive mates."

With little hope of either a husband or economic independence, young women in poverty easily drift into early, tentative, and sporadic sexual relationships. They pursue acceptance, love, and affection more desperately than young people in more affluent neighborhoods. Unlike middle-class girls, African-American or white, for whom sex is tied to aspiration and status and the motivation to avoid illegitimate pregnancy is great, for the young women of the ghetto, this kind of incentive simply doesn't exist.

When it comes to the role of welfare benefits, the general agreement on causes ends. Those believing that availability of welfare benefits has encouraged illegitimacy and that denial of these benefits would radically reduce it regard individual decision making as the key to understanding and preventing high rates of illegitimacy. This position assumes that the problems that poor and minority youngsters impose on themselves, their families, and the taxpayer are the product of conscious choices about engaging in sexual activity without effective contraception. Poor girls especially are viewed as "using pregnancy and childbearing as a ticket out of their parents' control, out of responsible behavior in completing school, and out of having to get a job." The pattern they are caught up in is seen as self-reinforcing and passed on from one generation to the next.

This line of reasoning seems not only plausible but comforting. If people are poor as the result of immoral or unwise behavior, if pregnancy is an option young women could reject if only they would choose to do so, then they can be held responsible for their situation and its consequences. Those who scrimp and save in order to marry and set up a household, the wives who bear the burdens of bringing in a second income while still fulfilling their traditional nurturing role, the couples who postpone having children until they can afford them feel amply justified in resenting the choices and behavior of the heedless and irresponsible.

The remedy flowing from this analysis is to deny welfare benefits and make it harder for young people to have babies they can't support. By threatening to cut off AFDC benefits, government would signal that no more children should be born to women unable to raise them without outside help. If children were hurt in the process, that would be justified by the long-term benefits of deterrence.

Joanne Barnhart, commissioner for Children, Youth and Families in the Bush administration, explained, not long after the 1994 election, that the new proposals were "driven by a world view that you have to write off the current generation to create the societal sea change we now need because none of the known interventions work." An underground sentiment fed by radio talk shows that focused special venom on welfare recipients who were black and Hispanic—presumably having large numbers of children and particularly undeserving of support—probably provided additional momentum to the groundswell of opposition to continuing AFDC benefits for unwed mothers.

"Conservatives might be willing to help children born out of wedlock if they could do so without helping the parents," wrote researchers Jencks and Edin, "but they would rather not help anyone than subsidize illegitimacy."

While it was clear that denying benefits would increase the number of children in poverty, no one could know the effect on illegitimacy. "Claims that eliminating welfare will virtually eliminate 'illegitimacy' are simultaneously insupportable and irrefutable by conventional social science," concluded Urban Institute researchers.

Those anticipating a sharp drop in out-of-wedlock births are likely to be disappointed. Financial calculations may be one, but only one consideration "in the sexual game that leads to illegitimate births," says Elijah Anderson, a sociologist who knows more than most about life at the bottom. The new welfare law may become part of the complex interplay of factors operating at both conscious and unconscious levels to determine whether a man and woman conceive a child out of wedlock, but for most, the denial of cash benefits is unlikely to be decisive.

- It is unlikely to be decisive among girls and women coerced into sexual relations. (Seventy-five percent of girls who have had intercourse before age 14 reported that it was involuntary; 44 percent of adolescent mothers in Washington State reported being raped; 20 percent of teenage mothers reported their babies were fathered by men who were six or more years older than they.)
- It is unlikely to be decisive among the many teenage mothers introduced to sexual experience by sexual abuse. (In a survey of 445 teenage mothers in Illinois, 61 percent reported a forced sexual experience—at an average age of eleven. Almost half the abusers were more than ten years older than the victims. Similar findings were reported in the Washington State survey: Two thirds of a sample of 535 teenage mothers had been sexually abused.)
- It is unlikely to be decisive among crack users, reported to have at least half again as many children as the average AFDC recipient.
- It is unlikely to be decisive among the majority of unmarried adolescents, who "drift" into pregnancy, "not seeking or planning for much of anything."

An alternative set of causal theories is based on the belief that while individual decision making is an important factor, it interacts with and is sometimes overwhelmed by social forces, particularly the diminished prospects of so many girls and boys growing up in concentrated and persistent poverty. These theories hold that, given the lengthening period that young people are at risk of pregnancy, and given the currently imperfect state of contraception, avoiding pregnancy is a complicated, challenging task that requires consistent dedication over an extended period of time. Even a fleeting step off the straight-and-narrow can allow a pregnancy to "just happen."

For young women with few alternatives and little hope, to whom a baby offers the promise of unconditional love, a chance to feel needed and valued, and a feeling of accomplishment, the calculus of choice is more complex than legislators and editorial writers like to admit. A recent report from the Institute of Medicine points out that because the human organism is designed to reproduce absent the utmost vigilance, the motivation to avoid unintended pregnancy must be extremely powerful if pregnancy is to be prevented. Those ambivalent about childbearing turn out to be at just as high a risk of having a child as those who positively desire to conceive. The IOM report concludes that "hopes and plans for a better adult life—*and reason to believe that the plans are realistic*" are what it will take to overcome the many obstacles to abstinence or successful contraception that poor young women face.

This conclusion is confirmed by considerable research showing that the teens most likely to become pregnant and give birth outside of marriage have both inherited disadvantages and contemporaneous reasons to feel discouraged. They come from families that are poor, or rural, or headed by a single parent, or part of a disadvantaged minority. Their "measured ability" is below average, they lack high aspirations for themselves, and they are not doing well at school. A high proportion of school-age girls who get pregnant actually drop out of school before they get pregnant. One study found that the girls who tested in the lowest 5 percent on a test of basic skills were *thirty-eight times* more likely to become an unmarried teenage mother than girls who tested in the top 5 percent.

Childbearing seems to offer a path to adulthood where few alternatives exist. A Massachusetts teenager put it to a focus group this way: "There's nothing going on; there's nothing that's going to happen. You aren't doing well in school, but you have a man. You are stuck in the projects, so you want to have a child."

Laurie Zabin of Johns Hopkins University, a researcher who knows as much about teen pregnancy as anyone, says the data are very clear: "As long as people don't have a vision of the future which having a baby at a very early age will jeopardize, they won't go to all the lengths necessary to prevent pregnancy."

Having observed that middle-class youth with a strong interest in their future do what it takes to avoid a pregnancy that would derail their plans, many pregnancy prevention programs try to convince poor youngsters that they do have a future worth postponing childbearing for. But, as sociologist Elijah Anderson points out, many inner-city youth are totally realistic in their belief that they have no future to derail. They know that postponing their first birth is unlikely to lead to a Wall Street partnership or an athletic scholarship—or even a stable marriage.

Those who have reason to believe otherwise act otherwise: Researchers Kristin Moore and Sandra Hofferth found that high school students enrolled in a college-preparatory curriculum (indicating not only high educational goals but probably that the school is fostering those goals) are just half as likely to have a child while still a teen than those not preparing for college—an effect that was even stronger among blacks than among whites.

This line of thinking suggests we are dealing less with simple failure of individual teenagers to control their sexual impulses than with the fact that "the major institutions of American life—families, schools, job markets, the medical system—are not working for them." When one looks at what is actually known about causes, the teen pregnancy issue—and even the illegitimacy issue—is "less about young women and their sex lives than it is about restricted horizons and the boundaries of hope."

How much will postponing childbearing help? William A. Galston, former White House adviser on family matters, has a favorite statistic: Americans who finish high school, reach age twenty, and get married before they have their first child have only an 8 percent chance that the child will grow up in poverty; but for those who don't do these three things before having their first child, the odds that their child will live in poverty rise to 79 percent.

Whether age itself is the crucial factor in determining outcomes for mother and child has become a matter of some debate. The conviction that these outcomes would change markedly if teenagers could be persuaded to delay childbearing until they were more mature is widely held and only occasionally challenged. Most recently it has been challenged by the contention that it isn't early childbearing that creates disadvantage and dependency; rather, it is disadvantage that makes women bear children at an early age. In her 1996 book, *Dubious Conceptions,* Kristin Luker, professor of sociology at the University of California, Berkeley, argues that even if large numbers of girls postponed their childbearing, the overall effects would be small because "the same social conditions that encourage teenagers to have babies also work to prevent them from ever being 'ready' to be parents in the way that a white, middle-class public might prefer.

Preexisting poverty, failure in school, a dearth of opportunities for personal and professional fulfillment . . . all lead both to early pregnancy and to impoverished lives." Parents who now have babies as teenagers would be no better prepared to nurture and support them a few years later in their lives because "the kinds of discouraged and disadvantaged women most at risk of having a baby in their teens are unlikely to become encouraged and advantaged . . . to bear healthy babies and become stably married . . . simply by postponing their first birth for a few years."

Of course, postponing childbearing for several years would carry the benefit of providing the baby with more mature mothering from someone no longer so much in the grip of her own adolescent needs. There is considerable research evidence that age itself is a crucial factor in outcomes for children of young teens. But Luker is probably right in contending that many damaging consequences of teenage parenting have more to do with the life circumstances of those who become pregnant as teenagers than they have to do with the age at which they become pregnant.

Long before they got pregnant, teenage mothers accumulated the risk factors associated with poor outcomes for themselves and their children: They were likely to be living in poverty, to have come from a single-parent family, to have been in trouble at school, to have been held back a grade, and to live in a bad neighborhood. Teenage parents, Luker insists, carry the disadvantages which lead to poor outcomes for them and their children and to high public costs, and these disadvantages would not be significantly modified if they had a few years more of discouraging life experiences before they became parents.

Many more experts are convinced that the timing of childbearing matters a lot. In that belief, a group of eminent national leaders has launched a national campaign, chaired by former New Jersey Governor Thomas Kean, which is aimed at supporting the values and actions that would result in a pregnancy-free adolescence for all. To encourage the postponing and planning of pregnancy and childbearing, the National Campaign to Prevent Teen Pregnancy is enlisting the help of media and other national leaders, supporting state and local action, focusing on how religion, culture, and public values influence teen pregnancy, and strengthening the knowledge base for prevention.

The president of the campaign, Isabel V. Sawhill, senior fellow at the Urban Institute with a distinguished professional career both behind and before her, sees this effort as one of the most challenging tasks she has ever addressed. She says that until we can turn around current high rates of first births to women who are teenagers, unmarried, or lacking a high school degree, "all our other efforts are almost doomed to failure." What would it take? "Adults who spend time with their own kids or mentor others', a more responsible media, a new social norm that says you should not bring a child into the world until you are fully prepared to be a parent, and more efforts to provide all young people, but especially the most disadvantaged, with reasons to avoid early pregnancy and parenting."

So what would effective prevention of illegitimacy really look like? We know a lot by now, from imaginative research and rich experience, about how to reduce high rates of illegitimacy and premature childbearing. But this knowledge has had little impact on policies and politics. Legislators' urgent desires for a single, simple remedy drives them to focus, as Christopher Jencks points out, on "the one policy lever they really control: government assistance for single mothers and their children." So they seek to eliminate those programs, or at the very least make them stingier.

But the evidence shows that what really works is a portfolio of remedies, not a single remedy. What really works is not a simple one-time fix.

In a comprehensive review of the knowledge base that could inform policies and programs to reduce teen pregnancy (commissioned by the National Task Force on Teen Pregnancy), Douglas Kirby found that single strategy programs don't help. To have a significant impact, it is necessary to address a large number of risk and protective factors over a long period of time.

The remedies that promise to reduce illegitimacy and welfare dependence include—at a minimum—the following:

- Those that assure young people of the prospect of a better future: That means high quality schooling to provide disadvantaged young men and women with the skills and motivation needed to succeed in a high-tech labor market; it also means the availability of decent jobs paying a living wage, and the connections that will link young people to job opportunities.
- Those that assure that young people will have the means of avoiding pregnancy: That means access to contraceptive services combined with education about sexuality, and—in many communities—access to the skills and support for postponing sexual activity.
- Those that assure young people of supportive families and com-

munities: That means rebuilding communities to support families in their child rearing and young people in their struggle toward a healthy adulthood and full participation in a society in which they have a stake; it also means the availability of parents and other adults investing time and energy in caring for, supervising, and mentoring children, in advocacy on their behalf, and in transmitting values and expectations.

• Those that create a climate that values children and child rearing: That means the creation of a national norm that every baby should be a wanted baby, and that all pregnancies should be actively desired by both parents at the time of conception; it also means supports to young parents, including family leave and access to high quality child care.

Obviously, these strategies go far beyond reform of the welfare system, but they represent the most promising steps to actually prevent welfare dependence—by directly decreasing the formation of single-parent families, and by helping to create the enriched lives and healthier communities that will in turn support further reductions in illegitimacy and welfare dependence.

Conclusion: "Some Good May Come of It"

When it became clear that President Clinton would sign the welfare repeal of 1996 into law, the astute political analyst E. J. Dionne wrote that "Some good may come of it, albeit at a high cost." With "welfare reform" out of the way, he thought, we can finally get beyond demagoguery and start talking about the issues that really matter: How to reduce poverty, joblessness, illegitimacy, and crime.

The unpopularity of AFDC was used by the Republicans in 1995 and 1996 to taint all antipoverty efforts, indeed all of government. But with AFDC gone, that may not work any more. As Mickey Kaus points out, "The Republicans may soon discover that the voters never really hated government, they just hated welfare." He predicts that active government could now be rebuilt on a more defensible foundation, because "Democrats have been liberated to meet the public's legitimate, unfilled expectations."

But of course it wasn't just an unpopular government program that was bothering the voters, it was also an unpopular group of beneficiaries. If the former welfare recipients began to be seen as struggling to make ends meet, ending up in shelters although they were doing what they could to help themselves and their children, valiantly trying to combine the roles of provider and nurturer but still not making it, might we not see a change in how Americans would view the need to help? Jencks writes that it would be "a grisly way of rebuilding support for compassion," but it could happen. The phony "welfare reform" of 1996 could, in some ironic way, open the door to real welfare reform. That would require widespread understanding of the causes of persistent and concentrated poverty. It would require a new recognition that making life miserable for welfare recipients and their children is not an antipoverty strategy. And it would mean a resolute commitment, by policy makers and citizens at every level, to the kind of welfare reform that emphasizes jobs and the supports that will enable people to take them and keep them, and to the development of the strategies that would strengthen families and schools and rebuild the social and physical fabric of the inner city.

7

Strengthening a Collapsing Child Protection System

AFTER TWENTY-FIVE YEARS on the Stanford law school faculty and three years in the counsel's office of the federal Department of Health and Human Services, Michael Wald was ready to put his theories to the test of harsh reality. He accepted San Francisco Mayor Willie Brown's invitation to become the city's director of human services. His first directive after being sworn in was that no young child was to be removed from home without his or her favorite stuffed animal or blanket. He wasn't just trying to ease a small fraction of the trauma of separation. He also was trying to suggest to his staff and to the public that these are children we are dealing with here, not just cases and numbers. In a tragically overwhelmed child welfare system, that has become too easy to forget.

The child welfare system, especially in the past decade, has become steadily less able to safeguard children and meet the escalating needs of desperate families in crisis. The most recent national data show that the number of children abused, neglected, or abandoned in the U.S. doubled between 1986 and 1993, from 1.4 million to 2.8 million in just seven years, and that the number of children who were seriously injured as a result of maltreatment quadrupled—rising from 143,000 to nearly 570,000. The number of children judged by the authorities to be faring so badly at the hands of their own families as to be taken from their homes is also rising steadily, now numbering about half a million. Many more are living informally with relatives or friends because their parents cannot care for them. The number of children who die annually at the hands of their "caretakers" is now about two thousand. And when a child dies a particularly horrible death as a result of abuse, it is usually possible to learn from the front page of the local newspaper that the local child welfare agency is in a state of disarray or total breakdown.

The reports about small children deliberately and gruesomely tortured over months and even years add to our sense of outrage—at those capable of such crimes and at the authorities, apparently impotent to prevent them.

The child welfare system is in collapse because it was never designed to deal with the current number of reports nor the more complex needs of families. The extraordinary increase in the number of parents using crack cocaine, the increase in poverty, the erosion of formal and informal supports, and the deteriorating employment situation of the unskilled all caught the system unprepared. In the 1970s and early 1980s, states responded to higher caseloads by hiring more staff. But by the end of the 1980s, as state budgets became tighter, funding was cut and the numbers and quality of staff diminished, although caseloads continued to rise and family problems were becoming more complicated. Some children were removed from home because the family couldn't pay the rent; others were left at home to face escalating violence.

Child welfare agencies were in turmoil. Controversy flared about what they were *supposed* to be doing, and they lacked the capacity to act on whatever they thought their mandate was. The controversy about when children should be removed from home, and when intensive services should be mobilized to keep a family together and a child safe, continued to rage, bursting from professional journals onto the evening news. Healthy babies still languish in hospitals for weeks, sometimes months for lack of foster homes and the services that would enable them to go home or be adopted. Children are left in foster care for years, often with many different families. One New York boy was placed in thirty-seven different homes in a period of two months. Another lived with seventeen different families in twenty-five days. In Illinois, which keeps the most reliable state data, the median time spent in the first foster care placement is nearly three years (thirteen months for white children, twenty-one months for Hispanic children, and fifty-five months—that's more than four and a half years—for African-American children.

State and local child protection systems have fallen so far short of doing what the law requires that twenty-one are operating under judicial supervision. Since the conservative attack on "welfare" of 1995 and 1996 quite deliberately attempted to lump together AFDC and the child welfare system to discredit both, child welfare reformers nervously wonder whether the system can be mended before the call to end it becomes irresistible. (Several earlier versions of the 1996 AFDC repeal, in fact, would also have repealed the federal responsibility for child protection.)

No one questions the high stakes. The devastating consequences of child maltreatment have been thoroughly documented. Whether one focuses on the tragedy of abandoned babies, tormented toddlers, or sexually abused schoolchildren; on the long-term effects of abuse and neglect; or on the apparent inability of public agencies to protect children from harm, the public's dismay is surely justified.

What Has Gone So Terribly Wrong?

"If the nation had deliberately designed a system that would frustrate the professionals who staff it, anger the public who finance it, and abandon the children who depend on it, it could not have done a better job than the present child welfare system," reported the National Commission on Children in 1991.

The child welfare system is, with some noteworthy exceptions, a system where everything that can go wrong has gone wrong.

- It is not protecting children from serious maltreatment, even death.
- It is receiving many more reports of abuse than it can look into or respond to with help. In most jurisdictions, agencies investigate only 40 to 60 percent of all reports coming to child abuse hotlines. Nationally, about 30 percent are substantiated.
- Children who should be removed from their homes to protect their safety are not removed; children who could safely remain at home are removed. Needed services and supports are typically not available either for families in which abuse could be prevented or for foster or adoptive families caring for seriously damaged children.
- Decisions on removing a child from home are made by caseworkers and judges who lack the time, support, guidance, and often training that would maximize the chances for wise decisions. (Paul Boland, presiding judge of Los Angeles County Juvenile Court, told the National Commission on Children that every day, "most judges have 35 to 40 cases on their individual calendars, and they have an average of 10 minutes to spend on each child's fate and each family's future.")

- Children for whom the child protective agency and the court assume responsibility may be moved from one placement to another, many inadequately supervised and supported, and languish in out-of-home care with no one making effective efforts to find a permanent place for them.
- Children legally free and ready for adoption often wait years for placement in an adoptive home, especially if the child is past infancy.

The biggest reasons that child welfare is in such disarray are a progressive narrowing of objectives as child abuse reports increase and funding does not, the problem of the swinging pendulum, and the lack of support for families in the world outside the child protection system.

The system narrowed its objectives. When the child welfare system was established as part of the 1935 Social Security Act, it was intended to protect and care for homeless and neglected children, and children "in danger of becoming delinquent." It was seen primarily as a way to provide the services and supports that would help parents meet their child-rearing responsibilities. When that was not enough to guarantee a child's safety, it was prepared to remove children from their parents and provide substitute care.

With the discovery of widespread incidents of "battered child syndrome" in the early 1960s and the ensuing mandated child-abuse reporting in the late 1970s, the system abruptly became solely a child protective system. It was now targeted on the plight of children classified as abused or neglected, who were then routinely removed from their families, pretty much regardless of the cause of the abuse or neglect. Many children were placed in institutions—often very expensive and far away from home—while others were cast into a foster care limbo, not available for adoption because nobody was paying attention. During this period the recognition grew that some of the trauma suffered by children removed from home was unnecessary and might have been avoided if anyone had been in a position to do preventive work with their families.

The federal child welfare legislation of 1980 represented an attempt to correct this situation with reforms designed to make substitute care less necessary and to keep children from being lost in the state's protective custody. The new laws mandated new procedural protections and "reasonable efforts" to keep families together where possible, to reconnect family ties that had been broken, or to make other permanent plans for children when adequate parental care could not be reestablished. Like many other federal mandates of this era, this one was underfunded. Its procedural protections massively increased paperwork burdens, introducing new rigidities that interfered with better service delivery. Nevertheless, the 1980 legislation succeeded, at least for a brief period, in reducing the number of children in institutions and in foster care, shortening the period of time children were in out-of-home placement, and increasing the number of children returned to their families or adopted.

By the end of the 1980s, the crack epidemic, growing poverty, and the deterioration of inner-city neighborhoods were turning those numbers in the wrong direction again. The cases coming to the child protection system (CPS) continued to increase not only in number but in severity. Large urban CPS programs were inundated with a type of child maltreatment they had not previously encountered. The safety issues associated with drug abuse were not well understood nor effectively responded to. Crack was so devastating to families because it was the first illicit drug used as much by women as by men. The New York City fatality review board found that among the children who died at the hands of their parents, three quarters of the parents were drug abusers.

The public demanded ever greater efforts to curb child abuse but was increasingly unwilling to fund them.

The result, according to child welfare expert Duncan Lindsey, was a continual narrowing of definitions of who should receive child welfare services. Children who weren't being beaten, sexually molested, starved, or tortured but were only in need of the services that child welfare agencies used to provide "began dropping through the holes of the protective services safety net." Child welfare services were organized more and more around investigation and less around helping a family with its problems. Families were often assessed repeatedly without ever getting any help. When allegations of abuse were not substantiated, the case was closed, regardless of how troubled the children and families. The family supportive services that might have alleviated the need for child protection were often cut to finance the protective services.

By 1989, a national survey by Columbia University social welfare scholars Sheila Kamerman and Al Kahn found that child welfare agencies had been changed from welfare agencies to protective services agencies, "whose function was to investigate the ever-increasing avalanche of child abuse reports." Requests for service or aid to families in distress or chronic crisis received low priority, and in some instances, no response at all. Kamerman and Kahn reported,

"In state after state, county after county, public officials described their child and family services as if there were only one function— child protection. Any other service was insignificant by comparison and had to be sacrificed or constricted to ensure an adequate child protection response."

As managers tried to deal with staff of whom a shrinking proportion were adequately trained, rules and paperwork increased exponentially. Soon the need to document every action and every decision meant that the paper flow among child welfare workers, supervisors, police, courts, and attorneys accounted for an expanding part of everyone's time. The job of the child welfare worker now consisted of investigations of allegations of child abuse, paperwork, and supervision of court orders, not the provision of services.

Professional associations sought to help front-line workers make their peace with their much constricted role. The American Public Welfare Association issued guidelines identifying services that should be considered as outside the domain of child protective services: CPS should not intervene if parents are unable to support their children adequately; teenage sex offenders should receive CPS assistance only if they themselves were currently abused or at risk of abuse; CPS should intervene in cases of teenage prostitution only if "the parent is directly involved in keeping the child in prostitution, or if the child has turned to prostitution as a means of escaping abuse or neglect."

The major risk factors, then, that if dealt with might prevent child abuse, neglect, and abandonment, and might reduce harm and suffering, had been defined out of the dominion of child protective services—without being defined *into* any other. No one should be deluded into thinking any differently. "The public perception in New York City is that the child welfare agency is meant to help families in distress when it is in fact not," said Linda Schleicher, director of policy for the union representing the city's child welfare workers in 1996. "It is simply not funded or set up to deal with poverty. It is mandated to investigate abuse and neglect. That's it."

The problem of the swinging pendulum. As the number of families in contact with the child protection system increased, the one-size-fits-all response became ever less tenable. Whether the problem was that the family had been evicted or their heat had been shut off, or that a child turned up in the emergency room with broken bones and cigarette burns on his back, the authorities could offer foster care and sometimes counseling, but that was it.

To leaders in the field, it seemed particularly egregious that there was no way to help families who might be able to get their lives together with a more intensive and flexible form of help than most child protection agencies could provide.

By the mid-1980s, the search for alternative ways to intervene began to focus on Homebuilders, a Tacoma, Washington, family services agency that had developed an intensive, home-based set of interventions. The Homebuilders intervention was developed on the premise that many troubled families would fare much better if the child welfare agency, in responding to whatever crisis precipitated the intervention, rather than simply removing a child from home, could offer the alternative of intensive, in-home services. Highly trained, highly professional Homebuilders staff were on call twenty-four hours a day, seven days a week. With a caseload of no more than two or three families, they could respond effectively to a full range of needs in ways previously unrecognized by child welfare workers.

As recounted in the story of Michigan's Families First in Chapter 3, Homebuilders' techniques were adopted by many agencies, and even some state systems were beginning to make room for this new way of working with families. Many children remained safely in their homes with strengthened families, and much unnecessary foster and institutional care was averted. That was the good news.

There were two pieces of bad news. One was that intensive family preservation services, instead of being seen as one valuable addition to the child welfare tool kit, were embraced by many as the new one-best-answer to troubled families, replacing the previous one-best-answer of removing the child.

The second piece of bad news was that many administrators and legislators ignored the details of implementation. Having become convinced that some children could be helped without being removed from their families, they came to believe that almost any mix of whatever social services might be available would do. They missed the fact that what had worked in the Homebuilders demonstrations was a painstakingly thought-out, carefully crafted, amply supervised set of intensive interventions backed up by services from other agencies not available in most communities. And so it came to be that, as the interest in the new way of working with families spread, almost simultaneously there were reports of negative outcomes from severely diluted and distorted implementations of the original, and the backlash set in. Family preservation and the 1980 child welfare amendments mandating "reasonable efforts" to keep families together were blamed in several particularly shocking deaths of children at the hands of their parents.

That's how the death of Joey Wallace, in April 1993, led to an increase in Chicago's foster care population.

Joey was three when he was killed by his mother, Amanda Wallace, not long after he had been returned to her from foster care. She killed him by wrapping an extension cord around his neck and hanging him from a transom. Amanda Wallace herself had been beaten and abused so badly that she had started running away from home when she was 7 years old. When she was 8 she was swallowing glass and nails, and stabbing herself bloody with needles. Before she was 9 she was sent to a foster home and subsequently to a mental hospital after setting fire to her bed.

At the time of her trial in Joey's death, her lawyer carried three cardboard boxes into the courtroom which contained just some of Amanda Wallace's mental hospital records. The psychiatrist at Elgin Mental Health Center, where she had been a resident at the time of Joey's birth, was on record saying that she should never have custody of this or any other baby. Three times the Illinois Department of Children and Family Services removed him from his mother, three times judges ordered him returned, against the advice of psychiatrists, who had warned that Amanda Wallace was mentally unstable and that she might well kill him, and of Joey's foster mother, who was also afraid that his mother would kill him, and had pleaded with child protection workers that he not be returned home. A family preservation worker had also recommended against keeping the child with his mother. He was returned to her when the family moved and the paperwork was lost.

And what was the reaction to this tale of horror? It was another rapid swing of the pendulum. There was no careful, thoughtful, detailed examination of how so much could have gone so wrong in the judicial system and in the Illinois child welfare agency. It was "family preservation" (described by *Newsweek* at the time as "a national policy to keep families together at almost any cost . . . even in the worst cases") that was blamed for leaving this child in danger. "Everyone in Chicago agrees that Joseph Wallace died because the system placed a parent's right above a child's," wrote *Newsweek*. When Elisa Izquierdo died at her parents' hands in November 1995 in New York City Mayor Giuliani said that New York's child protection system was "too rigidly focused on keeping families together."

Over the past ten years we have seen opinion shift wildly from one end of the spectrum to the other on the question of when it is better to remove a child from a troubled family, and when it is better to provide the services that could keep the child safely at home and the family intact. This is in part the result of the tendency among policy makers and the public to deal in extremes with such emotion-laden topics as child abuse. It is also the result of the squeeze on the child welfare system from increasing demands and diminishing resources. If there are not enough qualified, well-trained, well-supervised front-line staff to make thoughtful decisions, the decisions they do make are more likely to reflect some absolute, at one or another extreme.

And so the pendulum continues to swing. In the fourteen months after Joey Wallace's death, the foster population in Chicago soared 30 percent. Children were jammed into shelters, forced to sleep in welfare offices when the shelters overflowed, and placed in over-crowded foster homes, with inadequate screening of foster parents. The foster care panic that occurred in the name of protecting lives had the opposite effect. That year, more children died in foster homes than in any previous year.

After every high-profile tragedy, more children are taken away because the only alternative would be to do something about the overwhelmed and undertrained caseworkers and judges and about the missing supports.

The out-of-home-placement panic that follows the death of a child can't even be resisted in jurisdictions that are in the midst of reforming their child welfare systems. Gerry Zapata, who heads a network of neighborhood agencies providing services in a Los Angeles County reform effort, told me what happened in East Los Angeles in late 1995 after two children died: "The numbers taken away really shot up right after that. The department was getting really clobbered and they were clobbering the workers. So, in that East L.A. area where we are, for a while practically every kid that came in went into foster care."

Instead of focusing on the range of options needed to meet each child's and family's situation, the public debate pits the goal of safe-guarding children against the goal of strengthening families and becomes fixated on a false choice between family preservation and foster care.

Diminishing support for families from the world outside the child protection system. The child protection system having narrowed over the 1980s, and the narrowed mission having come to consume all available resources by the early 1990s, there were no public child welfare services left for troubled families outside the purview of the child protection system. In most jurisdictions, such problems as inadequate parenting, chronic neglect, inability to manage aggressive adolescents, and even severe emotional disturbance in child or parent had virtually no claim on public resources.

At the same time, support for ordinary family life was shrinking. Wage rates at the bottom of the income scale were plummeting, housing and nutrition programs were being cut, and poverty was becoming more concentrated. Both formal and informal supports for parenting and community life were harder and harder to come by.

Professionals and others encountering families in trouble increasingly referred them to CPS when they didn't know what else to do. The CPS doorway seemed to be one of the few remaining avenues for help. A CPS referral was at least "doing something." As social services of all kinds were cut back, even officials in other systems needing help with children or families found they couldn't get it unless they labeled the problem abuse or neglect. They persuaded state legislators to expand their statutory definitions of child abuse and neglect to include truancy (now labeled "educational neglect"), inadequate medical care (now labeled "medical neglect"), and failure to thrive (now labeled "emotional neglect").

But as referrals to CPS became ever more numerous, the help available diminished, with already strained resources going into investigations, not services. The reports coming into CPS now not only included the new categories of educational, medical, and emotional neglect but also, increasingly, serious physical abuse. The system found itself unable to respond appropriately either to families in serious trouble sorely needing intensive intervention, or to the families who needed a different kind of help than the constrained child protection agencies could offer.

As these factors converged, the painful paradox of the modern child welfare system emerged: A standardized, centralized, legalistic system, designed to respond to rare incidents of physical abuse, was overwhelmed by reports of a much wider array of problems. As a result, it could do justice neither to the most severe cases of physical abuse nor to the potential of preventing abuse and neglect.

Increasing poverty and the prospect of disaster compounded. The condition of the child welfare system continues to deteriorate as poverty, especially extreme poverty, increases. Most people at the front lines agree with Peter Digre, director of the Los Angeles

County Department of Children and Family Services, when he says, "What drives child abuse is poverty and destitution."

Digre's impression is supported by the data. The most comprehensive national study of child maltreatment compared families with an annual income of under $15,000 with families with an annual income of over $30,000. The survey found abuse to be fourteen times more common, and neglect to be forty-four times more common, in poor families. The study emphasized that the findings "cannot be plausibly explained on the basis of the higher visibility of lower income families to community professionals."

The situation is bound to get worse, not better, with the repeal of guaranteed income support for poor families with children and with other cutbacks in safety-net programs further eroding both formal and informal supports. The new world of diminished support for poor families is likely to drive more parents to such desperation that many will be at higher risk of abusing their children. Many more will be unable to care for their children, not because they are neglectful but because they lack the means to provide them with food, clothing, and shelter.

This of course raises the question of how the already overwhelmed child protection system is to deal with these children, as the 1995–96 congressional debate on welfare repeal recognized. Conservatives responded by proposing the return of orphanages. These politicians had perhaps forgotten—or never learned—that government initiated income support for needy families at the beginning of the twentieth century explicitly to avoid harming children by institutionalizing them.

Shortly after the 1994 congressional elections, Newt Gingrich invoked the orphanage as a way of dramatizing the deficiencies of the present system. He made it clear that if the withdrawal of welfare benefits left mothers unable to care for their children, it would be acceptable to remove these children from their mothers (who, he strongly implied, weren't taking good care of them anyway). They could be put in virtually any other form of care, including orphanages.

Gingrich deliberately invoked orphanages as an alternative to the welfare system—meaning both the income assistance (AFDC) system and the child protection/child welfare system. He suggested that both—or either; he wasn't particular—were symbolized by young mothers who would rather abandon their infants in a dumpster than care for them.

Members of the Gingrich circle did not try to hide their intent to manipulate the emotions of the public. Gingrich's friend and adviser, Vin Weber, explained, "If you get to the point where you've had a serious discussion of the need for orphanages, you have destroyed the standing of the welfare program. Newt used orphanages to illuminate his rejection of the existing welfare system. . . . Conservatives believe that the heart of the welfare system is that it's encouraging out-of-wedlock births, and that those children have a lot of pathology."

Chester Gibson, Gingrich's debate coach at West Georgia College, provided further clarification when he said that drawing the contrast between a dumpster and an orphanage is a "wonderfully vivid image" that makes people think that a radical alternative to the present system may not be such a bad idea.

It was not long before the manipulation of symbols included a deliberate confusion of poverty with child neglect. Even those who worried that orphanages might be Dickensian institutions incompatible with modern ideas of responsive child rearing could countenance them if they were persuaded that "the parents are so vile, that even an orphanage would be an improvement."

But in considering whether even an orphanage would be better than being raised by an uncaring, addicted, neglectful mother, we must remember that the orphanage alternative comes up in response to the prospect of mothers not being able to provide for their children *because they have been denied the money to provide for them,* not because they have mistreated their children. The children of addicted, neglectful mothers are *already* being taken away by the child welfare system. That is not at issue. At issue here are the children whose caretakers had become inadequate only as a result of *becoming poor.*

But even very smart observers failed to make that distinction in the immediate aftermath of the pronouncements that orphanages would solve the problem of families left destitute by welfare cutoffs. George Will asked that we recognize that "the serious idea being considered by serious people is that infants whose mothers are, say, 16, unmarried, uneducated, unemployed, addicted and abusive might be better off in institutions." Gertrude Himmelfarb wrote that orphanages were better than "the abusive, alcoholic, drug addicted, violence-prone family, or non-family, that is the normal habitat of many children."

A simple look at the cost figures shows that the debate about orphanages was more about symbols than programs. Douglas Besharov of the American Enterprise Institute calculated in December 1994 that the cost of orphanage care for the two children in the average welfare family would range from $72,000 to $144,000 per year. That would be four to nine times the amount the family was receiving currently in cash, food stamps, Medicaid, and other services.

As soon as the orphanage rhetoric began to seem a political liability, the debate returned to foster care as the solution for families becoming destitute as a result of welfare cuts. The inability of the child welfare system to deal with the children it already is responsible for did not seem to give the politicians much pause.

But neither an overwhelmed, overcrowded system nor the consensus first enunciated in the Theodore Roosevelt administration that "no child should be deprived of his family by reason of poverty alone" kept Representative Bill Archer, chair of the House Ways and Means Committee, from declaring that if you don't go to work "you lose your welfare benefits and if the children cannot be supported by you, they have to be put into foster homes." Poor women had been so successfully demonized that an extraordinary number of Americans were willing to believe that anyone who cannot support herself without help must be a poor mother who *deserves* to have her children removed from her care.

As we turn now to the reforms that could make the child protection system effective in protecting children and preventing abuse, neglect, and abandonment, we should be under no illusion that even a reformed system could cope with the doubled or tripled number of children who may be catapulted into poverty and the child protection system—not by neglectful mothers or fathers, but by a neglectful society.

Keeping Children Safe *and* Preventing Abuse and Neglect in a Reformed Child Welfare System

The need for fundamental reform of the child welfare system was readily apparent from the mid-1980s on. While the precise nature of the needed reforms was being debated, it was possible to discern a consensus around goals.

- Protecting and promoting children's safety should have highest priority.
- Maltreatment should be prevented before it occurs to the fullest extent possible, utilizing an ever-expanding and effective set of tools.

- Anyone engaging in the criminal act of willfully abusing a child should be reliably punished.
- Children should be able to grow up inside protective, decent families, preferably their own biological families, but if necessary in other, well-supported families.
- Families taking decent care of their children should be left alone unless they ask for help; if they do, they should be able to get it without being labeled abusive.
- The system should distinguish sensibly among situations where a family is in need of basic or informal support, where the family needs intensive professional services, and where a child should be removed from home.
- Children who must be removed from their homes should live in the least restrictive and most familylike setting consistent with their needs.

Those not immersed in the battles over child welfare reform might consider this list of goals both self-evident and uncontroversial. Yet struggles to redesign child welfare systems to reach these goals encounter formidable barriers. Current child protection approaches are mandated in federal and state law and deeply ingrained in policy and practice. Current services and approaches, while much criticized, have a constituency often resistant to change, including tens of thousands of caseworkers trained in traditional approaches. Many of them suffer from a "bureaucratic malaise" that routinely sabotages and undermines the agency's capacity to change. In addition, financial incentives encourage out-of-home placement, and the political stakes in changing child protective services are high: Politicians are reluctant to make changes that could be made to appear as lenient toward child abusers. Finally, public distrust of current child protection services is rooted in genuine skepticism about the willingness of reformers to make child safety their primary concern.

Each of these obstacles is being overcome somewhere, not easily and rapidly, but painstakingly and gradually.

Efforts now under way show that it is possible to take reforms beyond pilot programs to accomplish widely shared goals. We will look at examples of initiatives that are preventing maltreatment by supporting healthy development; helping families in trouble, and keeping children safe by assuring that the full range of needed tools is available and of high quality; creating new, neighborhood-based partnerships between child protective agencies and community organizations that can support troubled families and protect children;

and creating community-based safe havens for those who cannot live in family settings.

PREVENTING MALTREATMENT BY SUPPORTING HEALTHY DEVELOPMENT

Home visiting. Of the tools at the prevention end of the spectrum, perhaps the most promising is home visiting to families with newborns. As a strategy for promoting healthy births and child development and preventing child abuse, home-based services and family support through home visiting has had a long and proud history—in Europe, as well as earlier in this century under public health auspices in this country. Many efforts to revive home visiting in the U.S. are now under way, including the Healthy Families America initiative described in Chapter 2, which is furnishing support to families and acting as an early warning system so that intervention services can be provided before abuse occurs.

Prenatal care and family planning. Sensitive, enhanced prenatal care serves an even earlier preventive function, and has proven particularly effective when targeted at populations at risk. A Philadelphia initiative was able to significantly reduce the problem of hospital boarder babies by arranging for a public health nurse and a social worker to work intensively with each high-risk pregnant woman throughout the prenatal period. "We address what we can address and address it aggressively," says Dr. Michael R. Spence, professor of obstetrics at Allegheny University of the Health Sciences.

Family planning services, a still earlier preventive intervention, have never received much attention in the child protection context—a curious oversight since "intendedness" and "wantedness" of a pregnancy and a child are among the most crucial protections against child abuse and neglect. Family planning has never become a routine part of child welfare services, even though automatically offering clients such services would probably be far more cost-effective than parent education, which *is* routinely offered. Although many clients of the child protection system want more children, often to replace those taken away, probably many more mothers would be relieved to gain control over their fertility. The system's coolness toward family planning services may result from efforts to shy away from controversy, and from a fear that such services could be used coercively.

Comprehensive neighborhood-based supports. Neighborhood-based family support programs, like other approaches to promoting healthy development, have broader purposes, but also contribute to the goal of preventing maltreatment. Family support programs often include home visiting, parent education and, most typically, neighborhood-based drop-in centers. Family support centers give all comers—particularly mothers of young children—a warm welcome, and are an avenue to other forms of support. Whether parents come to talk with staff or with other mothers, to sew, or to get advice about child rearing or a medical mystery, they don't have to identify a problem as a reason to be there.

Increasingly, the family support movement is devoting its energies to making other settings, including schools, and entire systems, including education, child welfare, and juvenile justice, more supportive of families in the expectation of improving many family outcomes, with a reduction in child abuse and neglect among them.

NEW TOOLS FOR A FULL TOOL KIT

In most places, the tools that could both prevent maltreatment and protect children in serious trouble are simply not available. Frontline workers and agencies everywhere must typically select from a meager and depleted tool kit.

To meet today's expanding needs, the kit must be augmented. An augmented tool kit would mean that more children could safely be maintained at home, more children could safely be returned to their families, and more troubled children could thrive in foster and adoptive families. The augmented tool kit must include old tools generally no longer available, including in-home services for badly disorganized families not in crisis but with multiple, chronic problems; community-based services for adolescents who are disturbed, runaways, or in conflict with parents; services for families where parents are mentally retarded or mentally ill; and enriched, specialized, and intensive supports for foster families. It must also include new ways of working more respectfully and collaboratively with families, intensive services provided to families in their own homes, and treatment for adults abusing drugs or alcohol.

This last category has been so widely ignored in the child welfare context that some further discussion is warranted.

Treatment and assessment for parents abusing drugs or alcohol. Researchers and practitioners may not agree on either the numbers or the paths of causation, but most agree that the response to substance abuse in the child welfare system has been scandalously inadequate. When an alcohol or drug abuse problem is found in a family referred to the child protection system, the CPS worker—in a virtually uniform response—hands the parent a list of phone numbers of nearby treatment facilities, rarely accompanied by accurate information about waiting lists, costs, eligibility requirements, or arrangements for the care of children. The information is usually no more complete or helpful when accompanying a court order requiring the parent to secure treatment.

This paltry response is particularly tragic because it represents a missed opportunity of great magnitude. The insufficient information about services, some of which may not even be available or accessible, comes at the moment when the parent is most likely to respond to a demand to obtain treatment.

There has been a reluctance in both the child protection system and the alcohol and drug abuse treatment system to recognize how crucial it is to connect the two. Addiction, by diminishing self-control, profoundly diminishes the capacity to parent. Addiction can overwhelm the protective parental instinct. But substance abuse agencies do not see children and families as priorities, and child welfare agencies do not always recognize the threat to children's safety and well-being posed by substance abuse.

The hopeful news on this front is that we know now what we didn't know just ten years ago—that comprehensive treatment works. Although data is meager on treatment effects for individuals referred for treatment through the child welfare system, one study of drug-involved women with children found that 75 percent of those completing treatment remained drug free, and 84 percent of children participating in treatment with their mothers improved their school performance. It is also encouraging that the Center for Substance Abuse Treatment, in reviewing the results of comprehensive treatment programs, was able at least to document that these programs resulted in later savings—of cost avoided—of four to seven times as much as the cost of treatment.

The state of Delaware, with a federal waiver allowing it to use child welfare funds for substance-abuse treatment, was able to staff joint teams to serve families with children at risk of abuse or removal from home as a result of parental substance abuse. The state of Washington is doing joint training of staff from the Department of Alcohol and Drug Abuse and the Division of Child and Family Services. In California, Sacramento County was able substantially to increase the number of individuals receiving services, and to reduce waiting times for treatment of child welfare clients, at least in part because it now trains social workers, public health nurses, and neighborhood-based staff jointly in assessing and treating substance-abusing clients. In a pioneering, two-generational venture, Head

Start programs have received federal funds to address substance abuse problems among Head Start parents.

NEW PARTNERSHIPS WITH FAMILIES AND NEIGHBORHOODS

Probably the most urgently needed child protection reform begins with the recognition that agency-based services alone can never protect children, especially in depleted neighborhoods. Formal services can only supplement the protection and nurturance provided by families and communities. In response to a widespread sense that prevailing child welfare arrangements have been too far removed—physically, psychologically, and administratively—from the communities they serve, pioneering child welfare agencies are trying to establish partnerships with the ultimate child welfare system—families and neighborhoods.

New partnerships, becoming known as Community Partnerships for Child Protection, anchor help for troubled families in the neighborhood by strengthening both formal and informal supports.

Jerome G. Miller, the court-appointed receiver of the District of Columbia child welfare system, has said, "If we had churches involved, neighborhood groups and social workers who come from the same zip code, we'd know when a family was in trouble, and who could help."

The new partnerships emerging between child welfare agencies and communities involve significant departures from traditional policies and practices.

They are bringing mainstream funding to nonprofit community-based agencies, which have an entirely different connection with families and neighborhoods than do the agencies that have provided services in the past. Increasingly, the partnerships engage not only community-based organizations but parents and neighborhood residents. This allows them to help parents feel less isolated in their child rearing and to respond to a family's self-defined need for help. Partnerships increase the chances that neighbors will help neighbors, be it with a casserole, a crib, or a baby-sitter. At the same time, strong partnerships in the name of child safety between public and community-based agencies and parents and neighborhood residents can help to bridge the gulf of mistrust between public agencies and the community they serve.

Community Partnerships for Child Protection also mean that all the partners share responsibility—even when things go wrong. Most starkly, it means that all the partners show up even at the press conference if a child dies.

Frank Farrow of the Center for the Study of Social Policy sees the new partnerships and the new networks as possibly heralding a more widespread, more fundamental "re-evolution" of helping agencies. He believes that large-scale human service bureaucracies may actually be obsolete, and rather than being refashioned should be disassembled and replaced by more decentralized, flexible, and smaller-scale entities. Because the kind of standardized services that large agencies are used to dispensing no longer meet the need, these new forms of network service organization may be one early form of replacement.

Promising neighborhood-based child welfare initiatives are now emerging in many parts of the country. Of these I will describe one in Los Angeles and one in Cedar Rapids, Iowa, as well as two neighborhood-based foster care reforms, one in Brooklyn and one in Cleveland.

LOS ANGELES COUNTY PARTNERS WITH COMMUNITY-BASED NETWORKS

Los Angeles is one of the big cities that found its child protection system so beleaguered that reform became imperative. Many abused children in foster care were not being monitored as required by law, and the county was paying many millions of dollars in settlements to children who had been abused while in the county's custody.

After a yearlong study, a widely representative watchdog commission recommended that the County Department of Children and Family Services supplement existing interventions with more intensive family-centered services. "No longer," declared the commission, "would social workers be limited to two stark choices, to leave the kids with their families with minimal supervision or to send them to foster and group homes, where loving nurture is all too rare."

The Los Angeles County version of child welfare reform is distinguished first by its size—it has served ten thousand children in three years. Its comprehensive services and supports are available to families for a period of three months to a year at a somewhat less intensive level than the more crisis-driven family-based programs provide. Its biggest departure from the past is the networks of grassroots community organizations on which it is built.

Twenty-five networks were formed by the department, beginning with neighborhoods with the highest incidence of children removed from home as a result of abuse or neglect.

The department's decision to base the reformed system on community churches, Boys and Girls Clubs, day care centers, and other neighborhood organizations emerged from the way the leaders of this reform effort understand the problem of child abuse and neglect. They see it less as a product of individual failings than as embedded in life circumstances, poverty most especially, and they looked for groups that had the respect and trust of people in their neighborhoods.

Peter Digre is the official behind Los Angeles County's part of the reform effort. A former youth worker with a doctorate in urban ministry, Digre is described by Nancy Daly, chair of the watchdog commission, as "a passionate, caring professional, who had a vision and who wasn't afraid." Digre explains that, as poverty increases, so do child abuse and neglect. "Families get caught in a downward spiral: First their utilities are shut off, so they can't keep the milk for the baby cold. Then they get behind in their rent and move in with friends or relatives, who may have a criminal history. Forty percent of our families cannot find housing. Half can't find day care, so they can't work. Two thirds have drug problems."

Nancy Daly, who now heads a fifty-member citizens' advisory committee, agrees, and expresses great concern about the future. "More funding cuts will mean more abuse and more deaths," she says.

Clearly, many of the problems of families coming into the child welfare system could be solved by a more sensible system of economic supports to children and families at the state or federal level. But in the absence of such a system, Digre says, the problems of poverty and housing and drug abuse must somehow be dealt with, at the grass roots, where people live, if children are to be protected. Thus the Los Angeles reformers came to focus on building "the capacity of communities to support families over the long term," says Jacquelyn McCroskey of the L.A. County Children's Planning Council.

Soon the L.A. County Department of Children and Family Services was contracting with neighborhood agencies with strong connections to local families to establish the Los Angeles Family Preservation and Family Support Networks—collaborations of formal and nonformal resources acting together, under contract to the county. Lead agencies receive payment on the basis of a lump sum varying with the service needs of the family, then distribute the funds among agency partners to support a wide range of services, from substance abuse treatment to informal recreation programs.

The highest priority goes to keeping children safe. On a report of violent abuse, both a law-enforcement officer and a social worker visit the family, and the child is removed unless both agree that the child is safe. For children not in danger, the community networks come into play.

"There is no magic," Digre says. "You have to pay some serious money. Our people are visiting families anywhere from four to sixteen times a month. But it works."

In each neighborhood, public and private agencies, schools, churches, community development groups, and other neighborhood organizations come together to decide how they will form a network that will support and strengthen vulnerable families. Roles and responsibilities of each member are defined, and the agencies decide together on a lead agency. Lead agencies range from El Centro del Pueblo, a youth-advocacy program for gang members in north-central Los Angeles, to the Boys and Girls Clubs of San Fernando Valley and the Drew Child Development Corporation in south-central Los Angeles.

"These are the agencies that breathe in and out with what's going on in the neighborhood," says Digre. "You can't help the families we work with, with their unpredictable, chaotic lives, with the lack of transportation and lack of opportunities they face, unless you can get involved with them intensively and unless you're really hooked into the community." Illustrating the essence of the new public/private partnership, he told me of attending Sunday services in a church that was part of one of the networks. The pastor introduced to the congregation a family in crisis, and before the church emptied that morning, a dozen families had surrounded the harried mother and her children, each pledging some form of support.

In this way the networks are building on the strengths of resources that have not traditionally been a part of the publicly funded service system for vulnerable families. The front line of support for families now consists of people who have long lived or worked in these neighborhoods, who have a direct stake in helping these families and these neighborhoods succeed. In an effort to extend the reach of the networks, the Edna McConnell Clark Foundation is helping Los Angeles County to work with at least two of the networks in what they call a "diversion strategy" to provide help to families at an earlier stage, before a formal intervention would be necessary.

Daly says that neighborhood agencies stay with the families they work with. "Ultimately the families come to trust the agency and look to it as a resource. The next time there's a problem—before it gets big—your kids won't go to school or whatever, you turn to that agency for help because you see it as your friend."

Bruce Rubenstein, Los Angeles County's deputy director for community development, says the family's ongoing connections to neighborhood organizations help keep children safe. "Social isolation is one of the key factors in the most egregious cases of child abuse and homicide."

But no one has any illusions that community roots and community connections eliminate the need for professional expertise. The leader of one of the networks put it to me this way: "Just because I'm in the community and wish these families well and pray for them and want to be supportive, that's not necessarily enough. I've worked with people where there's a lot of pathology and who need a whole lot more help than that, so I am very sensitive to the issue that you just can't let every little non-profit that is out there in the community decide that the way to get some money is to become part of one of these networks. We have to have a set of standards that we are willing to be held to—standards of participation, standards of performance, and standards of professional consultation and supervision."

The biggest change from the past may be in how neighborhood-based services look from the perspective of the community. Dr. Xylina Bean, chief of neonatology at the King-Drew Medical Center, and director of Shield for Families, which put together one of the networks, says that these neighborhood-based organizations have a unique stake in the program. "When a community-based organization is involved," she says, "we are interested in the idea of longevity, we are interested in this actually being a program that's going to continue as part of the community. Not something that you're going to do for three or four years as an experiment or a demonstration, where you come out with some numbers and publish your article and say how wonderful it was, and then you move on to the next project. These organizations that are now involved, they are part of the community, and they derive their reason for existence from the community itself."

The new resources that have flowed to the neighborhood organizations have also strengthened the organizations' overall ability to serve the community, which was another reason community engagement was so important, according to Dr. Carolyn Reid-Green, chief executive officer of the Drew Child Development Corporation. With one in thirteen African-American children under court protection or probation, Dr. Reid-Green says, "We see our children's pain as having become an income stream for others, outside our community. Everywhere you look in child welfare, you see these large corporate agencies. And this was the first time that some grass-roots folks could get involved in a big way and could be sure that we would have staff that was really sensitive to what was happening with our families."

Even at this early stage, evaluators have found significant improvements in functioning among participating families: One-third fewer children are going into foster care in areas where the networks are operating. With 75 percent of the county covered by the networks, they have seen the number of child abuse deaths decrease from sixty-one in 1991 to forty-one in 1993, and the number is still dropping.

To support the networks and the new ways of working, the child welfare system in Los Angeles had to make significant administrative and fiscal changes. It had to change entrenched bureaucratic practices in how it allocated money and resources and in how it worked with community organizations. Budgeting and regulations had to be loosened to make sure that both funding and expertise would be available to the networks for up to a year of planning for their new roles; funds would flow to the networks to reflect various levels of care and intensity of services; and the community organizations would receive continuing, rapid feedback by becoming part of an information tracking system installed by the county.

From the outset of the county's efforts to make the child welfare system more responsive and more community based, Digre has been willing to take risks. The biggest was betting that neighborhood agencies close to the families they were to help would actually have the strength and stability to carry the heavy responsibility the county was placing on them. Of the twenty-four grassroots agencies the county contracted with in the first three years, most have received help to strengthen their own management capacity, and none has failed.

His second risk was betting he could square his unorthodox arrangements with the auditors. The county was paying for rent deposits and for cribs, for counselors and for outreach personnel, for risk assessment and for refrigerators. The county was partnering with police, schools, the probation department, child protection, and tiny neighborhood groups operating out of storefronts. Sitting atop a $772 million budget, with money coming from dozens of state and federal categorical programs, each with its own regulations governing expenses and reimbursement, Digre knows the stakes are high.

Sometimes the view from the bottom is not so rosy. One long-time observer of the Los Angeles human services scene says that even when there is someone in a leadership position willing to buck tradition, the grassroots agencies are left to deal with a system that takes four months to get a contract signed, "a system that is set up to prevent any kind of change." People working at the network level see evidence that county administrators do not uniformly support the reforms and often try to impose constraints that could bring them to an abrupt halt.

Digre is unfazed. When I ask whether the auditors and the accounting department are nipping at his heels, he displays the optimism that is his hallmark: "We just have to work together to balance flexibility and accountability!" He believes that by keeping their eyes on the prize of improved outcomes for children, he and his new grassroots colleagues will prevail.

CEDAR RAPIDS, IOWA, TAKES THE "PATCH" APPROACH TO NEIGHBORHOOD SERVICE DELIVERY

Taking its name from the British term for "neighborhood," Patch has staff from both public and private agencies working together in the neighborhood. Linda Winston, executive director of the local settlement house, says the biggest change from the past is that Patch workers, based in family resource centers, have become part of the neighborhood. "People recognize them on the sidewalk, and when they work together as part of a neighborhood cleanup campaign."

She believes that the strength of Patch is that the community knows its staff are there for the long haul. "People are saying maybe they can trust Patch and maybe they can go over there and talk about their problems honestly for a change, versus leaving two or three problems out of the dialogue because they are afraid of what might happen if they tell the truth."

The Patch team includes a public health nurse, a housing inspector, social workers from the local settlement house, and someone from the local child protection agency. All put heavy emphasis on interacting with the natural helping networks in the neighborhood, and they regard the team as an important resource for family and neighborhood. While all workers maintain their core professional roles, they value the flexibility of being able to stand in for one another and to work together with families. The child protection member of the team works with families only as part of the Patch team, not separately, and has come to be seen by residents as a resource, not an intrusion.

The neighborhood Patch teams are expanding as Cedar Rapids agencies continue to assign more staff to the neighborhoods. Family support workers based in the same family resource centers as Patch assist families with housing, health, education, and employment issues, as well as with child development. These workers also recruit families as "Neighborhood Partners," to act as mentors, providing support and advice to fragile families with whom they are linked.

The settlement house's Winston says the biggest change originating with Patch is the move away from "the old form of collaboration, in which everyone does his or her own thing but they all sort of do it in the same place, to the creation of a true partnership, where the success of one is the success of all." It used to be that the welfare worker would tell the mother to go to work, the child development specialist would tell her she should be home playing with the baby, and the mental health counselor would tell her she should be doing something about her alcohol abuse. Now, Winston says, when staff from the voluntary agencies sit down with one another and with child protection or probation workers and with the family, they supplement one another's understanding of a particular family's strengths and problems and are able to reinforce the help each provides.

Winston also expresses relief at how the new system allows all team members to solve small problems quickly and spend most of their time on serious situations. It used to be that when children came to school dirty, for example, the mother would be accused of neglect, a complaint would be filed with child protection, and a full-scale investigation would follow. It might be weeks before anyone offered any help. Now a family support worker can issue a Laundromat pass and arrange transportation to the Laundromat on the day the dirty clothes come to her attention. Similarly, a child protection worker worried about a family with a new baby can consult with the nurse home visitor seeing that family weekly before having to barge in with an investigative team.

The Patch system makes it possible for families to get help in the normal course of events from familiar people and places, says Frank Farrow, who works with the Cedar Rapids reform efforts on behalf of the Clark Foundation. He tells of a Cedar Rapids couple who fell far behind paying their bills when the husband was laid off from work and began drinking heavily. A friend who knew him from the neighborhood association's cleanup campaign realized the tension was beginning to affect the couple's three young children. The friend suggested he drop by at the Patch family resource center, which the neighborhood association had helped to start. There, the family obtained debt management counseling, cash to pay off the most urgent bills, and a start on job retraining that ultimately led to a new job.

The theoreticians' vision that has driven the Clark Foundation's support is becoming reality in Cedar Rapids. Interventions specifically designed to protect children are indeed becoming nested in a broader community system designed to support and strengthen families.

NEIGHBORHOOD-BASED FOSTER CARE IN BROOKLYN AND CLEVELAND

Another promising departure in making child welfare services more effective and more responsive is neighborhood-based foster care.

It is no coincidence that Sister Mary Paul at the Sunset Park Center for Family Life in Brooklyn was one of the first to call the current system of foster care placements "crazy." She knew it was crazy because she was in very close touch with the families of her community. Since 1978, Sister Mary Paul and her codirector, Sister Mary Geraldine, have provided comprehensive, family-supportive services in an atmosphere described by Dr. Brenda McGowan of the Columbia University School of Social Work as "one of friendliness, informality, and warmth . . . reminiscent of the old settlement houses."

As more and more children were removed from their homes in the late 1980s, Sister Mary Paul said it made no sense for them to be taken suddenly, in the middle of the night, with sibling groups broken up and placed all over the city and parents not knowing for weeks where their children were.

Going into foster care is never easy for any child, observes Sister Mary Paul, but it's a less drastic, less radical change if the child doesn't also have to cope with being plunged into a strange neighborhood, a different school, and the compounding losses of siblings and friends.

In 1988, with the help of the Foundation for Child Development, the Sunset Park Center set out to demonstrate the advantages of neighborhood foster care, so children could attend their regular schools, and siblings could be placed together or close enough to see each other daily. They also were determined to show they could successfully recruit local foster families, and that encouraging frequent contact between biological parents and foster parents brought long-term benefits.

In the model they evolved, biological and foster parents are helped to share parenting responsibilities, such as walking children to school or taking them to the doctor or the center's mother-child play group. Services are offered rapidly and intensively with the goal of normalizing and abbreviating the placement. When the child can be returned home, the center maintains responsibility for aftercare, ensuring continuity of relationships and monitoring of the home situation to assure the child's safety.

But persuading the city to utilize the innovative neighborhood service has, at least until recently, been a major problem. New York City's child welfare computers had never, of course, sorted cases by neighborhood, and the center had to rely on individual child welfare workers to identify children who should be placed in Sunset Park. Although city administrators pronounced themselves impressed with the program, the sisters don't always hear about the children from Sunset Park needing to be placed. Observes Sister Mary Geraldine, "It's almost as if the workers have to manually buck the system and remember to call us."

That lack of support from the formal system may be coming to an end. The reformist Commissioner of Children's Services appointed in 1996, Nicholas Scopetta, has announced plans to draw on the strategies that have succeeded in Los Angeles and in Sunset Park to keep children in their own neighborhoods when removed from home and to work closely with neighborhood organizations.

A similar effort to decentralize foster care to the neighborhood is under way in Cleveland under the auspices of the Cuyahoga County Department of Children and Family Services, showing again that public agencies can embed themselves into neighborhoods—even as much as a faith-based settlement house did in Brooklyn.

In Cleveland, children are also placed together with their siblings in their own neighborhood. With the help of the Annie E. Casey Foundation's Family to Family Initiative, the department has been trying to build bridges between birth families and foster families. Birth parents are able to share information—about favorite foods, bedtimes, dreams, and fears—to make the child's transition into foster care easier. Birth and foster mothers can speak daily, and foster parents can invite birth parents to take children to appointments and school events.

Judith Goodhand, executive director of the department, says that if foster parents know birth parents only as the cause of pain to their foster children and speak disparagingly about them to the children, they leave the children torn and confused, and unwittingly seed new conflicts for families that may be reunited. Goodhand says, "I've seen so many children over the years who were just devastated by the way their foster parents spoke about their birth parents. Not enough people in the traditional system appreciated the simple fact that the emotional bond between parent and child is a powerful force and that most children love their birth parents no matter who they are and what they do."

The department has also found that neighborhood-based foster care makes it easier to recruit foster families and enhances caseworkers' understanding of the neighborhood and its families. The neighborhood focus makes it easier to provide supports for foster families, such as afterschool programs, weekend programs, and respite care. The department's modern management-information system allows it to assign foster care families geographically, says Goodhand, "and the Casey Foundation's Family to Family Initiative has helped our agency to stop treating children as if they are statistics."

The reforms have had a visible impact, including a 29 percent increase in foster care homes, a one-third decrease in the number of children in residential institutions, and the end of keeping newborns in hospitals awaiting placement.

ESTABLISHING COMMUNITY-BASED SAFE HAVENS

The nation already has thousands of "congregate care facilities," currently housing some thirty thousand children, and will probably always need such institutions to care for children who need the specialized, stable, structured care that families may not be able to provide. Nan Dale, of The Children's Village, which provides residential treatment in a family setting, says, "After the second or third or fourth foster-care failure, when the child has set a fire, cut the cat's tail off, and attempted suicide, [somebody has to realize that] this kid needs treatment, and not just another foster home."

Serious discussion of the needs for new types of residential care has become difficult since the invocation of orphanages in efforts to discredit the child welfare system. However, given that infants, young children, and adolescents coming into the child welfare system are much more damaged than they used to be, and that many neighborhoods have become so unsupportive of families, many observers are taking a second look at the need for safe havens, including residential care in settings that would be not only in but part of the neighborhood they serve.

The big problem with residential institutions serving large numbers of poor and minority children is not only that institutions for the poor so often become poor institutions, but that the most fundamental child-rearing functions are almost impossible to carry out within institutional settings. Uri Bronfenbrenner, dean of child development scholars, has established that to grow up whole, be able to learn, and develop a conscience, children need to experience—especially in the early years—the *irrational love, attention, and commitment* of at least one adult. Bronfenbrenner summarizes volumes of studies: "Somebody has to be crazy about the kid." For that to happen within an institution, formidable obstacles must be overcome.

Professionals as well as community people are struggling to meet exactly that challenge, trying to find ways for people to live under one roof that is an integral part of a community and not removed from everything that makes a house a home.

Ideas worth exploring include those of Kent Amos, a former IBM executive, who over the years has taken more than eighty youngsters into his Washington, D.C., home, fed them, tutored them, guided them, and actually adopted many of them. As he goes around the community floating his ideas, he likes to ask principals and teachers from inner-city schools how many children in their student bodies and classrooms really shouldn't go home at the end of the school day. Having heard numbers as high as 40 percent, he says he'd like to see a place "within walking distance of the school, where these principals knew they could send their troubled kids to stay for a while, where they would be taken care of by neighbors—where even the adults might get some help in sorting out their problems." Amos visualizes a campus where families could learn "everything from academic and job skills to how to be a good neighbor," and where they could go for supervised study, recreation, or advice. He says such a place could transform lives by accommodating children, families, and single adults, with children spending some time with their families, some time in their own dorm.

John DiIulio, the Princeton professor who made himself famous by predicting an era of young "super-predators" just over the horizon, says kids from the roughest circumstances turn out all right if "they grow up believing that there are adults in their world who care desperately about their physical, emotional, and intellectual well-being, and who want nothing in return save love itself." To make sure that more kids will have such adults in their lives, he advocates "urban kibbutzim," connected to inner-city churches, staffed by inner-city residents, including retirees, subsidized with public funds, and held accountable for results rather than compliance with rules.

Of all the innovative safe havens, the most systematic attention, for good reason, has gone to Second Chance Homes for young mothers and their babies. The beauty of this idea is that it combines the structure of an institution with the presence of "someone who's crazy about the kid." Meant to provide unmarried teenage mothers a safe, structured, and supportive place to be with their babies, these Second Chance Homes are a new version of the nearly forgotten maternity homes that long ago provided community support for unmarried mothers.

The promoters of Second Chance Homes hope that a year or so in a supportive and structured setting could provide a powerful impetus for breaking an intergenerational cycle of early childbearing, school failure, long-term dependence, and risk of abuse and neglect.

Kathleen Sylvester, working under the auspices of Washington's Progressive Policy Institute to advance the idea of a federally supported network of such homes, says they would offer the four fundamental elements high-risk teen mothers need if they and their children are to have a realistic chance to succeed—nurturing and support, structure and discipline, socialization, and a safe place to be at a vulnerable time for both mother and child. The homes are intended to serve a population of young mothers who, along with their children, are at highest risk because they are predominantly poor, have done badly in school, and have highly unstable housing situations. Many of these young mothers were themselves badly nurtured and even abused, and many are in poor physical and mental health. Staff of the Second Chance Homes are able to help the young mothers by creating a sense of order, helping them learn to become good mothers, supporting continued education and job training, making sure they get needed health and mental health services, connecting them to mentors, offering protection from abusive and predatory men, and providing a sense of family. If things don't go well, they can also assist the child protection agency to make an informed judgment about any mother unlikely to be able to meet her child's needs over the long term.

A survey by Sylvester found fourteen Second Chance Homes in eleven states, in operation for several years, usually with a combination of private and public funding. Most accept teen mothers between ages fifteen and eighteen (some also accept girls in the last stages of pregnancy) and limit their stay to about two years. Among their achievements: healthier babies, high rates of high school and GED completion, successful transitions to employment and independent living, and dramatically reduced rates of second pregnancies. Another survey done by Kathleen Reich under the auspices of Harvard's Kennedy School of Government, found nine more such homes. Two examples described in both the Sylvester and Reich surveys can serve as prototypes:

Bridgeway is a private, nonprofit organization in Lakewood, Colorado, founded in 1986, operating three homes for sixteen previously homeless pregnant and parenting teenagers and their babies, and supervised by live-in houseparents. Bridgeway measures its success in a repeat-pregnancy rate of only 5 percent, compared with a 47 percent rate among teens in nearby Denver; in an 85 percent graduation rate from high school; and in 55 percent of its residents continuing on to post–high school education.

Seton Home in San Antonio, Texas, provides residential care for about thirty-five pregnant girls and teen mothers annually, in two cottages, each housing eight mothers and babies. Some residents enter voluntarily, some are referred by state agencies. The program specializes in serving teens who were previously homeless or in foster care. Many had been sexually abused as children. Success here is documented by 90 percent of babies born to residents weighing more than the national average for babies born to teens, and only 10 percent of residents becoming pregnant again within the following year.

The Federal Government Departs from Tradition in How It Works with States and Communities

The reform of human service systems occurring at state and local levels was, as we have seen, a product of pressures stemming from a new and spreading awareness that old ways were not providing effective responses to escalating human problems. This awareness was having an impact at the federal level as well.

Seven months into the first Clinton administration, Congress passed its first major piece of child welfare legislation in more than a decade. Its supporters viewed it as an unprecedented opportunity for the federal government to support states and communities in launching fundamental reforms of their child and family services systems. Fortunately, the billion-dollar legislation that could lay the groundwork for a new response to the crisis in child welfare landed in the laps of a group of officials whose vision extended beyond the usual bureaucratic concerns.

The two officials of the Department of Health and Human Services (DHHS) responsible for putting flesh on the bones of this legislation had come to Washington uniquely equipped for their task. Mary Jo Bane, then assistant secretary for Children and Families, and Olivia Golden, then commissioner of the Administration for Children, Youth, and Families (ACYF), had both held positions in state government. They had also been part of a multiyear series of seminars at Harvard's Kennedy School of Government, "Making the System Work for Poor Kids." The single biggest conclusion from those seminars was that improving child- and family-serving systems depended on untying the hands of front-line workers and community agencies. Bane and Golden, reflecting back, agree it was helpful to have internalized that conviction before it became their job to implement the new child welfare legislation.

It also helped that they were operating in the "Reinventing Government" climate set by Vice President Gore and the National Performance Review, which supported a more flexible approach to implementation than most predecessors would have dared to try.

The other source of influence that turned out to make a significant contribution was an ad hoc group of national organizations that brought together supporters of the legislation to provide help in the implementation process. Led by the Children's Defense Fund and the Center for the Study of Social Policy, the group convened meetings of state planning groups, prepared extensive materials, and kept in close touch with plans for implementation.

Department officials quickly decided to promote the new legislation as a way to reform child welfare and related systems, not as one more categorical program. They also rejected the hallowed bureaucratic practice of focusing all staff energy on writing regulations that would mandate a specific approach to service delivery. ("Mary Jo made it very clear that she didn't want this to be a group of feds closing the door and sitting down and writing the specs for the program," recalls one staff member.) Instead, the agency embarked on an unprecedented process of consultation, designed to allow federal officials systematically to listen to and learn from state and community groups. The process was led by Golden and by Carol Williams, associate commissioner of ACYF and head of the DHHS Children's Bureau. It included parents and community service providers who had never before been invited to the table with government officials.

Williams says that learning from the field through broad consultation was so important "because for a number of years this agency had been cut off from the field, and not encouraged to have dialogue with people in the field," she said. "The notion that we would use people actually delivering and receiving services as primary informants in the design of a strategy felt very different to people in communities, because we've micromanaged the wrong stuff over the last 15 or 20 years." After opening up the process, Williams explained, "the second thing we did was to push the state and local people to look at the whole service delivery system . . . to make child welfare planning much more open, much more thoughtful, and not just a bureaucratic submission of plans . . . and to really begin to do an analysis of how they'd like to shift resources."

State and community representatives were very clear about what they wanted from the federal government. They wanted the federal agency to articulate and disseminate a new vision and to provide training, technical assistance, and opportunities to learn from their peers. They didn't want a blueprint and they didn't want to be dictated to. And they wanted to be supported in devising flexible and innovative responses to local circumstances. Deborah Stark, Golden's special assistant, recalls, "We learned that at the federal level we couldn't be prescriptive, we really needed to define the principles, the goals, and the vision and then allow the flexibility so that the states and communities could devise specific and highly individualized strategies to get to agreed-upon outcomes."

State and community people were also clear that they relied on the federal officials to remove the categorical barriers in the way of providing services that were coordinated, easily accessible, and rooted in the community.

Because the original legislation allowed money and time for planning and for extensive community involvement, because it required an interagency focus and an outcomes orientation, and because of the way DHHS officials went about implementing it, the Family Preservation and Support Services legislation became a powerful force in helping child welfare programs and institutions to debureaucratize and form community partnerships in ways that would allow them to become more effective in serving vulnerable families and children.

Child Welfare in the Post–Welfare Repeal Era

As families previously dependent on welfare support begin to have their benefits terminated, the question becomes acute: How will the child protection system respond to the needs of children where parents are no longer eligible for income support but who cannot find or keep a job paying enough to house and care for their children? Finding an answer will be complicated, not only because of a lack of funds, but also because child protection systems are explicitly prohibited from providing ongoing housing or cash assistance, even if children are neglected as a result of economic deprivation.

Mary Jo Bane, who had responsibility for the federal government's child protection and income support systems until her resignation from HHS in 1996, believes that states, communities, and private agencies will soon have to respond by developing new approaches to child welfare. Such new approaches would go beyond the challenge of responding to more children coming into the child welfare system because of economic pressures, and would confront directly the fact that full-time unsubsidized employment is too ambitious a goal for some parents, especially in areas where jobs are scarce. It may fall to the child welfare system, suggests Bane, to establish a new national structure of long-term, ongoing assistance, possibly including federally supported structured-living situations.

Conclusions: The Real Reform of Child Welfare

The reform efforts show that society can do better, for at least two generations of young people caught in the turmoil of the times, than the child welfare system has done in the past. The reforms that promise to achieve widely shared goals have at least the following common elements:

- The staff of effective agencies are equipped with a full tool kit, including the formal and informal services and supports needed by biological, foster, and adoptive families.
- Promising reform efforts are building a new neighborhood base for services through partnerships with formal and informal neighborhood organizations for the combined purpose of protecting children, preventing abuse, and strengthening biological, foster, and adoptive families.
- Promising reform efforts operate under explicit and high-quality standards, with extensive training and continuing consultation and supervision, helping staff to select and use the best strategy for each child and family.
- Promising reform efforts continue to evolve over time; they develop or adapt new tools to meet new needs, at both the preventive and "deep" ends of the spectrum.
- Promising reform efforts recognize that the problem of child protection can't be solved only by reforms within the child protection system. Because child maltreatment is so closely related to forces that erode parental capacity—poverty, substance abuse, domestic

violence, parental isolation, and a general lack of family and community supports—efforts to reduce it become part of a more comprehensive commitment to improving child and family well-being.
- Every one of the promising community reform efforts has been led
by visionary local trailblazers and supported—conceptually and
financially—by the resources brought by outsiders. Private philanthropy, with the Clark and Casey Foundations in the lead, as well
as universities, advocates, professional organizations, and federal
and state governments, has provided leadership and has invested
heavily and successfully in establishing the climate and knowledge
base for the current, most promising child welfare reforms.

8

Educating America's Children

FOR MORE than two years, *Wall Street Journal* reporter Alex Kotlowitz hung out with two young boys in one of Chicago's most devastated public housing projects. He wrote their story in *There Are No Children Here,* a powerful book that provided a close look at growing up in a devastated inner-city neighborhood. At the end of the book, Kotlowitz explained his inability to maintain his journalistic detachment. His friendship with the boys and their family had become too important. "Anything I could do to assist them I did—and will continue to do" was the book's last sentence. And one of the first things he did was to use the earnings from the book so their mother could send both boys to private school.

Kotlowitz was not the first to discover that if you have money and want to alter the probable life trajectory of a ten-year-old inner-city African-American boy—early school failure, delinquency, drugs, prison, and perhaps premature death—the best single way is to get the child out of his neighborhood school. Entire organizations have been established for that purpose.

Some see as the moral of the story that public schools have failed and should therefore be turned over to the private market. However, most observers—including a majority of the American public—believe that the market cannot produce schools that fulfill the need to teach all children well. They fear, too, that if we remove the pillar of public schooling, we gravely weaken the foundations of democracy.

But even many who believe that America needs its public schools doubt that we know how to make them work, especially for those who need them most. After more than a decade of noisy, expensive, and contentious efforts at school reform, the public is worried about American education. In June 1996, an NBC/*Wall Street Journal* poll found education the number-one issue among American adults in deciding how to vote in the presidential election. A cross-section of Americans told pollsters in the fall of 1996 that fear of decline in the education system outranked their concerns about crime, welfare, and illegal drugs.

That Americans had decided that education was the nation's most important issue was conclusively confirmed when President Clinton, leader of the most poll-driven administration in American history, announced in his 1997 State of the Union address that education would be his number-one priority for the next four years.

The good news is that we do know how to make public education work. Now we need the national will—not just to do *something,* but to build systematically on the impressive, if sporadic, successes of the past to prepare all our children for productive, joyful lives in a prosperous America of the twenty-first century. We must act on four fronts:

- acknowledging the importance of the earliest years, we must assure that all children will arrive at school ready for school learning
- we must put together what we know about effective school reform by creating the internal and external conditions for schools to succeed
- we must create stronger community supports for school success
- we must bridge the void between school and work

The tasks are formidable, but we have reason to be optimistic. The knowledge culled from the struggles and successes of the past decade lay a firm foundation on which to build. And the nation's leaders, from the president to local community activists, seem ready to move.

Assuring That All Children Will Be Ready for School

In the past decade, brilliant new research into the physiology and chemistry of the brain has established that the first three years are more critical to the development of human capacities than any three that follow. Brain development, it turns out, occurs earlier and more rapidly, and is more vulnerable to babies' experiences, than anyone had previously thought. Whether babies are cuddled, played with, read to and protected from harm, and how adults talk, sing, and respond to them, actually determines the *structure* of their brains and the *number of synapses* they will be able to use in learning to read, do algebra, and feel sadness, guilt, and joy.

If all goes well, nature has decreed that some 950 *trillion* connections between brain cells will be made in the first months after birth. But if all does not go well, and the baby is abused, lives amid chaos, or is left to lie endlessly in her crib by a depressed mother or overwhelmed child care worker—that baby's brain will not develop the normal "wiring" she needs to get on with her developmental tasks.

What's more, child development researchers have found that the most ordinary daily experiences of young children shape their capacity to learn. The curriculum of the earliest years—how a baby is fed, diapered, talked to, held, and responded to—teaches lessons that turn out to be crucial to all that happens next. In the first months and years of life, babies learn

- whether they are loved and are important to the adults who care for them
- whether their most basic needs will be met or ignored
- whether it's worth making an effort to communicate and to understand
- whether it's worth making an effort to put two blocks on top of one another
- whether it's worth trying to make sense of their surroundings
- whether the world is a reasonably predictable place.

Totally mundane, routine experiences, it turns out, become the determinants of whether children will develop the brain power *and* the personal characteristics that enable them to learn in school: the curiosity, the confidence, the trust, the capacity to work at reaching a goal.

The babies who learned early on that their cries will not be answered, that their hunger will not be satisfied, that their efforts will not be applauded, that there is no one to count on, will arrive at school in grave danger of falling behind and of becoming discouraged, resentful, and disruptive.

The implications of both the brain research and the child development research are phenomenal. But they have been largely ignored in public policy. A 1994 Carnegie Corporation task force concluded that, based on what we now know about child development, America's neglect of the earliest years amounts to "a quiet crisis." What is at stake is not only the number of children who will grow up to live stunted lives but the costs to society of educating and supporting—

and imprisoning—the needlessly impaired adults these children are likely to become.

But since the drama of the early years plays out mainly in the intimate environment of the young child, is there really a role for public policy? This is the question that Americans have had such a hard time coming to grips with.

Our national failure to act on what we know about the early years is the product, at least in part, of our commitment to rugged individualism. The notion that every family should be able to care for its own, without outside help, has made the U.S. the only industrialized country in the world without universal preschools, paid parental leave, and income support for families with young children. Mothers, and often fathers, in most other countries get paid leave so they can stay home during the first year or eighteen months, when infants and toddlers have the greatest need for highly individualized attention. Preschoolers from age two or three in other countries usually are assured high-quality, developmentally oriented child care, often through the public schools. Children's medical care, with an emphasis on preventive health services, and income support for families with young children, are taken for granted as a valued investment in the future productivity of the nation.

In the U.S., where we seem to fear dependency among adults more than damage to children, our national support of poor families with young children is so meager that even before the welfare repeal of 1996, the U.S. had the highest proportion of children growing up in poverty in the industrialized world. One of ten U.S. children under three is growing up in "extreme" poverty—conditions in which it is almost impossible to give young children the responsive care and nurturing, both emotional and physical, their healthy development requires. Parents know very well, and the research confirms, that if they can't be sure where the next meal is coming from, and if the child care person they depend on has five infants to care for simultaneously, their young children won't receive the nurturing their brains and bodies and hearts require.

To the extent that the United States has a policy toward families with young children, it moves in two contradictory directions—one aimed at raising children's chances to succeed at school and in life, and the other at getting their mothers into gainful employment, regardless of whether that harms young children.

On the supportive track, we have been willing to acknowledge a limited societal stake in meeting poor children's developmental needs, and providing some of the services that will lead to school readiness. Having discovered more that thirty years ago that high quality preschool supports could raise the chances of school success for three- and four-year-olds in poor families, we created Head Start. Now that we know that the critical years start still earlier, the federal government initiated Early Head Start for children under three, and states have developed programs like North Carolina's Smart Start, and Vermont's Success by Six. But with some sporadic exceptions, including a minimal foray into unpaid family leave, and limited public support for a sprinkling of family resource centers, parents are pretty much on their own in trying to cope with their children's preschool needs.

On the getting-the-kids-out-of-the-way track, a separate set of policy rationales reflects our national eagerness to assure that young families not be dependent on public support. We acknowledge a limited societal stake in the child care that supports the transition from welfare to work, and in the child care needs of the working poor, but that support has been grudging. It has never reached all the families that need the help, and has been narrowly aimed at getting parents into the workforce regardless of the impact on children of poor quality child care, and is now pitting the child care needs of the welfare poor against those of the working poor. In our resolve that all young mothers be gainfully employed, we seem to be ready to put young children in any setting that will allow their mothers to leave them. We ignore research the suggests that during their first year infants are probably best cared for by their mothers, and countenance full-day child care arrangements that actually *put* children at risk.

The high-quality child care that is essential if children are not to be harmed while their mothers work has fallen scandalously short of meeting the need—even before additional mothers were propelled into the workforce by changes in the welfare laws.

A General Accounting Office report issued in 1995 confirms that existing federal child-care subsidy programs put more emphasis on parental employment than child development, with subsidies that are too low to cover the cost of centers that provide high-quality comprehensive services. A study of representative child care centers in four states found that only one in seven had "a level of child care quality that promotes healthy development and learning."

So we should not be surprised to learn that increasing numbers of children are coming to school unready for school learning. When the Carnegie Foundation for the Advancement of Teaching surveyed seven thousand kindergarten teachers about how well prepared the children in their classes were for school learning, the foundation characterized the results as "deeply troubling, ominous really." The teachers reported that 35 percent of the children could not be considered ready to learn. They didn't know their full names or that a pencil was something to write with. Some were so hungry for food or affection they could concentrate on nothing else. Experts estimate that in the inner cities the proportion of children not ready for school learning is more like 60 percent. These children not only fail to benefit from what school offers, but when there are several "unready" children in a classroom, the entire class of children suffers. Minneapolis kindergarten teacher Doris Williams says that as an experienced teacher she can handle one child who is unready for school, "but when I have two or three children like that, there is no way I can avoid shortchanging the whole class."

A Carnegie Corporation task force recommending a comprehensive learning strategy for America's children reported in 1996 that "Millions of preschoolers are spending precious years caught in a maze of unstable, substandard settings that compromise their chances of succeeding in school." The task force also found that high-quality care is least available to those whose children would derive the greatest benefits from it—the poor. The final report of the Quality 2000 Initiative concluded that U.S. child care settings "have so long been neglected that they are now among the worst services for children in Western society."

Focused on getting every low-income young mother into the workforce, we have become so short-sighted we forget that their children's child care experiences could jeopardize *their* futures and *their* chances to become self-sufficient.

The child care subsidies provided under the new 1996 welfare law fall sharply short of meeting the need. The new law significantly reduces the funding that can be used to improve program quality, although a 1994 study by the Families and Work Institute found that only 9 percent of more than two hundred "family child care" homes it studied—the most popular form of child care for very young children—provided high-quality care. Thirty-five percent were so inadequate as to be rated "growth harming."

Under the new welfare legislation, states may find that to assist the welfare poor they must divert child care funds that now enable the working poor to stay on the job. Some states are limiting child care payments to $30 a week. Young children are shuttled from one child care setting to another as the conditions that determine their parents' eligibility change. Policy analysts ask what we will have accomplished if, as the price of encouraging parental work, "society fosters child neglect by leaving children without care or with inadequate care."

Propelled by the new research findings, and by a serious national commitment—at least in rhetoric—to universal school readiness, pioneering individuals and communities in many parts of the country are plowing new ground in addressing the early childhood challenge. Two of the most promising developments are Avancé, in San Antonio, and Schools of the 21st Century.

AVANCÉ SPREADING THROUGH TEXAS

Avancé is among the best known of the community-based early childhood programs that work with two generations at once. Founded by Gloria Rodriguez, then a first-grade teacher, it began with a handful of mothers in San Antonio in 1973. Avancé is now operating in more than fifty sites, helping 5,500 low-income Texas families get their young children ready for school each year.

As a teacher, Rodriguez had been struck with the large number of low-income Hispanic children who had already been written off as early as the first grade as slow learners or uneducable. These children had never held a pencil, weren't fluent in either English or Spanish, and, says Rodriguez, "when you got close to them they thought you were going to hit them." Other teachers assumed that these children, who lacked the verbal and even motor skills that enable most middle-class children to start school eager for school learning, simply lacked intellectual potential. Dr. Rodriguez knew that it was not a problem of potential, but of early experience and aspirations. She explains that these children's parents valued education as the way out of poverty, but didn't know how to help their children to be ready to succeed at school. Before Avancé, they never expected their children to go further in school than they did—the seventh or eighth grade.

Building on the parents' love for their children, Avancé teaches parents not only that they can help their children learn from the moment they are born, but how. In workshops that also encourage making connections with neighbors and other families, parents learn to make simple, inexpensive toys that help to stimulate learning at home. Through weekly home visits, parenting workshops, and family support centers with on-site nurseries and top-notch early childhood programs, parents who have felt overwhelmed, depressed, and powerless gain control of their lives and radically change their own and their children's prospects. Avancé helps parents to complete their formal education, improve their English, and sometimes to control their anger. It also helps train and place them into jobs by working with local businesses and by hiring participants to work in the program.

Says one father, "We fell in love with Avancé because they treated us like a family and like friends. They helped me to look at myself: what I did then and what I'm doing now and what I want to do later. . . . Now I want more for my future and for my children." Many parents are struck by the difference between their older children and the younger ones raised with the help of Avancé. They say that the Avancé children have a passion for reading and seem to outshine their older brothers and sisters in academics. Avancé has won national acclaim not only for passing literacy from parent to child, but also for helping to reduce child abuse, mental health problems, and juvenile crime. In a population that had dropout rates of 70 and 80 and 90 percent, long-term follow-up studies show that 90 percent of Avancé children are graduating from high school and half go on to college.

SCHOOLS OF THE 21ST CENTURY

A model with strikingly similar purposes, but operating under entirely different auspices, was developed by Edward F. Zigler, eminent Yale University psychologist and one of the founders of Head Start. His "Schools of the 21st Century" makes the neighborhood public school the site of full-day high-quality child care for three-, four-, and five-year-olds, and the hub of a network of services—including home visiting and supports for family-day-care providers—for children under three and their families. Child care is also available before and after school and during vacations for children up to age twelve. A sliding-fee schedule makes it possible to serve all children, regardless of income.

Zigler reasons that now that well over half of the mothers of preschool children are in the workforce, the nation can no longer leave the question of out-of-home child care to luck or the vagaries of the marketplace. After all, he says, "When a parent selects a child care setting, he or she is not selecting a service that permits a parent to work, but rather an environment which is a major determinant of the development of the child." To Zigler this means that the nation needs a reliable and stable system of child care, based in a known and universal institution—the nation's elementary schools.

The model has already been adopted by four hundred schools in fourteen states. The great advantage of the idea is that the nation's schools provide, ready-made, part of the infrastructure for a massive program that could serve all the nation's children.

But some regard the public school infrastructure as a mixed blessing. Many don't trust the school system, some because they believe that it has failed in its original charge and should not have an additional, particularly delicate mission thrust upon it, some because they see schools as alien to their community, and some because they feel that education professionals do not now and never will understand and value the developmental needs of young children and their families.

Zigler agrees that most school people don't understand children under five, and therefore insists site coordinators be professionals trained in child development.

Concerns about making schools more responsive to young children and to families were part of the reason that Zigler joined with his Yale colleague, child psychiatrist and school reformer James Comer, in a joint venture. Comer had been working since 1968 to find ways of changing the climate of elementary schools to pay more attention to child development, to make the basic management of the school more participatory, and to reduce the dissonance between home and school by involving parents in the life of the school. Both innovators recognized that schools adopting the Comer approach (of which there are now six hundred) were a much better fit than most with the early childhood programs of the Schools of the 21st Century. In 1992 they decided to launch a new program, combining the philosophies of Zigler's Schools of the 21st Century with Comer's School Development approach to create a new model, cozily called the "CoZi" schools, of which there were fourteen by early 1997.

The Bowling Park Elementary School in Norfolk, Virginia, the first CoZi school in the country, serves 474 children from low-income housing projects in its "Comerized" elementary school and has added the Zigler features for the younger children and their families. It creates an atmosphere of nurturing that involves the entire school and family community. "By combining the programs we can serve the whole child during each stage of development," says Lorraine Flood, CoZi coordinator for Norfolk public schools. "We start working with families when the children are from zero to three years old. This fosters close bonds between children, their families, and the school."

Responding to needs identified by parents, Bowling Park is also offering adult education courses, a family breakfast club at which parents talk about children's books, a singing group, and a "room moms" program that puts parents into the classroom as teacher's aides. Parents also persuaded the principal to introduce school uniforms and now help launder them. The result of all these efforts, says Flood, is that children feel "connected to the school by a sense of order, and a sense of community." The more quantifiable results are higher test scores and a 97 percent attendance rate.

The Imperative Emerging from Early Childhood Successes

Oases of excellence like these exist in the midst of fragmented and contradictory policies and hopelessly inadequate funding. Public funds from federal, state, and local governments constitute only about one quarter of the total amount spent on early care and education, but federal subsidies alone come from ninety different programs located in eleven federal agencies and twenty offices. Parents as well as communities are left to make Herculean efforts to put together circumscribed pieces of child care and family supports that don't fit with each other or with family needs.

Many communities are now trying to help parents by patching together and strengthening what they have, and by expanding many wonderful local programs. They are making valiant efforts to pool funding from a variety of disparate sources to create a network of child development settings, from family child care homes to centers to Head Start programs. They are trying to offer high-quality, developmentally appropriate services at times and in places that fit families' needs to have children cared for during the hours parents are working while contributing to and not detracting from children's development. This means trained and well-compensated staffs, parents involved in meaningful planning and decision making, and support services to help strengthen parental capacity and parent-child bonds.

But it is still a morass.

As a member of three different national commissions that sought during the past four years to come up with a single model that communities throughout the country could adopt to solve the child care and school readiness problem, I can testify that there probably is no such thing. The more we learned about the complex and varied needs around the country, and the impressive, if spotty and fragmented, efforts now under way to meet them, the less confident we became that we could come up with one model for nationwide local implementation.

But when the findings from the new research on early development are superimposed on the nation's new welfare policies an unprecedented urgency arises, and we can no longer countenance our unsystematic, laissez-faire, free-lance approach to supporting healthy growth in the early years.

A nation that is determined that all children arrive at school ready for school learning, that understands that the earliest years carry the highest stakes, and that has decided as a matter of national policy that mothers of young children belong in the workplace and not at home, cannot shirk its national responsibility.

The rationale for a universal national early childhood policy can be based on economic calculations. Governor James Hunt of North Carolina says that the new research on early development will make it possible to explain to voters that in the absence of early intervention, "their schools aren't going to work for them, their technical training isn't going to work, other things we do later on aren't going to work fully unless we do this part right and do this at the appropriate time." And the rationale can be based on moral considerations: it is unconscionable for government to decree that mothers must leave their babies in the care of others without being able to assure that these babies' life prospects will not be damaged in the process.

Neither the market nor the ingenuity of individual communities can provide such assurance. We need a national framework within which states and the federal government assist communities to assure that young children will receive the responsive, nurturing, engaged care they need in their earliest years. This framework should be built on three solid foundation stones.

The first foundation stone would assure that all three- and four-year-olds have access to a setting that provides both a high-quality preschool experience and care for children during the hours their parents work, to assure that they will enter school ready for school learning. Schools would be a logical and attractive setting for such a universal preschool program, if such an initiative included a commitment to shape a preschool climate that would incorporate both the principles of child development and the full participation of families in preschool programming—along the lines that Professors Zigler and Comer have so successfully demonstrated. In some communities, the schools would be both the physical and administrative setting. In others, existing high-quality child care programs, including Head Start, could be the sponsors, as could community-based organizations such as those that operate the Beacons Schools in New York City (as described in Chapter 2).

The second foundation stone would provide the supports to families with infants and toddlers that would assure that they get the best possible start on life and on learning. These supports would be provided by community-based organizations, that already have a successful track record. Groups like Avancé, and others like HIPPY, Parents as Teachers, Early Head Start, and Healthy Families America, now providing home visiting, family support, and early-education services so successfully to a relatively small number of families, could offer a scaled-up version to so many more. What has been missing is a national commitment to doing what it takes to provide a place in every neighborhood—typically but not necessarily the neighborhood school—from which these programs could operate. They would receive technical assistance and subsidies to reach out to where the youngest children are, to provide supports to adults now caring for these children wherever they may be—at home, in family day care, in child care programs of all kinds—and to upgrade care wherever it is being provided.

The third foundation stone, of course, is assurance that all children will receive the health care they require during the early years. Several states are in the process of trying to provide this assurance, and the 105th Congress is considering several bipartisan proposals that would extend public and private health insurance to fill this void.

Just before the 1996 Democratic Convention, as polling made it clear that education was at the top of the voters' agenda, the president's advisers discussed proposing a national initiative to make a pre-kindergarten year a universal option for all children. I'm told by a White House aide that the idea was discarded as too expensive. It is now time to reconsider that idea, as a start on getting all children ready for formal learning, and combining it with systematic efforts to create a family-friendly place in every community from which services and supports would emanate that would reflect what we now know about the high stakes of the earliest years of life.

Now that we know how much can be done to set all young children on a trajectory to school success, we must act on what we know can be accomplished during this period of unmatched opportunity—and vulnerability.

After that, it's up to the schools themselves, to which we now turn.

Today's Schools: "Inadequate to the 21st Century"

It may seem strange that dissatisfaction with our education system stands at an all-time high when more youngsters are completing high school than ever before, and more are enrolling in college, when the average American has had more years of schooling, and when test scores of disadvantaged students have been climbing. In fact, contrary to popular belief, today's schoolchildren are performing in most subjects about as well as their parents and teachers did twenty-five years ago, and better in math and science. Most American schools are managing to hold the line academically, despite the tough challenges of higher child poverty rates, frayed communities and families, and a continual stream of immigrants.

The explanation for the general dissatisfaction is twofold: First, the schools seem to be failing in matters important to the public, such as maintaining order and discipline and teaching the basics. Second, the nation requires vastly more from the schools than it ever has before. Schools are being asked to educate all, not just some, and to much higher academic levels. If America's schools seem to be failing, it is because they are being asked to succeed in a task of unprecedented magnitude.

Today's education, concludes the Consortium on Productivity in the Schools, "is not low quality compared with the performance of the past, but inadequate quality to meet the needs of the 21st century."

For most of this century, except for the years of the Great Depression, anyone willing to work hard could find a job that paid enough to support a family. As a result, the vast majority could do without extensive formal education. It was also considered acceptable for elementary schools to "sort the pupils by their evident or probable destinies," as Harvard President Charles William Eliot explained in 1908. Children who had trouble learning because they were hungry, disturbed, distracted by problems at home, or deemed "unsuited" to serious education simply gave up on school or were pushed aside. By getting out of the way, these children helped to make the process of universal public education appear to be working smoothly. No one worried about the fact that the schools were not educating all students, because those who were not headed for college typically got jobs that were good enough to sustain a family.

Suddenly, however, beginning in the late 1970s, business leaders started saying the schools were not producing employees with the skills that American industry needed. In nearly every industry the spread of new technologies created demands for employees who knew how to do more than ever before. The schools that had seemed quite adequate in a prior era were not meeting the needs of a rapidly changing economy. Reports followed swiftly on one another declaring that a much greater proportion of children had to acquire high levels of academic skills. Society no longer could tolerate the continuing failure of large numbers of children from historically low-achieving neighborhoods.

Because of fundamental changes in the nature of work and the global economy, countries that educate high proportions of their children prosper. Those that don't fall behind. Individuals who come into adulthood with high skills prosper. Those who don't fall behind.

Economists Frank Levy and Richard Murnane found that high-wage companies look for six essential skills in hiring entry-level workers: the ability to do math and read at the ninth-grade level, to solve problems where hypotheses must be formed and tested, to work in groups, to communicate clearly, and to use personal computers for simple tasks. They also found that almost half the nation's seventeen-year-olds are leaving high school today without those skills.

The schools made some changes over the past two decades, but not the fundamental changes the new times demanded. They were able to increase the number of students taking tough academic courses and the proportion of high school graduates going on to college. They responded to the clamor to reduce the number of dropouts. The rate of youngsters completing high school rose slowly but steadily, from 82 percent in 1972 to 86 percent in 1993. Graduation rates for black youngsters increased from 74 percent in 1972 to just under 84 percent in 1993. But as school completion rates rose, one began to hear of shocking numbers of young people graduating from high school unable to read their own diplomas and lacking the competence needed for higher education or skilled employment.

The Chicago businessman and philanthropist Irving Harris, whose good works include devoting time, energy, and money to improving the lives of students at inner-city DuSable High School, tells an illuminating story. He had heard from DuSable's principal about the talented president of the student council, who was about to graduate and hoped to attend the Illinois Institute of Technology. Harris called the IIT director of admissions and offered to finance a scholarship to help this young man to achieve his dream. He received a return call with word that, although considered a good student at DuSable, the young man had tested at seventh-grade level, five grades below what IIT required. Had he been only two grade levels behind, the admissions director told Harris, IIT would have arranged for tutoring, but the five-year gap was judged too great to overcome.

In his moving book about life at New York's City College, *New Yorker* writer Richard Traub tells a similar story about graduates of the city's high schools, who were arriving at college so far behind that City College was virtually unable to help them. He describes the frustrations of teachers of remedial classes with New York City public school graduates who have "only the barest degree of literacy." A teacher posed the question to Traub: "Just how much can you remediate? Can you bring a student from a fourth-grade level to a twelfth-grade level in three semesters, when he's already eighteen years old?" Traub attributes the bulk of the problem to the culture of New York City's high schools, whose overwhelming imperative has been to graduate students, come what may. "Cynicism and despair were mingled with sympathy for the terrible problems with which the kids were burdened," said Traub, but the result has been that they are allowing students to graduate "in a state of virtual illiteracy."

The hard numbers bear out the anecdotal evidence. The National Assessment of Educational Progress found that in 1994, only 81 percent of American seventeen-year-olds (including 66 percent of blacks and 63 percent of Hispanics) could read well enough to generalize on the basis of a simple paragraph. Only 41 percent (including 22 percent of blacks and 20 percent of Hispanics) could understand a paragraph containing complicated information. Only 7 percent of the seventeen-year-olds could handle complex math problems involving algebra, and only 20 percent could write at an adequate level. The business leaders of the Committee for Economic Development interpret the results of those tests as signifying that fewer than half of all seventeen-year-olds have reading, writing, math, and problem-solving skills adequate for success in business, government, or higher education.

Comparisons with other industrialized countries have also been discouraging. Except for elementary school reading levels, where U.S. figures compare favorably with those of other countries, the U.S. is usually near the bottom. In case studies comparing U.S. urban schools with Japanese, Taiwanese, and Chinese urban schools, for example, the top American fifth graders had math scores comparable to those of the worst-performing Asian school.

To make matters worse, the gains made in closing the gap between minority and white students seem to be slipping away. Progress among minority elementary school students was quite remarkable between 1977 and 1988, probably because of programs funded by Title I of the Elementary and Secondary Education Act, bilingual education programs, Head Start, and other efforts to strengthen compensatory education. But that progress was not sustained after 1988, and the gap was reported in 1996 to be widening again. The reasons for the backsliding are unclear—perhaps because the national focus shifted away from the academic achievement of poor and minority children or because life outside school became increasingly hard for inner-city children.

What is clear, however, is that despite the energy invested in school reform, there has not been enough progress in closing the educational achievement gap for poor and minority children, especially those of the inner city. "The real sin in our achievement patterns," says Michael Timpane, former dean of Columbia University Teachers' College, "is the disparities we permit."

The disparities we permit are a sin on grounds of future labor market needs and opportunities, and on grounds of a democracy's commitment to equal opportunity. The disparities we permit are unacceptable because if the children growing up in families now stuck at the bottom are not educated effectively, we are doomed to live in two separate societies, with differences in income and color reinforced by differences in educational opportunity.

Our schools are not organized to counteract the forces of inequality. In a television conversation with David Gergen about his book *When Work Disappears*, William Julius Wilson described how inner-city youngsters who do not make eye contact with strangers are handicapped in seeking a retail job where they have to meet customers. The demeanor they have adopted to survive on the street is the demeanor they present to the prospective employer, with the result that they are shut out of mainstream employment. One set of remedies involves changing the neighborhood. Another is to change the schools. Schools where teachers know all the students, where discipline and a sense of order prevail can inculcate the fundamental skills that many children will not learn anywhere else. Inner-city schools do not now but could in the future radically change the long-term prospects of children growing up in neighborhoods where work has disappeared, and few adults have to get up on time and routinely cope with having to take instructions from a supervisor. Schools, ultimately, could radically change the long-term prospects of children whose socialization has been left in the hands of the gangs and the street.

Good schooling has never been as important as it is in this era of ever greater concentration of poverty and disadvantage.

Real School Reform May Be on the Way

Amid the swirling debate among politicians, parents, educators, and the public about the future of education, it's easy to miss how much the core of the school reform debate has shifted. Much of the conversation today, vastly more than ever before, is about what students should know and be able to do. This bodes well for the future of school reform in a pluralistic society committed to decentralized decision making, because we are beginning to focus on the purposes of schooling.

It's also easy to miss how much agreement has grown up in recent years among rival school reformers. The reformers themselves, as they compete for funding and followers, focus on the differences in their proposals. Yet actually a broad accord exists on the essential components of reform, the internal characteristics of schools that succeed, and the external conditions in which successful schools can be developed and sustained.

The reformers' agendas for change are remarkably compatible with those advocated by business leaders, national political leaders, the vast majority of state governors, and Presidents Bush and Clinton—as well as with emerging public beliefs about the purposes of schooling. My rendering of the consensus may not satisfy every reform champion, but we will see that enough agreement exists to provide clear guidance to the public and the policy makers.

WHAT HAS MADE SCHOOL REFORM SO HARD?

School reform has not had a happy history over the past decade. Three unpleasant realities help explain why there has been little to show for recent school reform efforts: the erosion of support from outside the schools, the encrusted bureaucracies in which the schools are embedded, and the public's distrust of the reformers' agenda.

The supports from family and community for learning and high achievement have crumbled. While today's schools are being asked to educate a much greater proportion of students at higher levels, the family and community environments of these children are eroding the habits of mind that form the basic underpinnings of school learning. Our schools were designed to educate students from families that put a high value on learning and had the capacity to meet their children's health, nutritional, and emotional needs. Today, however, the same schools are asked to educate children whose dreams have been shattered, whose families are trapped in poverty, ill health, and turmoil, and who speak a myriad of languages, sometimes not including English. Schools established to serve children from stable and safe neighborhoods are expected somehow to cope with children who move every few months, and grow up surrounded by violence, drugs, poverty, ill health, and destitution of both purse and spirit.

Profound changes in bureaucratic institutions are hard to make. Profound institutional change—change that matters because it affects the daily interactions of teachers and students—is hard to make. When profound change occurs, it is usually in one school at a time. Despite the pleas of prestigious national commissions, highly bureaucratized school systems have been unable to bring about the changes that would influence outcomes for children on a large scale. Richard Elmore, an expert on the problem of going beyond one school at a time, says, "We can produce many examples of how educational practice could look different, but we can produce few, if any, examples of large numbers of teachers engaging in these practices in large-scale institutions designed to deliver education to most children."

Deborah Meier agrees, from her perspective as a school reform practitioner. She says the schools "successful with students who would otherwise count among society's failures" tend to be one of a kind. Most of them flicker brightly for a while and gradually burn out. Meier, too, has thought deeply about why the successful exceptions so rarely become the norm. First, they require a lot of protection from the bureaucracy, and ultimately exhaust the capacity of the "godfatherly" individuals and institutions that have provided the necessary cover and nurturance. Second, their leaders burn out from their efforts to push past the roadblocks imposed by the system's need for control and order. School systems, after all, solve conflicts by invoking the rule that "If it's not good for everyone, it's not good for anyone." Exceptions, Meier argues, smack of favoritism and inefficiency, and as they become more visible, they create ever greater demands for compliance ("Why are they allowed to get away with this or that? Who do they think they are, anyway?").

Albert Shanker, late president of the American Federation of

Teachers, observed that educators trying to bring about change are "treated like traitors or outlaws for daring to move out of the lock-step and do something different."

The conclusion is inescapable: If the only way to sustain a successful school is to protect it from the system, you have to change the system. If the system's rules punish persons doing the right thing, and reward those doing the wrong thing, you have to figure out how to change the rules. And that, while possible, is very hard to do. It is especially hard to do when administrators remain convinced, by habit and tradition, that the only desirable "reform" is one that would uniformly impose new procedures on all the schools in a given jurisdiction. Administrators exercising top-down control fail to see that, as bureaucratic controls tighten, teacher commitment, satisfaction, and performance diminish.

The public doesn't trust the reformers. While the public and the reformers agree on the broad goals of education (to give children the knowledge and skills that they need in order to earn a living and to become responsible citizens) there has been a chasm in perceptions of how these goals are to be achieved. Unless this chasm is bridged, support for public education will continue to fray, perhaps soon to the breaking point.

The public is not prepared to give up on public education, according to opinion polls, but surveys show that the public is angry and frustrated about what it considers the frequent failure of schools to teach students the basics of reading, writing, spelling, and simple math.

"When someone observes a supermarket checkout person who cannot make change, that to them is authentic assessment," says Public Agenda President Deborah Wadsworth. "It convinces people that the basic skills are not being taught or learned, and they regard those basics not only as important in themselves but also as the foundation for more advanced learning. To promote 'higher order thinking skills' when kids can't make change seems to the public wrongheaded, if not absurd."

The public suspects reformers of "promoting fuzzy and experimental teaching techniques at the expense of the basics," and believes that reformers are ignoring concerns that schools be made safe, orderly, and "purposeful enough for learning to take place." According to Public Agenda surveys, the public doubts that putting more money into schools or school reform will produce better results and believes that much of the money now going into the schools is wasted. The public doubts the reformers' claim that "all children can learn" and that school success can be achieved—even in a good school—by children who come from troubled homes and violent neighborhoods.

Educators and supporters of public education run a great risk if they ignore these concerns. In the absence of clear evidence that public education is improving, voter and lawmaker support for the very idea of public schools could collapse. Furthermore, the changes needed are so profound that they can be made only if educators and the public unite around a common agenda.

As we shall see, an agenda around which the public and the reformers can agree is beginning to emerge.

Consensus About the Characteristics of Schools That Succeed

Considerable agreement is becoming apparent around the characteristics of successful schools, and especially those that are most successful with disadvantaged students. These schools share four characteristics: a clear focus on academic learning, ambitious professional development activities, a significant measure of autonomy in decision making, and an intentionally created sense of community.

Successful schools focus on academic learning as the central purpose of schooling. The most promising school reforms focus resolutely on academic achievement, on a mission of enhancing the intellectual quality of student learning, and on assuring that students are engaged in challenging academic work.

Successful schools have mobilized school staff around a clearly articulated, common vision focused on curriculum and instruction, improved achievement for all students, and teacher responsibility for student learning. A Rand study of thirteen schools serving poor, inner-city students found that the successful schools had a clear, uncomplicated mission: They all were focused on the experiences they intended to provide their students, and how they intended to influence student performance, attitudes, and behavior. These "focused" schools, especially at the high school level, occupy the opposite end of the spectrum from conventional suburban high schools, which have been characterized (at least by reformers) as "mushy, all-purpose institutions," shopping malls, and smorgasbords without basic academic purpose, where students spend as much time in athletics, driver education, general shop, and "life skills education" as in learning algebra, literature, and foreign languages.

Within the agreement on centrality of the academic mission, there are many variations in how school reformers define knowledge and learning. Most, though not all, build their reforms on the new findings from cognitive science about how the human mind acquires, retains, and uses knowledge. It was serendipitous that just as the schools were being pressured to teach smarter and better, researchers were coming out with remarkable discoveries about how children learn that would equip teachers to teach smarter and better. Cognitive scientists found that students do not simply "receive" new knowledge, they "construct" it, basing it on their own experience, previous knowledge, and understanding. Applying that insight widely to curricula and teaching practices is hard, requiring changes in the beliefs and skills of millions of classroom teachers. But research has already shown that teachers can learn to apply these insights, and teach differently and more effectively as they do.

Because facts provide some of the scaffolding for problem solving—the more you know the more you can learn—there is common ground between the cognitive scientists and conservative reformers, like E. D. Hirsch, who emphasizes the importance of children mastering a body of facts. "You can't learn only *how* to learn about the Civil War," Hirsch maintains. "To learn about any subject, you have to build on previous knowledge. The more books one reads about the Civil War, the easier they are to read because the main characters in the story become increasingly familiar."

Most reformers are trying to get away from rote learning—the assimilation, memorization, and repetition of isolated facts, devoid of connection to any broad scheme or context, without application to problems that engage students' interests. They differ in just how far away they seek to get from mastering facts like multiplication tables and historical dates, but most aim for a greater emphasis on student understanding of content. Most believe that deep understanding is most likely when students exercise some control over their own learning, rather than when they are expected to passively absorb knowledge purveyed by a teacher standing in front of the room. Learning works best, these reformers say, when students make judgments about what types of knowledge they need to solve a problem, when they construct and test their own explanations, and when they interact around interesting and difficult questions.

Some reformers consider it essential for instruction to be sufficiently individualized that students can learn and advance at their own pace. That represents a break with the tradition of holding time constant and letting mastery vary. (Every first grader spends the same amount of time over the same nine months at beginning reading, whether or not he has learned to read.) Most reformers now believe that students should be given the necessary time and resources to meet specific goals, whether learning to read or mastering fractions. Educator Lauren Resnick of the University of Pittsburgh points out that this does not mean repeating the classes a student failed the year before. It does mean no longer tolerating the present wide variation in knowledge and skills that students acquire during their allotted seat time in school. It means that the school makes available alternative ways of learning. That could be a different technique used by a classroom teacher or tutor, or a nonschool learning opportunity, including afterschool, weekend, and summer programs involving churches, settlement houses, youth organizations, or business internships.

Catholic high schools, which have generally been remarkably successful in educating inner-city children, implement their clear focus on academics by organizing around a core curriculum for all students, regardless of personal background or future educational plans, representing a "proactive view among faculty and administrators about what all students can and should learn." This highly focused academic organization probably accounts for much of the more equitable distribution of achievement found in Catholic high schools. The focused curriculum creates a less cumbersome work environment for students, faculty, and administrators and provides more opportunities for informal social interaction and greater commonality in student experiences.

Successful schools provide teachers with ambitious professional development activities. Because the newer conceptions of how children learn are such a far cry from what most teachers and principals have learned, practiced, and internalized over the years, the reformers see an intensive approach to professional development as the key to changing the school culture.

Paula Evans recalls that when she began teaching high school French in the late 1960s, her department head gave three commands: "Never talk to a student before class. Make sure the books have covers. Look for gum." Her professional development consisted of "a visit from my supervisor and advice to write at the board without turning my back to the class."

One has only to spend an hour in an ordinary classroom to understand the distance between much current practice and the vision of "authentic pedagogy," which aims at an in-depth understanding of what students are studying. The following description of a class period in a Savannah, Georgia, middle school is instructive:

Shortly after the bell rings, the teacher tells his students to hand in their homework and then announces that the lesson for the day is about amphibians and reptiles. Without further orientation, he dims the lights and turns on a *National Geographic* videotape. The technical quality of the production is good, but many of the students seem uninterested. As soon as the narration begins, a number put their heads down and after a few minutes some appear to be sleeping. At one point, the teacher looks up from the papers he is correcting to admonish the students to take notes. Only two students appear to be doing so.

From time to time the teacher gets up from his desk and goes to a student with a question about the homework that was just handed in. Each time he does this he talks loudly and drowns out the narration. This distraction is compounded a few minutes later when the loudspeaker barks, "James Stile, come to the office." The student leaves, but soon returns, disrupting the class with his comments. A quarter of the way through the period, a substitute teacher from next door bursts in, looking frightened and upset. She says loudly that she must use the intercom to call the office. Her kids are misbehaving and she needs help. All the while the narrator is describing the habits of amphibians and reptiles.

The class quiets down again after a few sharp commands from the teacher. Soon, however, a student with a late pass knocks at the door, which is now locked, and the teacher has to let the student in. The teacher resumes his loud conversations with individual students about their homework. . . .

With about five minutes to go in the period, he abruptly turns off the VCR and says the tape will be completed tomorrow. He offers no summary, nor does he seek any student questions about the subject which has just occupied 40 minutes of class time. He admonishes the students to "pay attention because you will have a worksheet on this." He begins returning the corrected homework, but is interrupted by the substitute teacher who had come in earlier. She apologizes for the previous interruption. "No problem," the science teacher says, but before he can resume returning the homework, the intercom interrupts for the fourth time with several announcements, concluding with a reminder that students return to their homeroom to get their report cards. This sends a wave of remarks and laughter through the class that makes further business impossible. Shortly after this, the bell rings and students charge into the hall.

Changing the teaching habits and classroom atmosphere illustrated in this story is not a simple task. David Hornbeck, superintendent of schools in Philadelphia, says, "None of us changes our thinking because a superintendent told us to—it takes sustained, intensive living, learning, coaching, and reflecting on good practice." It is hardly surprising, therefore, that effective staff development efforts are ambitious and far-reaching. According to the Consortium for Policy Research in Education, the best training occurs in settings that allow staff to function as a strong, professional, collaborative community. Effective professional development activities aim at more than conveying bits of information. Rather, they expect to cultivate the disposition of teachers to make necessary changes in practice and to encourage teachers' views of themselves as learners. They also provide opportunities for teachers to collaborate in planning and assessing their instruction and time to participate in learning opportunities outside the school.

Most successful school reformers emphasize the long-term nature of successful staff development efforts and the importance of feedback, trial and error, and problem solving over time. By contrast, most traditional staff development activities are short-term, often one-shot efforts to increase teachers' awareness of reforms, their familiarity with new curricula, or their ability to administer or score tests. These activities tend to be too short and to lack the follow-up necessary to develop the deep content and pedagogical knowledge necessary to meet new instructional goals. The Productivity Consortium found that today "the professional development of teachers is poorly aligned with teaching performance, operating as a ritual means to salary increases rather than as a means to support improved teaching."

Harvard social critic and school reformer Richard Elmore has concluded that the underlying weakness of conventional professional development activities is their incorrect assumption that if teachers had access to good ideas they would know how to put them into practice, "that teachers knew how to transform their own practice and that all they needed was access to new ideas about what to do." Elmore found that practice was unlikely to change "without some exposure to someone who could help the teachers to understand the difference between what they were doing and what they aspired to do" and without some way of their consulting regularly with others on problems of practice as they arose. His studies of schools struggling with reform suggest that because teachers need direct experience with the kind of practice they are expected to engage in, "it is probably unreasonable to expect teachers to transform their practices in response to big ideas without careful observation and sustained work with outsiders in their own classrooms, either by working with an expert or by being in an organization in which the practice is part of the air they breathe."

Harvard's Howard Gardner (of multiple intelligence fame) has put forth his notion of what professional development would consist of if one could imagine a very broad range of disparate reformers (such as Diane Ravitch, Chester Finn, E. D. Hirsch, Theodore Sizer, Henry Levin, and Deborah Meier) arriving at what he calls a "consensual compact." Their professional development efforts, as combined in Gardner's imagination, would be designed to

- assure that teachers actually believe that the new ideas were worth attempting and were of sufficient merit to warrant the scuttling of long-held beliefs and practices;
- help teachers develop the skills that would enable them to teach and assess progress in new ways;
- encourage teachers to think of themselves. not as implementers of someone else's philosophy, but as professionals who take responsibility for their own actions, as architects, doctors, and lawyers do.

The right kind of professional development activities bring about a fundamental change, says Henry Levin, who developed the Accelerated Schools approach to universal school success. "If you visit our schools, and see the teachers who three or four years ago looked like a perfectly ordinary group of teachers, what they're doing now is so extraordinary, you ask, 'Where do you get such great teachers?' But they were always there. That's the tragedy of our system—not using the talent that's in the schools."

Others focus on the inadequacies of the training that teachers receive at the very outset of their careers. American Federation of Teachers President Albert Shanker contended that every other profession has a better system of induction for new members than teachers. "Beginning teachers need a chance to learn what constitutes good practice with the help of accomplished colleagues instead of being forced to figure everything out for themselves." The National Commission on Teaching and America's Future likewise offered a "scathing indictment" of current practices of teacher education and the use of unqualified teachers in the classroom. The commission (which, significantly, included the presidents of the two national teachers' unions) in 1996 called on states to establish licensing and review procedures that would make it easier to remove incompetent teachers, establish mandatory standards, and develop pay plans that would reward knowledge and skills.

Successful schools have enough autonomy to support their mission. School reformers believe almost unanimously that individual schools must have sufficient autonomy over critical decisions, including staffing, leadership, budgets, scheduling, curriculum, and pedagogy, to allow them to pursue their mission and so they can be held accountable for the impact of their decisions. One comprehensive review of the research concluded that the strongest schools had "a well-defined mission, the authority to hire staff consistent with the mission, and effective leaders who kept the school on track," and that these characteristics were most often found in schools that were freed from conventional external constraints.

Effective schools are able to solve their own problems, to manage their external relationships, and to evolve in response to emerging needs and experience. Teachers can influence both policy and practice without being undermined by centrally mandated rules or standardized procedures.

Advocates of school autonomy recognize that individual schools have no such autonomy in Japan and Germany, which have excellent school systems. But pluralism and diversity are not as highly valued in those countries, and there is not as much controversy about the nature of effective schooling.

As the U.S. moves into the next century, allowing schools the freedom to make decisions at the school building level—about how students are grouped, how teachers relate to students and to each other, and how time is used—seems crucial to almost all reformers. But they also point out that the structural changes that schools would then be free to make do not automatically bring changes in teaching practice that will lead students to think differently and learn more. There are schools that have expended tremendous effort and resources on replacing forty-five-minute class periods with ninety-minute periods, only to find that teachers don't necessarily use longer classes to teach in fundamentally different ways. School autonomy boosts student achievement only when there is a strong strategic focus on curriculum and instruction.

Many reformers also stress the centrality of one specific structural feature—that many effective schools are small enough for teachers to know their students well, and to increase opportunities for communication and trust. Deborah Meier believes that schools should be small enough to allow faculty to sit around a table and to permit everyone who will be affected by a decision to be consulted. They should be small enough for schools and families to collaborate face to face over time, for children to feel and be safe, and "for phony data to be detectable by any interested participant." The research generally backs the view that smaller is better. The large schools that have been consistently effective (such as high schools of science or the performing arts) seem almost always to be organized around a shared purpose that is so clear and so widely accepted that there is less need for intimate interpersonal relations among the participants that smallness provides.

Many successful schools are intentional communities. There is increasing recognition that schools play a role that goes beyond transmitting skills and knowledge. They also convey values—some by default and some by intention. Many of the most successful schools see themselves less as bureaucratic institutions than as communal and socializing institutions, with a mission to prepare the young for productive participation in adult society.

The studies that have compared schools that focus explicitly on creating an intentional community with more typical schools whose missions are shaped by external policy makers and funders have found that the schools that are intentional communities are more likely to succeed than bureaucratically organized schools. And while schools creating intentional communities are often private, such schools could flourish in the public sector if school systems were adapted to be hospitable to them.

In the typical bureaucratically organized school, administrators govern in a top-down manner through formalized and standardized district-wide goals and procedures. Bureaucratic schools are essentially franchises, reflecting a standard model established by central authorities. Staff and students have little reason to consider the schools uniquely their own. The school offers little in the way of common goals to unify and bind the people who are parts of it. Students have a wide choice of courses and activities and are encouraged to pursue their individual interests and ambitions. Everything the school offers is the product of individualistic and competitive interests, and of the bureaucratic preferences of external funders and regulators. By conveying the sense that "no one fails here who shows up," bureaucratic schools perpetuate a silent conspiracy between school and community that mediocre academic achievement will be acceptable. Half of the high school students questioned in a recent Public Agenda survey said their schools didn't challenge them to do their best.

Schools that function as intentional communities differ from bureaucratic schools in organization, ethos and educational style.

- The intentional school exercises authority through strong social contracts that emphasize the responsibility that administrators, students, and teachers feel toward one another. The assumption is that teachers are motivated by their commitment to the school's mission, not controlled by central authorities.
- Intentional schools aggressively mold student attitudes and values; they do not see themselves as neutral transmitters of information and skills.
- Intentional schools in the inner city function as bridging institutions, joining empathy toward students and their families with a clear recognition of the demands of contemporary middle-class American life. Believing that "the school is of value to the disadvantaged student because it is culturally different," they help mediate the gulf between the intimacy of the family and the impersonalism of the world of work.
- Intentional schools focus on academic achievement and draw all students toward learning certain core skills in a common curriculum with strong academic content. All students are expected to meet high academic standards, to devote substantial effort to their schoolwork, and to engage in sustained, disciplined, and critical thought.

Catholic schools have established a reputation for creating intentional communities and succeeding with disadvantaged children, a fact that has sparked considerable controversy over whether the characteristics of Catholic schools—and others organized around an ideology of community—could be incorporated into more schools operating in the public sector.

A rigorous study of Catholic schools by Anthony Bryk of the University of Chicago and two colleagues concluded there is no reason why secular schools could not espouse a set of humanistic beliefs and social principles that would allow them to establish a compelling ethos similar to the one that Catholic schools have established and to obtain similarly beneficial results.

Evidence that this, in fact, has been done comes from the Central Park East elementary and secondary schools. Their founder, Deborah Meier, describes a school community based on mutual respect, close bonds between students and teachers, a strong sense of belonging, responsibility, and caring; a school community powerful enough to be compelling to young people, a club worth enlisting in. These characteristics seem to add up to precisely the set of humanistic beliefs and social principles that are the secular analog of the ethos of the Catholic schools.

The External Conditions That Sustain Successful Schools

While there is considerable agreement about the nature of schools that succeed in equipping all their students, including those from disadvantaged backgrounds, with the skills they need, disagreement remains about the external conditions under which those schools are likely to be developed and sustained.

Some believe that successful schools will thrive in large numbers only if they are turned over to the marketplace. The privatizers believe bureaucratic restraints on public schools are immutable, and that successful schools simply cannot survive within the public system.

Because so many of the impediments to fundamental reform are embedded in public school bureaucracies, the idea of turning schools over to the private sector seems attractive at first blush. And that is precisely the solution embraced by a handful of policy analysts, led by John Chubb and Terry Moe of the Brookings Institution; by education entrepreneurs such as the Edison Project and Education Alternatives, Inc.; and by many conservative politicians.

Chubb and Moe argue that excessive bureaucracy undermines the traits that make schools effective: rigorous and focused goals, strong educational leadership by principals, professionalism among teachers, and ambitious academic programs for all students. And they are absolutely right. They are also right in contending that schools need substantial autonomy to sustain these characteristics. But then they take a giant ideological leap, asserting that, because democratic control inevitably produces unrestrained bureaucracy, there is no way for successful schools to flourish unless they are put entirely "beyond the reach of public authority."

The idea of giving up on public schools, seen as expensive failures, has popular appeal, as many politicians have discovered. Hardly a day went by in the 1996 presidential campaign that Bob Dole didn't make a pitch for school vouchers so that "everyone in this audience would have the same right as Bill Clinton and Al Gore—the right to send your child to the school of your choice."

There are arguments against privatizing the schools on the grounds that the private market would be impossible to regulate and that there would never be sufficient profit in private schools to attract the necessary investment. But the real difficulty with privatization is that it would knock down one of the few remaining pillars supporting our democratic life. Schooling, after all, is both a private and a public good. It is a private good in that it enhances individual productivity and earnings, health and longevity, and access to information. As a public good, effective schooling provides students with a common set of values and knowledge. It creates citizens who can function democratically and contribute to national productivity. It helps distribute social and economic opportunity more fairly among persons from diverse racial, ethnic, and class origins. It reflects the stake all Americans have in tomorrow's citizens.

True enough, the public school pillar of our democratic life is already crumbling. To the extent that public education, in fact, does not function as an integrating community enterprise, it becomes exceedingly vulnerable to market takeover.

The alternative to dismantling the weakened public education pillar is to strengthen it. That means tackling the complex task of making bureaucracies support effective schools. Earlier in this book we saw the changes beginning in other public bureaucracies to permit front-line discretion and avoid rigidity and uniformity. Public institutions of many kinds are being adapted to operate in ways that produce successful outcomes for all children, including those who start with the odds against them.

No one disputes that the characteristics of effective schools are difficult to sustain within today's public system. The critical issue is whether a public system can be designed that would nurture—rather than damage—effective schools.

There is research and experience to suggest it can be done.

Four conditions are essential if the key features of success are to be sustained within large systems. (1) Accountability must be based on standards for student achievement. (2) Parents, teachers, and students must be able to exercise enough choice to allow the school to become an intentional community. (3) Schools must get help in selecting and implementing proven interventions. (4) Everyone involved must understand that no reform in isolation will bring improved outcomes—many changes must be aligned with one another.

These external conditions cannot create successful schools, but they can, in Deborah Meier's words, "stack the deck in favor of good schooling, so that great schools are more likely, good schools become ordinary practice, and poor schools get more quickly dealt with."

ACCOUNTABILITY BASED ON STANDARDS FOR STUDENT ACHIEVEMENT

"Standards are the starting point, the sine qua non, of school reform," said Louis Gerstner, chairman of IBM, at the 1996 Education Summit, which he co-chaired. Actually, he had been saying it
for a while. President Bill Clinton, on the other hand, had been
thinking the same thing, but not until his State of the Union speech
in 1997 did he actually *say* it, loud and clear: He would undertake
"a national crusade for education standards." Not only would education be his number-one priority for the next four years, but first on
his ten-point program would be "national standards, representing
what all our students must know to succeed in the knowledge economy of the twenty-first century."

It was a breathtaking victory for the proponents of national standards, who had been working toward the widespread acceptance of
student achievement standards for nearly a decade, a decade during
which national standards had several times been declared dead. After the president's ringing endorsement, it was unlikely they would
ever again become dormant, much less die.

The movement for national school achievement standards came to
public attention in 1989, when President George Bush and the nation's governors agreed at the first national education summit in
Williamsburg, Virginia, on six ambitious goals to improve education
and to stimulate public- and private-sector collaboration. The two
goals relating to academic achievement ("All students will leave
grades four, eight, and twelve having demonstrated competency over
challenging subject matter" and "U.S. students will be first in the
world in math and science achievement,") implied the establishment
of national standards to define what children are supposed to learn.

"The promise of standards prompted an unusual political convergence," Diane Ravitch, then assistant secretary of education, subsequently recalled. "People who worried most about excellence looked
to standards to raise achievement; people who worried most about
equality looked to standards to provide students with equal access to
challenging curricula and learning experiences. Together they forged
an unusual and effective alliance."

Strong, content-based standards could replace the old forms of
accountability, based on school compliance with prescribed procedures. Schools would be liberated from the detailed rules that
stemmed from the 1960s and 1970s, when "doing the procedurally
correct thing" replaced "doing the right thing." Reformers pinned
their hopes on trading accountability for autonomy. If desired out-

comes could be agreed upon, school boards and legislators might be deterred from micromanaging the processes of schooling.

Furthermore, clear goals and standards would not only stimulate improved performance but would persuade the public that something good was being accomplished in the schools. Standards would also heighten employer interest in grades and other measures of school performance in hiring noncollege-bound students.

Standards would assure that the right to elementary and secondary education meant more than a right to a seat in a public school. It would mean, agreed the AFT's Albert Shanker and the conservative educator E. D. Hirsch, the right to a high-quality education that gives all American children "the knowledge they will need to participate and prosper in American society."

Education reformers also looked to standards "to change the conversation," as educator Robert Slavin put it, so that teachers and administrators will talk more about what has to change, what they might be doing differently, in order to better meet the academic needs of their students.

But not long after school achievement standards came to public notice, the idea was fiercely attacked by those who saw in academic standards a threat to the American tradition of controlling schools locally.

"We're not going to give up local control just because some CEO says we need statewide standards," declared Governor Terry Branstead, the conservative Republican governor of Iowa.

Religious conservatives attacked standards because they opposed any role in education for anyone outside the local community, but also because of the bizarre content of some of the standards being proposed. Several state groups had seized on the standards idea as a vehicle for a looser, nonacademic agenda, which they defined so sloppily as to make the entire venture vulnerable. The proponents of standards had always intended they would reflect clearly defined, measurable academic skills. But drafting groups in Pennsylvania proposed such "standards" as "Students are to give examples of their own positive and negative personal impacts on the environment and assess their personal commitment to the environment" and "Students are to demonstrate the ability to bring about and adapt to change in their own lives." As the late Albert Shanker wrote, while other industrialized countries called for solving simultaneous linear equations, algebraically and by graph, Ohio's proposed outcomes included "maintaining physical, emotional and social well-being" and "establishing priorities to balance multiple life roles."

Many educators and their business allies were as appalled as the religious conservatives. And if right-wing attacks and an absence of rigor (to put it politely) among some state drafting bodies were not enough, not even all school reformers agreed on national standards. Theodore Sizer, founder of the Coalition of Essential Schools, was adamant that individual schools must be able to define their own outcomes. He believes national standards and assessments would be incompatible with the Coalition's view of the purposes of education: to create "informed skeptics," for whom a questioning attitude is more important than mastering a body of information.

Standards were also attacked in 1992 by a distinguished group of school reformers and civil rights activists, who issued a statement claiming that "any policy to establish benchmarks for achievement without creating equity in the educational resources available to children would be a cruel hoax." The opposition of many advocates for children, for the poor, and for minorities was understandable. National standards would surely reveal disparities in school achievement by race, income, and class. Knowing that these differences were the result of disinvestment in these children, their neighborhoods, and their schools, they feared that the differences would be interpreted instead as revealing a lack of effort or—worse yet—lack of potential among children never given a chance to succeed at school.

Advocates of standards tried to set the record straight, and to resuscitate the apparently moribund standards movement. (In a February 1995 talk at the Brookings Institution titled "The Short Unhappy Life of National Standards," Chester Finn, assistant secretary of education in the Bush administration, declared national education standards dead for the foreseeable future.) They argued that national standards are necessary to reflect the national interest in all children learning at high levels. As the Productivity Consortium puts it, "The effects of a weak education transcend state boundaries. . . . Those states with weak education systems contribute less to the country's economy and leave their youth, who often migrate to other states, less able to accommodate to economic change, more apt to need government assistance, and less apt to form stable families." David Hornbeck, among the earliest advocates of state and national standards, contends that "high standards for all is our best hope for overcoming widespread low expectations, which is the biggest barrier to all children achieving at high levels." The defenders of standards and new forms of assessment pointed out that explicit state and national standards would replace standards now implicitly set by textbook publishers and commercial test designers. They advised all concerned to distinguish between "vague, affective outcomes and clear academic standards" and to keep in mind the following criteria for setting standards:

- Standards must state clearly what students are supposed to know and be able to do, as in "Students should be able to use decimals, fractions, ratios and percents to analyze data from a survey."
- Standards must be clearly focused on measurable academic achievement and avoid adopting vague, value-laden "lifestyle" goals and objectives.
- Negotiations about standards must be aimed not at simply reaching agreement, but reaching agreement on high standards. (The process worked in California, says Diane Ravitch, because "the state's educational leadership did not compromise every difference by acceding to every demand," but was "willing to say no to inappropriate demands and pressures.")

In the hopes of being able to galvanize the public and educators around concrete proposals, a number of professional organizations began developing standards for what all students should know and be able to do. The New Standards Project, a consortium of states and school districts serving about half the nation's schoolchildren, was founded in 1990 with foundation support by education scholar Lauren Resnick of the University of Pittsburgh and Marc Tucker of the National Center for Education and the Economy. It developed standards and assessments based on standards of other countries, the views of professionals in the various disciplines, and public opinion about what students ought to know and be able to do. It also trained teachers in the use of the new assessment techniques.

In 1994, President Clinton confirmed—albeit rather softly—in a letter to Republican Governor Carroll A. Campbell of South Carolina that he wanted to be part of the standards consensus. He wrote, "The key to meaningful long-term education reform lies in clearly-stated national goals coupled with maximum feasible flexibility for states and localities to devise and implement their own plans for achieving those goals. Schools should be held accountable for results—not for complying with a discouraging maze of micromanaged bureaucratic prescriptions."

Resnick was by now meeting frequently with the nation's governors and advising them to "stop setting rules for how schools should be staffed, how time should be organized, how courses should be taught, and how money should be spent." By holding the schools to standards and letting them make their own decisions, she said, "You will have real public accountability, but a lean and nonintrusive bureaucracy." She told the governors that if they wanted a high school diploma in their state to mean more than that its owner attended school, most of the time, for twelve years, they had to raise their expectations. She pointed out that high school teachers feel trapped into making few demands and grading generously because so many students arrive barely able to read and completely mystified by basic arithmetic. "Somewhere between first and fifth grade," she said, "expectations of mediocrity become so firmly established that individual teachers, even whole schools, have trouble bucking the tide." If governors wanted to change this situation, she told them, someone would have to set clear standards of what students are expected to learn.

Evidence was beginning to come in that higher standards and new assessments, when coupled with consequences, were helping to motivate both students and teachers. In 1995, Milwaukee scrapped its math multiple-choice tests for one that forced students to apply math concepts and analytic thinking, and announced that students who failed would not graduate. Seventy-nine percent failed the first time the new test was given. Teachers, parents, and students were shocked and furious. The school board nearly retreated. But after several months, the community mobilized. Teachers put more emphasis on teaching problem-solving skills. High schools started after-school and Saturday tutoring. Churches and businesses offered supplies and tutors. Now more than 80 percent of the students are passing. High school principal Nancy Conner says, "This has been tough, but it proves these kids have the ability to do more than we have been expecting of them. If you could see their faces when they finally pass, you would know we're doing the right thing."

More and more public officials and others concerned with improving education in America came to see standards-based accountability as a critical underpinning for school reform. With the ends of education agreed upon, schools could give students the time needed to master the material. They could vary the means of seizing on children's interests, passions, and learning styles, as well as the school community's judgment about teaching styles. Neither children nor teachers would have to be treated like interchangeable parts. People afraid of outside control of schools could embrace standards as the least intrusive way of assuring accountability. Standards, wrote two former assistant secretaries of education in Republican administrations endorsing the Clinton proposal, would be a yardstick, not a harness.

Unlike some other reform ideas, school achievement standards were welcomed by most of the public. Three quarters of the respondents to a *U.S. News and World Report* poll in 1996 said academic standards should be raised. "Parents want to make sure in these anxious times that no matter where they live, [education] standards will be high," explained Celinda Lake, who conducted the survey. Furthermore, more than half of those polled said they wanted standards set at the national or state level. Even students agreed on the need for standards. In a study released by Public Agenda in February 1997, three fourths of high school students surveyed said that requiring students to learn more and making them pass tests before they could graduate would make students pay more attention to their studies.

In poll after poll, the American public has approved of national standards and even of a single national test. Ravitch suggests that national standards are popular because they imply to the public that the nation will somehow work together to improve achievement.

The widespread public support of standards may have helped the president to decide to take his bold stand in his 1997 State of the Union address, although Michael Cohen, special assistant to the president for education, says that neither Secretary of Education Richard Riley nor the president ever gave up on standards, even when they were given up for dead by others. They found that by focusing on assessing reading in fourth grade and math skills in the eighth grade, where consensus was substantial, they could avoid much of the destructive controversy of the past.

The resilience of the standards idea may be the most remarkable development in contemporary school reform efforts. Apparently Americans are willing to try to come to some agreement on what they want their children to learn. Resnick believes that at least 80 percent of the public agree on at least 80 percent of what children should be learning, which makes wide agreement on standards a realistic goal. Harvard's Elmore sees the new focus on the purposes of schooling as an auspicious development, because it provides a solid basis on which to build future school reform efforts.

On December 4, 1996, the New York City Schools Chancellor Rudy Crew proposed that the city adopt the English, math, and science standards developed by the New Standards Project. New York City was the first school district to adopt the proposed standards in their entirety—a remarkable action, considering that the New Standards standards are based not on the lowest common denominator, but rather on high expectations and achievement. As *The Christian Science Monitor* said in an editorial, "If a set of standards with national scope can be successfully applied in the Big Apple, the lumbering school reform movement could kick into higher gear."

By early 1997, forty-nine states (all except Iowa) were committed to setting statewide academic standards.

Not long after Crew's announcement, and just before the president made his ringing endorsement, Resnick told me she believes we are embarked on a new era. She said, "We've been focused for so long on how to make standards—we may be seeing the shift, at last, to a focus on how to meet them!"

PUBLIC SCHOOL CHOICE: MISSION-FOCUSED EDUCATION
WITHOUT PRIVATIZATION

If the combination of high standards and schools with distinctive visions of how to meet these standards are the key to higher levels of school achievement for all students, what are the conditions in which both standards and distinctive schools can flourish? Many reformers have concluded that distinctive schools can be sustained only in a system where parents, teachers, and students can choose their schools. Choice within the public school system can provide an environment in which schools with a distinctive character and vision of how to achieve school success can attract parents, teachers, and students who share that vision.

Since consensus is only beginning to emerge among leaders of reform, and has certainly not reached most of the public, about the *methods* of teaching and learning most likely to achieve important educational goals, choice allows teachers and families to select schools reflecting their values and beliefs about the means of education. With sufficient choices for parents, children, and teachers, schools can afford to be different from one another, with a distinctive character, emphasis, and style of operations that appeal to some but not all.

This way of thinking about good schools—that, in fact, one size does not fit all—is, of course, the direct opposite of what so many policy makers are looking for. It flies directly against the mind-set that seeks to shape schools by imposing structures and rules that can be simultaneously applied to all of them. In the bureaucratic mind-set—even the bureaucratic reform mind-set—standardization is seen as an organizational imperative. The particulars that set schools apart from one another are seen as imperfections needing repair. But if it is the particulars that lie at the heart of good schools and explain their surprising successes, the new rules have to be different in kind from the old rules.

The new rules would include uniform basic protections against conflicts of interest and discrimination on the basis of race or ethnic origin; they would make it possible for schools to come together on such resources as science labs, better managed at levels above the individual school. But the new rules would give successful schools power and responsibility to design their own particulars and thus, in Deborah Meier's formulation, to surround students with powerful adults in a position to act on their behalf in open and publicly responsible ways and committed to shared educational and ethical principles.

Public school choice programs are now in successful operation throughout the nation. By 1993, 11 percent of all American children were attending public schools their families had chosen. The newest and most rapidly growing movement to provide publicly accountable options to parents, students, and educators within the public system is one variation on choice: the charter school movement.

Charter schools formalize the autonomy and freedom from regulation that in the past was sporadically dispensed to occasional innovators. A charter, usually issued by the state or local school board, allows groups of parents, teachers, or community-based organizations to establish a school that operates autonomously, free from local district and state regulations except for basic civil rights and health and safety requirements. In return, the school agrees to be held accountable for improving student achievement.

By late 1996, twenty-five states had authorized nearly five hundred charter schools, with many more on the drawing board. Chester Finn, who visited thirty-five such schools in seven states, considers them "the most vibrant force in public education." He reported that some of the schools emphasized book-centered "core knowledge," while others stressed "learning by doing," but all were fulfilling parents' demands for safety, order, basic skills, and dedicated teachers.

No one can predict how much charter schools will grow. They may remain merely an escape valve for a small minority of teachers and parents who have a clear concept of how teaching and learning should occur, and therefore want to extricate their schools from regulation and school board oversight. Or charter schools could become the norm. In some communities, all public schools might eventually be operated by independent groups of teachers, parents, community organizations, teachers' unions, or independent nonprofits. Local school boards would evolve from operating a highly regulated bureaucracy to managing a system of individual schools, each with its own mission and clientele. The school board would be responsible for ensuring that there is a school for every student, that the claims made by schools are valid, that what students learn in elementary school fits with what they will learn in middle school and high school, and that health, safety, and nondiscrimination requirements are observed. Representing a balance of public and private interests in education, a reformed local school board could shut down a charter school where students were not achieving agreed-upon academic results.

Many people, however, still have an almost visceral antipathy toward the idea of school choice. They fear that, even within the public sector, it could be a forerunner of abandoning public schooling altogether. They worry that it will lead to further advantages for the haves at the expense of the have-nots. They may believe that distinctive schools with specialized objectives violate equality of educational opportunity and are therefore undemocratic. Because of evidence that better-educated and more affluent parents are more likely to take advantage of choice, they worry about the youngsters left behind. After more fortunate students are siphoned off, would the youngsters whose parents didn't exercise choice be confined to even worse schools? Is it really possible in a choice system to guard against segregation by race, class, ethnic background, and income?

The recurrent findings that the schools that succeed today, even with students from disadvantaged backgrounds, *are* distinctive, and are considered distinctive by students, parents, and staff, suggest the necessity of finding ways of assuring equity that don't rely on uniformity. Parochial schools, Montessori schools, schools that prepare youngsters for careers in science or the performing arts have all been successful at least in part because they are organized around what researcher Paul Hill calls an "integrative principle."

A school's integrative principle is the basis on which it works as a whole organization rather than an aggregate of uncoordinated events and individuals. A school's integrative principle encompasses its theory of instruction, teaching, and learning. It structures decisions about what student learning the school considers most important, how the school motivates students, what the school demands of students, how the school selects and socializes teachers, and how the school maintains the confidence of parents and the broader community. Because the integrative principle has implications for the school's hiring and socialization of teachers, its relationships with parents and public authority figures, as well as the experiences it creates for students, it can only be maintained if the school has the decision-making autonomy that charter schools are designed to grant.

Most charter school arrangements establish the conditions of autonomy that Hill and others have identified as characterizing the most effective schools: school resources come in lump sum form so that leaders are not forced to add new programs and abandon old ones to meet funders' changing priorities; they make possible the stability in leadership and staffing so a group of collaborators can stay together and learn together; they allow for freedom of movement among schools by staff and families so people can find a school with a particular approach to instruction that suits them, rather than having to stand and fight the approaches of others that differ from the one they prefer.

Charter schools remove many of the impediments that make it difficult for schools to control their resources and activities, to hold to a consistent line of action, and to deviate from traditional ways of doing things. Whereas in the prevailing system, legislators, courts, and school administrators can order schools to take on new tasks and operate in new ways, and thus make it impossible for them to integrate their activities around a coherent approach to teaching and to relations between staff, students, and the community, charters are designed to protect a school's distinctive identity.

School choice through charter schools, then, becomes a facilitating condition to enable distinctive schools to thrive. It does not create them. It does not substitute for carefully crafted reforms. It is not, as Richard Rothstein points out, "the 'invisible hand' that makes schools improve without the hard work of teachers, parents, administrators, and students."

Of course, if choice is to be exercised within the public school system, there must be restrictions to assure that the integrative principle will not be some form of racial, religious, or gender supremacy. Bryk and colleagues caution that the distinctiveness that promotes organizational excellence could also become "breeding grounds for intolerance and exclusivity." The crux of whether a public school choice system is ultimately supportive or destructive of democratic ideals, they suggest, is whether the distinctiveness is aligned with American democratic ideals. The character, goals, and operating styles that make these schools distinctive must be reconciled with traditional beliefs in public schools as the place where children learn to be part of a larger society.

No one, of course, knows whether that can actually be done if public school choice and charter schools continue to grow and spread, perhaps to dominate in some states and some school districts. You don't have to be a bureaucrat or a liberal ideologue to worry about the possibility that students and teachers will sort themselves out into small, like-minded groups, protected from ever having to rub shoulders with anyone very different from themselves. Some of the people who worry remember pre–World War II big-city schools as their introduction to the wider world, their opportunity to discover children with strange faces and unfamiliar clothes and speech. "Learning was serious business," one of my friends who went through the New York City public schools recalls; "the dreaded Regents Exams loomed mysteriously. The sons and daughters of the dry cleaner and the man who sold papers and tobacco went on to win full scholarships to Harvard and Yale and Wellesley." But most important, as she thinks back, was that her school allowed her "to come to know a wide sample of humanity, and to live history and democracy in action." It is the one period of her life, she says, when she had a sense "of our whole civilization and all its variety and possibilities."

Are we prepared to give all that up? I think we must give up some of it for now, for we have grown too contentious, and we cannot arrive at enough of a consensus about the means of education to rely on bureaucracies to shape schools that will be uniform in character and uniformly good in quality. Public school choice may be a stage we must go through before we can return to a system of common schools. But in the meantime, public school choice seems like a way to improve student outcomes, and thereby to fend off pressures for universal vouchers and the complete privatization of schooling.

Vouchers offer another approach to choice, with much greater risks to democracy, survival of the public schools, and to the overall quality of education. Some voucher plans limit vouchers to low-income students, who may use them to attend private schools, as in Milwaukee and Cleveland, where black Democrats and white Republicans joined in persuading state legislatures to enact the enabling legislation. The rationale advanced for providing vouchers to low-income families is that the public schools have failed poor students and vouchers can purchase a decent education for some of these students, while shaking up the system by investing in competition. A variation of limited vouchers would make a specified share of school revenues available to all families in neighborhoods where schools have failed and show no signs of improving.

It is hard, though, to see how most voucher proposals—which would provide $1,000 to $1,500 a year—would help low-income children get into private schools charging many times that amount. The vouchers' main effect would be to transfer public funds from public school parents to private school parents through a tax subsidy. They would also leave many more children behind in a public school system with diminished resources.

Universal vouchers, on the other hand, that allocate funds to private, public, and religious schools based on the number of students choosing to attend would cause "unmitigated disaster" for the public schools. Most observers believe that universal vouchers would cause torrents of funds to flow from public schools to subsidize the more expensive private schools. This system has already had a trial run in Chile, where disciples of Milton Friedman, the conservative Chicago economist who originally proposed unregulated vouchers, persuaded the Pinochet government to try it. Class differences in education exploded and test scores of lower income students plummeted.

ASSISTANCE TO SCHOOLS IN SELECTING AND IMPLEMENTING
PROVEN INNOVATIONS

Over the past several years, many individual schools have adopted or adapted one of a number of schoolwide reforms that have been developed elsewhere, usually with a sound research base, often supported by a national network. Examples include Robert Slavin's Success for All and Roots and Wings, James Comer's School Development Program, Ed Zigler's Schools of the 21st Century, Henry Levin's Accelerated Schools, and Ted Sizer's Coalition of Essential Schools. The national networks established by each of these reform streams—which provide implementation materials, continuing professional development, and an ongoing connection with supportive outsiders—currently make it possible for schools to succeed with these innovations even though they may not get a great deal of support from their own districts.

Robert Slavin has concluded from his experience that there is an urgent need to allow more schools to learn about, select, and implement models of research-based schoolwide reform. That process could be made much more effective in his view if school districts, states, and other intermediaries set up a continuing process of identifying programs and practices that have been found effective, and whose sponsors have designed the necessary materials, manuals, technical assistance, mentoring, and training systems to make them replicable. States or school districts would provide information about such models to schools and communities through conferences and other means, would identify funds and other resources that could support implementation and evaluation of the innovations, and would build capacity to further spread successful innovations.

For the components of school reform that are marketed and chosen in this way, it will not be enough just to disseminate a set of ideas and principles or to provide the supporting materials. The school that chooses to adopt the innovation must provide staff with enough time to learn how the new approach is intended to work, and to adapt it to the school's own circumstances. As we saw in the chapter on replication, successful scale-up seems to require an intermediary who maintains a strong, continuing relationship with the replicator to support professional development, to help legitimate the new norms and new practice, to assist in coping with the resistance to and the unexpected consequences of the innovations, to collaborate in developing midcourse corrections, and to establish the networks through which innovators can learn from one another, support one another, and achieve a sense of common purpose. Effective professional development activities are especially crucial to assure that teaching practice actually changes, by allowing for feedback, trial and error, and problem solving over time.

NO SILVER BULLET, BUT ALIGNED REFORMS

No one reform will work in isolation. Since 1909, when Paul Ehrlich discovered the "silver bullet" of salvarsan to treat syphilis, the search has been on to find an equally simple and specific cure for virtually every other ill known to humankind. The search for silver bullets has been particularly fervid in school reform, because the alternative of applying an infinite number of reform variations to America's 88,000 schools and fifteen thousand school districts is so profoundly daunting.

So we get reduced class size or school uniforms or volunteer reading tutors as *the* answer. The history of school reform can be seen as a history of mistaking parts of the education system for the whole, as educators, policy makers, and the public attribute all problems to whatever piece they happen to know, and are then disappointed by the limited impact of their solutions.

Unhappily for the reformer, the evidence suggests that *many* changes must be made—in individual schools and in the systems in which they operate. And the changes must be coherently aligned with one another. The Productivity Consortium warns that "any reform that tackles only a piece of the problem will fail."

The pressures to narrow the scope of change, to substitute visibility for depth and process for product, and to limit reforms to a single, isolated, or diluted component explain the usually disappointing results. Complex institutions, we must finally learn, cannot be changed one circumscribed piece at a time.

More challenging standards and assessments alone will not raise student achievement. They must be accompanied by improved curriculum, better-trained educators, changes in the organization and management of schools, and often more resources—especially in the schools that have been systematically underfunded.

Structural changes in schools alone don't improve student performance. They help only if they support dedicated teachers making changes in teaching practices to solve identified problems of teaching and learning.

Changes in process without attention to content have little payoff. One school district's staff, studied by Elmore and colleagues, was primarily focused on "getting schools engaged in the *process* of changing themselves." There was no attention to any particular areas of content or practice; resource teachers were told to engage teachers in something—anything—that "the teachers would find useful in their classrooms." Very little real change resulted.

Site-based management, when it is not accompanied by other reforms, tends simply to transfer the fights among interest groups from the district to the building level, with no impact on student achievement.

If assessment is not aligned with curricular goals and content, there are no strong signals to either teachers or students about what is important for teachers to teach and for students to learn. The absence of that alignment means teachers have to divide their time between teaching a curriculum that stresses certain knowledge and skills, on the one hand, and preparing students for tests that assess different knowledge and skills.

Neither less regulation nor even more money, in themselves, bring fundamental change unless schools make strategic use of the new flexibility or new funds. A natural experiment involving sixteen elementary schools serving poor children in east Austin, Texas, showed that money alone doesn't mean better education. In 1989, the schools were identified as in need of special help because of high absenteeism and low achievement scores. Each was given $300,000 a year for five years, in addition to normal school funding, as part of the resolution of a court desegregation case. Five years and $24 million later, both attendance and achievement remained at previous low levels in fourteen of the sixteen schools. But in the other two, attendance rates rose steadily until they were among the city's highest, and achievement test scores rose to equal the city's average. The difference? The fourteen schools had no strategy for using the new funds. Those that reduced class size didn't make other changes the smaller classes made possible. The superintendent said that even when class size was brought down to ten, "You'd have two rows of five students, and the teacher would still be sitting up there in the front of the room, and still using ditto sheets like before."

The two schools that raised achievement also used much of the extra money to lower class size, but took advantage of the smaller classes to use a reading and math curriculum that the rest of the district used only with gifted and talented children. The two successful schools provided professional development opportunities to help teachers learn to teach the new curriculum effectively. They did all this explictly in pursuit of raising student achievement and found ways to engage teachers, parents, and students in devising ways of reaching these goals.

Widespread school success, it is clear, does not depend on individual techniques, practices, or even structures. The most promising efforts show that simply improving parts of schools or implementing one or two elements of reform isn't enough; schooling needs to be comprehensively redesigned. Many changes must be made simultaneously and made to fit together. This does not mean that a single change, made because the school community has agreed on its importance, will not send out a helpful signal. Reduced class size, school uniforms, or volunteer reading tutors can be a first step to energize a group that doesn't recognize its ability to make changes. But any of those steps alone will not bring lasting improvement.

Of course the reforms that require simultaneous attention to many different fundamental elements are the hardest to bring about—in education as elsewhere. The research and demonstration results that come out of the hothouse consist of a rich array of changes that produce a rich array of improved results. Yet those innovations typically shrivel or die in the real world—particularly in the real world of schooling. There may be no other sector in which power is so widely dispersed and therefore so difficult to mobilize behind a complex agenda for change. Weighing into the process are

fifteen thousand local school districts, fifty state boards of education, concerned parents and taxpayers everywhere, teachers, administrators, and a gamut of interest groups from textbook publishers to janitors' unions. It is a formidable task, therefore, to gather the many reform pieces, align them, and mobilize support.

But, as we have seen, that task has been made easier by the newly emerging consensus around the purposes of education, in the form of standards. Nevertheless, a huge gap remains between how reformers and the public view education reform.

Closing the Gap Between the Perceptions of Reformers and the Public

Unless the voting, taxpaying public becomes convinced that school reformers are acting in their interest, the formidable task of fundamental school reform will remain undone. Educators and community and national leaders must make sure that the public becomes better informed about today's educational realities. Educators and school reformers must show they are responding to the public's wishes, including a commitment to safety, order, discipline, and student mastery of the basics.

What the public needs to know about rising expenditures and declining productivity. When Yale University president Benno Schmidt resigned to head the Edison Project and create a national chain of private schools, he explained that he had given up on public schools. He said, "We have roughly doubled per-pupil spending in public schools since 1965," but the "nation's investment in educational improvement has produced very little return." This claim is almost universally accepted and is echoed by experts, from school finance analysts to public policy gurus. It is used to make the case that public education funds are scandalously wasted and that there is no need for additional funding.

But it's not true.

The big increases in funding over the past thirty years have gone to special education and other programs whose effects do not and were never expected to show up in higher academic achievement scores. The share of all school expenditures for special education quadrupled between 1967 and 1991. Thirty-eight percent of the new money spent in the early 1990s went to special education.

The narrowing of the achievement gap between minority students and others that occurred between 1977 and 1992 is the more extraordinary since hardly any new money went to urban schools. The

slight growth in regular education spending that did occur (per pupil expenditures grew by a little over 1 percent per year) was much greater in suburban than in urban districts. In urban districts, per-pupil spending on regular education grew hardly at all and would have declined in real terms had the districts not cut back on operations, maintenance, and administration.

What the public needs to know about who can learn at high levels. There has been an American belief that what goes on at school won't make much difference, either because the capacity for learning is fixed at birth or because schools cannot overcome the disadvantages of students from uneducated or unsupportive families. Parents, policy makers, and taxpayers who believe that academic ability is a fixed quantity and school success preordained, who see schools functioning more as sorting mechanisms than as institutions that change destinies, will never be mobilized to support the changes that schools must make.

Educator Lauren Resnick believes Americans assume deep down that aptitude is paramount in learning and that aptitude is largely hereditary. She points out that few have considered the possibility that "effort actually creates ability, that people can become smart by working hard at the right kinds of learning tasks." Educational psychologist Jeff Howard agrees, and reports on how hard it is to convince people of the research that shows "smart is not something you just are; smart is something you can get to be." Thus, the school reformers' conclusion that all children can learn falls on deaf ears because at some level we have always "known" that it's not so. We have always "known" that innate ability sets the upper limits on a child's prospects for learning, and that the great majority of American children are too dim to learn challenging material.

These suspicions are reinforced, of course, by primitive beliefs about the distribution of ability by race and ethnic origin. So when we hear that inner-city students are doing badly at school, our first reaction is to find our prejudices confirmed, not to ask what the schools should be doing differently.

The new brain research of course raises new questions in this realm. If the first three years of experience determine the structure of the brain, are the children who were neglected or abused in those early years destined to be exceptions to the idea that all children can learn? There is considerable agreement among the experts on this point: If we miss early opportunities to promote healthy development, they say, later learning will be harder and slower. The experts report that "As children move into the second decade of life, it ap-

pears to be more difficult to bring about change." But they emphasize that it is not impossible. Studies of resilience show that children
growing up in deprivation can become successful learners if they
attend good schools and have supportive adults in their lives.

But lingering doubts that schools can really make a difference may
explain why Public Agenda found neither teachers nor the public
particularly concerned that children with the greatest need for expert instruction are least likely to get it because the best teachers
gravitate to the schools that teach children with the fewest educational problems. Disadvantaged children, according to education reformer Dennis Doyle, "have a better chance for an equal and rigorous education, and whatever advancement it may bring, in Paris or
Tokyo than in one of America's big cities." Lacking the faith that
our schools can make a difference and educate all children well, we
are not outraged.

Harvard's Howard Gardner ascribes some of the public's doubts
to the efforts of conservative forces "to gut the public school system
altogether," to the media's propensity to give much more attention
to critics of school reform than to the work of the reformers, and to
"the media's insatiable thirst for bad news and concomitant reluctance to chronicle success, except as a curiosity." Journalist Sara
Mosle points to the media's inclination, when it does have good
news from the world of education, to tell the story in terms of extraordinary teachers, "long dear to screenwriters and to the editors
of Sunday feature magazines." Many of these stories do help to
explode the myth that children of color or children from poor families can't learn. But they don't inform citizens about the broader
conditions of education and how they might be improved in more
than one classroom at a time.

As a matter of fact, the past decade has produced plenty of evidence that should persuade skeptics that school reform efforts can
change outcomes and prospects even among students whose life circumstances did not predispose them to school success.

One of the early miracle-worker stories, about teacher Marva
Collins on CBS's *60 Minutes,* was more interesting than most because *60 Minutes* took the unusual step of actually doing long-term
follow-up.

In 1979, *60 Minutes* aired its original story about Marva Collins,
the Chicago teacher who started her own elementary school on the
city's West Side. Viewers saw reporter Morley Safer making his way
past the familiar signs of big-city blight—the broken windows, the

burned-out buildings, the abandoned cars—until he reached the oasis of Marva Collins's classroom. She was teaching Chaucer's *Canterbury Tales* to attentive inner-city African-American sixth graders. The children told Safer about the authors they liked—Chaucer, Dante, Dostoyevsky, Booker T. Washington, and Hans Christian Andersen. Collins explained to Safer that with love, hard work, and no-nonsense teaching, inner-city children could compete academically with anyone.

Many viewers were skeptical, none more than Charles Murray. In his book, *The Bell Curve*, he argued that the Marva Collins kind of success story is too good to be true, that there is no hard evidence of her success, and that any gains her pupils made in elementary school would soon fade. So *60 Minutes* decided to check. Producers found thirty-three of the thirty-four students they had shown in that classroom sixteen years earlier, and flew a group of them back to Chicago.

Of the thirty-three former students located by *60 Minutes,* all were working or in school. One was a tailor who expects to be putting out his own line of clothes, one a police officer, two were corrections officers, one a restaurant buyer, one an office manager, one the owner of a transportation company, one an army officer, three were teachers, and one works in the state's attorney's office. Two were in law school and two were university students. And one, Erika Pace, whose family had been told before she got to Marva Collins that she was borderline retarded and would never learn to read, had just graduated from college *summa cum laude!*

Of course there are teachers and schools in every part of the country succeeding daily with children who would have been written off elsewhere. Many of the schools have been shaped and nurtured by a charismatic founder. If they are in the public sector, powerful protectors shield them from rigid rules and intrusive bureaucrats. Their experience is inspiring and makes clear that rotten outcomes are not preordained for the children of the inner city. But the individual successes do not answer the question of whether each miracle worker can change only one classroom of children at a time. Can outcomes also be changed when reform is scaled up to include large numbers of children and teachers and more than a single school? The answer to this question is only beginning to come in—because it is only very recently that school reformers have begun to address the problem of scale.

Success for All (described in Chapter 2), which aims at assuring that all children read easily by the time they leave third grade, has a carefully evaluated record of widespread effectiveness. Students in fifteen Success for All schools in seven states achieved higher reading levels, had better attendance, and were less likely to be placed in special education or retained a grade than their peers. And the gap between Success for All students' reading scores and their peers' has been increasing in each year of the program.

The Accelerated Schools Project of Henry Levin at Stanford University has expanded over nine years from its original two pilot schools to over seven hundred elementary and middle schools serving poverty populations in seven states. Where the program has been in place for more than two years, fewer children are retained a grade or placed in special education, and student achievement has progressed from below grade level to above grade level.

Findings like these are being repeated all over the country. They converge to demonstrate that school reform deep enough to affect student outcomes can occur on a large scale within the public school system, utilizing ordinary teachers.

What the public must know about the new skills children need and how they are most likely to acquire them. The public's understanding is crucial. It is the public that controls directly much of the money going to the schools, that will ultimately decide whether public schools should be abandoned to the marketplace, and that can support or impede reform in local schools. The new ideas about what students should know and be able to do, how students should be taught and how they should be assessed challenge the conceptions that students, parents, educators, the public, and policy makers are familiar and comfortable with. Many who are dubious about what's going on in the schools today have not grasped the enormous difference between the intellectual requirements of the economy of the future and the world of their own past. American students and parents express high levels of satisfaction with average, even mediocre educational performance, but employers and colleges don't. Many Americans are not aware that all children now need "a challenging and rigorous education . . . a thinking-oriented curriculum." That they must have had the experience of striving to understand something in depth and applying that understanding to new and unfamiliar situations. That many of the skills children need to learn cannot be assessed with multiple-choice tests.

Educators must become more responsive to public demands. Educators must provide evidence that they are aware of and share the public's demands for safety, order, and discipline in the schools, and for student mastery of the basics.

Public Agenda found that both teachers and the public consider lack of order a top problem in the schools, and both believe that neither teaching nor learning can occur without order. They yearn for a return of civility. "Large majorities of teachers and the public name restoring order in schools as a top priority. What's more, they share an agreed-upon agenda on how to accomplish this." Both teachers and the public support proposals to expel students who bring illegal drugs or weapons to school, and to remove "persistent troublemakers" from class.

My own view is that we need much better evidence than we now have about the effects of various ways of dealing with troublemakers and about how to educate the youngsters who may be expelled. In the meantime, I agree with Albert Shanker's advocacy of separate education facilities for chronically disruptive students. I share his fear that if schools continue to "allow the education of the majority of students in a class to be destroyed by one . . . there will be mounting pressure from parents for vouchers and for other alternatives to public schools, and that pressure will ultimately succeed."

As for the academic agenda, an overwhelming 98 percent of teachers and 92 percent of the public consider it essential that schools teach basic reading, writing, and math skills. Citizens want students to master "higher order" skills but only *after* they have mastered the basics. Teachers are as wary as the public about such teaching innovations as the early use of calculators, teaching composition without teaching spelling and grammar, and grouping students of different abilities together. Only a bare majority of the public agrees with educators that multiple-choice exams should be replaced with essays.

Educators are beginning to convince the public to think about what works in education in ways that better reflect new research and experience. They are also seeing the advantages of integrating the concerns of a skeptical public into their reform strategies.

We now turn to examine the role of schools in response to family and community breakdown, an arena still plagued by many unsolved conundrums.

Strengthening Community Supports for School Success

Stephen O'Connor, who tries to reach inner-city children by teaching creative writing, tells of a student who wrote about watching his father shot and killed. Another wrote about seeing her best friend killed as they walked together to the grocery store. A third wrote about being so badly neglected that she lost all her hair when she was seven. Mr. O'Connor says his greatest frustration is the "relentless intrusion of social problems into the classroom." He sees the poor performance of American students as "a symptom of our neglect of the many social crises that afflict our nation."

There is near unanimity that the intrusion of social problems into the classroom vastly complicates the job of schools but little agreement on solutions, or indeed on the extent the success of other reforms depends on finding those solutions.

Patricia Graham, former dean of the Harvard School of Education, says it is virtually impossible to reach academic goals when "so many children live in families and communities that are in utter disarray, when so many live in abject poverty without sufficient food, health care, or adequate housing . . . when so many children live in families and communities where learning has never been taken seriously, where books are never read, where television is watched extensively on a daily basis. . . ."

For children whose nonacademic needs are met at home, the schools are fundamentally working, even if they don't educate all children to their full potential. One study of Indo-Chinese refugee children showed them succeeding at school although they came from poor families because they had "the requisite familial and social supports" from home.

But ever fewer children come to school with "the requisite familial and social supports," and that is the crux of the problem. More and more children come to school from worlds that lessen their chance of success in school. Whether they are tired, hungry, sick, disruptive, unmotivated, undisciplined, disturbed, neglected, or abused, they arrive with problems that interfere with their own or others' learning.

In the past, extended family, neighbors, and teachers shared responsibility for children. The key was redundancy. Especially in minority neighborhoods, if a parent was unavailable, other adults were on hand to hurry a dawdling child to school, teach a new skill, or set another place at the table. Today, overstressed heads of single-parent families work long hours away from home and their neighborhood. Even churches and settlement houses have abandoned many depleted neighborhoods. Redundancy has been lost, and with it much of the mortar that kept children from falling between the cracks.

Teachers feel as though they are expected to pick up the pieces. They tell pollsters and focus groups that social problems are at the top of their concerns. A teacher in Connecticut says, "All the social problems of our communities have been thrown at the teacher. You have to be a psychologist, you have to be a nurse, you have to be a baby-sitter, and I've done all those jobs and more."

The wish, and often the need, to respond to children's urgent unmet needs saps the academic energies of teachers, students, and administrators. Students' problems, addressed or ignored, steal time from teaching and learning. Deborah Wadsworth of Public Agenda says "high standards, advanced knowledge, top-notch academic mastery seem to be routinely sacrificed in an ongoing educational triage." If classroom teachers turn out not to be fierce champions of high-level academic learning (and surveys show they are not), if they rank maintaining order, discipline, and civility in the classroom over achieving high academic standards (and surveys show they do), their mind-set and their training may be in part responsible, but surely the circumstances of large numbers of children with serious problems must play a big part. Principal Learie Phillip of Roosevelt High School in Washington, D.C., says that although he knows his main function is to be an instructional leader, he spends 60 to 70 percent of his time "monitoring the hallway to enforce discipline."

Teachers find it terribly difficult to teach students whose motivation to learn is not given a high priority by peers, families, and much of the broader culture.

A ten-year, three-university study of twenty thousand students from diverse backgrounds published in 1996 concluded that a teenage culture that frowns on school success will defeat every effort at school reform. The researchers may have overstated their point, because there are plenty of schools that have, in fact, triumphed over the teenage culture. They are right, however, in contending that it is hard to make everything else work—curriculum overhaul, tougher standards, improved professional development—if students do not come to school interested in learning.

This problem is not limited to but is particularly acute in the inner city.

The antiachievement ethic of schools in areas of concentrated poverty is troubling to both outsiders and inner-city residents. But it is not so hard to understand, says Geoffrey Canada, who returned to the Harlem of his childhood as director of the Rheedlen Centers for Children. "Many children feel that their lives are so harsh and so uncertain," he says, "that when they see a child doing well in school and adopting middle-class norms and attitudes it triggers the reaction 'You think I'm going to suffer a life of fear, fear for my future, fear for my very existence, and you're gonna just waltz through life and make it out of here? No way. You ought to feel pain and fear and doubt just like the rest of us.'"

The National Urban League's Hugh Price says that the negative pressures often reach the point where the minority youngsters who are succeeding at school try to hide their achievements: "At Ballou High School in Washington D.C. achievers were so embarrassed and intimidated that those who'd won academic honors were afraid to attend the awards ceremonies."

Canada, Price, and many other African-American leaders are engaged in significant new efforts to counteract these forces, and to persuade inner-city youngsters that, in Bob Herbert's words, "being smart, like being black, is nothing to be ashamed of."

Some educators respond to the difficulties of the era by arguing that higher rates of school success must await massive changes in society. They take comfort in the idea of schools as helpless in the face of powerful outside forces. As a Seattle teacher put it, "The school system isn't broken, society is broken." Paul Houston, executive director of the American Association of School Administrators, says it makes no sense to try to "fix" the schools. It is not schools, he argued, but "our society that is failing our children and . . . we cannot fix the schools outside of their societal context." Echoing the words of the late, highly respected education leader Ernest O. Boyer, he says, "We cannot have islands of academic excellence in a sea of community indifference."

The services, supports, and community connections that schools mobilized in the past have become inadequate. Efforts to get help for children with complex problems take away from teaching time and are unproductive when teachers lack the necessary time and training, when school counselors and school nurses are overwhelmed and lack the needed skills, and when community agencies are overwhelmed, inaccessible, or simply nonexistent.

SCHOOL RESPONSES TO FAMILY AND COMMUNITY BREAKDOWN

Many schools and school districts feel they cannot stand idly by, and must play a role in buffering children against the powerful outside forces that undermine their academic success. Most have proceeded by trial and error in a murky terrain. They respond in one or a combination of the following ways: (1) They have improvised and they have linked to whatever services are out there. (2) They have put their buildings and playgrounds at the disposal of the neighborhood. (3) They have become partners in efforts to reform services and build communities. (4) They have supported families as valued partners in promoting children's learning.

Schools that have tried to respond by *improvising and linking* to available health and social services have sometimes succeeded—but only in an environment where the services that were available came close to what was needed. In the main, improvising and linking have turned out to be weak solutions because what's out there to link with—mainly traditional categorical agencies—often can't provide the help that's required. Even when community agencies are persuaded to offer "one-stop shopping," making services available at the school, the relocated services often bring their old flaws with them. Locating services on school premises or strengthening referral networks do not, by themselves, make categorical services coherent. Relocation will not make impersonal and overspecialized services suddenly responsive to the complex needs of children, families, and communities.

Improvising and linking are also unlikely to be enough to assure that a dependable and appropriate set of services and supports will be in place for teachers to mobilize. Teachers who are unsure where to draw the boundary between responding to students' nonacademic needs in the interests of more effective teaching on the one hand, and becoming a therapist to their students on the other, need to know they can rely on high-quality backup services. Even a teacher trying only to be aware of the difficulties with which her students are contending can get into bad trouble, as the following story illustrates:

> Barbara Jenner, a teaching supervisor, observes that a new teacher is having difficulty teaching a twelve-year-old girl in her class. To model effective teacher behavior, Jenner puts her arm around the girl and says, "I just want you to know that I love you. Even when I'm annoyed at you, even when you do and say not nice things, I'll still love you." The girl begins to cry. Between sobs, the girl tells of being molested when she was nine, about being called ugly as long as she could remember, about being embarrassed by her frumpy clothes and her hair, about having to take care of two younger siblings while her mother worked a night job, of being too tired to do her homework, of being afraid to walk home after school. Ms. Jenner's heart sinks. She had reached this girl, gotten her to bare her soul, and in her own way to ask for help—help that she has no way of providing. "Beyond taking her home with me for good, there was absolutely nothing I could do about the plight of this child. For weeks I felt as though I had betrayed her."

This story suggests that it may be risky to reach out to students, showing that you care about them, in the absence of professional backup that can be trusted and rapidly mobilized.

Many schools *are putting their buildings and playgrounds at the disposal of the neighborhood,* and seem to be pleased with the results. Most expect a long-term payoff in higher rates of school success. Many parents and other residents feel connected to these schools in a way they never were before. Frequently the school building is the only facility in a depleted neighborhood with an avowed public purpose, and schools are the only functioning infrastructure, both physically and administratively. Schools that become community schools stay open evenings and weekends and often become hubs for neighborhood activities of many kinds. Unlike a welfare office or mental health center, schools are a nonstigmatizing setting (especially if parents feel free to come there for reasons other than that their child is in trouble).

Some of the most impressive successes have happened when community-based organizations arrange, directly or through intermediaries, to organize a full array of community services and supports on school grounds. Examples include the Beacon schools in New York City (see Chapter 2) and Caring Communities in Missouri (see Chapter 3). In the most promising developments, the school makes its physical facilities available, but the community-based organization mobilizes the services and supports and becomes the agent of the community's interests.

Recognizing that schools are rarely in a position to reform services on their own, many *schools have become partners in community efforts to reform services and build communities.* These schools are aware that, especially in depleted neighborhoods, school success requires more than just formal, specialized services. It also depends on the creation of informal helping networks, including church and social ties, family support services, youth development programs, mentoring, recreational opportunities, and strong bonds among adults. This recognition gives schools an important place at the table where community reform is being organized, but does not require them to take sole responsibility for its success.

In his involvement with school reform efforts, Frank Farrow says he has observed that teachers in schools that have become active partners in a community's concerted efforts to assure needed services and supports are in place are *less* likely to feel pressure to perform a social work role at the expense of academics. He encounters the teacher who is overwhelmed with having "to be everything to these students" *only* in schools that haven't gotten very far in sorting out their roles and those of other community institutions.

The experience of school staff in Missouri's Caring Communities schools supports Farrow's conclusion. There (see Chapter 3), teachers who had once been kept at arm's length by human service professionals, were trained to spot signs of trouble in their pupils—from slumps in classroom performance to depression—and to convey their concerns to Caring Communities coordinators. "The greatest accomplishment of Caring Communities is that I feel relieved of responsibility for social problems," said one teacher. "I can really teach."

Support of families for children's schools and learning is increasingly coming to be seen as crucial, and *schools are seeking out families as valued partners.* All children learn best when parents and teachers share similar visions, when there is a "sense of constancy" between home and school, says sociologist Sara Lawrence-Lightfoot. That sense of constancy, however, is much harder to achieve today than it used to be.

Urbanization, increased mobility, fewer informal connections at the church or supermarket, greater demands on parents' time, and more concentrated poverty have all widened the distance between home and school. The distance is of course greatest for children of parents whose class, race, education, and family income differ most from those of the school staff. Most poor and minority parents have a passionate regard for education. Yet they often don't know how to translate their yearning for their children's success at school into useful action. Many also are acutely aware of the antiacademic and antiachievement gospel to which their children are exposed, and would welcome school efforts to help them counter media and peer pressures.

Schools, in turn, even when they see the need for deeper parent involvement, may be discouraged because it often seems that there is no one out there to work with. Enlisting today's overwhelmed and overstressed—and sometimes alienated—parents requires more skill and ingenuity than ever before.

But slowly, schools are learning how to help more families—especially those who would not become involved on their own—to become and stay involved in their children's education. Research and experience have started to show how much impact family involvement can have on promoting the chances of success at school, especially when schools shift from inviting occasional attendance at PTA meetings to seeking genuine partnership with families.

School-family partnerships can increase student motivation and academic achievement. Even families long considered "unreachable" can be reached. When schools do make special efforts to bridge cultural and social gaps and enlist parents as allies, that partnership can overcome barriers of family structure, race, social class, parent education, and income.

The more ways schools offer parents to become partners, the more effective the connections become. Schools that build successful partnerships respect families, and often welcome them with special facilities for parents to meet with one another and school staff. These schools help parents monitor and assist their children's learning at home. They are in touch with parents about their children's work—when it's wonderful as well as when there are complaints. They use technology to improve communication with families—by giving teachers telephones, voice mail, and e-mail capacity. They enlist parents as volunteers in classrooms, libraries and offices, and for school trips and events. Many schools also now include parents in decision making and governance.

The evidence is now clear that the cycle of distrust between schools and communities can be broken, and that doing so has an impact on academic achievement. But while there is rapid movement in the right direction, only a minority of schools are acting vigorously on the belief that parents are valuable contributors to children's school learning.

LESSONS FROM SCHOOL-COMMUNITY CONNECTIONS

Although the picture of the place where schools, services, communities, and families intersect is still murky, at least four conclusions are supported by current experience.

1. *Schools can become islands of hope in otherwise devastated neighborhoods.* When schools and communities work together to give poor children the supports typically enjoyed by children in middle-class neighborhoods, they help children avoid a culture of failure. Schools can go far to become part of the community, to make families their allies, to respond to children and their families, and to acknowledge their complex lives. Schools can welcome community-based organizations and family support centers, and their buildings can become hubs for community services.

2. *Schools should not be asked to take responsibility for a service-reform and community-building agenda.* Society must put limits on the demands placed on schools. There is growing consensus

that it is costly and not wise to make beleaguered schools responsible for reforming services and the community infrastructure. They must become *part* of the solution but should not be required to *be* the solution or to be the lone leader in finding the solution.

Where an organization with deep roots in the community takes responsibility for arranging with a school to make its premises available to become a combination settlement house, center for reformed services and primary supports, and the headquarters of a neighborhood-wide community-building effort, that is an unalloyed plus that will ultimately be reflected in higher rates of student academic achievement. But asking a school to take responsibility for doing the same thing can have high costs in energy diverted from academic goals. In a major policy study, the business leaders of the Committee on Economic Development encouraged communities to *place* services in schools and to *deliver* services through schools, but insisted that the task of making appropriate services available should not become the *responsibility* of schools.

At the intersection of schools, services, and communities, it has been easier to know what needs to be done than to figure out and agree on who should do it. Because there is no institution in most communities that takes responsibility for improving outcomes among all the children of a given neighborhood or community, many have tried to assign that role to schools by default.

Especially in communities that have unraveled, where few other institutional resources remain, efforts to mobilize the supports that children need to succeed at school quickly come up against the absence of any entity that is both administratively and politically a logical repository of responsibility. Our distrust of government seems to have gone so far as to leave no public entity other than the schools we dare draw upon to address the missing services, supports, and community infrastructure. And yet, if we pile on the schools every burden no one else will assume, we risk finding that they are not educating our children properly.

What is needed is a broad entity that can take responsibility for the many supports needed for school success, and for the larger array of child outcomes that communities can agree on. Schools alone should not be expected to assume the task of finding or creating that entity; others in the community must help.

Obviously this is a challenge that goes well beyond school reform, but it is put in bold relief by the recognition that school success cannot be achieved by schools alone, and that there is no institution now in existence that could reasonably be asked, in all American communities, to step in to fill the vacuum.

In the meantime, urgent unanswered questions remain, as they must when the schools are trying to educate children put at risk by their environments. Should we applaud or protest when we read that Chicago teacher Corla Hawkins has enlisted her principal in converting unused school space into a dormitory to provide a home as well as a school for neglected children? (She says she knows that schools are supposed to be for academic learning, "but these kids have to come to school to get socks and gloves because they have nothing. . . .") Should we be grateful or disapproving of the principal who keeps in her office a closet full of clothes she can distribute, or a washing machine to launder students' clothes?

3. *Intermediaries can help.* One way that communities have filled the vacuum between what students need to succeed at school and the schools' limited capacity to meet those needs is through intermediaries capable of convening stakeholders, providing and analyzing data, and building local capacity for reform. Among the best known of the locally based intermediaries is Oakland's Urban Strategies Council. From its inception, the Urban Strategies Council has focused on supporting school success, especially among the poor and minority children who were being left behind, and has been able to link schools, services, and the community.

The Youth Development Institute of the Fund for the City of New York played a crucial intermediary role in developing and sustaining the Beacon schools, as we saw in Chapter 2. Another innovative intermediary is the California Partnership for Comprehensive, Integrated, School-linked Services, created by a consortium of foundations together with California's governor and the state superintendent of education. It has been able to help communities to use state "Healthy Start" funds to place services for children and families at or near school sites, and to make the current service-delivery system more comprehensive, integrated, flexible, and family focused.

4. *In the most depleted neighborhoods, services are not enough.* Services designed on the premise that individual defects are the problem and services the solution will help some children and even some of their families. Such services won't be enough, however, in schools where the majority of children in every classroom are burdened by multiple risk factors predisposing them to rotten

outcomes. Especially in neighborhoods where disadvantage is more than a private misfortune, requiring more than an expert to treat a series of individual "deficits," services, even when efficiently coordinated, are unlikely to be the answer. In these neighborhoods particularly, much experimentation is still needed to find the best ways to build on what we have learned about how communities can organize to support universal school success.

Forging the Essential Connections Between Schools and Work

We have seen that we know enough to set all young children on a trajectory to school success. We know the characteristics of schools that succeed, and the conditions that support effective schools. We also know enough to be able to bridge the void that now exists between school and work, to which we now turn.

America has the worst school-to-work transition process of any industrialized nation, says former Secretary of Labor Ray Marshall. Educator Lauren Resnick says the United States is locked into a "peculiarly dysfunctional relationship between education and work." William Julius Wilson reports that the failure to address the school-to-work transition for noncollege-bound youth has reached crisis proportions in the inner city.

What is going on here?

The problem this country has in helping young people go from school to work stems partly from our unsystematic approach to large social problems, but also from our democratic aspirations. Unlike Europeans, Americans like the idea of keeping options open well into adulthood. But we have not faced up to the cost of doing so in today's high-tech labor market. Hilary Pennington of Jobs for the Future told the Clinton Economic Conference in 1992 that young people not headed for college are on a path to nowhere. "Under the guise of opportunity and free choice, we leave them largely to flounder alone in the labor market, from low-wage job to dead-end job through their 20s."

Unintentionally, we have created a world in which the only reliable way to enter the workforce on a career track is through graduation from college. Resnick observes that while college graduates "are eased gently into economic and civic adulthood by our established institutions, public and private, the other three quarters are left to fend for themselves in an increasingly unfriendly and undependable world." Clearly, if only half of high school graduates even enter college, and only half of that group graduates, the vast majority never even have a shot at a career in the growing information economy.

The notion of bypassing this problem by increasing the number of young people who go to college is fanciful and wasteful. It is true that virtually all of the jobs of the future will require high skills. But they wouldn't all require a college education if the high schools taught what they are supposed to teach, and if there were better connections between high schools and the world of work.

Most inner-city high schools lack even the most rudimentary supports for students who are not on a college track. William Julius Wilson pointed out to the Clinton Economic Conference that school counselors rarely know of present and future labor market requirements. They have little time and less training to help high school students in danger of not finding a decent job to prepare for noncollege careers and to connect them with job opportunities.

Unlike employers in Germany and Japan, U.S. employers offering good jobs with a stable future and some chance for advancement usually do not hire workers straight out of high school. As a result, many young people drift from one short-term minimum-wage job to another, with frequent periods of unemployment in between. As Resnick points out, they get the message that "society doesn't need or want them as responsible adults. For many young people, drifting and lack of commitment become a way of life."

This is a big problem for all American youths, and especially minority youngsters. It is a major catastrophe in the inner city, where the jobless rate among black male high school dropouts ages sixteen to twenty-four is 70 percent! The fact that employers tend not to hire young people, even high school graduates, until they have reached their mid-twenties means, as Wilson puts it, that "for about six years, these kids are floundering around. . . . By October, several months after they graduate from high school in June, only about 42 percent of black kids have jobs compared with 69 percent of white kids. And in the inner city, the numbers are even worse. . . . So what do these kids do while they're waiting six years trying to survive?" A lot of them turn to drugs and crime.

Wilson's Chicago findings are echoed by a 1994 University of Pennsylvania survey of three thousand employers across the country, which found most companies afraid to hire young people, viewing them as unreliable workers. "We were surprised at just how much animosity there is toward young people in the employer community," said Robert Zemsky, co-director of the group that developed the survey and interviewed employers. "In the focus groups the response was almost scatological. It's not clear how much this really had to do with young people and how much it's just something in the culture now that young people get dumped upon. The trouble is if you dump on young people long enough, it becomes a self-fulfilling prophecy."

Geoffrey Canada reports the same thing happening to young people in Harlem. Because so many of the jobs available without high-level skills are gone, he says, "We have young people who start off at 14, 15, or 16, really excited about work . . . out with their working papers knocking on doors, and they find that there are no jobs. They become 17, 18, 19—the same thing. No jobs. And after a while, the resilient behavior you need to continue looking can be lost."

Most thoughtful observers believe that this appalling situation will not change until there is an entirely new system for making the school-to-work transition, with diverse pathways from one to the other. There may be no more urgent task for educators and business leaders than the creation of such a system.

A workable system would include many elements already operating separately somewhere:

- Apprenticeship opportunities using the workplace as a learning place, run by unions, trade associations, and schools. Learning takes place both in school and at the worksite.
- Career Academies, usually a school within a school, integrating academic and vocational instruction around a broad career theme.
- Cooperative education, providing part-time jobs during the school year, often coordinated with students' specific career interests.
- School-based enterprises, providing work and entrepreneurial experience in fields ranging from restaurants and child care to construction and auto repair.

Efforts along these lines are now being energized and supported by the federal School-to-Work Opportunities Act of 1994. The act is still limited to supporting demonstrations, and is not yet funded at a scale that would give it national impact on the school-to-work problem. But it does specify an unusual federal role. Unlike much past legislation, the act asks states to develop their own programs, to build on existing institutions, and to weave the various elements together into a coherent system. The act also encourages wide variability to reflect the diversity of community needs and people involved. Widely lauded as one of the least restrictive laws on the statute books, it uses performance standards to monitor the system without prescribing cumbersome rules and procedures.

The school-to-work legislation also enables communities to act on research showing the importance of a young person's close attachment to a caring and successful adult. That adult—a mentor, role model, and coach—supplements what teachers, neighbors, and family members provide, particularly when traditional community supports are lacking.

The results of promising demonstrations that started well before the passage of the act are now becoming available. Data from more than two hundred Career Academies now in operation nationwide show that they integrate academic and vocational instruction and provide work-based learning opportunities. They restructure high schools into smaller, more personalized schools and allow teachers more influence over their work. Ten Academies studied by the Manpower Demonstration Research Corporation varied in ways that underscored their ability to adapt to community needs and circumstances, and that enabled them to attract a wide range of students, ranging from those in danger of dropping out or performing poorly to those doing well in school. A study of another ten sites in California found that "Academy students had better attendance, failed fewer courses, earned more credits, got better grades, and were more likely to graduate than their peers in a comparison group."

The new school-to-work strategies recognize that most students learn best in context—when they see how knowledge is actually used outside the school, especially in a work setting. The workplace becomes a learning laboratory where young people can experience the relevance of school knowledge in the "real world." This perspective dovetails neatly with the new theoretical findings from cognitive research. Both the theory and the practice place a premium on dissolving the barrier between abstract and hands-on learning.

Today's big challenge in the school-to-work domain is, of course, the same as the challenge in every other arena with promising models. How do we go from a few precious examples to a system that will enable millions of students to move smoothly from school to work? The challenge is not only to expand the number of individual interventions but to create a coherent system. "Most places are doing one aspect," Hilary Pennington says. "They're working on changing the schools, or the workplace, or the post-secondary connection. The key implementation challenge is to help places move toward doing all three things well."

Wisconsin is probably closest to taking such a systematic approach. In his persuasive book, *Rethinking America,* journalist Hedrick Smith describes that state's comprehensive approach to the school-to-work transition. He tells the story of John Torinus, an entrepreneur who runs a high-tech graphics and printing business in West Bend, Wisconsin. Torinus had become concerned when he couldn't find qualified workers coming out of local high schools. "We had illiterates, people who couldn't read blueprints, people who couldn't do simple decimals," he said. Torinus was asked to join a group of businesspeople accompanying Governor Tommy Thompson's Commission on Youth on a trip to look at the German school-to-work system. He returned convinced that the German system is more democratic than the American system because "it develops the potential of more young people and puts more young people on track toward a solid economic future." Torinus and Wisconsin State Schools Superintendent Bert Grover collaborated to bring to Wisconsin the German training system. They found average high school students who were turned off by school itching to get into the work world. Collaborating with a local high school, they designed a world-standard curriculum, tying together academic and job skills and arranging for teenagers to study part-time and work part-time and receive pay for their work.

In 1992 Torinus took on his first eleven apprentices, eight more the following year, ten more the next. He said, "The results were astounding. Mediocre students started making the dean's list." After they graduated, Torinus hired every apprentice he could.

Wisconsin's dual-education program now sends 450 apprentices from eighty-five schools into more than two hundred businesses in nine different industries, from banking and health care to small business and manufacturing, linking education in the classroom with education at the work site. Smith observes, "These youngsters are treated like adults and expected to perform well at the workplace. They are also beginning to see their education as relevant to the world they want to grow up into. That changes their motivation—and their performance."

Coming Up: An Extraordinary Era in Education

We are embarking on an extraordinary era in education in America. The president and the people agree that we must have an education system adequate to meet the twenty-first-century needs of a prosperous, high-tech, democratic nation. We can now assure that parents and their babies in the earliest years will have the support they need so children will arrive at school with a zest for school learning. We can act now to make first one and then two years of pre-kindergarten education universal, and to make family supportive services available to every family with an infant or toddler. We must align what we know about school reform, including standards that will focus schools on academic learning, professional development to support effective teaching, and enough opportunities for choice within the public school system, to enable schools to become mission-oriented communities of effective learning. We must act on what we know to create stronger community supports for school success, and to bridge the void between school and work.

As never before, we can shape our education system in the years ahead to become the powerful instrument that will enable all America's children to become all they hope they can be, and more.

Part III

Rebuilding Communities

The next and final chapter describes seven place-based
neighborhood transformation initiatives. All have
created synergy by putting together a wealth of
knowledge and experience from many different domains.
They show how extraordinary, but still underestimated,
neighborhood transformation efforts could combine into
a major national strategy to combat poverty, rebuild the
inner city, and reverse the growth of an American
underclass.

9

Synergy: Putting It All Together to Transform Neighborhoods

WHEN LEGENDARY BUILDER James Rouse died on April 9, 1996, the obituaries on the network news and in the newspapers quoted his favorite saying, "Whatever ought to be, can be." Friends and colleagues had often heard him say it, and they cited it to justify calling Rouse a visionary. They cited it to explain his long string of extraordinary achievements, including Columbia, the town he founded in Maryland, and the "festival marketplaces" he invented— Harbor Place in Baltimore and Faneuil Hall in Boston. But most of all, they relied on it to explain how he came, in the last fifteen years of his life, to focus his boundless genius, determination, and inspiration on the transformation of inner-city neighborhoods.

I remember the first time I encountered Rouse's passion for changing the world. It was 1990, and he had gathered a few of us over dinner in a hotel dining room overlooking the Baltimore harbor to solicit advice on next steps for his work in Baltimore's Sandtown neighborhood. He asked us to join hands as he said grace, and then—his eyes shining—explained his purpose. He was determined to demonstrate that it was possible to transform life at the bottom, in neighborhoods like Sandtown, and that it would cost less to do this than not to do it. He told us that he was filled with horror at the lives people live at the bottom of the American city, and filled with hope that he could show that this need not be. He told us of his conviction that we cannot remain indifferent to the "largest aggregation of homeless, jobless, school dropouts, drug addicts, people living in misery in the civilized world." That the nation cannot survive as a world leader with millions of poor people living at the bottom; that unless we create a good life for low-income people, "we are dead as a country." And he was determined to prove that the downward spiral could be reversed.

We were a sophisticated group around that table, but we were awed by this man's determination. He must have misunderstood the silence because he went on, "When I talked about building Columbia, as an integrated city in the Maryland of the 1960s, they said I was crazy. But Columbia is thriving today as an integrated city. When I undertook Harbor Place in the late seventies, they said it wasn't possible to build a marketplace and get people to come back to the city. Baltimore was dead, the inner harbor was a stinking mess. Today eighteen million tourists come to the inner harbor every year. I'm just as convinced we can turn Sandtown around. We can because we must."

That is the message he was able to convey. Three years later, a Sandtown resident spoke to an interviewer about James Rouse. "The man has been inspired," he said. "He's on a mission and he cannot fail because he's been sent, and he will succeed just like we will, because he is God-sent." Rouse himself noted that he "feels the hand of the Lord" on his shoulder a lot of the time.

Here was a man both so practical and so spiritual that he could speak the language of Baltimore's mayor, of the city's poorest residents, and of his fellow businesspersons while feeling the Lord's hand. Rouse and the Enterprise Foundation he established with his wife, Patty Rouse, were ready to help the mayor and the neighborhood take on all the "sick systems" at once. Together they would show that seventy-two abandoned city blocks could be restored by building affordable housing and assuring public safety, by simultaneously improving the school, health, justice, and human services systems, and by providing job training and economic opportunity. Together they would show what could be done, because, he said, no one anywhere in America had yet tried "on a scale large enough or with the intensity to be effective" to bring about the breadth of change that was required.

Neighborhood transformation in areas of concentrated poverty was an idea so grand that it not only captured the imagination of America's most innovative developer but mobilized residents of neighborhoods across the country and leaders of government, philanthropy, and business. It energized, as we shall see, bankers, priests, community organizers, neighborhood residents, and a former president of the United States.

Efforts to transform depleted neighborhoods and restore hope to their inhabitants are under way in every part of the country. "Something is working," said the Committee for Economic Development in a 1995 policy study. "While the nation has been looking away, residents and grassroots institutions in many decaying neighborhoods have quietly begun to turn their communities around . . . [and to] offer new hope that the complex problems of the inner cities can be solved."

These unheralded local successes are improving lives and neighborhoods by reweaving the social fabric, building housing, increasing public safety, expanding opportunity, and equipping residents to take advantage of new opportunities. They differ from one another in auspices, operating style, and the range of activities they undertake. All are building on the lessons of past failures and successes, and on a wealth of new understanding about both problems and remedies. The leaders of these efforts, coming from all walks of life, seem fully aware of the complexity of the challenge they have undertaken. Despite the prevailing cynicism about the prospects of any organized efforts to do good on a large scale, they have committed their hearts and minds to the daunting task of transforming the neighborhoods that so much of the rest of America has given up on.

Rediscovering Community

Americans who agree on nothing else, writes William Raspberry, agree that we used to live in wonderful neighborhoods and communities. The neighborhoods that we who are middle-aged and older remember nostalgically may have been poor, seedy, segregated, and populated by the rejected and exploited, but they were our communities and we miss them.

My friend and colleague Marian Wright Edelman, founder and president of the Children's Defense Fund, reminisces about growing up in Bennettsville, South Carolina, in her wonderful book, *The Measure of Our Success: A Letter to My Children and Yours:*

> I went everywhere with my parents and was under the watchful eye of members of the congregation and community who were my extended family. They kept me when my parents went out of town, they reported on me and chided me when I strayed from the straight and narrow of community expectations, and they basked in and supported my achievements when I did well. Doing well, they made clear, meant high academic achievement, playing piano in Sunday school, participating in

other church activities, being helpful, displaying good manners, and reading.

Gil Walker's memories of his childhood in Gary, Indiana, also feature networks of adults engaged with children, promoting community values.

> I can remember, when I was coming up, walking home from school with my report card in my hand. Before I got home, five or six people wanted to see it. If it was a good report card, I got hugs, I got kisses. . . . If it was a bad report card, every one of those individuals said, 'Gil Walker, you know you could do better. . . .' "

Gil Walker now runs a midnight basketball program for young people who live in Chicago public housing as his way of trying to replace the lost networks he remembers.

So what happened to those communities?

They have been rapidly eroding all over the industrialized world. Some combination of the following have interacted to weaken community bonds everywhere:

- Fear of crime, violence, and disorder deters people from gathering informally in public spaces. Public parks and playgrounds seem more threatening than welcoming. Older people especially, traditionally the backbone of neighborhoods, are afraid to venture out of their homes. In many neighborhoods, vigilant mothers keep their children—even teenagers—at home to keep them safe.

- Rapid advances in transportation and communication, together with the requirements of the post-industrial economy and the attraction of the suburbs and mild climates, have required and allowed vast numbers of people to move far from their neighborhoods and families of origin. Mobility has become easy and frequent—for all but the poor and elderly and those marooned by racial prejudice.

- The women who used to organize the PTA, volunteer in hospitals, and operate as front-porch disciplinarians and supervisors of the street scene are elsewhere. Some left with the opening of professional and workplace opportunities from which they had been excluded. Many more entered the labor market out of economic necessity.

- With the increase of single-parent families, many parents (usually mothers) must be both nurturer and breadwinner, leaving little time for community relationships.

- Technology has made it unnecessary to leave home and mingle with others to see movies and plays and listen to music. We watch sports on television rather than play them with our children, friends, and neighbors, and we listen to intimate matters being discussed by Oprah's guests rather than our own.

- The scale of most institutions that touch our lives makes it harder to make connections. The corner grocery has been replaced by the supermarket, neighborhood stores by regional Wal-Marts, and even six-year-olds have to cope with elementary schools of two thousand children. Political institutions have become so large and so complex that most people have no chance to work together to solve small-scale problems, and feel they have no control over how their taxes are spent or how their children are taught.

For all these reasons and more, Americans feel less anchored, more adrift. Political philosopher Michael Sandel believes that the erosion of community lies at the heart of our contemporary discontent.

Robert F. Kennedy was one of the first American politicians to recognize that the loss of community was hurting us, individually and collectively. Not long before he was killed, he called attention to the destruction of "the thousand invisible strands of common experience and purpose, affection, and respect, which tie men to their fellows." He believed that the world beyond the neighborhood had become "impersonal and abstract . . . beyond the reach of individual control or even understanding." In his 1968 presidential campaign, he called for the restoration of community as "a place where people can see and know each other, where children can play and adults work together and join in the pleasures and responsibilities of the place where they live."

Without a sense of community, says John Gardner, "people lose the conviction they can improve the quality of their lives through their own efforts."

The loss of community, like most contemporary ills, hits the poorest the hardest. The decline of manufacturing, the disappearance of well-paid jobs for the unskilled, racial discrimination in both hiring and housing, the decreasing value of income supports, inferior and overwhelmed schools and services, the flight of the middle class to the suburbs, crack, the crack trade, and guns all have combined to form the inner-city deserts, inhospitable to healthy human development.

The influence of neighborhoods on families and life outcomes has long been apparent to people working at the front lines, but research in this area had been dormant for several decades. The documentation of connections was sparse. For many years, social scientists avoided studying connections between neighborhoods and individual outcomes. But the influence of neighborhoods became a hot topic again as part of the poverty-related research stimulated by the Social Science Research Council and by William Julius Wilson's 1987 book, *The Truly Disadvantaged*.

The new research began to document the connections between community conditions and high rates of youth violence, school failure, and childbearing by unmarried teenagers. These studies profoundly challenged the conventional wisdom—and the conclusions of earlier research—that life outcomes were determined just by what went on within the confines of the family.

- Conventional wisdom holds, and social policies are devised on the belief, that the quality of parenting depends on the information, skills, and resources which individuals bring to the child-rearing task. But the evidence now shows that neighborhoods profoundly affect how parents raise their children. When the streets are dangerous and disorderly, adults establish fewer connections with others, resulting in less supervision of children. "Normal" child rearing may be unachievable or even unwise for those trapped in the inner city. Child development experts advise mothers in the Robert Taylor Homes to let their babies crawl and explore, but the mothers know better, and keep their babies in their cribs to protect them from rat bites and rat poison. At the scene of a 1991 killing in Washington, DC, a police officer ordered a woman to remove a four-year-old who stood watching while the dead man's bloody torso was examined in full view of the crowd. The boy's grandmother protested that she was trying to teach the boy a lesson, "That's what you gotta do, show them real life. Don't honeycoat it."

- Conventional wisdom holds, and social policies are devised on the belief, that the values of inner-city residents are defective and produce high rates of young people unable to distinguish right from wrong. But researchers have found that in socially depleted neighborhoods, many residents have perfectly respectable values but are unable to transmit them for lack of a community structure to maintain effective social controls.

- High delinquency rates, educational failure, infant mortality, child abuse, adolescent substance abuse, and gang violence have been found to be related to the absence of neighborhood institutions

that promote healthy youth development, including primary supports like Little League, whether the neighborhood has high concentrations of single-parent families, and the number of unrelated adults who are available and willing to work with youth.
- The presence of affluent neighbors and the extent and concentration of neighborhood poverty are associated with a surprising array of outcomes, including rates of teenage pregnancy and school dropout, maternal depression, IQ, and the extent of aggression among five-year-olds.

The research makes clear, then, that the capacity of families to do their child-rearing job is powerfully dependent on the health of their communities. A few children, blessed with extraordinary resiliency or unflagging adult support will be able to beat the odds, but most children growing up in severely depleted neighborhoods face a daunting array of risks that greatly diminish their chances of escaping poor economic, educational, social, and health outcomes. Regardless of race, family composition, income, or natural endowment, as Harvard's Robert Putnam of *Bowling Alone* fame pithily puts it, "of two identical youths, the one unfortunate enough to live in a neighborhood whose social capital has eroded is more likely to end up hooked, booked, or dead."

A number of scholars have proposed that much of the devastating damage of ghetto life can best be explained by the theory of epidemics. Many inner cities, in this view, are neighborhoods that have experienced epidemics of social problems such as substance abuse, school dropout, adolescent pregnancy, and juvenile crime. The incidence of the social problems rises because they are contagious and are spread through peer influence, and peer influence reigns when countervailing social forces are weak. The epidemic theorists have found that when the number of high-status role models (professionals, managers, teachers) drops below a certain level, perhaps 5 percent, the neighborhood reaches a "tipping point," plunging almost overnight from relatively functional to wildly dysfunctional.

Because the proportion of poor persons living in extreme-poverty areas continues to increase, the damaging effects are being inflicted on an increasing number of children. As these children become parents, their children—in the absence of intervention—are destined to become the parents of yet another and larger generation of undereducated, underemployed, unlawful, and unaffiliated adults.

Increased crime and social disorder in depleted neighborhoods bring higher rates of fear, neighborhood dissatisfaction, and intentions to move out, which then lead to even further increases in social disorder.

The research documenting the effect of community conditions in determining individual and community outcomes has added urgency to efforts to intervene. It has also served as an important source of legitimation for current comprehensive community-building initiatives. The forerunners of these initiatives had no such validation. But it was a different era, and they seemed not to need either academic research to support their theories, or evidence of cost effectiveness to support their actions.

Past Efforts to Transform Neighborhoods, Fight Poverty, Build Community, and Improve Services

Experience with the antecedents of current initiatives provides some guideposts to what has worked—and even lessons about mistakes to avoid.

Settlement houses. The settlement houses were probably the earliest precursors of current neighborhood transformation efforts. They were brought to this country from England toward the end of the nineteenth century as a response to the spread of sweatshops, poverty, and sordid tenements in rapidly growing American cities. Jane Addams and other founders of the settlements believed that educated, upper-class men and women should move into poor neighborhoods and dispense educational and social services, organize social and instructional clubs, run day nurseries, provide recreational opportunities—and simultaneously agitate for better city services and new social legislation. The settlers at Hull House supported organized labor, the outlawing of child labor, and women's suffrage, and mobilized community residents in support of pocket parks, playgrounds, libraries, garbage collection, police and fire protection, and closing sewers.

Although ready to respond to the specific ills of individuals, the settlement leaders were committed to the neighborhood. They aimed to strengthen the fabric of the community, acting as brokers for newly arrived immigrants and helping them cope with "the endless difficulties of everyday life."

Settlement houses spread rapidly, especially in the East and Midwest. Their approach to assimilation and integration flourished, in large part because the industrial economy was growing rapidly and could pay a living wage to big-city newcomers, unskilled as well as skilled.

Welfare through patronage. Another response to the poverty and dislocation that the era's economic growth left in its wake was what sociologist Theda Skocpol calls the "patronage democracy" of urban political party machines. They sponsored "a sort of distributive, discretionary welfare regime" that delivered jobs, housing, food, and clothing, as well as contracts for public works basically as part of the party's efforts to tighten its hold on a district. The urban machines kept in close touch with the new industrial working class and its many problems of low income, uncertain employment, illness, and family disorganization.

George Washington Plunkitt of Manhattan's Tammany Hall explained the principles of patronage democracy to journalist William Riordan in 1905:

> "You go right down among the poor families. . . . If there's a fire on Ninth, Tenth, or Eleventh Avenue, for example, any hour of the day or night, I'm there with some of the election district captains as soon as the fire engines. If a family is burned out I don't ask whether they are Republicans or Democrats, and I don't refer them to the Charity Organization Society, which would investigate their case in a month or two and decide they were worthy of help about the time they are dead from starvation. I just get quarters for them, buy clothes for them, and fix them up until they get things runnin' again. It's philanthropy, but it's politics, too—mighty good politics."

The beginning of formalized social services. The Charity Organization Society that Plunkitt ridiculed operated in marked contrast to both the settlement houses and the party machines. It foreshadowed the family service agencies and the social work profession of the present day. Appalled by what they saw as indiscriminate giving of the settlements and political machines, and by the imprecise criteria they applied to assess needs for assistance, the charity societies emphasized coordination, investigation, and "scientific philanthropy."

Skocpol records that their work was based on the conviction that personal change among the poor was the key to the alleviation of poverty, and that change came about by offers of "carefully meted, individually targeted assistance and motivation to poor people who needed to be goaded toward self-improvement." The societies' motto was "Not alms but a friend"—a friend who determined what was best for the subject family, avoided pampering and multiple sources of help, and gave just enough to motivate but not enough to satisfy. Standardization, formalization, categorization, and special-ization in treating individual deficits became the hallmarks of the human service professions and ultimately of the overall design of public support for human services.

Help that was earlier offered on a model of the extended family—taking into account factors in the neighborhood as well as in the individual and family, and requiring sensitivity and commitment—was replaced by help from the expert professional, modeled on the physician's function to investigate, diagnose, and prescribe for the individual.

Neighborhoods rediscovered—from the Depression to the Kennedy era. The Great Depression of the 1930s and the social upheavals in its wake elicited a resurgence of interest in the neighborhood among urban sociologists, particularly in Chicago. Academics of the Chicago Area Project saw themselves as not only researchers but activists. They found antisocial behavior more the norm than the exception among neighborhood youth, and were convinced that the key to changing young people was to address the feelings of marginality, anomie, and powerlessness widespread among the community's adults. They extended the settlement vision by relying on community members and organizations, especially the church, to play major roles in enhancing residents' sense of control over their lives. They did not pressure the city for better services or address neglect by landlords, red-lining by banks, and related causes of community dispirit, perhaps, historian Robert Halpern suggests, because they accepted the idea that the residents were themselves responsible for the deteriorated condition of their community.

The emergence in the late 1930s and early 1940s of an external enemy and the leveling experience of World War II encouraged once again the notion of America as a classless society. But by the mid-1950s it had become clear that poverty would not somehow disappear of its own accord. Unemployment in the ghetto seemed to have become impervious to general economic prosperity. The inner city was no longer a way station to the mainstream—for many it was the end point.

By the early 1960s, the social landscape was being changed by the civil rights movement, and also by the emergence of large national foundations. The civil rights movement provided a vehicle, as Kenneth Clark pointed out, for urban African-Americans to reveal both "the extent of their hurt" and their growing strength. The large foundations provided new resources and new energy to respond to the claims for equal opportunity by excluded minorities, and to the deepening poverty of the inner city.

The most ambitious response was the Ford Foundation's Gray Areas program, conceived in 1959 and operational by 1961. Its architects, led by the Ford Foundation's legendary Paul Ylvisaker, believed that the political and social institutions of the preceding era, which had integrated generations of immigrants into the mainstream by providing education, jobs, and services, were incapable of dealing with the new migrants to big cities. They hoped to show how "all the institutions of social adaptation" could become part of the assimilation process and open opportunities for poor families moving into the cities from the rural south, Indian reservations, and the coal-mining hollows of Appalachia.

Social institutions that had become so bureaucratized that they had forgotten their purpose of mitigating the harshness of the marketplace for the most vulnerable would be brought together and persuaded by the dedicated leaders of the Gray Areas demonstrations to reexamine and reform their practices.

The optimism surrounding the Gray Areas work made it possible to enlist gifted young activists. Mayors pledged their cooperation. Later Ylvisaker reflected that "We had that beautiful running time of two or three years . . . the world wanted to solve the problems, the Ford Foundation was golden, Kennedy was in office and you could talk about the experimental programs that would become governmental programs."

It didn't last.

The mostly white and very professional leaders of the Gray Areas projects were challenged by groups of residents, mostly minority, increasingly militant, and already embittered by urban renewal. Halpern believes that the projects' difficulties signaled "the end of a long era of acquiescence among inner-city neighborhoods to externally initiated reform." The projects luxuriated in a long planning period, learning too late, says Mitchell Sviridoff, "that you have to be able to produce something fairly soon to achieve credibility." One more frustration arose when evaluators assumed—quite unrealistically—that they could deny interventions to some in order to test their effectiveness on others.

The Gray Areas projects also discovered that the enriched human services they were able to fund could play only a modest role in altering people's life situation and prospects, especially in the face of a receding labor market, an eroding tax base for urban schools, housing policies that intensified ghetto isolation, and historic patterns of racial discrimination.

The Great Society: Community Action and Model Cities. The Economic Opportunity Act, although launched at a time of economic growth and optimism, was from the outset shaped by resource constraints and the need for political compromise.

The group planning the War on Poverty in 1964 advocated a government jobs program as the centerpiece, in line with the recommendations of the government's economists as well as the country's activists. But, as we have already seen, President Johnson, leery of a large-scale jobs program that would have required a tax increase, rejected it out of hand.

Sargent Shriver, director of the new Office of Economic Opportunity, accommodated to the inevitable, rationalizing that "the problem was not jobs, it was people qualified to hold a job." That was a less expensive problem to solve. The OEO set about expanding economic opportunity to the extent that could be done by providing education, job training, student loans, health and legal services, and by involving the poor themselves in the design and administration of community antipoverty programs.

The designers of the Community Action Program did not much consider the early lessons of the Gray Areas Project or the other neighborhood-based initiatives of the early 1960s. Peter Marris and Martin Rein argued in 1973 that "those shaping the War on Poverty took the assumptions and strategies of the Gray Areas program for granted, [even though] many of these assumptions and strategies already were proving problematic in practice." It was not surprising, then, that the new community action agencies encountered many of the same difficulties—exacerbated by their greater visibility and their public funding.

Raucous complaints from mayors, governors, and members of Congress showed how hard it is to bring about fundamental change when using public funds—especially when the process involves setting up alternative political structures and funding litigation challenging the operation of government agencies. In many cities, the tensions between the local establishment and the newly "empowered" poor completely paralyzed the process.

It also became clear that the creation of a parallel service structure—the OEO's response to the difficulty of changing mainstream human service systems—was unlikely to become part of a local service-delivery network. The new federally funded services would not, it turned out, even become integrated with other federally funded programs.

But at least as destructive to the antipoverty purposes of community action as the hostility of urban mayors and the difficulty of reforming services was OEO's inability, as a result of the initial presidential decision, to respond to the need for jobs in areas where the economy was not growing.

These failings, however, should not obscure the biggest impact of the OEO's community action program: It drew a new cadre of previously excluded young people into the political mainstream. It "nourished and intensified a growing citizen's movement . . . and launched a new generation of minority leaders into public life." During their heyday, community action agencies "gave a generation of poor people a taste of having control over their own lives."

Together with the civil rights movement, community action was able to establish a climate of hope. Rosemary Bray, a black woman who had grown up on welfare to graduate from Yale University and become an editor of *The New York Times Book Review,* recalls her belief, coming of age in the 1960s, that with hard work she could accomplish anything. "That was the promise of the civil rights movement and the war on poverty—for millions of African-Americans the defining events of the 1960s. Caught up in the heady atmosphere of imminent change, our world was filled . . . with amazing images of black people engaged in the struggle for long-denied rights and freedoms."

But the images that meant hope to Rosemary Bray were an intolerable threat to Senator John Stennis. Furious public officials fought back. Continued congressional support was constantly made contingent on OEO Director Sargent Shriver's willingness to defund the most controversial programs.

The Johnson administration was ready to back off from the politically volatile Community Action Program, but reluctant to turn its back on the possibility of a national urban policy. According to historian Alice O'Connor, a coalition of urban legislators, liberal philanthropists, social scientists, and labor officials urged new Model Cities legislation that would make up for the failure of urban renewal while avoiding the political liabilities of Community Action. United Auto Workers President Walter Reuther wrote to President Johnson in 1965, calling for a massive investment in six demonstration sites to "stop the erosion of life in urban centers" by stimulating jobs, as did the TVA, while creating "architecturally beautiful and socially meaningful communities in large urban centers."

The new Department of Housing and Urban Development saw Model Cities as an important symbol of commitment to rebuilding the inner city. The Johnson administration promoted it as a response to the inner-city riots of 1965 and 1966. Attorney General Nicholas Katzenbach, at a Senate hearing on the Model Cities legislation, responded to allegations of conspiracies behind the riots: "The riots were indeed fomented by agitators—agitators named disease and despair, joblessness and hopelessness, [and] rat-infested housing."

The Model Cities vision was based on the premise that education and health and social services would not be enough, even when categorical programs were pulled together to make them more responsive to the needs of the poor. Housing construction and rehabilitation had to be added and resources had to be concentrated. The original legislative drafts posited initial funding of $500 million for six cities and housing that would be racially and economically integrated to help keep upwardly mobile blacks and whites tied to central-city neighborhoods.

Virtually none of the hopes for Model Cities was realized. The Vietnam War robbed it of the necessary funding, and the process of getting it through Congress robbed it of authority and targeting. Six cities became sixty-six, and soon 150. Provisions promoting residential integration were dropped. No one at the local level took the Model Cities planning process seriously. Ultimately, wrote Peter Edelman and Beryl Radin, "Model Cities became a lesson in the dissipation of limited resources."

The most profound lesson that came out of Gray Areas, Community Action, and Model Cities did not emerge until later. None of us fully realized at the time how powerfully the impact of the anti-poverty interventions was being undermined by economic developments of which we were only dimly aware. None of us fully understood that the massive deindustrialization then taking place would overwhelm even the most effective local initiatives.

Service reform through service integration. From the 1970s to the mid-1990s, reformers committed to fighting poverty and improving the lives of disadvantaged children were forced to become profoundly modest in their aspirations. Focusing on what could be done in a climate that seemed to rule out major change and large governmental expenditures, they attached their hopes to efforts to coordinate and integrate fragmented services. This strategy appealed to both liberals and conservatives because it addressed a problem everyone could see and agree on: accumulating evidence that services meant to improve the life prospects of the poor were often proving ineffective—at least in part because they were so fragmented.

Service integration was promoted by its fans as the way to modify the operations of specialized and bureaucratized service systems so they would meet complex family needs, improve access to services, and eliminate inefficiencies and duplication. Those who saw the problem as primarily logistical considered coordination of services important for the same reason that medical specialists coordinate their intervention—to avoid prescribing drugs that could combine to produce dangerous or even fatal effects. It also appealed to those seeking a managerial solution to perceived bureaucratic inefficiency or looking for a meshing of categorical programs to make them more effective for individuals with multiple problems.

Since 1971 there have been about two dozen major federal initiatives aimed at service integration. The National Governors' Association catalogued 150 service integration projects in forty states just in the one domain of promoting family self-sufficiency. Professional organizations, consultants, and federal agencies issued guidebooks and manuals, foundations required local projects to provide evidence of coordination, and new organizations were formed to encourage service integration, both within and across categorical systems. Local service providers complained increasingly of spending all their time at meetings to integrate services.

But very little changed in the face of the multiplicity of regulations and incompatible eligibility requirements, the professionalized, specialized, and bureaucratized mind-sets of program managers, and the limited funding and influence available to those trying to bring about integration.

Federally funded service integration efforts became ever more modest, but the barriers to providing coherent services grew. Each wave of reform had to contend with a more complex, inflexible, and fragmented human service system and with the cumulative disillusionment resulting from previous failures.

Some improvements were achieved, including case management within systems, especially in mental health. "One-stop shopping" was also widely embraced, often with schools as the common site for service location. These modifications in service delivery were possible because they required no major change. Co-location didn't require the co-locators to give up funds, authority, or turf. New case management arrangements reduced some of the hassles families faced in obtaining service, but also didn't require anyone to give up anything, because one set of case managers could always be super-imposed on another.

Cognizant of all of these difficulties, but convinced of the need for "greater boldness in efforts to bring about a meaningful integration of human services . . . and a basic restructuring in the way educational and human services are delivered," the Annie E. Casey Foundation in 1988 launched New Futures, perhaps the most ambitious of the service integration efforts of the past ten years.

The goal of New Futures was to help more at-risk youth to become productive adults by reducing dropout rates, improving academic performance, preventing teen pregnancies, and increasing the number of youth going on to jobs or college. The Casey strategy was to provide generous funding (averaging $10 million to each of five medium-size cities) over a period of five years to enable newly established collaborative governing bodies in these cities to restructure existing institutions to make services more responsive to the needs of youngsters of middle school age.

Seven years after the inception of New Futures, the Casey Foundation reluctantly concluded that comprehensive reform of service systems "is the path of most resistance." During the five-year grant period, youth outcomes did not, in fact, improve. In an unusually candid report on its experience, the Casey Foundation recognized that its challenge to communities to bring about comprehensive system reform was not met. The foundation concluded that "vested interests in current practice, fiscal constraints, and political risks" were able to undermine and minimalize system change.

The Casey Foundation promptly acted on the recognition that its strategies were not achieving their intended purpose, and its grant-making activities have since become "increasingly committed to combining system reform, policy innovation, community capacity building, and neighborhood investments . . . in community institutions." Its new funding priorities have put service integration into a much broader context, and have made the foundation a major force in today's efforts to strengthen families and institutions in distressed neighborhoods.

Community development corporations. During this same period, another social movement had begun, with significant implications for rebuilding inner-city neighborhoods and responding to America's urban crisis.

Community development corporations (CDCs) began in the 1960s but took root in the 1970s as urban neighborhoods began to disintegrate, and federal funding for subsidized housing began to dry up. CDCs have now become "one of the fastest-growing community-based institutions in inner-city America."

They are free-standing nonprofit, community-based organizations dedicated to the revitalization of a discrete—usually distressed—geographic area. They are governed by boards consisting of neighborhood residents and sometimes business and civic leaders. Their activities typically include the construction and rehabilitation of housing, but most also provide housing-related services, and some do community advocacy and organizing and provide some social services. Some also develop commercial real estate and try to bring capital into the neighborhood in support of neighborhood small business. Many have also become vehicles for residents to enter into social networks and address both neighborhood and individual needs.

Anna Faith Jones, president of the Boston Foundation, says, "Involving the people who live in the community that is to be developed is the radical underpinning of the entire movement. Unlike urban redevelopment and public housing, where government has come in as an outside force and built this housing and put people in it, you involve the people who live there in a process that says: What do we want to do here, in our own neighborhood?"

The early CDCs sprang up almost simultaneously in a number of cities in the latter half of the 1960s, perhaps out of frustration with some of the earlier attempts to impose solutions crafted far away. They got their first big shot in the arm in 1967 when Robert F. Kennedy, then senator from New York, began to push the idea of community development after a visit to the devastated Bedford-Stuyvesant neighborhood in Brooklyn.

Elsie Richardson, who moved into the first housing project in Bedford-Stuyvesant in 1950 and soon became a neighborhood activist, remembers helping to organize the senator's tour of the neighborhood: "We selected certain places to take him, to give him a feel of what was happening, good and bad. I recall there was a house on Atlantic Avenue, we knocked and this woman opened the door and she almost passed out. Bobby Kennedy? She was really in a state of shock. . . . There was a lot of tension around his visit. Whether this would be another political thing of walking through the community and nothing coming out of it. . . ."

Kennedy was clearly moved by the desolation he saw. After his walk around the neighborhood, visitors and residents met at a nearby YMCA. Judge Thomas Jones, one of the few black judges in the area, got up and asked Kennedy for a commitment. As he remembers it, "I said I'm glad you're here. I said your late brother, Jack Kennedy, had already seen these things. He knew these things, and you know these things. You were his Attorney General. I said, we're tired of being studied, Senator, and then I sat down. Some of them thought it was an angry thing to say. But I was sick and tired of being studied, and that's all I said. He wasn't disturbed by it. He said, 'I understand.' "

Kennedy returned to Washington knowing that federal support would be essential. He saw community development as "a way of turning the ghettos into the kind of launching pads for immigrant upward mobility that the Irish neighborhoods of Boston had been for Kennedy's own forebears." Beginning immediately after his visit, he worked with the people in Bedford-Stuyvesant on the initial plans and told his staff to draft legislation. Enlisting his fellow New York senator, Republican Jacob Javits, as co-sponsor, he was able to amend the Economic Opportunity Act to allocate funds to the Bedford-Stuyvesant Restoration Corporation, which became the prototype CDC. The partnership between neighborhood leaders and the corporate and philanthropic community, recalled Michael Sviridoff, would serve to free it of the "contentiousness . . . and complicating political baggage" of the Community Action Program. Symbolic of that partnership, Franklin Thomas, first head of the Bedford-Stuyvesant Restoration Corporation, moved from there to become president of the Ford Foundation.

Cutbacks in public funding ultimately weakened the Bedford-Stuyvesant Restoration Corporation, but for many years it did build the community, and it did build hope. As Judge Jones put it almost thirty years later, "It was empowerment of the people of my community, our community, with the help of the people who could unlock the doors, break up the logjams that were keeping us from achieving any democratic rights in our own community."

Over the next decade, the Ford Foundation funded CDCs heavily, with a total of $100 million in the late sixties and seventies. By the mid-seventies, Ford's contributions almost equaled those made by the federal government through Community Development Block Grants and Urban Development Action Grants. By the late 1970s, Ford was sufficiently convinced that CDCs were a promising anti-poverty strategy to create the Local Initiatives Support Corporation, a privately supported intermediary, to seek out promising CDCs and enlist investments from the private and public sectors.

By the early 1990s CDCs had developed more than 320,000 units of affordable housing. Their number mushroomed from one hundred in 1970 to more than two thousand by 1995. Many became sturdy institutions in otherwise unstable neighborhoods, and vehicles by which residents could address both neighborhood and individual needs.

Time for Synergy and Synthesis?

In this exploration of earlier reform efforts, we have seen how reform energy has careened between attempts to strengthen persons and places, between interventions to repair damage and to prevent damage, between reliance on personalized charity and impersonal public systems, and between strategies to restructure from the top down and from the bottom up. Often the quest has been for the one golden way to intervene that would be both simple and cheap.

In the past several years, a new and more sophisticated theme has begun to surface, perhaps signaling an emerging new synthesis. Clear-eyed funders, community activists, researchers, policy analysts, and legislators are beginning to see that no single strand of intervention can be counted on to produce significant results for populations in high-risk circumstances. They have seen that narrowly defined interventions can't triumph over the forces of destruction.

The new synthesis rejects addressing poverty, welfare, employment, education, child development, housing, and crime one at a time. It endorses the idea that the multiple and interrelated problems of poor neighborhoods require multiple and interrelated solutions. The new synthesizers are determined to reverse "the economic, social, and political marginalization that has turned the urban poor into an 'underclass' and their neighborhoods into battle zones." They refuse to "choose between addressing the structural and behavioral causes of neighborhood dysfunction, or between equipping the poor to leave unsupportive neighborhoods or making them better places to live." They insist on combining physical and economic development with service and education reform, and all of these with a commitment to building community institutions and social networks.

Not all of the community initiatives that label themselves as comprehensive neighborhood transformation efforts have been able to implement the ambitious agenda that the new synthesis implies, but, as we will see, the new synthesis is the belief system on which most of the new generation of initiatives is being built.

The neighborhood transformation projects now bubbling up in

cities around the country with support from public and philanthropic funds are rekindling long-dormant hope. They may also contain the clues to reversing the decline of America's inner cities and
the growth of a potentially permanent underclass.

While there has been a lot of trial and error, a lot of groping in the
dark, and much unjustified optimism about how much can be accomplished with severely constrained resources in very little time, a
great deal of useful experience is being accumulated that justifies the
hope that many attach to the new initiatives.

I have come to know and will tell the story of seven neighborhood
change efforts that illustrate the current surge of community rebuilding. They tell of different, and sometimes even conflicting, approaches to putting together much of what is known to work. Together they inspire wonder at the determination of Americans from
all walks of life to overcome enormous obstacles to make their
neighborhoods into decent places to live and bring up children.

Three of these stories contain the promise of truly transforming a
neighborhood—the one inspired by James Rouse in Baltimore, a
new venture capital approach involving five community development corporations in the once-forsaken South Bronx, and Savannah's journey from service reform to comprehensive community initiative. Two of the initiatives—in Atlanta and Boston—suggest to
me, though not to all observers, that not every approach to fighting
poverty and building communities is equally promising. The oldest
of the seven I describe, in Newark, New Jersey, shows how much
can be accomplished with a mix of opportunism and spirituality.
And the newest, the Empowerment Zones getting under way in eight
cities, provide some hints of what could be accomplished if the nation decided to take comprehensive community building to scale.

BALTIMORE'S COMMUNITY BUILDING IN PARTNERSHIP IN SANDTOWN-WINCHESTER

Before the transformation began, Sandtown-Winchester was about
as bleak as it gets. George Will, after a December 1995 visit, wrote
that when you saw the "winds whipping through gaping empty windows in abandoned rowhouses" you could easily conclude that
"spring never comes here."

An almost entirely African-American community, Sandtown has a
proud history. Cab Calloway was born here, and Thurgood Marshall had been a star at the local high school. But by the late 1980s,
Sandtown ranked among the worst areas in the city in its rates of
poverty, unemployment, school performance, teen pregnancy,

chronic illness, violent crime, and frequency of HIV-AIDS. Its rates of low birth-weight babies and infant mortality were four times the national average. Seventy percent of families were headed by single women. Half of all households had annual incomes under $11,000; a quarter had incomes under $5,000. Three quarters of Sandtown families lived in substandard housing, and eight hundred residential units stood vacant. Nine thousand tons of debris had to be trucked away before new housing could be built.

The Sandtown area was so forsaken that the major question raised by critics of the initiative was whether, for this highly visible and symbolically important community transformation effort, the Enterprise Foundation and the City of Baltimore should have picked a neighborhood that was less destitute.

Jim Rouse wanted the ultimate challenge of his life, and he got it. (*The Washington Post* quoted Rouse as saying, "We wanted a place that could be called a 'bottom' neighborhood, one with real human devastation, where people were really living in the worst possible conditions." The *Post* pronounced Sandtown to be "perfect" for this purpose.) If life in Sandtown could be changed, then surely nothing is impossible.

And life in Sandtown is changing.

The seeds of the initiative were sown when Sandtown residents confronted newly elected Baltimore Mayor Kurt Schmoke after a 1989 news conference where he had announced two new housing projects. As Leonard Jackson, Jr., a neighborhood resident, recalls, residents told Schmoke that unless he could curb crime, improve the schools, clean the streets, provide better health care, and fix other shoddy services, new housing would not make much difference.

The idea of combining physical development with social renewal struck a responsive chord with the mayor. He approached the Baltimore-based Enterprise Foundation, knowing it had been founded on the belief that housing alone was not enough to make a neighborhood a decent place to live, and was now seeking opportunities to focus its housing development capacity in a very poor neighborhood where both government and the community shared a similar vision. The mayor also knew that Enterprise had strong Baltimore ties, and that Rouse's personal reputation for promoting civil rights locally put Enterprise in a position of being respected by both city hall and the Sandtown community.

In early 1990, Mayor Schmoke convened a task force, representing the city, the Enterprise Foundation, a grassroots group called Baltimoreans United in Leadership Development (BUILD), and the

Sandtown community to examine ways in which they could join forces to transform Sandtown. Because Sandtown residents considered no single organization to have the capacity to become the lead partner from the community, the task force pulled together hundreds of residents and staff of public and private agencies to set up eight working groups, chaired or co-chaired by residents, focused on housing and physical development, economic development and employment, education, health care, substance abuse, family support services, crime and safety, and community pride and spirit.

Enterprise Foundation participants were given pause, early on, by the timidity of the aspirations that both residents and service providers brought to the "visioning" process. I remember being invited to meet with the group charged with developing health goals, and suggesting they aim higher than shortening the wait in the emergency room from all day to a few hours. Patrick Costigan, coordinating the process for the Enterprise Foundation, reflected later that residents and city agency staff alike had been conditioned by realities of neighborhood life and past revitalization efforts. "The harsh edges of everyday life made it hard to dream about good schools, nice housing or health care beyond the emergency room. Service providers, constrained by budget cutbacks and political mandates, were equally reluctant to think big in the visioning process."

City agencies and Enterprise brought in consultants and community leaders from elsewhere to "stretch the visioning." Enterprise raised private resources and the city delivered discretionary public funds. Although community leaders were suspicious and talked of broken promises from local government, the commitment of the energetic new mayor, the Enterprise Foundation's brokering, and the experience of working together began to overcome a history of neglect. As each of the partners delivered what they promised, a sense of trust began to emerge.

But progress in moving participants to think outside the traditional categories suddenly became a serious barrier in getting actual operations underway. None of the partners, says Costigan today, had the capacity to act on the boldness of the vision they had all committed to. The Enterprise Foundation was essentially a housing-oriented organization. Neighborhood service providers had been struggling for years to meet crisis needs and keep their agencies afloat. City government was similarly overwhelmed in the face of continuing federal and state budget cutbacks. No one could offer the expertise or the discretionary funding that would be required to bring about fundamental reforms in education, health care, and social services and to integrate these with one another and with activities aimed at community building and assuring public safety.

The planning groups tried to cross sector boundaries by agreeing on five goals, which would make the need to integrate become more obvious, and which might make it possible to resist the fierce magnetic pull of existing categories. They would prepare all children to succeed in school; prepare all young adults to enter the workforce or continue on to higher education; equip all families to support and care for themselves; enable all residents to live in a safe, nurturing environment; and empower the community to sustain an improved quality of life.

The formulation of these goals did indeed provide clarity and became a way to test program options by forcing the question of how a proposed program or activity could contribute to achieving one or more of the goals. The leadership tried, whenever possible, to couple planning with activities that met the immediate needs of residents and laid building blocks for longer-term change. Each project signaled that something was happening, each responded to a need identified in the community, and each contributed to the neighborhood's sense of ownership.

Residents were trained and employed as community advocates to recruit others to participate in program design and to bring their knowledge of the neighborhood to the transformation process. Some could reach out to young mothers. Others knew the streets and could relate to the long-term unemployed and the drug culture. One advocate was a high school dropout who proved particularly valuable in encouraging young people to stay in school. All had been unemployed at the time they were hired. Some were struggling with drug problems or hampered by criminal records. Most lacked the self-confidence to take the necessary steps for their own advancement. Yet each was able to connect to a particular place, culture, or subgroup within the neighborhood.

The program design process produced an ambitious plan to change virtually every aspect of community life in three to five years. At a large public meeting in March 1993, seventeen community leaders presented the plan, and the mayor capped the day of celebration by "pledging to see to it that every boarded-up house—and there are many—in the neighborhood is renovated within one year."

The transition to program implementation was immediate—but ill prepared, says Costigan. He compares it to running and winning a political campaign. "You're campaigning and campaigning, you get elected, and then the next morning you have to do it." Unlike the governing that follows victory in a political campaign, however, the transformation process had no established form, no precedents to follow. "Government and the private market had long ago failed Sandtown. The old systems were broken and dysfunctional. We had to build new capacity, new operating partnerships among community, government, and the private sector, and develop new resources. All that would take time, commitments, and money."

But the hundreds of residents who were now engaged in the process, as well as agency representatives and service providers, all expected quick action. They, and the early funders, wanted to see results. No one realized how hard and time-consuming it would be to nurture the neighborhood leadership and build the capacity of existing community organizations and service providers to implement the radically new program activities in ways that could sustain them over time.

By early 1996, there was, nevertheless, an impressive list of accomplishments:

- **The governing board:** Community Building in Partnership, Inc. (CBP) manages the transformation process. It includes representatives of the three founding partners, several business and professional people, and Sandtown residents, who hold ten of seventeen seats.
- **The physical changes:** The physical appearance of the neighborhood is being radically transformed. Two hundred twenty-seven Nehemiah town homes were built through the combined initiative of the Enterprise Foundation and Baltimoreans United in Leadership Development. Former President Carter led Sandtown Habitat to begin renovation on thirty homes for low-income purchasers. Six hundred units of public housing have been modernized, and one hundred new homes are under development. Twenty vegetable and flower gardens have replaced tons of debris removed from vacant lots, and three parks have been refurbished.
- **Education:** A "school readiness" pathway has been developed to assure that preschoolers will receive health care and appropriate developmental experiences in both home and school, including full-day kindergartens. The school system has agreed to a compact that will give the community unprecedented say about curriculum, hiring, and budgeting in the three Sandtown elementary schools. A new nationally proven curriculum (based on the "core knowledge" ideas of E. D. Hirsch) has been adopted, and professional development, preschool programs, and adult education are being

aligned with it. Management authority has been increasingly turned over to the principals and an education director, formerly with the Edison Project, who coordinates programming in all three area elementary schools.

- **Health care and human services:** Infant mortality has been reduced. Five formerly competing health care providers are providing comprehensive, high-quality primary care to all neighborhood residents, regardless of ability to pay. Three school-based clinics have opened and eventually will serve all children up to the age of eighteen, and all pregnant women and children ages zero through three have access to health care and supports.

  Aggressive outreach by a team of "family advocates" helps individuals and entire families obtain health services, and residents have been trained to monitor the health of their neighbors. New prevention and intervention programs are helping adults at risk for or suffering from arthritis or high blood pressure. A church-sponsored clinic reaches patients who have been unable to receive care through established providers. The rate of HIV-AIDS infection has decreased with the introduction of a needle exchange program, and a local hospital has placed a substance abuse treatment program directly in the neighborhood. A management information system is being introduced to coordinate client tracking and service delivery.

- **Jobs:** More than two hundred residents have been employed in CBP community improvement activities, and another five hundred have gotten jobs through Sandtown Works, a neighborhood-based assessment, training, and placement center operated by CBP. Six hundred more have been assessed and/or trained. A church-sponsored employment placement center that opened in early 1995 has helped find jobs for an additional 150 residents. School dropouts are developing construction skills and completing their education in federally supported YouthBuild and YouthCorps programs. Plans are under way to work with the estimated fifteen hundred residents who have severe obstacles to overcome, such as drug addiction or criminal records, before they can obtain jobs that pay a living wage.

- **Community building and quality-of-life services and supports:** A new community support center for families and at-risk youth has been opened in the neighborhood that offers youth recreational activities, outreach and support to families in crisis through a family advocate program, peer supports for struggling individuals and families, emergency services, senior activities, and adult education.

More than one hundred block captains have been organized to fight crime. Fifteen known crack houses have been closed through a cooperative effort of block clubs, police, and the courts. Pop Warner Football and Little Leagues have blossomed on a playing field formerly controlled by drug dealers. Shopping choices are multiplying with the opening of two new drugstores in the neighborhood, which for twenty years had none, and work is beginning on a marketplace offering foods, crafts, and entertainment. Residents have taken more control over local zoning matters, rejecting undesirable commercial and retail proposals.

A new community spirit is palpable. A series of regular community events has begun to evolve, including an annual Pumpkin Patch festival attended by thousands of children, Thanksgiving and Christmas food drives, an Easter egg hunt, a summer fun festival, and regular cleanups. Over seventeen hundred residents are newly registered to vote. And a community newspaper, *The Sandtown Viewpoint,* is distributed neighborhood-wide each month.

Nearly one hundred residents serve in some type of community advocate position, from health care, youth services, and family support to education and communications. These positions are becoming stepping stones into the labor market for residents once thought to have no skills.

The Sandtown experience has shown that a three-way partnership which includes the public sector, the neighborhood, and an "enabling" organization like the Enterprise Foundation can provide a solid basis for neighborhood change, overcoming a legacy of mistrust. The three partners have been able to work through past adversarial relationships, enabling them to leverage millions of dollars in public funds.

Targeting reform efforts and resources on a single neighborhood clearly carries political risks, especially to a relatively new mayor. Schmoke had reason to be wary of focusing so much attention on a single neighborhood of ten thousand people in a city with a population of nearly three quarters of a million. He had to be concerned both with the risk of failure and with the perception of favoritism. By visibly associating himself with the CBP effort, his leadership and management abilities could be judged harshly if things didn't go well.

The Enterprise Foundation was able to help mitigate these risks. With the significant resources it committed, it helped leverage additional private funding from national foundations and corporations. In this way the mayor was not perceived as favoring Sandtown with scarce public resources as much as he was seen attracting significant resources to Sandtown that otherwise would not be available to Baltimore.

The Sandtown experience has also shown how difficult it is to obtain funding on terms that encourage rather than undermine coherent neighborhood transformation efforts. With funding from nearly seventy different sources supporting over 110 different programs and projects, the job of securing, matching, tracking, and reporting on these activities is formidable (and underfunded, as most funders are reluctant to support the administrative costs of managing a large, multidimensional program). In part because funders want evidence of results that correspond to their categorical mandate and can be attributed to their funding, the paperwork requires four full-time staff and 10 to 20 percent of the time of all program managers.

But the paperwork burdens aren't the worst of it. The most destructive effects of current constraints are on programming. To respond to community needs in a coherent way, CBP leaders tried to design an initiative that crosses traditional categorical boundaries, but to get funding they had to break into pieces what they had so laboriously cobbled together. They had to submit grant requests that would conform to traditional programmatic categories, separating health services from employment, youth development from education, and family support from community building.

When CBP got HUD money for a family development center to be located in public housing, it took many months of negotiations to get permission for it to serve the entire neighborhood, including some people who didn't live in public housing. Similarly, HHS regulations prohibit outreach workers funded by its Healthy Start program to be trained to offer vital information about human service and employment programs to the clients they see for health promotion purposes.

Ronica Houston, who became executive director of CBP in 1995, laments that "everybody is trained in such a categorical mode, it's almost impossible to escape."

Despite all the difficulties, the stirrings in Sandtown are beginning to bring James Rouse's dream to life. But the Sandtown story also teaches that commitment, dedication, and inspiration may not be enough if funding and technical assistance can be obtained only on terms that are such a poor fit with comprehensive initiatives. Powerful forces that combine to undermine ambitious initiatives could be better resisted if new organizations like CBP had access to both funding and technical assistance offered on terms that meshed better with the needs of comprehensive neighborhood transformation efforts.

CCRP AND THE SOUTH BRONX CDCS: VENTURE CAPITAL
AND A FAIRY GODMOTHER

Since the 1950s, the South Bronx's claim to fame has been its devastation.

The Bronx had been a fine place to live, with the access it provided to good jobs in Manhattan, until after World War II, when industries in search of cheaper workers started to leave. Thousands of job seekers from the rural South and the Caribbean arrived in the 1950s and '60s, just as the jobs were going the other way.

As drugs, crime, and violence took over in the 1960s and early '70s, the residents of the Bronx who had a choice left. "Landlords too began to leave, many torching their buildings for the insurance money as a parting gesture," wrote Patrick Breslin in *Smithsonian*. "The banks and insurance companies left. More and more buildings burned, and then wrecking balls and bulldozers knocked down the hollow hulks."

That was when the South Bronx really became famous. *The New York Times* called it "the nation's most infamous symbol of urban blight . . . a bombed out relic and a synonym for hopelessness and decay." It became the premier site of photo opportunities to symbolize all that had gone wrong in America's inner cities. President Carter visited a charred and abandoned Charlotte Street in 1977 to illustrate his concern with the urban crisis. Ronald Reagan came while campaigning in 1980 to say he had not "seen anything that looked like this since London after the Blitz."

Then came the South Bronx miracle.

"In a city full of surprises, few are as striking as the contrast between the 20 year old image of the burned-out South Bronx, and the reality after what officials call the nation's largest urban rebuilding effort," wrote *The New York Times* in its news columns. "Take a Sunday drive," the *Times* editorialized, "and you will be surprised to see that the burned-out Bronx is largely gone."

Burned-out buildings have been replaced by apartment houses with curtains on the windows and—on the spring day when I was visiting—parents pushing baby carriages and children playing on the sidewalk. There are streets with new two-story houses with lawns and gardens and window boxes filled with flowers.

Charlotte Street itself had become a new kind of photo op: a development of eighty-nine single-family homes on grassy lots that look as though they had been flown in from Southern California. Some have wooden decks complete with barbecues.

Joe Santiago, a heating and air-conditioning engineer, grows pears, peaches, and apples in his backyard. "It's like a piece of the country inside the city," he says.

"The kids love it, they can play in the yard, and I don't have to worry," says Alexandra Immanuel, a nurse who came to New York from St. Lucia as a teenager. "The neighbors are good," she says, "everybody looks out for each other here."

The resurrection of the South Bronx has been going on since 1986. Abandoned buildings are rare, and nineteen thousand apartments have been rehabilitated. More than 2,500 new houses have been built for working-class home buyers and two thousand more are under construction.

The heroes of this story, editorialized *The New York Times* in 1995, are "the not-for-profit community development corporations that build and rehabilitate the buildings and who counsel the first-time home buyers who make up just about all of the new owners." Most of the construction was performed not by conventional for-profit developers but by the community development corporations (CDCs) described earlier in this chapter. Supported by sophisticated national intermediary organizations and aided in recent years by federal tax credits for low-income housing, several CDCs became a particularly potent force in the South Bronx.

Anyone who doubted that something really big was happening had only to look at *Business Week*'s year-end predictions for 1995, which were declaring Orange County *Out* and the South Bronx *In*.

But the housing revival was not, initially, matched in other spheres. The public schools were still as bad as they ever were, one third of adults didn't have a high school degree, one quarter couldn't read at a fourth grade level, one half had no history of labor force participation, and crime was rampant.

If there was one person in New York who was in a position to recognize the paradox of a miraculous physical renaissance occurring in the midst of woefully inadequate human supports, it was Anita Miller.

A one-time banker (she had been CEO of a New Jersey savings bank and acting chairman of the Federal Home Loan Bank Board in the Carter Administration), Miller had been intimately involved with South Bronx CDCs as a program officer at the Ford Foundation and later as program director at the Local Initiatives Support Corporation. Well connected to everyone who mattered in both the public and private sectors, Anita Miller not only recognized the paradox but was bursting to do something about it.

The opportunity came from Edward Skloot, executive director of the New York-based Surdna Foundation. Surdna had been supporting a lot of community development, and Skloot had been wanting to explore a broadened conception of community revitalization. Miller and Skloot together began to puzzle out how Surdna and other foundations might be able to help CDCs to build on their successes and to move beyond housing to become effective agents for comprehensive revitalization of neighborhoods. Early in 1991, Skloot asked Miller to do a feasibility study.

Miller not only recognized the opportunity and the need, she also recognized the difficulty. She and Skloot were convinced you had to start with a solid base in the community, and they concluded that the CDCs could provide that in a way that no other entity could. CDCs that had run large-scale housing programs had the community ties and the experience that gave them credibility in the neighborhood. And that credibility put them in a unique position to take on a far-reaching revitalization strategy.

But Miller also thought very carefully about what supports these CDCs would need to enable them to take on the broader agenda when there were no readily available sources of flexible money with which to attract and knit together many categorical and hard-to-use programs. She also knew that it would be difficult, if not impossible, for each CDC, operating in isolation, "to create a program with sufficient substance to satisfy funders while at the same time leaving participants with sufficient latitude to design their own efforts."

In the summer of 1991, Miller and Skloot proposed to the Surdna Foundation board that it launch, together with other funders, a large-scale effort, to be known as the Comprehensive Community Revitalization Program (CCRP). The CCRP would help selected CDCs to develop their capacity to take on a substantially expanded role and would act as an intermediary to make up for the defects in the existing arrangements to provide funding, technical assistance, time, and expertise.

Anita Miller's own role was critical from the outset. "She was the A-quality management that the initial funders banked on even before the CCRP strategy was fully developed," says Mike Sviridoff.

She would also be counselor, sounding board, devil's advocate, co-strategist, and link to government and other influential leaders. And it was her insight that the key to achieving an ambitious community agenda, in the South Bronx at least, was to provide socially entrepreneurial organizations that were well rooted in the community with a source of what was essentially venture capital. Through CCRP, the South Bronx CDCs would have ready access to funds that could be used flexibly and quickly to leverage additional funds and to support the core activities it was so difficult to fund from other sources. Through CCRP, the South Bronx CDCs could choose from a far better selection of experts and good ideas and best practices than they could identify on their own.

In essence, CCRP would be the fairy godmother that would have eased the struggles that made it so hard for Pat Costigan and his CBP colleagues to be effective.

In the fall of 1991 the Surdna Foundation committed $3 million to the CCRP plan. By 1996 a total of twelve foundations and two banks had contributed more than $8 million to support the initiatives with flexible money.

In choosing its CDC partners, CCRP decided to "start with the strong and make them stronger." The partnership began in 1992, with teams of residents, local agencies, and business interests coming together to plan the physical space in their neighborhoods. Miller had several reasons to put an early emphasis on physical planning. First, there was a devastating vacuum: No one else was doing this kind of planning. The city was filling every open space with housing projects, and no one else was making sure that vital neighborhoods would emerge from the ashes of the South Bronx. Second, it seemed important to engage people who lived and worked in the CCRP neighborhoods in a concrete task that required real, big decisions rather than by trying to work out a collaborative process in the abstract. Third, this would be an opportunity to establish a new precedent in how residents and CDCs could work together with local government and with outside experts.

Through months of intensive planning and outreach, CDC-led groups considered where parks, playgrounds, and health and child care facilities should be located, what kind of housing should be built on remaining vacant sites, what stores and banking would be needed, and where physical improvement and resident-police collaboration could deter crime. In involving professional urban planners, Miller made sure that the experts saw themselves, and were seen by the neighborhood people, as expert *helpers*—not as the people who would be calling the shots.

The "Quality of Life Physical Planning" was completed in 1994 at a cost of over $200,000. CCRP published a handsome graphic illustration of each community's vision for its neighborhood (which received the American Planning Association's first annual Presidential Award) and an idealized poster map showing housing, parks, playgrounds, medical facilities, and retail commerce. The professional planners and staff from The Trust for Public Land continue to work with each neighborhood's planning task force to assist in implementing the plans. Participating CDCs have attracted more than $3 million—largely in public moneys—for twelve different projects to rehabilitate old parks and playgrounds and to create new ones. Vacant lots have been turned into community gardens, and residents have removed tons of debris and been involved in cleaning up sections of the Bronx River. Three more open-space projects are receiving over $600,000 in grants and technical assistance from the federal Urban Resources Partnership Program.

With $150,000 in start-up money from CCRP, the Mid-Bronx Desperadoes Community Housing Corporation was able to begin work on a supermarket and shopping center complex that is expected to bring three hundred jobs into the community and significantly improve access to affordable goods for area residents. By mid-1996 MBD had been able to leverage $4.6 million in equity for the estimated $27 million project.

The CDCs continued to move beyond their traditional roles to bring disparate elements of their communities together to identify and address common needs. Through CCRP-funded outreach workers, each CDC has expanded its community organizing efforts—spending more time talking and listening to local citizens, and engaging them both to plan and participate in new programs.

When public safety emerged as a major CDC concern, CCRP organized a workshop with law enforcement officials and contracted with neighborhood security experts from the Citizens Committee for New York City to work with the CDCs. Today CDC staff, resident councils, and tenant associations are collaborating with local police and the district attorney's office to improve police accountability and communications and to involve residents in strategies aimed at reducing crime and increasing their sense of security.

CCRP has helped the CDCs to build the kind of management capacity that enables them to make a series of separate programs and projects add up to more than the sum of their parts. A cadre of consultants based in established agencies but committed to providing specialized assistance to CDCs on high-priority issues help with job training and placement, recreation, and maintaining a sophisticated management information system.

The family-oriented activities of the Mount Hope CDC illustrate how far beyond housing these CDCs have gone.

Before families receive their keys to move into the once abandoned but now transformed Mount Hope apartment houses, they meet with Mount Hope housing social workers. They discuss their housing, education, income, and employment histories, their health problems, and their children's special needs. They also talk about whom the family counts on for social support—relatives, friends, churches, etc. The social workers, who occupy the ground floor in one of six buildings (where 60 percent of the 261 units are occupied by formerly homeless families), make occasional home visits and help connect residents to appropriate supports.

Soon after the association with CCRP began, Mount Hope was able to supplement its counseling efforts with HIPPY, the Home Instructional Program for Pre-School Youngsters, which ultimately became the centerpiece of the CDC's family support services. HIPPY is an innovative child and family development program model founded in Israel and brought to the U.S. in the early 1980s by the National Council of Jewish Women with the support of Hillary Rodham Clinton in her capacity as wife of the governor of Arkansas. HIPPY boosts the prospects of at-risk toddlers by working with their parents at home to allow them to become more effective early teachers of their young children.

Mount Hope launched its HIPPY program for fifty families in the fall of 1994. Within a year enrollment doubled, and Mount Hope now uses HIPPY as the vehicle to connect resident families with one another and with whatever assistance they require. Area parents, trained as HIPPY outreach workers, have become particularly good at reaching isolated families.

Through outreach, tenants associations, tenant counseling, and a new self-awareness curriculum, it became clear that an alarming number of Mount Hope residents had suffered from domestic violence and seemed to have no safe place to turn. They reported that police were often unhelpful when called for assistance. In response, Mount Hope first conducted training for staff, then launched a support group for tenants who have suffered domestic violence, and acted to ensure better response to domestic violence disputes from the police.

While creating an elaborate social support system to help new residents transform their lives, Mount Hope's organizing and community development efforts are dramatically transforming the neighborhood surrounding its thirty-eight buildings with new parks, playgrounds, a thrift store, a credit union, and a new primary health care center operated by the Institute for Urban Family Health, a nonprofit affiliated with nearby Bronx-Lebanon Hospital. Not only does the new medical practice provide residents long-overdue access to primary health care, its doctors have given preference to local residents in staffing the clinic, and also sit on the board of the local HIPPY program. Mount Hope provides the services of one of its Spanish-speaking caseworkers to help in responding to nonmedical problems uncovered in the course of working with patients and their families.

Another example of how effective the South Bronx CDCs have become in integrating people-oriented and place-oriented interventions comes from the Mid Bronx Senior Citizens Council's CDC. Having made its reputation in developing 1,580 units of housing, Mid Bronx Seniors identified economic development and child care as top-priority needs in its community planning process. It is now immersed in efforts to provide child care for neighborhood preschoolers while helping their parents find work and providing care for their grandparents.

In 1994, after extensive networking, and with technical assistance support from CCRP, Mid Bronx Seniors became the sponsors of a new Head Start program. It soon became clear that while the Head Start program was serving the children well, no one was helping program parents with their needs for job training. Further networking resulted in a connection with Toby Herr, who had been working in Chicago on ways of combining Head Start with a self-sufficiency program for parents. Ricky Granetz, who was working with CCRP partners on employment issues, helped Mid Bronx Seniors to adapt key elements of Herr's approach at Project Match to the specific circumstances of the mid Bronx and secured funding from the Foundation for Child Development, which has a special interest in programs that work with parents and children simultaneously. Herr says that the flexibility and human development orientation of CCRP and Mid Bronx Seniors was a perfect fit with Project Match's basic elements of effectiveness.

The headquarters of Mid Bronx Seniors is now in the Andrew Freeman Home, which is being transformed into a family support center with the help of a $675,000 New York State award for capital improvements. My own visit to the ornate old mansion on the Grand Concourse, owned by the CDC and site of many of its activities, was dazzling. The Head Start kids were on the first floor with teachers, parents, aides, and trainees bustling about. The second floor—looking nothing like any facility for the aged I had ever seen—is home to some ninety elderly residents, alert and involved, and looking forward to seeing the little ones later in the day. The second floor is also where the meeting rooms and a library are, and where I met with the director, Jeannette Puryear, and senior staff of the Mid Bronx Seniors CDC and learned about some of the other activities. Among these is Healthy Living Systems, a catering venture housed in the renovated kitchen, which simultaneously provides meals to the Head Start children and parents and staff, to the elderly residents, and to the homebound elderly in the neighborhood. The catering business has trained and employed more than two dozen local residents and helps the staff learn about the barriers that residents have to overcome to be able to get jobs in less protected environments. "We try to give people the time they need to learn," says Puryear. "They need time to make mistakes and learn from them so they can acquire the problem-solving skills they need to surmount the complexities of becoming self-sufficient in a community like this one!"

With its capacity to synthesize experience from all of its sites, CCRP is in a particularly good position to help the CDCs to develop programs in response to emerging needs. After their earliest emphasis on physical planning, the South Bronx CDCs have been moving toward an ever-increasing focus on jobs.

When it began its self-sufficiency initiative, CCRP contracted with America Works, perhaps the best known of the New York job-training and placement agencies. It soon became apparent that this was not going to be a good fit. Isolated and fearful residents of CDC neighborhoods did not always act on recommended referrals, and America Works was rejecting too high a proportion of the clients the CDCs were referring. Part of the problem was that the CDCs had not developed the capacity to assess job readiness. The other part of the problem, explains Miller, was that America Works achieves its excellent placement record by focusing on people who speak good English, have solid presentation skills, and are basically job-ready. The high rate of rejections turned out to undermine the entire effort. Miller says that "you just can't afford to have rejects here—this population has had too much experience with being rejected." She was convinced that the CDCs needed to create or gain access to a culture prepared "to come up with whatever it takes to support people in their journey to self-sufficiency."

As ever in their problem-solving mode, Miller and the CDCs decided to turn to Federated Employment Guidance Services (FEGS), a respected job-training and mental health agency, which assigned staff to work with the CDCs to develop employment programs that took into account the many different kinds of supports that would be needed, including English-as-a-Second-Language training and GED classes; training of social service staff in employment-oriented and assessment skills; developing new models for the transition from welfare to work; and putting together a comprehensive on-line database listing 2,500 educational, vocational, and job-training/placement programs throughout New York City.

The CDCs have been able to fill a void in welfare-to-work programs by creating neighborhood-based employment services within each CDC that can engage the hard to reach and help them to prepare for, acquire, and retain suitable jobs. The CDCs will provide intensive post-placement support to newly employed residents every week for twelve weeks and then every month for a year.

One last aspect of the CCRP-CDC partnership strikes me as important to understand: the nature of the relationship between the initiative and the community residents, which emphasizes the residents' role as engaged citizens.

In analyzing the success of CCRP, Mitchell Sviridoff and William Ryan identify four possible styles of engagement between neighborhood residents and any given community-based initiative: The resident may be seen as *client,* the passive recipient of services provided by experts. The resident may be regarded as *empowered political activist,* the diametric opposite of the client, where the needs of the neighborhood are understood as resulting primarily from an imbalance of power. A third possibility is to view the resident as *policy maker,* which Sviridoff and Ryan consider problematic, because only a small fraction of a community's residents will have the time or inclination to participate in this way. The fourth possibility, which is the choice they believe CCRP has made, is to relate to the resident as *engaged citizen.* "It is the process of creating connections between residents and the local institutions that shape the life of their community. . . . It is widespread resident involvement that is best suited to the job of stabilizing or turning a community around and sustaining the progress. The more residents engage, the more they build up networks, contacts, trust and standards—all ingredients essential to a community's problem solving capacity." And, as

Robert Putnam argues, the more collective problem-solving a community does, the better it becomes at collective problem solving.

Sviridoff and Ryan believe, and I agree, that CCRP has been highly successful in connecting people to one another, not as clients or beneficiaries, not as participants in a contest for power or as policy makers, but as resources for one another. When they see the results of their planning, they see themselves not as consumers but as contributors. Vigorously engaged with one another, learning that together, by their own efforts, they can change their community and the course of their own and their children's lives, residents throughout the South Bronx seem indeed to be functioning as engaged citizens.

THE SAVANNAH YOUTH FUTURES AUTHORITY: A LONG JOURNEY WITHOUT A ROAD MAP

There were eight of us in the airport meeting room: Otis Johnson, a founder and the director of the Savannah Youth Futures Authority, his two colleagues, Arthur "Don" Mendonsa and Mary Willoughby, and five of us who had converged from various parts of the country to learn as much as we could about the Savannah experience. About halfway through our conversation, Otis Johnson suddenly said, "If we could just go back to the beginning, knowing what we know now!" He wasn't the first pioneer to have learned from hard-won experience, but his comment made me especially eager that others could learn enough from the Savannah experience that the journey might be made less arduous.

The Savannah story begins as a tale of service integration. Ten years later, the story is far from ended, but now contains compelling evidence that the combination of service reforms with community development is proving to be very powerful.

Otis Johnson dates the beginning of the journey as October 8, 1986, when Savannah city manager, Don Mendonsa, spoke to an upper-middle-class Savannah church audience about the city's "invisible population." He proposed to make it visible. He told of the 35,000 citizens who live in Savannah's inner city, suffering from racial discrimination, from the indifference of the majority community, and from the lack of any community initiative to improve the quality of their lives. He reported that the predominantly African-American residents of the inner city are victims in 90 percent of the city's homicides, almost 90 percent of the rapes, and nearly 80 percent of the assaults. And he warned that unless the entire community worked together for fundamental change, "we must be prepared to accept and live with the injury that is done to the quality of our lives as consequence of the conditions of their lives."

When Mendonsa took his message to the city council three weeks later, it struck council member Otis Johnson as welcome, if overdue. A professor of social work with a PhD in social welfare from Brandeis University, and one-time organizer for the Savannah Model Cities and Community Action programs, Johnson had just been elected to his second term as alderman and was intensely interested in stimulating action on Mendonsa's proposals. In discussions over the next several months, the two worried together about the difficulty of mobilizing community leaders on these issues. Not long after, as if in direct response to their concern, they each received from the mayor copies of a letter that had just come from the Annie E. Casey Foundation, inviting Savannah to become one of ten cities to receive a planning grant to compete for a much larger sum as part of the foundation's New Futures initiative. They were particularly pleased because, in order to participate, Savannah would be required to make a high-level leadership commitment to make the fundamental changes necessary to improve outcomes for high-risk youth.

Mendonsa has since retired as city manager, but he and Johnson are still working together today. From the outset, they shared the assumptions on which the Casey Foundation built New Futures:

- that building a collaborative governing body could change the delivery of human services, because the collaborative would be able to collect and use data specific to the community about such crucial social issues as teen parenting, school success, and teen idleness; key stakeholders would agree on measurable outcomes and on who had to do what to achieve them;
- that new awareness of the problem, together with a $10-million-dollar grant over five years, would provide the necessary motivation and incentive for change;
- that a focus on middle-school children was the optimal place to begin;
- that once it became apparent that no one agency could succeed in improving the crucial outcomes in isolation, collaboration among stakeholders would follow;
- that once the collaborative was empowered to "take on long established public institutions on behalf of disadvantaged youth," existing institutions would adopt case management and other restructuring to make services more responsive to the needs of youngsters.

Savannah won the five-year Casey grant in the spring of 1988 and persuaded the Georgia General Assembly to create a new public/private agency, the Youth Futures Authority (YFA), to develop and implement a comprehensive plan for youth in Savannah. The YFA would include four members appointed by the city, county, and school board, and three appointed by state commissioners.

The relationship between the YFA and the schools was rocky from the outset. There was a lot of jockeying for position and control with the school superintendent, and the schools were unhappy with YFA's interest in bringing about fundamental changes in schooling. The schools were looking to the collaborative for add-on funding for add-on programs—not for pressure to change how they did things. The schools were also uncomfortable with the YFA's collection and analysis of data on the school experience of children, disaggregated across race and gender lines. The data showed black boys to be at the bottom of every distribution, from truancy and suspension to course failure and dropping out.

Despite the schools' unhappiness, Mendonsa feels it was essential to get the data out. "If we had not aired our dirty linen in public, showing these astounding failure rates, I'm not sure we would have had as much support from the public as we've gotten."

Another early difficulty was that the main intervention the design called for—case managers assigned to youngsters identified as at risk—turned out to be very weak. The case managers were overworked, seriously circumscribed in their contacts with the youngsters, and unequipped to develop the strategies or to mobilize the resources that might change young lives. They were supposed to make at least three attempts a month to see their students face to face, but these meetings were usually very short and tended to take place in school hallways or lunchrooms. Even when meaningful relationships developed in these circumstances, case managers often were unable to stay with a particular child as their responsibilities changed. When case managers made a referral for more intensive or specialized services, nothing happened unless a parent followed through.

One case manager tried to get a summer job for Tonya, one of her charges, but found that the family's income made Tonya ineligible for one program and that she was too young for another. Then she discovered that Tonya shouldn't be working over the summer anyway, because she was supposed to go to summer school to avoid having to repeat seventh grade. It was midsummer when the case manager learned that Tonya was not in summer school, because the number of unexcused absences she had accumulated during the previous school year made her ineligible.

As very little seemed to be changing at either the individual or institutional level, YFA began to reassess. After two and a half years, the members of the authority became convinced that the problems they were trying to deal with didn't begin in middle school. If a significant proportion of black children are already two years behind in sixth grade, and if each year ninety black boys are suspended from school *while they are still in first grade,* surely any effective intervention would have to start much earlier—perhaps with prenatal care for the mother. And the object of intervention would have to be not just the individual child but the entire family—and even the entire school.

These insights shaped phase two of the Savannah initiative. The focus shifted from efforts to remediate past failures to preventing youths from acquiring multiple risk factors. Savannah won a Healthy Start grant to improve prenatal care for high-risk pregnant women, took steps to strengthen parenting skills and to expand access to quality preschool experiences, and to set up an adolescent health network.

Pressures to take on a broader agenda also increased as it became clear that a partnership between the schools and the chamber of commerce, known as the Savannah Compact, was not bearing fruit. Over 130 companies had agreed to provide mentors, to sponsor workplace visits, and to hire and provide remedial instruction to the 30 percent of seniors who wanted full-time employment after graduation and were functioning at least at a tenth-grade level. The board of education, for its part, promised to increase the number of students ready for full-time jobs. The businesses, it turned out, never had to deliver on their promises of jobs or remedial instruction because not enough of the graduating seniors had reached a tenth-grade level of performance.

Even as phase two was going into operation, it was clear that the outcomes the New Futures grant had hoped to impact were not improving conditions in Savannah or in any of the other New Futures sites. Johnson, Mendonsa, and several of their YFA colleagues came to realize that their goals would not be achieved unless they further expanded their domain.

"Because of the difficulties we encountered, we had to keep evolving," explains Johnson. "The goal and the vision remain the same: improving outcomes for children and families. But to get there, we had to take on much more, which is how—even though we started by doing services reform—we evolved into a comprehensive community initiative."

Casey provided two more years of funding to help YFA to expand its scope, and agreed that YFA would devise its own strategies to reflect its experience and its deeper understanding of what it would take to change outcomes. While the Casey Foundation had been quite correct in assuming that key stakeholders in the participating cities would be able to agree on measurable outcomes, they turned out to be overoptimistic in thinking that agreement that *something* should be done could be readily converted into agreement about *what* should be done. Neither cause nor remedy for the major problems was self-evident, and, according to two of the evaluators of New Futures, "in the absence of agreement about remedies, a profusion of proposals competed with each other for recognition and funding."

Mary Willoughby, YFA senior planner, confirms there was a "disconnect between the desired outcomes and the constrained repertoire of interventions." As Johnson put it, "We know the end point, the vision that drives us, but we have no road map showing how to get there."

But they were building theories. They were trying to follow, Willoughby said, "the chain of evidence." And first among the theories that informed their work in this phase was that "physical, economic, social, and human capital strategies had to be integrated," and that had to be done at the neighborhood level.

Two years earlier, Mendonsa had worked with the police department to produce a series of maps that showed the geographic overlap in the location of crimes, violence, delinquency, fires, substandard housing, female-headed households, poverty, infant mortality, and teenage parenting. The maps showed clearly that the city's social ills were concentrated in a four-square-mile section just south of the downtown business district, labeled "Area C." The residents of the area were hardly delighted by the notoriety they received, noting that theirs was the only neighborhood in town known by its police label. But they were also aware that the notoriety might be the route to mobilizing action. The YFA people were convinced that the maps were "worth a thousand words" in pointing out how directly neighborhood is implicated in all the outcomes of great concern, and in creating a consensus around the necessity of targeting interventions on the Area C neighborhood.

This is, in fact, exactly what has happened. For the first time, Area C now hosts its own police precinct. It has become the site of a new drug task force and a U.S. Department of Justice Weed and Seed program (designed to "weed out" the criminal element and "seed" the area with prevention services). In 1993 the area became one of five new sites of Columbia University's Children at Risk program to prevent substance abuse, known in Savannah as the Uhuru (freedom) project.

The YFA work was gradually achieving a much sharper focus. Johnson says, "We're flooded with Requests for Proposals, but we've stopped chasing dollars. We're not interested unless the offer fits our plans."

And the plans are to engage in "comprehensive community building" with the Area C residents, with a series of family resource centers as the physical manifestation of the concept. The first of these, the St. Pius X Family Resource Center, in an airy and inviting renovated one-time school building, opened on April 18, 1994. A multitude of services are located at the center, including health and mental health, nutrition, eligibility for income support, and the Uhuru family advocates. As important, the center is also home to a collection of activities that welcomes participants from throughout the neighborhood without their having to define a problem to participate. These include a soccer league, the Girl Scouts, Boys and Girls Clubs, conflict resolution classes, information and referral services, and a child development center for infants, toddlers, and preschool children. The hope is that the family resource center will become part of the everyday life of the neighborhood, and that it will be powerful enough to create a new culture in which staff feel that their primary responsibility is to the community, not their agency.

The center takes seriously the role of clients themselves in defining their needs. It is governed largely by community representatives, most of whom are active in other neighborhood activities and have status in the community. Many see the center as evolving to become a cornerstone of the community, showcasing local talent and sponsoring cultural programs such as African dance and arts.

A theme that runs increasingly through current YFA planning is an Afrocentric emphasis on the integrity of community, family, and the individual. Community leaders contend that middle-American values of self-reliance, self-discipline, good work habits, healthy ambition, and the reinforcement of family and community ties are made more accessible to the children and families of the neighborhood within an Afrocentric framework.

Johnson, Mendonsa, and Willoughby all believe if they can show that the existence of the family resource center, with its reoriented and enhanced services and supports and its community-building activities, actually changes outcomes among its participants, they could get the depth of support needed to change life outcomes among all children at risk in Savannah. If they could document a clear reduction in infant mortality or crime, in the number of new offenders, or in the disparities between black and white children's health or school readiness, they are convinced they could change Savannah.

Promising data are beginning to come in. Black infant mortality has dropped by nearly 45 percent since 1992. Births to black teens have dropped 12 percent. Foster care placements are down almost 25 percent over the past two years.

And why do Johnson and colleagues believe that they will be able to go to scale once they have documented impressive outcomes, when so many wonderful interventions remain, at best, an oasis? That's where the power of the YFA comes in, they say. Earlier models didn't have the structure of a ready-made public/private authority that could take what they had developed in the hothouse into the real world.

The fact that YFA is a new public/private entity created by the state legislature is so important, Johnson says, because the present structure doesn't work. "If the representatives on the school board from my community were doing what they were supposed to do, and were raising the issues that they should be raising, we wouldn't need a special school committee in my neighborhood. If the representatives on the city council from my community were raising the zoning issues which would keep outsiders from doing whatever they want in Area C, we wouldn't need a special housing and zoning committee in that neighborhood. The structure that is in place, the legitimate structure, is the problem. Because it is not representing the interests of the people."

Johnson has also thought deeply about the mix of people that should constitute a governing entity like the YFA. "To improve life in these communities you can't have an either/or philosophy: that it either has to be dominated by the people in the community or by the power brokers connected to the government. Neighborhood people, because they've been disempowered, don't have the wherewithal to move a comprehensive social change agenda by themselves, and need other stakeholders in government, in the business sector, and in the service sector as partners. There are too many outside factors impinging on neighborhoods for them to totally change their physical, social, and economic conditions by themselves, without enlisting significant other stakeholders."

Mendonsa concurs, and adds that the other difficulty with existing governmental structures is that they are set up categorically, and not set up to accomplish common goals. "We have to figure out a better design, so that on issues of housing, public order, crime, and economic development, government could deal with neighborhoods much more coherently."

And if they succeed in changing lives in Savannah, and if they can prove that they have done so, would the nation have the capacity to do it everywhere? Otis Johnson has thought about that, too. "If the will were there to make these [inner city] communities livable, then a lot of this discussion about capacity wouldn't be necessary. When the Russians sent up Sputnik, this country didn't have the capacity to match that feat. But the will was there. And the competition between Russia and the U.S. provided an opportunity to exert that will, and to agree on the expectation that in X number of years we will have a man on the moon. We built that capacity, and we did it. If this country ever develops the will, if we agree that we are not going to allow these conditions in any neighborhood, then I think we will build the capacity to do it."

A FORMER PRESIDENT AND A PROCESS-HEAVY, STRATEGY-LIGHT ATLANTA PROJECT

In 1991, former President Jimmy Carter promised to lead Atlanta in a campaign against the "devastating social problems associated with urban poverty." Rallying Atlantans to the inner-city cause, he suggested it would be embarrassing to host the Olympic Games amid urban decay. But when the Olympics came to Atlanta in 1996, not much had changed. Probably in deference to Carter's noble intentions, there were murmurs, but no shouts, asking why there was so little to show for $33 million and five years of effort.

"The greatest problem in the nation is that rich, powerful and secure people like us don't help poor people," President Carter had told *The Wall Street Journal* in 1992. "Somewhere in God's world there needs to be one major urban community that can successfully address these problems." The auguries seemed good for this antipoverty effort of unparalleled scale, which would mobilize government, business, citizen volunteers, universities and churches, as well as neighborhood residents. The bold Atlanta Project drew the attention of metropolitan leaders across the country, hungry for guidance on how to reverse the decay of their inner cities. In the months after the announcement, inquiries came in from Philadelphia, Milwaukee, San Francisco, New York City, Washington, D.C., Austin, Little Rock, and Los Angeles. The outpouring of demand persuaded the former president to expand his horizon and create the America Project to help other cities begin parallel efforts. By early 1995, more than two hundred delegations had come to Atlanta to study the project's techniques and results.

The Atlanta Project was organized around twenty neighborhood "clusters," each selecting two individuals, paid by the project, to represent its needs to the project's advisory board and secretariat. Each cluster would be paired with one of Atlanta's institutions of higher learning and a major Atlanta corporation. These were the only stipulations. Carter and his colleagues were determined not to repeat past mistakes of inventing programs on high and foisting them on low-income communities.

It was the bottom-up nature of the initiative that Carter emphasized in meeting with a small group from the National Community Building Network visiting the Atlanta Project headquarters on November 15, 1993. "I have seen so many programs designed by brilliant people, and they have all failed because we didn't allow the people to whom the programs were directed to decide," he said. "The neighborhoods have to be able to decide and we have to show that people of different races and with different backgrounds can work together."

Dan Sweat, a prominent member of Atlanta's white business establishment who was the project coordinator in its early years, underscored the point: "Unlike past efforts, corporate America is not trying to impose its own solutions."

In retrospect, it seems as though the ex-president and the Atlanta Project might have overlearned one valuable lesson to the exclusion of several other, equally important ones. Leery of dictating to those they intended to help, the project leaders leaned far over backward in providing only a blank slate and a process—and no substantive guidance. The process at the heart of the project, according to an early announcement, was based on "connecting people with people—rich with poor, young with old, and people of all ethnic racial and religious origins in a way that will enrich the lives of all involved." The idea was for people to connect not only spiritually and socially but also electronically through an elaborate communications system, donated by IBM, to link the twenty neighborhood clusters with each other and with headquarters.

On my visit I was dazzled by the sophistication of the futuristic communications network but disappointed to find it being used primarily to deal with logistical details. One neighborhood cluster signaled that it lacked a volunteer for tutoring on Monday afternoons, another that it needed more coloring books for a preschool session. The illusion of activity created by high-tech communications seemed to obscure the need for strategic thinking about solving fundamental problems.

My concern about the lack of strategic thinking was reinforced by my visit to a vocational high school. A guidance counselor proudly showed me the bank of computers for student use in a vocational guidance area. But they were programmed with only generic information on vocations, and included no local or regional data on job availability or projections of future industry demand. The school was part of a cluster paired with Delta Airlines. Several Delta executives were expected to sign up for tutoring, but no one knew of any arrangement with Delta to employ graduates of the school.

So much time and energy were going into establishing the clusters, identifying community leaders, and making sure that all planning came from the neighborhoods that the process was in danger of collapsing under its own weight.

"The Atlanta Project was beginning to look a bit like General McClellan's Union army—all preparation and no action," observed the *Atlanta Constitution* ominously.

About eighteen months into the operation, with few visible results from the efforts of so many earnest citizens, the staff decided on a citywide immunization campaign. On April 17 and 18, 1993, seven thousand volunteers knocked on tens of thousands of doors to spread the word that parents should bring their preschool children to free clinics for vaccinations. The *Atlanta Constitution* described the impact of the volunteer campaign as "astonishing."

But an ambitious citywide weekend mobilization proved easier to bring about than day-to-day change in the neighborhoods. The first evaluation report pointed out that while the vaccination campaign had indeed been successful, the project had done less well in enlisting volunteers for long-term tasks such as tutoring in the public schools. The evaluators also found a lack of strategic thinking and action. "A large amount of time and money has been spent on projects that bear little or no relationship to the project's goals," the report said. "Too many neighborhood projects have focused on health fairs, taking children on trips to museums and other 'feel good' activities that have had little effect on creating jobs or alleviating other aspects of poverty."

Five years from its inception, the Atlanta Project scaled down its operations and ended its support of the cluster offices. Jimmy Carter expected some neighborhoods to continue their relationships with their corporate and university partners. He pledged that he and his wife would continue their participation.

The one neighborhood office that stayed in business, independently of the Atlanta Project since mid-1996, provides an impressive illustration of how the clusters were meant to work. Joan Walsh, who wrote about the Atlanta Project for the Rockefeller Foundation, attributes the success of the Therrell cluster to its three leaders—Nick Snider, Helen Catron, and Eric Flowers. Snider was executive vice president of United Parcel Service in 1992 when he joined the project as corporate advisor. Before long he stunned his UPS colleagues by deciding to work with the cluster full-time. His partner, cluster coordinator Helen Catron, had run Head Start programs in Chicago under Mayor Richard Daley. Catron, who is African-American, says that Snider, who is white, ran into residents' doubts about his motives for working in an almost exclusively black neighborhood. He dealt with that by rolling up his sleeves and going to work—"harder than anyone could believe." Catron says, "He went to all the meetings. He listened, he didn't just talk. He was never condescending."

Eric Flowers, a graduate of Therrell High School, West Point graduate, and Desert Storm veteran, became the third of the leadership trio. He showed up one day, volunteering to start a Therrell alumni mentoring program. Catron and Snider persuaded him to stay and become assistant cluster coordinator, initially working with young people on violence prevention.

The three helped the cluster to organize an independent, nonprofit corporation and to establish a family resource center called The Family Tree. The center will provide cultural and recreation activities and become the site of a coordinated array of student and family services. UPS, the Casey Foundation, and the Carter Center have together committed a million dollars to support the center, to be run jointly by Flowers (now the cluster coordinator) and science teacher Adrienne Doanes, who had been active in the cluster from the beginning as chair of the education committee. Catron says she is proud of what they are leaving behind, but regrets that few other clusters can boast a similar legacy. She thinks it was a mistake to provide so little training and direction for cluster coordinators, and to think that five years would be a realistic time frame for community change.

As an outside observer, it strikes me that Catron is right, and that much more would have been achieved if the energy released by the ex-president's call for transcending race, class, and economic lines had been combined with more strategic thinking. The Atlanta Project's theories of change—let the neighborhoods decide, and get people of different races and backgrounds working together—were incomplete. Strategies were never linked with outcomes. Seeds may have been planted that have yet to sprout, but for now, the successes that have been achieved have been more a matter of happenstance than design.

A RELIGIOUS MISSION AND STRATEGIC OPPORTUNISM IN NEWARK

Newark's New Community Corporation is widely considered the country's most successful community development corporation. Its origin goes back to July 14, 1967, when a Newark cab driver was stopped by two police officers for passing their double-parked cruiser on 15th Avenue. Before booking him for tailgating and driving the wrong way on a one-way street, the officers beat him brutally in public view. Black taxi drivers quickly spread the word around the city over their radios. Five days of bloody rioting followed, leaving twenty-three dead and more than one thousand injured.

Life magazine called it "the predictable insurrection." If the riot was predictable, given the severe poverty and miserable living conditions of Newark's black residents, very little had been done to prevent it, even though Newark's business leaders had released a study seven months earlier calling Newark's problems "more grave and pressing than those of perhaps any city in the nation."

Once a bustling commercial hub where immigrant families could gain their bearings before moving on to the middle class, Newark had become an emblem of urban decay, with the lowest per capita income of any American city. Entire sections of Newark's Central Ward had been abandoned even before 1967. As in the South Bronx, most of the rest was soon leveled by arsonists or by urban renewal.

Aftershocks, including heightened racial tensions and declining investment in the city, can still be felt in Newark today. But not within the walls of the restored Gothic church where, in 1994, I sipped flavored iced tea and listened to a young man playing classical music while waiting for my appointment with the founder and director of New Community, Monsignor William Linder. The breathtaking building houses the corporation's offices, a health spa, a sandwich shop, a fine restaurant, and a group medical practice, all looking out on an atrium where people sit, talk, and eat accompanied by music from the grand piano. "Good food and music are a means of attracting people from the university and medical center and neighborhood businesses into our community, a way of combating the trend toward ever greater isolation between the haves and have-nots," explained Monsignor Linder later.

Monsignor Linder came to Newark in 1963 as a priest at Queen of Angels parish in the Central Ward. An activist unafraid of controversy, with early connections to the Southern Christian Leadership Conference, the benign-looking Linder has been called "a guerrilla on behalf of the community."

In the months following the 1967 disorders, community activists gathered at Father Linder's church and decided to create an organization to rebuild the abandoned wasteland that was central Newark, and channel the anger of its residents into community development, housing, and supportive services. They formed a board and called their dream the New Community Corporation. They visited innovative housing developments throughout the Northeast and worked with architects on plans for housing that would meet the needs of low-income families like their own. That meant homes that looked like homes—only a few stories high, roomy and comfortable, appropriate for raising families—a sharp departure for inner-city, low-income housing.

The first buildings were completed in 1975. Each apartment had an outside entrance and all were built around a common courtyard, with the kitchen designed so parents could look out and watch their children at play.

That was the beginning. Today NCC consists of thirty legal entities, including six for-profit enterprises. It owns and manages 2,500 new or refurbished apartments housing more than 6,500 residents in nine locations. It operates transitional housing along with an array of social services for homeless families, teen mothers, victims of domestic violence, and abused or neglected children awaiting permanent placement. It runs a credit union, a scholarship fund, and after-school, summer, and teen-parent programs. NCC also provides day care services for more than six hundred children in seven "Babyland" sites, which include a Head Start program and a center for HIV-positive children. NCC health services include a group health clinic, medical transportation services, a home health care service with more than four hundred patients, and a 180-bed nursing home.

NCC employs residents to supply support services for its retail ventures, including a one-hundred-person security force, a staff of carpenters, plumbers, painters, and others to maintain the properties, and a sewing center that provides uniforms and other items for NCC employees. By 1993, NCC was one of only ten Newark corporations employing more than one thousand people.

Like other flexible, lithe, fast-on-their-feet community initiatives, NCC provides a hospitable setting for adapting interventions developed elsewhere. Thus, in the fall of 1993, it added to its extensive job training and placement efforts a new partnership with the Center for Employment Training, the highly acclaimed program based in San Jose, California, to help low-skilled residents move to at least moderately skilled employment. The program emphasizes making training resemble work experience as much as possible. That is particularly suited to the NCC setting, since trainees can apprentice in construction work, carpentry, electrical work, and health services as part of activities already under way at NCC.

Intensive support services are a mainstay of the CET-NCC partnership. Trainee Kevin Edwards, who describes himself as a recovering addict, says, "I've had some difficult times, but the folks here really care about us. A teacher will call your house if you don't come to class." Even more important, the support often continues for months after a graduate is hired. Kathy Spivey, NCC's director of staff development, makes sure of that. In fifteen years as a regional director of human resources for McDonald's, she learned that one reason managers try to avoid hiring someone from a training program is the high probability of failure when there is no support mechanism. In the past ten years, the NCC employment center has been able to place more than nine thousand applicants.

NCC's most visible accomplishment is probably its Pathmark Shopping Center, opened in 1990, the only major supermarket to be built in the Central Ward since the 1967 riots. To establish Pathmark, NCC fought in court and city hall to acquire the land, and assembled $16 million in financing through state and federal grants, commercial loans, loans from two foundations, its own equity, and the social investment of religious communities. The shopping center employs 325 workers, and dozens of local residents who got their starts in the Bergen Street Pathmark have subsequently transferred to other Pathmarks.

Fifty thousand shoppers come to the Pathmark each week, and the Pathmark corporation reports that, square foot for square foot, revenue is double the national average. Two thirds of profits from the store go to NCC, which invests them back into the community's job-training and housing programs.

Because of its long and rich experience, NCC has been widely studied. Most observers identify as principal characteristics NCC's toughness, responsiveness, ability to seize opportunities while remaining committed to its mission, and its spiritual underpinnings.

Stories of NCC toughness abound. Bill Brooks, vice president for corporate responsibility of Prudential Insurance, says, "When Bill Linder comes in here I don't know whether to duck, sew up my pockets, or leave town. He is very likely to go away with what he is seeking." A city official who frequently deals with NCC observes that "NCC people turn around their Roman collars when they come in here. They play hardball." Linder says that's a good reputation to have. "You have to get the reputation that you can't be stopped. That took us fifteen years. It's only then that you can break their silly rules!"

NCC's director of development, Raymond Codey, likes to tell the story of Harmony House, an apartment complex for the homeless designed by NCC with the help of the giant pet food company, Hartz Mountain Industries. As they were ready to break ground, HUD, which held title to the land, announced that its approval would take six more months.

"We politely left the meeting and we broke ground at eight o'clock the next morning," Codey smilingly recalls. "We built the building and sent HUD a picture and . . . 'freaked out' would be a bad choice of words, but they were extremely upset. We got Secretary Kemp to call HUD's Newark office and tell them to wake up and smell the coffee, that helping people to help the homeless is what their mission is all about. They resolved the situation within an hour."

One of NCC's greatest strengths has clearly been its ability to respond to the changing needs of its community. "Fifteen years ago," recalls Joe Chaneyfield, vice president of the board and New Community Homes tenant, "we had no plans to build a shopping center, a nursing home, or a homeless shelter. But, as these needs arise, we rise to the needs." Chaneyfield's explanation is a simple but accurate summary of how NCC has done business over the past twenty years.

The trust that permeates relationships among the many parts of NCC is clearly based on a shared sense of overarching mission. So important is the organization's success to its leaders, Linder points out, that even relatives of board members can be fired for incompetence without a complaint from the board.

The religious component is fundamental. Linder says that hardly anyone appreciates how alienated low-income people are from secular institutions. It is Christian social teachings, he says, that give people in the organization a sense of their power by helping them see there is something bigger than the institutions they are up against. He explains he is not talking about sectarian beliefs. Most people who make up New Community are not Catholic. He speaks of his religious roots as growing more out of the civil rights movement than the Church, and says his theology focuses more on bringing social justice to the poor here on earth than in the hereafter.

The real secret of New Community's success may lie in the way it has combined religion and opportunism. When Karl Koechlin, who wrote his master's dissertation about NCC, told Linder this was the conclusion he had come to, Linder agreed, but added that it was the religious component that *allowed* NCC to be opportunistic. Grounded on religious teachings of social justice, NCC can adapt and shift as opportunities present themselves without fear of losing its way. Its social justice goals keep it focused. As Koechlin describes it, "NCC's ability to learn about its environment allows it to see what is possible; its moral perspective, influenced heavily by Christian teaching, enables it to see what is necessary."

SHIFTING POWER TO THE DUDLEY STREET NEIGHBORHOOD IN BOSTON

The director of Boston's Dudley Street Rebuilding Community Initiative, May Louie, told a group of us in January 1997, "We believe in power, and we believe that the people who live in the neighborhood should have the most to say about what happens there." The distribution of power between neighborhood residents and outsiders was, from the very start, central to the development of Dudley Street Neighborhood Initiative. The impoverished multiracial, multiethnic neighborhood had long felt abused by the city of Boston. First, it was urban renewal in the 1960s. Then, when the neighborhood tried to buck the disinvestment, arson, and "redlining" of the 1970s by proposing a partnership with the city, city officials simply laughed.

Evangelical Baptist minister Reverend Paul Bothwell recalls a city representative telling a committee from the neighborhood, "This city don't make partnerships with nobody! We don't need partnerships! We do what we want to do and we'll do it in our time!"

With the highest concentration of vacant land in Boston, the Dudley Street neighborhood had become a dumping ground for illegal toxic waste, abandoned cars, and three illegal commercial trash-transfer stations. An official city report found neighborhood decay to be the result of pressures from developers, the inability to get mortgages, the exodus of stable-income residents, and a decline in property values, creating a sense of entrapment for those who remained. Yet neither the city nor the downtown business interests were about to come to the aid of the Dudley residents.

Resentment of Boston's establishment ran so high that when Boston's Riley Foundation came to a neighborhood meeting in early 1985 to unveil a well-funded, long-term revitalization proposal, the residents flat-out rejected it because it would not be run by neighborhood residents. The meeting made it clear: Whatever was done would be governed by a board on which residents of the area would be a majority, with equal representation for the neighborhood's four major cultures—black, Cape Verdean, Latino, and white.

Foundation board members agreed, convinced by what they heard at the meeting that the neighborhood improvement they sought could best be brought about by a strategy of community and individual empowerment.

At DSNI, resident involvement meant resident control. And resident control meant that the funders would declare their willingness to give up control of the agenda-setting process. As board member—and subsequent executive director—Rogelia Whittington tells it, DSNI leaders go to foundations on this premise: "You're contributing to something here, but it's not your agenda. If it's your agenda, we don't want your money. But if you want to support our agenda, this is what we plan to do and this is how we plan to do it." One longtime member of the DSNI Human Development Committee, Najwa Abdul-Tawwab, explained that going along with a funder's agenda would be selling out. If the funder isn't willing to "do it the way we want it done . . . we're not going to do it."

This outlook has given DSNI its distinctive character. DSNI has been able to get foundation funds on its own terms, but not public categorical funds, which typically require a commitment to provide certain specified services or to work toward certain specified or negotiated outcomes. Hence, it is not surprising that DSNI's major achievements have been in community building and in the politics of physical revitalization rather than service provision or reform.

The first of DSNI's dramatic victories was the city's agreement, following a vigorous, neighborhood-wide campaign, to clean up the long dumped-upon vacant lots. ("The stench, which for so many years had hung over the neighborhood, was lifted!") When DSNI went to the local newspapers with lists of abandoned cars, city tow trucks began to appear. That happened in 1986. The following year DSNI got a commuter rail stop to downtown Boston restored.

In 1987, DSNI turned up the heat in its "Don't Dump on Us"

campaign, demanding the closing of the illegal trash-transfer stations that were breeding grounds for rats, mosquitoes, odor, and disease. Ché Madyun, newly elected DSNI president, declared, "There is nothing that says that just because you don't have a lot of money you should live in filth." Residents met, picketed, and finally marched to the mayor's office. They were thrilled to hear Mayor Ray Flynn tell his lawyers to stop stalling and shut the trash-transfer stations down. When the operators continued dumping, the mayor led a team of city officials to the trash stations and padlocked the gates.

Father Walter Waldron of St. Patrick's Church says, "When some of the trash folks were trashed—closed down—it became acceptable to believe that if *they* could be changed, then so could other things."

These victories were about more than physical renewal. They were also about changing residents' perceptions of their neighborhood and of their own power to change the conditions in which they live.

Among the residents' central concerns was control of the area's vacant land. They worried about becoming part of the gentrification sweep that had displaced low-income residents of Boston's South End. The vacant land was concentrated in a sixty-four-acre tract known as the Triangle in the heart of the neighborhood. There was no way to develop a coherent piece of property because half the packets of land were owned by the city and half were privately owned, mostly under municipal liens or tax-foreclosure petitions. Most lots were too small to develop, and foreclosing on the properties, one by one, would be prohibitively expensive and time-consuming.

DSNI's pro bono consultants and lawyers unearthed an obscure provision in state law holding that a public entity—in this instance the Boston Redevelopment Authority—could exercise the power of eminent domain and authorize an urban development corporation to acquire land for the purpose of developing low- and moderate-income housing. DSNI staff and board faced two big questions: Dared they make an ally out of eminent domain, the traditional enemy of the poor, used a decade earlier by public agencies to displace low-income residents to make way for luxury high-rises as part of urban renewal? Second, what was the chance of convincing the city to grant this kind of sovereign authority to a low-income-neighborhood group?

Having decided to make the bold move, board and staff developed a sophisticated political strategy. They targeted the mayor's office, the Boston Redevelopment Authority, the city's Public Facilities Department, and private developers, any one of which could squash the deal. The mayor's eagerness to be the first in the nation to grant the right of eminent domain to a nonprofit neighborhood group proved decisive.

Even with the mayor's support, it took a year, a lot of politicking, and organizing under the slogan, "Take a stand, own the land." On November 10, 1988, the Redevelopment Authority Board, its reluctant unanimous vote taken under considerable pressure, announced to a cheering Dudley Street crowd that eminent domain had been granted. The following week the business organ, *Banker and Tradesman,* editorialized, "There is nothing new about community residents uniting to influence the thrust of development in their neighborhoods. What is very new, however, is a community-based group that doesn't have just the ability to influence development, but the authority to control it, as well."

DSNI developed a comprehensive community revitalization plan that was adopted by the City of Boston as its official plan for the neighborhood. It received a $2 million loan from the Ford Foundation to buy vacant land for redevelopment.

DSNI leaders used the momentum of its land triumph to launch other initiatives. They obtained new traffic lights and better mass transit. They created a human services collaborative, and put up a mural celebrating community unity and diversity. They set up after-school programs and summer camps, built gardens and playgrounds and a neighborhood park, renovated more than three hundred housing units, constructed seventy-seven new single-family and cooperative homes, and are working on plans to construct some two hundred more units.

Interviews with DSNI board members made clear that their most strongly held belief—their overriding theory of change—was that community and individual empowerment was the only road to a better life for the neighborhood's people. They saw means and ends as virtually identical—a better life being defined as overcoming disenfranchisement and powerlessness, and being achieved by overcoming disenfranchisement and powerlessness. They saw individual activities as validated by the fact that the neighborhood had chosen them. Other goals, such as lower poverty rates and crime rates, would similarly be reached through community and individual empowerment.

DSNI activists cite the teachings of social critic John McKnight to explain their reluctance to focus on other goals like lowering rates of teenage pregnancy and school dropouts. McKnight holds that since service dollars are focused on meeting needs, "local leaders are, in effect, being forced to denigrate their neighbors and their community by highlighting their problems and deficiencies." DSNI leaders are skeptical of becoming involved with human service agencies, which they see as responding only to symptoms. "And treating symptoms doesn't cure problems. It just maintains them and sometimes proliferates them, and keeps them here."

In the spectrum of community initiatives, DSNI is probably at the extreme end of emphasizing process over product. In the words of its first executive director, Peter Medoff, it believes that "in the long run, the products will be more and better if the process is empowering." Medoff held that DSNI made the city of Boston more responsive to its citizens and taught city officials to "recognize the value of neighborhood expertise and vision." In a book about DSNI, published after his untimely death, Medoff wrote, "Where there was once powerlessness, there is community control. There is Dudley pride."

I was able to witness Dudley pride for myself, in 1996, at its twelfth anniversary celebration, which also featured the premiere of an award-winning documentary film about DSNI. It was a gala evening, with ethnic food from more cultures than I could count or recognize, and more joy among the many hundreds of revelers than seemed conceivable in a community that was still so depleted.

It was a great celebration and a wonderful evening. Next day, no longer under its spell, I thought about the children of Dudley Street, still not receiving the education needed to make it in a high-tech economy, about the high rates of unemployment, and about how the community still believes that the police invent charges to humiliate neighborhood youth by strip-searching them in public places. I couldn't help wondering whether, despite its impressive victories, the neighborhood was paying a price in adopting an ideology that limited its ability—so far at least—to engage with the police, the social service system, the education system, the job training system, or economic development to impact more profoundly the lives of neighborhood residents.

EMPOWERMENT ZONES: A NEWCOMER WITH MOMENTOUS POTENTIAL

Deborah Wright, CEO of the Upper Manhattan Empowerment Zone, says that the federal Empowerment Zone legislation is a statement that inner cities matter to the future of this country.

Authorized by Congress in 1993, the Empowerment Zones (EZs)

are the government's most comprehensive effort in thirty years to rebuild areas of persistent poverty. EZs are indeed remarkable, both for their symbolism and their potential.

Most unusually, the design of the federal program makes use of the lessons of past experience. Cities are not told what to do, but asked what they could and would do to revive their most distressed neighborhoods, with a pledge of federal help in getting it done. The legislation foresees a long-term (ten-year) scope, legitimizes the neighborhood as a locus of change, and mandates simultaneous investment in economic and human development, community building, and service reform. It encourages the use of EZ funds to leverage money from other sources, and requires involvement of community residents, businesses, and local institutions—a much broader array of participants than the initiatives of the War on Poverty included. And it targets the bulk of its funds on just eight cities and three rural areas.

In addition to tax benefits and tax credits, the staples of past efforts to regenerate depressed areas, each of the distressed communities designated an Empowerment Zone is entitled to $100 million in social services funds. (A designation as an Enterprise Community went to sixty urban and thirty-three rural communities as a sort of consolation prize with fewer benefits.) The designers of the legislation had also learned from the past that communities would need help in making federal funding easier to use, and made it possible for federal agencies to waive specific program requirements so that funds from different programs could be combined and reallocated. Communities were encouraged to identify bureaucratic impediments to better program design and service delivery. To help local communities negotiate their way through the maze of federal programs, President Clinton created a high-level interagency structure, the Community Empowerment Board (chaired by Vice President Al Gore and including the heads of seventeen federal agencies). State and local government were encouraged to take analogous steps.

If this process achieves its promise, it will shatter precedent and enable communities to use federal resources more coherently and therefore more effectively than in the past. Policies of economic uplift for inner-city neighborhoods, from housing to business development, from public safety to service reform, have traditionally been, according to former Philadelphia Councilman Ed Schwartz, "a bureaucratic nightmare." Getting the federal act together would go far toward making this initiative succeed where past efforts have failed.

Perhaps reflecting confidence that this could indeed happen, HUD designed an unusually promising approach to evaluation. The criteria for assessing success are based on the local vision for the community's transformation, but also include "key dimensions of community transformation that are common to all sites, or that are so important to national objectives that they shall be documented consistently for all . . . communities."

The communities that would receive EZ awards were chosen in December 1994, but some encountered early snags, arising primarily from disagreements about the composition and powers of governing boards. There were also some hopeful early signs. In October 1994, anticipating formal designation of the Harlem-South Bronx area as an EZ, Fleet Bank announced $70 million in low-interest loans for the area. Fleet Bank's James Murphy said, "Harlem's coming back, and the EZ deserves a lot of credit."

A month after the EZs were designated, urban affairs columnist Neal Peirce reported that the competition had "already sparked a wave of local partnerships and commitments that's worth many times any Federal cash or tax benefit."

By early 1996, the private sector in Detroit had already pledged $2 billion to the EZ, including a $750 million investment from the Chrysler Corporation in a new engine plant and a $200 million investment from General Motors to expand and improve an existing assembly plant in the zone. Local universities and colleges also responded with targeted plans for job training, work readiness, and education programs.

In Philadelphia, a commercial glass-making company that had left for the suburbs seven years ago is returning, bringing all forty-eight jobs back with it. A soldering business based in Malaysia will expand into the U.S., with the Philadelphia zone as its base. At least one and possibly two Pathmark supermarkets will be moving into the Philadelphia zone, with jobs for several hundred people who live there.

By mid-1996, the Harlem EZ reported being "flooded" with applications to share in the more than $250 million to be distributed to businesses and not-for-profit social agencies over ten years that were prepared to contribute to the revitalization of the area. The applicants include the Gap ("We think Harlem is retailing's best kept secret"); a marina that would build 105 new boat slips at the northern tip of Manhattan; a restaurateur hoping to resurrect the jazz club where bebop was born; Greyhound Bus Lines, which proposed to build an employee training center; and the Sony Corporation, seeking a partnership with Magic Johnson to build a multiplex cinema, a health club, a rooftop skating rink, and stores to make it the largest retail complex in Harlem, and, with five hundred workers, its largest commercial employer.

But looming over these hopeful developments was the threat of cutbacks in antipoverty and urban programs. A Columbia University report indicated that EZ executives were "deeply concerned that Federal and state budget reductions would . . . seriously undermine the EZ program and have especially detrimental effects on the EZs' capacity to improve conditions for children and families." Many worried that EZs would be expected to make up for service cuts and that funding cuts would diminish the EZs comprehensive approach to community development.

The potential of the Empowerment Zones, whose realization depends on developments that cannot yet be foreseen, is enormous. The potential is greater because the legislation incorporated past lessons learned; because EZs appeal to both conservatives and liberals; and because—as we will see at the end of this chapter—the EZs could serve as the vehicle for a massive infusion of investment to resurrect the nation's inner cities.

Community Rebuilding: Something Important Is Happening

The community rebuilding efforts I have just described add up to an extraordinary social development with stunning implications for the future.

Why have these developments gone unheralded? Why have they received virtually no national recognition?

Perhaps the main culprit in accounting for their getting so little notice is the general conviction that nothing works, that all major social problems have become intractable. In addition, enough past efforts at urban revitalization have failed that many of those who might have led or supported such efforts have turned their attention elsewhere. Further, because these initiatives really are local, they come to wider attention only spasmodically, and without being related to any larger social movement. Many proponents of these initiatives, aware of the inadequacy of current funding and the fragility of long-term support, sense the depth of the public's skepticism and are hesitant to raise expectations. When little signs of hope do appear in a magazine feature or on the network news, they pop up in decontextualized randomness, and can't break through the barriers of disbelief.

But a careful look at the evidence, from both research and experience, suggests that these developments deserve far more attention than they have been getting. The evidence suggests we know enough about what works in putting together effective interventions in targeted neighborhoods that we could make comprehensive place-based interventions into a promising response to the deepest problems of America's inner cities.

Successful systematic efforts to change the circumstances of life in the inner city have several common elements that are now widely agreed upon.

The Elements of Successful Community-rebuilding Initiatives

1. *Successful initiatives combine action in the economic, service, education, physical development, and community-building domains.* The hallmark of the new community initiatives is the determination to go beyond fixing individual problems. They set out "to foster a fundamental transformation of poor neighborhoods, and of the circumstances and opportunities of individuals and families who live there." They reflect the conviction that past efforts have been fundamentally flawed because they attempted to address the many problems clustered among people in poverty just one problem at a time.

Even service agencies were finding that services alone could not respond to many families' most urgent needs. A 1991 survey of member agencies of Family Services of America found that while the problems contributing to family distress overwhelmingly included housing, crime, poverty, and difficulties at school, agencies responded by offering the families psychological counseling nearly 90 percent of the time.

There are signs that more and more communities all over the country are beginning to respond to deteriorating neighborhood conditions by blurring the sharp divisions among prevailing categorical programs and among prevailing ideological divides. Earlier arguments between the adherents of economic versus behavioral explanations, and between service-based or opportunity-based remedies, are beginning to subside as more people come to see these arguments as unproductive and the either/or choices as moot. More recognize that the well-being of children, families, and communities are inseparable. People most concerned about the inadequate economic-opportunity structure, and people most concerned about individual inadequacies that make it impossible for those left behind to take advantage of whatever opportunities are available, are beginning to see it is no more productive to be blind to one as to the other.

More and more initiatives are adopting a broad, noncategorical, nonideological, comprehensive approach. The leaders of these initiatives may argue endlessly about how comprehensive an array of activities an initiative has to be committed to in order to call itself comprehensive, but the crucial common principle seems to be that they all share a *comprehensive mind-set.*

They distinguish between a comprehensive mind-set and a comprehensive mandate. A comprehensive mandate from the funder, which includes a laundry list of separate programs and activities that the nascent initiative is expected to launch all at once, is not only overwhelming to staffs and boards but makes it impossible to respond to community needs and demands as they emerge. Harold Richman, director of the Chapin Hall Center for Children and co-chair of the Roundtable for Comprehensive Community Initiatives, says that a comprehensive mandate can paralyze an initiative, force it into excessively lengthy planning, or lead it to function at such a superficial level that it is entirely ineffective just so it can say, yes, at least we've picked something from column A, something from column B, and something from column C.

The most promising initiatives all use—and are encouraged by their funders to use—a comprehensive lens as they survey both problems and opportunities. They all understand the necessity and the effectiveness of working simultaneously on economic and physical development, service and educational reform, and community building. But they are strategic in choosing where to begin, in sequencing their activities, and in how much they take on at once.

2. *Successful initiatives rely on a community's own resources and strengths as the foundation for designing change initiatives.* Successful community-based change initiatives reflect the specific assets, needs, institutional relationships, and power structures of individual communities. There is no one model of neighborhood transformation that could be applied everywhere. Designing the neighborhood change effort to fit individual communities is closely linked to the process of community building.

Community building, which has become such an important element of effective community initiatives, is more an orientation than a technique, more a mission than a program, more an outlook than an activity. It catalyzes a process of change grounded in local life and priorities. Community building addresses the developmental needs of individuals, families, and organizations within the neighborhood. It changes the nature of the relationship between the neighborhood and the systems outside its boundaries. A community's own strengths—whether they are found in churches, block clubs, local leadership, or its problem-solving abilities—are seen as central. Community building is based on the belief that inner-city residents and institutions can and must be primary actors in efforts to solve the problems of their neighborhoods.

In her report on community building for the Rockefeller Foundation, Joan Walsh emphasizes that the community building movement is resolutely inclusive and multiracial. She sees it "as much an attempt to complete the business of the civil rights movement as of the War on Poverty."

The meanings of community building are and will continue to be many and varied. They include efforts to create "a political impact on large impersonal forces," as the Empowerment Zones are trying to do to make up for the loss of industrial jobs, and as DSNI was able to do to stop Boston trash haulers from dumping trash in its neighborhood. They also include efforts to enhance "the capacity of individuals to believe that they can change the course of their own lives by their own efforts," as when neighborhood residents make decisions as part of a neighborhood governance entity. They all have in common the recognition that because the problems of individuals and families in the inner city did not arise in isolation from neighborhood conditions, addressing these problems requires strengthening the norms, supports, and problem-solving resources that link individuals to one another and to institutions of their community. They all agree, in the words of one community activist, that "community building is the long-term agenda of building the capacity in these communities to take on whatever agenda pops up."

They seek to increase community effectiveness in securing public and private goods and services allocated from outside the neighborhood on grounds of equity and expanding opportunity, as a means of empowering the community as a whole, and to assure that the neighborhood's residents will be prepared for employment, parenting, and otherwise to function in mainstream society.

Community building activities focus on rebuilding the social fabric of the neighborhood to provide residents with the benefits of community, which John Gardner defines as "security, a sense of identity and belonging, a framework of shared assumptions and values, a network of caring individuals, the experience of being needed . . . and responding to need." The strategies for operationalizing this goal vary, but all "aim to increase the density of social interaction and communication in the service of neighborhood improvement."

Efforts to reduce social disorder and physical "incivilities," such as broken windows, trash, public drinking, and prostitution, are also part of community building. They are undertaken in the expectation of improving directly the quality of neighborhood life and of discouraging potential offenders who may be deterred by the knowledge that residents are battling deterioration and are not indifferent to what goes on in the neighborhood.

Effective community-building activities often bring the social control and nurturance that can compete with gangs as a basis for social organization for young people. By connecting adults with one another and with youth, community-building activities such as mentoring and organized supervision of afterschool and nighttime educational and recreational programs are able to strengthen informal social controls by building an extensive set of obligations, expectations, and social networks.

3. *Successful initiatives draw extensively on outside resources, including public and private funds, professional expertise, and new partnerships that bring clout and influence.* If there seems to be a contradiction between relying on a local community's own resources and strengths while drawing on outside resources, the paradox is more apparent than real.

Many problems facing inner-city residents arise from powerful economic forces and from deficiencies in key public systems that originate far beyond the borders of distressed communities. That is why these neighborhoods cannot turn themselves around without being able to draw on funding, experience, expertise, and influence from outside the neighborhood.

The alternative to leaving depleted neighborhoods entirely on their own is not to revert back to a discredited model of dictating change from the top down. Effective interventions aimed at transforming neighborhoods require a new relationship between insiders and outsiders that allows for the flow of information and wisdom to go in both directions.

Potential sources of outside help are trying to get beyond past misunderstandings about what they can usefully contribute. Many had earlier taken a posture that implied, "If you don't want us to tell you what to do, OK, we're out of here. If you reject our mandates, we won't offer you our wisdom. If you reject our agenda, we won't offer you our assistance." Outsiders are learning that while there is very little that they can usefully mandate, they have a great deal to offer in a two-way relationship.

Among the most useful functions that outsiders are now performing in support of community-based initiatives are the following:

- *They provide funding.* They aim to make their money available in amounts and under conditions that are reasonably related to the objectives to be achieved. That means making funds available early in the process, and for a sufficiently long and predictable period. It also means making funding available in support of non-categorical activities (such as management, planning, and interdisciplinary training).
- *They provide clout* that can remove or reduce obstacles (political, bureaucratic, regulatory) that have interfered with the design and implementation of a coherent set of interventions. Outsiders can offer political influence and connections to decision makers, inaccessible to purely bottom-up efforts, especially in mobilizing additional resources.
- *They provide technical assistance.* They may help initiatives to arrange training for staff in community building, new forms of professional practice, and program management. They are able to mobilize and broker needed expertise, especially when it falls within a single domain.

There is a broad consensus around the three common elements of successful community initiatives I have just described. I believe that successful initiatives also share a fourth element, one around which there is less consensus:

4. *Effective initiatives are designed and operated on the basis of one or more plausible theories of change.* Plausible theories of change cover a wide range of possibilities, but all connect activities or interventions with important outcomes. Systematic collections of theories of change illuminate what is worth doing, shed light on promising ways to sequence change efforts, can suggest what is not worth doing, and help participants to inject intentionality and purpose into their activities.

Says one CCI director, enunciating a plausible theory of change, "I've really come to believe that jobs are the key, and that everything we do has to be organized around pathways to work—pathways that start as far back as prenatal care and school readiness, but that ultimately connect up with increasing the number of young adults that are productively employed."

Another plausible theory of change is one distilled by an evaluator of several comprehensive community-based initiatives. She has concluded that direct interventions to control violence and disorder and to assure public safety are not only essential to successful community building, but must be put in place at an early stage, because violence and disorder often produce barriers of distrust among neighbors, prevent families from entering into the life of the community, and drive out the middle-class home owners and elderly residents who may be left in a deteriorating neighborhood. By reducing neighborhood violence and disorder it is possible to increase parental effectiveness and resident participation, lower the stress and uncertainty of daily life, and increase the economic viability of the area by making it more attractive to investors.

Another theory of change found in many community-building activities: When residents of depleted neighborhoods undertake activities that perceptibly change the conditions of their lives (getting a new traffic light installed or closing down the hated trash-transfer stations), they gain a sense of increased "intentionality," the conviction that they can change the course of their lives by their own efforts. That increases their effectiveness as parents, helps them support their children's efforts to succeed at school, and is more likely to make them part of informal social networks that build social capital.

Another plausible theory of change connects improved outcomes for adolescents, including lower rates of teenage childbearing and youth crime, and higher rates of school success, with schools that maintain high standards, offer youngsters diverse opportunities to learn and to succeed, and provide them with opportunities to form sustained and trusting relationships with caring adults.

A last example of a plausible theory of change has to do with the intensity and scope of the intervention. Many informed observers believe that to transform communities of concentrated disadvantage, investments and strategies for change must be mobilized at a high level of intensity. They believe that interventions applied in the usual small doses are unlikely to be effective. Wrote Herbert Stein, chairman of the Council of Economic Advisers in the Nixon and Ford administrations: "The streets may need to become not a little safer, but much safer before investment is attracted [to depleted neighborhoods]. A big program may be much more effective per dollar and per unit of effort than a little one."

Each of these theories is, of course, totally compatible with the others, and all five could be utilized by a single initiative. All five are plausible, and therefore useful.

The idea that all comprehensive initiatives should operate on one or more plausible theories of change may strike the reader as self-evident. (Although it is not an idea that is universally accepted—recall the twenty-nine directors of youth development projects in the Midwest in Chapter 5, twenty-eight of whom couldn't come up with a theory to explain their activities.) What is crucial here is the suggestion that the field of community revitalization has moved beyond the point where any random activity can be considered to be as likely to be effective as any other.

The implication is that because some theories of change are more promising than others, generic information about promising theories of change should be collected, analyzed, and disseminated. It is around this proposition, that the time has come for all involved with comprehensive community initiatives to think and act more strategically, that the controversy arises. Some believe not only that a thousand flowers should be allowed to bloom, but that in community building efforts, no seeds brought in—or even recommended—by outsiders will ever take root and bloom. Others believe, as I do, that progress among community initiatives would occur more rapidly and more predictably if people working in individual neighborhoods could draw on a rich collection of rigorous knowledge, gleaned from both research and experience. Such a knowledge base could help local people in making judgments to distinguish plausible from implausible theories, promising from unpromising theories, and likely from unlikely links between activities and outcomes.

The reason for the lack of consensus around this proposition is that the available evidence which could contribute to this knowledge base is generally suggestive but not certain. When this lack of certainty is combined with an overinterpretation of what it means to respect local knowledge and local circumstances, it is easy to conclude that not very much that is worth knowing can be known from outside a specific neighborhood.

It is a strange phenomenon that when people finally learn the crucial lesson that it is important to pay attention to community and neighborhood, and that it is unproductive to impose rigid blueprints from the top, they often just flip to the mirror image of the construct they left behind, and believe that everything has to be known, discovered, and done exclusively from the bottom up. Neither extreme turns out to be very functional. Better to let go of the notion that everything has to be either bottom up or top down, and to adopt an interactive process.

Once one conceives of the process as a continuing series of conversations between outsiders and insiders—between top and bottom—it makes sense to invest in maximizing the knowledge that outsiders can contribute to the conversation. Knowledge that is probably but not certainly correct is not only worthy of being introduced into the conversation but can be immensely helpful. As we discovered in Chapter 2, when it comes to reinventing wheels, each community may have to construct its own, but it is still possible to save a lot of time, money, and energy, and to increase the chances of coming up with an effective set of interventions, by providing local entrepreneurs and activists with the formula for calculating the circumference of the wheel and with information about the materials that have been found by others to work well in constructing the spokes. The formula for the circumference is a factual piece of information, known to the outsider with certainty; information about how others have constructed the spokes might be more speculative but would nevertheless be helpful, in that the new initiative would have some hypotheses to work with rather than having to start at square one.

Geoffrey Canada, who has been involved with New York's Beacon schools, asked a group of leaders of the comprehensive community initiatives movement, Why can't we be more aggressive about what we know?

I think we can and should.

To be more aggressive about what we know, we first have to be more systematic in assembling and trying to understand what we know.

Then we might be able to identify not only plausible theories, but even implausible theories.

It may be that the disappointing performance of the early years of the Atlanta Project can best be explained by the weakness of the theory on which it was founded. Although it was advanced by a respected former president of the United States, the notion that poverty and homelessness could be successfully attacked primarily by "connecting people with people" has to be seen as highly romantic. Showing that "people of different races and with different backgrounds can work together" is certainly part of revitalizing poor neighborhoods and of building community, but we know enough to say that can't be the whole of it. Monsignor Linder of the New Communities Corporation in Newark says that he tried to tell a delegation from the Atlanta Project about the importance of focusing directly on economic development, but "they didn't seem to get it." He had the impression that the Atlanta Project wasn't hospitable to an institutional change agenda, especially one that might involve a certain amount of conflict.

What would it take to confidently identify some theories of change as more promising than others? A systematic review of existing evidence would probably point to specific arenas within which one could draw fairly sturdy generalizations. Starting with some high-priority outcomes that are relatively easy to measure as an end point (such as higher rates of school success, employment, and public safety), one would probably discover that research and experience suggest that the pathways with a high probability of leading to such outcomes can be identified and are not infinite in number.

Other arenas would be much more complicated and controversial because comparatively less data is available and political and value issues are more salient. The arenas in which it would be harder to make progress include questions of whether building community capacity should be seen as a valued outcome or primarily as a means to an end, and how to resolve the tension between pressures to achieve tangible, visible, measurable outcomes and building community capacity. Other difficult questions arise around the trade-offs between acting in domains where the connections are fairly clear and those where they are not. (If a representative community group puts a higher priority on the design and painting of a neighborhood mural than on an early childhood education program, is there a basis for an outsider to suggest that the group consider reversing the priorities?) Under what circumstances should some objective judgment about the activities an initiative might undertake, or their sequence, be introduced into the process of local decision making?

However such questions are resolved, I think it is extremely important for the further development of comprehensive community initiatives that the most knowledgeable and thoughtful participants and observers of the process not shy away from trying to uncover and synthesize as much information as possible—and then draw generalizations from it. The funders, designers, and operators of these initiatives should be able to draw on the greatest possible body of relevant and accessible knowledge so that their own local decision making becomes as highly informed and strategic as it is possible to make it.

Creating the Conditions Under Which Comprehensive Initiatives Can Be Improved, Sustained, and Expanded

The concentrations of poor, welfare-dependent, single-parent families that have come to define most inner-city neighborhoods resulted almost entirely from policies devised from far away.

The disappearance of well-paid jobs for the less skilled that accompanied the decline of manufacturing, racial discrimination affecting both hiring and home ownership, the decreasing value of income supports, and inferior, overwhelmed schools and services all are beyond the control of inner-city residents, and all have combined to form inner-city devastation. Furthermore, many government policies, including urban renewal and decisions about the location and design of public housing, that might have buffered the negative effects of changing economic and residential patterns, actually exacerbated them.

Too many of the problems found in deprived communities cannot be corrected without changes that can be made only outside of those communities, affecting jobs, service systems, the placement of housing and commercial development, public transportation, education, and the allocation of resources.

Community initiatives cannot succeed without a great deal more help from outside than they can now obtain. (Some observers, including historian Alice O'Connor, doubt that community initiatives can succeed at all in the absence of policies that promote greater income equality, jobs for low-skilled workers, and the enforcement of antidiscrimination policies in employment and housing.)

The missing supports needed to create the conditions under which comprehensive initiatives can be improved, sustained, and expanded into more depleted neighborhoods, include

- the availability of continually updated and evolving information about what works
- new forms of "nontechnical" technical assistance
- connections to political clout to influence decisions that affect neighborhood lives but are made in distant places
- more appropriate and higher levels of funding.

Information about what works. Funders, designers, and managers of neighborhood transformation initiatives need continually updated information about what works in the context of comprehensive community-based interventions. Research and experience have taught us much about which theories of change are plausible and which ones are better than others. Not every lone initiative should have to start from scratch in making judgments about what would work in a given community at a given stage of development.

But there has been a widespread reluctance to aggressively assemble, analyze, and disseminate what is, in fact, known. There seems to be an institutional reticence problem, growing out of the overlearned lesson that mandates imposed from above don't work. But it is also true that not every organizing auspice is as good as any other, that not every starting point is as good as any other, that some outcomes are more important than others, that some activities are much more likely than others to accomplish specified purposes, and that some theories of change are better than others. Leaving local initiatives to painstakingly make these discoveries on their own, or to never make them at all, has been a wasteful process and will interfere with further progress in spreading these initiatives.

Most wasteful of all has been the absence of well-funded, concerted attempts to learn systematically from current experience and to disseminate that learning to those responsible for community-change initiatives, to those who make relevant policy in the private and public sector, and to the general public.

There has been no mechanism to distill the lessons from current experience to reach the general public with information about these promising strategies that could lay the groundwork for vigorous, large-scale policy and programmatic change—at the level of the neighborhood, the city, the state, and the nation—to turn around the disintegration of the nation's inner cities.

"Nontechnical," noncategorical technical assistance. The prevailing kinds of technical assistance now available are, with very few exceptions, technical. Technical means not political, not committed. Technical means distant and neutral. Harvard's Ron Ferguson, who has worked with a variety of community-based reform efforts, says that what these fragile initiatives need is "friendly" technical assistance, just as they need friendly research and evaluation. They need technical assistance allies, who will join with them in solving problems and in figuring out what they need in order to be most effective. They need a virtually unknown form of technical assistance, which enhances the capacity of a local organization to choose and build its own programs. Unlike the outside experts, who make a brief foray into the community and leave, the new breed of technical-assistance providers stick around and get to know the community in which they are working. The Urban Strategies Council, perhaps the most

experienced locally based provider of "nontechnical" technical assistance in the country, has found that a large part of its success in assisting neighborhood groups in Oakland is that "we see each other in restaurants and the supermarket over the months, and even years."

A second problem with the prevailing kinds of technical assistance is that they are, with very few exceptions, every bit as fragmented, as categorical, as crisis oriented, and as mired in short-term and circumscribed ways of thinking as the systems these neighborhood initiatives are trying to reform and supplant. It is easy to obtain technical assistance to solve a specific, categorical problem, but it is almost impossible to obtain the assistance that takes into account the importance (and messiness) of building local capacity in a particular setting, and that can deal with the issues that cross disciplines and helping systems.

Most outside experts are able to help only with discrete pieces of a comprehensive agenda. You can get a preschool education expert, and a child care expert, and a school reform expert, but very few who understand the connections between the three. And if you want help on relating all these to a community-organizing and housing-rehabilitation effort, you will find even fewer people with the requisite expertise.

A community that is determined to set its own agenda also needs help, as Angela Blackwell, founder of the Urban Strategies Council, points out, in learning not to be afraid of data, in not leaving the gathering, analysis, and utilization of data to distant professionals, in building its capacity to understand data and use it strategically, to forge partnerships, to resolve conflicts and make connections both inside and outside the neighborhood. That kind of help is hard to come by from most current sources of technical assistance.

Political clout to influence decisions that affect neighborhood lives. Connections to decision makers that are inaccessible to purely bottom-up efforts are needed 1) to address larger structural issues, including economic development, the creation of and connection to public and nonprofit sector jobs, and the control of the weapons, violence, and drugs that disrupt community life; 2) to mobilize new sources of funding and other resources (such as mentors from outside the neighborhood); 3) to bring about the systems reforms that could modify policies that interfere with the effectiveness of community initiatives; and 4) to mobilize widespread public understanding and support for comprehensive community initiatives as an effective way to combat poverty and rebuild inner cities.

Changing the conditions of funding. The biggest single obstacle faced by comprehensive community initiatives is the excruciatingly poor fit between their funding needs on the one hand, and the amounts of money available to them and the terms on which they can get it on the other.

Well-informed observers disagree about the extent to which the solution of this problem depends on changes in the conditions attached to obtaining money, in the ability to leverage and reallocate existing resources, or in the amounts of money available to these initiatives. But all agree that whether or not substantial new funds become available, it is essential to change the way resources are now deployed.

No one disagrees that the circumstances that now govern funding of comprehensive initiatives must be fundamentally changed. Not only do they force community development organizations to devote inordinate amounts of time to "grant grubbing," and applying and reporting to many different sources, but because funding is so complex, it becomes the domain of a few experts and is ultimately disempowering of grassroots participants.

Even a foundation-funded conference on lessons learned from comprehensive urban development projects concluded that foundations are more likely to contribute to than reduce the prevailing fragmentation of services, with their emphasis on categorical, short-term funding, their focus on the new and innovative, and their reluctance to develop collaborative mechanisms among themselves.

One director says that to make foundation funding more supportive of comprehensive initiatives "would require turning the funding world upside down, where funders would match their support to the interests of individual communities, instead of each funder asking every community to match community needs to a particular foundation's interests."

Many initiative leaders contrast the foundation rhetoric about service integration with their funding performance. "When they come right down to it," one director told me, "the foundations want their funds absolutely focused on health care, or absolutely focused on early childhood education. Those are the outcomes they want tracked, and they want documentation that connects the specific outcomes they are interested in to the specific activities they funded. There are a few exceptions to that, but there are a lot more horror stories than exceptions."

This director adds that she has also found, to her great dismay, that when the foundations "finally get serious about the need for an integrated program, they set up their own integrated program. If you ask for money to help you with a program that has already been defined by a community and its partners, forget it, because they don't want to fund anything that doesn't have their imprimatur on it from the outset."

Leaders of some local efforts say that dealing with public funders is even more difficult than dealing with foundations. Lynn Videka-Sherman reports that settlement houses that are trying to become more comprehensive are continuously frustrated by the red tape involved in obtaining public funding for social services, because funding regulations work against program coordination. Congressional mandates are of course particularly hard to match up with local needs. Angela Blackwell cites the example of augmented Head Start funds coming to Oakland to be used to serve more four-year-olds, despite the Oakland Urban Strategies Council having determined that the greatest need for additional funding was in serving one- to three-year-olds.

Perhaps the most important reason to change the conditions under which money to support comprehensive neighborhood initiatives becomes available is not only that fragmented, categorical funding is hard for local initiatives to use, but that it acts like a magnet, pulling people and programs back to the episodic, piece-meal, incoherent, crisis-oriented, unresponsive interventions they have been charged to get away from.

Leveraging or obtaining new funds. Many observers believe that if comprehensive initiatives had to continue operating with present conditions and levels of funding held constant, they could probably limp along, and chalk up some useful accomplishments.

But their impact would fall far short of their potential. And finite quantities of time, energy, hope, and money would be inefficiently expended.

If, on the other hand, comprehensive initiatives were to become part of a national strategy to save America's inner cities, neither current levels nor current sources of funding would come close to meeting the need. If federal and state legislators, philanthropies, community leaders, and the general public were to recognize the seriousness of the current crisis of America's inner cities, and the growing gap between the prosperity of America's have and have-nots, it would be necessary to devise new investment strategies.

Rationale for a new investment strategy. At a time of public skepticism about any major thrust to improve life among the poor, especially if it involves government and large amounts of money, the burden of proof that the investment will be worthwhile is a heavy one. Talented economists and public policy analysts have tried to make the case that spending more now on comprehensive interventions in areas of concentrated poverty will save much larger amounts later. Most efforts have involved estimates comparing the cost of comprehensive neighborhood transformation with the cost of doing nothing more than is currently being done in those neighborhoods. This method is sometimes called "the cost of failure" analysis. (Vermont, Georgia, and Nebraska are calling it "the cost of bad results.") The argument this analysis makes is that because strategic current expenditures will save more money later, increasing current spending is both economically efficient and socially desirable.

Charles Bruner and colleagues at Iowa's Child and Family Policy Center estimated the potential savings (realized through saved prison and welfare expenditures and increased tax revenues) resulting from improving child and family outcomes through known effective interventions in Allegheny County, Pennsylvania. Compared with the cost of the interventions, they calculated that a return on investment by a ratio of three to one would be conservative.

The Enterprise Foundation calculates that if investments in the neighborhood transformation process in Sandtown-Winchester brought Sandtown families to the social, education, and economic level of families in the average low-income Baltimore neighborhood, a public/private investment of $40 million over ten years in the transformation process would result in public sector savings in the next twenty years of more than $110 million dollars.

One difficulty with an argument based on long-term savings is that it entails many assumptions that cannot be made precisely because they involve predictions of the future in areas where data are scarce. But that difficulty can be partially overcome, suggests Anthony Downs of the Brookings Institution, by asking several reputable analysts to make careful, conservative estimates.

The much bigger difficulty is that the institutions called upon to spend more now are not the same institutions as will realize the savings later. And most institutions—especially publicly funded ones—are far more driven by short-term-spending pressures than by the prospect of long-run savings. Downs suggests two possible solutions to this difficulty: a philanthropic version and a public sector version.

In the philanthropic version, the investors are not motivated by financial gain. They are identifying their institutional interests with the good of society as a whole, and making their contributions in the hope of reducing future expenditures by the entire society. Here the argument is conceptually convincing but not of great practical import, since the philanthropic sector cannot come up with money in the amounts that would be required if comprehensive community revitalization were to become a major instrument of national urban policy.

Downs's public sector version starts with the reality that because key public institutions are fragmented into many specialized parts, the benefits of current spending are rarely reaped by the agency that does the spending (even if increased spending on early education, family support, or community building succeeds in reducing adolescent childbearing and violent crime, and the long-term savings will have been realized by the welfare and criminal justice systems). He goes on to show that public officials elected for two- or four- or even six-year terms are unlikely to consider investments with a twenty-year payoff very high on their public policy agenda. Although society as a whole would gain from the strategy of spending more today to reap large savings in the future, the problem is that "society as a whole is not an operating entity in charge of particular institutions." This analysis prompts Downs to ask whether it would be possible to create public sector institutions with the appropriate structure and incentives by giving a single institution combined responsibility for a wide range of funding streams with a wide range of purposes, and by insulating the officials of that institution from the pressures that compel them to focus on short-term results.

The Empowerment Zones suggests Downs, could be the "overarching public institution which encompasses a broad range of specialized functions" that might have the political legitimacy "to combine, rearrange, and reallocate both federal and local public fund flows." He believes the EZs might represent a "public institutional structure much more likely to be influenced by the approach and the arguments embodied in the investment model than any other in sight."

Downs's analysis leads one to speculate that some combination of his philanthropic model and expanding the conceptual, administrative, and financial reach of the Empowerment Zones apparatus might be superior to either alone, and might indeed provide a structure capable of channeling funds to comprehensive community initiatives under conditions and in amounts that could begin to meet the need.

STRUCTURES TO SUPPORT THE LARGE-SCALE DEVELOPMENT OF
COMPREHENSIVE NEIGHBORHOOD TRANSFORMATION EFFORTS

Two kinds of structures are now needed to provide ongoing outside support to both public and private comprehensive neighborhood transformation efforts, one that is local, and the other national.

Locally-based intermediaries. Several successful models of local intermediaries now exist. One is the Comprehensive Community Revitalization Program, which—as we have seen—has been able to vastly expand the activities and effectiveness of five community development corporations in the South Bronx by providing coherent and timely funding, useful "nontechnical" technical assistance, and connections to political clout and influence.

A second form of successful local intermediary, this one with a broader purpose than the support of comprehensive community interventions, is exemplified by Oakland's Urban Strategies Council. Many current recommendations for how local intermediaries might function—whether at the national, regional, or local level—are based on the experience of the Urban Strategies Council, and on the work of its offshoot, the National Community Building Support Center. Most agree that local intermediaries should encompass the complexity and ecology of urban distress and solutions while being flexible and opportunistic about points of intervention; they should be guided by a clear, overarching vision and be able to translate the neighborhood and public sector to each other; they should utilize sound research as a convening and mobilizing tool; and they should work with all parts of the community to develop realistic strategies for systems change and in creating a power base from which reforms can occur.

A third form of locally based intermediary is linked to a local community foundation or other entities viewed as nonpartisan, long-term stakeholders in the community's future.

National intermediaries. In my view, a new intermediary that would take responsibility for functions that can be effectively performed only at the national level is now needed to create the conditions under which comprehensive neighborhood transformation efforts can be improved, sustained, and expanded into many more depleted neighborhoods. No entity is now performing those functions. It remains to be invented—or created by joining existing institutions in some entirely new way.

Richard Nathan, director of the Rockefeller Institute of Government, believes that homegrown neighborhood transformation efforts cannot long survive without the support of a national entity, "a new national center of gravity . . . providing a critical mass of intellectual talent and leadership," to strengthen the nonprofit community-based organizations so critical to the social and economic development of urban areas.

While there are institutions currently doing pieces of this job in the course of generating and testing ideas, surfacing and exchanging lessons, and providing local organizations with technical assistance and consultation, there is no single venue with a central strategic capacity focused on encouraging the spread of high-quality comprehensive community initiatives. There is no venue now operating on a sufficiently large scale and with a clear enough focus to capture the lessons of experience with neighborhood transformation, and systematically assemble, distill, analyze, and disseminate them for the express purpose of being built upon. There is no venue in which these lessons are being combined with the findings of research to influence policy and program design, to shape future expansion, experimentation, and research. There is no venue with the capacity and the mandate to reach the general public with information about the promising strategies that could lay the groundwork for vigorous, large-scale policy and programmatic change to turn around the disintegration of the nation's inner cities.

There has been no national mechanism from which to exercise the political influence that is inaccessible to grassroots comprehensive initiatives. There has been no national mechanism that could address the need for public and private funders to come together to develop common applications for funding, and common reporting forms. There has been no auspice to bring funders together to do joint or coordinated funding of neighborhood-based efforts. There has been no venue for expanding the understanding, at the national level, of government agencies, professional associations, and advocacy groups about the potential of neighborhood-based transformation, and about the changes needed in existing programs, policies, funding, and training that could support these local efforts.

There are precedents for setting up institutions that would accomplish these tasks, though most have operated in more narrowly defined areas than comprehensive community initiatives.

When the Ford Foundation thought it was important to learn more about how to improve programs to help long-term, hard-core-unemployed persons make the transition to stable employment, and to leverage more federal demonstration funds, it set up the Manpower Development Research Corporation (MDRC) with a mandate to do the most rigorous possible research to assess the impact of a variety of interventions on different population groups. The Ford Foundation also charged MDRC to design and fund interventions for the express purpose of maximizing the total state of knowledge about what was promising and successful, and to construct the mechanisms that could capture the lessons from both successes and failures to influence further program development and large-scale policy change.

Another national intermediary, the Local Initiatives Support Corporation (LISC), was created in 1979, as part of the Ford Foundation's efforts to spread and support community development corporations by generating and supplying capital. With the support of several foundations, LISC seeks out promising CDCs and enlists project investments from the private and public sectors to help them become more effective. The Enterprise Foundation has performed a similar national intermediary function since 1983. In 1993 the Rockefeller Foundation led a number of foundations to establish a new entity, the National Community Development Initiative, which aims at expanding the community building potential of community development corporations by infusing intermediaries with large amounts of new money, to be used primarily for housing development.

Another partial analog to what is now needed in the comprehensive community initiative field is Public/Private Ventures (P/PV). Created in 1977 to design, test, and study initiatives in the youth employment field, it has now broadened its scope to support the development of effective programs and policies to increase a wide range of opportunities for low-income young people. P/PV has shown it is possible to deal rigorously with the public demand for hard outcomes in the youth development field, which—as in the neighborhood transformation field—are difficult to define and document, and which even the best interventions do not produce very quickly.

I believe the time has come for a public-private partnership to create a new entity—standing alone or as part of an existing institution, or joining several institutions in a network—to perform the essential functions not now being carried out. The designated entity (the British would call it a QANGO—a quasi-autonomous nongovernmental organization) would become the source of reliable knowledge to guide communities in undertaking neighborhood transformation; to shape future expansion, experimentation, and research; and to inform the public about what's working and why in community building and neighborhood transformation, about the projected costs and savings of these efforts, and about how the nation could support promising large-scale policy and programmatic initiatives that could turn around the disintegration of the nation's inner cities.

Community Revitalization Is Worth Doing Even Though It Is Not a Quick or Simple Fix

Among those who know the comprehensive neighborhood transformation field best, there is considerable difference of opinion about how fast to scale up. Many are concerned that the nation's capacity to support these complex ventures is not extensive enough to assure that all the initiatives now in operation will succeed, much less to support a doubling or tripling of their number. Others fear that in this era of skepticism about our ability to act together on behalf of the common good, we will not be able to raise the requisite resources, and that any push to scale up will result in diluted and weakened interventions.

It is my view that we now know enough to at least take some big steps forward by putting in place the structures and supports outlined above, so we would be prepared in another five years to begin to address inner-city problems on a scale that compares with the enormity and urgency of the need.

In the long-term, comprehensive neighborhood transformation could—alongside new macroeconomic policies and other measures to restore opportunity to people now stuck at the bottom—become a major national strategy to combat poverty, rebuild the inner city, and reverse the growth of the underclass.

We Can Achieve
Our Common Purpose

I HAVE TRIED TO PAINT a picture of the possible. I have tried in this book to give all of us—voters, taxpayers, neighborhood and corporate leaders, front-line professionals, philanthropists, legislators, policy analysts, bureaucrats, and skeptics—good, solid reasons, compelling reasons, to conclude that we are not helpless in the face of our most urgent social problems. Whether we believe that the most urgent of these problems is the poverty of the inner city, the failure of urban schools, juvenile crime, or too many children born without two parents to cherish and protect them, the evidence I have assembled tells us that we are not helpless.

All Americans can participate in creating the large-scale changes that are now needed to rebuild America. There are many ways to help, many ways to heal. But this book has been less about individual contributions than about what our society can do through government and through America's abundance of voluntary institutions. Those who engage in community service or serve as mentors to youngsters who desperately need a caring adult meet critical needs and send out ripples of hope as they enlist in a purpose that extends beyond self-interest. Their work is essential. But when this nation faces big problems, it solves them not only through individual effort, but also through our ability to combine in common purpose.

It is at the institutional level, especially where government is involved, that we have been so stuck. It is at the institutional level that we as an organized citizenry must find better ways to help and to heal.

Over the past several decades, as major public programs and systems became outmoded, feeble, and often futile, the tools for fixing or replacing them also became outmoded. Budget deficits, the growing power of special interests, and a profound misunderstanding of the causes of our troubles paralyzed the forces of renewal. Americans lost confidence in their ability to act together to solve urgent social problems.

I believe this book gives us reason to think we can become unstuck, and shows some of the ways.

Every one of us can be part of the process of becoming unstuck. As voters or community leaders, as legislators, policy analysts, or philanthropists, we can have some say over how money is allocated and rules are made. As teachers, social workers, job trainers, community organizers, bureaucrats, board members, labor or business leaders or volunteers, we can have some say over how the daily tasks of some institution are conducted. As academics or journalists we can have some say about what trends and what events get attention, what the public and professionals-to-be are taught about what matters, and what is defined as useful knowledge. As parents who dream of a better future for our children, we can have some say over the supports provided to families, and to the schools and other institutions that will help determine the opportunities our children will have as they grow into adulthood.

Eight strategies emerge from the promising initiatives described in this book that can help guide our efforts. The first four strategies come out of the first four chapters.

- Recognize the Seven Attributes of Highly Effective Programs and the environments that will support them.
- In spreading what works, distinguish thoughtfully between the essentials that can indeed be replicated and the components that must be adapted locally. Break Through the Hidden Ceiling on Scale by creating the conditions in which effective interventions will thrive.
- Don't look only for programmatic innovations. Instead, find ways to surmount obstacles to fundamental systems change so that the attributes of successful demonstrations can become the norms of mainstream systems. Tame bureaucracies by finding new ways to balance bureaucratic protections against the imperative of accomplishing public purposes.
- In undertaking major initiatives, make sure that funders, managers, front-line staff, and program participants agree on valued out-

comes. Make sure that all stakeholders understand how the initiative's activities and investments are related to outcomes, so that they will be able to use results to judge success.

In Chapters 6, 7, and 8 I looked at how these strategies are being applied in efforts to reform three systems—welfare, child protection, and education—and found that none of these systems can achieve its objectives by relying only on what can be done from *within* the system. Higher rates of self-sufficient adults require more than welfare reform. Higher rates of children protected against abuse and neglect require more than child protection reform. Higher rates of children succeeding at school require more than school reform. In every one of these systems, reformers found that they had to make substantial and highly strategic changes in how front-line staff and managers went about their daily business to leave behind the rigidities of the past. But that wasn't enough. They also had to reach outside the formal systems boundaries and establish partnerships with citizens and communities to achieve the system's objectives in improving outcomes for children and families.

Four more strategies emerge from examining efforts to achieve synergy by putting together what works and building communities. What we have learned can guide future efforts to sustain, strengthen, and expand comprehensive neighborhood initiatives:

- The time has come to give up searching for a single intervention that will be the one-time fix—the lifetime inoculation—that will protect against the effects of growing up in neighborhoods of despair, violence, and unemployment, in neighborhoods without decent schools, safe streets, stable families, or a sense of community. Forget about selecting among economic development, public safety, physical rehabilitation, community building, education reform, or service reform in an effort to find the single most promising way to intervene. In trying to carve out a manageable piece of the problem, try slicing in a different dimension. Look for opportunities to impact a neighborhood or a neighborhood institution, not just opportunities to impact a circumscribed problem with a circumscribed solution. Take a broader view.
- Forget about getting results overnight and be prepared to build for a future your generation may not see. Take a longer view.
- Recognize that intensity and critical mass may be crucial. Especially in areas of concentrated disadvantage, make sure interventions operate at a high enough level of intensity and with a broad enough scope to capture the imagination of participants and the

public. Create the synergy that can bring about real change and tip a neighborhood toward becoming functional.

- Forget about choosing between bottom-up and top-down approaches. Depleted inner-city neighborhoods cannot turn themselves around without very substantial help from outside the neighborhood. But neither can outsiders impose solutions. Effective neighborhood transformation requires that community-based organizations be able to draw on funding, expertise, and influence from outside, and that outsiders be able to draw on information, expertise, and wisdom that can come only from the neighborhood itself.

These eight strategies will, I believe, help us rebuild a society in which all our children can come into adulthood loving and loved, competent and productive, caring and cared for. At heart, that is what this book is about.

We now know what children need from their immediate surroundings if they are to develop into healthy adults. They need adults (at least one, and preferably two) who are consistently nurturing, enjoying, teaching, coping, and loving, adults who take responsibility for their children and hold their children's well-being to be as important as their own. They need to have their physical needs provided for, to be protected from harm, and to have the early experiences that leave them eager for school learning and diligent enough to succeed. The inner-city youngsters growing up surrounded by people who haven't made it need mature adults who can convince them they have a future worth struggling for.

Society must be able to count on parents to have the moral sense, the beliefs, and the capacity to assume those responsibilities. But, as we give heavy weight to relying on parents to carry out their obligations, we must also be aware that *individual parents cannot meet their responsibilities in our complex, twenty-first-century world without support from outside.* Collectively, we must make sure that the societal structures that can support families, and that can strengthen communities, are in place.

Our society is in jeopardy because not enough of our arrangements for providing those supports are in place and working.

Whether a home visitor comes to relieve the anxieties of a new mother, whether high-quality child care is available when both parents go to work, whether parents can get jobs that pay enough for decent housing and food, whether a competent doctor can be quickly reached when the baby has a fever, whether the neighborhood is safe from gunfire and gangs, whether a depressed mother can find the help that will allow her to care for her children, whether an addicted father can get treatment, whether there is reason for children to work hard at school, whether an adolescent has somewhere to go in the afternoon that doesn't automatically propel him or her into trouble, whether there is a path to follow that leads from school to work, whether there is reason for youngsters to be confident of a productive future *are all determined beyond the four walls where parenting takes place.* All require collective, and often governmental, action. All require us to think beyond whether government should be large or small, and to think instead about how government can function effectively, often in partnership with the private sector, to enable parents and communities to function effectively.

This analysis leads us to embrace the conservative tenet of personal responsibility and obligation while, at the same time, we embrace the liberal tenet that there are common purposes we cannot achieve without government. And we embrace simultaneously the nonpartisan tenet that if government doesn't work, it must be made to work.

And where is the money to come from? Part of the answer lies in doing the calculations showing that many of the interventions portrayed in these pages save many times their cost in the long run. The other part of the answer lies in coming to see that we may have to reorder our spending priorities because we dare not write off any of America's children, families, and inner-city communities.

We can act now to assure that the children and families who live today with little hope will not be abandoned in the hostile territory of inner cities, where work and community have disappeared and anomie reigns. We can act now to assure that they can become part of the American dream in the next century. With more robust and systematic support to sustain reformed programs and community initiatives, we can begin to move our victories from the small scale to the medium scale. We will not have to depend exclusively on local heroes to circumvent every obstacle and every barrier that our systems have put in their way. We can gather the credible evidence that common purposes are indeed being achieved, and thereby begin to restore confidence in reformed public and private institutions, systems, and partnerships.

We will then be better able to make the large-scale changes that would convert today's innovative front-line practices, piecemeal policy reforms, and sporadic community-building efforts into the prevailing norms that will constitute tomorrow's revitalized Public Purpose Sector.

All of us can join together in pursuing this agenda, across boundaries that have separated us by ideology, class, and race, and that have separated politicians, professionals, and bureaucrats from one another and from the communities they serve. Together we can rebuild the public trust, recognizing our interdependence, knowing that we are caught, in the words of Martin Luther King, Jr., "in an inescapable network of mutuality." Together we can be sustained by the conviction that we have the resources—material, intellectual and spiritual—to assure that every American family can expect its children to grow up with hope in their hearts and a realistic expectation that they will participate in the American dream. Together we can share, and together we can achieve, our Common Purpose.

Notes

INTRODUCTION

p. xvi **trust the government in Washington:** *Washington Post*/Kaiser Family Foundation/Harvard University survey, reported on in Morin, Richard and Dan Balz. "Americans Losing Trust in Each Other and Institutions." *Washington Post,* 28 January 1996.

p. xvi **gap between rich and poor:** Bernstein, Aaron. "Inequality: How the Gap Between Rich and Poor Hurts the Economy." *Business Week,* August 15, 1994.

p. xvi **greatest income disparity of any modern democratic nation:** Rattner, Steven. "Leaky Boats on the Rising Tide." *New York Times,* 29 August 1995.

p. xvi **median wages of American men fallen steadily:** Thurow, Lester C. "Companies Merge; Families Break Up." *New York Times,* 3 September 1995.

p. xvi **cushion the effects of harsh economic forces:** Timothy Smeeding quoted by Bradsher, Keith. "Gap in Wealth in US Called Widest in West." *New York Times,* 17 April 1995.

p. xvii **more children live in poverty in the U.S.:** Smeeding, Timothy with L. Rainwater. "Doing Poorly: The Real Income of American Children in a Comparative Perspective." LIS Working Paper #127, July 1995.

p. xvii **"quietly seceding from the rest of the nation":** Reich, Robert B. "Secession of the Successful." *New York Times Magazine,* 20 January 1991.

p. xvii **life expectancy lower . . . in Third World countries:** Wilson, William Julius. *When Work Disappears: The World of the New Urban Poor.* New York: Knopf, 1996.

p. xviii **Raspberry quote:** Raspberry, William. "We're Not Bad Guys, Just Doubtful." *Washington Post,* 17 March 1992.

p. xviii **"federal government can't do the job right":** Morin, Richard. "A United Opinion: Government Doesn't Do a Very Good Job." *Washington Post,* 11 October 1995.

p. xviii **Rivlin quote:** Rivlin, Alice. *Reviving the American Dream: The Economy,*

The States, and the Federal Government. Washington, DC: Brookings Institution, 1992. P. 179.

pp. xviii–xix Roper Poll: Zinmeister, Karl. "Indicators." *The American Enterprise,* March/April 1995.

p. xix Blendon quote: "PBS The NewsHour with Jim Lehrer," February 5, 1996.

p. xix Fallows quote: Fallows, James. *Breaking the News: How the Media Undermine American Democracy.* New York: Pantheon, 1996.

p. xix election night poll: *Washington Post*/Kaiser Family Foundation/Harvard University survey, reported on in *New York Times,* 16 November 1994.

pp. xix–xx numbers and proportions for 1995: *Analytical Perspectives.* Budget of the U. S. Government, Office of Management and Budget, Fiscal Year 96. Table 6.2. (Percentages do not add to 100, as these are selected categories only.)

p. xx Rowen quote: Rowen, Hobart. "What Your Taxes Actually Buy." *Washington Post,* 29 December 1994.

p. xx Dionne quote: Dionne, E. J. *Why Americans Hate Politics.* New York: Simon & Schuster, 1991.

p. xx Schlesinger quote: Schlesinger Jr., Arthur. "Wake up, Liberals, Your Time Has Come." *Washington Post,* May 1, 1988. Daniel P. Moynihan also took note of this phenomenon when he wrote in 1990, "The Reagan deficits are doing their intended work, providing an automatic obstacle to any new program." Moynihan, Daniel Patrick. "Another War—the One on Poverty—Is Over Too" *New York Times,* July 1990.

p. xx only a minor portion went to poor families with children: The most massive increases in government spending were accounted for by health costs, and went primarily to providers of health care to the aged and disabled, including hospitals, nursing homes, and physicians.

p. xx Jencks quote: Jencks, Christopher. *Rethinking Social Policy: Race, Poverty, and the Underclass.* New York: HarperCollins, 1992. P. 79.

p. xx "nothing has worked": DeParle, Jason. "Debris of Past Failures Impeded Poverty Policy." *New York Times,* 7 November 1993.

p. xx "poverty won": Ibid.

p. xxi We won the war against poverty of the aged: 1995 data show that the poverty rate for the aged, which has been declining steadily since 1967, is now the lowest for any age group. U. S. Census Bureau, Income and Poverty 1995, data released September 26, 1996.

p. xxi We shrank the health gap between the haves and the have-nots: U. S. Department of Health and Human Services. *Trends in the Well-Being of America's Children and Youth: 1996.* Washington, DC, 1996.

p. xxi chances that someone who was sick would see a doctor: Mayer, Susan and Christopher Jencks. "War on Poverty: No Apologies, Please." *New York Times,* 9 November 1995.

p. xxi reduced infant mortality in Beaufort, South Carolina: Milbank, Dana. "Up from Hunger. War on Poverty Won Some Battles as Return to Poor Region Shows." *Wall Street Journal,* 30 October 1995.

p. xxi Twice as many black and Hispanic children could read proficiently: National Center for Education Statistics. NAEP, "1992 Trends in Academic Progress."

p. xxi proportion of seventeen-year-olds with very low reading and math scores has fallen: Mayer and Jencks, November 9, 1995.

p. xxi The gap between black and white students' proficiency in both reading and

math narrowed: National Center for Education Statistics. NAEP, "1992 Trends in Academic Progress."

p. xxii **Bookbinder quote:** Bookbinder, Hyman. "America's War on Poverty, Untold Stories from the Front Lines." Produced by Blackside, Inc., presented by WGBH Boston, January 16, 1995.

p. xxii **alternative to social indifference:** Margolis, Richard J. "Sometimes, Something Seems to Work." *New York Times Book Review,* 3 February 1985.

p. xxii **Monroe quote:** Blackside, Inc. "America's War on Poverty." PBS, January 15, 1995.

p. xxii **jobs . . . that paid enough to support a family:** Tobin, James. "Poverty in Relation to Macroeconomic Trends, Cycles, and Policies." In Danziger, Sheldon H., Gary D. Sandefur and Daniel Weinberg. *Confronting Poverty: Prescriptions for Change.* New York: Harvard University Press, 1994.

p. xxiii **increasing poverty among the least well off:** These long-term trends, including the declining share of income received by those in the bottom quintile, are continuing. U. S. Census Bureau, Income and Poverty 1995, data released September 26, 1996.

p. xxiii **computer-driven equipment:** Swasy, Alecia and Carol Hymowitz. "The Workplace Revolution." *Wall Street Journal,* 9 February 1990.

p. xxiii **76 percent had not completed high school:** Zuckerman, Mortimer B. on "The Charlie Rose Show," September 14, 1995.

p. xxiii **hasn't hired anyone from the local high schools:** Joint Center for Political Studies. "Inner City Males: Recent Research and Its Policy Implications," 1988.

p. xxiii **employer view of young black males:** Wilson, 1996.

p. xxiii **jobless ghetto of the inner city was being created:** Wilson, 1996 and Wilson, William Julius. *The Truly Disadvantaged: The Inner City, the Underclass, and Public Policy.* Chicago: University of Chicago Press, 1987.

p. xxiii **hastened the deterioration of the ghetto:** Massey, Douglas. "American Apartheid: Segregation and the Making of the Underclass." *American Journal of Sociology* 96 (2). Pp. 329–57.

p. xxiv **unreliable economic providers:** The inner-city black men interviewed by Wilson's team often complained about how suspicious women were of their intentions, and how difficult it was to find women who are supportive of partners with a low living standard. Wilson, 1996.

p. xxiv **Anderson quote:** Anderson, Elijah. "Abolish Welfare—And Then What?" *Washington Post,* 31 December 1993.

p. xxiv **Ferguson quote:** Ferguson, Ronald F. and Mary S. Jackson. "Black Male Youth and Drugs: How Racial Prejudice, Parents and Peers Affect Vulnerability." Harvard University, Malcolm Wiener Center for Social Policy, John F. Kennedy School of Government, September 1992.

pp. xxiv–xxv **adopt an anti-achievement ethic at school:** Canada, Geoffrey. *fist stick knife gun: A Personal History of Violence in America.* Boston: Beacon Press, 1995. Pp. 149–50.

p. xxv **They do not trust . . . "helping" professionals:** Ferguson and Jackson, 1992.

p. xxv **the system has rejected them:** Terry Williams quoted by Wilson, William Julius. "Imagine Life Without a Future." *Los Angeles Times,* 6 May 1992.

p. xxv **the deference they feel they deserve:** Anderson, Elijah. "The Code of the Streets." *Atlantic Monthly,* May 1994.

p. xxv **higher rates of employment among recent immigrants:** Considerable research documents that race-conscious decisions by employers about hiring and location have barred low-skilled black males from jobs open to immigrants and Hispanic Americans. The majority of employers are much more likely to hire immigrants and Hispanics than blacks, in part because the former are more likely to be embedded in complex migration networks, and to be employed in the first place. Mincy, Ronald B. "The Underclass: Concept, Controversy, and Evidence." In Danziger, Sandefur and Weinberg, 1994. P. 145. Also see Krogh, Marilyn. "A Description of the Work Histories of Fathers in the Inner City of Chicago." Chicago Urban Poverty and Family Life Conference, Chicago, IL, October 10–12, 1991, cited in Wilson, William Julius. "Race, Class, and Poverty in Urban America: A Comparative Perspective." United Way of New York Lecture, April 30, 1992, New York, NY. Interviews by Jan Rosenberg and Philip Kasinitz in Red Hook, Brooklyn, found employers hire friends of employees. Rosenberg and Kasinitz, "Why Enterprise Zones Will Not Work," *City Journal,* Autumn 1993.

p. xxv **Glazer quote:** Glazer, Nathan. "The Amoral Center." *The Responsive Community,* Fall 1996.

p. xxvi **Murray quote:** Murray, Charles. "The Legacy of the 60s." *Commentary,* July 1992.

p. xxvi **Meier quote:** Interview with Lianne Hansen, National Public Radio, September 24, 1995.

CHAPTER 1   What Works and Why We Have So Little of It

p. 3 **"most remarkable results for poor youths":** Dugger, Celia. "For Young, a Guiding Hand Out of Ghetto." *New York Times,* 9 March 1995.

p. 3 **"investments in disadvantaged youths can work":** "A Youth Program That Worked." *New York Times,* 20 March 1995.

p. 3 **QOP results:** Hahn, Andrew. "Evaluation of the Quantum Opportunities Program (QOP). Did the Program Work?" Brandeis University, June 1994.

p. 4 **the watered-down program:** Schorr, Lisbeth. *Within Our Reach: Breaking the Cycle of Disadvantage.* New York: Anchor Books, 1989. According to David Racine of Replication and Program Strategies, Inc., the home visiting program subsequently was transferred from the health department to the social services department, which was able to resume operating it based on the original design.

p. 4 **extensive follow-up found . . . no impact:** Rogers, Mary M., Mary D. Peoples-Sheps and James R. Sorenson. "Translating Research into MCH Service: Comparison of a Pilot Project and a Large-Scale Resource Mothers Program." Public Health Reports, Vol. 110, September/October 1995. Pp. 563–69.

p. 5 **Description of QOP:** Center for Human Resources. "Quantum Opportunities Program: A Brief on the QOP Pilot Program," Brandeis University, September 1995.

pp. 5–6 **Study of experimental Oregon program:** Herr, Toby, Robert Halpern and Suzanne L. Wagner. "Something Old, Something New: A Case Study of the Post-Employment Services Demonstration in Oregon." Chicago: Project Match, Erikson Institute, November 1995.

p. 6 **staff . . . take on an extended role:** Whelage, Gary E. *Reducing the Risk: Schools as Communities of Support.* New York: Falmer Press, 1989.

p. 6 **think beyond professional services:** Kinney, Jill, Kathy Strand, Marge

Hagerup and Charles Bruner. "Beyond the Buzzwords: Key Principles in Effective Frontline Practice." Falls Church, VA: National Center for Service Integration, 1994.

p. 6 some place to turn in a time of crisis: Rosenfeld, Jona M., Donald A. Schön and Israel J. Sykes. *Out from Under: Lessons from Projects for Inaptly Served Children and Families.* Jerusalem: JDC-Brookdale Institute of Gerontology and Human Development, March 1995.

p. 6 high proportion of first jobs end within six months: 57 percent of AFDC recipients from the Cabrini-Green housing projects lost their first job within six months. Alan M. Hershey, LaDonna Pavotti, "Turning Job Finders into Job Keepers." Paper prepared for Conference on Welfare to Work sponsored by the Center for the Future of Children, February 21–22, 1996.

p. 6 pioneering state . . . child health initiatives: Bruner, C. and J. M. Perrin. "More Than Health Insurance: State Initiatives to Improve Maternal and Child Health." New York: Milbank Memorial Fund, 1995.

p. 7 what is happening to the children: That this is far from the norm has been documented in a survey of substance abuse treatment agencies, which found that "in most counties and states, there isn't even a box on the form which tracks whether adults in treatment have children." Gardner, Sid and Nancy Young. "The Implications of Alcohol and Other Drug-related Problems for Community-wide Family Support Systems." Draft paper prepared for Kennedy School Executive Session on the Future of Child Protective Services, November 1996.

p. 7 support families' capacities to raise strong children: Stephens, Susan A., Sally A. Leiderman, Wendy C. Wolf and Patrick T. McCarthy. "Building Capacity for System Reform." Bala Cynwyd, PA: Center for Assessment and Policy Development, 1995.

p. 8 " 'best practices' are whatever works in a given context": Nothdurft, William E. "Out from Under: Policy Lessons from a Quarter Century of Wars on Poverty." Washington, DC: The Council of State Policy and Planning Agencies, 1990.

p. 8 mobilize community members: Hess, Peg, Brenda McGowan and Carol H. Meyer. "Practitioners' Perspective on Family and Child Services." In Kahn, Alfred J. and Sheila B. Kamerman. *Children & Their Families in Big Cities: Strategies for Service Reform.* New York: Columbia School of Social Work, 1996.

p. 8 sites . . . produced its own version: Hirota, Janice M. "Children at Risk: An Interim Report on Organizational Structure and Dynamics." New York: Center on Addiction and Substance Abuse at Columbia University, February 1995.

p. 8 problems . . . rooted in a lack of resources: Hess, McGowan and Meyer, 1996.

p. 8 successful corporations: Peters, Thomas J. and Robert H. Waterman. *In Search of Excellence: Lessons from America's Best-Run Companies.* New York: Harper & Row, 1982.

p. 8 fad of the moment: Management expert Peter Drucker says than an organization's mission should be abandoned only if it has been achieved. *Non Profit World,* July/August 1991.

p. 8 create a compelling ethos: The Coalition of Essential Schools. "What Research Suggests About Essential School Ideas." Coalition of Essential Schools, *Horace,* Vol. 11, No. 3, January 1995. Bryk, Anthony S. and M. E. Driscoll. *The High School as Community: Contextual Influences, and Consequences for Students and*

Teachers. Madison: University of Wisconsin-Madison, National Center on Effective Secondary Schools, 1988. Chubb, J. E. and T. M. Moe. *Politics, Markets, and America's Schools.* Washington, DC: Brookings Institution, 1990.

p. 9 able to continue evolving: The National Research Council's recent review of what is known and what can be done about violence in urban America recommended allowing programs to evolve on the basis of experience. National Research Council. *Violence in Urban America: Mobilizing a Response.* Washington, DC: National Academy Press, 1994.

p. 9 shared view of the . . . organization's principal goals: DiIulio, John J., Jr. *Deregulating the Public Service: Can Government Be Improved?* Washington, DC: Brookings Institution, 1994. Pp. 73–74.

pp. 9–10 Skills of leaders of prize-winning programs: Golden, Olivia, quoted in Schorr, Lisbeth and Deborah Both. "Attributes of Effective Services for Young Children: A Brief Survey of Current Knowledge and Its Implications for Program and Policy Development." In Effective Services for Young Children: Report of a Workshop. Washington, DC: National Academy Press, 1991.

p. 10 support from their managers: Charles Bruner, quoted in ibid.

p. 10 Adams quote: Bill Moyers Special, "What Can We Do About Violence?" PBS, January 9, 1995.

p. 11 relationships . . . most important: Karen Pittman speaking at meeting of International Youth Foundation Board, July 20, 1995.

p. 11 relationships with caring adults . . . central to . . . effectiveness: National Research Council. *Losing Generations: Adolescents in High Risk Settings.* Washington, DC: National Academy Press, 1993.

p. 11 Comer re: people who have given up on helping systems: Comer, James P. "Educating Poor Minority Children." *Scientific American,* 1988 259(5):42–48. Studies of program effectiveness repeatedly stress the "centrality of human relationships," and of drawing disadvantaged populations into "a sense of membership in the community," Lightfoot, Sara Lawrence. "Visions of a Better Way: A Black Appraisal of Public Schooling." Report of the Committee on Policy for Racial Justice, Joint Center for Political Studies, 1989. Also Whelage, Gary E. *Reducing the Risk: Schools as Communities of Support.* New York: Falmer Press, 1989.

p. 11 Ferguson quote: Ferguson, Ronald F. "How Professionals in Community-Based Programs Perceive and Respond to the Needs of Black Male Youth." In Mincy, Ronald B. (ed.). *Nurturing Young Black Males.* Washington, DC: Urban Institute Press, 1994.

p. 11 Head Start study: Nolan, Timothy M. "What Really Makes Head Start Work? You *May* Be Surprised!" Milwaukee, WI: Learning Plus Press, 1991.

p. 11 relationship that helps to turn lives around: The Center for the Study of Social Policy found that "It is the accessibility, intensity, and empowering nature of the relationship between the worker and an individual or family that helps motivate family members, enables them to take responsibility for necessary changes, and results in more effective use of services." "A Framework for Child Welfare Reform." Unpublished paper, prepared for the Annie E. Casey Foundation. Greenwich, CT: December 1987.

p. 11 improving student achievement: McLaughlin, Milbrey and Joan E. Talbert. "Contexts That Matter for Teaching and Learning." Palo Alto, CA: Center for Research on the Context of Secondary School Teaching, 1993.

p. 11 fourth grader: Noblit, George W. and Dwight L. Rogers. "Creating Caring in Schools," a paper prepared for the Lilly Endowment Research Grants Program on Youth and Caring Conference, Key Biscayne, FL: February 26–27, 1992.

p. 12 crucial to his success: Adams says, "It's wrong to think that I could deal effectively with a lot of kids—six or seven hundred kids—because I couldn't run an effective family if I had 700 children."

p. 12 Wilkes quote: Urban Strategies Council, *Connections: Linking Youth with Caring Adults,* 1989.

p. 12 Synthesis of . . . research on mentoring: Sipe, Cynthia L. *Mentoring: A Synthesis of P/PV's Research: 1988–95.* Public/Private Ventures, 1996.

p. 13 practitioners elicit client strengths: Kinney, Strand, Hagerup and Bruner, 1994.

p. 13 "problem-solving exchange": Nelson, Douglas. "Joining Forces for Change—Family Support in the '90s." Family Resource Coalition 1994 National Conference, Chicago, IL, May 6, 1994.

p. 13 Handler quote: Handler, Joel. *Down from Bureaucracy: Ambiguities in Privatization and Empowerment.* Princeton: Princeton University Press, 1996. Pp. 213–15.

pp. 13–14 Schön description of new practitioners' collaborative stance: Schön, Don. Memo to Yona Rosenfeld, January 30, 1993.

p. 14 Shawn Satterfield quote: Ferguson in Mincy, 1994.

p. 14 Stoneman quote: Interview with Dorothy Stoneman, October 31, 1994.

p. 14 YouthBuild evaluation: Ferguson, Ronald and Philip Clay. "YouthBuild in Developmental Perspective: A Formative Evaluation of the YouthBuild Demonstration Project." Cambridge, MA: MIT Department of Urban Studies and Planning, September 1996.

p. 14 YouthBuild staff going beyond the call of duty: Ferguson, Ronald F. and Jason C. Snipes. "The Counselor's Role in Helping Youth Through Developmental Tasks and Stages in YouthBuild." Paper prepared for 1995 HUD Counselors' Training.

pp. 15–16 Quotes from Opportunity to Succeed participants and Joe Califano: "CBS Sunday Morning," March 31, 1990.

p. 16 Spiritual approach . . . an important key to change: Farrow, Frank. "System Change at the Neighborhood Level: Creating Better Futures for Children, Youth, and Families." Washington, DC: Center for the Study of Social Policy. Prepared for National Leadership Symposium on Community Strategies for Children and Families, February 14–16, 1996.

p. 16 Woodson quote: Raspberry, William. "The Power of Spirituality." *Washington Post,* 7 December 1992.

p. 16 conservatives may turn away from . . . secular means and Loury quote: Sandel, Michael J. *Democracy's Discontent: America in Search of a Public Philosophy.* Cambridge: Harvard University Press, 1996.

pp. 16–17 Oliver quote: "This Week with David Brinkley." ABC, December 25, 1994.

p. 17 the possibility of redemption: Chanoff, David. "Street Redeemer, James Galipeau." *New York Times Magazine,* 13 November 1994.

p. 17 P/PV quote: Conservation Company and Public/Private Ventures. "Building from Strength: Replication as a Strategy for Expanding Social Programs That Work." Philadelphia: Replication and Program Services, 1994.

p. 17 Light quote: Light, Paul. "Creating Innovating Organizations in the Public

Sector: A Summary of Findings from the Surviving Innovation Project." Paper prepared for delivery at the annual meetings of the Association of Policy Analysis and Management, Pittsburgh, October 31–November 2, 1997.

p. 18 Tucker quote: Tucker, Marc on "Crisis: Urban Education, Making the System Work." New York, 1990.

p. 19 conditions that are still exceedingly rare: The condition of large-scale reform as described by the University of California's Sid Gardner: "Sustained political attention where the norm is sporadic crisis management. . . . community-wide planning where the norm is political targeting. . . . greater discretion at the level of the line worker where the norm is rule-bound bureaucracy. . . . long-term support where the norm is short-run savings. . . . comprehensiveness where the norms are programmatic, categorical, and professionally myopic." Gardner, Sid. "Elements and Contexts of Community-based, Cross-systems Reform."

p. 19 when the model . . . become[s] the norm: Cutler, Ira. "The Role of Finance Reform in Comprehensive Service Initiatives." Washington, DC: The Finance Project, 1994.

p. 20 Maryland state official quote: *Washington Post,* 25 March 1996.

CHAPTER 2 Spreading What Works Beyond the Hothouse

p. 22 McDonald's success story: Halberstam, David. *The Fifties.* New York: Ballantine, 1994. P. 171; Drucker, Stephen. "Who Is the Best Restaurateur in America?" *New York Times Magazine,* March 10, 1996. Charles Stewart Mott Foundation, Annual Report 1990. "Replication: Sowing Seeds of Hope." Flint, MI. McDonald's today still specifies the color of the toilet paper in the rest rooms. Young, Dennis R. "An Interview with Peter F. Drucker." San Francisco: Jossey Bass, *Nonprofit Management & Leadership,* Vol. 2, No. 3, Spring 1992.

pp. 22–23 Drucker quote: Young, 1992. P. 301.

p. 23 Memo calling for mass production in the human services: Circulated by the AAAS's Initiative for Children, and greeted by Professor Harvey Brooks as consistent with the "rich literature on this subject from the applied natural sciences and engineering, including medicine," and as "very original and ambitious, but [sic] well worth a serious try."

p. 23 "figure out how to replicate that": Clinton, Bill. "Remarks by the President in Blue Ribbon Ceremony," May 14, 1993.

p. 23 "our enduring problem in America in public life": Remarks by the President-elect, meeting with governors, January 19, 1993.

pp. 23–24 Quotes from *Primary Colors:* Klein, Joe, *Primary Colors.* New York: Random House, 1996. Pp. 18–19.

p. 24 Converting innovative exceptions into the prevailing rule: Richard Elmore of the Harvard Graduate School of Education writes that the central dilemma of education reform is that "we can produce many examples of how educational practice could look different, but we can produce few, if any, examples of large numbers of teachers engaging in these practices in large-scale institutions designed to deliver education to most children." Elmore, Richard F. "Getting to Scale with Good Educational Practice." Cambridge: *Harvard Education Review,* Spring 1996. William Morrill, president of Mathtech, Inc., says the same thing about human services. "With respect to individual projects in communities, we can, at this micro level—with enough imagination, energy, and resources—do almost anything once.

. . . But it is at the replication stage . . . where we have gotten into trouble and seem unable to make much progress." Morrill, William A. "Getting Beyond the Micro Gee Whiz: Can Innovative Service Change the Service System?" In Kahn, Alfred J. and Sheila B. Kamerman. *Children & Their Families in Big Cities: Strategies for Service Reform.* New York: Columbia University, 1996.

p. 24 at much the same rate as those that didn't work: These were the findings of a review by the Conservation Company and Public/Private Ventures. Conservation Company and Public/Private Ventures. "Building from Strength: Replication as a Strategy for Expanding Social Programs That Work." Philadelphia: Replication and Program Services, 1994.

p. 25 "into the intergovernmental system": Personal communication from David Racine, July 18, 1996.

p. 25 Demonstrations masking disinvestment: Memo from Don Schön, December 17, 1992.

p. 27 "tricking the system": Cutler, Ira. "The Role of Finance Reform in Comprehensive Service Initiatives." Washington, DC: The Finance Project, 1994.

p. 27 "the safety valve to stave off systems change": Heather Weiss, at a meeting of the Working Group on Early Life, Harvard University, October 12, 1993.

p. 27 make the system . . . more resistant to change: Smale quoted by Sviridoff, Mitchell and William Ryan. "Prospects and Strategies for Community-Centered Family Service." Paper prepared for Family Service America, 1995.

p. 27 Foundations . . . overemphasizing innovation: Charles Stewart Mott Foundation Annual Report, 1990. Also Conservation Company and Public/Private Ventures, 1994. The Mott Foundation report on replication concluded that "the need to press for public support for effective programs gets short shrift in the grantmaking process." Berlin, Gordon, quoted in Mott report: "There is a tendency for foundations not to stick with anything. . . . Foundations will start to develop something and say, 'Well, we showed this worked, and now we're moving on to the next thing.' "

p. 27 began to focus directly on the replication issue: Mott Foundation Annual Report, 1990.

p. 29 Racine quote: Personal communication, July 18, 1996.

p. 29 Schön quote: Memo from Don Schön, MIT, to Jack Habib, JDC, Israel, December 17, 1992.

p. 29 Herr quote: Herr, Toby. "Balancing Deeper and Wider." Rensselaerville Institute: *Innovating,* Vol. 2, No. 3, Spring 1992.

p. 29 assumed . . . a "good product" would become part of a mainstream system: Elmore, Spring 1996.

p. 30 Haskins quote: Collins, James. "The Day Care Dilemma." *Time,* February 3, 1997.

p. 30 Lieberman quote: Olson, Lynn. *Education Week,* November 11, 1994.

p. 32 Description of YouthBuild: Unless otherwise indicated, the information about YouthBuild comes from interviews with Dorothy Stoneman on October 31, 1994, and July 23, 1996; interim reports from Dorothy Stoneman; 1995 and 1995 issues of *The YouthBuild Bulletin;* May 23, 1995, letter to Lisbeth Schorr from Dorothy Stoneman; January 12, 1996, letter from Dorothy Stoneman; and Ferguson, Ronald and Philip Clay. "YouthBuild in Developmental Perspective: A Formative Evaluation of the YouthBuild Demonstration Project." Cambridge: MIT Department of Urban Studies and Planning, September 1996.

p. 34 Stoneman's quote re "gives a lot of people hope": Seltzer, Anne-Marie. "YouthBuild: a National Service and Community Development Program That Says Yes to Teenagers." *Radcliffe Quarterly,* December 1993.

p. 40 Healthy Families America and Hawaii's Healthy Start: Information about Healthy Families Indiana not otherwise attributed comes from visits and interviews conducted by Judith Tolmach Silber during the month of March 1995.

p. 41 Effects of home visiting: David and Lucille Packard Foundation. "Home Visiting." Los Altos, CA: Center for the Future of Children, Vol. 3, No. 3, Winter 1993.

p. 41 "We don't have a dime . . .": Healthy Families America was providing training, technical assistance, training materials, monitoring, and evaluation, but no start-up funds.

p. 41 one Indiana child died as a result of abuse or neglect: Impink, Rhonda Vickery and Joanne B. Martin. "Facilitating a Collaborative Partnership for Healthy Families Indiana." Unpublished paper, October 3, 1994.

p. 41 incidence of abuse . . . an entirely unexpected zero: *The APSAC Advisor,* Vol. 6, No. 4, 1993.

p. 42 NCPCA's leadership was ready for a reappraisal: Daro, Deborah. "Child Maltreatment Research: Implications for Program Design." In *Child Abuse, Child Development and Social Policy.* Dante Cicchetti and Sheree L. Toth (eds.). Norwood, NJ: Ablex Publishing Company, 1993.

p. 42 GAO report: U. S. Government, General Accounting Office. "Home Visiting: A Promising Early Intervention Strategy for At-Risk Families." GAO/HRD-90-83, July 11, 1990.

p. 42 U.S. Advisory Board report: U.S. Advisory Board on Child Abuse and Neglect. Richard Krugman, chair. "Child Abuse and Neglect: Critical First Steps in Response to a National Emergency." U.S. Department of Health and Human Services, August 1990.

p. 42 offered a million dollars toward that end: Personal conversation with Anne Cohn Donnelly, March 17, 1995.

p. 43 array of services tailored to each family's needs: Research supports the comprehensiveness of this approach. A recent review of research found that "the most significant benefits have been achieved in home visiting programs that attempt to address a broad array of needs of children and their parents." Packard Foundation. "Home Visiting." P. 9.

p. 44 transition . . . to a statewide program with public funding: By 1991, Hawaii's Healthy Start had expanded to 11 sites, had an annual budget of $7 million. In 1992 Healthy Start was screening 52 percent of all newborns throughout the islands.

p. 44 Critical program elements: Healthy Families America. "Critical Elements for Effective Home Visitor Services," February 1996.

p. 44 "selling an approach, not a model": HFA Program Planning Packet includes sample budgets, possible funding sources, staff recruitment techniques, training agenda, evaluation techniques, and site descriptions.

p. 45 certifying programs: HFA also provides training and technical assistance to states that do not have HFA sites to integrate and improve the quality of existing services.

p. 45 model for . . . uncategorical use of categorical funds: Personal conversation with Peter Edelman, then Assistant Secretary for Planning and Evaluation, Department of Health and Human Services, June 1996.

p. 46 Step Ahead councils also serve as the governance mechanism: To assure community collaboration, local Healthy Families projects are required to obtain endorsement of local Step Ahead councils in applying for funding from the state's Healthy Families Fund.

p. 46 97 percent of the families had no reported incidents of abuse or neglect: Among the first year's success stories: Darlene B. was eighteen years old when she gave birth to her second baby. A member of a Fort Wayne gang, she had been arrested for vandalism and running away from home, expelled from high school and several times remanded to the Youth Center. Frequent bitter fights with her mother kept Darlene, her two children, and her motorcycle on the move. Living wherever she could find refuge, her lifestyle posed a serious danger to her children. Despite (or because of) her precarious future, Darlene initially wanted no part of Healthy Families. After three months of fruitless pursuit, the Family Support worker drew her into conversation long enough to learn that Darlene had once wanted to be a nurse. Told that her dream was not impossible, Darlene began to listen. She joined Healthy Families, is now enrolled in a Graduate Equivalency Degree (GED) program, and works part time in a nursing home—a recognized entry-level position in her career field. She is living at home again and saving money to get a place of her own. The new stability in her life has vastly increased the prospects of a safe and stable home life for her children.

p. 47 Schools as Beacons of Hope: The story of the Beacon schools draws on materials prepared by Richard Mendel, interviews by Mendel with Michele Cahill of the Youth Development Institute and Richard Murphy, formerly New York City Commissioner of Youth Services. Also my visit to Countee Cullen, and interviews with Geoffrey Canada, Shawn Dove, and Joseph Stewart on October 17, 1994, other conversations with Geoffrey Canada, as well as the following materials: Canada, Geoffrey. *first stick knife gun: A Personal History of Violence in America.* Boston: Beacon Press, 1995. Canada, Geoffrey. "Monsters." *New York Times,* 17 December 1992. Videotape, "Victory Over Violence." Cahill, Michele, Jacqueline Perry, Marlene Wright and Avra Rice. "A Documentation Report on the New York City Beacons Initiative." New York: Youth Development Institute, December 1993, and Cohen, Deborah L. "Live and Learn." *Education Week,* June 7, 1995.

p. 48 ten initial Beacons were selected: Just as the grantees were chosen, their funds were nearly eliminated when the "Safe Streets, Safe Cities" budget was targeted for deep cuts in response to a city-wide fiscal crunch. But Mayor Dinkins stood by the Beacons program. It is said he had to decide between a prison barge in New York Harbor to handle the overcrowding in city jails or Beacon schools, and he chose Beacons.

p. 49 "to give them a hug, to hold their hand": Bob Herbert quoting Canada. "Men and Jobs." *New York Times,* 30 September 1996.

p. 50 "We set those limits": Bob Herbert quoting Stewart. "Take the A Train." *New York Times,* 27 September 1996.

p. 56 Success for All in Learning to Read and Learning to Replicate: This description of Success for All is based on correspondence from Robert Slavin, March 1, 1995; personal conversations with Robert Slavin, June 1, 1995, July 18, 1996, and October 22, 1996, and the following materials: Slavin, Robert E., Lawrence J. Dolan and Nancy A. Madden. "Scaling Up: Lessons Learned in the Dissemination of Success for All." Center for Research and Education of Students Placed at Risk. Johns Hopkins University, December 1994; Madden, Nancy A., Robert E. Slavin, Nancy L. Karweit and Barbara J. Livermon. "Restructuring the Urban Elementary School." *Educational Leadership,* February 1989. Center for Research on Effective Schooling for Disadvantaged Students. "Success for All Improves Reading Performance in Sites Across Nation." Baltimore: Johns Hopkins University. CDS, March 1994.

p. 57 "It makes no sense": Slavin quoted in Manzo, Kathleen Kennedy and Joetta L. Sack. "Teacher Training Seen Key to Improving Reading in Early Grades." *Education Week,* February 26, 1997.

p. 60 "ad-hoc entrepreneurial efforts": "Building from Strength: Replication as a Strategy for Expanding Social Programs That Work." Philadelphia: Replication and Program Services, 1994.

p. 60 combine the replication . . . with the adaptation: This is also the conclusion that Replication and Program Services, Inc., comes to. The term they use to describe this process is "adaptive replication."

p. 61 "that force reformers back toward the status quo": Morrill, in Kahn and Kamerman, 1996.

p. 64 Lynn quote: Duke University. "Research on Innovations in State and Local Government." The Governor's Center at Duke University, 1992 Conferences. P. 11.

CHAPTER 3 Taming Bureaucracies to Support What Works

pp. 65–67 The story of Leticia Johnson: This is a true story, adapted from Sanders, Joelle. *Before Their Time: Four Generations of Teenage Mothers.* New York: Harcourt Brace Jovanovich, 1991.

p. 68 Kelman quote: Kelman, Steven. "The Renewal of the Public Sector." *The American Prospect,* Summer 1990.

p. 69 every restraint . . . arises from someone's demand for it: Wilson, James Q. *Bureaucracy: What Government Agencies Do and Why They Do It.* New York: Basic Books, 1989.

p. 69 Appropriations . . . made without benefit of budgets: Barzelay, Michael. *Breaking Through Bureaucracy: A New Vision for Managing in Government.* Berkeley, CA: University of California, 1992. P. 3.

p. 69 "robbing . . . as they cemented . . . political control": Tolchin, Martin. "The Citizen as Customer." *New York Times Book Review,* March 8, 1992.

p. 69 from . . . anybody who happened to need protection or favors: Blum, John M., Edmund S. Morgan, Willie Lee Rose, Arthur M. Schlesinger, Jr., Kenneth M. Stampp and C. Vann Woodward (eds.). *The National Experience: A History of the United States.* Fifth Edition. New York: Harcourt Brace Jovanovich, 1968.

p. 69 Plunkitt quote: Tolchin, 1992.

p. 69 ". . . to root out . . . patronage": Skocpol, Theda. *Protecting Soldiers and Mothers: The Political Origins of Social Policy in the United States.* Cambridge: Harvard University Press, 1992.

p. 70 consistent application of universal rules: Barzelay, 1992. Pp. 4–5.

p. 70 reformers . . . loathed corruption more than they loved efficiency: DiIulio, John J. Jr. *Deregulating the Public Service: Can Government Be Improved?* Washington, DC: Brookings Institution, 1994.

p. 70 "new national institutions were needed": This paragraph on federal-state relations based on the seminal book by Alice Rivlin, *Reviving the American Dream: The Economy, the States, and the Federal Government.* Washington, DC: Brookings Institution, 1992.

p. 71 Califano quote: Califano, Joseph A. Jr. "How Great Was the Great Society?" Address at "The Great Society: A 20-Year Critique." The Lyndon B Johnson Auditorium, LBJ Library, University of Texas, April 19, 1985.

p. 71 Rivlin quote: Rivlin, 1992.

p. 71 more controls and clearances: Kaufman, Herbert. *The Administrative Behavior of Federal Bureau Chiefs.* Washington, DC: Brookings Institution, 1981. P. 192.

p. 71 layers of decision making: Light, Paul C. *Thickening Government: Federal Hierarchy and the Diffusion of Accountability.* Washington, DC: Brookings Institution, 1995.

p. 72 further limit agency discretion: Wilson, 1989.

p. 72 Gore quote: National Performance Review. *From Red Tape to Results: Creating a Government That Works Better and Costs Less.* Washington, DC: September 7, 1993.

p. 72 Inspector General quoted by Philip K. Howard. *The Death of Common Sense: How Law Is Suffocating America.* New York: Random House, 1994. P. 96.

p. 73 discretion . . . "an open invitation to abuse": Altshuler, Alan A. "Bureaucratic Innovation, Democratic Accountability, and Political Incentives." In Altshuler, Alan A. and Robert D. Behn (eds.). *Innovation in American Government.* In press. Brookings Institution, 1997.

p. 74 Bureaucracy resulting from categorical funding: This section on categorical funding is informed throughout by a paper by Sid Gardner, "Reform Options for the Intergovernmental Funding System: Decategorization Policy Issues," produced under the auspices of the Roundtable on Comprehensive Community Initiatives for Children and Families of the Aspen Institute.

pp. 74–75 Gardner quote: Gardner, Sid. "Failure by Fragmentation." *California Tomorrow,* Fall 1989. Pp. 18–25.

p. 75 Califano quote: Califano, April 19, 1985.

p. 75 "a coordinated system would emerge": Edelman, Peter B. and Beryl Radin. Introduction to "Serving Children and Families Effectively: How the Past Can Help Chart the Future." Washington, DC: Education and Human Services Consortium, 1991.

p. 75 "the porkiest of the pork": The unnamed Nixon Administration official is quoted by Peterson, George E. "A Block Grant Approach to Welfare Reform." In Sawhill, Isabel. "Welfare Reform: An Analysis of the Issues." Washington, DC: Urban Institute, 1995.

p. 76 $200 toward purchase of a washing machine: As Michael Lipsky points out, distribution of public benefits in our society is driven primarily by concerns about equity, and equity is interpreted to require not only rigid eligibility criteria but also rigid rules to assure that people in similar situations receive identical responses. Lipsky, Michael and Stephen Ratheb Smith. "Nonprofit Organizations, Government, and the Welfare State." *Political Science Quarterly,* Vol. 104, No. 4, 1989–90. Pp. 625–48.

Resolution of the equity-responsiveness dilemma may lie in rejecting overly broad categories, within which equity is maintained, and overly narrow interpretations of what it means to treat people equitably. The family that would receive help in purchasing a washing machine could be seen, *in the ways that matter,* to be quite unlike the other families in the Homebuilders' case load.

For it costs dearly in lost effectiveness not to heed Robert Theobald's warning that it sometimes seems "we'd rather have a system that pretends to be equitable, while doing great harm, than one that makes mistakes while saving human beings." Robert Theobald quoted by Raspberry, William. "Charity Closer to Home." *Washington Post,* 23 January 1995.

p. 76 cash to . . . cope with unexpected contingencies: The most important determinants of success in what line workers actually do when they meet clients (which should be the litmus test for an effective public policy) are flexibility and freedom from normal federal categorical program constraints, according to Gordon Berlin, formerly Deputy Commissioner of Welfare, New York City. From Berlin, Gordon. "The New Poverty Among Families: A Service Decategorization Response." New York: MDRC, 1993.

pp. 76–77 strict rules . . . undermine responsiveness: A willingness to rethink the proper balance between equity and flexibility is apparently not universal among lawyers for the poor. As Philip Howard tells the story in his book, *The Death of Common Sense,* New York City had put aside some funds to advance rent payments to families who were threatened with eviction because they had fallen behind on paying rent for reasons beyond their control. The advances were made at the discretion of individual welfare personnel. Legal Aid lawyers, representing clients who were turned down, sued on the basis that not everyone was treated the same.

p. 77 Golden re reconciling safeguarding quality with responsiveness: Personal communication from Olivia Golden, March 18, 1996.

p. 77 whether four home visits in the course of a year made any difference: Bruner, Charles and George Oster (eds.). "Family Development and Self-Sufficiency Demonstration Grant Program. Proceedings of the Program Implementation Workshop: A Focus on Iowa's Support Programs." Des Moines, IA: Child and Family Policy Center, February 17, 1989.

p. 77 Parents as Teachers has spread to forty-seven states . . . makes monthly home visits: Information as of December 1, 1996, from Parents as Teachers National Center, St. Louis, MO.

p. 77 Centralized control . . . "the lifeblood of efficient administration": Barzelay, 1992.

p. 78 discretion and local variation . . . as illicit: Elmore, Richard F. "Backward Mapping: Implementation Research and Policy Decisions." *Political Science Quarterly,* Vol. 95, No. 4, Winter 1979–80.

p. 78 cumbersome rules to control their subordinates: DiIulio, John J. Jr., Gerald Harvey, and Donald F. Kettl. *Improving Government Performance: An Owner's Manual.* Washington, DC: Brookings Institution, 1993. P. 27.

p. 78 Gore quote: National Performance Review, 1993.

p. 78 variability and discretion . . . are often assets: Both Richard Elmore of the Harvard Graduate School of Education and John DiIulio of Princeton University and the Brookings Institution argue this point in widely different contexts. Elmore, Winter 1979–80. P. 610. DiIulio, 1994.

p. 79 maximizing discretion . . . where the problem is most immediate: Richard Elmore has written that "the problem-solving ability of complex systems depends not on hierarchical control but on maximizing discretion at the point where the problem is most immediate," Elmore, Winter 1979–80. P. 605.

p. 79 limit the flexibility of people at the front lines: Elmore, 1979–80. P. 610. DiIulio, 1994. DiIulio, Harvey, and Kettl, 1993.

p. 79 Elmore quote: Elmore, 1979–80. P. 610.

p. 79 rushing to abandon hierarchical forms: Heckscher, Charles. "Can Business Beat Bureaucracy?" *The American Prospect,* Spring 1991. P. 114.

p. 79 Quote of James Houghton, late chairman of Corning Glass: Houghton, James R. "The Age of Hierarchy Is Over." *New York Times,* 24 September 1989.

p. 79 insights . . . not . . . adopted in the public sector: Yankelovich, Daniel. "Three Destructive Trends: Can They Be Reversed?" Paper presented to the National Civic League's 100th National Conference on Governance. November 11, 1994.

p. 79 "solving problems by adopting rules": Wilson, 1989.

pp. 79–80 De Tocqueville quote: Alexis de Tocqueville, quoted in DiIulio, 1994. P. 24.

p. 80 Manning quote: In Wilson, 1989. P. 30.

p. 80 more staff . . . needed to administer: Barzelay, 1992. P. 124.

p. 80 more managers . . . needed to enforce: Wilson, 1989. P. 133.

p. 80 capacity to tackle new problems is sapped: DiIulio, Harvey, and Kettl, 1993. P. 81.

p. 80 they become paralyzed: A panel of seventeen assistant secretaries, convened by the National Academy of Public Administration, agreed that "government has become entwined in elaborate management control systems and the accretion of progressively more detailed administrative procedures," with the result that now "procedures overwhelm substance." Wilson in DiIulio, 1994. P. 46.

p. 80 Gore quote: National Performance Review, 1993.

p. 80 paperwork demands . . . a serious morale-breaker: Hess, Peg, Brenda McGowan, and Carol H. Meyer. "Practitioner's Perspectives on Family and Child Services." In Kahn and Kamerman, 1996.

p. 81 Gardner findings: Gardner, 1994.

p. 81 not to help . . . find and pay for permanent housing: Messinger, Ruth W. "Out of Hotels, into Homes." *New York Times,* 7 August 1993.

p. 81 "his mental illness had not yet progressed far enough": Jane Waldfogel presentation to John F. Kennedy School Executive Session on New Paradigms for Child Protection Services, October 10, 1994.

p. 82 "the 'walk-in' was turned away": Hagedorn, John M. *Forsaking Our Children: Bureaucracy and Reform in the Child Welfare System.* Chicago: Lake View Press, 1995. P. 120.

p. 82 the father was doing nothing "wrong": *New York Times,* 12 May 1995. This story has a more promising ending than the others: When Jose Jr. was fifteen years old, he moved out. Mr. Sanchez went to the Children's Aid Society, which assigned a social worker who got to know both father and son, persuaded the school to evaluate Jose Jr. and—on the basis of psychiatric advice—to provide him with special education services. Father and son both got counseling, and young Jose has moved back home, is getting along better with his father, and is getting passing grades in all but one class at school.

p. 82 IEL findings: Dunkle, Margaret. "A Bottom-Up Look at Welfare Reform:

What Happens When Policymakers Apply for Assistance from the Programs They Created?" *Education Week,* November 29, 1995.

pp. 82–83 Hagedorn Milwaukee story: Hagedorn, 1995. P. 101.

p. 83 children . . . moved from one child care setting to another: Marcia Myers presentation at conference on Welfare Reform and Child Development, Board on Children and Families, National Academy of Sciences, December 5, 1994.

p. 83 what auditors count: "The auditors' vigilance (invisible to the policy community, yet religiously scouring case files for missing documentation) is a root cause of bureaucracy preoccupied with eligibility verification and re-verification," writes Gordon Berlin, formerly Deputy Commissioner of Welfare, New York City. "Fighting disallowances and protecting against them consume large blocks of local officials' time. Documenting eligibility occupies the bulk of case-workers' time. Maintaining a client and service focus quickly becomes a secondary priority." Berlin, 1993.

p. 83 Jessie Hall quote: Haveman, Judith. "Red Tape May Snarl Turnover of Welfare." *Washington Post,* 20 March 1995.

p. 83 Dunkle quote: Dunkle, November 29, 1995.

p. 84 "exquisitely specific contexts": This is Patricia A. Graham's term.

p. 84 Quindlen quote: Quindlen, Anna. *New York Times,* 21 September 1991.

p. 84 Starr quote: Starr, Paul. "Liberalism After Socialism." *The American Prospect,* Fall 1991. Pp. 70–80.

pp. 84–85 Devolution description and Clinton quote: Cook, Gareth. "Devolution Chic." *Washington Monthly,* April 1995.

p. 85 Goldsmith quote: Goldsmith, Steve. "Revamping Welfare, Rebuilding Lives." *New York Times,* 4 August 1996.

p. 85 Kondratas quote: Haveman, Judith. "Scholars Question Whether Welfare Shift Is Reform." *Washington Post,* 20 April 1995.

p. 85 Devolution does not . . . : Between 1970 and 1992, employment in state government grew by 64 percent while the federal civilian work force declined as a percentage of the U.S. population. During the same period, state legislative expenditures increased by 117 percent while federal expenditures increased by 19 percent. Cook, April 1995.

pp. 85–86 child health initiative findings: Newacheck, Paul W., Dana C. Hughes, Claire Brindis, and Neal Halfon. "Decategorizing Health Services: Interim Findings from the Robert Wood Johnson Foundation's Child Health Initiative." The People-to-People Foundation: *Health Affairs,* Vol. 14, No. 3, 1995. Child Health Initiative Grantees Meeting, New Orleans, LA, October 18, 1996.

p. 86 vastly strengthened capacity of states: Rivlin, 1992. P. 84.

p. 86 Dionne quote: Dionne, E. J. "The New, New, New Federalism." *Washington Post,* 7 March 1995.

p. 87 "flexibility" of civil service rules that allow a worker: Hagedorn, 1995. P. 53.

p. 88 MDRC service integration findings: Manpower Demonstration Research Corporation. "Lives of Promise, Lives of Pain: Young Mothers After New Chance." np: MDRC, 1994.

p. 88 actually needed were new social policies: Kahn, Alfred J. and Sheila B. Kamerman. "Integrating Services Integration: An Overview of Initiatives, Issues, and Possibilities." National Center for Children in Poverty, Columbia University School of Public Health, September 1992.

p. 88 Wilson quote: Dubnick, Melvin J. "A Coup Against King Bureaucracy?" In DiIulio, 1994.

pp. 88–89 Privatization has become the 1990s elixir and Starr quote: Starr, Paul. "The Limits of Privatization." Washington, DC: Economic Policy Institute, n.d. Starr also writes that supporters of privatization prescribe it as a tonic for efficiency and economic growth, an appetite suppressant for the federal budget, a vaccine against bureaucratic empire-building, and a booster for individual freedom.

p. 89 The most committed privatizers: Kettl, Donald F. "The Myths, Realities, and Challenges of Privatization." In Thompson, Frank J. (ed.), *Revitalizing State and Local Public Service*. San Francisco: Jossey Bass, 1993.

p. 89 optimistic version of the privatization argument and *Reinventing Government* quote: Osborne, David and Ted Gaebler. *Reinventing Government: How the Entrepreneurial Spirit Is Transforming the Public Sector*. New York: Penguin, 1993.

p. 89 making government more entrepreneurial: Urging the entrepreneurial, debureaucratizing spirit in the executive branch of government is not enough, especially when it is not supported in the legislative branch. When the U.S. Forest Service decided to "empower" managers in the field to deploy resources where needed and to use discretion to solve problems on their own, morale and productivity soared. But Congress eventually forced the Forest Service to abandon its reform, because "Congressmen view their jobs as deciding where the money goes, [and there is] no indication that they intend to change their roles." *New Republic*, October 11, 1993.

p. 89 bipartisan answer to every challenge: Shenk, Joshua Wolf. "The Perils of Privatization." *Washington Monthly*, May 1995.

p. 89 most . . . public money for social services is spent through private non-profit contractors: Kettl in Thompson, 1993.

p. 89 government . . . principal source of nonprofit human service agency financing: Salamon, Lester M. *Partners in Public Service: Government-Nonprofit Relations in the Modern Welfare State*. Baltimore: Johns Hopkins University Press, 1995.

p. 90 Conditions in which contracting out brings benefits: Donahue (Donahue, John. *The Privatization Decision: Public Ends, Private Means*. New York: Basic Books, 1989); Gormley (Gormley, William T. Jr. "Privatization Revisited." Paper prepared for the Twentieth Century Fund Conference on Privatization, New York, May 4, 1993); and Kettl, 1993, have all come to similar conclusions on this point.

p. 90 conditions of meaningful competition . . . unlikely . . . in . . . human services: Handler, Joel F. *Down from Bureaucracy: Ambiguities in Privatization and Empowerment*. Princeton, NJ: Princeton University Press, 1996. P. 137.

p. 90 lack of qualified providers inhibits competition: In a study of Massachusetts Department of Social Services contracting with nonprofits (1,700 contracts), nonprofits came to have no existence apart from government programs; government had to continually prop up inefficient and mismanaged organizations to maintain continuity for clients, and the performance of the nonprofits differed little from that of public agencies.

p. 90 "monopolistic behavior on the part of its contractors": In the mid-1980s the Massachusetts Department of Mental Health negotiated over 2,000 separate contracts with over 500 vendors, which aimed to give the state flexibility by avoiding bureaucratic rigidities, to lower costs by avoiding civil service and union requirements, and to achieve greater responsiveness to local needs. A study of the process found that the aims of the contracting had not been realized. Kettl in Thompson, 1993. P. 263.

p. 90 Goldsmith quote: Johnson, Dirk. "In Privatizing City Services, It's Now 'Indy-a-First-Place.' " *New York Times*, 2 March 1995.

p. 90 Kettl quote re advantages of contracting out: Kettl in Thompson, 1993. P. 266.

p. 90 Handler quote re greater flexibility: Handler, 1996. P. 137.

p. 90 "shift away from flexibility": Lipsky and Smith, 1989–90. Pp. 625–48.

p. 90 Handler re "organizations . . . indistinguishable": Handler, 1996. P. 160.

p. 91 model had to be standardized: Presentation of Bruce Guernsey, Robert Wood Johnson Foundation School-Based Health Centers, at Conference on What Works of the Colorado Foundation for Families and Children, March 29, 1996, Denver, CO.

p. 92 those needing . . . service are not the customers: The most important customers of police chiefs and child protective service professionals are their overseers, because they are using public resources to produce public results. Moore, Mark in DiIulio, 1994. P. 229.

p. 92 Handler re "claims . . . not plausible": Handler, 1996. Pp. 120, 170.

p. 92 CEOs who have gone from large corporations to government: Graham, T. Allison Jr. "Public and Private Management: Are They Fundamentally Alike in All Unimportant Respects?" In Stillman, Richard J. II. *Public Administration.* Boston: Houghton Mifflin, 1992.

p. 92 Government has intrinsic responsibility for pursuing the public interest: Kettl in DiIulio, 1994. P. 186.

p. 92 nation is more than a giant market: Kuttner, Robert. "After Solidarity." *The American Prospect*, May–June 1996.

p. 92 give up at our peril community institutions: Sandel, Michael J. *Democracy's Discontent: America in Search of a Public Policy.* Cambridge: Harvard University Press, 1996.

p. 93 "nimble" public institutions: Kuttner, May–June 1996.

p. 93 Governor Cuomo quote: "Meet the Press," NBC News, April 7, 1996.

p. 93 most of the money raised by charities: Wolpert, Julian. "Delusions of Charity." *The American Prospect*, Fall 1995. Pp. 86–88.

p. 93 donations to organizations providing human services: Of the ten categories tracked by the American Association of Fundraising Council, only "human services" has decreased in the last two years. Kaplan, Ann E. (ed.) *Giving USA.* New York: AAFRC Trust for Philanthropy, 1996.

p. 93 Daly and Bailey quotes: Van Beima, David. "Can Charity Fill the Gap?" *Time*, December 4, 1995.

pp. 93–94 coalition of religious leaders: Jeter, Jon. "Welfare Plan Rebuffed by Md. Clerics." *Washington Post*, 12 December 1996.

p. 94 Analyses prepared for Independent Sector: Abramson, Alan J. and Lester M. Salamon. "The Nonprofit Sector and the Federal Budget: Update as of December 1996." Washington, DC: The Aspen Institute and Johns Hopkins University, 1996.

p. 94 Olasky ideas: Olasky, Marvin N. *The Tragedy of American Compassion.* Washington, DC: Regnery, 1992. Julian Wolpert in *The American Prospect* ("Delusions of Charity," Fall 1995), and Van Biema, December 4, 1995, provide an easy guide to Olasky's thinking.

p. 95 **Wilson quote:** Wilson, 1989. P. 376.

p. 95 **Altshuler on characteristics of government bureaucracy:** Altshuler, in press.

p. 95 **Kelman on renewal of public sector:** Kelman, Summer 1990.

p. 96 **Missouri's Caring Communities:** The on-site interviews, reporting, and writing about Missouri's Caring Communities on which this section is based were done by Deborah Cohen, then assistant editor of *Education Week,* between August 1 and December 31, 1995, and supplemented by conversations between Lisbeth Schorr and Gary Stangler in 1996, and by Center for the Study of Social Policy. "Profiles of Missouri's Community Partnerships and Caring Communities." CSSP, December, 1996.

p. 100 **Family Investment Trust:** The trust is funded by several foundations, including the Annie E. Casey Foundation, the Edna McConnell Clark Foundation, the Danforth Foundation, the Greater Kansas City Community Foundation and Affiliated Trusts, and the Marion Ewing Kauffman Foundation, and receives technical assistance from the Center for the Study of Social Policy in Washington, DC.

p. 103 **New York Networks for School Renewal:** Description based on materials provided by and conversations with Beth Lief, President and CEO, Fund for New York City Public Education, and Deborah Meier.

p. 103 **Meier quotes generalizing from her experience:** Meier, Deborah. *The Power of Their Ideas: Lessons for America from a Small School in Harlem.* Boston: Beacon Press, 1995.

p. 104 **first New Visions Schools:** Fund for NYC Public Education, "New Visions Schools," January and April 1992.

p. 107 **Michigan's Statewide Move Beyond Bureaucracy to Protect Children:** Where not otherwise indicated, the information on the Michigan Families First program was obtained through interviews with Families First staff, directors, and clients; and with Michigan State Social Services staff, by Judith Tolmach Silber of the Human Service Collaborative on a visit to Michigan on November 6–9, 1995.

p. 110 **impossible to maintain the flexible operating conditions . . . without contracting out:** Because of an unresolved dispute with the public service employees union about overtime, hiring procedures, and work rules, Kelly believes that, even if the legislation had not required the department to operate through private agencies, Families First would have had to contract services to private agencies. The United Auto Workers, which represents DSS employees in Michigan, alleges that the Families First decision to use contract employees violates Michigan's civil service regulations. The case, which is still in litigation, has aroused considerable hostility, with some contending that the union is attempting to discourage DSS employees from referring cases to Families First. (In a New York City family-based program, Family Ties, a public service employees union representing Family Ties employees sued to challenge the nontraditional work requirements, such as that workers be on call twenty-four hours a day, seven days a week.)

p. 110 **unless standards were rigorously enforced:** In Illinois, each local provider designed its own version of family-based services. There were no uniform standards to help workers assess child safety, there was no basic model and no practice standards, and many programs were understaffed, with poorly trained workers.

p. 112 **Families First impact on systems:** Department of Mental Health. "Systems Reform for Children and Their Families: A Report to the Michigan Human Service Directors." Lansing, MI: Department of Mental Health, March 6, 1995. Michigan Department of Social Services. " 'Strong Families/Safe Children': Michigan's Plan for Family Preservation and Support" (P.L. 103-66). Lansing, MI: Michigan Department of Social Services, 1995.

pp. 112–13 Effects on families and children: Michigan Department of Social Services. "Families First Handbook." Lansing, MI: Michigan Department of Social Services, 1995. Between 1988 and 1995, two children whose families were receiving Families First services died as a result of parental abuse. The state director of social services and other senior officials accepted responsibility for the tragedies; they pointed out that thoughtful planning, meticulous administrative oversight, exhaustive training, low case loads, and an adequate budget had kept Michigan tragedies to a minimum, and pledged to work harder and to learn from mistakes that were made.

p. 113 functions that must be standardized from the top down: There are, of course, important public functions whose standardized processes and responses are the mark of excellence. Such functions include the Social Security Administration's determination of benefits and payments, the Internal Revenue Service's calculation of income taxes owed, and the criteria used by air traffic controllers for determining at what altitude a given plane should be flying. In none of these examples would fewer standards or greater front-line discretion enhance the quality of the agency's performance.

CHAPTER 4   A New Focus on Results

p. 115 New Focus on Results: This chapter reflects the contributions of long-time collaborators in my work on outcomes accountability, Frank Farrow, David Hornbeck, and Sara Watson.

p. 116 Wilson quote: Wilson, James Q. "Can the Bureaucracy Be Deregulated? Lessons from Government Agencies." In DiIulio, John J. Jr., *Deregulating the Public Service: Can Government Be Improved?* Washington, DC: Brookings Institution, 1994. P. 58.

p. 117 "reinventing government" proposals: Osborne, David and Ted Gaebler. *Reinventing Government: How the Entrepreneurial Spirit Is Transforming the Public Sector.* New York: Penguin, 1993.

p. 117 Rivlin quotes: Rivlin, Alice M. *Systematic Thinking for Social Action.* Washington, DC: Brookings Institution, 1971. Pp. 65, 140–41.

p. 118 Clinton quote "If the government rewards": President Bill Clinton, January 24, 1995.

p. 118 Kettl quote: Kettl, Donald F. "Deregulating at the Boundaries." In John J. DiIulio, Jr. (ed.), 1994.

p. 118 Staff performance improves: Barzelay, Michael. *Breaking Through Bureaucracy: A New Vision for Managing in Government.* Berkeley, CA: University of California, 1992. P. 128.

p. 118 outcomes accountability . . . replacing . . . mutual distrust: Dyer, Barbara. "The Oregon Option: Early Lessons from a Performance Partnership Contributing to an Emerging Practice of Results-Driven Accountability." Alliance for Redesigning Government, August 1996.

pp. 118–19 focus on outcomes [by] New York City Police Department: Lardner, James. "The New Blue Line," *New York Times Magazine,* 9 February 1997.

p. 119 strengthened ethical core: Gardner, Sid. "Kissing Babies and Kissing Off Families." Speech given at Concord, MA: April 26, 1995.

p. 120 **Bredekamp quote:** Memorandum from Sue Bredekamp to Sharon Lynn Kagan, Michael Levine, Valora Washington, May 8, 1995.

p. 121 mastery shows up on "school readiness" tests: Many leaders in early education are convinced that whatever outcome measures are selected to document school readiness will, in Harvard professor Sheldon White's words, "mislabel, miscategorize, and stigmatize children" by measuring only narrow cognitive development. Sheldon White at Carnegie Conference, June 1, 1995; also Kagan, Sharon Lynn. "By the Bucket: Achieving Results for Young Children." National Governors' Association Issue Brief, May 19, 1995.

p. 123 **ambitious goals:** Pittman, K. and S. Zeldin, "Evaluating Youth Development in Programs and Communities: The Need for an Integrated Framework and Collaborative Strategy." Washington, DC: Center for Youth Development and Policy Research, 1992.

p. 124 **proposed draft standards:** Independent Regulatory Review Commission, *Pennsylvania Bulletin,* Part II (Mechanicsburg, PA: Fry Communications, Vol. 21, No. 44, November 2, 1991). "State Board of Education School Profiles; Curriculum; Vocational-Technical Education." P. 5222.

p. 125 **"process creep":** Osborne and Gaebler, 1993. P. 350.

p. 126 **capture the full effects of . . . excellent interventions:** Derek Bok, former president of Harvard University and author of *The State of the Nation* (Harvard University Press, 1997), concludes that we must, in measuring outcomes, remember that we should not try to force all socially useful activities into the Procrustean bed of pure outcomes accountability. (Personal communication from Professor Bok, July 24, 1996.)

p. 127 **Meier quote:** Sachar, Emily. "New York City Roundtable: Which Way to Quality Schools?" Ford Foundation Report, Summer–Fall 1966.

p. 127 **legitimacy through a local consensus-building process:** Philadelphia school superintendent David Hornbeck contends that if the results of outcomes-based accountability are to have "hard-edged consequences," extensive participation and consultation should be followed by final decisions made by bodies at a higher or broader level of governance than those being held accountable. The opposing argument is made by Charles Bruner of the Iowa Child and Family Policy Center, who has struggled with this issue both as state legislator and advisor to local programs. Bruner argues that, if the accountability system is to be regarded as fair, useful, and legitimate, those charged with achieving outcomes must be involved in the outcomes selection process. Sid Gardner, of the Center for Collaboration for Children at the University of California in Fullerton, believes that a consensus-building process is essential because the selection of outcomes is not primarily a technical but a political problem. Young, N. K., S. L. Gardner and S. M. Coley. "Getting to Outcomes in Integrated Service Delivery Models." In "Making a Difference: Moving to Outcome-Based Accountability for Comprehensive Service Reforms." Falls Church, VA: National Center for Service Integration Resource Brief 7, 1994.

p. 127 **decision making will become more outcome oriented:** Some contend it is impossible to introduce outcomes-based rationality into decision making. In his classic text on federal budgeting, *The Politics of the Budgetary Process,* Aaron Wildavsky contended that a rational budget process was impossible because politicians and the public won't accept rational reports on results. Walters, Jonathan. "The Benchmarking Craze." *Governing,* April 1994. P. 33.

p. 129 **they called it their "Achilles' heel":** Macy, Christina H. "The Oregon

Option: A Federal-State-Local Partnership for Better Results." A Report to the Annie E. Casey Foundation. Baltimore, MD: The Annie E. Casey Foundation, 1996.

p. 129 data in . . . small areas: In the vanguard of the work on neighborhood level indicators are the National Neighborhood Indicators Project at the Urban Institute, the Information Infrastructure Project at the Chapin Hall Center for Children, the Foundation for Child Development, Chris Moore at Child Trends, researcher Claudia Coulton at Case Western Reserve University, and the Office of the Assistant Secretary for Research and Evaluation of the U.S. Department of Health and Human Services.

p. 129 child and family functioning: The Federal Interagency Forum on Child and Family Statistics is developing a core list of indicators for which federal data are currently available to produce an annual report on a limited number of indicators that best capture the conditions facing American children and youth.

p. 129 measures of community change: Among those at the forefront of this work are Thomas Burns at OMG, Abe Wandersman at the University of South Carolina, Claudia Coulton at Case Western Reserve, and the Evaluation Steering Committee of the Aspen Institute's Roundtable on Comprehensive Community Initiatives, which is developing an "Annotated Catalog of Outcomes and Measures for Use in [Planning and] Evaluating CCIs."

p. 130 identification of interim milestones: The difficulty of obtaining timely outcomes information contributed to the decision to cancel the proposed Children's Initiative of the Pew Charitable Trusts. The coordinator of the external review team wrote that "To build the public and political will to continue, projects must be able to demonstrate results in a credible way. State officials developing The Children's Initiative recognized that data on enhanced outcomes were critical to expansion, but such data were unlikely to be available within the important early years of the project." Krauskopf, James A. "Overcoming Obstacles to Implementing Reform of Family and Children's Services." Paper prepared for the annual meeting of the Association for Public Policy Analysis and Management, Chicago, October 1994.

p. 130 long before a program is "proud": Campbell, D. T. "Problems for the Experimenting Society in the Interface between Evaluation and Service Providers." In *America's Family Support Programs: Perspectives and Prospects*. Kagan, S. L., D. R. Powell, B. Weissbourd, and E. Zigler (eds.). New Haven: Yale University Press, in press.

p. 131 causal connections cannot be established with certainty: University of Wisconsin demographer Larry Bumpass advised the National Academic of Science's Board on Children and Families to stay away from trying to establish links among interventions, strategies, interim markers, and long-term outcomes, contending that science isn't far enough along to provide the causal models that would justify making such connections. (Board meeting of November 4, 1994.)

p. 131 to achieve a more systematic understanding: The Evaluation Steering Committee of the Aspen Roundtable on Comprehensive Community Initiatives has been discussing a much less ambitious version of this idea, a "Michelin Guide" to interim indicators, that would assess the degree of confidence with which the hypothesized connection between interim indicators and long-term outcomes measures could be linked, all along the causal chain. The idea would be to distinguish among the connections that seem to be fairly well established, those where the evidence is weaker and the hypothesized connections urgently need to be tested, and those where even promising hypotheses are lacking.

p. 132 Wyse quote: Carlin, Peter. "Future State." *Northwest* magazine, January 13, 1991.

p. 133 1994 Board report: Oregon Progress Board. "Oregon Benchmarks: Standards for Measuring Statewide Progress and Institutional Performance." Salem, OR: Oregon Progress Board, December 1994.

p. 133 programs directly tied to the Benchmarks: National Center for Service Integration. "Oregon Case Study." From Steps Along an Uncertain Path, 1996.

p. 133 mobilize citizens in . . . collaborative action toward . . . outcomes: One dramatic example came from Tillamook County, which had reduced its teen pregnancy rate by nearly 75 percent between 1990 and 1994, from one of the highest to the lowest rate in Oregon, by undertaking multiple strategies with multiple partners over multiple years. Luke, Jeff and Kathryn Neville. "Teenage Pregnancy Prevention: A Case Study of the Tillamook County Experience." Discussion draft, September 10, 1996.

p. 133 Dyer quote: Dyer, August 1996.

p. 134 fewer restrictions on how they achieve these results: Council of Chief State School Officers. Ensuring Student Success Through Collaboration: Issue Brief. "Moving Toward Accountability for Results," Summer 1995. Cutler, Ira. "The Role of Finance Reform in Comprehensive Service Initiatives." Washington, DC: The Finance Project, 1994.

p. 134 Governor Roberts quotes: Peirce, Neal. "Oregon Gains More First for Citizen Participation." Washington Post Writers Group, 1992.

p. 134 Roberts quote re giant step: Lindsay, Dave. "Accord to Give Oregon More Autonomy in Running Programs." *Education Week,* December 14, 1994.

p. 134 Rivlin quote: Goshko, John M. "To Cut Red Tape, Oregon Experiments with Federal Aid." *Washington Post,* 6 August 1995.

p. 134 new processes . . . institutionalized: Altshuler, A., in press.

pp. 134–35 Morrill proposal: Morrill, William A. "Getting Beyond the Micro Gee Whiz: Can Innovative Service Change the Service System?" In Kahn and Kamerman, 1996.

p. 135 other federal efforts: The Government Performance and Results Act requires all executive agencies to submit a five-year strategic plan specifying goals and objectives by September 30, 1997. Performance Partnership Grants offers states broad, flexible funding and greater control over expenditure priorities in return for greater accountability for results.

p. 135 community collaboratives . . . taking responsibility: The largest single effort to shift to an outcomes orientation in the nonprofit sector has been undertaken by United Way of America (UWA). Also many states are negotiating with local collaboratives on the outcomes and indicators for which the local collaborative will be held accountable, the rate of progress expected, and the consequences for performance above or below expectations. The community then develops the strategies to achieve its goals. (See Watson, Sara. "Beyond Lists: Moving to Results-Based Accountability." Washington, DC: Center for the Study of Social Policy, January 1996.)

p. 136 Mother Teresa quote: Sharon Lynn Kagan at Wingspread Conference: "Going-to-scale with a Comprehensive Services Strategy." May 3–5, 1993.

p. 136 **The largest gamble in social policy:** Interview with David Frost, PBS, March 28, 1997.

p. 137 **monitoring changes in the well-being of children and their families:** "Assessing the New Federalism." Urban Institute, Policy and Research Report, Spring 1996.

p. 138 **urging journalists . . . to learn and write about the massive policy changes:** *The Children's Beat,* Vol. 4, No. 1. Casey Journalism Center for Children and Families, University of Maryland, Fall 1996. The earliest reports of the effects of the new policies have indeed come from journalists. For example, the *Chicago Tribune* of 24 February 1997 reported that in Wisconsin, which is ahead of most other states in implementing welfare benefits cutoffs, shelters were overflowing, and that homelessness had reached emergency proportions, especially among women and children. (Jouzaitis, Carol. "Cold Reality of Welfare Reform.")

CHAPTER 5   **Finding Out What Works**

p. 140 **Moynihan-Lipset-Coleman story:** Daniel Patrick Moynihan, "James S. Coleman: Moved by the Data, Not Doctrine," *New York Times Magazine,* 31 December 1995. Peter Rossi, another eminent sociologist and onetime colleague of Coleman's and Moynihan's, disagrees with their interpretation of the study's results as meaning "It's all family." He believes that "there were school effects which Coleman and Moynihan neglected to see." Personal communication, July 29, 1996.

p. 140 **"social change . . . more difficult than anyone had thought":** Moynihan, ibid.

p. 142 **McGrory report on Senate Finance Committee hearing:** McGrory, Mary. "Lonelier Than Usual at the Top." *Washington Post,* 11 November 1994.

p. 142 **looking for answers in all the wrong places:** Martin Gerry, Assistant Secretary for Policy and Evaluation in the Department of Health and Human Services in the Bush administration, likes to say the reason Lisbeth Schorr could find all the successful programs she wrote about in *Within Our Reach* was that she didn't rely exclusively on the formal evaluation literature to figure out what works. He's right.

p. 143 **Rivlin warning:** Rivlin, Alice. Discussion of "Payoffs of Evaluation Research," in Abt, Clark C. (ed.), *The Evaluation of Social Programs.* Beverly Hills: Sage Publications, 1979.

p. 143 **premade treatment quote:** Williams, Harold S., Arthur Y. Webb and William J. Philips. *Outcome Funding: A New Approach to Targeting Grantmaking.* Rensselaerville, NY: Rensselaerville Institute, 1991.

p. 143 **Kagan "square peg" quote:** "Getting Smart, Getting Real." Report of the Annie E. Casey Foundation's Research and Evaluation Conference, 1996.

p. 144 **interventions that change only one thing at a time:** Aaron, Henry J. "Strategy versus Tactics in Designing Social Policy." Talk delivered at Brandeis University, 1992.

p. 144 **interventions that . . . are anathema to the traditional evaluator:** Kubisch, Anne C. et al. "Voices from the Field: Learning from Comprehensive Community Initiatives." Washington, DC: Aspen Institute, 1995. Also Knapp, Michael S. "How Shall We Study Comprehensive, Collaborative Services for Children and Families?" *Educational Researcher,* Vol. 24, No. 4, pp. 5–16, May 1995.

p. 144 **evaluations use an experimental design:** O'Connor, Alice. "Evaluating

Comprehensive Community Initiatives: A View from History." In *New Approaches to Evaluating Community Initiatives: Concepts, Methods, and Contexts.* J. P. Connell, A. C. Kubisch, L. B. Schorr, and C. H. Weiss (eds.). Washington, DC: Aspen Institute, 1995.

p. 144 Sawhill quote re future evaluations: Sawhill, Isabel V. "Poverty in the US: Why Is It So Persistent?" *Journal of Economic Literature,* September 1988.

p. 145 if their program did not fit: At the first meeting of the evaluation steering committee of the Roundtable on Comprehensive Community Initiatives in October 1993, Peter H. Rossi, eminent sociologist and evaluator, responded to the posited mismatch between the most promising interventions and prevailing evaluation approaches by contending that if such a mismatch did indeed exist, the program design would have to change. More recently, he has written that "The problem is not that 'conventional evaluation' approaches are out of synchrony with comprehensive community initiatives, but that comprehensive community initiatives are not evaluable . . . [because they are] amorphous interventions whose procedures are unspecified and whose outcomes cannot be identified." He believes that they could mature and become evaluable over time. Memorandum to Anne Kubisch and Karen L. Fulbright-Anderson, June 2, 1996.

p. 145 Pressures . . . distorted program design: When the Casey Foundation started planning its New Futures service reform initiative, it decided not to compromise program design to fit the requirements of an experimental or quasi-experimental evaluation design because no comparable groups of participants or institutions could be identified; matched pairs of cities were not available because sites were chosen precisely because of their "unique promise as 'cities ready to change' "; and matched schools were not available because sites were to focus their efforts on schools with the greatest concentrations of at-risk students. "Imposing a uniform 'treatment' across sites would have undermined the Foundation's conviction that local problems are best solved by local solutions." Also, cities were encouraged to refine their interventions and change them over time in response to feedback that could improve them. Appendix re methodology: See The Challenge of Evaluating Change, Center for the Study of Social Policy. "Building New Futures for At-Risk Youth." Washington, DC: CSSP, May 1995.

p. 145 local variation would render the intervention neither evaluable nor replicable: Meeting of Robert Wood Johnson Advisory Committee on Project BEGIN, Chicago, May 25, 1994. Hoerger, Thomas K., Jackqueline L. Teague, Edward C. Norton and Judy M. Thorn. "Project BEGIN: Does It Pay to Intervene in Early Childhood?" Research Triangle Park, NC: Research Triangle Institute, January 1996. Department of Health and Human Services. "Project BEGIN: Statement of Work from the Request for Proposals 200-94-0828(P)." The Centers for Disease Control and Prevention, which was collaborating with the Robert Wood Johnson Foundation in planning and evaluating Project Begin, subsequently informed the advisory committee, in June 1996, that it had decided against implementing the project because those responsible were no longer certain that "our program of research made the best possible use of the limited dollars available for the study of these issues." Letter from Edward A. Brann, M.D., Director, Project Begin, June 10, 1996.

pp. 145–46 Minow conclusion: Minow, Martha. "Learning from Experience: The Impact of Research About Family Support Programs on Public Policy." *University of Pennsylvania Law Review,* Vol. 143, No. 1, November 1994.

p. 146 **Richman quote:** Meeting of Grantmakers for Children and Youth, Atlanta, GA, January 13, 1994.

p. 146 **if he has a neighbor who is a churchgoer:** Case, Anne C. and Lawrence F. Katz. "The Company You Keep: The Effects of Family and Neighborhood on Disadvantaged Youths." Cambridge, MA; National Bureau of Economic Research, May 1991. Also Putnam, Robert D. "The Prosperous Community: Social Capital and Public Life." *The American Prospect,* Spring 1993. Pp. 35–42.

p. 146 **a variety of evaluation approaches:** Traditional, method-driven evaluation is described by Chen and Rossi as standardized, with the same research principles applied across different types of programs in different settings; simplifying the evaluation task by narrowing down critical issues, such as threats to internal validity in the experimental paradigm; with quality judged by the prestige of the particular method used and of how closely the evaluation follows the research principles of that method. Chen and Rossi, "Introduction: Integrating Theory into Evaluation Practice." In Chen and Rossi, *Using Theory to Improve Program and Policy Evaluations,* 1992.

p. 146 **Hollister on "the nectar of the gods":** Hollister, Robinson G. and Jennifer Hill. "Problems in the Evaluation of Community-Wide Initiatives." In Connell et al., 1995.

p. 147 **broader evaluation mind-set:** Weiss, Carol Hirschon. "Nothing as Practical as Good Theory: Exploring Theory-Based Evaluation for Comprehensive Community Initiatives for Children and Families." In Connell et al., 1995.

p. 147 **Knapp quote re conceptual maps:** Knapp, May 1995.

p. 147 **powerful tools . . . not statistical but conceptual:** Furstenberg, Frank F. and Mary Elizabeth Hughes. "The Influence of Neighborhoods on Children's Development: A Theoretical Perspective and a Research Agenda." Paper prepared for the conference Indicators of Children's Well-Being, Bethesda, MD, 17–18 November 1994.

p. 147 **Carol H. Weiss . . . one of the pioneers:** Weiss, Carol H. *Evaluation Research: Methods of Assessing Program Effectiveness.* Englewood Cliffs, NJ: Prentice-Hall, 1972.

pp. 147–48 **Weiss explanation of theory-based evaluation:** Weiss. In Connell et al., 1995.

p. 148 **twenty-nine directors of youth development projects:** I am not providing the source for these quotations in order not to embarrass the foundation that sponsored this very interesting survey, or the grantees who responded so openly.

p. 149 **pathbreaking application of a theory-based evaluation:** Bloom, Howard S. and Susan P. Bloom. "Research Design Issues and Options for Jobs-Plus." Paper commissioned to provide a framework for developing a research design for the Jobs-Plus Initiative being launched by the Manpower Demonstration Research Corporation in partnership with the U. S. Department of Housing and Urban Development and the Rockefeller Foundation, March 1996.

p. 150 **people responsible for programs:** This was the observation of Peter Bell when he was president of the Edna McConnell Clark Foundation. "1993 Report of the President." New York: Edna McConnell Clark Foundation.

p. 150 **Usher re moving from adversarial to supportive evaluation:** Usher, Charles L. "Improving Evaluability Through Self-Evaluation." *Evaluation Practice,* Vol. 16, No. 1, 1995. Pp. 59–68.

p. 151 **Ferguson re inside evaluator:** Ferguson, Ronald F. "Four Proposals in

Response to Brown's Essay on Evaluation." In Stone, Rebecca (ed.). "Core Issues in Comprehensive Community-Building Initiatives." Chicago: Chapin Hall Center for Children, 1996. P. 60.

p. 152 evaluator . . . as an engaged participant: Prudence Brown, who has written extensively on the changing role of evaluators, suggests that they should be working not only more collaboratively with sponsors and implementers within individual initiatives, but also across initiatives. She believes that the time has come to "create a learning culture" that would support learning across initiatives, and a more collaborative attitude among evaluators. This would require overcoming the qualms about external scrutiny of models before they are refined, and encouraging evaluators, now set up to compete with each other, to share their experience. By combining strong conceptualization and good descriptions with comparable measurements, we could begin to build cumulative knowledge across sites about pathways to change, and make clearer cross-site analytic comparisons leading to the kind of generalizations on which significantly improved policies and programs could be built. Brown, Prudence. "The Role of the Evaluator in Comprehensive Community Initiatives." In Connell et al., 1995.

p. 152 Usher quote re "constructively critical": Usher, 1995. Pp. 59–68.

p. 152 they are using multiple methods and perspectives: An excellent example of the new, more comprehensive approach to evaluation is the plan to assess state and local efforts to improve results for families and children drawn up for the Missouri Family Investment Trust by the Center for the Study of Social Policy (described in "Evaluating Successful Results for Missouri's Children and Families," Washington, DC: CSSP, December 1995). It was clear from the outset that traditional evaluation tools would not suffice, because (1) individuals could not be randomly assigned to treatment and control groups since the sites aimed to improve the lives of everyone in the community; (2) comparison communities that were similar but not launching an intervention could not be identified; and (3) there was no uniform "treatment" to evaluate since communities were being encouraged to design their own strategies for achieving core results. CSSP worked with several of the evaluators pioneering new approaches to evaluation to develop a strategy that would include (1) intensive technical assistance to local sites to help them specify the results they seek and strategies to be used; (2) information systems to provide timely feedback on the indicators that measure changes in each of the six core results; (3) an evaluation team to collect and analyze information showing changes in service systems likely to lead to improved results, and to analyze aggregate information across sites; and (4) assistance to selected sites to study aspects of their intervention using comparison groups and experimental methods to permit a more certain attribution of change to specific local activities.

p. 152 Bryk re subjecting soft idea to rigorous scrutiny: Bryk, Anthony S., Valerie E. Hill, and Peter B. Holland. *Catholic Schools and the Common Good.* Cambridge, MA: Harvard University Press, 1993.

p. 152 more usable information: No one disputes that random assignment of individuals to treatment and control groups is the best counter-factual (i.e., the answer to the question of what would have happened had there been no intervention). But there are more and more instances where that is not an option, because so many of the most promising interventions "aim to affect all residents in the community—and many depend on this 'saturation' to build support for the initiative." (Kubisch, 1995.) Comparison communities are often not an option because communities are not selected randomly for the intervention, and communities change rapidly in crucial but unpredictable ways. In one study that relied on comparison communities for the counter-factual to test an intervention aimed at increasing rates of school completion, one of the comparison communities experienced a sudden surge of economic development, and the school system of the other was fundamentally altered by court-ordered desegregation. Peter Rossi says there are circumstances when "phantom" controls have to be used, where experts use their prior knowledge to estimate what would have happened without the program. Personal communication, July 29, 1996.

p. 152 "results . . . moving in the desired direction": Furano, Kathryn, Linda Z. Jucovy, David P. Racine, and Thomas J. Smith. "The Essential Connection: Using Evaluation to Identify Programs Worth Replicating." Philadelphia, PA: Replication and Program Strategies, Fall 1995.

p. 153 Schön re combating "epistemological nihilism in public affairs": Schön, Don. *Beyond the Stable State.* New York: Random House, 1971.

p. 153 Baltimore quote: David Baltimore, letter to *The New Yorker,* January 27, 1997.

p. 153 Darman re guide to social policy in the twenty-first century: Richard Darman. "Riverboat Gambling with Government." *New York Times Magazine,* 1 December 1996.

CHAPTER 6   Beyond Welfare Repeal: Real Welfare Reform

p. 158 how much harm will come to children: These were the predictions of Mary Jo Bane in "Welfare as We Might Know It." *The American Prospect,* January–February 1997, No. 30.

p. 158 "When he promised crowds to 'end welfare as we know it,' they went wild": Borger, Gloria. "Clinton's Hard Sell on Welfare." *U.S. News & World Report,* July 19, 1993.

p. 158 40 percent of Clinton's paid campaign advertising mentioned ending welfare: Gibbs, Nancy. "The Vicious Cycle." *Time,* June 20, 1994.

p. 158 Ellwood's 1988 book . . . argued: Ellwood, David T. *Poor Support: Poverty in the American Family.* New York: Basic Books, 1988.

p. 159 whether . . . "audiences were cheering something quite different": Herbert, Bob. "Welfare Stampede." *New York Times,* 13 November 1995.

p. 159 Clinton quote re "we will help you, but we want you to change": Page, Clarence. "The Flip Side of Welfare 'Reform.'" *Washington Times,* 12 February 1992.

p. 160 the detailed plan . . . would cost much more: Herbert, ibid.

p. 160 "nasty secrets": Borger, ibid.

p. 160 Elwood re slogans: Personal conversation with David Ellwood, October 27, 1995.

p. 160 approval was still at 82 percent of respondents still approved: Ellwood, David T. "Welfare Reform as I Knew It." *The American Prospect,* May–June 1996.

p. 160 91 percent would support a plan: Ibid.

p. 161 Massing quote: Massing, Michael. "Ghetto Blasting." *The New Yorker,* January 16, 1995.

p. 161 Jencks and Edin quote: Jencks, Christopher, and Kathryn Edin. "Do Poor

Women Have a Right to Bear Children?" *The American Prospect,* Number 20, Winter 1995.

p. 161 **Drew quote re postponement:** Drew, Elizabeth. *Showdown.* New York: Simon & Schuster, 1996.

p. 161 **welfare debate . . . shifted from work to illegitimacy:** Ibid.

p. 162 **Weisberg quote:** Weisberg, Jacob. *In Defense of Government.* New York: Scribner, 1996.

p. 162 **Dionne re heart of Republican strategy:** Dionne, E. J. *They Only Look Dead: Why Progressives Will Dominate the Next Political Era.* New York: Simon & Schuster, 1996.

p. 162 **No one told the stories of struggling families saved from destitution:** Few politicians dared speak for the many families that had been kept intact through some terrible times, and prevented from going hungry and homeless by the discredited welfare system.

p. 162 **Clinton quote re "hardworking Americans":** Radio address by the President to the nation, December 10, 1994. (Italics mine.)

p. 162 **"rescue millions of Americans out of a corrupt welfare system":** Herbert, Bob. "The Mouths of Babes." *New York Times,* 22 June 1996. Quoting Clay Shaw.

p. 163 **$55 billion of federal aid to the poor:** Isabel Sawhill of the Urban Institute describes it as a redistribution of income from the poor to the rest of us.

p. 163 **DeParle quote re making both worse:** DeParle, Jason on "The Charlie Rose Show," July 31, 1996.

p. 163 **Bishop May quote:** "Some Look at the Welfare Plan with Hope, but Others Are Fearful." *New York Times,* 4 August 1996.

p. 164 **a Chicago woman named Mary Ann Moore:** DeParle, Jason. "Better Work Than Welfare." *New York Times Magazine,* 18 December 1994, and personal conversation with Jason DeParle, December 1995.

p. 166 **largest . . . category of past welfare recipients:** Bane, Mary Jo. "Welfare Reform Issue Paper" prepared for the February 26, 1994, meeting of the Working Group on Welfare Reform, Family Support and Independence. P. 9.

p. 167 **Gueron re most women on welfare:** Eckholm, Eric. "Solutions on Welfare: They All Cost Money . . ." Last of six articles, "Rethinking Welfare." *New York Times,* 26 July 1992.

p. 167 **study of welfare mothers in Chicago:** Twentieth Century Fund. "Welfare Reform: The Basics. A Twentieth Century Fund Guide to the Issues." New York: Twentieth Century Fund, 1995.

p. 167 **Moore quote:** DeParle, December 18, 1994.

p. 167 **Hobbs quote:** Vobejda, Barbara. "Welfare's Next Challenge: Sustained Employment." *Washington Post,* 22 September 1996.

pp. 167–68 **Jencks/Edin quote:** Jencks, Christopher, and Kathryn Edin, 1995.

p. 168 **none . . . considered eligible for the armed forces:** Zill, Nicholas. "Characteristics of AFDC Recipients That Bear on Their Fitness for Work Requirements Under Welfare Reform." Presented at American Enterprise Institute for Public Policy Research, December 15, 1993. Washington DC. A demonstration of the importance of cognitive capacity came out of the 1966 "natural experiment" when Secretary of Defense Robert McNamara lowered the armed services entrance requirements to admit 100,000 men who scored below the usual standard, hoping that the military's structured training would make up for their weak skills. However, they flunked out of basic training, were court-martialed, and prematurely discharged at twice the usual rate, and failed the army's electronics, communications, medical technician, and mechanical repair courses at four to seven times the average rate. Many army manpower experts thought the results would have been different if extra resources had been provided to train these men. Evans, David. "Losing Battle." *National Review,* June 30, 1986.

p. 168 72 percent . . . scored in the bottom quartile: Burtless, Gary. "Welfare Recipients' Prospects for Employment: Labor Market and Job Skills." Final Draft, January 31, 1996. Washington, DC: The Brookings Institution.

p. 168 "insurmountable barriers to employment": Haveman, Robert. "From Welfare to Work: Problems and Pitfalls." University of Wisconsin-Madison, Institute for Research on Poverty. *Focus,* Vol. 18, No. 1, Special Issue 1996.

p. 168 significantly handicapped . . . by their abuse of alcohol and/or illicit drugs: These estimates, reported by the General Accounting Office, the Inspector General of the Department of Health and Human Services, and the Center on Addiction and Substance Abuse at Columbia University, are all based on the National Household Survey on Drug Abuse, USDHHS.

pp. 168–69 Taylor Institute study re male violence . . . undermined women's efforts: Raphael, Jody. "Domestic Violence: Telling the Untold Welfare-to-Work Story." Chicago: Taylor Institute, 1995.

p. 169 Texas and California . . . had waiting lists . . . for day care: Twentieth Century Fund, 1995.

p. 169 Goldsmith quote: Goldsmith said that "the immense variety of problems experienced by those who apply for government assistance" can only be addressed by a system that has the necessary "flexibility and heart." *New York Times,* 4 August 1996.

p. 169 how impervious the 1996 welfare legislation was to empirical information: Tom Corbett of the University of Wisconsin Institute for Research on Poverty said, "Welfare is such an emotional issue, and raises such fundamental questions about what kind of society we want, that the debate becomes driven by norms, values, biases, stereotypes and passions. Reason and rationality get squeezed out." Joyce Foundation. "Work in Progress," September 1996.

p. 169 Offner quote: Offner, Paul. "Unlearned Lessons About Welfare." *Washington Post,* 25 July 1996.

p. 170 "fathers are virtually invisible": Nelson quoted in Holmes, Steven A. "Low-Wage Fathers and the Welfare Debate." *New York Times,* 25 April 1995.

p. 170 Offner re men "lounge around the street corners": Offner quoted in Thompson, Tracy. "Unhitched but Hardly Independent." *Washington Post,* 13 May 1995.

p. 170 households headed by women increased . . . economic fortunes of young men declined: Casey Foundation, Annie E. "Kids Count Data Book 1995." Baltimore, MD: The Annie E. Casey Foundation, 1995.

p. 170 Herr description of Project Match: Joyce Foundation. "Work in Progress."

p. 171 Herr re human growth and development: Herr, Toby. "Balancing Deeper and Wider." Rensselaerville Institute: *Innovating,* Vol. 2, No. 3, Spring 1992.

p. 171 "A welfare-to-work system that reflects what we know": Herr, Toby, Suzanne L. Wagner and Robert Halpern. "Making the Shoe Fit: Creating a Work-Prep System for a Large and Diverse Population." Chicago: Project Match, December 1996.

p. 173 Reporting on the demonstration, Herr and her colleagues observe: Herr,

Toby, Robert Halpern and Suzanne L. Wagner. "Something Old, Something New: A Case Study of the Post-Employment Services Demonstration in Oregon." Chicago: Project Match, Erikson Institute, November 1995. Also see the excellent report on the four post-employment demonstration sites in Haimson, J., A. Hershey and A. Rangaranjan. "Providing Services to Promote Job Retention." Princeton, NJ: Mathematica Policy Research, Inc., December 1995.

p. 174 analysis of the first year's experience in the four . . . sites: Hershey, Alan M. (Mathematica) and LaDonna Pavetti (Urban Institute). "Turning Job Finders into Job Keepers: The Challenge of Sustaining Employment." In "From Welfare to Work." *The Future of Children,* Vol. 7, No. 1, Center for the Future of Children, Spring 1997, Palo Alto, CA.

pp. 175–76 Wilson re "jobs network system has broken down," need for job information and placement centers: Wilson, 1996; also Wilson, William Julius on "The Charlie Rose Show," September 23, 1996.

p. 176 Lessons for supporting the transition to work: Gueron, Judith M. and Edward Pauly. *From Welfare to Work,* Russell Sage Foundation, 1991. Kamerman, Sheila B. and Alfred J. Kahn (series eds.). *Planning a State Welfare Strategy Under Waivers of Block Grants.* New York: Columbia University School of Social Work, 1996. The Urban Institute. "Lessons from Five State Welfare Reform Initiatives." Washington, DC: The Urban Institute Policy and Research Report, Winter 1995–96. The Rockefeller Foundation. "Into the Working World: Research Findings from the Minority Single Parent Program." New York: The Rockefeller Foundation, 1990. Alter, Catherine and Jan L. Losby. "Evaluation of Iowa's FaDSS Program: A Family Support Program for Long-Term Welfare Recipients." Iowa City, IA: Institute for Social and Economic Development, December 1995.

p. 177 work is likely to be unstable: Jencks, Christopher. "The Hidden Paradox of Welfare Reform." *The American Prospect,* No. 32, May–June 1997.

p. 177 academics estimate . . . number of poor jobless: Gans, Herbert J. *The War Against the Poor,* New York: Basic Books, 1995. Wilson quoted by Jack E. White, "Let Them Eat Birthday Cake," *Time,* September 2, 1996. Yale Professors Harvey, Marmor, and Mashaw believe that the idea of forcing unskilled mothers into the labor market is an outright scam under prevailing conditions. They liken it to sending 100 hungry dogs to chase 90 bones, with the 10 dogs who end up without bones being found lazy and unmotivated. Harvey, Marmor, and Mashaw. "Gingrich's Time Bomb." *The American Prospect,* Spring 1995.

p. 178 Harlem study re fourteen people pursuing every new fast food job: Newman, Katherine S. "Working Poor: Low Wage Employment in the Lives of Harlem Youth." In *Transitions Through Adolescence: Interpersonal Domains and Context.* J. Graber, J. Brooks-Gunn, and A. Petersen (eds.). Pp. 323–44. Mahwah, NJ: Erlbaum Associates, 1996. Also Newman, Katherine S. "What Inner-City Jobs for Welfare Moms?" *New York Times,* 20 May 1995.

p. 178 Employers . . . prefer immigrants: Danziger, Sandra K. and Sheldon Danziger. "Will Welfare Recipients Find Work When Welfare Ends?" Washington, DC: Urban Institute Welfare Reform Briefs, No. 12, June 1995.

p. 178 employers . . . choose ethnic and immigrant newspapers: Wilson, 1996.

p. 178 four thousand hopeful applicants: Swarns, Rachel L. "4,000 Hearts Full of Hope Line up for 700 Jobs." *New York Times,* 19 March 1997.

p. 178 labor market . . . unable to employ less-skilled: Danziger, Sheldon H.

and Peter Gottschalk. *America Unequal.* Cambridge: Harvard University Press, 1995.

p. 179 **Hugh Price re jobs for residents of neighborhoods . . . with high unemployment:** Quoted in Holmes, Steven A. "A Rights Leader Minimizes Racism as a Poverty Factor." *New York Times,* 24 July 1994.

p. 179 **Moynihan recently recalled the 1964 cabinet meeting:** Moynihan, Daniel P. "When Principle Is at Issue." *Washington Post,* 4 July 1996.

p. 179 **according to critic Mickey Kaus:** Kaus, Mickey. "Reflections on the Moynihan Report." *American Enterprise,* January/February 1995.

p. 180 **cities becoming "almost unlivable":** This is Elijah Anderson's prediction in Anderson, "Abolish Welfare—And Then What?" *Washington Post,* 31 December 1993.

p. 180 **Edelman proposed . . . a combined public and private job creation effort:** Edelman, Peter. "The Worst Thing Bill Clinton Has Done." *Atlantic Monthly,* March 1997.

p. 181 **Edin/Lein research on poor single working mothers:** Jencks and Edin, Winter 1995. Also see Edin, Kathryn, and Laura Lein, *Making Ends Meet,* in press.

p. 181 **if health insurance . . . available . . . , welfare caseloads would go down:** Moffitt, Robert and Bobbie Wolfe. "The Effect of the Medicaid Program on Welfare Participation and Labor Supply." *Review of Economics and Statistics,* November–December 1992.

p. 181 **EITC . . . "is life support":** Bluestone, Barry and Teresa Ghilarducci. "Rewarding Work: Feasible Antipoverty Policy." *The American Prospect,* May–June 1996.

p. 181 **Reagan praise of EITC:** Ibid.

p. 182 **Moynihan re helping a welfare client into the work force:** Moynihan, Daniel Patrick. "Congress Builds a Coffin." *New York Review of Books,* January 11, 1996.

p. 182 **Mead quote re Wisconsin:** Quoted in ibid.

p. 182 **costs of . . . effective employment support:** Haveman, *Focus,* 1996.

p. 183 **Deardourff report on how children fare at the hands of state governments:** Deardourff, John D. "Guarantees for the Children." *Washington Post,* 9 June 1996.

p. 183 **Mary Jo Bane re incentives to states:** Bane, Mary Jo. "Stand By for Casualties." *New York Times,* 10 November 1996.

pp. 183–84 **Bane re for-profits driven by cost-considerations:** Bane. *The American Prospect,* January–February 1997.

p. 184 **Sawhill quote:** Sawhill, Isabel V. "Welfare Reform: An Analysis of the Issues." Washington, DC: Urban Institute, 1995. P. xiv.

p. 184 **Peterson quote re spiraling parsimony:** Peterson, George E. In Sawhill, ibid.

p. 184 **more than a third of the states:** Jencks, 1997.

p. 184 **latest Urban Institute estimates:** Sawhill, 1995.

p. 185 **Feelings about disintegrating values . . . originate in the post–World War II affluence:** Yankelovich, Daniel. "How Changes in the Economy Are Reshaping American Values." In Aaron, Henry J., Thomas E. Mann and Timothy Taylor (eds.). *Values and Public Policy.* Washington, DC: Brookings Institution, 1994. Pp. 16–53. Also see Furstenberg, Frank Jr. "New Patterns of Family Life." Remarks to the trustees of the Zellerbach Family Fund, San Francisco, November 19, 1992.

p. 185 **decline of marriage might be bad for children:** Popenoe, David. "On the

Decline of Marriage." In *The Children's Beat,* Casey Journalism Center for Children and Families, Vol. 3, No. 1, Fall 1995.

p. 185 assurance that . . . every child had a claim on some adult male's earnings and protection: Jencks, Christopher. *Rethinking Social Policy: Race, Poverty, and the Underclass.* New York: HarperCollins, 1992.

p. 185 teenage parenting became . . . a "lightning rod": Luker, Kristin. *Dubious Conceptions: The Politics of Teenage Pregnancy.* Cambridge, MA: Harvard University Press, 1996.

p. 186 poverty and curtailed parental education that . . . accompany single and teenage parenthood: About half of children in single mother families live in families with incomes below the poverty level (U. S. Bureau of the Census, 1991a). Teenage mothers have lower levels of lifetime educational attainment. Maynard, Rebecca A. (ed.). "Kids Having Kids: A Robin Hood Foundation Special Report on the Costs of Adolescent Childbearing." New York: Robin Hood Foundation, 1996. Adolescent mothers who drop out of school were typically not doing well in school and dropped out even before they became pregnant. *Sex and America's Teenagers.* New York: The Alan Guttmacher Institute, 1994. P. 59.

p. 186 children of unmarried teen mothers: Maynard, 1996. Aber, J. Lawrence, Lisa J. Berlin, Jeanne Brooks-Gunn, and John M. Love. "Enhancing Comprehensive Community Initiatives: A Social Science Model of Early Childhood Development Within the Community." Draft, July 1996. Prepared for the Roundtable on Comprehensive Community Initiatives of the Aspen Institute.

p. 186 early childbearing as . . . antecedent to . . . poverty and dependency: Guttmacher Institute, 1994. P. 59.

p. 186 if she is single, the prospects for her children: McLanahan, Sara and G. Sandefur. *Growing up with a Single Parent.* Cambridge MA: Harvard University Press, 1994.

p. 186 spend time in jail: McLanahan, Sara. "On the American Family." In *The Children's Beat,* Casey Journalism Center for Children and Families, Vol. 3, No. 1, Fall 1995.

p. 186 paid employment as adults: Garfinkel, Irwin and Sara McLanahan. "Single-Mother Families, Economic Insecurity, and Government Policy." In Danziger, Sheldon H., Gary D. Sandefur and Daniel Weinberg. *Confronting Poverty: Prescriptions for Change.* New York: Harvard University Press, 1994. P. 207.

p. 187 proportion of births: Advance Report of Final Natality Statistics, 1994. National Center for Health Statistics, 1996. Most recently, both nonmarital birth rates and teen birth rates have been going down, without anyone knowing quite why. Between 1991 and 1995 teenage births dropped slightly nationally and in 46 states. The pace of the increase in nonmarital births as a whole, which had been increasing fairly steadily since 1940, slowed in the 1990s, and births outside of marriage actually decreased between 1994 and 1995 for the first time since 1978. National Center for Health Statistics, DHHS, Report to Congress on Out-of-Wedlock Childbearing, 1995.

p. 187 in other countries . . . cohabiting couples: Bumpass, L. and J. Sweet. "Children's Experience in Single-Parent Families: Implications of Cohabitation and Marital Transitions. *Family Planning Perspectives,* 1989, 21. Pp. 256–60.

p. 187 Other nations . . . provide greater support: Skolnick, Arlene and Stacey Rosencrantz. "The New Crusade for the Old Family." *The American Prospect,* Summer 94.

p. 187 U.S. . . . less successful in reducing poverty through income-transfer programs: Danziger, Sandefur and Weinberg, 1994. P. 209.

p. 187 U.S. . . . teen birthrate is higher: Maynard, 1996.

p. 187 U.S. . . . teen birthrate among whites alone: National Center for Health Statistics, 1966, and United Nations, *1993 Demographic Yearbook*, 1995.

p. 188 age of initiation of sexual activity: Bachrach, Christine A., Stephanie J. Ventura, Susan F. Newcomer and William D. Mosher. "What Is Happening to Out-Of-Wedlock Childbearing?" American Enterprise Institute and Henry J. Kaiser Family Foundation Seminar Series on Sexuality and American Social Policy, Washington, DC, March 10, 1995.

p. 188 majority . . . do not marry the fathers of their children: Maynard, 1996.

p. 188 Fewer employed males with decent incomes . . . meant fewer marriages: This phenomenon was particularly marked among black men in the inner city, who often complained about how suspicious women were of their intentions, and how difficult it was to find women who are supportive of partners with a low living standard. Wilson, 1996.

p. 188 as . . . jobs diminished, "the behavior of . . . white men . . . came to resemble that of blacks and Hispanics: Sullivan, Mercer. "Patterns of AFDC Use in a Comparative Ethnographic Study of Young Fathers and Their Children in Three Low Income Neighborhoods." Paper prepared for the Office of the Assistant Secretary for Planning and Evaluation, U. S. Department of Health and Human Services, 1990.

p. 188 With little hope of . . . husband or economic independence . . . incentive simply doesn't exist: Wilson, 1996.

p. 189 Poor girls . . . viewed as "using pregnancy and childbearing": Dodson, Lisa. "We Could Be Your Daughters: Girls, Sexuality and Pregnancy in Low-Income America." Cambridge, MA; Radcliffe Public Policy Institute, 1996.

p. 189 resenting the . . . behavior of the . . . irresponsible: Luker, 1996.

p. 189 Barnhart quote: Institute of Medicine, National Academy of Sciences Board on Children and Families meeting on welfare reform, December 5, 1994.

p. 189 the groundswell of opposition to continuing AFDC benefits for unwed mothers: Like underground sentiments of all kinds, this one was unaffected by the facts. It ignored the following facts: (1) the increase in unmarried teen births has been steadiest among white teens, increasing more than threefold since 1970. Ventura, S. J., J. A. Martin, and S. M. Taffel. Advance Report of Final Natality Statistics, 1993. Monthly Vital Statistics Report, Vol. 44, No. 3 (Suppl.), 1995. (2) Most industrialized nations have witnessed the same dramatic increases in nonmarital births since 1960 as the U. S. Twentieth Century Fund, 1995. (3) In 73 percent of AFDC families, there are only 1 or 2 children; the average size of AFDC families, (counting the mother) has gone down from 4.0 in 1969 to 2.9 in 1992. Bachrach et al., March 10, 1995.

pp. 189–90 "rather not help anyone than subsidize illegitimacy": Jencks and Edin, Winter 1995.

p. 190 Conclusion of Urban Institute researchers: Sonenstein, Freya L. and Gregory Acs. "Teenage Childbearing: The Trends and Their Implications." Washington, DC: Urban Institute, Welfare Reform Briefs, No. 13, June 1995.

p. 190 Financial calculations . . . only one consideration: Anderson, E. *Sexuality, Poverty, and the Inner City.* Menlo Park, CA: Henry J. Kaiser Family Foundation, 1994.

p. 190 girls and women coerced into sexual relations: 75 percent involuntary: Guttmacher Institute, 1994. P. 59. Twentieth Century Fund, 1995. 44 percent raped: Boyer, Debra and David Fine. "Sexual Abuse as a Factor in Adolescent Pregnancy and Child Maltreatment." *Family Planning Perspectives,* Vol. 24, No. 1, January/February 1992. P. 7. 20 percent fathered by older men: Landry, David J. and J. D. Forrest. "How Old Are U.S. Fathers?" *Family Planning Perspectives,* Vol. 27, No. 4, July/August 1995.

p. 190 teenage mothers introduced to sexual experience by . . . abuse: Illinois survey: Gershenson, Harold P., Judith S. Musick, Holly S. Ruch-Ross, Vicki Magee, Katherine Kamiya Rubino, and Deborah Rosenberg. "The Prevalence of Coercive Sexual Experience Among Teenage Mothers." *Journal of Interpersonal Violence,* Vol. 4, No. 2, June 1989. Pp. 204–9. Twentieth Century Fund, 1995. Washington State survey: *Family Planning Perspectives,* 24 (1), January/February 1992.

p. 190 crack users: Besharov, Douglas J. "On Welfare Trends." Casey Journalism Center for Children and Families. *The Children's Beat,* Fall 1995.

p. 190 adolescents who "drift" into pregnancy: Moore, Kristin A. Statement . . . before the United States Senate Committee on Finance, March 14, 1995.

p. 191 IOM report conclusion: *The Best Intentions: Unintended Pregnancy and the Well-Being of Children and Families.* Institute of Medicine. Washington DC: National Academy Press, 1995. (Italics mine.)

p. 191 drop out of school before they get pregnant: Luker, Kristin, 1991.

p. 191 girls who tested . . . lowest . . . on a test of basic skills: Berlin, Gordon and Andrew Sum. "Toward a More Perfect Union: Basic Skills, Poor Families, and Our Economic Future." New York: Ford Foundation, 1988.

p. 191 Massachusetts teenager quote: Dodson, 1996.

p. 192 students enrolled in a college-preparatory curriculum: Moore, Kristin and Sandra Hofferth. "Factors Affecting Early Family Formation: A Path Model." *Population and Environment,* Vol. 3, No. 1, 1980. Pp. 73–98.

p. 192 "restricted horizons and the boundaries of hope": Luker, 1991.

pp. 192–93 Luker argument: Ibid.

p. 194 Sawhill quote: Personal communication from Dr. Sawhill, March 19, 1997.

p. 194 "the one policy lever they really control": Jencks, 1997.

p. 194 comprehensive review of the knowledge base: Kirby, Douglas. "No Easy Answers: Research Findings on Programs to Reduce Teen Pregnancy." Washington, DC: The National Campaign to Prevent Teen Pregnancy, March 1997.

p. 194 support for postponing sexual activity: Douglas Kirby, who has studied a range of pregnancy prevention efforts, believes that comprehensive programs like the highly visible "Best Friends," which offers peer support, adult mentors, annual awards, and fitness activities, holds much greater promise that "just say no abstinence programs." Howard, Bill. " 'Best Friends' Snag $50 Million for 'No-Sex Ed,' " *Youth Today.* March/April 1997, vol 6, no. 2.

p. 195 Dionne re issues that really matter: Dionne, E. J. "In the Wake of a Bogus Bill." *Washington Post,* 5 August 1996.

p. 195 Kaus quote re "they just hated welfare": Kaus, Mickey. "The Revival of Liberalism." *New York Times,* 9 August 1996.

p. 196 "a grisly way of rebuilding support": Jencks, 1997.

CHAPTER 7 Strengthening a Collapsing Child Protection System

p. 197 most recent national data: U. S. Department of Health and Human Services, Administration for Children and Families, National Center on Child Abuse and Neglect. *The Third National Incidence Study of Child Abuse and Neglect* (NIS-3), September 1996. (These numbers are controversial and have been challenged as overstating the problem and based on questionable methodology. Anyone interested in the degree of passion aroused by the quest for reliable numbers should refer to the exchange in *Slate* of October 4, 1996, October 25, 1996, and November 11, 1996.)

p. 197 children . . . taken from their homes: Official HHS reports indicate that the number of children in the publicly funded foster care system rose from 262,000 in 1982 to 442,000 in 1992. Recent state data indicate that, since 1992, foster placements have continued to increase, with the result that nationally the number of children in out-of-home care is likely to exceed 500,000 in 1996. HHS. "Trends," 1996.

p. 198 child welfare agency . . . in a state of disarray: In many jurisdictions about half of the families in which a death occurred were known to a child welfare agency. A New York City review of child fatalities concluded that "in a third of the cases the Child Welfare Administration's own neglect either allowed or contributed to the tragedy." Stoesz, David and Howard Jacob Karger. "Suffer the Children." *Washington Monthly,* June 1996.

p. 198 system . . . never designed to deal with . . . complex needs of families: GAO, September 1995.

p. 198 caught the system unprepared: U. S. Advisory Board on Child Abuse and Neglect, Krugman, Richard, chair. "Child Abuse and Neglect: Critical First Steps in Response to a National Emergency." U. S. Department of Health and Human Services, Office of Human Development Services, August 1990. P. 20.

p. 198 state budgets became tighter: Besharov, Douglas J. and Lisa A. Laumann. "Child Abuse Reporting." *Social Science and Modern Society,* Vol. 33, No. 4, May/June 1996.

p. 198 babies . . . languish in hospitals: Preston, Jennifer. "In New Jersey, Infants Languish in Hospitals." *New York Times,* 16 September 1996.

p. 198 thirty-seven homes . . . seventeen different families: Stoesz and Karger, 1996.

p. 198 Illinois data re time in foster care: Goerge, Robert, Fred Wulczyn, Allen Harden, *An Update from the Multistate Foster Care Data Archive: Foster Care Dynamics 1983–1993.* University of Chicago, Chapin Hall Center for Children, n.d.

p. 198 twenty-one are operating under judicial supervision: Pear, Robert. "Many States Fail to Meet Mandates on Child Welfare." *New York Times,* 17 March 1996.

p. 199 The devastating consequences of child maltreatment: Children who have been abused or neglected are more likely to be arrested for violent crime; to do badly at school; to abuse drugs or alcohol and run away as adolescents; to engage in physical aggression and antisocial behavior; and to abuse their own children. Recent research has also found that physical abuse, like vigorous shaking of an infant, can produce changes in brain chemistry that "may be the route by which a brutalized child becomes a violent adult." Researchers at the University of Montreal believe that brain changes resulting from abuse may be responsible for the inability of boys to inhibit bad behavior, even if they know they'll be punished for it. "They don't seem to be able to stop themselves." Having been abused as a child increased the probability of arrest as a juvenile by more than half, and of arrest for a violent crime by 38 percent. Widom, Cathy S. "The Cycle of Violence." Research in brief (National Institute of Justice Research, U. S. Department of Justice), October 1992. National Research Council, Panel on Research on Child Abuse and Neglect. *Understanding Child Abuse and Neglect.* Washington, DC: National Academy Press, 1993. P. 212. Goleman, Daniel. "Early Violence Leaves Its Mark on the Brain." *New York Times,* 3 October 1995.

p. 199 the public's dismay is surely justified: The U. S. Advisory Board on Child Abuse and Neglect contends that no other problem has greater power to cause or exacerbate a range of social ills, and that the failures of the child protection system represent "not only a moral lapse but also the threat of disintegration of the nation's social fabric." 1991 report of the U. S. Advisory Board on Child Abuse and Neglect.

p. 199 National Commission quote: National Commission on Children. "Beyond Rhetoric: A New American Agenda for Children and Families." Washington, DC: GPO, 1991.

p. 199 more reports . . . than it can look into: Wells, S., J. Fluke, J. Downing and C. H. Brown. "Final Report: Screening in Child Protective Services." Washington, DC: ABA, 1989. Also Children's Defense Fund. "The State of America's Children, 1995." Washington, DC: 1995.

p. 199 Judge Boland quote: National Commission, 1991.

p. 200 children . . . ready for adoption often wait years: Of foster children who were legally free and awaiting adoption in 1990, 46 percent had been waiting two years or longer. Spar, Karen. "Foster Care and Adoption Statistics." Congressional Research Service, 105th Congress, n.d.

p. 200 When the child welfare system was established: Lindsey, Duncan. *The Welfare of Children.* New York: Oxford University Press, 1995.

p. 200 federal child welfare legislation of 1980: Kamerman, S. B. and A. J. Kahn. "Social Services for Children, Youth and Families in the United States." *Children and Youth Services Review,* 12, 1990. Pp. 1–184.

p. 201 New York City fatality review board found: Besharov, Douglas J. "Hot to Save Children." *New York Times,* 14 January 1996.

p. 201 Lindsey re narrowing definitions: Lindsey, 1995.

p. 201 services . . . organized . . . around investigation: Besharov, Douglas J. "The Children of Crack: A Status Report." *Public Welfare,* Winter 1996.

p. 201 family supportive services . . . cut to finance the protective services: Lindsey, 1995.

p. 201 national survey by Kamerman and Kahn: Kamerman and Kahn, 1990.

p. 202 paperwork increased exponentially: Farrow, Frank. "Child Protection: Building Community Partnerships." Paper prepared for Harvard Kennedy School Executive Session on New Paradigms for Child Protective Services, November 1996. Also Hagedorn, John M. *Forsaking Our Children: Bureaucracy and Reform in the Child Welfare System.* Chicago: Lake View Press, 1995.

p. 202 American Public Welfare Association guidelines re services outside the domain of child protection: NAPCWA Guidelines. *Public Welfare,* Summer 1988.

p. 202 **Schleicher quote:** Sexton, Joe. "Child Welfare Chief Provides a Glimpse at Decentralization." *New York Times,* 8 September 1996.

p. 204 **The story of Joey Wallace and his mother:** Bellows, Joel J., John J. Casey, Roy E. Hofer. "The Report of the Independent Committee to Inquire into the Practices, Processes, and Proceedings in the Juvenile Court as They Relate to the Joseph Wallace Cases," October 1, 1993. Also Ingrassia, Michele and John McCormick. "Why Leave Children with Bad Parents?" *Newsweek,* April 25, 1994. Terry, Don. "Mother Sentenced to Life in a Killing That Shook Chicago." *New York Times,* 26 July 1996.

p. 204 *Newsweek* **quotes:** Ingrassia and McCormick. Ibid.

p. 204 **Giuliani quote:** In Wexler, Richard. "Beware the Pitfalls of Foster Care." *New York Times,* 21 January 1996.

p. 205 **more children died in foster homes:** Kendall, Peter, and Terry Wilson. "Boy's Death Casts Shadow on Foster Care." *Chicago Tribune,* 28 February 1995.

p. 205 **panic . . . in jurisdictions . . . reforming their . . . systems:** Interview with Los Angeles network participants, September 10, 1996.

pp. 205–6 **no public child welfare services left for troubled families:** Kamerman, Sheila and Alfred J. Kahn. "If CPS Is Driving Child Welfare—Where Do We Go from Here?" *Public Welfare,* Winter 1993.

p. 207 **comprehensive national study of child maltreatment:** U. S. Department of Health and Human Services, Administration for Children and Families, National Center on Child Abuse and Neglect. *The Third National Incidence Study of Child Abuse and Neglect* (NIS-3), September 1996. Chapter 5, pp. 2–17; Summary: Chapter 8, pp. 10–11.

p. 207 **to avoid harming children by institutionalizing them:** Twentieth Century Fund, 1995.

p. 208 **Weber re orphanages:** Drew, Elizabeth, 1996.

p. 208 **Gibson re "wonderfully vivid image":** Gibson, Chester on C-Span, January 2, 1995.

p. 208 **"the parents are so vile . . .":** Wexler, Richard. "A Warehouse Is Not a Home." *New York Times,* 18 March 1995.

p. 208 **Will quote:** Will, George. "About Those 'Orphanages.' " *Newsweek,* December 12, 1994.

p. 208 **Himmelfarb quote:** Himmelfarb, Gertrude. "The Victorians Get a Bad Rap." *Washington Post,* 9 January 1995.

p. 208 **debate about orphanages . . . more about symbols:** As Mary Jo Bane points out, early versions of the Republican welfare bill would have allowed states to use block grant money for orphanages, "in stark recognition of the facts that some families would be denied assistance entirely and that not all parents would successfully meet the challenges of the new requirement." The word "orphanage" was quickly removed from subsequent versions of the bill in response to fierce Democratic attacks, but the underlying problem was never addressed. Bane, 1997.

p. 208–9 **Besharov on cost of orphanage care:** Besharov, Douglas J. "Orphanages Aren't Welfare Reform." *New York Times,* 20 December 1994. Ronald A. Feldman, dean of Columbia University School of Social Work, and formerly deputy director of Boys Town, explains that costs are so high because at Boys Town, which Speaker Gingrich held up as a model orphanage, well-trained husband-and-wife teams spend twenty-four hours a day with the children, all the time supervised by mental health professionals. Costs there run between $50,000 and $55,000 per child. Feldman, Ronald A. "What You Can't Learn from Boys Town." *Washington Post,* 13 December 1994.

p. 209 Archer quote: Scheer, Robert. "Returning to Bad Old Days of Orphanages." *Los Angeles Times,* 11 December 1994.

p. 209 Goals of a reformed child welfare system: The entire rest of this chapter has been heavily influenced by the discussions in which I participated as a member of the Harvard Kennedy School's Executive Session on New Paradigms for Child Protective Services 1994–97, and the materials produced as part of that effort. I have relied particularly on the November 1996 paper by Frank Farrow, "Child Protection: Building Community Partnerships."

p. 209 consensus around goals: This list of goals draws on recent recommendations of the U.S. Advisory Board on Child Abuse and Neglect, the vision statements put forward as part of reform efforts in Florida, Missouri, and Hawaii, and discussions of the Harvard Kennedy School Executive Sessions on New Paradigms for Child Protective Services 1994–97. The only real divergence from the consensus is probably that professionals believe not all maltreatment, not even all serious maltreatment, can be prevented before it occurs, whereas the public looks forward to the day when no children, certainly no children known to child protective agencies, will suffer harm at the hands of their caretakers.

p. 210 financial incentives [for] out-of-home placement: The National Commission on Children found that children often are removed from their families "prematurely or unnecessarily" because federal aid formulas give states "a strong financial incentive" to do so rather than provide services to keep families together. National Commission on Children, 1991.

p. 211 Spence quote: Preston, Jennifer, 1996.

p. 211 Family planning . . . never . . . a routine part of child welfare services: Besharov, Winter 1996.

p. 212 old tools . . . no longer available: Kamerman and Kahn, 1990.

p. 212 Treatment for adults abusing drugs or alcohol: This section is based primarily on "The Implications of Alcohol and Other Drug-related Problems for Community-wide Family Support Systems," by Gardner, Sid and Nancy K. Young. Paper prepared for the Kennedy School Executive Session on New Paradigms for Child Protective Services, November 1996.

p. 213 the threat . . . posed by substance abuse: Sid Gardner and Nancy Young, among the few experts who have looked carefully at the intersection between child protection and substance abuse, point out that child welfare agencies have been reluctant to face up to the reality of cases where substance abuse and child abuse or neglect combine so destructively "that a 'no chances' rule should apply, and termination of parental rights should be virtually automatic." Gardner and Young, November 1996. Also Wald, Michael S. "Termination of Parental Rights." In *When Drug Addicts Have Children.* Douglas Besharov (ed.). Child Welfare League of America, 1994. P. 198. Horn, Wade. "Implications for Policy-making." In Besharov, 1994. A complicating problem is that the two systems have separately ticking clocks. Both fail to recognize what is at stake. The substance abuse agency sees the importance of giving an adult a second, third, or fourth chance; the child welfare agency sees an addicted parent's devastating inability to protect his or her child.

p. 213 results of . . . treatment programs: Center for Substance Abuse Treatment. "Study of Grantees Administered by the Women and Children's branch."

Rockville, MD: Center for Substance Abuse Treatment, 1995. Also Young, Nancy K. "Alcohol and Other Drug Treatment: Policy Choices in Welfare Reform." Washington, DC: Center for Substance Abuse Treatment and the National Association of Alcohol and Drug Abuse Directors, 1996.

p. 214 the ultimate child welfare system—families and neighborhoods: The U.S. Advisory Board on Child Abuse and Neglect called for a child protection system redesigned to support even the most troubled and impoverished neighborhoods and families, with new arrangements that would "strengthen neighborhoods so that people are involved with each other as a community and that adults feel competent as parents, empowered to protect the safety of their own children, and responsible for supporting each other." U.S. Department of Health and Human Services. U.S. Advisory Board on Child Abuse and Neglect. "Neighbors Helping Neighbors: A New National Strategy for the Protection of Children." USDHHS, September 1993.

p. 214 Community Partnerships for Child Protection: A term that came out of the Edna McConnell Clark Foundation's child protection initiative and the Harvard Kennedy School's Executive Session on Child Protective Services.

p. 214 Miller quote: Lewin, Tamar. "Child Welfare Is Slow to Improve Despite Court Order." *New York Times*, 30 December 1995.

p. 215 Los Angeles County partners with community-based networks: Except where otherwise indicated, information about the Los Angeles County child welfare reform comes from interviews with Peter Digre on March 21, 1996, with a group of Los Angeles network participants assembled by Carolyn Reid-Green on September 10, 1996, and with Nancy Daly on March 6, 1996. Also from Hornblower, Margot. "Fixing the System." *Time*, December 11, 1995; Howard, Bill. "How LA's Pete Digre Clips Foster Care Spiral. *Youth Today*, Vol. 4, No. 5, September/October 95; personal communication from Jacquelyn McCroskey, February 13, 1996; and Farrow, Frank. "System Change at the Neighborhood Level: Creating Better Futures for Children, Youth, and Families." Washington, DC: Center for the Study of Social Policy, February 1996; Noble, Kenneth B. "In Push to Transform Agency, a Child Welfare Official Looks West." *New York Times*, 12 November 1996.

p. 218 need for professional expertise: Participant in L.A. meeting, September 10, 1996.

p. 218 Dr. Xylina Bean quote: L.A. meeting, September 10, 1996.

p. 219 evaluators . . . found significant improvements . . . among participating families: Meezan, William and Jacquelyn McCroskey. "Improving Family Functioning Through Family Preservation Services: Results of the Los Angeles Experiment." *Family Preservation Journal*, February 1996.

p. 220 the "Patch" approach to neighborhood service delivery: The description of the Cedar Rapids Patch program is based on conversation with Linda Winston and Marc Baty on June 13, 1995, interview with Charles Bruner in February 1996, and Frank Farrow. "System Change at the Neighborhood Level: Creating Better Futures for Children, Youth, and Families." Washington, DC: Center for the Study of Social Policy, February 1996.

p. 222 Sunset Park Center for Family Life neighborhood foster care demonstration: Unless otherwise indicated, based on: Hess, Peg, Brenda G. McGowan, Carol H. Meyer, "Practitioners Perspectives on Family and Child Services." In Kahn, Alfred J. and Sheila B. Kamerman, 1996. McGowan, Brenda G. with Alfred J. Kahn and Sheila B. Kamerman. "Social Services for Children, Youth and Families: The New York City Study." New York: Columbia University School of Social Work,

June 1990. Lerner, Steve. "The Geography of Foster Care: Keeping the Children in the Neighborhood." New York: Foundation for Child Development, February 1990. AEC *Focus.* "Center for Family Life at Sunset Park." Baltimore, MD: Annie E. Casey Foundation, Fall, 1995.

p. 222 **parents not knowing . . . where their children were:** Steve Lerner, in his Foundation for Child Development publication about neighborhood-based foster care at Sunset Park, tells of the New York City mother of eight, dying of AIDS, who wanted to see her children one last time. But the children, it turned out, had been placed in seven different foster homes run by different agencies scattered around the city. By the time they could be found and assembled, the mother had died.

p. 223 **reformist Commissioner . . . has announced plans:** Russakoff, Dale. "Protector of NY City's Children Knows 'the System' Well." *New York Times,* 19 December 1996.

p. 223 **effort to decentralize foster care . . . in Cleveland:** AEC *Focus.* "Building Bridges for Families in Cuyahoga County." Baltimore, MD: Annie E. Casey Foundation, Fall, 1995. Materials provided by the Annie E. Casey Foundation Family to Family Initiative, and by Cuyahoga County Department of Children and Family Services.

p. 224 **"congregate care facilities":** Besharov and Laumann, 1996.

p. 224 **Nan Dale on residential treatment:** Weisman, Mary-Lou. "When Parents Are Not in the Best Interests of the Child." *Atlantic Monthly,* July 1994.

p. 225 **Amos quote:** Raspberry, William. "Children Who Shouldn't Go Home from School." *Washington Post,* 12 December 1994.

p. 225 **DiIulio quote:** DiIulio, John J. "The Plain, Ugly Truth About Welfare." *Washington Post,* 15 January 1995.

pp. 225–26 **Second Chance Homes:** Much of this section on Second Chance Homes is based on Sylvester, Kathleen. "Second-Chance Homes." Progressive Policy Institute. Washington, DC: Policy Briefing, June 23, 1995. Also on Reich, Kathleen. "Improving Outcomes for Mother and Child: A Review of the Massachusetts Teen Living Program."

p. 227 **The federal government departs from tradition:** Information in this section based on conversations by the author with Olivia Golden, HHS, MaryLee Allen, Children's Defense Fund, and Frank Farrow, Center for the Study of Social Policy; interviews conducted by Patricia Savage with Carolyn Williams, July 25, 1995, and Deborah Stark, July 13, 1995; and submission by the Department of HHS to the Kennedy School Innovations in Government Award.

p. 228 **ad hoc group of national organizations:** Help included periodic memoranda with recommendations and rulemaking suggestions, and an elaborate planning guide, "Making Strategic Use of the Family Preservation and Support Services Program: A Guide for Planning." Published in October 1994, prepared by the Center for the Study of Social Policy and the Children's Defense Fund, and reviewed by the members of the ad hoc group.

p. 229 **Child welfare in the post-welfare repeal era:** Bane, 1997.

CHAPTER 8   Educating America's Children

p. 232 **Entire organizations have been established for that purpose:** A Better Chance, the oldest of these, seeks out talented and motivated children of color, and places 2,100 annually in the nation's top preparatory schools. Nine out of ten go on to graduate from college.

p. 232 majority of the American public: A Princeton Survey Research Associates poll for *Newsweek* found that the public disapproved spending reductions in K–12 education programs in greater numbers than it opposed spending cuts in Medicaid, the environment, defense, or farm price supports (June 1995).

p. 233 education the number-one issue among American adults: Murnane, Richard J. and Frank Levy. "Why Money Matters Sometimes: A Two-Part Management Lesson from West Austin, TX." *Education Week,* September 11, 1996.

p. 233 education system outranked . . . concerns about crime, welfare, and illegal drugs: These were the results of polls taken by Gallup/CNN/*USA Today,* and by Robert Teeter and Peter Hart for NBC News/*Wall Street Journal.*

p. 234 950 *trillion* connections between brain cells: Kolb, B. "Brain Development, Plasticity, and Behavior." *American Psychologist* 44(9), 1989. Pp. 1203–12.

p. 234 baby's brain will not develop the normal "wiring": Carnegie Corporation of New York. "Starting Points: Meeting the Needs of Our Youngest Children." New York: Carnegie Corporation, 1994. Chugani, H., M. E. Phelps and J. C. Mazziotta. "Positron Emission Tomography Study of Human Brain Functional Development." *Annals of Neurology,* 22(4), 1987. P. 495.

p. 234 In the first months and years of life, babies learn: Zero to Three. "Heart Start: The Emotional Foundations of School Readiness." Executive Summary. Arlington, VA: National Center for Clinical Infant Programs, 1992.

p. 234 "a quiet crisis": Carnegie Corporation of New York. "Starting Points," 1994.

p. 235 U.S. the only industrialized country in the world: Wilson, 1996, p. 215.

p. 236 GAO report re more emphasis on parental employment than child development: Government Accounting Office. "Early Childhood Centers: Services to Prepare Children for School Often Limited." Washington, DC: GAO/HEHS-95-21.

p. 236 study of . . . child care centers in four states: Cost, Quality, and Child Outcomes Study Team. "Cost, Quality, and Child Outcomes in Child Care Centers, Executive Summary." Second Edition. Denver: Economics Department, University of Colorado at Denver, 1995.

p. 236 Carnegie Foundation survey of kindergarten teachers: Boyer, Ernest L. "Ready to Learn." New York: Carnegie Foundation for the Advancement of Teaching, 1991.

p. 237 In the inner cities the proportion of children not ready for school learning: Personal communication, Edward F. Zigler, February 19, 1997.

p. 237 Williams quote: Harris, Irving B. *Children in Jeopardy: Can We Break the Cycle of Poverty?* New Haven: Yale University Press, 1996. P. 9.

p. 237 Carnegie Corporation task force findings: Carnegie Corporation of New York. "Years of Promise: A Comprehensive Learning Strategy for America's Children." New York: Carnegie Corporation, 1996.

p. 237 "the worst services for children in Western society": Kagan, S. L. and N. E. Cohen. "Solving the Quality Problem: A Vision for the Early Child Care and Education System. A Final Report of the Quality 2000 Initiative." New Haven: Yale University Press, in press.

p. 237 only 9 percent of . . . "family child care" homes . . . provided high-quality care: Families and Work Institute. "The Study of Children in Family Child Care and Relative Care." New York: Families and Work Institute, 1994.

p. 237 states may . . . divert child care funds: Kamerman, Sheila B. and Alfred J. Kahn (eds.). "Child Care in the Context of Welfare Reform." New York: Columbia University School of Social Work, 1997.

pp. 237–38 Policy analysts ask what we will have accomplished: Kamerman and Kahn, 1997.

p. 238 Avancé: Based on personal conversations with Gloria Rodriguez; Avancé, Inc., New Replication Initiatives, March 27, 1995, and other materials provided by Avancé; also on Deborah L. Cohen. "Teach their Parents Well." *Education Week,* October 19, 1994, and Stephen Shames. *Pursuing the Dream: What Helps Children and Their Families Succeed.* Chicago: Family Resource Coalition, 1997.

p. 239 Schools of the 21st Century: The description of the Zigler Schools of the 21st century and the Comer/Zigler CoZi schools are based on Zigler, Edward F. "School of the 21st Century: A Step Towards a Solution." *Florida's Child,* Spring 1989. Materials provided by the Bush Center in Child Development and Social Policy and the Norfolk public schools. "21st Century and Comer Meet in Norfolk." *Child Care ActioNews,* May–June 1994. Also Kagan, Sharon L. and Edward F. Zigler (eds.). *Early Schooling: The National Debate.* New Haven: Yale University Press, 1987.

p. 241 quantifiable results: Hornblower, Margot. "It Takes a School." *Time,* June 3, 1996.

p. 241 federal subsidies . . . from ninety different programs: Carnegie Corporation, 1996.

p. 241 efforts to pool funding from . . . disparate sources: As we have seen, most federal and state funding streams contribute to, rather than help communities overcome, existing fragmentation, although some of the newer federal legislation, such as the Empowerment Zones and the Family Preservation and Support Act, explicitly make funds available for broad-based community strategies.

p. 241 create a network of child development settings: Head Start programs play a unique role in the planning process in many communities. They need new partners because many are able to offer only part-day services, while many of the families they serve need full-day programs. Head Start's federal-to-local funding structure, originally designed to maintain maximum local autonomy and flexibility, was for many years its strength. But with the growth of state preschool initiatives, the greater need for full-day programs, and momentum building for collaborative approaches to funding and delivering early-childhood services, local Head Start programs are increasingly joining others in efforts to develop more choices and more coherence.

p. 241 three different national commissions: Two were advisory councils to the Secretary of Health and Human Services, asked to help plan the future of Head Start and Early Head Start, respectively. The third was a task force established by the Carnegie Corporation to report to the American public on how the nation could best meet the needs of young children.

p. 242 mothers of young children belong in the workplace: Although the federal welfare law allows states to exempt mothers of infants from work requirements for a year, early indications are that states are not taking advantage of the provision, and requiring mothers to start job search or job training regardless of how young their children may be.

p. 243 proposing . . . a pre-kindergarten year a universal option: Morris, Dick. *Behind the Oval Office.* New York: Random House, 1997.

p. 244 schoolchildren are performing . . . as well as their parents . . . did: "Slight Rise in Math and Science Scores, Less in Reading." *New York Times,* 13 October 1996.

p. 244 schools are managing to hold the line academically: Carnegie Corporation, 1996.

p. 244 "inadequate . . . to meet the needs of the 21st century": Consortium on Productivity in the Schools. "Using What We Have to Get the Schools We Need." New York: Columbia University, 1995.

p. 244 schools were not educating all: Graham, Patricia Albjerg. "Assimilation, Adjustment, and Access." In Ravitch, Diane and M. A. Vinovskis (eds.). *Learning from the Past: What History Teaches Us About School Reform,* Baltimore, MD: Johns Hopkins University Press, 1995.

p. 245 children had to acquire high levels of academic skills: One of the first books to document the mismatch between what the economy needs and what the schools were providing was *Thinking for a Living,* by Ray Marshall and Marc Tucker. New York: Basic Books, 1992.

p. 245 Individuals [without skills] fall behind: Graduating from high school reduces the probability of being on welfare by 50 percent, and reduces the probability of being unemployed by one third. "AAHE/Education Trust Conference Report Reveals Troubling Trends for Low-Income and Minority Students." American Association for Higher Education, October 26, 1995. Over a lifetime, high school dropouts will earn $812,000 less than college graduates, and $2,404,000 less than individuals with professional degrees. Bureau of the Census Statistical Brief. More Education Means Higher Career Earnings, SB 94-17, August 1994.

p. 245 six essential skills: Murnane, Richard J. and Frank Levy. *Teaching the New Basic Skills.* New York: Free Press, 1996.

p. 245 rate of youngsters completing high school rose: Coley, Richard S. "Dreams Deferred: High School Dropouts in the United States." Policy Information Center, Educational Testing Service, 1995.

p. 245 Graduation rates for black youngsters increased: National Center for Education Statistics. "Dropout Rates in the United States, 1993." National Center for Education Statistics, September 1994.

pp. 245–46 Irving Harris story re DuSable High School: Personal communication from Irving Harris, October 30, 1995.

p. 246 Traub story about graduates of New York City high schools at City College: Traub, James. *City on a Hill: Testing the American Dream at City College.* Reading, MA: Addison-Wesley, 1994. P. 109.

p. 246 hard numbers bear out the anecdotal evidence . . . understand a paragraph containing complicated information: National Center for Education Statistics. "Report in Brief, NAEP 1994 Trends in Acadmic Progress."

p. 246 write at an adequate level: Committee for Economic Development. "CED and Education: National Impact and Next Steps. A CED Symposium." Washington, DC: CED, 1991.

p. 246 Comparisons with other . . . countries: LaPointe, A., N. Mead and J. Askew. *Learning Mathematics.* Princeton, NJ: Educational Testing Service, 1992. LaPointe, A., J. Askew and N. Mead. *Learning Science.* Princeton, NJ: Educational Testing Service, 1992. Also Carnegie Corporation, 1996.

p. 247 Progress among minority . . . students . . . between 1977 and 1988:

Personal communication from Archie LaPointe, Director, Center for Assessment of the Educational Testing Service, December 1, 1995.

p. 247 gap . . . widening again: "Building a Nation of Learners, 1996." Report of the National Education Goals Panel. Washington DC: November 1996.

p. 247 reasons for . . . backsliding: Ibid. Also Kati Haycock, director of the Educational Trust, American Association for Higher Education. Quoted in Applebome, Peter. "Minorities Falling Behind in Student Achievement." *New York Times,* 29 December 1996.

p. 247 not . . . enough progress in closing the . . . achievement gap: Timpane, P. Michael. "The Uncertain Progress of Education Reform, 1983–94." In Zigler, Edward F., Sharon Lynn Kagan, and Nancy W. Hall (eds.). *Children, Families and Government: Preparing for the Twenty-First Century.* New York: Cambridge University Press, 1996.

p. 247 "real sin in our achievement patterns": Personal communication from Michael Timpane, December 12, 1996.

p. 249 destitution of both purse and spirit: This is the description of the new challenge to schools in the Committee for Economic Development report, "Putting Learning First: Governing and Managing the Schools for High Achievement." New York: Committee for Economic Development, 1994.

p. 249 Elmore quote: Elmore, Richard F. "Getting to Scale with Good Educational Practice." Cambridge: *Harvard Education Review,* Spring 1996.

p. 249 Deborah Meier reflections on why successful exceptions rarely become the norm: "Can the Odds Be Changed?" Draft by D. Meier, July 1996; also personal conversations with Meier, July 1996.

pp. 249–50 Shanker quote: Quoted by Nathan, Joe. "The Charter School Movement is Growing Because It's Working." *Education Week,* February 19, 1997.

p. 250 administrators . . . convinced . . . that the only desirable "reform": Hill, Paul, Gaile E. Foster and Tamar Gendler. *High Schools with Character.* Santa Monica, CA: Rand Corporation, August 1990.

p. 250 Administrators exercising top-down control: Lee, Valerie E., Julia B. Smith and Robert G. Croniger. "Another Look at High School Restructuring." Issues in Restructuring Schools Report No. 9, Fall 1995. Center on Organization and Restructuring of Schools.

p. 250 the public and . . . reformers agree on the broad goals: Consortium on Productivity, 1995. P. 3.

p. 250 The public is not prepared to give up on public education: In the recent past, polls show that the public disapproves of reducing federal funding for education, and considers education as the top legislative priority. *Washington Post*-ABC News poll; Times Mirror Center for the People and the Press; NBC News/*Wall Street Journal.*

p. 250 Wadsworth quote: Wadsworth, Deborah. "Bridging the Divide: What the Public Is Telling Educators Could Help Resuscitate School Reform." *Education Week,* November 30, 1994.

pp. 250–51 public doubts the reformers' claim: Johnson, Jean and John Immerwahr. "First Things First: What Americans Expect from the Public Schools." New York: Public Agenda, 1994.

p. 251 Successful schools have mobilized school staff: Consortium on Productivity (consisting of University of Pennsylvania, Harvard University, Stanford, University of Michigan, and University of Wisconsin), 1995.

p. 251 conventional suburban high schools . . . characterized: "mushy, all-purpose institutions" where "students chose easier and easier courses that asked less and less of them." Shanker, Albert. "Would Parents Really Opt for Excellence?" *New York Times,* 10 February 1991. "shopping malls": the term popularized by Ted Sizer from Powell, A., E. Farrar, and D. Cohen. *The Shopping Mall High School.* Boston: Houghton Mifflin, 1985.

p. 252 teachers can learn to apply these insights: Timpane, Michael. "Thoughts on Cognitive Science and Education," November 27, 1996.

p. 252 the more you know the more you can learn: Ravitch, Diane. *National Standards in American Education.* Washington, DC: Brookings Institution, 1995. Pp. 103–5.

p. 252 Hirsch quote: Hirsch, E. D. Jr. *The Schools We Need & Why We Don't Have Them.* New York: Doubleday, 1996.

p. 252 away from rote learning . . . [toward] deep understanding: Elmore, Richard F. *Restructuring in the Classroom: Teaching, Learning, and School Organization.* San Francisco: Jossey-Bass, 1996.

p. 252 instruction . . . sufficiently individualized: Doyle, Dennis P., and Susan Pimental. "Setting Standards, Meeting Standards: Creating High Performance Schools." Coalition for Goals 2000.

p. 253 does not mean repeating the classes: Resnick, Lauren. "From Aptitude to Effort: A New Foundation for Our Schools." *Daedalus,* Vol. 124, No. 4, Fall 1995. Pp. 55–62.

p. 253 alternative ways of learning: Consortium on Productivity in the Schools, 1995.

p. 253 Catholic high schools . . . organiz[ed] around a core curriculum: Bryk, Anthony S., Valerie E. Lee and Peter B. Holland. *Catholic Schools and the Common Good.* Cambridge, MA: Harvard University Press, 1993.

p. 253 Evans quote: Evans, Paula. "Getting Beyond Chewing Gum and Book Covers." *Education Week,* October 19, 1994.

pp. 253–54 Savannah middle school story: Whelage, Gary. In "Building New Futures for At-Risk Youth: Findings from a Five Year, Multi-Site Evaluation." Washington, DC: Center for the Study of Social Policy, 1996. P. 62.

p. 255 effective staff development efforts are ambitious: Consortium for Policy Research in Education. "Public Policy and School Reform: A Research Summary." CPRE Research Report Series Report #36, 1996. Similarly, the seven different school reform initiatives funded by NASDC all produced professional development efforts that are "coherent, reinforcing a long-term vision for change and advancing progress toward higher student achievement." New American Schools Development Corporation. "Lessons Learned." In *A Thousand Actions, Annual Report, 1994/1995.*

p. 255 professional development of teachers is poorly aligned: Consortium on Productivity, 1995.

pp. 255–56 Elmore on professional development: Elmore, 1996. Elmore worries that school reformers are not paying enough attention to providing teachers with access to the knowledge and skills that are crucial for change. He believes that altering teaching practice necessarily means putting teachers in some kind of new relationship with people who have more knowledge and skill than they do, which, for many teachers, means "a new way of thinking about their role as practitioners."

p. 256 Gardner on combined reformers' professional development efforts: Gardner, Howard. "Limited Visions, Limited Means: Two Obstacles to Meaningful Education Reform." *Daedalus,* Vol. 124, No. 4, Fall 1995. Pp. 101–5.

p. 256 **Levin on professional development:** Merrow Report, "Early Learning." Aired on PBS September 6, 1996.

p. 256 **Shanker quote:** Shanker, Albert. "Where We Stand: The Real Solution." *New York Times,* 29 September 1996.

p. 257 **so they can be held accountable:** Conversation with Deborah Meier, July 1996.

p. 257 **review of research re strongest schools:** Newman, Fred M. and Gary G. Whelage. "Successful School Restructuring: A Report to the Public and Educators." Madison, WI: Center on Organization and Restructuring of Schools, 1995.

p. 257 **structural changes . . . do not automatically bring changes in teaching practice:** CPRE conclusion based on five years of research on public policy and school reform. Consortium for Policy Research in Education, 1996.

pp. 257–58 **Meier quote:** Conversation with Deborah Meier, July 1996.

p. 258 **research . . . that smaller is better:** Viadero, Debra. "By the Numbers: Ideal High School Size Found to be 600 to 900." *Education Week,* April 4, 1996.

p. 258 **intentional communities . . . more likely to succeed:** Lee et al., Fall 1995. This included a review of the following studies: one of 13 urban high schools conducted by the Rand Corporation; one a 12-year, multi-university study of Catholic high schools; and the third, also a multi-university study, analyzing data from 820 secondary schools and 12,000 students around the nation.

p. 258 **bureaucratic schools perpetuate a silent conspiracy . . . that mediocre academic achievement will be acceptable:** Bryk, quoted in Consortium on Productivity, 1995.

p. 258 **high school students . . . in . . . Public Agenda survey:** Bradley, Ann. "Survey Reveals Teens Yearn for High Standards." *Education Week,* February 12, 1997.

p. 259 **teachers motivated by . . . commitment:** Lee et al., Fall 1995.

p. 259 **schools . . . as bridging institutions:** Bryk et al., 1993. p. 317.

p. 259 **learning certain core skills:** Lee et al., Fall 1995.

p. 259 **secular schools could . . . establish a compelling ethos:** Bryk et al., 1993.

p. 260 **Chubb and Moe argument:** Chubb, J. E. and T. M. Moe. *Politics, Markets, and America's Schools.* Washington, DC: Brookings Institution, 1990.

p. 261 **as a public good, effective schooling:** Levin, Henry M. "Education as a Public and Private Good." Association for Public Policy Analysis and Management. *Journal of Policy Analysis and Management,* Vol. 6, No. 4, 1987. pp. 628–42.

p. 261 **research and experience . . . suggest it can be done:** The major finding of the Rand Corporation study of big-city high schools was that the key features of successful schools can be made available to all students, even the most disadvantaged, and can be sustained within public school systems. Hill, Foster, and Gendler, 1990.

p. 261 **"stack the deck in favor of good schooling":** Meier, 1996.

p. 262 **school achievement standards came to public attention:** Ravitch, 1995.

p. 262 **Ravitch quote:** Ibid.

p. 262 **"doing the procedurally correct thing.":** Grant, G. "Schools That Make an Imprint: Creating a Strong Positive Ethos." In Bunzel, J. H. (ed.). *Challenge to American Schools.* New York: Oxford University Press, 1985.

p. 263 Slavin re changing the conversation: Robert E. Slavin at meeting of the Consortium for Policy Research in Education. Philadelphia, October 22, 1996

pp. 263–64 Shanker on outcomes: Shanker, Albert. "Outrageous Outcomes." *New York Times,* 12 September 1993.

p. 264 Sizer on outcomes: Sizer, Theodore R. "An Unsettling Conversation." *Education Week,* September 18, 1996.

p. 264 Standards . . . attacked . . . would be a "cruel hoax": "Prominent Educators Oppose National Tests." *New York Times,* 29 January 1992.

p. 264 "effects of a weak education transcend state boundaries": Consortium on Productivity, 1995.

p. 264 Hornbeck quote: Personal communication from David Hornbeck, November 15, 1996.

p. 265 criteria for setting standards: Composite of recommendations of Resnick, Lauren B. "Making High School Count." In M. Higginbotham (ed.). "What Governors Need to Know About Education reform." Washington, DC: National Governors' Association, pp. 85–98. Committee for Economic Development, 1994. Ravitch, 1995.

p. 265 Ravitch re California process: Ravitch, 1995.

p. 265 Clinton letter to Campbell: Ibid.

pp. 265–66 Resnick to governors: Resnick. In Higginbotham, 1995.

p. 266 Conner quote: Sanches, Rene. "The Hard Truths of Higher Standards." *Washington Post,* 23 February 1997.

p. 266 could vary the means: Doyle, Dennis P. and Susan Pimental with the assistance of Alison Auerbach. "Setting Standards, Meeting Standards: Creating High Performance Schools." Coalition for Goals 2000.

p. 267 a yardstick, not a harness: Finn, Chester E. and Diane Ravitch. *Washington Post,* 25 February 1997.

p. 267 standards . . . welcomed by . . . public: Schroff, Joannie. "The Case for Tough Standards." *U.S. News & World Report,* April 1, 1996.

p. 267 students agreed on the need for standards: Bradley, Ann. "Survey Reveals Teens Yearn for High Standards." *Education Week,* February 12, 1997.

p. 267 public . . . approved of national standards: Ravitch, 1995.

p. 267 neither . . . Riley nor the president ever gave up: Personal communication from Michael Cohen, February 11, 1997.

p. 267 Resnick re 80 percent of the public, Elmore re focus on the purposes of schooling: Personal communication from Lauren Resnick, January 16, 1997; personal communication from Richard Elmore, January 17, 1997.

p. 268 *Monitor* editorial: "Smart Move in Big Apple." *Christian Science Monitor,* 6 January 1997.

p. 268 Resnick quote: Personal communication, January 16, 1997.

p. 268 schools . . . that appeal to some but not all: Meier, 1996.

p. 269 seen as imperfections needing repair: Bryk, Lee and Holland, 1993.

p. 269 new rules: Consortium on Productivity, 1995. Meier, 1996.

p. 269 11 percent of all American children: National Center for Education Statistics, "Education Policy Issues: Statistical Perspectives. Use of School Choice," June 1995.

p. 269 charter schools: Committee for Economic Development, 1994.

p. 269 Finn on charter schools: Finn, Chester E. Jr. "Teachers vs. Education." *New York Times,* 24 August 1996.

p. 270 a reformed . . . school board: Millot, Marc Dean, Paul T. Hill and Robin Lake. "Charter Schools: Escape or Reform?" *Education Week,* June 5, 1996.

p. 270 better-educated . . . parents . . . more likely to take advantage of choice: The Carnegie Foundation for the Advancement of Teaching. "School Choice." Princeton, NJ: Carnegie Foundation for the Advancement of Teaching, 1992. P. 15.

p. 270 Paul Hill's description of a school's "integrative principle": Hill, Paul T. "The Integrative Principle: What it is, Why it Matters, and Why Public Schools have Difficulty Getting and Keeping it." Paper prepared for presentation at the 1997 Annual Convention of the American Educatonal Research Association, Chicago, IL, March 25, 1997.

p. 271 not "the 'invisible hand' ": Rothstein, Richard. Introduction. *School Choice: Examining the Evidence.* Edith Rasell and Richard Rothstein (eds.). Washington DC: Economic Policy Institute, 1993.

p. 272 Universal vouchers: Judis, John B. "Bad Choice." *New Republic,* September 30, 1996.

pp. 273–74 Slavin recommendations re schoolwide reforms: Slavin, Robert E. "District Strategies to Support School Change." Memorandum prepared for October 22, 1996, meeting of the Consortium for Policy Research in Education.

p. 275 "any reform that tackles only a piece of the problem will fail": Consortium on Productivity, 1995.

p. 275 standards . . . alone will not raise . . . achievement: Consortium for Policy Research in Education, 1996.

p. 275 changes in teaching . . . to solve identified problems: Elmore, 1996.

p. 275 absence of . . . alignment: Consortium for Policy Research in Education, 1996.

p. 275 make strategic use of the new flexibility or new funds: Consortium for Policy Research in Education, 1996.

p. 275 natural experiment involving sixteen elementary schools . . . in east Austin, Texas: Murnane and Levy, September 11, 1996.

p. 276 schooling needs to be comprehensively redesigned: Newman and Whelage, 1995. Elmore, 1996.

p. 277 Schmidt quote: This story is told in Rothstein, Richard. "Where's the Money Gone." Washington DC: *Economic Policy Institute,* 1995.

p. 277 claim . . . echoed by experts: Rothstein (ibid.) cites school finance expert Allan Odden, a Brookings report by John Chubb and Eric Hanishek, and Irving Kristol as examples.

p. 277 Analysis of funding increases: Rothstein, 1995.

p. 278 Resnick quote: Resnick, Fall 1995. Pp. 55–62.

p. 278 "smart is something you can get to be." Howard, Jeff. "You Can't Get There from Here: The Need for a New Logic in Education Reform." *Daedalus,* Vol. 124, No. 4, Fall 1995. Pp. 85–92.

p. 278 agreement among the experts: Shore, Rima. "Rethinking the Brain: New Insights into Early Development." New York: Families and Work Institute, 1997.

p. 279 the fewest educational problems: Resnick. *Daedalus,* 1995. Pp. 55–62.

p. 279 Doyle quote: Doyle and Pimental.

p. 279 Gardner re public doubts: Gardner, Fall 1995. Pp. 101–5.

p. 279 story in terms of extraordinary teachers: Mosle, Sara. "What We Talk About When We Talk About Education." *New Republic,* June 17, 1996.

pp. 279–80 Marva Collins story: CBS News. *60 Minutes*, September 24, 1995. "Too Good to Be True?" *60 Minutes* also asked Dr. Guy Stuart, a Chicago statistician, to compare the thirty-three former students with a similarly constituted comparison group. Dr. Stuart projected that, in a group with comparable backgrounds, one would have been murdered, at least two would be in prison, and at least five would be on welfare.

pp. 280–81 Success for All results: Slavin, Robert E., Nancy A. Madden, Lawrence J. Dolan and Barbara A. Wasik. "Success for All: A Summary of Research." *Journal of Education for Students Placed at Risk,* Vol. I (1), Pp. 41–76. Also, Center for Research on the Education of Students Placed at Risk. Research and Development Report, October 1996, No. 1. "Roots and Wings" extends the original Success for All reading program to include math, science, and social studies. It now operates in 37 schools, and a study found students in Maryland Roots and Wings schools have improved at two to three times the rate of their counterparts. This despite the fact that the Roots and Wings population included many more children in poverty than the comparison population and moved at a rate twice the state average. New American Schools Development Corporation, 1994/1995.

p. 281 Accelerated Schools results: Levin, December 1994.

p. 281 Findings . . . repeated all over the country: For example, similarly encouraging findings come from Charlotte, North Carolina. Five years after systemwide school reform began, SAT scores were up by a record-breaking 27 points, there was a fivefold increase in the number of African-American students taking Advanced Placement courses, and the gap between black and white student achievement narrowed markedly. Doyle and Pimental, 1996.

p. 281 new ideas . . . challenge [old] conceptions: Consortium for Policy Research in Education, 1996.

p. 281 children . . . need ". . . a thinking-oriented curriculum": Ravitch, 1995.

p. 281 experience of striving to understand: Gardner, Fall 1995. Pp. 101–5.

p. 281 cannot be assessed with multiple-choice tests: Ravitch, 1995.

p. 282 if persistent troublemakers were removed from class: Johnson and Immerwahr, 1994.

p. 282 Shanker quote: Shanker, Albert. "Education Reform: What's Not Being Said." *Daedalus,* Vol. 124, No. 4, Fall 1995. *American Education: Still Separate, Still Unequal.*

p. 282 "higher order" skills . . . *after* they have mastered the basics: Immerwahr, John and Jean Johnson. "Americans' Views on Standards: An Assessment by Public Agenda." Public Agenda. New York: 1996.

p. 282 Teachers . . . wary . . . about . . . innovations: Farkas, Steve and Jean Johnson. "Given the Circumstances: Teachers Talk About Public Education Today." Public Agenda. New York: 1996.

p. 282 multiple-choice exams . . . replaced: Johnson and Immerwahr, 1994.

p. 283 O'Connor quote: O'Connor, Stephen. "Problems Schools Can't Solve." *New York Times,* 26 March 1996.

p. 283 Graham quote: Graham, Patricia Albjerg. "What America Has Expected of Its Schools Over the Past Century." In Ravitch, Diane and Maris A. Vinovskis (eds.). *Learning from the Past: What History Teaches Us About School Reform.* Baltimore, MD: Johns Hopkins University Press, 1995.

p. 283 study of Indo-Chinese refugee children: Caplan, Nathan, Marcella H.

Choy and John K. Whitmore. "Indochinese Refugee Families and Academic Achievement." *Scientific American,* Vol. 266, No. 2, February 1992. Pp. 36–42.

p. 284 **Connecticut teacher quote:** Farkas and Johnson, 1996.

p. 284 **Wadsworth quote:** Ibid.

pp. 284–85 **Canada quote:** Canada, 1995.

p. 285 **Price quote:** Herbert, Bob. "A Word to the Wise." *New York Times,* 14 February 1997.

p. 285 **Herbert quote:** Ibid.

p. 285 **Seattle teacher quote:** Farkas and Johnson, 1996.

p. 285 **Houston quote:** Houston, Paul. D. "School Reform Through a Wide-Angle Lens: The Consideration of Context." *Daedalus,* Vol. 124, No. 4., Fall 1995. Pp. 169–72.

p. 286 **difficulties with which her students are contending:** That great educator, former U.S. Commissioner of Education Harold Howe, observes, "It is clearly unreasonable to expect teachers to be responsible for the many non-school problems of children, but they should be aware of the pressures and difficulties with which their students are contending." Howe, Harold. "Priority Strategies for Improved Learning." *Daedalus,* Vol. 124, No. 4, Fall 1995.

p. 286 **Jenner story:** Smith, Ralph R. and Michelle Fine. "Toward Community-Responsive Schools." In Building Strong Communities: Strategies for Urban Change conference report. Cleveland: May 13–15, 1992. Ralph Smith and Michelle Fine, who tell this story, believe that it helps to explain why one senses in schools the same detachment one observes in hospital emergency rooms. The detachment may alienate teachers from their work and may estrange them from students and families, but at least it helps to keep the teacher from becoming overwhelmed.

p. 288 **Support of families . . . coming to be seen as crucial:** Delgado-Gaitan, Concha. "School Matters in the Maxican-American Home: Socializing Children to Education." *American Educational Research Journal* 29 (Fall). Pp. 495–513.

p. 288 **Lawrence-Lightfoot quote:** Lawrence-Lightfoot, Sara. *Worlds Apart.* New York: Basic Books, 1978.

p. 288 **to become and stay involved in their children's education:** Epstein, Joyce L. "School and Family Partnerships." In Encyclopedia of Educational Research. Sixth Edition. M. Alkin (ed.). New York: Macmillan, 1992.

p. 289 **Even families long considered "unreachable" can be reached:** Epstein, 1992. Also Henderson, Anne T. and Nancy Berla (eds.). "A New Generation of Evidence: The Family Is Critical to Student Achievement." Washington, DC: National Committee for Citizens in Education.

p. 289 **partnership can overcome barriers:** Epstein, 1992.

p. 289 **cycle of distrust between schools and communities can be broken:** Stone, Clarence and Kathryn Doherty. "Schools in the Local Community Development System." Paper presented at National Community Development Policy Analysis Network research conference. Washington, DC: Brookings Institution, November 15, 1996.

p. 289 **only a minority of schools:** Davies, Don. "The 10th School, Where School-Family-Community Partnerships Flourish." *Education Week,* July 10, 1996.

p. 289 **help children avoid a culture of failure:** Comer, James, Norris Haynes, Edward T. Joyner and Michael Ben-Avie (eds.). *Rallying the Whole Village: The Comer Process of Reforming Education.* New York: Teachers College Press, 1966.

p. 290 **making . . . services available should not become the *responsibility of*** *schools:* Committee for Economic Development, 1994. Educators and community leaders trying to come to grips with the schools-services-communities conundrum under other auspices have reached similar conclusions: Shore, Rima. "Moving the Ladder: Toward a New Community Vision." Report based on the workshop on "Schooling and Families: New Demands, New Responses," held at the Aspen Institute, Aspen, CO, August 6–13, 1994, and Woodrum, Arlie. "A Ladder All Kids Can Climb: Implementing a New Community Vision." Unpublished paper. November 13, 1995.

p. 291 **educate children put at risk by their environments:** This is the formulation of Joy Dryfoos in her excellent book, *Full-Service Schools.* San Francisco: Jossey Bass, 1994.

p. 291 **Urban Strategies Council . . . focused on supporting school success:** Urban Strategies Council reports include "Good Education in Oakland: Strategies for Positive Change," September 1990; "Good Education in Oakland: Preparing for Positive Change," October 1991; and "Partnership for Change: Linking Schools, Services and the Community to Serve Oakland Youth," 1992.

p. 291 **California Partnership:** The California Partnership for Comprehensive, Integrated School-linked Services brings together the skills, experience, and resources of state government and the California foundation community. A third kind of intermediary, the University of Chicago's Center for School Improvement, provides an unusually intensive form of assistance to seven extremely disadvantaged Chicago schools.

p. 292 **neighborhoods where disadvantage is more than a private misfortune:** These questions are discussed with great insight in Stone, Calvin and Gary Whelage. "Community Collaboration and the Restructuring of Schools." Center on Organization and Restructuring of Schools, 1992.

p. 292 **Pennington quote:** Pennington, Hilary C. speaking at the Clinton-Gore Economic Conference in Little Rock, Arkansas, December 14–15, 1992. *President Clinton's New Beginning.* New York: Donald I. Fine, 1992.

p. 292 **"three quarters are left to fend for themselves":** Resnick, Lauren B. "Schooling and the Workplace: What Relationship?" Prepared for Aspen Institute Conference, "Preparing Youth for the 21st Century." Palm Beach, FL: February 16–19, 1996.

p. 293 **Wilson re school counselors:** Wilson, William Julius, speaking at the Clinton-Gore Economic Conference in Little Rock, Arkansas, December 14–15, 1992.

p. 293 **Resnick quote:** Resnick, February 16–19, 1996.

p. 293 **jobless rate among black male high school dropouts:** Wilson, 1996.

p. 293 **black kids have jobs compared with . . . white kids:** Data from U.S. Bureau of Labor Statistics. "Nearly Three-Fifths of High School Graduates of 1988 Enrolled in College." U.S. Department of Labor news release, 89-308, June 1989.

p. 293 **A lot of them turn to drugs and crime:** Wilson, William Julius, on NBC News "Meet the Press," February 19, 1995. In his book, *When Work Disappears.* Wilson illustrates the point with an interview with a thirty-five-year-old unemployed man, who told a University of Chicago interviewer, "I'm a cocaine dealer 'cause I can't get a decent-ass job. What other choices do I have? I have to feed my family. . . . Do I work? I work. . . . I been working since I was fifteen years old. I had to work to take care of my mother and father and my sisters. See, so can't, can't nobody bring me that bullshit about I ain't looked for no job. . . ."

pp. 293–94 Zemsky quote: In "National Survey Shows a Rift Between Schools and Business. *New York Times,* 20 February, 1995.

p. 294 Canada quote: Geoffrey Canada conversation with Bob Herbert. "Men and Jobs." *New York Times,* 30 September 1996.

p. 295 Career Academies studied by Manpower Demonstration Research Corporation: Kemple, James and JoAnn Leah Rock. "Career Academies: Early Implementation Lessons from a 10 Site Evaluation," 1996.

p. 295 A study of another ten sites in California: Olson, Lynn. "On the Career Track." *Education Week.* Vol. 13, February 23, 1994.

p. 295 workplace becomes a learning laboratory: These are the observations of Sam Halperin, who headed the 1980s work that called attention to the plight of non-college-bound youth. Halperin, Samuel. "School-to-Work: A Larger Vision." American Youth Policy Forum, November 4, 1994.

p. 295 dovetails . . . with new findings from cognitive research: Berryman, Sue E. and Thomas R. Bailey. *The Double Helix of Education and the Economy.* New York: Teachers College, Columbia University, 1992.

p. 295 Pennington quote: Olson, Lynn. "Bridging the Gap." *Education Week,* January 26, 1994.

p. 296 Smith description of Wisconsin systematic approach: Smith, Hedrick. *Rethinking America: Innovative Strategies and Partnerships in Business and Education.* New York: Avon, 1996.

CHAPTER 9   Synergy: Putting It All Together to Transform Neighborhoods

p. 303 Efforts to transform depleted neighborhoods are under way: Locally based efforts aimed at strengthening neighborhoods probably number about 3,000. Of these about 250 are committed to a comprehensive agenda.

p. 303 "Something is working," said the Committee for Economic Development: Committee for Economic Development. "Rebuilding Inner-City Communities: A New Approach to the Nation's Urban Crisis." Washington, DC: CED, 1995.

p. 303 they were our communities and we miss them. Raspberry, William. *Washington Post,* 10 April 1995.

p. 304 vigilant mothers keep their children—even teenagers—at home to keep them safe: Furstenberg, Frank F. Jr. "How Families Manage Risk and Opportunity in Dangerous Neighborhoods." In Wilson, William Julius (ed.). *Sociology and the Public Agenda.* Newbury Park: Sage Publications, 1993. Pp. 231–58.

p. 304 Technology has made it unnecessary: Putnam, Robert D. "Bowling Alone: Democracy in America at the End of the Twentieth Century." Harvard University, 1994.

p. 305 Sandel re erosion of community: Sandel, Michael J. *Democracy's Discontent: America in Search of a Public Philosophy.* Cambridge: Harvard University Press, 1996.

p. 305 Kennedy quote: Ibid.

p. 305 influence of neighborhoods on families: Furstenberg, Frank F. Jr. and Mary Elizabeth Hughes. "The Influence of Neighborhoods on Children's Development: A Theoretical Perspective and a Research Agenda." Conference Indicators of Children's Well-Being. Bethesda, MD: November 17–18, 1994.

p. 306 The documentation of connections was sparse: A review by Jencks and Mayer found few sturdy statistical effects of poor neighborhoods. Jencks, Christopher and Susan Mayer. "The Social Consequences of Growing Up in a Poor Neighborhood. In Lynn, L. E. and M. G. H. McGeary (eds.). *Inner-City Poverty in the United States.* Washington, DC: National Academy Press, 1990.

p. 306 social scientists avoided studying connections between neighborhoods and individual outcomes: They may have been deterred by how poorly the complexity of the task fit with their quest for unambiguous results. "Methodologically," declared the National Research Council, "it is difficult to identify causal relationships between complex social settings and individual behavioral outcomes, and most results are open to more than one explanation." National Research Council, Panel on High Risk Youth, Commission on Behavioral and Social Sciences and Education. *Losing Generations: Adolescents in High-Risk Settings.* Washington, DC: National Academy Press, 1993.

p. 306 the influence of neighborhoods became a hot topic again: Furstenberg and Hughes, 1994.

p. 306 neighborhoods profoundly affect how parents raise their children: Aber, Larry, Lisa Berlin, Jeanne Brooks-Gunn and Robert Granger. "The Role of Comprehensive Community Initiatives in Enhancing Early Childhood Development." Manuscript in preparation. Washington, DC: The Aspen Institute. Jarrett, R. "Bringing Families Back In: Neighborhoods' Effects on Child Development." In Brooks-Gunn, J., G. J. Duncan and J. L. Aber (eds.). *Neighborhood Poverty: Context and Consequences for Children: Conceptual, Methodological, and Policy Approaches to Studying Neighborhoods.* Vol. 2. New York: Russell Sage Foundation, in press. Klebanov, P. K., J. Brooks-Gunn, L. Chase-Lansdale and R. Gordon. "The Intersection of the Neighborhood and Home Environment and Its Influence on Young Children." In Brooks-Gunn, Duncan and Aber, in press.

p. 306 adults establish fewer connections: Coulton, Claudia C. "Effects of Neighborhoods on Families and Children: Implications for Services." In Kahn and Kamerman, 1996. P. 104.

p. 306 "Don't honeycoat it": "In D.C. Neighborhood, Two Killings in a Half Hour." *Washington Post,* 7 December 1991.

p. 306 residents have . . . respectable values: Sampson, Robert J. "The Community." In Wilson, James Q. and Joan Petersilia (eds.). *Crime: Twenty-eight Leading Experts Look at the Most Pressing Problem of Our Time.* San Francisco: Institute for Contemporary Studies, 1995.

pp. 306–307 neighborhood institutions that promote healthy youth development: Connell, James P., J. Lawrence Aber and Gary Walker. "How Do Urban Communities Affect Youth? Using Social Science to Inform the Design and Evaluation of Comprehensive Community Initiatives." In Connell et al., 1995. Also Sampson, 1995.

p. 307 affluent neighbors and . . . neighborhood poverty . . . associated with . . . outcomes: Aber et al.; Jarrett, R.; Klebanov et al.

p. 307 child rearing . . . powerfully dependent on the health of . . . communities: Nelson, Douglas. Introduction to *Kids Count Data Book.* Baltimore: Annie E. Casey Foundation, 1994.

p. 307 children growing up in severely depleted neighborhoods face a daunting array of risks: Nelson, Douglas. Executive Director's Message, The Annie E. Casey Foundation 1994 Annual Report. Baltimore; The Annie E. Casey Foundation.

p. 307 Putnam quote: Putnam, Robert D. "The Prosperous Community: Social Capital and Public Life." *The American Prospect,* No. 13, Spring 1993. Based on research of Case and Katz: Case, Anne C. and Lawrence F. Katz. "The Company

You Keep: The Effects of Family and Neighborhood on Disadvantaged Youths." Cambridge, MA: National Bureau of Economic Research, May 1991.

p. 307 **peer influence reigns when countervailing social forces are weak:** This is the formulation of Jonathan Crane. "The Epidemic Theory of Ghettos and Neighborhood Effects on Dropping Out and Teenage Childbearing." *American Journal of Sociology,* vol. 96, No. 5, 1991. Pp. 1226–59.

p. 307 **the neighborhood reaches a "tipping point":** Gladwell, Malcolm. *The New Yorker,* June 3, 1996

p. 307 **damaging effects . . . inflicted on an increasing number of children:** Kasarda, J. "Inner-City Concentrated Poverty and Neighborhood Distress: 1970 to 1990." Housing Policy Debate 4, 1993. Pp. 253–302.

pp. 307–308 **Increased crime and social disorder in depleted neighborhoods:** Sampson, Robert J. "What 'Community' Supplies." NCDPAN meeting, November 15, 1996.

p. 308 **Past efforts to transform neighborhoods:** In recounting the antecedents of current efforts I am enormously indebted to Robert Halpern's superb history of neighborhood initiatives. As will be apparent from these endnotes, his splendid 1995 book, *Rebuilding the Inner City,* provided invaluable understanding as well as information.

p. 308 **Settlement house history:** Skocpol, Theda. *Protecting Soldiers and Mothers: The Political Origins of Social Policy in the United States.* Cambridge: Harvard University Press, 1992.

p. 308 **settlers at Hull House:** Specht, Harry and Mark Courtney. *Unfaithful Angels: How Social Work Has Abandoned Its Mission.* New York: Free Press, 1994.

p. 308 **mobilized community residents:** Halpern, 1995.

p. 308 **settlement leaders . . . committed to the neighborhood:** Ibid.

p. 309 **urban machines kept in close touch with the new industrial working class:** Skocpol, 1992.

p. 309 **Plunkitt quote:** Tolchin, Martin. "The Citizen as Customer." *New York Times Book Review,* 8 March, 1992.

p. 309 **Appalled by . . . indiscriminate giving and imprecise criteria for assistance:** Putnam, Marian C. "Friendly Visiting." In Proceedings of the Thirty-seventh Conference of Charities and Corrections. Fort Wayne, IN: Archer Printing Co, 1910. Pp. 1–28.

p. 309 **Skocpol re "carefully meted, individually targeted assistance":** Skocpol, 1992.

p. 309 **"Not alms but a friend":** Richman, Harold. Unpublished paper, January 1995.

p. 310 **replaced by help from the expert professional:** Mary Richmond, the founder of the Charity Organization Society, advocated "the gathering of evidence, or investigation . . . to arrive at as exact a definition as possible of the social situation and personality of a given client." Richmond, Mary E. *Social Diagnosis.* New York: Russell Sage, 1917. Quoted by Halpern, 1995.

p. 310 **the residents were . . . responsible:** Halpern, 1995.

p. 310 **World War II encouraged . . . the notion of America as a classless society:** Halpern, 1995. Quoting Patterson, James. *America's Struggle Against Poverty.* Cambridge: Harvard University Press, 1986. P. 57.

p. 310 **poverty would not . . . disappear of its own accord . . . inner city no longer a way station to the mainstream:** Halpern, 1995.

p. 310 Clark re "the extent of their hurt" and their growing strength: Clark, Kenneth, *Dark Ghetto*. New York: Harper & Row, 1965. Cited in Halpern, 1995.

p. 311 Gray Areas program: Jackson, Mario-Rosario and Peter Marris. "Comprehensive Community Initiatives: Overview of an Emerging Community Improvement Orientation." Baltimore, MD: The Development Training Institute, January 1996.

p. 311 Ylvisaker quote: Halpern, 1995.

p. 311 white . . . professional leaders of Gray Areas projects . . . challenged by . . . residents: Halpern, 1995. Urban renewal had bulldozed neighborhoods, especially black neighborhoods—hence its nickname, "Negro removal"—and replaced them with highways, high-priced housing developments, and municipal office complexes that looked wonderful when planners presented them at Chamber of Commerce meetings but, when built, only hastened the city's decline. Lemann, Nicholas. "The Myth of Community Development." *New York Times Magazine*, 9 January 1994.

p. 311 Sviridoff quote: Sviridoff at focus group organized by Roundtable on Comprehensive Community Initiatives, Aspen Institute, New York City, June 6, 1995.

p. 311 One more frustration: Jackson and Marris, 1996.

p. 311 enriched human services . . . could play only a modest role: Halpern, 1995.

p. 312 Johnson rejection of jobs program: Moynihan, Daniel P. "When Principle Is at Issue." *Washington Post*, 4 July 1996.

p. 312 Shriver quote: Blackside, Inc. "America's War on Poverty," PBS, January 16, 1995.

p. 312 Peter Marris and Martin Rein re "those shaping the War on Poverty": Marris and Rein, *Dilemmas of Social Reform*. London: Routledge and Kegan Paul, 1973. Quoted in Halpern, 1995.

p. 312 when the [change] process involves setting up alternative political structures: Edelman, Peter and Beryl A. Radin. "Serving Children and Families Effectively: How the Past Can Help Chart the Future." Washington, DC: Education and Human Services Consortium, 1991.

p. 313 at least as destructive . . . was OEO's inability . . . to respond to the need for jobs: O'Connor, Alice. "Federal Policy in Poor Communities: A Brief History." Paper prepared for the NCDPAN Fall 1996 Conference, November 1996.

p. 313 biggest impact of the OEO's community action program: Katz, Michael B. *The Undeserving Poor: From the War on Poverty to the War on Welfare*. New York: Pantheon Books, 1989.

p. 313 community action agencies "gave a generation of poor people a taste of having control over their own lives": Edelman and Radin, 1991.

p. 313 Rosemary Bray: Bray, Rosemary. "So How Did I Get Here?" In Lavelle, Robert (ed.). *America's New War on Poverty*. San Francisco: KQED Books, 1995.

p. 313 congressional support . . . contingent on . . . Shriver's willingness to defund . . . controversial programs: These included the Child Development Group of Mississippi (the state's grassroots Head Start program) and California Rural Legal Assistance, the program that incurred Governor Ronald Reagan's wrath for its representation of migrant workers against California growers.

p. 313 Reuther quote: Quoted by O'Connor, November 1996.

p. 314 Katzenbach quote: Halpern, 1995.

p. 314 The Model Cities vision: Edelman and Radin, 1991.

p. 314 original legislative drafts posited initial funding of $500 million for six cities: Halpern, 1995.

p. 314 No one . . . took the Model Cities planning process seriously: Halpern, 1995. Edelman and Radin, 1991.

p. 314 "Model Cities became a lesson in the dissipation of limited resources": Ibid.

p. 314 anti-poverty interventions . . . undermined by . . . massive deindustrialization: Mitchell Sviridoff, who led New Haven's efforts under both Gray Areas and Community Action auspices, recently went back to New Haven. "Every factory in the New Haven of the early '60s is gone. Winchester, that employed five to ten thousand people, Sargent's Hardware that employed two thousand people, New Haven Clock—you name it, it's gone. The aircraft industry, forty to fifty thousand people, is down to ten thousand. The earthquake of de-industrialization . . . And back then no city was prepared to counteract it with anything but a services strategy . . . Sviridoff at Roundtable on Comprehensive Community Initiatives, June 6, 1995.

p. 315 Those who saw the problem as primarily logistical: Sviridoff, Mitchell and William Ryan. "Investing in Community: Lessons and Implications of the Comprehensive Community Revitalization Program." New York: Comprehensive Community Revitalization Program, January 1996.

p. 315 It also appealed to those seeking a managerial solution: John McKnight, quoted by Peirce, Neal and Carol Steinbach. Paper on Grassroots Initiatives prepared for the John T. and Catherine D. MacArthur Foundation.

p. 315 looking for a meshing of categorical programs: Kahn and Kamerman, 1996. P. 13.

p. 315 two dozen major federal initiatives: Department of Health and Human Services, Office of the Inspector General. "Services Integration: A Twenty-Year Retrospective." OEI-01-91-00580. Washington, DC: 1991.

p. 315 150 service integration projects in 40 states: McCart, Linda. "Developing Innovative Programs to Support Families." Annapolis Junction, MD: National Governors' Association, 1992.

p. 315 very little changed: Department of Health and Human Services, OEI-01-91-00580. 1991.

p. 315 Federally funded service integration efforts: Agranoff, Robert. "Human Services Integration: Past and Present Challenges in Public Administration." *Public Administration Review,* November/December 1991; 51 (6). Pp. 533–42.

p. 315 reform had to contend with a more complex, inflexible, and fragmented system: Halpern, Robert. "Supportive Services for Families in Poverty: Dilemmas of Reform." *Social Service Review,* September 1991, 65 (3). Pp. 343–64.

p. 315 cumulative disillusionment resulting from previous failures: At this point, both the HHS inspector general and the General Accounting Office counseled retreat. "Given the enormity of the barriers they face, service integration efforts that seek major institutional reform should be initiated selectively, if at all," said the inspector general. The GAO, while noting that the "current delivery system has been unable to adequately address the multiple needs of at-risk families," urged caution and pointed up the great risk of failure of "initiatives that call for state and local governments to make fundamental changes in service-delivery systems." United States General Accounting Office. "Integrating Human Services: Linking At-

Risk Families with Services More Successful Than System Reform Efforts." US GAO; Gaithersburg, MD: 1992. GAO/HRD-92-108.

p. 316 convinced of the need for "greater boldness . . . and a basic restructuring": Nelson, Doug in A.E.C. *Focus.* Baltimore, MD: Annie E. Casey Foundation, n.d.

p. 316 The Casey strategy: Center for the Study of Social Policy. "Building New Futures for At-Risk Youth." Washington, DC: CSSP, May 1995.

p. 316 youth outcomes did not, in fact, improve . . . "vested interests" undermined: Casey Foundation, Annie E. "The Path of Most Resistance: Reflections on Lessons Learned from New Futures." Baltimore, MD: Annie E. Casey Foundation, August 1995.

p. 316 The Casey Foundation promptly acted: Nelson, Douglas W. "Executive Director's Message." 1995 Annual Report, Annie E. Casey Foundation.

p. 317 CDCs . . . "one of the fastest-growing community-based institutions in inner-city America": Committee for Economic Development, 1995.

p. 317 dedicated to the revitalization of a discrete . . . geographic area: Halpern, 1995.

p. 317 governed by boards . . . of residents and sometimes business and civic leaders: Sviridoff, Michael. "The Seeds of Urban Renewal." *The Public Interest,* Winter 1994.

p. 317 Some also develop commercial real estate: Committee for Economic Development, 1995.

p. 317 Anna Faith Jones quote: Pratt Institute. "Building Hope," video, 1994.

p. 317 Richardson quote: Ibid.

p. 318 Judge Jones quote: Ibid.

p. 318 Kennedy saw community development: Medoff, Peter and Holly Sklar. *Street of Hope: The Fall and Rise of an Urban Neighborhood.* Boston: South End Press, 1994.

p. 318 Sviridoff quote: Sviridoff, Winter 1994.

p. 318 Judge Jones quote: "Building Hope," 1994.

p. 318 Ford created the Local Initiatives Support Corporation: Sviridoff, Winter 1994.

pp. 318–19 Their number mushroomed from 100 in 1970 to more than 2000: Committee for Economic Development, 1995.

p. 319 narrowly defined interventions can't triumph: A major study by the CED also concluded that past efforts failed because they addressed poverty, welfare, unemployment, inadequate education, substandard housing, and crime one at a time, ignoring that "the co-existence of problems within a neighborhood creates a mutually reinforcing process of decay that limits the effectiveness of each narrowly focused initiative."

p. 319 poor neighborhoods require multiple and interrelated solutions: From review of community initiatives by Jackson and Marris, January 1996.

p. 319 It refuses to "choose between structural and behavioral causes": From review of community initiatives by Walsh, Joan. "Stories of Renewal: Community Building and the Future of Urban America." New York: The Rockefeller Foundation, January 1997.

p. 319 It insists on combining physical and economic development with service and education reform: From review of community initiatives by Committee for

Economic Development, 1995. The excellent recent report from Joan Walsh for the Rockefeller Foundation, "Stories of Renewal," comes to the same conclusion.

p. 319 **Not all of the community initiatives:** A review of the field for the Urban Institute suggests that the new synthesis is more likely to be found in rhetoric than in reality. The authors, Maria Jackson and Peter Marris, believe that even those engaged in comprehensive initiatives do not fully grasp that a comprehensive strategy will require extensive policy and institutional reform efforts "to compensate for the shortcomings of institutions intended to integrate people into the economic opportunity structure (such as schools), as well as efforts to eradicate destructive individual behaviors." Jackson and Marris, 1996.

p. 320 **Sandtown-Winchester:** Unless otherwise indicated, this description is based on conversations with James Rouse and Pat Costigan and on meetings with staff and boards of the Enterprise Foundation and of CBP between 1991 and 1996; a conversation with Ronica Houston on July 17, 1996; the Interim Evaluation Report submitted by the Conservation Company in October 1995; and on "Building Community Solutions" by Pat Costigan, February 7, 1997. I am particularly indebted to Pat Costigan for sharing his thoughtful reflections with me, and for allowing me to make use of them.

p. 320 **Will quote:** Will, George. "An Urban Resuscitation." *Washington Post,* 31 December 1995.

p. 321 *The Washington Post* **quoted Rouse . . . pronounced Sandtown to be "perfect" for this purpose:** Gugliotta, Guy. "Rebuilding a Community from the Bottom Up." *Washington Post,* 4 January 1993.

p. 321 **residents told Schmoke that . . . new housing would not make much difference:** Rankin, Robert A. "Helping Residents Rebuild a Blighted Community." *Philadelphia Inquirer,* 24 May 1992.

p. 322 **Costigan quote:** Costigan, February 7, 1997.

p. 323 **the mayor capped the day of celebration:** Michael Fletcher. "Mayor Pledges Changes in Sandtown." *Baltimore Sun,* 7 March 1993.

p. 325 **Management authority has been increasingly turned over to the principals:** Walsh, 1997.

p. 328 **CCRP and the South Bronx:** In putting together this story of CCRP, I had the help of researcher/writer Richard Mendel, and many hours of conversations with Anita Miller, who was most generous with her time, insights, and wisdom. She also provided me with extensive materials, including CCRP reports and the annual assessments prepared by OMG, Inc. Ricki Granetz of FEGS was a wonderful guide to CCRP programming; the senior staff of the Mid Bronx Seniors CDC made my visit there highly informative; and Wanda McLain, CCRP assistant project director, took me on an extraordinary South Bronx tour.

p. 328 **Thousands of job seekers . . . arrived:** Breslin, Patrick. "On These Sidewalks of New York, the Sun Is Shining Again." *Smithsonian,* March 1995.

p. 328 **Landlords . . . began to leave . . . buildings burned:** Ibid.

p. 328 *The New York Times* **called it "the nation's most infamous symbol of urban blight":** "A Bronx Miracle." *New York Times,* 12 March 1995.

p. 328 **President Carter visited . . . Charlotte Street:** Purdy, Matthew. "Left to Die, the South Bronx Rises from Decades of Decay." *New York Times,* 13 November 1994.

p. 328 **Ronald Reagan came:** Ibid.

p. 328 **"the contrast between . . . the burned-out South Bronx:** Ibid.

p. 328 "the burned-out Bronx is largely gone": *New York Times,* 12 March 1995.

p. 329 Santiago quote: Purdy, 1994.

p. 329 Immanuel quote: Breslin, 1995.

p. 329 The heroes . . . are "the not-for-profit community development corporations": *New York Times,* 12 March 1995.

p. 329 declaring Orange County *Out* and the South Bronx *In.:* Dunkin, Amy. "Hey, Is That Sonny Bono Driving a VW Bug?" *Business Week,* December 26, 1994.

p. 329 housing revival not matched in other spheres: Purdy, 1994. Also Halpern, 1995.

p. 330 CDCs . . . in a unique position to take on a far-reaching revitalization strategy: Miller, Anita. "Comprehensive Community Revitalization: A Demonstration Program in the South Bronx." Report to the Surdna Foundation. November 25, 1991.

p. 330 what supports . . . CDCs would need . . . to take on the broader agenda: Ibid.

p. 331 CCRP decided to "start with the strong and make them stronger": Sviridoff and Ryan, 1996.

p. 332 CCRP has helped the CDCs to build . . . management capacity: Ibid.

p. 336 CCRP-CDC partnership . . . emphasizes the residents' role as engaged citizens: Sviridoff and Ryan believe that it is in this sphere where the "underlying values" of an initiative can be identified, and that the key to understanding CCRP is its distinctive preference for engaging residents as "engaged citizens." Ibid.

p. 337 Savannah Youth Futures Authority: In putting together the YFA story, I have relied on what I learned from a meeting with Otis Johnson, Don Mendonsa, and Mary Willoughby in Charlotte, North Carolina, on March 13, 1995, under the auspices of the Evaluation Steering Committee of the Roundtable on Comprehensive Community Initiatives, and from listening very carefully to Otis Johnson whenever I have heard him speak—in many different settings—over a period of years. My information and understanding were expanded by the following materials: Casey Foundation, Annie E. "The Path of Most Resistance: Reflections on Lessons Learned from New Futures." Baltimore, MD: Casey Foundation, August 1995. Center for the Study of Social Policy. "Building New Futures for At-Risk Youth." Washington, DC: CSSP, May 1995. Halpern, 1995. Hirota, Janice. "Children at Risk: An Interim Report on Organizational Structure and Dynamics." New York: Center on Addiction and Substance Abuse at Columbia University, February 1995. Johnson, Otis S. "The FRC: What Are We Trying to Do?" Chatham-Savannah Youth Futures Authority, June 1994. Johnson, Otis S. "Savannah's New Futures Initiative: Getting to the Root of the Dandelion." In Council of Chief State School Officers. "Ensuring Student Success Through Collaboration: Summer Institute Papers and Recommendations of the Council of Chief State School Officers." Washington, DC: CCSSO, 1992. White, Julie A. and Gary Whelage. "Community Collaboration: If It Is Such a Good Idea, Why Is It So Hard to Do?" *Education Evaluation and Policy Analysis,* Vol. 17, No. 1, Spring 1995. Youth Futures Authority. "Chatham-Savannah Youth Futures Authority: Summary of Three Phases of Development."

p. 341 "in the absence of agreement about remedies . . .": White and Whelage, Spring 1995.

p. 343 **Promising data are beginning to come in:** Walsh, 1997.

p. 344 **a Process-heavy, Strategy-light Atlanta Project:** My information and understanding of the Atlanta Project, except as otherwise indicated, are based on two visits, one on November 15, 1993, and the other on October 12, 1994, conversations with leaders of The Atlanta Project and The America Project, a visit to one of the clusters, and extensive materials provided by the Project.

p. 344 **Rallying Atlantans to the inner-city cause:** Booth, William. "Olympian Goal in Atlanta." *Washington Post,* 7 June 1992.

p. 344 **Carter quote:** "Carter's Atlanta Project Is Reviving a Dream to Curb Rampant Poverty in King's Hometown." *Wall Street Journal,* 20 January 1992.

p. 345 **The outpouring of demand persuaded the former President to . . . create an America Project:** Peirce, Neal R. "Using the Atlanta Project Model, Carter Hopes to Build on Strength." *Philadelphia Inquirer,* 19 October 1992.

p. 345 **more than 200 delegations had come to Atlanta to study the project's techniques:** Bailey, Anne Lowrey. "Critical Report Leads Jimmy Carter's Atlanta Anti-Poverty Drive to Make Changes." *Education Week,* March 1995.

p. 345 **Sweat quote:** Sweat, Dan E. and Jacquelyn A. Anthony. "The Role of Corporations in Urban Revitalization." *National Civic Review,* Summer-Fall 1995.

p. 345 **The process at the heart of the project:** News from the Carter Center, January 7, 1992.

p. 346 *Atlanta Constitution* **quotes:** "Atlanta Project Pulled It Off." *Atlanta Constitution,* 5 May 1993.

p. 346 **"Too many neighborhood projects have focused on . . . 'feel good' activities:** Bailey, March 1995.

p. 347 **it was a mistake to provide so little training and direction:** Story of the Therrell cluster from Walsh, 1997.

p. 348 **Newark's New Community Corporation:** from an afternoon spent with Monsignor Linder and a visit to the neighborhood on October 18, 1994, and many materials I was able to collect from and about NCC. The most helpful of these were the superb thesis about NCC and Monsignor Linder by Karl Koerchlin of the MIT Urban Studies program, and the thorough description of NCC by Janice Hirota, done for the Children at Risk program of the Center on Addiction and Substance Abuse.

p. 349 **Linder "a guerrilla on behalf of the community":** Hirota, February 1995.

p. 349 **homes that looked like homes:** "In Our Hands, Breaking the Cycle of Despair." *Nonprofit World.* Vol. 8, No. 3, May-June 1990.

p. 349 **NCC consists of 30 legal entities:** Kukla, Barbara. "New Community Corp." *Star-Ledger,* 19 October 1992.

p. 350 **By 1993, NCC was one of only ten Newark corporations employing more than 1,000 people:** Hirota, 1995.

p. 350 **Kathy Spivey, NCC's director of staff development, makes sure:** Reardon, Christopher. "Career Ladders." Ford Foundation Report, Spring 1995.

p. 350 **In the past ten years, the NCC employment center has been able to place more than 9,000 applicants:** Linder, William J. NCC: "A Community Development Corporation." Paper prepared for Columbia University seminar, Children and Their Families in Big Cities, October 17, 1994.

p. 350 **profits from the store go . . . back into the community:** Revkin, Andrew C. "A Market Scores a Success in Newark." *New York Times,* 30 April 1995.

p. 351 **Codey quote:** Sylvia Lewis. "Tough Love Works in Newark." Planning, American Planning Association, October 1993.

p. 352 **Shifting power to DSNI:** Information about DSNI comes primarily from extensive interviewing and visiting by Patricia Savage, who studied DSNI (as well as the NFI project in Milwaukee) during the winter of 1994 and spring of 1995, as part of a Harvard Kennedy School of Government Policy Analysis Exercise designed to illuminate the characteristics of sustainable community-based initiatives. Also from the marvelous history of DSNI in Medoff, Peter and Holly Sklar. *Streets of Hope: The Fall and Rise of an Urban Neighborhood.* Boston: South End Press, 1994, from conversations with Sandy Jebrell and Miriam Shark at the Casey Foundation, and from the presentation by May Louie, manager of DSNI's Rebuilding Communities Initiative, to the Roundtable on Comprehensive Community Initiatives on January 28, 1997.

p. 352 **Bothwell quote:** Medoff and Sklar, 1994.

p. 354 **power of eminent domain:** The power of eminent domain authorizes taking "property for public use without the owner's consent upon making just compensation."

p. 357 **traditionally . . . "a bureaucratic nightmare":** Schwartz, Ed. "Reviving Community Development." *The American Prospect,* Fall 1994.

p. 358 **"key dimensions of community transformation":** USDHUD Request for Proposal to Evaluate Empowerment Zones and Enterprise Communities, October 27, 1995.

p. 358 **Murphy quote:** *Time,* October 10, 1994.

p. 358 **Peirce quote:** Peirce, Neal R. "Here's to the Empowerment Zones: Are They the Last Urban Initiative?" *Philadelphia Inquirer,* 30 January 1995.

p. 358 **two Pathmark supermarkets will be moving into the Philadelphia zone:** HUD *EZ/EC News,* August 1996. P. 3.

p. 358 **applicants include the Gap . . . a marina . . . a restaurateur:** *New York Times,* 20 August 1996.

p. 359 **EZ executives were "deeply concerned":** Fuchs, Esther and J. Philip Thompson. "Urban Community Initiatives and Shifting Federal Policy: The Case of the Empowerment Zones." In Kahn and Kamerman, 1996.

p. 360 **They set out "to foster a fundamental transformation of poor neighborhoods":** Kubisch, Anne C., P. Brown, R. Chaskin, J. Hirota, M. Joseph, H. Richman and M. Roberts. *Voices from the Field: Learning from Comprehensive Community Initiatives.* Washington, DC: Aspen Institute, in press.

p. 361 **Harold Richman re comprehensive mandate:** Richman at focus group organized by Roundtable on Comprehensive Community Initiatives, June 6, 1995.

p. 361 **most promising initiatives all use . . . a comprehensive lens:** "Comprehensive lens" is Prudence Brown's term.

p. 361 **no one model of neighborhood transformation:** Jackson and Marris, 1996.

p. 361 **It catalyzes a process of change:** The many aspects of community building are documented by the following: Kubisch et al., in press. Committee for Economic Development, 1995. Walsh, 1997. Sviridoff and Ryan, 1995. Halpern, 1995.

p. 362 **Gardner quote:** Gardner, John W. "Building Community." Prepared for the Leadership Studies Program of Independent Sector, September 1991.

pp. 362–63 **all "aim to increase the density of social interaction":** Brown, Prudence and Harold A. Richman. "Communities and Neighborhoods: How Can Existing Research Inform and Shape Current Urban Change Initiatives?" Background memorandum prepared for the Social Science Research Council Policy Conference on Persistent Poverty, November 9–10, 1993. Washington, DC.

p. 363 Community building activities often aim at reducing social disorder and physical "incivilities": Sampson in J. Q. Wilson, 1995. Also Kelling, George L. and Catherine M. Coles. *Fixing Broken Windows: Restoring Order and Reducing Crime in Our Communities.* New York: The Free Press, 1996.

p. 363 strengthen informal social controls by building social networks: Sampson, 1996.

p. 364 CCI director quote: Pat Costigan, personal communication, May 1996.

p. 365 By reducing neighborhood violence and disorder: Coulton in Kahn and Kamerman, 1996.

p. 365 when residents . . . undertake activities that perceptibly change the conditions of their lives: Brown and Richman, 1993.

p. 365 Another plausible theory of change connects improved outcomes for adolescents: Connell, J. P. and A. C. Kubisch. "Applying a Theory of Change Approach to the Evaluation of Comprehensive Community Initiatives." In *New Approaches to Evaluating Community Initiatives,* Vol. II, forthcoming.

p. 365 investments and strategies for change must be mobilized: Nelson, Executive Director's Message, 1995.

p. 365 Stein quote: Stein, Herbert. "The $50 Billion Option." *Wall Street Journal,* 12 June, 1992. Stein has sociological backing for this conclusion in epidemic theorist Jonathan Crane's observation that "A policy intervention that is large but not quite large enough is little better than no intervention at all: if the policy fails to reduce the incidence of a problem enough, that problem will tend to revert back to a high level of incidence on its own." Crane, 1991.

p. 367 Canada question: Meeting of the Roundtable on Comprehensive Community Initiatives, January 29, 1997.

p. 369 government policies that might have buffered the negative effects: Henry Cisneros speaking at the Urban Institute, November 11, 1993.

p. 369 changes that can only be made outside of those communities: "One cannot segregate, neglect, and isolate a neighborhood for 30 or 40 years, and then turn around and ask it to draw on its 'latent' resources." Halpern, 1995.

p. 369 O'Connor doubts: O'Connor, November 1996.

p. 371 almost impossible to obtain the assistance that takes into account: Kubisch, Anne C. "Comprehensive Community Initiatives: Lessons in Neighborhood Transformation." *Shelterforce,* January/February 1996.

p. 371 Blackwell quote: A. Blackwell, speaking at Urban Institute, November 17, 1993.

p. 372 funding is so complex, it becomes the domain of a few experts: Peter Dreier at National Community Development Policy Analysis Network research conference, Washington, DC: The Brookings Institution, November 15, 1996.

p. 372 foundations are more likely to contribute to than reduce the prevailing fragmentation of services: "Lessons from Comprehensive Urban Development Projects." Conference sponsored by the Robert Wood Johnson Foundation, July 30, 1993.

pp. 372–73 when the foundations . . . "get serious about the need for an integrated program": Confidential source. Sid Gardner of the California Center for Collaboration for Children adds that grantees are frustrated by the tendency of funders to relabel problems (from youth development to teenage pregnancy prevention to violence prevention) and make new grants without regard to ongoing community efforts to work with the same population or in the same neighborhood on the same problem under an outmoded name. Rather than create competing, parallel new programs and new collaborative entities, Gardner suggests that funders would do better to be less parochial and to build on and strengthen existing community activities.

p. 373 Videka-Sherman: Videka-Sherman, Lynn. "New-Style Settlement Houses." A survey of the new-style settlement houses. Albany, NY: Rockefeller Institute, 1992.

p. 374 Talented economists and public policy analysts have tried to make the case: These include the Enterprise Foundation, Anthony Downs at the Brookings Institution, Walt Rostow at the Austin Project, Robert Solow working with the Children's Defense Fund, and Charles Bruner at the Child and Family Policy Center in Iowa, to name just a few.

p. 374 Charles Bruner and colleagues . . . estimated the potential savings: Bruner, Charles, Stephen Scott and Martha Steketee. "Allegheny County Study: Potential Returns on Investment from a Comprehensive Family Center Approach in High-Risk Neighborhoods." Background paper, Child and Family Policy Center, January 1996.

p. 376 they should be guided by a clear overarching vision: Jackson and Marris, 1996.

pp. 376–77 Nathan quote: Nathan, Richard. "Urban Revitalization—From the Ground Up: A Proposal for a National Community," December 1, 1992.

p. 377 institutions currently doing pieces of this job: To cite only a few examples: The Center for the Study of Social Policy, which has provided assistance to community change efforts throughout the country, has called for a new kind of intermediary, because "future initiatives need to be able to learn about what interventions are most likely to achieve agreed upon goals, need to know more about how to mobilize diverse community interests and get them to work together, about the technical aspects of program implementation and financing strategies, and about how to change institutions." Center for the Study of Social Policy, May 1995. The Center for Community Change helps low-income people "develop the power and capacity needed to influence the policies and institutions that affect them and their communities." Center for Community Change. "Prepared for the Future: 1995 Annual Report." Washington, DC: Author, 1996. The Chapin Hall Center for Children at the University of Chicago "develops and tests new ideas, generates and analyzes information, and examines policies, programs, and practices that affect children, families, and communities." Chapin Hall Center for Children. "The Power of Knowing." Chicago, 1996. The Roundtable on Comprehensive Community Initiatives for Children and Families, affiliated with the Aspen Institute, was created for the purpose of sharing the lessons emerging from current CCIs, but does not have a mandate to use its systematic learning to expand the field.

p. 378 Another national intermediary: An Urban Institute study of community development corporations reported in June 1993 that "the rise of the national, state, and local intermediaries is the single most important story of the nonprofit development sector in the 1980s." The study cited the mobilization of capital, the provision of technical assistance, and the legitimation of CDCs as the three most important functions performed by the intermediaries.

Selected Bibliography

Aber, J. Lawrence, Lisa J. Berlin, Jeanne Brooks-Gunn, and John M. Love. "Enhancing Comprehensive Community Initiatives: A Social Science Model of Early Childhood Development Within the Community." July 1996. Prepared for the Roundtable on Comprehensive Community Initiatives for Children and Families, Aspen Institute.

Allison, Graham T. "Public and Private Management: Are They Fundamentally Alike in All Unimportant Aspects?" In Stillman, Richard J. III, ed., *Public Administration: Concepts and Cases,* 5th ed. Boston: Houghton Mifflin, 1992.

Altshuler, Alan A. "Bureaucratic Innovation, Democratic Accountability, and Political Incentives." In Altshuler, Alan A. and Robert D. Behn, eds., *Innovation in American Government.* In press.

Anderson, Elijah. "The Code of the Streets." *The Atlantic Monthly,* May 1994.

Bachrach, Christine A., Stephanie J. Ventura, Susan F. Newcomer, and William D. Mosher. "What Is Happening to Out-of-Wedlock Childbearing?" Paper presented at the American Enterprise Institute and Henry J. Kaiser Family Foundation Seminar Series on Sexuality and American Social Policy, Washington, DC, March 20, 1995.

Bane, Mary Jo. "Welfare As We Might Know It." *The American Prospect,* 30 (January–February 1997) 47–53.

Barzelay, Michael. *Breaking Through Bureaucracy: A New Vision for Managing in Government.* Berkeley, CA: University of California, 1992.

Behrman, R. E., ed. "The Future of Children: School-Linked Services." Los Altos, CA: Packard Foundation, The Center for the Future of Children, 2 (1), Spring 1992.

Berryman, Sue E. and Thomas R. Bailey. *The Double Helix of Education & the Economy.* New York: Columbia Teachers College, Institute of Education and the Economy, 1992.

Besharov, Douglas J. and Lisa A. Laumann. "Child Abuse Reporting." *Social Science and Modern Society,* Vol. 33, No. 4, May/June 1996.

Bluestone, Barry and Teresa Ghilarducci. "Rewarding Work: Feasible Antipoverty Policy." *The American Prospect,* May–June 1996.

Bobo, Lawrence and Ryan A. Smith. "Antipoverty Policy, Affirmative Action, and Racial Attitudes." In Danziger, Sheldon H., Gary D. Sandefur, and Daniel H. Weinberg, *Confronting Poverty: Prescriptions for Change.* New York: Harvard University Press, 1994.

Boyer, Debra and David Fine. "Sexual Abuse as a Factor in Adolescent Pregnancy and Child Maltreatment." *Family Planning Perspectives,* Vol. 24, No. 1, January/February 1992.

Boyer, Ernest L. *Ready to Learn: A Mandate for the Nation.* Princeton: Carnegie Foundation for the Advancement of Teaching, 1991.

Brooks-Gunn, J., G. J. Duncan, P. K. Klebanov, and N. Sealand. "Do Neighborhoods Influence Child and Adolescent Behavior?" *American Journal of Sociology* (1993), 99 (2): 353–395.

Brown, Prudence. "The Role of the Evaluator in Comprehensive Community Initiatives." In Connell, James P., Anne C. Kubish, Lisbeth B. Schorr, and Carol Weiss, *New Approaches to Evaluating Community Initiatives: Concepts, Methods, and Contexts.* Washington, DC: Aspen Institute, 1995.

Brown, Sarah S. and Leon Eisenberg, eds. *The Best Intentions: Unintended Pregnancy and the Well-Being of Children and Families.* Washington, DC: National Academy Press, 1995.

Bruner, C. and J. M. Perrin. *More Than Health Insurance: State Initiatives to Improve Maternal and Child Health.* New York: Milbank Memorial Fund, 1995.

Bruner, Charles, Stephen Scott, and Martha Steketee. "Allegheny County Study: Potential Returns on Investment from a Comprehensive Family Center Approach in High-Risk Neighborhoods." Background paper. Des Moines, IA: Child and Family Policy Center, January 1996.

Bryk, Anthony S. and M. E. Driscoll. *The High School as Community: Contextual Influences, and Consequences for Students and Teachers.* Madison: University of Wisconsin-Madison, National Center on Effective Secondary Schools, 1988.

Bryk, Anthony S., Valerie E. Hill, and Peter B. Holland. *Catholic Schools and the Common Good.* Cambridge, MA: Harvard University Press, 1993.

Canada, Geoffrey. *fist stick knife gun: A Personal History of Violence in America.* Boston: Beacon Press, 1995.

Caplan, Nathan, Marcella H. Choy, and John K. Whitmore. "Indochinese Refugee Families and Academic Achievement." *Scientific American,* 266(2)(February 1992): 36–42.

Carnegie Corporation of New York. "Years of Promise: A Comprehensive Learning Strategy for America's Children." New York: Carnegie Corporation, 1996.

———. "Starting Points: Meeting the Needs of Our Youngest Children." New York: Carnegie Corporation, 1994.

Carter, Stephen. *The Culture of Disbelief: How American Law and Politics Trivialize Religious Devotion.* New York: Anchor Books, 1993.

Case, Anne C. and Lawrence F. Katz. "The Company You Keep: The Effects of Family and Neighborhood on Disadvantaged Youths." Cambridge, MA: National Bureau of Economic Research, May 1991.

Annie E. Casey Foundation. "Kids Count Data Book 1996." Baltimore: The Annie E. Casey Foundation, 1996.

————. "The Path of Most Resistance. Reflections on Lessons Learned from New Futures." Baltimore: The Annie E. Casey Foundation, August 1995.

Center for Research on Effective Schooling for Disadvantaged Students. "Success for All Improves Reading Performance in Sites Across Nation." Johns Hopkins University: CDS, March 1994.

Center for the Study of Social Policy. "Building New Futures for At-Risk Youth." Washington, DC: CSSP, May 1995.

Center for the Study of Social Policy and Children's Defense Fund. "Making Strategic Use of the Family Preservation and Support Services Program: A Guide for Planning." Washington, DC: October 1994.

Chen, Huey-Tsyh. *Theory-Driven Evaluations*. Newbury Park, CA: Sage Publications, 1990.

Chen, Huey-Tsyh and Peter H. Rossi. *Using Theory to Improve Program and Policy Evaluations*. New York: Greenwood Press, 1992.

Children's Aid Society. "Building a Community School: A Revolutionary Design in Public Education. New York: Children's Aid Society, 1993.

Children's Defense Fund. "The State of America's Children Yearbook 1996." Washington, DC: Children's Defense Fund, 1996.

————. "Young Families: Suffering an Economic Freefall." Washington, DC: Children's Defense Fund, September 1994.

Chubb, J. E. and T. M. Moe. *Politics, Markets, and America's Schools*. Washington, DC: Brookings Institution, 1990.

Comer, James, Norris Haynes, Edward T. Joyner, and Michael Ben-Avie, eds. *Rallying the Whole Village: The Comer Process of Reforming Education*. New York: Teachers College Press, 1966.

Committee for Economic Development. "Rebuilding Inner-City Communities: A New Approach to the Nation's Urban Crisis." Washington, DC: Committee for Economic Development, nd.

————. Research and Policy Committee. "Putting Learning First: Governing and Managing the Schools for High Achievement." New York: Committee for Economic Development, 1994.

Connell, James P. and Anne C. Kubisch. "Applying a Theory of Change Approach to the Evaluation of Comprehensive Community Initiatives: Progress, Prospects and Problems." In *New Approaches to Evaluating Community Initiatives,* Vol. II. New York: Roundtable on Comprehensive Community Initiatives, forthcoming.

Connell, James P., J. Lawrence Aber, and Gary Walker. "How Do Urban Communities Affect Youth? Using Social Science to Inform the Design and Evaluation of Comprehensive Community Initiatives." In Connell, et al, 1995.

Connell, James P., Anne C. Kubisch, Lisbeth B. Schorr, and Carol Weiss. *New Approaches to Evaluating Community Initiatives: Concepts, Methods, and Contexts*. Washington, DC: The Aspen Institute, 1995.

Conservation Company and Public/Private Ventures. "Building from Strength: Replication as a Strategy for Expanding Social Programs That Work." Philadelphia: Replication and Program Services, 1994.

Consortium for Policy Research in Education. "Public Policy and School Reform: A Research Summary." CPRE Research Report Series Report #36, 1996.

Coulton, Claudia C. "Effects of Neighborhoods on Families and Children: Implications for Services." In Kahn, Alfred J. and Sheila B. Kamerman, *Children & Their*

Families in Big Cities: Strategies for Service Reform. New York: Columbia University School of Social Work, 1996.

Coulton, Claudia, Jill E. Korbin, and Marilyn Su. "Measuring Neighborhood Context for Young Children in an Urban Area." Cleveland, OH: Case Western Reserve, June 1995.

Crane, J. "The Epidemic Theory of Ghettos and Neighborhood Effects on Dropping Out and Teenage Childbearing." *American Journal of Sociology,* 96 (5): 1226–1259. 1991.

Cutler, Ira. "The Role of Finance Reform in Comprehensive Service Initiatives." Washington, DC: The Finance Project, 1994.

Danziger, Sandra K. and Sheldon Danziger. "Will Welfare Recipients Find Work When Welfare Ends?" Washington, DC: Urban Institute Welfare Reform Briefs Number 12, June 1995.

Danziger, Sheldon H. and Peter Gottschalk. *America Unequal.* Cambridge, MA: Harvard University Press, 1995.

Danziger, Sheldon H., Gary D. Sandefur, and Daniel Weinberg. *Confronting Poverty: Prescriptions for Change.* New York: Harvard University Press, 1994.

Darman, Richard. "Riverboat Gambling with Government." *New York Times Magazine,* 1 December 1996.

Daro, Deborah. "Child Maltreatment Research: Implications for Program Design." In *Child Abuse, Child Development and Social Policy,* Dante Cicchetti and Sheree L. Toth, eds. Norwood, NJ: Ablex Publishing Company, 1993.

Davies, Don. "The 10th School: Where School-Family-Partnerships Flourish." *Education Week,* 10 July 1996.

Delgado-Gaitan, Concha. "School Matters in the Mexican-American Home: Socializing Children to Education." *American Educational Research Journal,* 29 (Fall): 495–513.

DiIulio, John J., Jr. *Deregulating the Public Service: Can Government Be Improved?* Washington, DC: Brookings Institution, 1994.

DiIulio, John J., Jr., Gerald Garvey, and Donald F. Kettl. *Improving Government Performance: An Owner's Manual.* Washington, DC: Brookings Institution, 1993.

Dionne, E. J. *They Only Look Dead: Why Progressives Will Dominate the Next Political Era.* New York: Simon & Schuster, 1996.

———. *Why Americans Hate Politics.* New York: Simon & Schuster, 1991.

Dodson, Lisa. "We Could Be Your Daughters: Girls, Sexuality and Pregnancy in Low-Income America." Cambridge, MA: Radcliffe Public Policy Institute, 1996.

Drew, Elizabeth. *Showdown.* New York: Simon & Schuster, 1996.

Drucker, Peter F. "Really Reinventing Government." *Atlantic Monthly:* February 1995.

———. *Managing the Non-Profit Organization: Principles and Practices.* New York: HarperCollins, 1990.

Dryfoos, Joy. *Full-Service Schools.* San Francisco: Jossey Bass, 1994.

Dubnick, Melvin J. "A Coup Against King Bureaucracy?" In DiIulio, John J., Jr., *Deregulating the Public Service: Can Government Be Improved?* Washington, DC: Brookings Institution, 1994.

Duncan, G. J., J. Brooks-Gunn, and P. K. Klebanov. "Economic Deprivation and Early-Childhood Development." *Child Development,* 65(2): 296–318. 1994.

Dunkle, Margaret. "A Bottom-Up Look at Welfare Reform: What Happens When

Policymakers Apply for Assistance from the Programs They Created?" *Education Week*, 15(13)(November 29, 1995).

Dyer, Barbara R. "The Oregon Option: Early Lessons from a Performance Partnership Contributing to an Emerging Practice of Results-Driven Accountability." Alliance for Redesigning Government, August 1996.

Earls, Felton and Maya Carlson. "Promoting Human Capability as an Alternative to Early Crime Prevention." In *Integrating Crime Prevention Strategies: Propensity and Opportunity*, P-OH, Wikstrom, R. V. Clarke, and J. McCord. Stockholm, Sweden: National Council on Crime Prevention. 141–168. 1995.

Edelman, Peter. "The Worst Thing Bill Clinton Has Done." *The Atlantic Monthly*, March 1997.

Edelman, Peter B. and Beryl A. Radin. "Serving Children and Families Effectively: How the Past Can Help Chart the Future." Washington, DC: Education and Human Services Consortium, 1991.

Elmore, Richard F. "Getting to Scale with Good Educational Practice." Cambridge, MA: *Harvard Education Review*, Spring 96.

———. "Backward Mapping: Implementation Research and Policy Decisions." *Political Science Quarterly*, 95(4)(Winter 1979–80.)

Elmore, Richard F., Penelope L. Peterson, and Sarah J. McCarthey. *Restructuring in the Classroom: Teaching, Learning, and School Organization*. San Francisco: Jossey-Bass, 1996.

Ellwood, David T. "Welfare Reform As I Knew It." *The American Prospect*, May–June 1996.

———. *Poor Support: Poverty in the American Family*. New York: Basic Books, 1988.

Epstein, Joyce L. "School and Family Partnerships." In *Encyclopedia of Educational Research*, Sixth Edition, M. Alkin, ed. New York: Macmillan, 1992.

Evans, David. "Losing Battle." *National Review*, June 30, 1986.

Fallows, James. "Markets Can't Do Everything." *The Washington Monthly*, January/February 1996.

———. *Breaking the News: How the Media Undermine American Democracy*. New York: Pantheon, 1996.

Families and Work Institute. "The Study of Children in Family Child Care and Relative Care." New York: Families and Work Institute, 1994.

Farkas, Steve and Jean Johnson. "Given the Circumstances: Teachers Talk About Public Education Today." New York: Public Agenda, 1996.

Farrow, Frank. "Child Protection: Building Community Partnerships." Prepared for the Harvard Kennedy School of Government Executive Session on New Paradigms for Child Protection, 1997.

———. "System Change at the Neighborhood Level: Creating Better Futures for Children, Youth, and Families." Washington, DC: Center for the Study of Social Policy, February 1996.

Ferguson, Ronald F. "How Professionals in Community-Based Programs Perceive and Respond to the Needs of Black Male Youth." In Mincy, Ronald B., ed., *Nurturing Young Black Males*. Washington, DC: Urban Institute Press, 1994.

Ferguson, Ronald F. and Philip L. Clay. *YouthBuild in Developmental Perspective*, Cambridge: MIT Department of Urban Studies and Planning, 1996.

Ferguson, Ronald F. and Mary S. Jackson. "Black Male Youth and Drugs: How Racial Prejudice, Parents and Peers Affect Vulnerability." Cambridge, MA: Harvard University, Malcolm Wiener Center for Social Policy, John F. Kennedy School of Government, September 1992.

Foundation for Child Development. Sheila Smith, volume ed. Irving E. Sigel, series ed. *Two Generation Programs for Families in Poverty: A New Intervention Strategy*. Norwood, NJ: Ablex Publishing Corp., 1995.

Frank, Robert H. and Philip J. Cook. *The Winner-Take-All Society*. New York: The Free Press, 1995.

Furano, Kathryn, Linda Z. Jucovy, David P. Racine, and Thomas J. Smith. "The Essential Connection: Using Evaluation to Identify Programs Worth Replicating." Philadelphia, PA: Replication and Program Strategies, Fall 1995.

Furstenberg, Frank F. and Mary Elizabeth Hughes. "The Influence of Neighborhoods on Children's Development: A Theoretical Perspective and a Research Agenda." Paper presented at conference on Indicators of Children's Well-Being, Bethesda, MD, November 17–18, 1994.

Furstenberg, Frank F., Jr. "How Families Manage Risk and Opportunity in Dangerous Neighborhoods." In Wilson, William Julius, ed., *Sociology and the Public Agenda*. Newbury Park, CA: Sage Publications, 1993.

Gardner, Howard. "Limited Visions, Limited Means: Two Obstacles to Meaningful Education Reform." *Daedalus,* Vol. 124, No. 4, Fall 1995, 101–105.

Gardner, Sid. "Reform Options for the Intergovernmental Funding System: Decategorization Policy Issues." Washington, DC: The Finance Project, 1994.

Garfinkel, Irwin and Sara McLanahan. "Single-Mother Families, Economic Insecurity, and Government Policy." In Danziger, Sheldon H., Gary D. Sandefur, and Daniel Weinberg, *Confronting Poverty: Prescriptions for Change*. New York: Harvard University Press, 1994.

Gershenson, Harold P., Judith S. Musick, Holly S. Ruch-Ross, Vicki Magee, Katherine Kamiya Rubino, and Deborah Rosenberg. "The Prevalence of Coercive Sexual Experience Among Teenage Mothers." *Journal of Interpersonal Violence,* 4(2)(June 1989).

Golden, Olivia. *Poor Children and Welfare Reform*. Westport, CT: Auburn House, 1992.

Goldsmith, Stephen. "Revamping Welfare, Rebuilding Lives." *New York Times* Op-Ed, 4 August 1996.

Gomby, Deanna S. and Patricia H. Shiono. "Estimating the Number of Substance-Exposed Infants." *The Future of Children,* 1(1)(Spring 1991): 17–25.

Gore, Al. *Common Sense Government Works Better and Costs Less*. New York: Random House, 1995.

Gormley, William T., Jr. "Privatization Revisited." Paper prepared for the Twentieth Century Fund Conference on Privatization, New York, NY, May 4, 1993.

Government Accounting Office. "At-Risk and Delinquent Youth: Multiple Federal Programs Raise Efficiency Questions." GAO/HEHS-96-34. Washington, DC: Government Accounting Office, March 1996.

———. "Welfare Dependency: Coordinated Community Efforts Can Better Serve Young At-Risk Girls." Washington, DC: Government Accounting Office, May 1995.

———. "Community Development: Comprehensive Approaches Address Multiple Needs but Are Challenging to Implement." GAO/DRCED/HEHS-96-69. Washington, DC: GAO, February 1995.

——. "Early Childhood Centers: Services to Prepare Children for School Often Limited." GAO/HEHS-95-21. Washington, DC: GAO, 1995.

Graham, Patricia Albjerg. "What America Has Expected of Its Schools over the Past Century." In Ravitch, Diane and M. A. Vinovskis, eds., *Learning from the Past: What History Teaches Us About School Reform.* Baltimore, Md: The Johns Hopkins University Press, 1995.

The Alan Guttmacher Institute. "Sex and America's Teenagers." New York: 1994.

Hagedorn, John M. *Forsaking Our Children: Bureaucracy and Reform in the Child Welfare System.* Chicago: Lake View Press, 1995.

Halpern, Robert. *Rebuilding the Inner City: A History of Neighborhood Initiatives to Address Poverty in the United States.* New York: Columbia University Press, 1995.

——. "Supportive Services for Families in Poverty: Dilemmas of Reform." *Social Service Review,* September 1991, 65(3): 343–364.

Handler, Joel. *Down from Bureaucracy: Ambiguities in Privatization and Empowerment.* Princeton: Princeton University Press, 1996.

——. *The Conditions of Discretion: Autonomy, Community, Bureaucracy.* New York: Russell Sage, 1986.

Harris, Irving B. *Children in Jeopardy: Can We Break the Cycle of Poverty?* New Haven: Yale University Press, 1996.

Harvey, Philip, Theodore R. Marmor, and Jerry L. Mashaw. "Gingrich's Time Bomb." *The American Prospect,* Spring 1995: 44–52.

Haveman, Robert. "From Welfare to Work: Problems and Pitfalls." University of Wisconsin-Madison, Institute for Research on Poverty. *FOCUS,* 18(1). Special Issue 1996.

Haveman, Robert and Barbara Wolfe. *Succeeding Generations: The Effects of Investments in Children.* New York: Russell Sage Foundation, 1994.

Heclo, Hugh. "Poverty Politics." In Danziger, Sheldon H., Gary D. Sandefur, and Daniel Weinberg. *Confronting Poverty: Prescriptions for Change.* New York: Harvard University Press, 1994.

Herr, Toby. "Balancing Deeper and Wider." Rennselaerville Institute: *Innovating,* 2(3). Spring 1992.

Herr, Toby and Robert Halpern. "Changing What Counts: Re-Thinking the Journey Out of Welfare." Evanston, IL: Northwestern University, April 1991.

Herr, Toby, Robert Halpern, and Suzanne L. Wagner. "Something Old, Something New: A Case Study of the Post-Employment Services Demonstration in Oregon." Chicago: Erikson Institute, November 1995.

Herr, Toby, Robert Halpern, and Ria Majeske. "Bridging the Worlds of Head Start and Welfare-to-Work: Building a Two-Generation Self-Sufficiency Program from the Ground Up." Chicago: Project Match, 1993.

Hershey, Alan M. and LaDonna Pavetti. "Turning Job Finders into Job Keepers: The Challenge of Sustaining Employment." In *The Future of Children: From Welfare to Work.* Los Altos, CA: Packard Foundation, Spring 1997.

Hess, Peg, Brenda McGowan, and Carol H. Meyer. "Practitioners' Perspective on Family and Child Services." In Kahn, Alfred J. and Sheila B. Kamerman, *Children & Their Families in Big Cities: Strategies for Service Reform.* New York: Columbia School of Social Work, 1996.

Hill, Paul and Josephine Bonan. "Decentralization and Accountability in Public Education." Santa Monica: Rand Corporation, 1991.

Hill, Paul, Gaile E. Foster, and Tamar Gendler. "High Schools with Character." Santa Monica: Rand Corporation, August 1990.

Hirsch, E. D., Jr. *The Schools We Need.* New York: Doubleday, 1996.

Hollister, Robinson G. and Jennifer Hill. "Problems in the Evaluation of Community-Wide Initiatives." In Connell, et al, 1995.

Howard, Jeff. "You Can't Get There from Here: The Need for a New Logic in Education Reform." *Daedalus,* 124(4)(Fall 1995): 85–92.

Howard, Philip K. *The Death of Common Sense: How Law Is Suffocating America.* New York: Random House, 1994.

Hughes, Dana C., Neal Halfon, Claire D. Brindis, and Paul W. Newacheck. "Improving Children's Access to Health Care: The Role of Decategorization." The Robert Wood Johnson Foundation Child Health Initiative, February 8, 1996.

Immerwahr, John and Jean Johnson. "Americans' Views on Standards: An Assessment by Public Agenda." New York: Public Agenda, 1996.

Jarrett, R. "Bringing Families Back In: Neighborhoods' Effects on Child Development." In Brooks-Gunn, J., G. J. Duncan, and J. L. Aber, eds., *Neighborhood Poverty: Context and Consequences for Children: Conceptual, Methodological, and Policy Approaches to Studying Neighborhoods,* Vol. 2. New York: Russell Sage Foundation, in press.

Jehl, J. and M. Kirst. "Getting Ready to Provide School-Linked Services: What Schools Must Do." In R. E. Behrman, ed., *The Future of Children,* 2(1): 95–106. Los Altos, CA: Packard Foundation, 1992.

Jencks, Christopher. *Rethinking Social Policy: Race, Poverty, and the Underclass.* New York: HarperCollins, 1992.

Jencks, Christopher and Kathryn Edin. "Do Poor Women Have a Right to Bear Children?" *The American Prospect,* Winter 1995.

Jencks, Christopher and Susan Mayer. "The Social Consequences of Growing Up in a Poor Neighborhood." In Lynn, L. E. and M. G. H. McGeary, eds., *Inner-City Poverty in the United States.* Washington, DC: National Academy Press, 1990.

Johnson, Jean and John Immerwahr. "First Things First: What Americans Expect from the Public Schools." New York: Public Agenda, 1994.

Kagan, Sharon L. and N. E. Cohen. "Solving the Quality Problem: A Vision for the Early Child Care and Education System. A Final Report of the Quality 2000 Initiative." New Haven: Yale University Press, in press.

Kagan, Sharon L. and Bernice Weissbourd. "Toward a New Normative System of Family Support." In Kagan, Sharon L. and Bernice Weissbourd. *Putting Families First: America's Family Support Movement and the Challenge of Change.* San Francisco: Jossey-Bass, 1994.

Kahn, Alfred J. and Sheila B. Kamerman. *Children & Their Families in Big Cities: Strategies for Service Reform.* New York: Columbia University, 1996.

Kamerman, Sheila B. and Alfred J. Kahn, eds. "Child Care in the Context of Welfare Reform." New York: Columbia University, 1997.

———. *Planning a State Welfare Strategy Under Waivers of Block Grants.* New York: Columbia University, 1996.

———. "Social Services for Children, Youth and Families in the United States." Special Issue of *Children and Youth Services Review,* 12. 1990.

Kasarda, J. "Inner-City Concentrated Poverty and Neighborhood Distress: 1970 to 1990." *Housing Policy Debate,* 4: 253–302. 1993.

Katz, Michael B. *The Undeserving Poor: From the War on Poverty to the War on Welfare.* New York: Pantheon, 1989.

Kaus, Mickey. *The End of Equality.* New York: Basic Books, 1992.

Kelman, Steven. "The Renewal of the Public Sector." *The American Prospect,* Summer 1990.

———. *Making Public Policy: A Hopeful View of American Government.* New York: Basic Books, 1987.

Kemple, James J. and JoAnn Leah Roack. "Career Academies: Early Implementation Lessons from a 10-Site Evaluation." New York: MDRC, July 1996.

Kettl, Donald F. "The Myths, Realities, and Challenges of Privatization." In Thompson, Frank J., ed., *Revitalizing State and Local Public Service: Strengthening Performance, Accountability, and Citizen Confidence.* San Francisco: Jossey-Bass, 1993.

Kinney, Jill, Kathy Strand, Marge Hagerup, and Charles Bruner. "Beyond the Buzzwords: Key Principles in Effective Frontline Practice." Falls Church, VA: NCSI, 1994.

Klebanov, P. K., J. Brooks-Gunn, and G. J. Duncan. "Does Neighborhood and Family Poverty Affect the Mothers' Parenting, Mental Health, and Social Support?" *Journal of Marriage and the Family,* 56(2): 441–455. 1994.

Klebanov, P. K., J. Brooks-Gunn, L. Chase-Lansdale, and R. Gordon. "The Intersection of the Neighborhood and Home Environment and Its Influence on Young Children." In Brooks-Gunn, J., G. Duncan, and J. L. Aber, eds., *Neighborhood Poverty: Context and Consequences for Children. Six Studies of Children in Families and Neighborhoods,* Vol. 1. New York: Russell Sage Foundation Press, in press.

Knapp, Michael S. "How Shall We Study Comprehensive, Collaborative Services for Children and Families?" *Educational Researcher,* 24(4): 5–16. May 1995.

Kubisch, Anne C. "Comprehensive Community Initiatives: Lessons in Neighborhood Transformation." *Shelterforce,* January/February 1996.

Kubisch, Anne C., P. Brown, R. Chaskin, J. Hirota, M. Joseph, H. Richman, and M. Roberts. "Voices from the Field: Learning from Comprehensive Community Initiatives." Washington, DC: The Aspen Institute, in press.

Kuttner, Robert. "After Solidarity." *The American Prospect,* No. 26, May–June 1996.

Lardner, James. "The New Blue Line." *New York Times Magazine,* 9 February 1997.

Lawrence-Lightfoot, Sara. *The Good High School: Portraits of Character and Culture.* New York: Basic Books, 1983.

———. *Worlds Apart.* New York: Basic Books, 1978.

Lee, Valerie E., Anthony S. Bryk, and J. B. Smith. "High School Organization and Its Effects on Teachers and Students: An Interpretive Summary of the Research." In W. H. Clune and J. F. Witte, eds., *Choice and Control in American Education,* Vol. 1. Philadelphia: Falmer, 1990.

Lemann, Nicholas. "The Myth of Community Development." *New York Times Magazine,* 9 January 1994.

———. *The Promised Land.* New York: Random House, 1991.

Lerman, Robert. "Increasing the Employment and Earnings of Welfare Recipients." In Sawhill, Isabel V., ed., "Welfare Reform: An Analysis of the Issues." Washington, DC: The Urban Institute, 1995.

Lerner, Steve. "The Geography of Foster Care: Keeping the Children in the Neighborhood." New York: Foundation for Child Development, February 1990.

Levin, Henry M. *Accelerating Elementary Education for Disadvantaged Students. School Success for Children at Risk*. Orlando, FL: Harcourt Brace Jovanovich, 1988.

———. "Education as a Public and Private Good." *Journal of Policy Analysis and Management*, 6(4): 628–641. 1987.

Levitan, Sar A. "Evaluation of Federal Social Programs: An Uncertain Impact." Washington, DC: Center for Social Policy Studies, June 1992.

Light, Paul. "Creating Innovating Organizations in the Public Sector: A Summary of Findings from the Surviving Innovation Project." Paper prepared for delivery at the annual meeting of the Association of Policy Analysis and Management, Pittsburgh, October 31–November 2, 1997.

Lindsey, Duncan. *The Welfare of Children*. New York: Oxford University Press, 1995.

Lipsky, Michael and Steven Rathgeb Smith. "Nonprofit Organizations, Government, and the Welfare State." *Political Science Quarterly*, 104(4)(1989–1990): 625–648.

Love, John M., Lawrence Aber, and Jeanne Brooks-Gunn. "Strategies for Assessing Community Progress Toward Achieving the First National Educational Goal." Princeton: Mathematica Policy Research, October 31, 1994.

Luker, Kristin. *Dubious Conceptions: The Politics of Teenage Pregnancy*. Cambridge, MA: Harvard University Press, 1996.

Macy, Christina H. "The Oregon Option: A Federal-State-Local Partnership for Better Results." Baltimore, MD: The Annie E. Casey Foundation, nd.

Madden, Nancy A., Robert E. Slavin, Nancy L. Karweit, and Barbara J. Livermon. "Restructuring the Urban Elementary School." *Educational Leadership*, February 1989.

Madden, Nancy A., Robert E. Slavin, Nancy L. Karweit, Barbara J. Livermon, and L. Dolan. "Success for All: Effects on Student Achievement, Retentions, and Special Education Referrals." Baltimore, MD: Johns Hopkins University, Center for Research on Elementary and Middle Schools, 1988.

Manpower Demonstration Research Corporation. "Lives of Promise, Lives of Pain: Young Mothers After New Chance." New York: MDRC, 1994.

Marshall, Ray and Marc Tucker. *Thinking for a Living*. New York: Basic Books, 1992.

Massey, Douglas. "American Apartheid: Segregation and the Making of the Underclass." *American Journal of Sociology*, 96(2): 329–357.

———. "The Age of Extremes: Concentrated Affluence and Poverty in the 21st Century." Presidential Address, Population Association of America, New Orleans, Louisiana, May 10, 1996.

McGowan, Brenda G., with Alfred J. Kahn and Sheila B. Kamerman. *Social Services for Children, Youth and Families: The New York City Study*. New York: Columbia University School of Social Work, June 1990.

McKnight, John. *The Careless Society: Community and Its Counterfeits*. New York: Basic Books, 1995.

McLanahan, Sara and G. Sandefur. *Growing Up with a Single Parent*. Cambridge, MA: Harvard University Press, 1994.

McLaughlin, Milbrey and Joan E. Talbert. "Contexts That Matter for Teaching and

Learning." Palo Alto, CA: Center for Research on the Context of Secondary School Teaching, 1993.

McLoyd, V. C. "The Impact of Economic Hardship on Black Families and Children: Psychological Distress, Parenting, and Socioemotional Development." *Child Development,* 61(1990): 311–346.

Medoff, Peter and Holly Sklar. *Streets of Hope: The Fall and Rise of an Urban Neighborhood.* Boston: South End Press, 1994.

Meier, Deborah. *The Power of Their Ideas: Lessons for America from a Small School in Harlem.* Boston: Beacon Press, 1995.

Melaville, A., M. Blank, and G. Asayesh. "Together We Can: A Guide for Crafting a Profamily System of Education and Human Services." Washington, DC: US Department of Education and US Department of Health and Human Services, 1993.

Mincy, Ronald B. *Nurturing Young Black Males.* Washington, DC: Urban Institute Press, 1994.

———. "The Underclass: Concept, Controversy, and Evidence." In Danziger, Sheldon H., Gary D. Sandefur and Daniel Weinberg, *Confronting Poverty: Prescriptions for Change.* New York: Harvard University Press, 1994.

Minow, Martha. "Learning from Experience: The Impact of Research About Family Support Programs on Public Policy." *University of Pennsylvania Law Review,* 143(1)(November 1994).

Moffitt, Robert A. "Evaluating the New State Welfare Reforms." Madison, WI: Institute for Research on Poverty, 1996.

Moore, Kristin and Sandra Hofferth. "Factors Affecting Early Family Formation: A Path Model." *Population and Environment,* 3(1)(1980): 73–98.

Moore, Kristin, Brent C. Miller, Barbara W. Sugland, Donna Ruane Morrison, Dana A. Glei, and Connie Blumenthal. "Beginning Too Soon: Adolescent Sexual Behavior, Pregnancy, and Parenthood." Washington, DC: Child Trends, 1995.

Morrill, William A. "Getting Beyond the Micro Gee Whiz: Can Innovative Service Change the Service System?" In Kahn, Alfred J. and Sheila B. Kamerman, *Children & Their Families in Big Cities. Strategies for Service Reform.* New York: Columbia University, 1996.

Morrow, Kristine V. and Melanie B. Styles. "Building Relationships with Youth in Program Settings. A Study of Big Brothers/Big Sisters." Philadelphia: Public/Private Ventures, May 1995.

Moss, Philip and Chris Tilly. "Why Black Men Are Doing Worse in the Labor Market." New York: Social Science Research Council, 1992.

Moynihan, Daniel P. *Miles to Go: A Personal History of Social Policy.* Cambridge: Harvard University Press, 1996.

———. "Congress Builds a Coffin." *Congressional Record,* December 12, 1995.

Murnane, Richard J. and Frank Levy. "Why Money Matters Sometimes: A Two-Part Management Lesson from East Austin, Texas." *Education Week,* September 11, 1996.

———. *Teaching the New Basic Skills.* New York: Free Press, 1996.

Murray, Charles. "The Legacy of the 60s." *Commentary,* July 1992.

Nathan, Richard. "Urban Revitalization—From the Ground Up: A Proposal for a National Community." Rockefeller Institute of Government. December 1, 1992.

National Center on Education and the Economy. *America's Choice: High Skills or Low Wages!* Rochester, NY: NCEE, June 1990.

National Commission on Children. "Beyond Rhetoric: A New American Agenda for Children and Families." Washington, DC: GPO, 1991.

National Performance Review. "From Red Tape to Results: Creating a Government That Works Better and Costs Less." Washington, DC: September 7, 1993.

National Research Council. "Violence in Urban America: Mobilizing a Response." Washington, DC: National Academy Press, 1994.

National Research Council, Panel on Research on Child Abuse and Neglect. *Understanding Child Abuse and Neglect.* Washington, DC: National Academy Press, 1993.

National Research Council, Panel on High Risk Youth. *Losing Generations: Adolescents in High-Risk Settings.* Washington, DC: National Academy Press, 1993.

Newacheck, Paul W., Dana C. Hughes, Claire Brindis, and Neal Halfon. "Decategorizing Health Services: Interim Findings from the Robert Wood Johnson Foundation's Child Health Initiative." The People-to-People Foundation; *Health Affairs,* Vol. 14, No. 3, 1995.

Newman, Fred M. and Gary G. Whelage. "Successful School Restructuring: A Report to the Public and Educators." Madison, WI: Center on Organization and Restructuring of Schools, 1995.

Nightingale, Demetra Smith and Pamela Holcomb. "Increasing Employment: Success of Alternative Strategies." In *The Future of Children: From Welfare to Work.* Los Altos, CA: Packard Foundation, 1997.

Nothdurft, William E. "Out from Under: Policy Lessons from a Quarter Century of Wars on Poverty." Washington, DC: The Council of State Policy and Planning Agencies, 1990.

O'Connor, Alice. "Federal Policy in Poor Communities: A Brief History." Paper prepared for the NCDPAN Fall 1996 Conference, November 1996.

——. "Evaluating Comprehensive Community Initiatives: A View from History." In Connell, et al, 1995.

Olasky, Marvin N. *The Tragedy of American Compassion.* Washington, DC: Regnery, 1992.

Oregon Progress Board. "Oregon Benchmarks: Standards for Measuring Statewide Progress and Institutional Performance." Salem, OR: Oregon Progress Board, December 1994.

Osborne, David and Ted Gaebler. *Reinventing Government: How the Entrepreneurial Spirit Is Transforming the Public Sector.* NY: Penguin, 1993.

David and Lucille Packard Foundation. "The Future of Children: Home Visiting." Los Altos, CA: Packard Foundation, Winter 1993.

——. "The Future of Children: School Linked Services." Los Altos, CA: Packard Foundation, 1992.

Patton, Michael Q., Margaret J. Bringewatt, Jeanne L. Campbell, Thomas A. Dewar, and Marsha Mueller. "The Aid to Families in Poverty Program: A Synthesis of Themes, Patterns and Lessons Learned." Minneapolis: The McKnight Foundation, April 1993.

Pavetti, LaDonna. "Who Is Affected by Time Limits?" Washington, DC: Urban Institute, Welfare Reform Briefs Number 7, May 1995.

Peters, Thomas J. and Robert H. Waterman. *In Search of Excellence: Lessons from America's Best-Run Companies.* New York: Harper and Row, 1982.

Peterson, George E. "A Block Grant Approach to Welfare Reform." In Sawhill,

Isabel V., "Welfare Reform: An Analysis of the Issues." Washington, DC: Urban Institute, 1995.

Public/Private Ventures. "Strengthening Social Infrastructure for Successful Teenage Development and Transition to Adulthood." Philadelphia, PA: Public/Private Ventures, April 1993.

Putnam, Robert D. "The Prosperous Community: Social Capital and Public Life." *The American Prospect,* Spring 1993.

Raphael, Jody. "Domestic Violence: Telling the Untold Welfare-to-Work Story." Chicago: Taylor Institute, 1995.

Rasel, Edith and Richard Rothstein, eds. *School Choice: Examining the Evidence.* Washington, DC: Economic Policy Institute, 1993.

Rauch, Jonathan. "Demosclerosis." *National Journal,* September 5, 1992.

Ravitch, Diane. *National Standards in American Education: A Citizen's Guide.* Washington, DC: Brookings Institution, 1995.

Reich, Robert. "Secession of the Successful." *New York Times Magazine,* 20 January 1991.

Replication and Program Services. "Lessons Learned to Date." Philadelphia: Replication and Program Services, nd.

Resnick, Lauren B. "From Aptitude to Effort: A New Foundation for Our Schools." *Daedalus,* 124(4)(Fall 1995): 55–62.

———. "Making High School Count." In Higginbotham, M., ed., *What Governors Need to Know About Education Reform.* Washington, DC: National Governors' Association, 85–98.

Rivlin, Alice M. *Reviving the American Dream: The Economy, the States, and the Federal Government.* Washington, DC: Brookings Institution, 1992.

———. *Systematic Thinking for Social Action.* Washington, DC: Brookings Institution, 1971.

Rogers, Mary M., Mary D. Peoples-Sheps, and James R. Sorenson. "Translating Research into MCH Service: Comparison of a Pilot Project and a Large-Scale Resource Mothers Program." *Public Health Reports,* September/October 1995, 110: 563–569.

Rosenfeld, Jona M., Donald A. Schon, and Israel Sykes. *Out from Under: Lessons from Projects for Inaptly Served Children and Families.* Jerusalem: JDC-Brookdale Institute of Gerontology and Human Development, March 1995.

Rossi, Peter H. "The Iron Law of Evaluation and Other Metallic Rules." In Miller, J. and M. Lewis, eds., *Research in Social Problems and Public Policy,* Vol. 4. Greenwich, CT: JAI Press, 1987.

Rothstein, Richard. "Where's the Money Gone? Changes in the Level and Composition of Education Spending." Washington, DC: Economic Policy Institute, 1995.

Salamon, Lester M. *Partners in Public Service: Government-Nonprofit Relations in the Modern Welfare State.* Baltimore, MD: Johns Hopkins University Press, 1995.

Sampson, Robert J. "What 'Community' Supplies." Paper presented at National Community Development Policy Analysis Network research conference. Washington, DC: Brookings Institution, November 15, 1996.

———. "The Community." In Wilson, James Q. and Joan Petersilia, eds., *Crime: Twenty-eight Leading Experts Look at the Most Pressing Problem of Our Time.* San Francisco: Institute for Contemporary Studies, 1995.

Sandel, Michael J. *Democracy's Discontent: America in Search of a Public Philosophy.* Cambridge: Harvard University Press, 1996.

Sander, Joelle. *Before Their Time: Four Generations of Teenage Mothers.* New York: Harcourt Brace Jovanovich, 1991.

Sawhill, Isabel V. "Opportunity in America." Washington, DC: Urban Institute, August 1995.

———. "Welfare Reform: An Analysis of the Issues." Washington, DC: Urban Institute, 1995.

Schön, Donald A. *Beyond the Stable State.* New York: Random House, 1971.

Schorr, Lisbeth B. *Within Our Reach: Breaking the Cycle of Disadvantage.* New York: Anchor Books, 1989.

Schorr, Lisbeth and Deborah Both. "Attributes of Effective Services for Young Children: A Brief Survey of Current Knowledge and Its Implications for Program and Policy Development." In *Effective Services for Young Children: Report of a Workshop.* Washington, DC: National Academy Press, 1991.

Schwartz, Ed. "Reviving Community Development." *The American Prospect,* Fall 1994, No. 19.

Shanker, Albert. "Education Reform: What's Not Being Said." In *Daedalus,* Fall 1995, Vol. 124, No. 4, *American Education: Still Separate, Still Unequal.*

Shenk, Joshua Wolf. "The Public Schools' Last Hurrah?" *The Washington Monthly,* March 1996: 8–17.

Sherman, Arloc. *Wasting America's Future: The Children's Defense Fund Report on the Costs of Child Poverty.* Boston, MA: Beacon Press, 1994.

Skolnick, Arlene and Stacey Rosencrantz. "The New Crusade for the Old Family." *The American Prospect,* Summer 1994.

Slavin, Robert E., Mancy A. Madden, Lawrence J. Dolan, and Barbara A. Wasik. "Success for All: A Summary of Research." *Journal of Education for Students Placed at Risk,* I(1): 41–76.

Smith, Hedrick. *Rethinking America: Innovative Strategies and Partnerships in Business and Education.* New York: Avon, 1996.

Smith, Ralph. "Help the Children, Fix the System." *Penn Law Journal,* 27(1)(February 1992): 21–23.

Sonenstein, Freya L. and Gregory Acs. "Teenage Childbearing: The Trends and Their Implications." Washington, DC: Urban Institute, Welfare Reform Briefs 13, June 1995.

Sonenstein, Freya, Leighton Ku, and Barbara Cohen. "Promising Prevention Programs for Children." Washington, DC: Urban Institute, March 1991.

Starr, Paul. "The Limits of Privatization." Washington, DC: Economic Policy Institute, nd.

———. "Liberalism After Socialism." *The American Prospect,* Fall 1991: 70–80.

Stephens, Sally A., Sally A. Leiderman, Wendy C. Wolf, and Patrick T. McCarthy. "Building Capacity for System Reform." Bala Cynwyd, PA: Center for Assessment and Policy Development, 1995.

Stewart, Charles, Mott Foundation. "Replication: Sowing Seeds of Hope." Flint, MI: Mott Foundation, 1990.

Stone, Calvin and Gary Wehlage. "Community Collaboration and the Restructuring of Schools." Center on Organization and Restructuring of Schools, University of Wisconsin.

Stone, Clarence, Kathryn Doherty, Cheryl Jones, and Timothy Ross. "Schools and

Disadvantaged Neighborhoods: The Community Development Challenge." Paper presented at National Community Development Policy Analysis Network research conference. Washington, DC: Brookings Institution, November 15, 1996.

Sullivan, Mercer L. "More Than Housing: How Community Development Corporations Go About Changing Lives and Neighborhoods." Revised. New York: Community Development Center, New School for Social Research, 1993.

———. "Patterns of AFDC Use in a Comparative Ethnographic Study of Young Fathers and Their Children in Three Low Income Neighborhoods." Paper prepared for the Office of the Assistant Secretary for Planning and Evaluation. Washington, DC: US Department of Health and Human Services, 1990.

Sviridoff, Mitchell. "The Seeds of Urban Renewal." *The Public Interest,* Winter 1994: 82–103.

Sviridoff, Mitchell and William Ryan. "Investing in Community: Lessons and Implications of the Comprehensive Community Revitalization Program." New York: Comprehensive Community Revitalization Program, January 1996.

Sylvester, Kathleen. "Second-Chance Homes." Washington, DC: Progressive Policy Institute, June 23, 1995.

Tobin, James. "Poverty in Relation to Macroeconomic Trends, Cycles, and Policies." In Danziger, Sheldon H., Gary D. Sandefur, and Daniel Weinberg. *Confronting Poverty: Prescriptions for Change.* New York: Harvard University Press, 1994.

Traub, James. *City on a Hill: Testing the American Dream at City College.* Reading, MA: Addison-Wesley, 1994.

Twentieth Century Fund. "Welfare Reform: The Basics. A Twentieth Century Fund Guide to the Issues." New York: Twentieth Century Fund, 1995.

Tyack, David. "Health and Social Services in Public Schools: Historical Perspectives." In *The Future of Children: School-Linked Services,* Los Altos, CA: Packard Foundation, 1992.

US Advisory Board on Child Abuse and Neglect. "A Nation's Shame: Fatal Child Abuse and Neglect in the US." Washington, DC: US Department of Health and Human Services, Office of Human Development Services, April 1995.

———. "Neighbors Helping Neighbors: A New National Strategy for the Protection of Children." Washington, DC: US Department of Health and Human Services, September 1993.

US Department of Education. "Putting the Pieces Together: Comprehensive School-Linked Strategies for Children and Families." Washington, DC: US Department of Education, May 1996.

US Department of Education, Office of the Undersecretary. "Urban and Suburban/Rural Special Strategies of Educating Disadvantaged Children." Prepared under contract by The Johns Hopkins University and Abt Associates. Washington, DC: US Department of Education, nd.

US Department of Health and Human Services. *Trends in the Well-Being of America's Children and Youth: 1996.* Washington, DC: Department of Health and Human Services, 1996.

———. *Report to Congress on Out-of-Wedlock Childbearing.* Washington, DC: Department of Health and Human Services, September 1995.

———. "The Statement of the Advisory Committee on Services for Families with Infants and Toddlers." Washington, DC: Department of Health and Human Services, September 1994.

————. "Creating a 21st Century Head Start: Final Report of the Advisory Committee on Head Start Quality and Expansion." Washington, DC: Department of Health and Human Services, December 1993.

————. "Services Integration: a Twenty-Year Retrospective." OEI-01-91-00580. Washington, DC: 1991.

Urban Institute. "Assessing the New Federalism." Washington, DC: Urban Institute Policy and Research Report, 1996.

————. "Lessons from Five State Welfare Reform Initiatives." Washington, DC: Urban Institute Policy and Research Report, 1995.

————. "Widening Wage Inequality." Washington, DC: Urban Institute Policy and Research Report, 1995.

Usher, Charles L. "Improving Evaluability Through Self-Evaluation." *Evaluation Practice*, 16(1)(1995): 59–68.

Ventura, Stephanie. "Births to Unmarried Mothers: United States, 1980–92." National Center for Health Statistics. *Vital Health Statistics*, 21(53) (1995): 10.

Ventura, Stephanie J., Joyce A. Martin, T. J. Mathews, and Sally C. Clarke. "Advance Report of Final Natality Statistics, 1994." Washington, DC: National Center for Health Statistics. June 24, 1996.

Videka-Sherman, Lynn. "New-Style Settlement Houses." Albany, NY: Rockefeller Institute Bulletin, 1992.

Wald, Michael S. "Termination of Parental Rights." In *When Drug Addicts Have Children,* Douglas J. Besharov, ed. Washington, DC: Child Welfare League of America, 1994.

Walsh, Joan. "Stories of Renewal: Community Building and the Future of Urban America." New York: The Rockefeller Foundation, January 1997.

Weisberg, Jacob. *In Defense of Government: The Fall and Rise of Public Trust.* New York: Scribner, 1996.

Weiss, Carol Hirschon. "Nothing as Practical as Good Theory: Exploring Theory-Based Evaluation for Comprehensive Community Initiatives for Children and Families." In Connell, et al, 1995.

————. "Evaluation Research: Methods of Assessing Program Effectiveness." Englewood Cliffs, NJ: Prentice-Hall, 1972.

Weissbourd, Bernice. "The Evolution of the Family Resource Movement." In Kagan, Sharon L. and Bernice Weissbourd, *Putting Families First: America's Family Support Movement and the Challenge of Change.* San Francisco: Jossey-Bass, 1994.

Weissbourd, Richard. "Making the System Work for Poor Children." Cambridge, MA: Harvard University, Kennedy School of Government, November 1991.

White, Julie A. and Gary Whelage. "Community Collaboration: If It Is Such a Good Idea, Why Is It So Hard to Do?" *Education Evaluation and Policy Analysis,* 17(1)(Spring 1995).

Wilkins, Roger. "Don't Blame the Great Society." *The Progressive,* July 1992.

Williams, Harold S., Arthur Y. Webb, and William J. Philips. *Outcome Funding: A New Approach to Targeted Grantmaking.* Rensselaerville, NY: Rensselaerville Institute, 1991.

Wilson, James Q. "Can the Bureaucracy Be Deregulated? Lessons from Government Agencies." In DiIulio, John J., Jr., *Deregulating the Public Service: Can Government Be Improved?* Washington, DC: Brookings Institution, 1994.

————. *On Character.* Washington, DC: The AEI Press, 1991.

————. *Bureaucracy: What Government Agencies Do and Why They Do It.* New York: Basic Books, 1989.

Wilson, William Julius. *When Work Disappears: The World of the New Urban Poor.* New York: Knopf, 1996.

————, *The Truly Disadvantaged: The Inner City, The Underclass, and Public Policy.* Chicago: University of Chicago, 1987.

Wolff, Edward N. *Top Heavy: A Study of the Increasing Inequality of Wealth in America.* New York: Twentieth Century Fund, 1995.

Wynn, Joan, Joan Costello, Robert Halpern, and Harold Richman. "Children, Families, and Communities: A New Approach to Social Services." Chicago: Chapin Hall Center for Children, 1994.

Yankelovich, Daniel. "How Changes in the Economy Are Reshaping American Values." In Aaron, Henry J., Thomas E. Mann, and Timothy Taylor, eds., *Values and Public Policy.* Washington, DC: Brookings Institution, 1994.

Zero to Three. "Heart Start: The Emotional Foundations of School Readiness." Arlington, VA: National Center for Clinical Infant Programs, 1992.

Zill, Nicholas. "Characteristics of AFDC Recipients that Bear on Their Fitness for Work Requirements Under Welfare Reform." Paper presented at American Enterprise Institute for Public Policy Research. Washington, DC, December 12, 1993.

Acknowledgments

THE AUTHOR of a wide-ranging book like this one incurs even more obligations than most. I would not have dared to try to encompass the cutting-edge work in the many fields I was determined to include without the generous help of an extraordinarily knowledgeable group of friends and colleagues. I would not have been able to make sense of what I was learning without the probing conversations that so many of these friends and colleagues were willing to engage in over the years, and without their willingness to read what I had written, examine it through the lens of their experience, point out the thin spots, and help me learn more.

I am profoundly grateful to Peter Edelman, who went well beyond the requirements of deep friendship to read and thoughtfully critique every bit of what I wrote—even when the manuscript was twice its final length, and even when my need for his wisdom came in the midst of a maelstrom of other demands on him.

My good friend and colleague Harold Richman carried draft chapters on many transatlantic trips, and skipped in-flight movies to read them. The astute comments he sent back from distant corners of the world, reflecting his rich knowledge and original insights, were invaluable.

When I followed up on Derek Bok's casual offer of two years earlier to read my manuscript, he was as good as his word, even though he was finishing his own book at the time. He read everything I sent him, assessed it with a cool and practiced eye, and sent me back to the drawing board on several issues. I thank him and hope he will agree that the final product is considerably improved as a result.

Because the essence of my book is distilled from the hard-won experience of individuals in communities throughout the country, I owe much to those who generously took the time to help me understand their work. These are the people who are providing effective services, supports, and education, who are reforming systems, who are spreading successful interventions and are building communities. My warmest thanks go to Dorothy Stoneman, Peggy Eagan, Anne Cohn Donnelly, Geoffrey Canada, Shawn Dove, Joseph Stewart, Robert Slavin, Khatib Waheed, Gary Stangler, Deborah Meier, Beth Lief, Susan Kelly, Toby Herr, Peter Digre, Carolyn Reid-Green, Xylina Bean, Gerry Zapata, Linda Winston, Marc Baty, Sister Mary Paul Janchill, Patrick Costigan, Anita Miller, Joyce Puryear, Otis Johnson, Don Mendonsa, Mary Willoughby, Monsignor William Linder, Rose Asera, Kalyn Culler Cohen, Katy Schneider, Yoland Trevino, Peggy Funkhauser, Linda Radigan, Mary Nelson, and Michael Daniels. (I am no less grateful to those in this group whose projects got left on the cutting room floor when the manuscript outgrew its maximum size. They will recognize that their insights and experience are incorporated in this book, even if their stories are not.)

I needed the help of many more individuals to weave what I learned from these pioneers into sturdy fabric. Don Schön, David Racine, Michelle Cahill, Toby Herr, Richard Elmore, and Robert Slavin—from their very different perspectives—helped me to appreciate the full spectrum of replication issues. Carol Weiss, Anne Kubisch, Jim Connell, and Peter Rossi—from *their* very different perspectives—helped me wend my way into the evaluation world. The chapter on results-based accountability reflects nearly a decade of conversations—verbal and written—with Frank Farrow, David Hornbeck, Sara Watson, Charles Bruner, and Sid Gardner. I got many new insights about bureaucracies from Steven Kelman, Elihu Katz, Lisa Mihaly, Olivia Golden, and the writings of James Q. Wilson.

I am indebted to my embattled welfare reform tutors, David Ellwood, Mary Jo Bane, and Peter Edelman. As I have over the years, I depended on Sarah Brown's insights on the issues of teenage pregnancy and unintended childbearing issues. David Hornbeck, Michael Timpane, Deborah Meier, Lauren Resnick, and Richard Elmore were spectacular education mentors. I also relied heavily on their writings, and on the writings of Tony Bryk and Paul Hill. I got excellent advice on the challenges and opportunities in the early childhood field from Julius Richmond, David Hamburg, Edward Zigler, Olivia Golden, Bernice Weissbourd, Eleanor Stokes Szanton, Michael Levine, and Joan Lombardi. In child welfare, my education came from Frank Farrow, the members of the Harvard Kennedy Executive Session on Child Protective Services, my fellow advisory council members and the staff of the Edna McConnell Clark Foundation Program on Children, and the writings of Sheila Kamerman and Alfred Kahn.

My understanding of the history, theory, and challenges of neighborhood disintegration and community building was vastly expanded by the writings of William Julius Wilson, Elijah Anderson, Geoffrey Canada, Robert Halpern, Joan Walsh, and Alice O'Connor. Anne Kubisch took great pains to be sure I had my facts straight; and my comprehension of the intricacies of neighborhood transformation was vastly enriched by continuing dialogues with her and other colleagues on the Roundtable for Comprehensive Community Initiatives, particularly Harold Richman, Karen Fulbright-Anderson, Angela Blackwell, Barbara Blum, Peter Edelman, John Gardner, Sid Gardner, Craig Howard, Otis Johnson, Ralph Smith, and the late James Rouse.

I had valuable writing and interviewing help from Richard Mendel (on the Beacon Schools), Judith Tolmach Silber (on Michigan's Families First and Healthy Families Indiana), and Deborah Cohen (on Caring Communities and early childhood). Patricia Savage was diligent both as my research assistant and prior to that in her study of the Dudley Street Neighborhood Initiative in Boston and the Neighborhood and Families Initiative in Milwaukee as part of her Policy Analysis Exercise at Harvard's Kennedy School of Government.

My superb assistant, Meg Saunders, was prodigious in keeping track of sources, protecting me from distractions, rescuing me and the manuscript from technological disasters, and miraculously pulling needed facts and figures out of cyberspace.

Roger Scholl, my valued editor at Doubleday/Anchor, managed to overcome every obstacle to smooth my manuscript's journey to publication. In the final crunch, he and I prevailed for last-minute editing help on three fine journalists: my husband, Daniel Schorr, my son, Jonathan Schorr, and Richard Wexler. I am grateful to them for being willing to put their vast skills at our disposal under intense time pressure.

The Annie E. Casey Foundation was not only generous but patient in supporting the work that led to this book, and I am especially grateful to Douglas Nelson and Ralph Smith for their confidence in me. An idyllic month at the Rockefeller Foundation's study center in Bellagio, Italy, added significant momentum to the book's progress, as did additional support from the Joyce Foundation and the John T. and Catherine MacArthur Foundation.

I was able to sail relatively smoothly across the rough seas that a work like this encounters because I had a most extraordinary support group. I could always count on an attentive ear and wise counsel from my husband Dan, my son Jonathan, and my daughter Lisa; from my agent who became my trusted friend, Timothy Seldes; from my longtime mentor, Julius Richmond; and from my close friends Anne Kubisch, Ruth Caplin, Sarah Lawrence-Lightfoot, and Judith Silber. They and my friend Judith Viorst, a world-class support group all by herself, were always there to talk me through the obstacles that sometimes seemed insurmountable, and to convince me that it could actually be done.

And, lastly, I thank my mother, who is, at ninety-two, my longest-term supporter of all.

Index

ABOUT THE AUTHOR

LISBETH B. SCHORR is Lecturer in Social Medicine at Harvard University and Director of the Harvard University Project on Effective Interventions. She cochairs the Roundtable on Comprehensive Community Initiatives for Children and Families of the Aspen Institute.

Ms. Schorr has woven many strands of experience with social policy and human service programs together to become a national authority on improving the future of disadvantaged children and their families and communities and a leader in major national efforts on behalf of children and youth. Her previous, widely acclaimed, book, *Within Our Reach: Breaking the Cycle of Disadvantage*, was published by Doubleday in 1988.

She lives in Washington, D.C., with her husband, Daniel Schorr, senior correspondent for National Public Radio. The Schorrs have two grown children, Jonathan and Lisa.

WILLIAM JULIUS WILSON, Malcolm Wiener Professor of Social Policy at Harvard University, is one of the nation's most influential sociologists, and author, most recently, of *When Work Disappears: The World of the New Urban Poor*.